**ELEVENTH EDITION**

# The Enjoyment of Music

## SHORTER VERSION

ELEVENTH EDITION

# The Enjoyment of Music

## An Introduction to Perceptive Listening

### SHORTER VERSION

**Kristine Forney**

*Professor of Music,*
*California State University, Long Beach*

**Joseph Machlis**

*Late Professor Emeritus,*
*Queens College of the City University of New York*

W. W. NORTON & COMPANY • NEW YORK • LONDON

**W. W. Norton & Company** has been independent since its founding in 1923, when William Warder Norton and Margaret D. Herter Norton first published lectures delivered at the People's Institute, the adult education division of New York City's Cooper Union. The firm soon expanded its program beyond the Institute, publishing books by celebrated academics from America and abroad. By mid-century, the two major pillars of Norton's publishing program—trade books and college texts—were firmly established. In the 1950s, the Norton family transferred control of the company to its employees, and today—with a staff of 400 and a comparable number of trade, college, and professional titles published each year—W. W. Norton & Company stands as the largest and oldest publishing house owned wholly by its employees.

for Earle Fenton Palmer

Editor: Maribeth Payne

Developmental, Project, and Copy Editor: Kathryn Talalay

Managing Editor, College: Marian Johnson

Electronic Media Editor: Steve Hoge

Marketing Manager: Amber Chow

Photo Editor: Junenoire Mitchell

Photo Researcher: Julie Tesser

Ancillary Editor: Allison Courtney Hirschey

Editorial Assistant: Ariella Foss

Art Director: Hope Miller Goodell

Designer: Lisa Buckley Design

Senior Production Manager: Jane Searle

Music Typesetter: David Botwinik

Page Layout: Carole Desnoes

Cover Design: Joan Greenfield

Indexer: Marilyn Bliss

Composition: TexTech International

Manufacturing: Courier, Kendallville

**Library of Congress Cataloging-in-Publication Data**
Forney, Kristine.
The enjoyment of music: an introduction to perceptive listening / Kristine Forney, Joseph Machlis. — 11th ed., shorter version
p. cm.
Includes index.
**ISBN: 978-0-393-93415-1 (pbk.)**
1. Music appreciation. I. Machlis, Joseph, 1906–1998. II. Title.
MT90.M23 2011b
780—dc22          2010038437
W. W. Norton & Company, Inc., 500 Fifth Avenue, New York, NY 10110
www.norton.com
W. W. Norton & Company Ltd., Castle House, 75 / 76 Wells Street, London W1T 3QT
2 3 4 5 6 7 8 9 0

# Contents

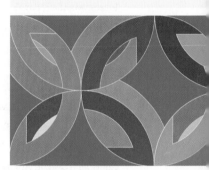

## Part I  Materials of Music     3

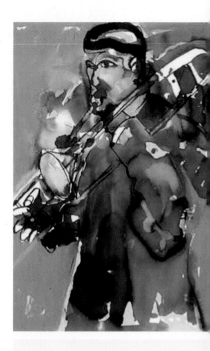

# Listening Guides

# Listening Activities

# Here & There, Then & Now

# Online Video and iMusic Examples

## ⊚ Videos

**Orchestra and Chamber Music Videos**

Bach: Contrapunctus I, from *The Art of Fugue* (string quartet)

Beethoven: Symphony No. 5 in C minor, I

Mozart: Concerto for Piano and Orchestra in G major, K. 453, I

Mozart: *Eine kleine Nachtmusik*, I

Sousa: *Washington Post March* (concert band)

Tchaikovsky: Symphony No. 5 in E minor, III

Telemann: *Tafelmusik*, selections (Baroque orchestra)

**Metropolitan Opera Videos**

Adams: *Doctor Atomic*, selections

Berg: *Wozzeck*, Act III, selections

Bizet: *Habanera*, from *Carmen*

Mozart: *Don Giovanni*, Act I, selections

Puccini: *Un bel dì*, from *Madame Butterfly*

Verdi: *Rigoletto*, Act III, selections

Wagner: *Die Walküre*, Act III, selections

## ⊚ iMusic

*(alphabetical listing)*

*Amazing Grace* (traditional hymn, UK)

*America* (patriotic song)

*Avaz of Bayate Esfahan* (Iran)

Bach, J. S.: *Brandenburg Concerto* No. 1, I

Bach, J.S.: Cantata 56, "Endlich, endlich wird mein Joch"

Bach, J. S.: Contrapunctus I, from *The Art of Fugue*

Bach, J. S.: Contrapunctus I, theme (original)

Bach, J. S.: Contrapunctus I, theme (inversion)

Bach, J. S.: Contrapunctus I, theme (retrograde)

Bach, J. S.: Contrapunctus I, theme (retrograde inversion)

Bach, J. S.: Contrapunctus I, theme (augmentation)

Bach, J. S.: Contrapunctus I, theme (diminution)

Bach, J. S.: *Jesu, Joy of Man's Desiring*

Bach, J. S.: Sarabande, from Cello Suite No. 2

Bach, J. S.: Toccata in D minor

*Battle Hymn of the Republic* (Civil War song)

Beethoven: *Für Elise*

Beethoven: *Moonlight* Sonata, Adagio

Beethoven: *Ode to Joy*, from Symphony No. 9, IV

Beethoven: *Pathetique* Sonata, I

Beethoven: Symphony No. 5, I

Berg: *Wozzeck*, Act I, Scene 1

Berlioz: *Symphonie fantastique*, I (*idée fixe*)

Bernstein: *Tonight*, from *West Side Story*

*Bhimpalasi* (North India)

Bizet: *Toreador Song*, from *Carmen*

Brahms: *Lullaby*

Brahms: Symphony No. 1, IV

Brahms: Symphony No. 4, IV

Call to Prayer (*Adhan*): *Blessings on the Prophet*

Catán: Interlude, from *Rappaccini's Daughter*

*El Cihualteco* (Mexico, mariachi song)

Chopin: Prelude in E minor, Op. 28, No. 4

Chopin: Prelude in B-flat minor, Op. 28, No. 16

Chopin: Prelude in A minor, Op. 29, No. 2

Debussy: *Jeux de vagues,* from *La mer*

*Dougla Dance* (Trinidad)

Foster: *Camptown Races*

Foster: *Oh, Susannah!*

*Gankino horo* (Bulgaria)

*Gota* (Ghana, West Africa)

# Preface

## *The Enjoyment of Music* Package

**Accessible and engaging, the Eleventh Edition of *The Enjoyment of Music* reflects how today's students learn, listen to, and live with music.**

*The Enjoyment of Music* is a remarkable resource for the study of music appreciation and literature. This book is a classic—it's been around for more than half a century—but its contents and pedagogical approach are very much up-to-date, featuring appealing music, the latest scholarship, an eye-catching design, and an unparalleled package of electronic ancillaries. This preface introduces some of the important features in the text, on the CDs, and online. Understanding these resources will enhance listening, help study skills, and improve performance in class.

## Using the Book

*The Enjoyment of Music* is designed for maximum readability. The narrative is accompanied by many useful and instructive features that will help in the study of music:

- A **varied repertory** broadly represents classical masters, including music by women and living composers, as well as jazz, rock, musical theater, film music, and non-Western musical styles.

- **Key Points**, at the beginning of each chapter, provide a brief summary of the terms and main ideas in each chapter.

- **Marginal sideheads** identify key terms defined in the text and focus attention on important concepts.

- **Marginal icons**, placed throughout the book, indicate the relevant online (StudySpace) resources. These include references to iMusic examples and Videos (see p. xvii) streamed on Study Space as well as an icon that points out Global music content 🌐.

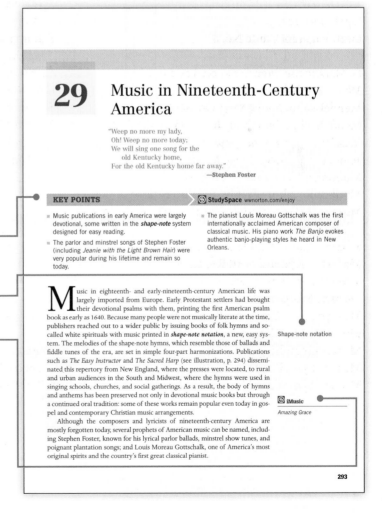

### 29 Music in Nineteenth-Century America

"Weep no more my lady,
Oh! Weep no more today;
We will sing one song for the
old Kentucky home,
For the old Kentucky home far away."
—Stephen Foster

**KEY POINTS**  StudySpace wwnorton.com/enjoy

- Music publications in early America were largely devotional, some written in the **shape-note** system designed for easy reading.
- The parlor and minstrel songs of Stephen Foster (including *Jeanie with the Light Brown Hair*) were very popular during his lifetime and remain so today.
- The pianist Louis Moreau Gottschalk was the first internationally acclaimed American composer of classical music. His piano work *The Banjo* evokes authentic banjo-playing styles he heard in New Orleans.

Music in eighteenth- and early-nineteenth-century American life was largely imported from Europe. Early Protestant settlers had brought their devotional psalms with them, printing the first American psalm book as early as 1640. Because many people were not musically literate at the time, publishers reached out to a wider public by issuing books of folk hymns and so-called white spirituals with music printed in **shape-note notation**, a new, easy system. The melodies of the shape-note hymns, which resemble those of ballads and fiddle tunes of the era, are set in simple four-part harmonizations. Publications such as *The Easy Instructor* and *The Sacred Harp* (see illustration, p. 294) disseminated this repertory from New England, where the presses were located, to rural and urban audiences in the South and Midwest, where the hymns were used in singing schools, churches, and social gatherings. As a result, the body of hymns and anthems has been preserved not only in devotional music books but through a continued oral tradition: some of these works remain popular even today in gospel and contemporary Christian music arrangements.

Although the composers and lyricists of nineteenth-century America are mostly forgotten today, several prophets of American music can be named, including Stephen Foster, known for his lyrical parlor ballads, minstrel show tunes, and poignant plantation songs; and Louis Moreau Gottschalk, one of America's most original spirits and the country's first great classical pianist.

Shape-note notation

iMusic
*Amazing Grace*

293

- **Here & There, Then & Now (HTTN) boxes** connects the musical past to the present while showing the role music plays in everyday life and culture—then and now—and from around the world—here and there.

- **By the way . . . (Btw) boxes** are informational items that answer questions frequently asked by students.

---

**7    Here & There, Then & Now**

## Chopin and the Salon

Although Chopin's music is central to the modern concert pianist's repertory—and thus a mainstay of today's concert hall performance—he composed for the more intimate atmosphere of the salon, or drawing room (the word derives from the French *salle*, or room). Like the Italian academies of earlier centuries (see p. 135), the Parisian salon was conceived as a gathering of musicians, artists, and intellectuals who shared similar interests and tastes, and was hosted by a wealthy aristocrat, often a woman.

It was also a place where professional performers and artists could mingle freely with amateurs. But Chopin, who arrived in Paris with "but one ducat in my pocket," found that although the wealthy clientele were eager to be entertained by him—and receive lessons from him as well—they

A Parisian salon concert depicted by **James Tissot** (1836–1902).

for every American town or village to one in England."

Americans were huge consumers of published sheet music as well, craving songs and piano music of limited to moderate difficulty playable by amateurs. Chopin's music was a natural answer to this demand. His dances, especially waltzes and marches, were relatively uncomplicated and technically fairly easy. (You may know the so-called *Minute* Waltz

in towns and cities across the United States as the principal venue for concert life, and especially piano performances.

Today, solo piano recitals and chamber music are still the most popular forms of classical music performed in private homes or salons. This kind of venue is preferred for intimate events, often for fund-raising purposes, sponsored by women's clubs and arts organizations. But in the world of popular music, some super-

---

**By the way . . .**

### How Did Mozart Die?

For more than two centuries, there has been speculation about what led to Mozart's sudden death at the age of thirty-five. The theory that he was poisoned by his rival Salieri—either medically or psychologically—was the main theme of the controversial play *Amadeus* (1979) by Peter Schaffer, adapted in 1984 into an Academy Award-winning movie. Other popular theories include malpractice on the part of his physician, rheumatic fever, heart disease, and even trichinosis from eating undercooked pork chops. Not long ago, DNA specialists thought they had found Mozart's skull. Unfortunately, there was no DNA match between this relic and that of his close relatives, which made it impossible to make any definitive analysis of the cause of his death. Medical specialists suggest that Mozart may have died of a more common problem: a streptococcal infection, possibly a bad case of strep throat that led to edema (a swelling in parts of the body) and kidney failure. According to historical records, there was a spike in such cases in Vienna among young men in the months surrounding Mozart's death. We may never know for sure, since no remains of the composer are extant for modern forensic testing.

---

**Meet the Performers**

### The Silk Road Ensemble

"The music leapt across national boundaries in a strange and wonderful way. We were reminded that multi-culturalism has been a reality for many contemporary musicians for a very long time."

Meet the Silk Road Ensemble, established by cellist Yo-Yo Ma in 2000 as part of the Silk Road Project—an artistic, cultural, and education organization with a vision of connecting the world's neighborhoods by bringing together artists and audiences around the globe. Now some sixty members strong, the ensemble includes not only musicians but also visual artists and storytellers from more than twenty countries along the ancient trade route that linked China with the West. The group, a part of the Silk Road Project, shares a unique perspective on the relationship between the traditional and the innovative in music, both Eastern and Western. In formal concerts and informal workshops given at universities and museums throughout the world, the ensemble promotes artistic exchange and cross-cultural awareness through music.

The ensemble performs on diverse traditional instruments, such as the Chinese pipa (a lute, see illustration

of Wu Man on right), the Japanese shakuhachi (a bamboo flute), the Indian tabla (a pair of small hand drums), and the Galician, or Spanish bagpipe. The group has been actively commissioning new works from composers and arrangers to keep their musical traditions alive in the modern world. The group's most recent recording, *Traditions and Transformations: Sounds of Silk Road Chicago*, won a 2009 Grammy Award.

**Check out these recordings by the Silk Road Ensemble:** Pipa Concerto by Lou Harrison, from *Traditions and Transformations: Sounds of Silk Road Chicago* (Yo-Yo Ma, cello; Wu Man, pipa; Chicago Symphony Orchestra, Alan Gilbert and Miguel Harth-Bedoya, conductors)

---

- **Meet the Performers boxes** introduce some of the world's most famous musicians and recommend recordings and videos.

- **Full-color photographs** and illustrations bring to life the figures and events discussed in the text.

- **Listening Guides** for each piece offer moment-by-moment descriptions of the works. (See About the Listening Guides, p. xxiv.)

- **What to Listen For boxes**, featured in each Listening Guide (see p. xxv), offer helpful suggestions for what to focus on in the music. These are organized by musical element, and each element is color-coded throughout the book.

---

**Hildegard of Bingen (1098–1179)**

**Hildegard of Bingen** was the daughter of a noble couple who promised her, as their tenth child, to the service of the church as a tithe (giving one tenth of what one owns). Raised by a religious recluse, she lived in a stone cell with one window and took vows at the age of fourteen. From childhood, Hildegard experienced visions, which intensified in later life. She was reportedly able to foretell the future.

With the death of her teacher, Hildegard became the head of the religious community and, around the year 1150, founded a new convent in Rupertsberg, Germany. Her reported miracles and prophecies made her famous throughout Europe: popes, kings, and priests sought her advice on political and religious issues. Moved to record her visions, she noted after a particular vision in 1141, that when "the heavens were opened and a blinding light of exceptional brilliance flowed through my flame," she understood fully the meaning of the scriptures. Although never officially canonized, Hildegard is regarded as a saint by the church.

Her collected music forms a liturgical cycle for the different feasts throughout the church year. Her highly original style resembles Gregorian chant but is full of expressive leaps and melismas that clearly convey the meaning of the words.

**Major Works:** poetry collection and visions entitled *Scivias* (*Know the Way*), one volume of religious poetry set to music (*Symphony of the Harmony of Celestial Revelations*), a sung morality play (*The Play of the Virtues*), and scientific and medical writings.

**iMusic:** Kyrie

The priest Volmar records Hildegard of Bingen's visions. The image, a miniature, is from her poetry collection *Scivias* (1141–51).

- **Composer biographies** are set off from the text's narrative for quick reference, along with a list of each composer's major works by genre.

### A Chant to the Virgin by Hildegard

Hildegard set many of her texts to music; her poetry is characterized by brilliant imagery and creative language. Some of her songs celebrate the lives of local saints such as Saint Rupert, the patron of her monastery, while many praise the Virgin Mary, comparing her to a blossoming flower or branch and celebrating her purity. Our example is an Alleluia (Listening Guide 3, p. 88), a movement from the Mass Proper, to be sung on a feast day for the Virgin. The chant is three-part, with the choral *Alleluia* framing the solo verse at the beginning and end. One of Hildegard's musical signatures can be heard here: an occasional

*In Her Own Words*

The words I speak come from no human mouth; I saw and heard them in visions sent to me. . . . I have no confidence in my own capacities—I reach out my hand to God that He may carry me along as a feather borne weightlessly by the wind.

- **In Her/His Own Words (IHOW),** placed throughout the text, offer informative and relevant quotes from composers and important historical figures.

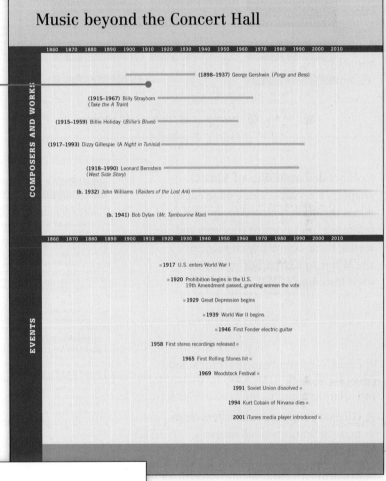

- **Timelines**, placed at the beginnings of each Part Opener, provide a chronological orientation for world events as well as for principal literary and artistic figures and composers.

- **Preludes** provide overviews of major artistic and intellectual trends in each historical period.

- **Critical Thinking** questions appear at the end of each chapter, raising issues for further study.

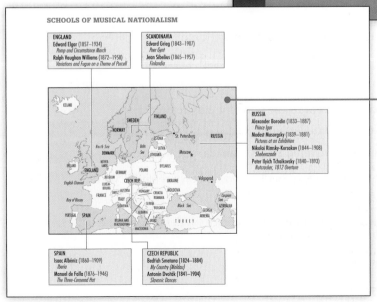

- **Maps** throughout the book reinforce the location and names of composers associated with major musical centers.

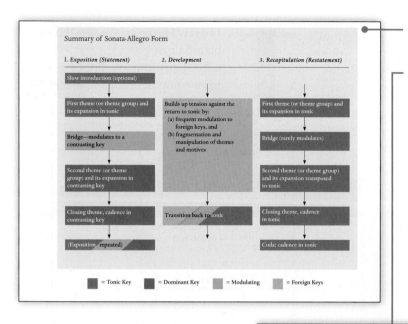

• **Colorful charts** visually reinforce concepts presented in the text.

• **Listening Activities** appear throughout the book to reinforce musical concepts using short iMusic excerpts.

• Color-coded **Materials of Music** chapters are visible along page edges when the book is closed for quick reference to important concepts and terms; these colors match those in the **What to Listen For** sections of each Listening Guide.

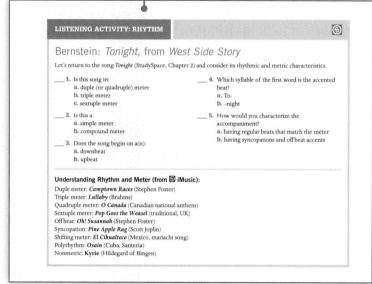

Other useful reference tools are included in the text as well:

• A **Glossary** (Appendix II) offers clear, concise definitions of all musical terms.

• A **Musical Notation** section (Appendix I) provides explanations of musical symbols used for pitch and rhythm.

• A **Table of Listening Guides and Recordings** (inside the front and back covers) provides quick reference for locating Listening Guides in the book, as well as pieces on the recording packages.

• All **iMusic and Video examples** are listed in the front of the book for easy reference.

• The **World map** (at the back of the book) offers a quick view of continents, countries, and major cities. Inserts provide detail on Europe, the United States, Canada, and Mexico.

• **World music examples** from iMusic and the main repertory are indexed on a separate World map (see p. xxiii).

• The **Index** (at the back of the book) gives the page numbers in boldface for definitions, and in italics for illustrations.

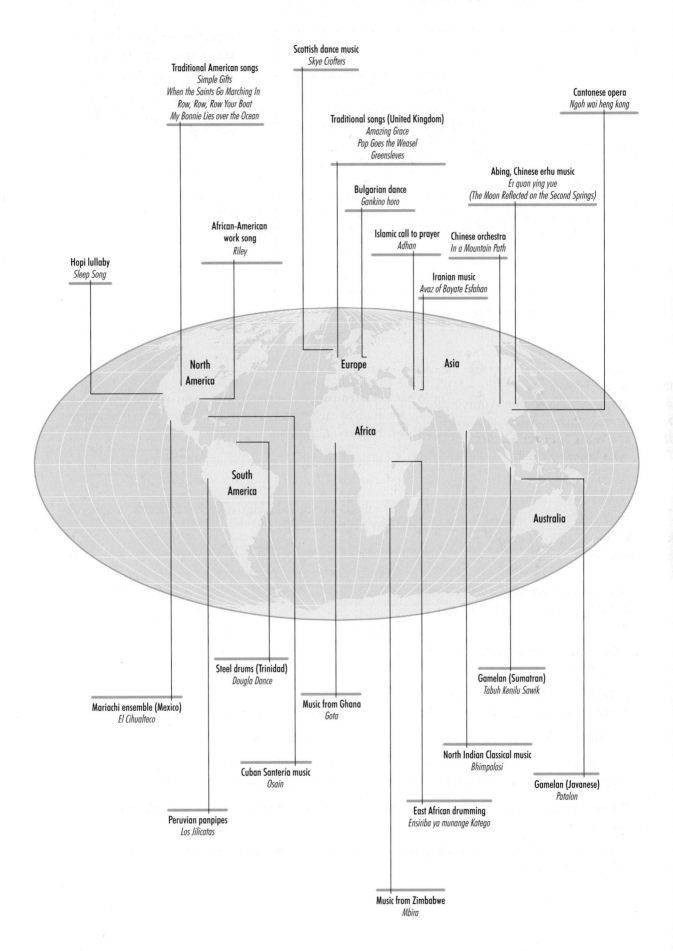

Scottish dance music
*Skye Crofters*

Traditional American songs
*Simple Gifts*
*When the Saints Go Marching In*
*Row, Row, Row Your Boat*
*My Bonnie Lies over the Ocean*

Cantonese opera
*Ngoh wai heng kong*

Traditional songs (United Kingdom)
*Amazing Grace*
*Pop Goes the Weasel*
*Greensleves*

Abing, Chinese erhu music
*Er quan ying yue*
*(The Moon Reflected on the Second Springs)*

Bulgarian dance
*Gankino horo*

African-American
work song
*Riley*

Islamic call to prayer
*Adhan*

Chinese orchestra
*In a Mountain Path*

Iranian music
*Avaz of Bayate Esfahan*

Hopi lullaby
*Sleep Song*

North
America

Europe

Asia

Africa

South
America

Australia

Steel drums (Trinidad)
*Dougla Dance*

Gamelan (Sumatran)
*Tabuh Kenilu Sawik*

Mariachi ensemble (Mexico)
*El Cihualteco*

Music from Ghana
*Gota*

North Indian Classical music
*Bhimpalasi*

Cuban Santería music
*Osain*

Gamelan (Javanese)
*Patalon*

Peruvian panpipes
*Los Jilicatas*

East African drumming
*Ensiriba ya munange Katego*

Music from Zimbabwe
*Mbira*

# About the Listening Guides

The **Listening Guides** are an important feature of the textbook; use them while listening to the recordings. The guides are easy to follow and will enhance your knowledge and appreciation of each piece. Refer to the sample **Listening Guide** and numbers on the facing page while reading through the following points:

**1** The recording locator, boxed in the upper-right-hand corner of each Listening Guide, provides CD and track numbers for both the 8-CD set (to accompany *The Enjoyment of Music*), in white, and the 4-CD set (to accompany the Shorter version), in yellow. The Shorter repertory is also on the recordings DVD and streamed from the website (StudySpace).

**2** There are interactive Listening Guides (**iLGs**) for all works in the Shorter on both the DVD and StudySpace (streaming). iLGs launch automatically from DVD or streaming—just load to go.

**3** The composer and title of each piece is followed by some basic information about the work, including its date and genre

**4** The total duration of each piece is to the right of the title.

**5** The **What to Listen For** box highlights how to focus your listening by drawing attention to each musical element. The Elements of music are color-coded throughout the book.

**6** CD track numbers, boxed and running down the left side of each Listening Guide, coordinate the CD tracks with the music and text.

**7** Cumulative timings, starting from zero in each movement, are provided throughout the Listening Guide.

**8** Texts and translations (when appropriate) are given for all vocal works.

**9** A moment-by-moment description of events helps you follow the musical selection throughout.

**10** Short examples of the main musical theme(s) are provided.

**11** At the end of many Listening Guides, you are referred to an **Online Listening Quiz** about the work.

**LISTENING GUIDE 30**  **2** ⓢ | DVD | **CD 5 (32–33)** | CD 2 (62–63) **1**

**3** Foster: *Jeanie with the Light Brown Hair*  **4** 3:03

**DATE:** 1854

**GENRE:** Parlor song

**5** **WHAT TO LISTEN FOR:**

| | | | |
|---|---|---|---|
| Melody | Wavelike (descending, then ascending); syllabic setting | Form | Strophic; with each verse in **A-A'-B-A** song form |
| Rhythm/ Meter | Moderate tempo in broad quadruple meter; free ascending cadenza in each verse | Performing Forces | 2 soprano voices in alternation and duet; accompanied by hammer dulcimer |
| Harmony | Major key, simple block- and broken-chord accompaniment | Text | 2-verse poem by Stephen Foster |
| Texture | Homophonic (some polyphony in duet) | | |

**6** ⟦32⟧ 0:00  **Introduction**

**7** 0:16  **Verse 1**  **9**

| | |
|---|---|
| I dream of Jeanie with the light brown hair, Borne, like a vapor, on the summer air! | **A section** |
| I see her tripping where the bright streams play, **8** Happy as the daisies that dance on her way. | **A' section** (varied). |
| Many were the wild notes her merry voice would pour, Many were the blithe birds that warbled them o'er; | **B section** Slows down, ascending cadenza. |
| Oh! I dream of Jeanie with the light brown hair, Floating like a vapor, on the soft summer air. | **A section** returns. |

1:28  **Interlude**

⟦33⟧ 1:37  **Verse 2** (alternating singers and in a duet)

| | |
|---|---|
| I long for Jeanie with the daydawn smile, Radiant in gladness, warm with winning guile; | **A section** |
| I hear her melodies, like joys gone by, Sighing round my heart o'er the fond hopes that die; | **A' section** (varied). Sung as duet. |
| Sighing like the night wind and sobbing like the rain, Wailing for the lost one that comes not again; | **B section** Slows down, ascending cadenza. |
| Oh! I long for Jeanine, and my heart bows low Never more to find her where the bright waters flow. | **A section** returns (unison). Sung as duet. |

2:50  Brief postlude

Opening of Verse 1, with descending melodic line:

I  dream  of  Jea - nie  with  the  light  brown  hair,  **10**

**B section**, with wavelike line:

Ma - ny  were  the  wild  notes  her  mer - ry  voice  would  pour.

**11** ⓢ **Now try the Listening Quiz.**

# To The Student

**This texbook provides you with the most innovative resources on the market.**

## Print Resources

The *Enjoyment of Music* is coordinated with various print and emedia resources. In addition to **StudySpace** (described below), Norton offers a pedagogically rich array of ancillary materials unique to this text, for use by both student and teacher:

### The Norton Recordings

Available in several formats, the Norton Recordings offer maximum flexibility at exceptional values:

- 8-CD set (corresponding to ENJ11 Full version), with track points. The CDs do not have Interactive Listening Guides ( iLGs)
- 4-CD set (corresponding to ENJ11 Shorter version), with track points. The CDs do not have iLGs
- Shorter repertoire as mp3s on DVD, with iLGs
- Shorter repertoire as streaming, with iLGs

### The Norton Scores

This two-volume anthology includes scores for nearly all the works on the Norton Recordings. A unique highlighting system—long a hallmark of this collection— assists you in following full orchestral scores and provides stylistic commentary for each piece. These scores are essential for instructor use in the classroom and for the preparation of lectures as well.

### The Study Guide

This workbook provides reviews, quizzes, drills, and listening exercises, as well as experiential activities that emphasize listening to popular, traditional, and non-Western music.

## StudySpace: Your Place for Successful Learning

StudySpace tells you what you should know, shows you what you still need to review, and then gives you an organized plan to master the material.

This easy-to-navigate website offers an impressive range of exercises, interactive learning tools, assessments, and review materials. Each student who purchases a new copy of *Enjoyment* will have access to **StudySpace** content that includes:

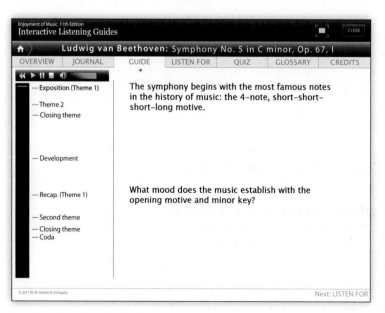

An Interactive Listening Guide.

**LISTENING TOOLS AND ACTIVITIES**

- **Listening Activities and Listening Quizzes integrate musical examples**. The Listening Activities will help you hear differences in styles and genres. The Listening Quizzes couple questions with musical excerpts to help identify the most important aspects of each work in Playlist. (Playlist refers to the core repertory in the book.)

- **iMusic examples**. These examples, both excerpts and longer works, are available as comparative examples and integrated into *Listening Activities* that will assist you in better understanding musical concepts, styles, and genres.

- **Materials of Music Interactive**. These activities provide interactive experience to explore the elements of music, from Melody, Rhythm, Harmony, Form and Texture, to audio/video demonstrations of the instruments of the orchestra.

- ***Britten, The Young Person's Guide to the Orchestra.*** This performance is accompanied by an interactive Listening Guide and introduces students to the instruments of the orchestra.

- **Interactive Listening Guides (iLGs).** Designed for lecture presentation and individual study, these new iLGs have been revised and reconfigured. Their focus is on discovering the music and then analyzing it with prompts that focus on the essential elements.

  The iLGs are available with the recordings in two formats: DVD and streaming. Each format can be purchased, separately or with the textbook, at a savings. No installation is required. All iLGs are just a click away, driven from a menu on the DVD or from the Playlist section of each chapter on StudySpace. The DVD also provides access to mp3 files that you can drag from the disc into iTunes, iPod, iPhone, iTouch, iPad, or other music player or device.

**VIDEOS**

- **Metropolitan Opera Video**. From the stage of New York City's Metropolitan Opera, top-quality performances of scenes from *Don Giovanni, Carmen, Die Walküre, Rigoletto, Madame Butterfly, Wozzeck,* and *Doctor Atomic* provide a one-of-a-kind theatrical experience.

- **Orchestra and Chamber Music Videos.** StudySpace offers some select orchestra and chamber music videos, including movements from Mozart's *Eine kleine Nachtmusik,* Beethoven's Symphony No. 5, Tchaikovsky's Symphony No. 5, Brittens's *Young Person's Guide to the Orchestra,* and others.

**ASSESSMENT AND REVIEW**

- **Quiz+** One of the strongest features of our StudySpace websites, Quiz+ takes online assessment to the next level. Quiz+ doesn't just tell you how well you did; it also shows you how to do better.

- Also included are **Chapter Outlines, FlashCards,** and **overviews of Composers, Musical Eras and Transitions,** and **HTTN** materials from the book for handy online reference. Relevant iMusic excerpts are hotlinked from the HTTN as well as throughout the textbook.

Additional premium content, including streaming music, interactive Listening Guides (see the description above), and an eBook, can also be accessed with the StudySpace *Plus* option.

# To the Instructor: What's New

*The Enjoyment of Music,* Eleventh Edition, presents a comprehensive pedagogical package that integrates innovative technological resources with the textbook and recordings. Be sure to review the previous section (pp. xxvi-xxvii) addressed to the student, for a description of these teaching materials. We have many new pedagogical features in this Eleventh Edition that will assist you and your students. Here is a more specific overview of the repertory changes and other features:

- 97 works with Listening Guides (62 in Shorter), 27 are new to this edition

- Enhanced coverage of contemporary art music:
    **John Corigliano** song cycle: *Mr. Tambourine Man: Seven Songs of Bob Dylan* (2003)
    **Jennifer Higdon** orchestral tone poem: *blue cathedral* (2000)
    **John Adams** opera: excerpts from *Doctor Atomic* (2005)

- Enhanced coverage of wind band music:
    **Ives:** *Country Band March* (band version)
    Streamed video of **Sousa's** *Washington Post March*

- Enhanced coverage of popular and rock music:
    Listening Activities focused on several "classic" rock selections (Bob Dylan, Rolling Stones, and Nirvana)
    Meet the Performers boxes for several important rock groups and performers

- World/traditional music examples with comparisons to Western classical music in Listening Activities:
    **Cantonese opera** with **Puccini:** *Madame Butterfly*
    **Mexican mariachi music** with **Revueltas:** *Homage to Federico García Lorca*
    **Javanese gamelan music** with **Cage:** *Sonatas and Interludes*
    **Chinese traditional music** with **Sheng:** *China Dreams*
    Many more brief comparisons in Listening Activities throughout the book

- New, more accessible, and highly teachable works include:
    **Medieval** *Sumer* **canon**
    **Arcadelt:** *Il bianco e dolce cigno*
    **Purcell:** *Dido and Aeneas,* sailor's dance and chorus
    **Haydn:** *Emperor* **Quartet**
    **Mozart:** *Don Giovanni,* excerpts including Catalog Aria
    **Chopin:** Mazurka in B-flat minor, Op. 24, No. 4
    **Stephen Foster:** *Jeanie with the Light Brown Hair*
    **Grieg:** *Peer Gynt, Morning Mood* and *In the Hall of the Mountain King*
    **Verdi:** Requiem, excerpt
    **Orff:** *O fortuna,* from *Carmina burana*
    **Copland:** *Appalachian Spring,* including *Simple Gifts* variations
    **Gershwin:** *Summertime,* from *Porgy and Bess*

- Excellent coverage of women musicians spanning the entire chronology of the book:
    Middle Ages: **Hildegard of Bingen chant**
    Early Baroque: **Barbara Strozzi aria**

Romantic: **Fanny Mendelssohn piano work**
Twentieth century: **Billie Holiday**, *Billie's Blues*
Twenty-first century: **Jennifer Higdon symphonic work**

- Various types of **Listening Activities** assist student learning:
  To reinforce each element of music
  To overview all historical periods
  To compare genres within an era and from one era to the next
  To compare styles between consecutive eras
  To explore other examples of a genre included in the book
  To compare Western art music with non-Western styles
  To preview styles and genres to come in the book

- New **Here & There, Then & Now** boxes enhance various types of connections between:
  Historical eras and modern life
  Western and non-Western cultures and traditions
  Art music and more popular styles
  Music and other disciplines (politics, science, technology, American and world history, gender studies)

- Rich collection of over 140 **iMusic** examples for comparison of styles includes:
  Well-known folk songs
  Familiar classical masterworks
  Traditional and art music from various non-Western cultures

- **Meet the Performers** boxes introduce a wide range of living (or recently deceased) musicians:

  Wynton Marsalis, trumpet and composer
  Lang Lang, piano
  Luciano Pavarotti, tenor
  Anoushka Shankar, sitar
  Yo-Yo Ma, cello
  James Galway, flute
  Carole Jantsch, tuba
  Evelyn Glennie, percussion
  The King's Singers, vocal group
  The Ying Quartet, string quartet
  Gustavo Dudamel, conductor

  Mikhail Baryshikov, dancer
  United States Marine Band
  Martha Graham, choreographer and dancer
  Billie Holiday, jazz singer
  Duke Ellington, jazz composer and piano
  Leontyne Price, soprano
  Bob Dylan, folk and rock singer
  Mick Jagger, rock singer/guitarist
  Nirvana, rock group
  Laurie Anderson, performance artist

- A new series of **By the way . . . (Btw)** boxes will engage students with interesting questions, including:

  Is It Noise or Music?
  Why All Those Foreign Terms?
  Did Women Sing Sacred Music?
  Who Were Vivaldi's Student?
  How Did Mozart Die?
  Why Did Beethoven Go Deaf?

  Who Is the Elfking?
  How Could Stravinsky's Ballet Have Caused a Riot?
  "Who cares if you listen?"
  Why Is Woodstock So Important?

# Instructor Resources

*The Enjoyment of Music* **is accompanied by a comprehensive set of instructor resources that make music appreciation easy to teach.**

## For Lecture and Presention

*Interactive Listening Guides* (see above for the details)
Designed for lecture presentation and individual study; operates from a DVD.

*Norton Opera Sampler DVD*
In a groundbreaking collaboration, Norton and the Metropolitan Opera have made available a DVD of opera videos correlated to the repertory in ENJ11. Over two hours of top-quality, live performances are now available to ENJ users—to Instructors on DVD and to students, who will be able to access these works, streamed from StudySpace (registration code required).

*Instruments of the Orchestra DVD*
Recorded at the Eastman School of Music, this DVD shows all the instruments of the orchestra—forty-five of them, including eleven percussion instruments—in action. Ideal for classroom use, this easily manageable, high-quality, full-screen DVD allows instructors to select video clips alphabetically or by instrument family and includes complete descriptions of each instrument. The videos are also available online at StudySpace.

*Instructor's Resource Discs (2-DVD Set)*
This helpful classroom presentation tool features enhanced Lecture PowerPoint slides (for Shorter only) that include a suggested classroom-lecture script in the notes field; a separate set of art PowerPoints with all the photographs, art, paintings, and drawn figures from the text; PowerPoint-ready *Instruments of the Orchestra* videos; 143 mp3 excerpts from the *Musical Example Bank;* and *Orchestral Performances* videos (see p. xvii).

*Instructor's Resource Manual*
Available in a downloadable format, this resource includes an overview of ancillaries to accompany *The Enjoyment of Music;* suggested approaches to teaching, a sample course syllabus and exam schedule; resources (books, videos, recordings) for enhancing key units; chapter outlines, and answers to Study Guide questions.

*Music Example Bank*
This unique and highly useful ancillary consists of four fully indexed audio CDs that illustrate—with examples from classical, folk, and popular music—the musical concepts discussed in the text.

# For Assessment

*Quiz+* takes online assessment to the next level (see above for details)

### Test Bank and Computerized Test-Bank in ExamView® Format

Featuring over 2,000 multiple-choice, true/false, and essay questions, the Test Bank is available in Microsoft Word and in ExamView® formats that enable the instructor to edit questions and add new ones.

### Norton Gradebook

With the free, easy-to-use Norton gradebook, instructors can easily access Study Space student quiz results and avoid email inbox clutter. No course setup required. For more information and an audio tour of the gradebook, visit www.wwnorton. com/college/nrl/gradebook

# For Course Management

### Coursepacks

Available at no cost to professors or students, Norton coursepacks for online or hybrid courses are available in a variety of formats, including all versions of Blackboard and WebCT. Content includes chapter-based assignments, test banks and quizzes, interactive learning tools, and selected content from the StudySpace website.

### Downloadable Instructor's Resources (wwnorton.com/instructors)

Instructional content for use in lecture and distance education, including the instructor's resource manual, coursepacks, test-item files, PowerPoint lecture slides, images, figures, and more.

So what's new in the Eleventh Edition? As you can see, more than ever! Updated and innovative technological materials, improved pedagogical resources, an engaging selection of composers, compositions and genres, as well as appealing visual and aural stimulation—all within the package of teaching materials on which you have come to depend. You will find a greater breadth of musical styles than ever before, and music repertory that speaks to today's student in a diverse, multicultural society. Although this text focuses on the Western art tradition, it addresses issues and events in the contemporary world and demonstrates the compelling influence of all styles of music—traditional, popular, and world—on the Western masters. The Eleventh Edition of *The Enjoyment of Music* combines an authoritative text, a stimulating new design that integrates text, pedagogy, and online resources, and an unparalleled package of print and online ancillaries. The result is an exceptional teaching—and learning—package.

Any project of this size is dependent on the expertise and assistance of many individuals to make it a success. First, we wish to acknowledge the many loyal users of *The Enjoyment of Music* who have taken the time to comment on the text and ancillary package. As always, their suggestions help us shape each new edition. We also wish to thank those instructors who participated in focus groups held at the University of California, Santa Barbara, and at California State University, Long Beach. These forums encouraged a free exchange of ideas on teaching methods, repertory, and the instructional use of technology.

The list of specialists who offered their expertise to this text continues to grow. In addition to those acknowledged in the last several editions, whose insights have helped shape the book, we wish to thank Roger Hickman (California State University, Long Beach), for updating the chapter on film music in this edition; Mandy Jo Smith, Erica Ann Watson, and Richard Luke Hannington (California State University, Long Beach) for their assistance with updating the rock chapter; Dolores Hsu (University of California, Santa Barbara), for her advice on the Chinese erhu work; Bahram Osqueezadeh (University of California, Santa Barbara), for his transcription of an Iranian santur piece and for his image included in the text; Mark Scatterday (Eastman School of Music), for producing the video clips of the Instruments of the Orchestra; the Eastman School of Music students who performed in the instrument videos; special thanks to the Metropolitan Opera for making their video excerpts available to us; Gregory Maldonado (California State University, Long Beach), for providing audio and video segments performed by the Los Angeles Baroque Orchestra; the Americus Brass Band (many members of which are CSU Long Beach alumni, Richard Birkemeier, director), for commissioned recording of five iMusic examples; the CSU Long Beach Opera, Orchestra, Choral, Woodwind, Brass, Wind, and Percussion programs (David Anglin, Johannes Müller-Stosch, Jonathan Talberg, John Barcellona, Robert Frear, John A. Carnahan, Michael Carney, directors), for recording many iMusic examples; Rychard Cooper (California State University, Long Beach), for his expert editing of music and video examples; David Garrett (Los Angeles Philharmonic), for licensing his performance of the Sarabande to Bach's Second Cello Suite; Allan Bevan (University of Calgary), for licensing his arrangement of *O Canada;* and David Düsing, for a specially commissioned arrangement of *Simple Gifts.*

The team assembled to prepare the ancillary materials accompanying this edition is unparalleled: it includes Jesse Fillerup (University of Mary Washington), author of the new interactive Listening Guides; John Husser (Virginia Technological Institute and State University), who designed and programmed the listening guides; James Forney (St. Lawrence University) and Tom Laskey (Sony Special Products), who assembled, licensed, and mastered the recording package; Roger Hickman (California State University, Long Beach), who prepared the commentary for the Norton Scores, assisted with recording selection and coordination with the scores, and who updated and edited the Test Bank File; Melissa Lesbines (Appalachian State University), for the StudySpace chapter outlines; Alicia Doyle (California State University, Long Beach), who created the Materials of Music Interactive module, and who prepared new online quiz questions, the new Instructor's Resource Manual, and PowerPoint slides for classroom presentation; Jeff Donovick and Christiane Vínet Fraser (St. Petersburg College), also for the Instructor's Resource Disc PowerPoints; Peter Hesterman (Eastern Illinois University) and John Miller (North Dakota State University), for their creative software design for the Materials of Music Interactive module; Gregory Maldonado (California State University, Long Beach), who highlighted the new scores for this edition; and my husband, William Prizer (University of California, Santa Barbara), who assisted in more ways than can possibly be named.

This new edition would not have been realized without the capable assistance of the exceptional W. W. Norton team. We owe profound thanks to Maribeth Payne, music editor at W. W. Norton, for her heartfelt dedication and counsel to the whole project; to Kathy Talalay, for her expert copyediting and project management, as well as her patience, encouragement, and advice; to electronic media editor Steve Hoge, for creating and coordinating our outstanding media package; to Courtney Hirschey, for her able editing of *The Norton Scores* and her coordination of many of the ancillaries; to Ariella Foss for overseeing innumerable details of the package; to Lisa Buckley, for her inviting and elegant design; to Hope Miller Goodell, for carefully shepherding all elements through the design process; to Trish Marx, Junenoire Mitchell, and Julie Tesser for their assistance with selecting and licensing the illustrations; to Carole Desnoes, for her artistic layout and incomparable sense of how things fit together; to Jane Searle, for her expert oversight of the production for the entire *Enjoyment* package; and to Amber Chow for her insightful marketing strategies. I would also like to thank Marilyn Bliss, for her thorough index; Barbara Necol, for her expert proofreading; David Botwinik, for his skilled music typesetting; and John McCausland, for his attractive maps.

We wish finally to express our deep appreciation to three former music editors at Norton—Michael Ochs, Claire Brook, and David Hamilton—who over the years have guided and inspired *The Enjoyment of Music* to its continued success.

Kristine Forney
Joseph Machlis

ELEVENTH EDITION

# The Enjoyment of Music

**SHORTER VERSION**

# Overview

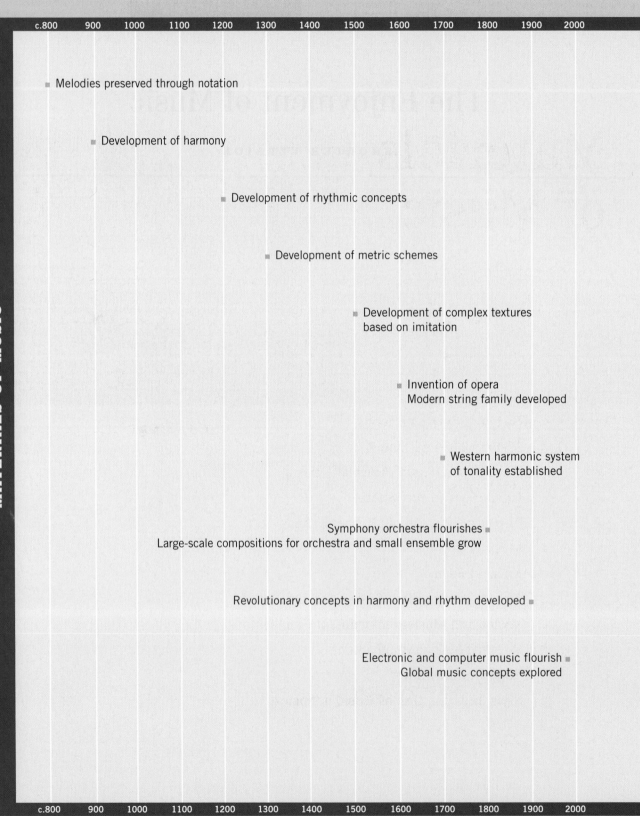

c.800  900  1000  1100  1200  1300  1400  1500  1600  1700  1800  1900  2000

Melodies preserved through notation

Development of harmony

Development of rhythmic concepts

Development of metric schemes

Development of complex textures
based on imitation

Invention of opera
Modern string family developed

Western harmonic system
of tonality established

Symphony orchestra flourishes
Large-scale compositions for orchestra and small ensemble grow

Revolutionary concepts in harmony and rhythm developed

Electronic and computer music flourish
Global music concepts explored

c.800  900  1000  1100  1200  1300  1400  1500  1600  1700  1800  1900  2000

# Materials of Music

Frank Stella (b. 1936), *Lac Laronge III*, 1969.

# Listening to Music Today

"Ah, music . . . a magic beyond all we do here!"

**—Albus Dumbledore, Headmaster,
Hogwarts School of Witchcraft and Wizardry**

Like any new endeavor, it takes practice to become an experienced listener. We often "listen" to music as a background to another activity—perhaps studying or for relaxation. In either case, we are probably not concentrating on the music. This type of "partial listening" is normal and appealing, but here we want to develop listening skills that expand your musical memory.

It is important to hear music in live performance, for nothing can equal the excitement of a live concert. The crowded hall, the visual and aural stimulation of a performance, and even the element of unpredictability—of what might happen on a particular night—all contribute to the unique communicative powers of people making music. There are, however, certain traditions surrounding concerts and concertgoing: these include the way performers dress, the appropriate moments to applaud, and even choosing good seats. These aspects of performance differ between art music and popular music concerts. Understanding the differing traditions—and knowing what to expect—will contribute to your enjoyment of the musical event.

This young man is listening to music on his MP3 player and using his laptop.

## Attending Concerts

You probably have a rich choice of musical events available regardless of where you live. To explore concerts in your area, check with the Music Department for on-campus concerts, read local and college newspapers for a calendar of upcoming events, or consult websites for nearby concert venues and calendars.

Ticket prices vary, depending on the event. For university events, tickets are usually reasonable (under $20). For a performance in a major concert hall, you will probably pay more, generally $35 to over $100, depending on the location of your seat. Today, most new concert halls are constructed so that virtually all the seats are satisfactory. Where you choose your seats depends on the type of the event. For small chamber groups, front orchestra seats, close to the performers, are best. For large ensembles—orchestras and operas, or even popular concerts—the best places are probably near the middle of the hall or in the balcony, where you also have a good view. For some concerts, you may need to purchase tickets in advance, either by phone or online, paying with a credit card. Be sure to ask for student discounts when appropriate.

Before you attend a concert, you may want to prepare by doing some reading. First, find out what works will be performed at the upcoming concert. Then check your textbook, **StudySpace**, and the Internet for information about the composers, works, genres, or styles. It is especially important to read about an opera before the performance because it may be sung in the original language (e.g., Italian).

What you chose to wear to a concert should depend on the degree of formality and the location of the event. Whatever the occasion, you should be neatly attired out of respect for the performers.

Plan to arrive at least twenty minutes before a concert starts, and even earlier if it is open seating or you must pick up your ticket at the box office. Be sure to get a concert program from the usher and read about the music and the performers before the event begins. Translations into English of vocal texts are generally provided as well. If you arrive late, after the concert has begun, you will not be able to enter the hall until after the first piece is finished or an appropriate break in the music occurs. Be respectful of the performers and those around you by not talking and not leaving your seat except at intermission (the break that usually occurs about halfway through the performance).

Inclement weather does not keep these concertgoers from enjoying the Berlin Philharmonic Orchestra's performance at this open-air amphitheater in Berlin.

## LISTENING ACTIVITY: A PREVIEW

 CD 7 (37–40) | CD 4 (10–13)

# Carl Orff: *O fortuna*, from *Carmina burana*

This short, exciting excerpt from a twentieth-century work by Carl Orff introduces us to the various elements that make up music. Orff's work may sound familiar—it has been used extensively in various media, including radio, TV commercials, *The Simpsons*, and movies like *Natural Born Killers*, among others.

### WHAT TO LISTEN FOR:

| | | | |
|---|---|---|---|
| Melody | One main melodic line; the range (highness and lowness) changes throughout | Expression | Changing tempos (pace) and dynamics (volume) to create drama |
| Rhythm/Meter | Accented pulses (beats) grouped in slow-moving triple divisions (difficult to count) | Performing Forces | Large choir and orchestra |
| Harmony | Harsh, jarring combinations of sound; a single sustained low pitch | Timbre | A mixed choir of women and men's voices with orchestra; frequent interjections by loud percussion (drums and metallic gongs) and brass (trumpets) |
| Texture | Interest focused on a single line with all parts moving together; then a new rhythmic idea appears under the tune | | |
| Form | Repetition is the main organizing feature, as other elements shift throughout | Text | Latin text in 3 verses; originally a medieval poem about fate and *Fortuna,* the Roman goddess of luck |

> **SUMMARY: ATTENDING CONCERTS**
>
> ■ Consult websites, your local and college newspapers, the Music Department, and bulletin boards on campus to learn about upcoming concerts in your area.
> ■ Determine if you must purchase your tickets in advance or at the door.
> ■ Read about the works in advance in your textbook or on the Internet.
> ■ Consider what to wear; your attire should suit the occasion.
> ■ Arrive early to purchase or pick up your ticket and to get a good seat.
> ■ Review the program before the concert starts to learn about the music.
> ■ Be respectful to the performers and those sitting near you by not making noise.
> ■ Follow the program carefully to know when to applaud.
> ■ Be aware of and respectful of concert hall traditions.
> ■ Above all, enjoy the event!

## The Concert Program

**Understanding the program**

One key aspect of attending a concert is understanding the program. A sample program for a university orchestra concert appears on page 7. The concert opens with an overture, with a familiar title based on Shakespeare's well-known play *A Midsummer Night's Dream*. We will see later that some works have a literary basis that helps interpret the composer's ideas. Felix Mendelssohn's dates establish him as an early Romantic master. (We will review style periods of music in Chapter 11).

The concert continues with a symphony by Mozart, of whom you have undoubtedly heard. We can deduce by the title that Mozart wrote many symphonies; what we would not know immediately is that this one (No. 41) is his last. The symphony is in four sections, or movements, with contrasting tempo indications for each movement. (You can read more about the tempo terms in Chapter 7 and the multimovement instrumental cycle and the forms of individual movements in Chapter 21.)

After the intermission, the second half of the concert will be devoted to a single work—a piano concerto by the late-nineteenth-century Russian composer Tchaikovsky. This concerto is in three movements, again a standard format (fast-slow-fast). The tempo markings are, however, much more descriptive than those for the Mozart symphony, using words like *maestoso* (majestic), *con spirito* (with spirit), and *con fuoco* (with fire). This is typical of the Romantic era, as is the work's somber minor key. In the concerto, your interest will be drawn sometimes to the soloist, performing virtuoso passages, and at other times to the orchestra.

In addition to the works being performed, the printed program may include short notes about each composition and biographical sketches about the soloist and conductor.

*In His Own Words*

The life of the arts is close to the center of a nation's purpose, and is a test of the quality of a nation's civilization.

—*John F. Kennedy*

## During the Performance

**Concert etiquette**

There are certain concert conventions of which you should be aware. The house lights are usually dimmed just before the concert begins. Make sure your cell phone is turned off and that you do not make noise with candy wrappers or shuffling papers if you are taking notes. It is customary to applaud at the entrances of performers, soloists, and conductors. In an orchestra concert, the concertmaster (the first violinist) will make an entrance and then tune the orchestra by asking the oboe player to play a pitch, to which all the instruments tune in turn. When the orchestra falls silent, the conductor enters, and the performance begins.

## PROGRAM

Overture to *A Midsummer Night's Dream*                    Felix Mendelssohn
                                                           (1809–1847)

Symphony No. 41 in C major, K. 551 (*Jupiter*)             W. A. Mozart
    I.      Allegro vivace                    (1756–1791)
    II.     Andante cantabile
    III.    Menuetto (Allegretto) & Trio
    IV.    Finale: Molto allegro

### Intermission

Concerto No. 1 for Piano and Orchestra                     P. I. Tchaikovsky
in B-flat minor, Op. 23                                    (1840–1893)
    I.      Allegro non troppo e molto maestoso;
         Allegro con spirito
    II.     Andantino simplice; Prestissimo; Tempo I
    III.    Allegro con fuoco

Barbara Allen, piano

The University Symphony Orchestra
Eugene Castillo, conductor

*In Her Own Words*

Applause is the fulfillment . . . . Once you get on the stage, everything is right. I feel the most beautiful, complete, fulfilled.

—*Leontyne Price*

Knowing when to applaud during a concert is part of the necessary etiquette. Generally, the audience claps after complete works such as a symphony, a concerto, a sonata, or a song cycle, rather than between movements of a multimovement work. Sometimes, short works are grouped together on the program, suggesting that they are a set. In this case, applause is generally suitable at the close

## Meet the Performers

### Wynton Marsalis

"The jazz band works best when participation is shaped by intelligent communication."

Meet trumpeter Wynton Marsalis (born 1961), one of the most successful jazz and classical players today. Born in New Orleans to a musical family, Marsalis showed an early aptitude for music, performing with church, jazz, and classical ensembles throughout his youth. His talent won him a brass scholarship to the Berkshire Music Center at Tanglewood in Lenox, Massachusetts, after which he attended the renowned Juilliard School in New York City. His early jazz training with the Art Blakey Band taught him that jazz is a democratic endeavor, in which all players should be treated equally and carry their own weight.

Marsalis has contributed much to the modern revitalization of jazz through his lectures, workshops, and performances. His untiring efforts have rekindled interest in the genre, including the legendary masters, whose recordings he has sought to reissue.

Wynton Marsalis is equally at home playing both jazz and classical genres, as well as his own crossover compositions. In 1997, he became the first jazz artist to win the Pulitzer Prize in music (for his epic opera, *Blood on the Fields*). A recent ambitious work entitled *All Rise* (2002) combines a jazz band, a gospel choir, and a symphony orchestra, and his newest recording, *He and She* (2009), uses spoken words with music to explore the timeless relationship between men and women.

**Check out these Wynton Marsalis recordings:** "Cried, Shouted, Then Sung," from the album *All Rise*; Haydn Trumpet Concerto (CD set)

### Lang Lang

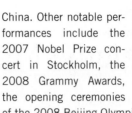

> "Each note that you play says something. If you are not inspired when you play, then you can just forget about it."

Meet Lang Lang (born 1982), a young Chinese pianist called "the hottest artist on the classical music planet" by the *New York Times*. Lang Lang began studying music at the age of three (after seeing a *Tom and Jerry* cartoon on TV, where Tom was playing Liszt's *Hungarian Rhapsody* No. 2) and began winning competitions at the age of five. At nine, he won the prestigious Tchaikovsky International Young Musicians Competition. He is also an accomplished writer: in 2008 he published an acclaimed and soul-bearing autobiography entitled *Journey of a Thousand Miles,* which has been translated into eight languages.

Lang Lang performs worldwide, with major orchestras and as a soloist. Some of these performances were as a United Nations International Goodwill Ambassador, in which he raised funds for the earthquake victims in China. Other notable performances include the 2007 Nobel Prize concert in Stockholm, the 2008 Grammy Awards, the opening ceremonies of the 2008 Beijing Olympic Games, and *The Oprah Winfrey Show*. Lang Lang is particularly committed to sharing the beauty of classical music with young musicians and through his own outreach program, the Lang Lang International Music Foundation.

**Check out these Lang Lang recordings:** Etude, Op. 10, No. 3 (*Tristesse*), by Frédéric Chopin; *Yellow River Concerto: Prelude: The Song of the Yellow River Boatman,* written by a group of Chinese composers

---

of the group. If you are unsure, follow the lead of others in the audience. At the opera the conventions are a little different; the audience might interrupt with applause after a particularly fine delivery of an aria or an ensemble number.

**Onstage decorum**    You might be surprised at the formality of the performers' dress. It is traditional for ensemble players to wear black—long dresses or black pants and tops for the women, tuxedos or tails for the men—to minimize visual distraction. Soloists, however, often dress more colorfully.

Other formal traditions prevail for concerts. For example, the entire orchestra may stand at the entrance of the conductor, and a small group, such as a string quartet, will often bow to the audience in unison. The performers often do not speak to the audience until the close of the program—although this tradition is changing—and then only if an additional piece is demanded by extended applause.

**Encore**    In this case, the ***encore*** (French for "again," and used for an added piece) is generally announced. Some musicians perform long, complex works from memory (see Meet the Performers box, above). To do so requires intense concentration and many arduous hours of study and practice before the concert.

You will undoubtedly sense an aura of suspense surrounding concerts. You should try to take full advantage of the opportunities available—try something completely unfamiliar, perhaps the opera or the symphony, and continue enjoying concerts of whatever music you already like.

For more information about concertgoing and for sample concert reports visit **StudySpace** at wwnorton.com/enjoy.

# 1 Melody: Musical Line

> "It is the melody which is the charm of music, and it is that which is most difficult to produce. The invention of a fine melody is a work of genius."
>
> —Joseph Haydn

## KEY POINTS

> **StudySpace** wwnorton.com/enjoy

- A *melody* is the line, or tune, in music.
- Each melody is unique in *contour* (how it moves up and down) and in *range*, or span of pitches.
- An *interval* is the distance between any two pitches. A melody that moves in small, connected intervals is *conjunct*, while one that moves by leaps is *disjunct*.
- The units that make up a melody are *phrases*; phrases end in resting places called *cadences*.
- A melody may be accompanied by a secondary melody, or a *countermelody*.

Melody is the element in music that appeals most directly to the listener. We know a good melody when we hear one, and we recognize its power to move us. We will see that melody is a universal concept shared by most musical cultures of the world.

A *melody* is a succession of single pitches that we perceive as a recognizable whole. We relate to the pitches of a melody in the same way we hear the words of a sentence—not singly but as an entire cohesive thought. Each melody has its own distinct character based on its range, contour, and movement. A melody goes up and down, with one pitch being higher or lower than another; its *range* is the distance between the lowest and highest notes. This span can be very narrow, as in a children's song that is easy to sing, or very wide, as in some

This apartment building in Vejle, Denmark, called The Wave, is designed by architect Henning Larsen to blend in with the surrounding environment of hills and a fjord. Its wavelike shape resembles that heard in many melodies.

9

### By the way . . .

#### Is It Noise or Music?

While a sound without distinct pitch might be classified as noise, a musical sound generally has perceivable and measurable pitch determined by its **frequency** (number of vibrations per second). This pitch depends on the length or size of a vibrating object. For example, a short string vibrates faster (at a higher frequency) than a long string (which has a lower frequency). This is why a violin sounds higher than a double bass. We represent each pitch with a symbol (called a **note**) placed on a staff. This symbol designates the frequency and the **duration**, or length of time. A musical sound is also perceived at a certain volume (its loudness or softness, called **amplitude**), and with a distinct quality known as **tone color** or **timbre**. This is how we distinguish voices from instruments, and a trumpet from a piano. We will see that the distinction between noise and music has become blurred in modern times.

melodies played on an instrument. Although this distance can be measured in numbers of notes, we will describe range in approximate terms—narrow, medium, or wide.

The **contour** of a melody is its overall shape as it turns upward, downward, or remains static. We can visualize a melody in a line graph, resulting in an ascending or descending line, an arch, or a wave (see Melodic Examples below).

The distance between any two pitches of a melody is called an **interval**. Melodies that move principally by small intervals in a joined, connected manner are called **conjunct**, while those that move in larger, disconnected intervals are described as **disjunct**. The movement of a melody does not necessarily remain the same throughout: it may, for example, begin with a small range and conjunct motion and, as it develops, expand its range and become more disjunct.

# The Structure of Melody

The component units of a melody are like parts of a sentence. A **phrase** in music, as in language, is a unit of meaning within a larger structure. The phrase ends in a resting place, or **cadence,** which punctuates the music in the same way that a comma or period punctuates a sentence. The cadence may be inconclusive, leaving the listener with the impression that more is to come, or it may sound final, giving the listener the sense that the melody has reached the end. The cadence is where a singer or instrumentalist pauses to draw a breath.

If the melody has words, the text lines and the musical phrases will generally coincide. Let's consider the well-known hymn *Amazing Grace* (see opposite). Its four phrases, both the text and the music, are of equal length, and the rhyme

## MELODIC EXAMPLES

ⓔ iMusic iMaterials

***Ode to Joy*** (Beethoven, Symphony No. 9)
Range: narrow (5-note span)
Contour: wavelike
Movement: conjunct

***Joy to the World*** (Christmas carol)
Range: medium (8-note span)
Contour: descending
Movement: conjunct, then a few leaps

***The Star-Spangled Banner*** (U.S. national anthem)
Range: wide (10-note span)
Contour: wavelike
Movement: disjunct (many wide leaps)

## MELODIC PHRASES AND CADENCES

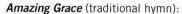 iMusic iMaterials

*Amazing Grace* (traditional hymn):
4 text phrases = 4 musical phrases
Final cadence = end of verse

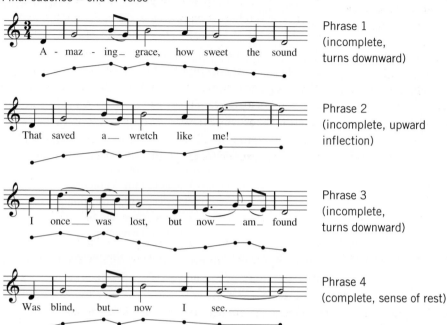

Phrase 1
(incomplete,
turns downward)

Phrase 2
(incomplete, upward
inflection)

Phrase 3
(incomplete,
turns downward)

Phrase 4
(complete, sense of rest)

Line is as important in art as in music. Notice how the eye is drawn to the disjunct movement implied in the mobile sculpture from 1955, by **Alexander Calder** (1898–1976).

scheme of the text is *a-b-a-b*. (The ***rhyme scheme*** of a poem describes the similarity in sound of the last syllables in each line). The first three cadences (at the end of each of the first three phrases) are inconclusive, or incomplete; notice the upward inflection like a question at the end of the second phrase. The fourth phrase, with its final downward motion, provides the answer; it gives the listener a sense of closure.

In order to maintain the listener's interest, a melody must be shaped carefully, either by the composer or by the performer who invents it on the spot.

What makes a striking effect is the ***climax***, the high point in a melodic line, which usually represents a peak in intensity as well as in range. Sing through, or listen to, *The Star-Spangled Banner* and note its climax in the last stirring phrase, when the line rises to the words "O'er the land of the free."

More complex music can feature several simultaneous melodies. Sometimes the relative importance of one melody over the other is clear, and the added tune is called a ***countermelody*** (literally, "against a melody"). You may have heard the famous high-range countermelody played by the piccolos (see p. 48) in the famous *Stars and Stripes* march by John Phillip Sousa (see p. 321). In other styles, each

 iMusic

*The Star-Spangled Banner*

Countermelody

 iMusic

*Stars and Stripes Forever*

# Bernstein: *Tonight*, from *West Side Story*

Let's try out your understanding of some terms relating to melody by listening to this familiar musical theater song (StudySpace, Chapter 1). Here's the text to help you follow along:

> Tonight, tonight, won't be just any night, tonight there will be no morning star.
> Tonight, tonight, I'll see my love tonight, and for us, stars will stop where they are.
> Today the minutes seem like hours, the hours go so slowly, and still the sky is light.
> Oh moon, grow bright, and make this endless day endless night.

Now try out your understanding of terms related to melody in the activity below.

____ **1.** Which term best describes the opening of the melody?
  **a.** conjunct
  **b.** disjunct
  **c.** static

____ **2.** How many melodic phrases, each ending with a sustained cadence note, are in this verse?
  **a.** two
  **b.** four
  **c.** ten

____ **3.** On which two words at cadences do the phrases seem most incomplete, where you know there is more to come?
  **a.** star   **c.** light
  **b.** are    **d.** night

____ **4.** Two changes occur on the line beginning with "Today." Pick the two below that you hear.
  **a.** the melody becomes more conjunct
  **b.** a countermelody is heard in the violins
  **c.** the melody becomes more disjunct
  **d.** the phrasing becomes irregular

____ **5.** Would you say the range of this melody is:
  **a.** narrow
  **b.** medium
  **c.** wide

____ **6.** Where do you think the melody's climax occurs?
  **a.** near the beginning
  **b.** in the middle
  **c.** at the end

**Understanding Melody (from 🎵 iMusic):**

Conjunct movement, small range: *America* (patriotic song)
Disjunct movement, large range: *Ride of the Valkyries* (Wagner)
Wavelike contour: *La Marseilleise* (French national anthem)
Regular phrasing/cadence: *My Bonnie Lies over the Ocean* (folk song)
Countermelody: *Stars and Stripes Forever*, Trio (Sousa)

melodic line is of seemingly equal importance, as we will note in our discussion of musical texture. For much of the music we will study, melody is the most basic element of communication between the composer or performer and the listener.

### Critical Thinking

**1.** What makes a melody particularly memorable?

**2.** How does the structure of a melody compare with the form of a sentence?

# 2 Rhythm and Meter: Musical Time

> "I got rhythm, I got music . . ."
>
> —**Ira Gershwin**

## KEY POINTS

> **StudySpace** wwnorton.com/enjoy

- **Rhythm** is what moves music forward in time.
- **Meter,** marked off in **measures,** organizes the **beats** (the basic units) in music.
- Measures often begin with a strong **downbeat.**
- **Simple meters**—duple, triple, and quadruple—are the most common.

- **Compound meters** subdivide each beat into three, rather than two, subbeats.
- Rhythmic complexities occur with **upbeats, offbeats, syncopation,** and **polyrhythm.**
- **Additive meters** are used in some world musics.
- Some music is **nonmetric** or has an obscured pulse.

Music is propelled forward by **rhythm,** the movement of music in time. Each individual note has a length, or duration—some long and some short. The **beat** is the basic unit of rhythm—it is a regular pulse that divides time into equal segments. Some beats are stronger than others—we perceive these as **accented** beats. In much of the Western music we hear, these strong beats occur at regular intervals—every other beat, every third beat, every fourth, and so on—and thus we hear groupings of two, three, four. These organizing patterns of rhythmic pulses are called **meters** and, in notation, are marked off in **measures**. Each measure contains a fixed number of beats, and the first beat in a measure receives the strongest accent. Measures are marked off by **measure lines**, regular vertical lines through the staff (on which the music is notated; see p. A4).

**Beat**

**Meter and measure**

Meter organizes the flow of rhythm in music. In Western music, its patterns are simple, paralleling the alternating accents heard in poetry. Consider, for example, this well-known stanza by the American poet Robert Frost. It has a meter that alternates a strong beat with a weak one (this is iambic meter, sounding like da DUM, da DUM, da DUM, da DUM). A metrical reading of the poem will bring out the regular pattern of accented (′) and unaccented (-) syllables:

> The wōods ́are lóve-lȳ, dárk ānd déep.
>
> But Ī have próm-is-és tō kéep,
>
> And mīles tō gó be-fóre Ī sléep,
>
> And mīles tō gó be-fóre Ī sléep,

*In His Own Words*

Rhythm and motion, not the element of feeling, are the foundations of musical art.

—*Igor Stravinsky*

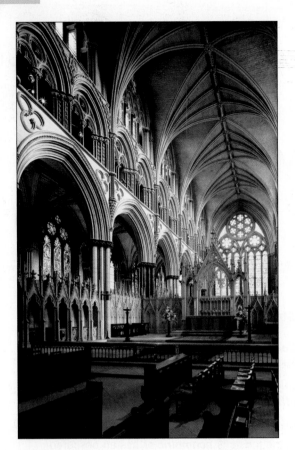

The duple subdivisions of the bays above the vaulted arches in Lincoln Cathedral (c. 1282) in England can be compared to simple meters in music.

# Metrical Patterns

You will hear the regularly recurring patterns of two, three, or four beats in much of the music we will study. As in poetry, these patterns, or meters, depend on the regular recurrence of an accent. In music, the first accented beat of each pattern is known as a *downbeat*, referring to the downward stroke of a conductor's hand (see conducting patterns, p. 58). The most basic pattern, known as *duple meter*, alternates a strong downbeat with a weak beat: ONE-two, ONE-two, or, in marching, LEFT-right, LEFT-right.

*Triple meter*, another basic pattern, has three beats to a measure—one strong beat and two weak ones (ONE-two-three). This meter is traditionally associated with dances such as the waltz and the minuet.

*Quadruple meter* contains four beats to the measure, with a primary accent on the first beat and a secondary accent on the third. Although it is sometimes difficult to distinguish duple and quadruple meter, quadruple meter usually has a broader feeling.

Meters in which the beat has duple subdivisions are called *simple meters*. However, in some patterns, the beat is divided into three; these are known as *compound meters*. The most common compound meter is *sextuple meter*, which has six beats to the measure, with accents on beats one and four (ONE-two-three, FOUR-five-six). Marked by a gently flowing effect, this pattern is often found in lullabies and nursery rhymes:

Lit – tle Boy Blue, come blow your horn, the

sheep's in the meadow, the cow's in the corn.

The examples opposite illustrate the four basic patterns. Not all pieces begin on a downbeat (or beat one). For example, *Greensleeves* is in sextuple meter and begins with an *upbeat*, that is, the last beat of the measure. (Notice that the Frost poem given earlier is in duple meter and begins with an upbeat on "the.")

**Syncopation**    Composers have devised a number of ways to keep the recurrent accent from becoming monotonous. The most common technique is *syncopation*, a deliberate upsetting of the normal pattern of accents. Instead of falling on the strong beat of the measure, the accent is shifted to a weak beat or to an *offbeat* (in between the stronger beats). Syncopation is a device used in the music of all centuries and is particularly characteristic of the African-American dance rhythms out of which jazz developed. The example on page 15 illustrates the technique.

Syncopation is only one technique that throws off the regular patterns. A composition may change meters during its course. Indeed, certain twentieth-century pieces shift meters nearly every measure. Another technique is the simultaneous use of rhythmic patterns that conflict with the underlying beat, such as "two against three" or "three against four"—in a piano piece, for example, the left hand might play two notes to a beat, while the right hand plays three notes to the same beat. **Polyrhythm**    This is called *polyrhythm* ("many rhythms") and occurs frequently in the music of many African cultures as well as in jazz and rock. In some non-Western musics, the **Additive meter**    rhythmic organization is even more complex, based on an *additive meter*, or group-

## EXAMPLES OF METERS

⊙ **iMusic  iMaterials**

ˊ = primary accent        ˇ = secondary accent        ‾ = unaccented beat

**Duple meter:** *Ah! vous dirai-je, maman* (Mozart), same tune as
  *Twinkle, Twinkle, Little Star* (children's song):

|  | ˊ | ‾ | ˊ | ‾ | ˊ | ‾ | ˊ | ‾ |
|---|---|---|---|---|---|---|---|---|
| Accents: | Twin- | kle, | twin- | kle, | lit- | tle | star.__ |  |
| Meter: | 1 | 2  \| 1 | 2  \| 1 | 2  \| 1 | 2 \| |

**Triple meter:** *America* (patriotic song):

| ˊ | ‾ | ‾ | ˊ | | ‾ | ‾ |
|---|---|---|---|---|---|---|
| My | coun- | try | 'tis____ | | of | thee. |
| 1 | 2 | 3  \| | 1 | 2 | | 3  \| |

| ˊ | ‾ | ‾ | ˊ | | ‾ | ‾ |
|---|---|---|---|---|---|---|
| Sweet | land | of | li- | - | ber- | ty |
| 1 | 2 | 3  \| | 1 | 2 | | 3  \| |

**Quadruple meter:** *Battle Hymn of the Republic* (Civil War song):

| ˊ | ‾ | ˇ | ‾ | ˊ | ‾ | ˇ | ‾ | ˊ | ‾ | ˇ | ‾ | ˊ | ‾ | ˇ | ‾ |
|---|---|---|---|---|---|---|---|---|---|---|---|---|---|---|---|
| Glo - ry, glo-ry hal- le - lu - - - jah!    Glo - ry, glo-ry hal- le - lu - - - jah! |
| 1  2  3  4    \|1  2  3  4 \|1  2  3  4    \|1  2  3  4\| |

**Sextuple meter:** *Greensleeves* (folk song, UK)

‾ ˊ‾ ‾  ˇ ‾  ‾  ˊ‾ ‾  ˇ ‾  ‾  ˊ‾ ‾  ˇ ‾  ‾  ˊ ‾ ‾    ˇˇ ‾
A- las my love, you do me wrong, to cast me off  dis - cour-teous – ly,
6 \|1  2  3 4 5  6   \|1 2 3  4  5   6 \|1  2 3   4 5 6  \|1  2  3      4  5  6

ing of irregular numbers of beats that add up to a larger overall pattern. For example, a rhythmic pattern of fourteen beats common in the music of India divides
into groupings of 2 + 4 + 4 + 4. We will see that certain folk styles employ similar
additive patterns of accents.

Some music moves without any strong sense of beat or meter. We might say
that such a work is **nonmetric** (this is the case in the chants of the early Christian
church) or that the pulse is veiled or weak, with the music moving in a floating
rhythm that typifies certain non-Western styles.

**Nonmetric**

Like meter in music, basic
repeated patterns can be
found in nature, such as in
this chambered nautilus shell.

## SYNCOPATION

***Swing Low, Sweet Chariot*** (African-American spiritual):
Try singing or speaking this song in time with a regular beat.
(Note that the words in the first measure fall between the beats.)

Swing low,_____ sweet char i- ot,_____
1            2      | 1      2        |

comin' for to car-ry me    home    _____
1          2      | 1      2        |

Time is a crucial dimension in music. This is the element that binds together the parts within the whole: the notes within the measure and the measure within the phrase. It is thereby the most fundamental element of music.

### Critical Thinking

**1.** How do composers vary rhythm and meter to keep the music interesting?

**2.** Do you find rhythm in Western music to be simple or complex? Explain your answer.

## LISTENING ACTIVITY: RHYTHM

Ⓢ

# Bernstein: *Tonight*, from *West Side Story*

Let's return to the song *Tonight* (StudySpace, Chapter 2) and consider its rhythmic and metric characteristics.

____ **1.** Is this song in:
    **a.** duple (or quadruple) meter
    **b.** triple meter
    **c.** sextuple meter

____ **2.** Is this a:
    **a.** simple meter
    **b.** compound meter

____ **3.** Does the song begin on a(n):
    **a.** downbeat
    **b.** upbeat

____ **4.** Which syllable of the first word is the accented beat?
    **a.** To-
    **b.** –night

____ **5.** How would you characterize the accompaniment?
    **a.** having regular beats that match the meter
    **b.** having syncopations and offbeat accents

### Understanding Rhythm and Meter (from Ⓢ iMusic):

Duple meter: ***Camptown Races*** (Stephen Foster)
Triple meter: ***Lullaby*** (Brahms)
Quadruple meter: ***O Canada*** (Canadian national anthem)
Sextuple meter: ***Pop Goes the Weasel*** (traditional, UK)
Offbeat: ***Oh! Susannah*** (Stephen Foster)
Syncopation: ***Pine Apple Rag*** (Scott Joplin)
Shifting meter: ***El Cihualteco*** (Mexico, mariachi song)
Polyrhythm: ***Osain*** (Cuba, Santería)
Nonmetric: ***Kyrie*** (Hildegard of Bingen)

# 3 Harmony: Musical Space

"We have learned to express the more delicate nuances of feeling by penetrating more deeply into the mysteries of harmony."

—**Robert Schumann**

## KEY POINTS

**StudySpace** wwnorton.com/enjoy

- **Harmony** describes the vertical events in music, or how they sound together.

- A **chord** is the simultaneous sounding of three or more pitches; chords are built from a particular **scale,** or sequence of pitches.

- The most common chord in Western music is a **triad,** which has three notes built on alternate pitches of a scale.

- Most Western music is based on **major** or **minor scales,** from which melody and harmony are derived.

- The **tonic** is the central tone around which a melody and its harmonies are built; this principle of organization is called **tonality.**

- **Dissonance** is created by an unstable, or discordant, combination of tones. **Consonance** occurs with a resolution of dissonance, producing a stable or restful sound.

To the linear movement of the melody, harmony adds another dimension: depth. Harmony is the simultaneous combination of sounds. It can be compared to the concept of perspective in painting (see p. 18). Not all musics of the world rely on harmony, but it is central to most Western styles.

Harmony determines the relationships of intervals and chords. We know that an **interval** is the distance between any two tones. Intervals can occur successively or simultaneously. When three or more tones are sounded together, a **chord** is produced. **Harmony** describes the simultaneous sounding of notes to form chords and the progression from one chord to the next. Harmony therefore implies movement and progression. It is the progression of harmony in a musical work that creates a feeling of order and unity.

*Interval and chord*

The intervals from which chords and melodies are built are chosen from a particular collection of pitches arranged in ascending or descending order known as a **scale**. To the tones of the scale we assign syllables, *do-re-mi-fa-sol-la-ti-do,* or numbers, 1–2–3–4–5–6–7–8. An interval of eight notes is called an **octave**.

*Scale and octave*

| Do | re | mi | fa | sol | la | ti | do |
|----|----|----|----|-----|----|----|----|
| 1 | 2 | 3 | 4 | 5 | 6 | 7 | 8 |

Octave

The most common chord in Western music, a particular combination of three tones, is known as a **triad**. Such a chord may be built on any note of the scale by combining every other note. For example, a triad built on the first tone of a scale

*Triad*

**17**

consists of the first, third, and fifth pitches of the scale *(do-mi-sol);* on the second degree, steps 2–4–6 *(re-fa-la);* and so on. The triad is a basic formation in our music. In the example below, the melody of *Camptown Races* is harmonized with triads. We can see at a glance how melody is the horizontal aspect of music, while harmony, comprising blocks of tones (the chords), constitutes the vertical. Melody and harmony do not function independently of one another. On the contrary, the melody suggests the harmony that goes with it, and each constantly influences the other.

*In His Own Words*

Do you know that our soul is composed of harmony?

—*Leonardo da Vinci*

# The Organization of Harmony

In all music, regardless of the style, certain tones assume greater importance than others. In most Western music, the first note of the scale, *do,* is considered the

Tonic

*tonic* and serves as a home base around which the others revolve and to which they ultimately gravitate. We observed this principle at work earlier with the tune *Amazing Grace* (p. 11), noting that it does not have a final cadence, or stopping point, until its last phrase. It is this sense of a home base that helps us recognize when a piece of music ends.

The principle of organization around a central tone, the tonic, is called *tonality.* The scale chosen as the basis of a piece determines the identity of the tonic and the tonality. Two different types of scales predominate in Western music written between about 1650 and 1900: major and minor. Each scale has a distinct sound because of its unique combination of intervals, which we will discuss in Chapter 4.

Harmony lends a sense of depth to music, as perspective does in this photograph, by **Fernand Ivaldi**, of a view down a tree-lined canal in France.

# Consonance and Dissonance

The movement of harmony toward resolution is the dynamic force in Western music. As music moves in time, we feel moments of tension and release. The tension is a perceived instability that results from **dissonance**, a combination of tones that sounds discordant, in need of resolution. Dissonance introduces conflict into

**EXAMPLE OF HARMONY**                                    ⊙ iMusic iMaterials

*Camptown Races* (Stephen Foster):

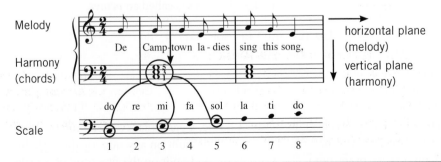

music in the same way that suspense creates tension in drama. Dissonance resolves in **consonance,** a concordant, or agreeable, combination of musical tones that provides a sense of relaxation and fulfillment. At their extremes, dissonance can sound harsh, while consonance is more pleasing to the ear. Each complements the other, and each is a necessary part of the artistic whole.

Harmony appeared much later historically than melody, and its development took place largely in Western music. In many Asian cultures, harmony is relatively simple, consisting of a single sustained tone, called a **drone,** against which melodic and rhythmic complexities unfold. This harmonic principle also occurs in some European folk music, where, for example, a bagpipe might play one or more accompanying drones to a lively dance tune.

Our system of harmony has advanced steadily over the past millennium (harmony was first introduced around the year 900), continually responding to new needs. Composers have tested the rules as they have experimented with innovative sounds and procedures. Yet their goal remains the same: to impose order on sound, organizing the pitches so that we perceive a unified idea.

Just as dissonance provides tension in music, this image of global researchers sunbathing on the edge of a frozen fjord in the arctic to emphasize the dramatic rate of global warming is discordant to the eye.

## Critical Thinking

**1.** How does dissonance make the listener feel, and why?

**2.** How is melody a horizontal idea while harmony is a vertical concept?

---

### LISTENING ACTIVITY: HARMONY

## Haydn: *Surprise* Symphony, second movement

Let's listen to this orchestral work (StudySpace, Chapter 3) to review the qualities of harmony and the concept of tonality. Then answer the questions in the activity below.

____ **1.** How many phrases do you hear before the loud "surprise" chord?
  **a.** two
  **b.** four
  **c.** six

____ **2.** How would you describe the harmony?
  **a.** simple, chords following the melody
  **b.** complex, more independent from the melody

____ **3.** Would you consider this selection's harmony more:
  **a.** consonant
  **b.** dissonant

____ **4.** Do you think the opening is in a:
  **a.** major key (sounding cheery)
  **b.** minor key (sounding sad)

### Understanding Harmony (from 🅢 iMusic):

Octave: *Prelude in E minor* (Chopin)
Chord: *If I Had a Hammer* (Pete Seeger)
Triad: *Pop Goes the Weasel* (traditional, UK)
Tonic: *Camptown Races* (Stephen Foster)
Major scale; tonality: *Joy to the World* (Christmas carol)

Minor scale and tonality: *Moonlight* **Sonata** (Beethoven)
Consonance: *America* (patriotic song)
Dissonance: *"In the lovely month of May"* (Schumann)
Drone: *Skye Crofters* (bagpipe, Scottish dance music)

# 4 The Organization of Musical Sounds

"If only the world could feel the power of harmony."
—W. A. Mozart

## KEY POINTS

> **StudySpace** wwnorton.com/enjoy

- An *octave* is the interval spanning eight notes of the scale. In Western music, the octave is divided into twelve *half steps*, the smallest interval used; two half steps make a *whole step*.

- The *chromatic scale* is made up of these twelve half steps, while a *diatonic scale* is built on patterns of seven whole and half steps that form *major* and *minor scales*.

- A *sharp* (♯) is a symbol that raises a tone by a half step; a *flat* (♭) lowers a tone by a half step.

- Other scale types are used around the world, built on different numbers of pitches and sometimes using *microtones*, which are intervals smaller than half steps.

- The *tonic chord*, built on the first scale tone, is the home base to which *active chords* (*dominant* and *subdominant*) need to resolve.

- Composers can shift the pitch level of an entire work (*transposition*) or change the center, or *key*, during a work (*modulation*).

We have seen how melody and harmony are two of the essential building blocks of musical compositions. Now we can consider how they function together to construct a musical system, both in the West and elsewhere.

Pitch names for notes are the first seven letters of the alphabet (A through G), which repeat when we reach an octave. As we've noted, an *octave* is an interval spanning eight notes of the scale. When we hear any two notes an octave apart sounding together, we recognize that the two tones sound "the same." (We give these two notes the same pitch name: for example, C and C an octave higher.)

*Octave*

One important variable in the different languages of music around the world is the way the octave is divided. In Western music, it is divided into twelve equal semitones, or *half steps*; from these are built the major and minor scales (each with a different combination of seven notes), which have constituted the basis of this musical language for nearly four hundred years.

*Half steps*

## The Formation of Major and Minor Scales

The twelve half steps that make up the octave constitute what is known as the *chromatic scale*. You can see these twelve half steps on the keyboard (see p. 21), counting all the white and black keys from C to the C above it. Virtually all West-

*Chromatic scale*

## NAMES OF TONES AND INTERVALS   ⊚ iMaterials

2 half steps  = 1 whole step
  C–C# ⟶ = 1 half step
  C#–D ⟶ = 1 half step
  C–D ⟶ = 1 whole step

| D♭ C# | E♭ D# | | G♭ F# | A♭ G# | B♭ A# | | |
|---|---|---|---|---|---|---|---|
| *do* C 1 | *re* D 2 | *mi* E 3 | *fa* F 4 | *sol* G 5 | *la* A 6 | *ti* B 7 | *do* C 8 |

⎣————————— octave —————————⎦

Tones of the chromatic scale
  12 half steps = 1 octave

Ascending form of chromatic scale (with sharps):

Descending form of chromatic scale (with flats):

ern music, no matter how intricate, is made up of the same twelve tones and their duplications in higher and lower octaves.

You will notice that the black keys on the piano are named in relation to their white-key neighbors. The black key between C and D can be called C sharp (#) or D flat (♭), depending on the context of the music. This plan applies to all the black keys. Thus a **sharp** raises a tone by a half step, and a **flat** lowers a tone a half step. Note that the distance between C and D is two half steps, or one **whole step** (the sum of two half steps).

We introduced the notion in Chapter 3 that certain tones in music assume greater importance than others; in Western music, the first tone of the scale, the **tonic**, is the home base to which the music gravitates. Two main scale types—major and minor—function within this organizational system known as **tonality**. When we listen to a composition in the **key** of C major, we hear a piece built around the central tone C, using the harmonies formed from the C-major scale. Tonality is the basic harmonic principle at work in most Western music written from around 1600 to 1900.

## The Major Scale

The major scale is the most familiar sequence of pitches. You can produce a C-major scale (*do-re-mi-fa-sol-la-ti-do*) by playing only the white keys on the piano from one pitch, C to the next C. Looking at the keyboard you will notice that there is no black key between E and F (*mi-fa*) or between B and C (*ti-do*). These tones are a half step apart, while the other white keys are a whole step apart. Consequently, a major scale is created by a specific pattern of whole (W) and half (H) steps— (W-W-H-W-W-W-H)—and can be built with this pattern starting on any pitch.

Within each major scale are certain relationships based on tension and resolution. One of the most important is the thrust of the seventh tone to the eighth (*ti* resolving to *do*). Similarly, we feel resolution when *re* moves to *do; fa* gravitates to

*In His Own Words*

There are only twelve tones. You must treat them carefully.

—*Paul Hindemith*

## PATTERN OF MAJOR AND MINOR SCALES

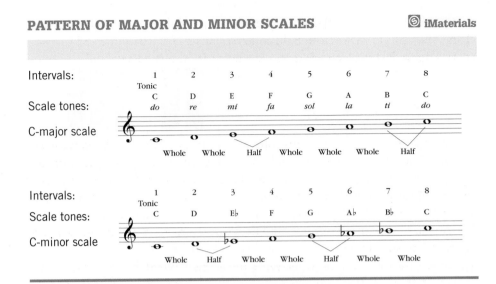

*mi;* and *la* descends to *sol.* We can hear some of these relationships at work in the beginning of the well-known carol *Joy to the World.* It starts on the tonic (*Joy*), then descends and pauses on the dominant (*world*), after which it continues downward, feeling a strong pull to the final *do* (on the word *come;* see melody on p. 10). Most important of all, the major scale defines two poles of traditional harmony: the tonic (*do*), the point of ultimate rest; and the fifth note, the dominant (*sol*), which represents the active harmony. Tonic going to dominant and returning to tonic is a basic progression of harmony in Western music.

## The Minor Scale

ⓢ **iMusic**

Bach: *The Art of Fugue,* theme

The minor scale sounds quite different from the major. One reason is that it has a lowered, or flatted, third degree. Therefore, in the scale of C minor, there is an E flat rather than the E natural (white key E) of the major scale; the interval C to E flat is smaller than the interval C to E in the major. The minor scale is very different from the major scale in mood and coloring. In the famous Bach theme to *The Art of Fugue,* we hear the smaller third interval right at the onset, as the melody outlines a minor third, then descends in a minor scale. The intervals of the minor scale (W-H-W-W-H-W-W) are shown in the table above.

# Diatonic and Chromatic Scales

Diatonic

Chromatic

Music in a major or minor key focuses on the seven tones of the respective scale and is therefore considered *diatonic.* In diatonic music, both the melody and the harmony are firmly rooted in the key. But some compositions introduce other tones that are foreign to the scale, drawing from the full gamut of the twelve half-steps that span the octave. These works are considered *chromatic* (meaning

ⓢ **iMusic**

*Joy to the World*

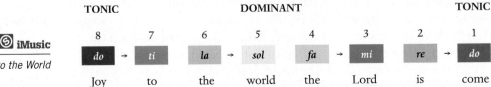

color). Romantic-era composers explored the possibilities of chromaticism to charge their music with emotion. In contrast, music of the Baroque and Classical eras is largely diatonic, centering on a key note and its related harmonies.

## Other Scale Types

The Western musical system is only one way to structure music. The musical languages of other cultures often divide the octave differently, producing different scale patterns. Among the most common is the ***pentatonic***, or five-note, scale, used in some African, Asian, and Native American musics. Pentatonic scales can be formed in a number of patterns, each with its own unique quality of sound. Another non-Western scale type is ***tritonic***, a three-note pattern found in the music of some African cultures.

Some scales are not easily playable on Western instruments because they employ intervals smaller than our half step. Such intervals, known as ***microtones***, may sound "off-key" to Western ears. One way of producing microtonal music is by an ***inflection*** of a pitch, or making a brief microtonal dip or rise from the original pitch; this technique, similar to that of the "blue note" in jazz (see Chapter 40), makes possible a host of subtle pitch changes.

Thus it is the musical system and the tones chosen in that system that determine the sound and character of each work, whether classical, popular, or traditional. They are what make Western music sound familiar to us and why sometimes the music of other cultures may sound foreign to us.

**Pentatonic**

**Tritonic**

**Microtones**

## The Major-Minor System

Just as melodies have inherent active and rest notes, so do the harmonies supporting them. The three-note chord, or ***triad***, built on the first scale tone is called the ***tonic***, or I chord, and serves as a point of rest. The rest chord is counterposed

**Tonic**

**Sophie Taeuber-Arp** (1889–1943), *Composition in Circles and Overlapping Angles* (1930). The overlapping and repeated shapes in this artwork can be compared, in music, to new pitch levels or to modulations to another key.

**Active and rest chords**

against other chords, which are active. The **_active chords_** in turn seek to be completed, or resolved, in the **_rest chord_**. This striving for resolution is the dynamic force in Western music, providing a forward direction and goal.

**Dominant**

The fifth scale step (*sol*), the **_dominant_** (V), forms the chief active chord, which has a feeling of restlessness and seeks to resolve to the tonic. The triad built on the

**Subdominant**

fourth scale step (*fa*) is known as the **_subdominant_** (IV). The movement from the subdominant to the tonic (IV to I) is familiar from the chords accompanying the "Amen" sung at the close of many hymns.

These three basic triads are enough to harmonize many simple tunes. The Civil War song *Battle Hymn of the Republic* is a good example:

**iMusic iMaterials**

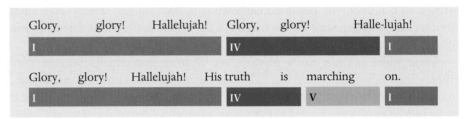

# The Key as a Form-Building Element

The three main chords of a musical work—tonic (I), dominant (V), and subdominant (IV)—are the foundations over which melodies and harmonic progressions unfold. Thus the key becomes a prime factor for musical unity.

At the same time, contrast between keys adds welcome variety. Composers begin by establishing the home key, then change to a related key, perhaps the dom-

**Modulation**

inant, through a process known as **_modulation_**. In so doing, they create tension, because the dominant key is unstable compared to the tonic. This tension requires resolution, which is provided by the return to the home key.

The progression, or movement, from home key to contrasting key and back outlines the basic musical pattern of statement-departure-return. The home key provides unity; the foreign key ensures variety and contrast.

The twelve major and twelve minor keys may be compared to rooms in a house, with the modulations equivalent to corridors leading from one to the other. A composer establishes the home key, then shapes the passage of modulation—the "corridor"—into a key area that is not far away from the starting point. Alternately, composers may take an entire work and set it, or transpose it, in a new key. This is convenient when a song's original key is too high or low to sing or play easily. You could begin on a different pitch and shift all the tones a uniform distance to a differ-

**Transposition**

ent level through the process known as **_transposition_**. In this way, the same song can be sung in various keys by differing voice ranges (soprano, alto, tenor, or bass).

Although we are not always conscious of key centers and chord progressions while we are listening to music, these basic principles are deeply ingrained in our responses. We perceive and react to the tension and resolution provided by the movement of harmony, and we can sense how composers have used the harmonic system to give a coherent shape and meaning to their works.

*In His Own Words*

If only the world could feel the power of harmony.

— W. A. Mozart

### Critical Thinking

**1.** What makes major scales different from minor ones? How does each scale type sound?

**2.** Why do we perceive some chords as active and others as points of rest?

## LISTENING ACTIVITY: MUSICAL SCALES AND KEY

First, let's listen to these two songs (StudySpace, Chapter 4) to see if you can hear the difference between a melody built on a *diatonic scale* and one that uses many *chromatic pitches*, not part of the seven-note scale. We can also check our sense of tonality with these examples in the activity below.

> **a.** Brahms: *Lullaby*
> **b.** Schumann: "In the lovely month of May"

_____ **1.** Which song uses more chromatic notes in the piano accompaniment?

_____ **3.** Which song feels like it is more clearly focused around a key center?

_____ **2.** Which song has a more diatonic melody (listen to one complete verse)?

_____ **4.** Which song feels as though it does *not* resolve to its key center at the end?

Now let's check your ability to recognize the difference in mood heard in *major* versus *minor keys*. Listen to the two iMusic examples below, both dances by Mozart, and answer the following questions.

> **c.** Mozart: Symphony No. 40, III
> **d.** Mozart: *Eine kleine Nachtmusik*, III

_____ **5.** Which example sounds more somber, suggesting it might be in a minor key?

_____ **6.** Leaving tempo aside, which selection sounds brighter, suggesting a major key?

### Understanding Scale and Tonality (from ⊚ iMusic):

Major scale and tonality: *Eine kleine Nachtmusik,* I (Mozart)
Minor scale and tonality: **Toccata in D minor** (Bach)
Pentatonic/heptatonic scale and microtonal intervals: *Bhimpalási* (North India)
Tritonic scale: *Sleep Song* (Hopi lullaby)
Modulation: *Eine kleine Nachtmusik* (Mozart), I (during first minute, modulates from G major to D major)

# 5 Musical Texture

"The composer . . . joins Heaven and Earth with threads of sound."

—**Alan Hovhaness**

## KEY POINTS

⑤ **StudySpace** wwnorton.com/enjoy

- ■ *Texture* refers to the interweaving of the melodic lines with harmony in music.

- ■ The simplest texture is *monophony,* or single-voiced music without accompaniment.

- ■ *Heterophony* refers to multiple voices elaborating the same melody at the same time.

- ■ *Polyphony* describes a many-voiced texture based on *counterpoint*—one line set against another.

- ■ *Homophony* occurs when one melodic voice is prominent over the accompanying lines, or voices.

- ■ *Imitation*—when a melodic idea is presented in one voice, then restated in another—is a common unifying technique in polyphony; *canons* and *rounds* are two types of strictly imitative works.

Line and texture are the subject of **Paul Klee**'s (1879–1940) painting *Neighborhood of the Florentine Villas* (1926).

## Types of Texture

Melodic lines may be thought of as the various threads that make up the musical fabric, or the *texture*. The simplest texture is *monophony,* or single-voiced. ("Voice" refers to an individual part or line, even when we are talking about instrumental music.) Here, the melody is heard without any harmonic accompaniment or other melodic lines. It may be accompanied by rhythm and percussion instruments that embellish it, but interest is focused on the single melodic line rather than on any harmony. Until about a thousand years ago, the Western music we know about was monophonic, as some music of the Far and Middle East still is today.

One type of texture widely found outside the tradition of Western art music is based on two or more voices (lines) simultaneously elaborating the same melody, usually in an improvised performance. Called *heterophony,* this technique usually results in a melody combined with an ornamented version of itself. It can be heard too in some folk music as well as in jazz and spirituals, where *improvisation* (in which some of the music is created on the spot) is central to performance.

Distinct from heterophony is *polyphony* ("many-voiced" texture), in which two or more different melodic lines are combined, thus distributing melodic interest among all the parts. Polyphonic texture is based on *counterpoint*, that is, one musical line set against another.

In another commonly heard texture, *homophony,* a single voice takes over the melodic interest, while the accompanying lines are subordinate. Normally, they become blocks of harmony, the chords that support, color, and enhance the principal line. Here, the listener's interest is directed to a single melodic line, but this is

## EXAMPLES OF MUSICAL TEXTURE

iMusic iMaterials

**Monophonic:** 1 melodic line, no accompaniment (performed solo, then chorus).
Hildegard of Bingen: **Kyrie** (chant):

**Heterophonic:** *When the Saints Go Marching In* (traditional, America).
Notice in the recording how the voice and instruments all elaborate on this one line:

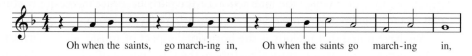

**Polyphonic:** 2 independent melodic lines combined.
Bach: Organ chorale prelude, *Jesu, Joy of Man's Desiring* (example begins 20 seconds into recording):

**Homophonic:** 1 melody with subordinate accompaniment.
Haydn: **Surprise** *Symphony No. 94, II*

**Homorhythmic:** a type of homophonic texture in which all voices move together, with the same words.
Handel: **"Hallelujah Chorus,"** opening, from *Messiah*:

| Rhythm | | | |
|---|---|---|---|
| Soprano | Hal - le - lu-jah, | Hal - le - lu-jah, | Hal-le - lu - jah, |
| Alto | Hal - le - lu-jah, | Hal - le - lu-jah, | Hal-le - lu - jah, |
| Tenor | Hal - le - lu-jah, | Hal - le - lu-jah, | Hal-le - lu - jah, |
| Bass | Hal - le - lu-jah, | Hal - le - lu-jah, | Hal-le - lu - jah, |

conceived in relation to harmony. Homophonic texture is heard when a pianist plays a melody in the right hand while the left sounds the chords, or when a singer or violinist carries the tune against a harmonic accompaniment on the piano. Homophonic texture, then, is based on harmony, just as polyphonic texture is based on counterpoint.

*Homorhythm*

Finally, there is **homorhythm,** a kind of homophony where all the voices, or lines, move together in the same rhythm. When there is text, all words are clearly sounded together. Like homophonic structure, it is based on harmony moving in synchronization with a melody.

A composition need not use one texture exclusively throughout. For example, a large-scale work may begin by presenting a melody with accompanying lines (homophony), after which the interaction of the parts becomes increasingly complex as more independent melodies enter (creating polyphony).

We have noted that melody is the horizontal aspect of music, while harmony is the vertical. Comparing musical texture to the cross weave of a fabric makes the interplay of the parts clear. The horizontal threads, the melodies, are held together by the vertical threads, the harmonies. Out of their interaction comes a texture that may be light or heavy, coarse or fine.

# Contrapuntal Devices

*Imitation*

When several independent lines are combined (in polyphony), one method that composers use to give unity and shape to the texture is **imitation,** in which a melodic idea is presented in one voice and then restated in another. While the imitating voice restates the melody, the first voice continues with new material. Thus, in addition to the vertical and horizontal threads in musical texture, a third, diagonal line results from imitation (see example below).

*Canon and round*

The duration of the imitation may be brief or it may last the entire work. A strictly imitative work is known as a **canon.** The simplest and most familiar form of canon is a **round,** in which each voice enters in succession with the same melody that can be repeated endlessly. Well-known examples include *Row, Row, Row Your Boat* and *Frère Jacques (Are You Sleeping?).* In the example below, the round begins with one voice singing "Row, row, row your boat," then another voice joins it in imitation, followed by a third voice and finally a fourth, creating a four-part polyphonic texture.

Round: *Row, Row, Row Your Boat* (in 4-voice imitation):  🎵 iMusic iMaterials

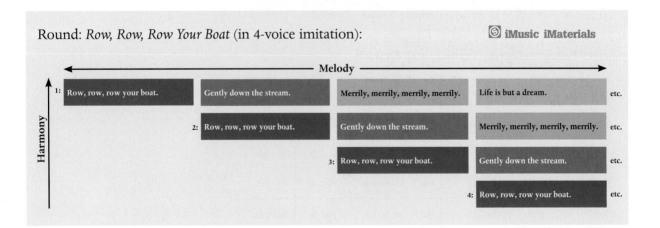

# Musical Texture and the Listener

Different textures require different kinds of listening. Monophonic music has only one focus—the single line of melody unfolding in real time. In homophonic music, the primary focus is on the main melody with subordinate harmonies as accompaniment. Indeed, much of the music we have heard since childhood—including many traditional and popular styles—consists of melody and accompanying chords. Homorhythmic texture is easily recognizable as well, in its simple, vertical conception and hymnlike movement. Here, the melody is still the most obvious line. Polyphonic music, with several independent melodies woven together, requires more experienced listening. The simplest polyphonic texture is the round. With practice, we can hear the roles of individual voices and determine how they relate to each other, providing texture throughout a musical work.

## Critical Thinking

**1.** How does texture in music compare with the weave of a fabric?

**2.** What role does imitation play in determining musical texture?

---

**LISTENING ACTIVITY: TEXTURE**

## Handel: "Hallelujah Chorus" from *Messiah*

Listen to Handel's famous "Hallelujah Chorus"(StudySpace, Chapter 5) to hear changing textures. Then complete the activity below.

____ **1.** At the opening, the chorus sings the word "Hallelujah" in a(n) _____ texture.
  **a.** imitative
  **b.** homorhythmic

____ **2.** At the words "For the Lord God Omnipotent reigneth," the texture changes to:
  **a.** monophonic
  **b.** homophonic

____ **3.** When two ideas are combined ("Hallelujah" and "For the Lord Omnipotent"), the texture becomes:
  **a.** homophonic
  **b.** polyphonic

---

### Understanding Texture (from ⊙ iMusic):

Monophonic texture: **Toccata in D minor**, opening (Bach)
Homophonic texture: ***Surprise* Symphony No. 94, II** (Haydn)
Homorhythmic texture: **Alla hornpipe**, from *Water Music* (Handel)
Heterophonic texture: *Los Jilicatas* (Peru, panpipes)
Changing texture: *Simple Gifts* (Shaker hymn)
Polyphonic texture: *Brandenburg Concerto* **No. 1, I** (Bach)
Imitation: **Contrapunctus 1**, from *The Art of Fugue* (Bach)

# 6 Musical Form

> "The principal function of form is to advance our understanding. It is the organization of a piece that helps the listener to keep the idea in mind, to follow its development, its growth, its elaboration, its fate."
>
> —**Arnold Schoenberg**

## KEY POINTS

⑤ **StudySpace** wwnorton.com/enjoy

- **Form** is the organizing principle in music; its basic elements are repetition, contrast, and variation.
- **Strophic form**, common in songs, features repeated music for each stanza of text.
- **Binary form** (**A-B**) and **ternary form** (**A-B-A**) are basic structures in music.
- A **theme** is a melodic idea in a large-scale work and can be broken into small, component fragments (**motives**). A **sequence** results when a motive is repeated at a different pitch.

- Many cultures use **call-and-response** (or **responsorial**) music, a repetitive style involving a soloist and a group. Some music is created spontaneously in performance, through **improvisation**.
- An **ostinato** is the repetition of a short melodic, rhythmic, or harmonic pattern.
- Large-scale compositions, such as symphonies and sonatas, are divided into sections, or **movements**.

**F**orm refers to a work's structure or shape, the way the elements of a composition have been combined, or balanced, by the composer to make it understandable to the listener. In all the arts, a balance is required between unity and variety, symmetry and asymmetry, activity and rest. Nature too has embodied this balance in the forms of plant and animal life and in what is perhaps the supreme achievement—the human form.

## Structure and Design in Music

Repetition and contrast

Music of all cultures mirrors life in its basic structural elements of **repetition** and **contrast**—the familiar and the new. Repetition fixes the material in our minds and satisfies our need for the familiar, while contrast stimulates our interest and feeds our desire for change. Every kind of musical work, from a nursery rhyme to a symphony, has a conscious structure. One of the most common in vocal music, both popular and classical, is **strophic form**, in which the same melody is repeated with each stanza of the text. In this structure, while the music within a stanza offers contrast, its repetition also binds the song together.

Strophic form

Variation

One principle of form that falls between repetition and contrast is **variation**, where some aspects of the music are altered but the original is still recognizable.

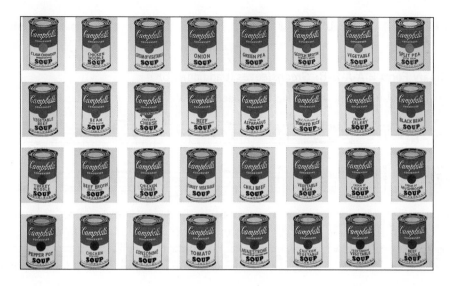

This famous painting by **Andy Warhol** (1928–1987) entitled *32 Campbell Soup Cans* shows the reliance of artists on the basic elements of repetition and variation.

We hear this formal technique when we listen to a new arrangement of a well-known popular song: the tune is recognizable, but many features of the version we know may be changed. All musical structures are based in one way or another on repetition and contrast. The forms, however, are not fixed molds into which composers pour their material. What makes each piece of music unique is the way the composer adapts a general plan to create a wholly individual combination. Performers sometimes participate in shaping a composition. In works based mostly on *improvisation* (pieces created spontaneously in performance—typical of jazz, rock, and in certain non-Western styles), all the elements described above—repetition, contrast, and variation—play a role. We will see that in jazz, musicians organize their improvised melodies within a highly structured, pre-established harmonic pattern, time frame, and melodic outline that is understood by all the performers. In many parts of Asia, improvisation is a refined and classical art, where the seemingly free and rhapsodic spinning out of the music is tied to a prescribed musical process that results in a lacework of variations. Thus, even when a piece is created on the spot, a balance of structural principles is present.

Improvisation

*In His Own Words*

Improvisation is not the expression of accident but rather of the accumulated yearnings, dreams, and wisdom of our very soul.

—*Yehudi Menuhin*

## Two-Part and Three-Part Form

There are two basic structural patterns found in art and in music. Two-part, or *binary* form, is based on a statement and a departure, without a return to the complete opening section. Three-part, or *ternary*, form extends the idea of statement and departure by bringing back the first section. Formal patterns are generally outlined with letters: binary form as **A-B** and ternary form as **A-B-A** (illustrated in the chart on p. 32).

Both two-part and three-part forms are common in short pieces such as songs and dances. Ternary form, with its logical symmetry and its balance of the outer sections against the contrasting middle one, constitutes a clear-cut formation that is favored by architects and painters as well as musicians.

## The Building Blocks of Form

When a melodic idea is used as a building block in the construction of a larger musical work, we call it a *theme*. The introduction of a theme and its elaboration    Theme

## BINARY AND TERNARY FORM

**Binary Form = A-A-B-B:** *Greensleeves* (traditional, UK)

Statement **A** (repeated with varied final cadences):

Departure **B** (with different cadences):

**Ternary Form = A-B-A:** *Simple Gifts* (Shaker hymn)

Statement **A** (repeated):

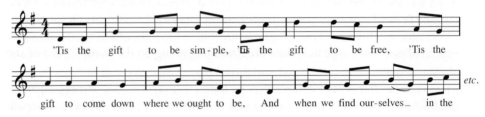

Departure **B** (ending resembles **A** with new text):

Repeated Statement **A**:

is the essence of musical thinking. This process of growth has its parallel in writing, when an idea—a topic sentence—is stated at the beginning of a paragraph and enlarged upon and developed by the author. Just as each sentence leads logically from one to the next, every phrase in a musical work takes up where the one before left off and continues convincingly to the next. The expansion of a theme, achieved by varying its melodic outline, rhythm, or harmony, is considered **Thematic development**   *thematic development*. This is one of the most important techniques in musical composition and requires both imagination and craft on the part of the creator.

The use of thematic development is generally too complex for short pieces, where a simple contrast between sections and modest expansion of material usually supply the necessary continuity. But thematic development is necessary in larger forms of music, where it provides clarity, coherence, and logic.

Certain procedures aid the process of musical development. The simplest is repetition, which may be either exact or varied. Or the idea may be restated at a higher or lower pitch level; this restatement is known as a *sequence*. A melody, or theme, can be broken up into its component parts, or motives. A *motive* is the smallest fragment of a theme that forms a melodic-rhythmic unit. Motives are the cells of musical growth, which, when repeated, varied, and combined into new patterns, impart the qualities of evolution and expansion. These musical building blocks can be seen even in simple songs, such as the popular national tune *America* (see below). In this piece, the opening three-note motive ("My country") is repeated in sequence (at a different pitch level) on the words "Sweet land of." A longer melodic idea is treated sequentially in the second line of the work, where the musical phrase "Land where my fathers died" is repeated one note lower beginning on the words "Land of the pilgrim's pride."

Whatever the length or style of a composition, it will show the principles of repetition and contrast, of unity and variety. One formal practice based on repetition and heard in music throughout much of the world is *call-and-response*, or

The Gare de Saint-Exupéry, a modern train station in Lyon, France, designed by the Spanish architect Santiago Calatrava, shows the importance of symmetrical patterns in architecture.

## MOTIVE AND SEQUENCES

 iMusic iMaterials

*America* (also *God Save the Queen*):

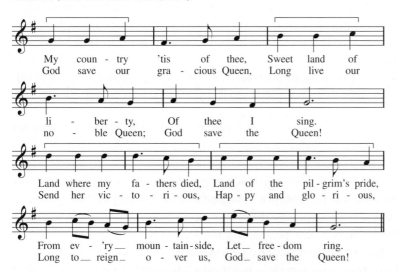

(Brackets show repeated motives at different pitch levels, or in sequences.)

## LISTENING ACTIVITY: MUSICAL FORM

# Tchaikovsky: *March*, from *The Nutcracker*

Listen to the march from the popular ballet *The Nutcracker* (StudySpace, Chapter 6) to test your ability in hearing the form, or structure, of a composition. Then complete the questions below.

____ **1.** The opening section sounds marchlike, with accented beats and alternations between instrumental groups. Eventually, a total change of character marks a short, new section. At approximately which time interval from the beginning does this appear?

    **a.** 30 seconds
    **b.** just after 1 minute.

____ **2.** Which elements below seem to change (choose as many as apply)?

    **a.** instruments    **c.** tempo
    **b.** meter    **d.** mood

____ **3.** When the opening section returns, is it exactly the same?

    **a.** yes
    **b.** no

____ **4.** Which best describes the overall form of this march?

    **a.** binary (**A-A-B-B**)
    **b.** ternary (**A-B-A**)

____ **5.** Which of these formal elements do you hear?

    **a.** repetition
    **b.** contrast
    **c.** variation

**Understanding Form (from 🎵 iMusic):**

Variation: ***Pop Goes the Weasel*** (traditional, UK)
Improvisation: ***Amazing Grace*** (traditional hymn)
Strophic form: ***Lullaby*** (Brahms)
Binary form: **Minuet in D** (*Anna Magdelena Notebook*)
Motive and sequence: **Symphony No. 5** (Beethoven)
Responsorial: **If I Had a Hammer** (Pete Seeger)

---

**Responsorial performance**

***responsorial music***. This style of performance, predominant in early Western church music, is also common in music of African, Native American, and African-American cultures, and involves a singing leader who is imitated by a chorus of followers. Another widely used structural procedure linked to the principle of repetition is ***ostinato,*** a short musical pattern—melodic, rhythmic, or harmonic—that is repeated throughout a work or a major section of a composition. One well-known work that uses this technique is the Pachelbel Canon in D in which rich string lines unfold gradually over an ever-present bass pattern. This unifying technique is especially prevalent in popular styles such as blues, jazz, rock, and rap, which rely on repeated harmonies that provide a scaffolding for musical development.

🎵 **iMusic**

Pachelbel: Canon in D

**Movement**

Music composition is an organic form in which the individual tones are bound together within a phrase, the phrases within a section, the sections within a ***movement*** (a complete, comparatively independent division of a large-scale work), and the movements within the work as a whole—just as a novel binds together the individual words, phrases, sentences, paragraphs, chapters, and parts.

### Critical Thinking

**1.** Why do composers need to think about form in music?

**2.** How is a larger form constructed from small ideas in music?

# 7 Musical Expression: Tempo and Dynamics

> "Any composition must necessarily possess its unique tempo. . . . A piece of mine can survive almost anything but a wrong or uncertain tempo."
>
> **—Igor Stravinsky**

## KEY POINTS

**StudySpace** wwnorton.com/enjoy

- **Tempo** is the rate of speed, or pace, of the music.
- We use Italian terms to describe musical tempo: some of the most common are **allegro** (fast), **moderato** (moderate), **adagio** (quite slow), **accelerando** (speeding up), and **ritardando** (slowing down).
- **Dynamics** describe the volume, or how loud or soft the music is played; Italian terms for dynamics include **forte** (loud) and **piano** (soft).
- Composers indicate tempo and dynamics in music as a means of expression.

## The Pace of Music

We know that most Western music has steady beats underlying the movement; whether these occur slowly or rapidly determines the **tempo,** or rate of speed, of the music. Consequently, the flow of music in time involves meter patterns, governing the groupings and relative emphasis of the beats, and tempo.

Tempo carries emotional implications. We hurry our speech in moments of agitation or eagerness. Vigor and gaiety are associated with a brisk speed, just as despair usually demands a slow one. Music is a temporal art (one that moves in time), therefore its pace is of prime importance, drawing from listeners responses that are both physical and psychological.

Because of the close connection between tempo and mood, tempo markings indicate the character of the music as well as the pace. The markings, along with other indications of expression, are traditionally given in Italian. This practice reflects the domination of Italian music in Europe during the period from around 1600 to 1750, when performance directions were established. Here are some of the most common tempo markings:

| | | | |
|---|---|---|---|
| *grave* | solemn (very, very slow) | *moderato* | moderate |
| *largo* | broad (very slow) | *allegro* | fast (cheerful) |
| *adagio* | quite slow | *vivace* | lively |
| *andante* | a walking pace | *presto* | very fast |

Frequently, we also encounter modifiers such as *molto* (very), *meno* (less), *poco* (a little), and *non troppo* (not too much). Also important are terms indicating a change of tempo, among them *accelerando* (getting faster), *ritardando* (holding back, getting slower), and *a tempo* (in time, or returning to the original pace).

# Loudness and Softness

**Dynamics** denote the volume (degree of loudness or softness) at which music is played. Like tempo, dynamics can affect our emotional response. The main dynamic indications, listed below, are based on the Italian words for soft *(piano)* and loud *(forte)*.

| | |
|---|---|
| *pianissimo* (***pp***) | very soft |
| *piano* (***p***) | soft |
| *mezzo piano* (***mp***) | moderately soft |
| *mezzo forte* (***mf***) | moderately loud |
| *forte* (***f***) | loud |
| *fortissimo* (***ff***) | very loud |

Directions to change the dynamics, either suddenly or gradually, are also indicated by words or signs. Here are some of the most common ones:

| | |
|---|---|
| *crescendo* | (<): growing louder |
| *decrescendo* or *diminuendo* | (>): growing softer |
| *sforzando* (***sf***) | "forcing": accent on a single note or chord; also shown by an accent (>) |

Speed and movement are easily perceived in this photograph of the 2002 Tour de France. Here, the cyclists are racing toward the finish on Paris's famous Avenue des Champs-Élysées.

Dynamics in music may be compared to light and shade in this photograph of the sun shining through a forest of trees.

# Tempo and Dynamics as Elements of Musical Expression

The composer adds markings for tempo and dynamics to help shape the expressive content of a work. We will see that these expression marks increased in number during the late eighteenth and nineteenth centuries, when composers tried to make their intentions known ever more precisely, until in the early twentieth century when few decisions were left to the performer.

If tempo and dynamics are the domain of the composer, what is the role of performers and conductors in interpreting a musical work? Performance directions can be somewhat imprecise—what is loud or fast to one performer may be moderate in volume and tempo to another. Even when composers give precise tempo markings in their scores (the exact number of beats per minute), performers have the final say in choosing a tempo that best delivers the message of the music. And for the many styles of music—non-Western, folk, and popular, among others—that do not rely on composer directions or even printed music, the performer takes full responsibility for interpreting the music.

## *In His Own Words*

Voices, instruments, and all possible sounds—even silence itself—must tend toward one goal, which is expression.

—*C. W. Gluck*

### TEMPO AND DYNAMICS IN A MUSICAL SCORE    ⓢ **iMusic iMaterials**

Beethoven: **Symphony No. 5**, opening:

Tempo: Fast (*Allegro*) with vigor (*con brio*)
Dynamics: Very loud (*fortissimo*), then soft (*piano*)

# Haydn: *Surprise* Symphony, second movement

Let's return to this slow movement from Haydn's *Surprise* Symphony (StudySpace, Chapter 7), to determine how expressive devices like tempo and dynamics affect our response to the music. Then complete the activity below.

___ 1. Which best describes the tempo of the work?
   **a.** very slow
   **b.** walking pace
   **c.** very lively

___ 2. Based on your reply above, which Italian tempo designation best suits this work?
   **a.** Largo
   **b.** Andante
   **c.** Vivace

___ 3. Which best describes the volume changes heard near the opening?
   **a.** soft, then louder, then very loud
   **b.** soft, then softer, then very loud
   **c.** loud, then softer, then even softer

___ 4. Based on your reply to question 3, which Italian terms best describe the dynamics at the opening ?
   **a.** *piano, pianissimo, fortissimo*
   **b.** *piano, mezzo forte, fortissimo*
   **c.** *forte, piano, pianissimo*

___ 5. What makes the "surprise" in the title?
   **a.** loud chord
   **b.** faster tempo
   **c.** slowing of the tempo

## Understanding Tempo and Dynamics (from ⊚ iMusic):

**TEMPOS:**
*Adagio*: **Clarinet Concerto** (Mozart)
*Andante*: **Lullaby** (Brahms)
*Moderato*: **Für Elise** (Beethoven)
*Allegro*: **Symphony No. 5** (Beethoven)
*Presto*: **William Tell Overture** (Rossini)

**DYNAMICS:**
*Pianissimo*: **Moonlight Sonata** (Beethoven)
*Piano*: **Clarinet Concerto** (Mozart)
*Forte*: **Eine kleine Nachtmusik**, III (Mozart)
*Fortissimo*: **Ode to Joy** (Beethoven)
*Crescendo*: **William Tell Overture** (Rossini)
Changing dynamics: **Toreador Song**, from **Carmen** (Bizet)

## Critical Thinking

**1.** How does tempo affect our response to music?

**2.** How do dynamics influence our response to music?

**3.** What role does the performer take in expressing the music?

# 8 Voices and Musical Instrument Families

"It was my idea to make my voice work in the same way as a trombone or violin—not sounding like them but 'playing' the voice like those instruments."

**—Frank Sinatra**

**KEY POINTS**

**StudySpace** wwnorton.com/enjoy

- Properties of sound include pitch, duration, volume, and *timbre*, or *tone color*.

- An *instrument* generates vibrations and transmits them into the air.

- The human voice can be categorized into various ranges, including *soprano* and *alto* for female voices, and *tenor* and *bass* for male voices.

- The world instrument classification system divides into *aerophones* (such as flutes or horns), *chordophones* (such as violins or guitars), *idiophones* (such as bells or cymbals) and *membranophones* (drums).

## Musical Timbre

We know that musical tone has pitch, duration, and volume. A fourth property of sound—known as *tone color*, or *timbre*—accounts for the striking differences in the sound quality of instruments. It is what makes a trumpet sound altogether different from a guitar or a drum. Timbre is influenced by a number of factors, such as the size, shape, and proportions of the instrument, the material from which it is made, and the manner in which the vibration is produced. A string, for example, may be bowed, plucked, or struck.

People produce music vocally (by singing or chanting) or by playing a musical instrument. An *instrument* is a mechanism that generates musical vibrations and launches them into the air. Each voice type and instrument has a limited melodic range (the distance from the lowest to the highest tone) and dynamic range (the degree of softness or loudness beyond which the voice or instrument cannot go). We describe a specific area in the range of an instrument or voice, such as low, middle, or high, as its *register*.

**Instrument**

*In Their Own Words*

If you can walk you can dance. If you can talk you can sing.

—*Zimbabwe proverb*

## The Voice as Instrument

The human voice is the most natural of all musical instruments; it is also one of the most widely used—all cultures have some form of vocal music. Each person's voice

### Luciano Pavarotti

*"Am I afraid of high notes? Of course I am afraid. What sane man is not?"*

Meet Luciano Pavarotti (1935–2007), one of the greatest operatic tenors of all times. He is deservedly the most famous of The Three Tenors (the other two are Plácido Domingo and José Carreras), whose concerts and media events have brought operatic favorites to the masses.

Born in Modena, Italy, to a working-class family, Pavarotti first dreamed of becoming a professional soccer player but soon turned his focus toward teaching and music. He began singing in local opera houses, making his debut at Milan's famous La Scala in 1965, singing the lead role in the powerful drama *La bohème* by Puccini. His shining career in opera and as a soloist, as well as his focus on humanitarian issues (working with the Red Cross and for refugees), took him across continents and into the hearts of people around the globe.

Pavarotti's final performance was at the 2006 Winter Olympics in Turin, Italy, where he thrilled hundreds of thousands with Puccini's beloved aria *Nessun dorma*. He died in 2007 of pancreatic cancer, a legend in his own time. One only has to watch him sing to understand his passion for music-making.

**Check out these recordings by Pavarotti:** *Nessun dorma*, from the opera *Turandot*, and *La donna è mobile*, from the opera *Rigoletto*, both on the album *Pavarotti's Greatest Hits*; *O sole mio*, from the album *Best of the Three Tenors*

---

has a particular quality, or character, and range. Our standard designations for vocal ranges, from highest to lowest, are **soprano, mezzo-soprano**, and **alto** (short for **contralto**) for female voices, and **tenor, baritone**, and **bass** for male voices.

In earlier eras, Western social and religious customs severely restricted women's participation in public musical events. Thus young boys, and occasionally adult males with soprano- or alto-range voices, sang female roles in church music and on the stage. In the sixteenth century, women singers came into prominence in secular (nonreligious) music. Tenors were most often featured as soloists in early opera; the lower male voices, baritone and bass, became popular soloists in the eighteenth century. In other cultures, the sound of women's voices has always been preferred for certain styles of music: lullabies, for example, are often the domain of women.

Throughout the ages, the human voice has served as a model for instrument builders and players who have sought to duplicate its lyric beauty, expressiveness, and ability to produce **vibrato** (a throbbing effect) on their instruments.

## The World of Musical Instruments

The diversity of musical instruments played around the world defies description. Since every conceivable method of sound production is used, and every possible raw material employed, it would be impossible to list them all here. However, specialists have devised a method of classifying instruments that is based solely on the way their sound

A European bagpipe (aerophone) often used in folk music, sounds a drone under the melodic line.

## Meet the Performers

### Anoushka Shankar

"I love playing with other people because you become part of a greater musical endeavor."

Meet Anoushka Shankar (born 1981), the daughter of the preeminent sitar player Ravi Shankar and an extremely talented musician in her own right. She performed widely with her father throughout her childhood and signed a recording contract of her own at the age of sixteen, releasing her first album, *Anoushka*, in 1998. Her most recent album is *Breathing under Water* (2007), which mixes classical sitar and electonica beats, performed with her half-sister Norah Jones, Sting, and her father. In 2002 she played a concert with her father in memory of Beatle George Harrison, who studied sitar with Ravi Shankar.

A recipient of numerous awards, Anoushka is clearly a rising star in the music world and the obvious successor to her father's legacy. Along with the British rock group Jethro Tull, she organized "A Billion Hands" Concert in 2008 as a benefit for victims of the attacks in Mumbai, India. "As a musician, this is how I speak, how I express the anger within me." Anoushka is also a strong supporter of animal rights.

**Check out this Anoushka Shankar recording:** *Oceanic, Part 2,* performed with Ravi Shankar, on the album *Breathing under Water*

---

is generated. The system uses four basic categories. *Aerophones* produce sound by using air. Common instruments in this grouping are flutes, whistles, accordions, bagpipes, and horns—in short, nearly any wind instrument. *Chordophones* are instruments that produce sound from a vibrating string stretched between two points. The string may be set in motion by bowing, plucking, or striking, so the instruments are as disparate as the violin, harp, guitar, Chinese hammered dulcimer (yangquin), and Indian sitar (see illustration above).

*Idiophones* produce sound from the substance of the instrument itself. They may be struck, shaken, scraped, or rubbed. Examples of idiophones are bells, rattles, xylophones, and cymbals—in other words, a wide variety of percussion instruments. *Membranophones* are drum-type instruments that are sounded from tightly stretched membranes. These instruments can be struck, plucked, rubbed, or even sung into, thus setting the skin in vibration.

**Aerophones**

**Chordophones**

**Idiophones**

(Left) A Chinese band, with children playing cymbals (idiophones).

(Right) A drum (membranophone) ensemble from Burundi in Central Africa.

# Simple Gifts (traditional hymn), arranged for choir

Listen to the choral work *Simple Gifts* (StudySpace, Chapter 8) to see if you can hear the different vocal timbres as they enter one by one. Then complete the activity below.

___ **1.** Which of these vocal parts is a high men's voice range?
  **a.** sopranos   **c.** tenors
  **b.** altos       **d.** basses

___ **2.** Which vocal section begins the song?
  **a.** sopranos   **c.** tenors
  **b.** altos       **d.** basses

___ **3.** Which vocal section enters next?
  **a.** sopranos   **c.** tenors
  **b.** altos       **d.** basses

___ **4.** In the quick alternation between men and women on the words " 'Tis the gift," which group sings this idea first?
  **a.** men's voices
  **b.** women's voices

Listen to the examples below from around the world (StudySpace, Chapter 8) and determine which sound production method(s) is used for each. You may select more than one answer, if two instrument types are heard.

  **a.** blown   **b.** bowed   **c.** struck

___ **5.** *Avaz of Bayete Esfahan* (Iran)

___ **6.** *Dougla Dance* (Trinidad)

___ **7.** *Skye Crofters* (Scotland)

___ **8.** *In a Mountain Path* (China)

___ **9.** *Los Jilicatas* (Peru)

---

### Understanding Voices and World Instruments (from ⊚ iMusic):

**VOICES:**
Soprano: *Lullaby* (Brahms)
Mezzo-soprano: *Amazing Grace* (traditional hymn)
Tenor: *Tonight*, from *West Side Story* (Bernstein)
Baritone: *Toreador Song*, from *Carmen* (Bizet)
Vocal quartet (soprano, alto, tenor, bass): *Row, Row, Row Your Boat*

**INSTRUMENTS:**
Aerophones: *Los Jilicatas* (panpipes, Peru)
            *Skye Crofters* (bagpipe, Scotland)
Idiophones: *Dougla Dance* (steel drums, Trinidad)
            *Tabuh Kenilu Sawik* (gongs, Indonesia)
Chordophones: *Avaz of Bayate Esfahan* (santur, Iran)
              *In a Mountain Path* (bowed erhu, China)
Membranophones: *Gota* (drums, Ghana, West Africa)
                *Bhimpalási* (tabla, North India)

In the next chapter, we will review the instruments used most frequently in Western music. Throughout the book, however, you will learn about other instruments associated with popular and art music cultures around the world that have influenced the Western tradition.

### Critical Thinking

**1.** How do we differentiate the sound of a particular voice or instrument?

**2.** How does the scientific classification system organize world instruments?

# 9 Western Musical Instruments

"In music, instruments perform the function of the colors employed in painting."

—Honoré De Balzac

## KEY POINTS

> ⑥ **StudySpace** wwnorton.com/enjoy

- The four families of Western instruments are *strings*, *woodwinds*, *brass*, and *percussion*.
- String instruments (chordophones) are sounded by *bowing* and *plucking*.
- Bowed strings include *violin*, *viola*, *cello*, and *double bass*; plucked strings include *harp* and *guitar*.
- Woodwind instruments (aerophones) include *flute*, *oboe*, *clarinet*, *bassoon*, and *saxophone*.

- Brass instruments (aerophones) include *trumpet*, *French horn*, *trombone*, and *tuba*.
- Percussion instruments include idiophones (*xylophone*, *cymbals*, *triangle*) and membranophones (*timpani*, *bass drum*); some instruments are pitched (*chimes*) while others are unpitched (*tambourine*).
- Keyboard instruments, such as *piano* and *organ*, do not fit neatly into the Western classification system.

The instruments of the Western world—and especially those of the orchestra—may be categorized into four familiar groups: strings, woodwinds, brass, and percussion. We will see, however, that all woodwinds are not made of wood, nor do they share a common means of sound production. Furthermore, certain instruments do not fit neatly into any of these convenient categories (the piano, for example, is both a string and a percussion instrument).

## String Instruments

The string family, all chordophones, includes two types of instruments: those that are *bowed* and those that are *plucked*. The bowed string family has four principal members: violin, viola, violoncello, and double bass, each with four strings (double basses sometimes have five) that are set vibrating by drawing a bow across them. The bow is held in the right hand, while the left hand is used to "stop" the string by pressing a finger down at a particular point, thereby leaving a certain portion of the string free to vibrate. By stopping the string at another point, the performer changes the length of the vibrating portion, and with it the rate of vibration and the pitch.

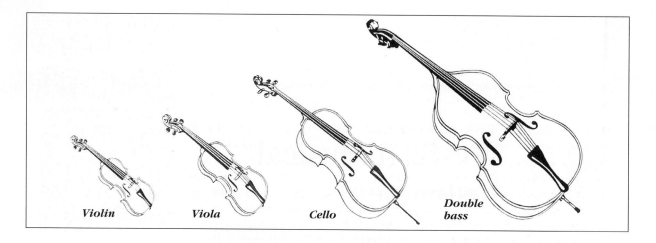

Violin   Viola   Cello   Double bass

Violin

The **violin** evolved to its present form at the hands of the brilliant instrument makers who flourished in Italy from around 1600 to 1750 (see Btw, p. 131). It is capable of brilliance and dramatic effect, subtle nuances from soft to loud, and great agility in rapid passages throughout its extremely wide range.

Viola

The **viola** is somewhat larger than the violin and thus has a lower range. Its strings are longer, thicker, and heavier. The tone is husky in the low register, somber and penetrating in the high. It often fills in the harmony, or it often may double another part. One instrument is said to **double** (reinforce) another when it plays the same notes an octave higher or lower.

Cello

The **violoncello**, popularly known as **cello,** is lower in range than the viola and is notable for its singing quality and its dark resonance in the low register. Cellos often play the melody and they enrich the sound with their full timbre.

Double bass

The **double bass,** known also as a **contrabass** or **bass viol,** is the lowest of the string instruments of the orchestra. Accordingly, it plays the bass part—that is, the foundation of the harmony. Its deep tones support the cello part an octave lower.

These four string instruments constitute the core or "heart of the orchestra," a designation that indicates the section's versatility and importance.

Orchestral string instruments can be played in many styles and can produce

(Left) Violinist Hilary Hahn.

(Right) Julie Barnes Spring, harpist for the Toronto Symphony Orchestra.

## Yo-Yo Ma

*"When you learn something from people, or from a culture, you accept it as a gift, and it is your lifelong commitment to preserve it and build on it."*

Meet Yo-Yo Ma (born 1955), the revered virtuoso cellist who organized the Silk Road Project, which brings together musicians from across the globe. This French-born, Chinese-American musician began studying cello at age four and performed for President John F. Kennedy in 1962, when he was only seven. Forty-seven years later, he performed for another president, Barack Obama, at his inauguration in January 2009, debuting John Williams's *Air and Simple Gifts.*

Yo-Yo Ma studied at Columbia and Harvard universities, after which he pursued a highly successful solo career. His recordings have won innumerable Grammy awards, some for recordings that defy categorization because they encompass so many genres. He is committed to educating people about all kinds of music: his Silk Road recordings feature music heard along the trade routes that connect Asia with other continents; his Appalachian recordings celebrate the traditional music of the mountainous regions of the southeastern United States; and his recent *Songs of Joy & Peace* features popular, classical, sacred, and secular music for world holidays.

**Check out these recordings by Yo-Yo Ma:** *Air and Simple Gifts,* by John Williams; *Allemande,* from Suite for Solo Cello, No 1 in G major, by J. S. Bach

---

**Special effects**

many special effects. They excel at playing *legato* (smoothly, connecting the notes) as well as the opposite, *staccato* (with notes short and detached). A special effect, *pizzicato* (plucked), is created when a performer plucks the string with a finger instead of using the bow. *Vibrato,* a throbbing effect, is achieved by a rapid wrist-and-finger movement on the string that slightly alters the pitch. For a *glissando,* a finger of the left hand slides along the string while the right hand draws the bow, thereby sounding all the pitches under the left-hand finger, in one swooping sound. *Tremolo,* the rapid repetition of a tone through a quick up-and-down movement of the bow, is associated with suspense and excitement. No less important is the *trill,* a rapid alternation between a tone and one adjacent to it.

String instruments are capable of playing several tones simultaneously, thereby producing harmony: *double-stopping* means playing two strings at once; playing three or four strings together is called *triple-* or *quadruple-stopping.* Another effect is created by the *mute,* a small attachment that fits over the bridge, muffling the sound. *Harmonics* are crystalline tones in a very high register that are produced by lightly touching the string at certain points while the bow is drawn across the string.

**Harp**

Two popular plucked string instruments are the harp and the guitar. The *harp* is one of the oldest of musical instruments, with a home in many cultures outside Europe. Its plucked strings, whose pitches are changed by means of pedals, produce an ethereal tone. Chords on the harp are frequently played in broken form—that is, the tones are sounded one after another instead of simultaneously. From this technique comes the term *arpeggio,* which means a broken chord (*arpa* is Italian for "harp"). Arpeggios can be created in a variety of ways on many instruments.

**Guitar**

The *guitar,* another old instrument, dating back at least to the Middle Ages, probably originated in the Middle East. A favorite solo instrument, it is associated today with folk and popular music as well as classical styles. The standard *acoustic* (as opposed to electric) *guitar* is made of wood and has a fretted fingerboard and six nylon strings, which are plucked with the fingers of the right hand or with a pick. The *electric guitar,* an electronically amplified instrument capable of many

(Left) Milt Hinton playing the double bass.

(Right) Guitarist Carlos Santana, during the 50th International Song Festival in Chile, February 2009.

specialized techniques, comes in two main types: the hollow-bodied (or electro-acoustic), favored by jazz and popular musicians, and the solid-bodied, used more often by rock musicians. Related to the guitar are such traditional instruments as the *banjo* and *mandolin*.

 **Video**

# Woodwind Instruments

Woodwind instruments (aerophones) produce sound with a column of air vibrating within a pipe that has fingerholes along its length. When one or another of these holes is opened or closed, the length of the vibrating air column within the pipe is changed. Woodwind players are capable of remarkable agility on their instruments by means of an intricate mechanism of keys arranged to suit the natural position of the fingers.

This group is less homogeneous than the strings. Nowadays woodwinds are not necessarily made of wood, and they employ several different methods of setting up

Oboe players in an orchestra.

## Meet the Performers

### James Galway

*"I do not consider myself as having mastered the flute, but I get a real kick out of trying."*

Meet Sir James Galway (born 1939), the "man with the golden flute." Born in Northern Ireland, Galway had a highly successful career as an orchestral flutist until 1975, when he decided to focus on solo concerts. Since then, he has enjoyed an international reputation, performing with leading orchestras and chamber groups as well as in pop concerts across every continent. Along the way, he has played for the British Royal family, three American presidents, the pope, and even the empress of Japan. He has also performed with a wide range of musicians such as Ray Charles, Elton John, Joni Mitchell, Stevie Wonder, the traditional Irish music group The Chieftains, and Pink Floyd. His list of awards is staggering, including several Grammys, being knighted by Queen Elizabeth II in 2001, and inducted into the Hollywood Bowl Hall of Fame in 2008. At age seventy, he still performs regularly.

Galway is dedicated to various humanitarian and charitable causes and especially to the education of young flutists. He is currently collaborating with a major flute manufacturer to produce a new, high-quality student instrument, to be called "the Galway Spirit."

**Check out these recordings by James Galway:**
*Badinerie,* from Orchestral Suite No. 2 in B minor, by J. S. Bach; *The Dark Island,* from the album *The Celtic Minstrel* (with The Chieftians)

---

vibration: blowing across a mouth hole (flute family), blowing into a mouthpiece that has a single reed (clarinet and saxophone families), or blowing into a mouthpiece fitted with a double reed (oboe and bassoon families). They do, however, have one important feature in common: the holes in their pipes. In addition, their timbres are such that composers think of them and write for them as a group.

The ***flute*** is the soprano voice of the woodwind family. Its tone is cool and velvety in the expressive low register, and often brilliant in the upper part of its range. The present-day flute, made of a metal alloy rather than wood, is a cylindrical tube, closed at one end, that is held horizontally. The player blows across a mouth hole cut in the side of the pipe near the closed end. The flute is used frequently as a melody instrument—its timbre stands out against the orchestra—and offers the

**Flute**

(Left) Bassoon players in an orchestra.

(Right) Richard Stolzman playing the clarinet in Carnegie Hall.

performer great versatility in playing rapid repeated notes, scales, and trills. The *piccolo* (from the Italian *flauto piccolo,* "little flute") is actually the highest pitched instrument in the orchestra. In its upper register, it takes on a shrillness that is easily heard even when the orchestra is playing *fortissimo.*

**Oboe**

The *oboe* continues to be made of wood. The player blows directly into a double reed, which consists of two thin strips of cane bound together with a narrow passage for air. The oboe's timbre, generally described as nasal and reedy, is often associated with pastoral effects and nostalgic moods. The oboe traditionally sounds the tuning note for the other instruments of the orchestra. The *English horn* is an alto oboe. Its wooden tube is wider and longer than that of the oboe and ends in a pear-shaped opening called a *bell,* which largely accounts for its soft, expressive timbre.

**Clarinet**

The *clarinet* has a single reed, a small thin piece of cane fastened against its chisel-shaped mouthpiece. The instrument possesses a smooth, liquid tone, as well as a remarkably wide range in pitch and volume. It too has an easy command of rapid scales, trills, and repeated notes. The *bass clarinet,* one octave lower in range than the clarinet, has a rich dark tone and a wide dynamic range.

**Bassoon**

The *bassoon,* another double-reed instrument, possesses a tone that is weighty in the low register and reedy and intense in the upper. Capable of a hollow-sounding staccato and wide leaps that can sound humorous, it is at the same time a highly expressive instrument. The *contrabassoon* produces the lowest tone of the wood-winds. Its function in the woodwind section of supplying a foundation for the harmony may be compared with that of the double bass among the strings.

**Saxophone**

The *saxophone,* invented by the Belgian Adolphe Sax in 1840, is the most recent of the woodwind instruments. It was created by combining the features of several other instruments—the single reed of the clarinet along with a conical bore and the metal body of the brass instruments. There are various sizes of saxophone: the most common are soprano, alto, tenor, and baritone. Used only occasionally in the orchestra, the saxophone had become the characteristic instrument of the jazz band by the 1920s, and it has remained a favorite sound in popular music today.

⊚ **Video**

# Brass Instruments

The main instruments of the brass family (also aerophones) are the trumpet, French horn (or horn), trombone, and tuba. All these instruments have cup-shaped mouthpieces attached to a length of metal tubing that flares at the end into a bell. The column of air within the tube is set vibrating by the tightly stretched lips of the player, which are buzzed together. Going from one pitch to another involves not only mechanical means, such as a slide or valves, but also muscular control to vary the pressure of the lips and breath. Brass and woodwind instrument players often speak about their *embouchure,* referring to the entire oral mechanism of lips, lower facial muscles, and jaw.

Robert Frear plays trumpet with a student group.

Trumpets and horns were widely used in the ancient world. At first, they were fashioned from animal horns and tusks and were used chiefly for religious ceremonies and military signals.

The *trumpet,* highest in pitch of the brass family, possesses a brilliant, clear timbre. It is often associated with ceremonial display. The trumpet can also be muted, using a pear-shaped, metal or cardboard device that is inserted in the bell to achieve a muffled, buzzy sound. The *French horn* is descended from the ancient hunting horn. Its mellow resonance can be mysteriously remote in soft passages and sonorous in loud ones. The muted horn has a distant sound. The horn is played with the right hand inserted in the bell and is sometimes "stopped" by plugging

(Left) Joshua Redman playing tenor saxophone.

(Right) The French horn section of the orchestra.

the bell with the hand, producing an eerie and rasping quality. The timbre of the horn blends well with woodwinds, brasses, and strings.

The *trombone*—the Italian word means "large trumpet"—has a full and rich sound in the tenor range. In place of valves, it features a movable U-shaped slide that alters the length of the vibrating air column in the tube. The *tuba* is the bass instrument of the brass family. Like the string bass and contrabassoon, it furnishes the foundation for the harmony. The tuba adds depth to the orchestral tone, and a dark resonance ranging from velvety softness to a rumbling growl.

Trombone

Tuba

Other brass instruments are used in concert and brass bands as well as marching bands. Among these is the *cornet*, which is similar to the trumpet. In the

## Meet the Performers

### Carol Jantsch

"I always knew I was sort of ahead of the game."

Meet Carol Jantsch (born 1985), the principal tuba player in the Philadelphia Orchestra. After studying piano and euphonium (a smaller tuba-like instrument), she settled on the tuba, graduating *summa cum laude* from the University of Michigan in 2006. While a senior there, she auditioned for and won the prestigious orchestra seat at the young age of twenty. She is not only the youngest member of the Philadelphia Orchestra but also the first woman to earn a tuba position in a major U.S. orchestra. Jantsch certainly defied the odds in this male-dominated profession, besting nearly two hundred competitors with her lyrical playing and luxurious sound. The orchestra's conductor insists she plays the unwieldy tuba "like a flute." While some believe women do not have sufficient lung capacity to play the tuba, Jantsch found hers measures up with her male counterparts.

Carol Jantsch has performed as a soloist with numerous orchestras as well as with the United States Marine Band. She is in demand as an instructor for various workshops and also teaches at the Curtis Institute, one of the premier music conservatories in America. In 2009, she released her first solo recording, entitled *Cascades*. She is a competitor in her leisure time as well, participating in Ultimate Frisbee tournaments and even in a tuba-throwing competition in Finland.

**Check out these recordings from Carol Jantsch's album *Cascades*:** *Scaramouche,* by Milhaud; Suite for Two Guitars by Piazzolla, arranged for tuba.

Trombonist Isrea Butler.

early twentieth century, the cornet was very popular in concert bands. The **bugle,** which evolved from the military (or field) trumpet of early times, has a powerful tone that carries well in the open air. Since it has no valves, it is able to sound only certain tones of the scale, which accounts for the familiar pattern of duty calls in the army. The **fluegelhorn,** often used in jazz and brass bands, is really a valved bugle with a wide bell. The **euphonium** is a tenor-range instrument whose shape resembles the tuba. And the **sousaphone,** an adaptation of the tuba designed by the American bandmaster John Philip Sousa (see p. 321), features a forward bell and is coiled to rest over the shoulder of the marching player.

## Percussion Instruments

⊚ **Video**

The percussion instruments of the orchestra are used to accentuate the rhythm, generate excitement at the climaxes, and inject splashes of color into the orchestral sound.

The percussion family (encompassing a vast array of idiophones and membranophones) is divided into two categories: instruments capable of producing definite pitches, and those that produce an indefinite pitch. In the former group are the **Timpani** **timpani,** or **kettledrums,** which are generally played in sets of two or four. The timpani has a hemispheric copper shell across which is stretched a "head" of plastic or calfskin held in place by a metal ring. A pedal mechanism enables the player to change the tension of the head, and with it the pitch. The instrument is played with two padded sticks. Its dynamic range extends from a mysterious rumble to a thunderous roll. The timpani first arrived in Western Europe from the Middle East, where Turks on horseback used them in combination with trumpets (see HTTN 2, p. 87).

**Xylophone** Also among the pitched percussion instruments are several members of the **xylophone** family; instruments of this general type are used in Africa, Southeast Asia, and throughout the Americas. The xylophone consists of tuned blocks of wood laid out in the shape of a keyboard. Struck with mallets with hard heads, the instrument produces a dry, crisp sound. The **marimba** is a more mellow xylophone of African origin. The **vibraphone,** used in jazz as well as art music, combines the principle of the xylophone with resonators, each containing revolving disks operated by electric motors that produce an exaggerated vibrato.

The **glockenspiel** (German for "set of bells") consists of a series of horizontal tuned steel bars of various sizes, which when struck produce a bright, metallic, bell-like sound. The **celesta,** a kind of glockenspiel that is operated by means of a keyboard, resembles a miniature upright piano. The steel plates are struck by small hammers to produce a sound like a music box. **Chimes,** or **tubular bells,** a set of tuned metal tubes of various lengths suspended from a frame and struck with a hammer, are frequently called on to simulate church bells.

**Indefinite pitch** The percussion instruments that do not produce a definite pitch include the **snare drum** (or **side drum**), a small cylindrical drum with two heads (top and bottom) stretched over a shell of wood or metal and played with two drumsticks. This instrument owes its brilliant tone to the vibrations of the lower head against taut snares (strings). The **tenor drum,** larger in size, has a wooden shell and no snares. The **bass drum** is played with a large soft-headed stick and produces a low, heavy sound. The **tom-tom** is a colloquial name given to Native American or African drums of indefinite pitch. The **tambourine** is a round, hand-held drum with "jingles"—little metal plates—inserted in its rim. The player can strike the drum

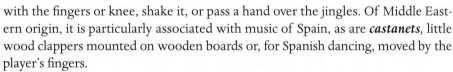

### Evelyn Glennie

*"Hearing is a form of touch. You feel it through your body, and sometimes it almost hits your face."*

Meet Dame Evelyn Glennie (born 1965), a Scottish performer and the first person in modern times to make a career as a virtuoso solo percussionist. Glennie's father played the accordion in a country dance band, and thus she began her music studies by learning folk tunes of her native Scotland. In addition to her classical training in London, she plays the Highland bagpipe and the harmonica, and collects percussion instruments from around the world.

Glennie has enjoyed a spectacular career as an international soloist, often performing works written for her. She gives over one hundred concerts a year as well as numerous workshops for students. It is not surprising that Glennie has received some eighty international awards, including the Dame Commander award from Britain's Queen Elizabeth II. She has recorded classical music as well as with the Icelandic singer Björk (on her album *Tele-*gram) and banjo virtuoso Béla Fleck.

What is so striking about Evelyn Glennie's career is that she is profoundly deaf: she hears very little and "feels" the music through her bare feet in performance, relying on her visual memory of the music, then playing instinctively. Her influence is felt not only through her innovative performances but also through her teaching and her exploration of the world of sound therapy as a means of communication.

**Check out these recordings by Evelyn Glennie:** *UFO,* by Michael Daugherty, with the Colorado Symphony Orchestra, Marin Alsop, conductor; Works by J. S. Bach, with Béla Fleck, banjo, on the album *Perpetual Motion*

with the fingers or knee, shake it, or pass a hand over the jingles. Of Middle Eastern origin, it is particularly associated with music of Spain, as are **castanets**, little wood clappers mounted on wooden boards or, for Spanish dancing, moved by the player's fingers.

The **triangle** is a slender rod of steel bent into a three-cornered shape; when struck with a steel beater, it gives off a bright, tinkling sound. **Cymbals** came to the West from central Asia during the Middle Ages. They consist of two large circular brass plates of equal size, which when struck against each other produce a shattering sound. The **gong** and the **tam-tam** are both broad circular disks of metal, suspended to a frame so as to hang freely. The tam-tam is a flat gong of indefinite pitch; however, the bossed gong, with a raised metal center, has a definite pitch. When struck with a heavy drumstick, it produces a deep roar. The gong has found its widest use in the Far East and Southeast Asia, where it is central to the ensemble known as the **gamelan** (see p. 400).

# Keyboard Instruments

A modern grand piano.

The **piano** was originally known as the **pianoforte,** Italian for "soft-loud" (see Btw, p. 36) which suggests its wide dynamic range and capacity for nuance. Its strings are struck with hammers controlled by a keyboard mechanism. The piano cannot sustain tone as well as the string and wind instruments, but in the hands of a fine performer, it is capable of producing a singing melody.

The piano has a notable capacity for brilliant scales, arpeggios, trills, rapid passages, and octaves, as well as chords. Its range from

lowest to highest pitch spans more than seven octaves, or eighty-eight semitones. It has several pedals that govern the length of time a string vibrates as well as its volume.

**Organic**

The *organ* is a type of wind instrument. The air flow to each of its many pipes is controlled by the organist from a console containing two or more keyboards and a pedal keyboard played by the feet. The organ's multicolored sonority can easily fill a huge space. Electronic keyboards, or synthesizers, capable of imitating pipe organs and other timbres, have become commonplace. (On early organ types and their music, see p. 140.)

**Harpsichord**

Another early keyboard instrument, much used in the Baroque era, is the *harpsichord*. Its sound is produced by quills that pluck its metal strings (see p. 140). The instruments described in this and the previous chapter form a vivid and diversified group, which can be heard and viewed through the Video module at StudySpace. To composers, performers, and listeners alike, they offer an endless variety of colors and shades of expression.

 **Video**

Musical Instruments

### Critical Thinking

**1.** Why are the woodwinds a less unified instrument family than the brass instruments?

**2.** Why are piano and organ difficult instruments to place in one instrument family?

---

**LISTENING ACTIVITY: WESTERN INSTRUMENTS**

## Britten: *The Young Person's Guide to the Orchestra*

We will consider this orchestral work in detail in the next chapter. Let's just listen to the first two minutes (StudySpace, Chapter 9) to see if you can recognize the different families of Western instruments when you hear them.

After the opening, the main theme is played by each instrument family alone. In what order do the families play the theme?

| | | |
|---|---|---|
| 1st | _____ | **a.** strings |
| 2nd | _____ | **b.** percussion |
| 3rd | _____ | **c.** woodwinds |
| final | _____ | **d.** brass |

### Understanding Instruments and Instrument Families (from 🔊 iMusic):

Strings: **Canon in D** (Pachelbel)
Woodwinds: **Woodwind Quintet, Op. 88, No. 2** (Reicha)
Brass: **Contrapunctus I**, from *The Art of Fugue* (Bach)
Percussion (bass drum, cymbals, glockenspiel): *Stars and Stripes Forever* (Sousa)
Cornet: *Oh, Susannah!* (Stephen Foster)
Guitar: *Greensleeves* (folk song, UK)
Piano: *Spring Song* (Mendelssohn)
Organ: **Toccata in D minor** (Bach)
Harpsichord: **Minuet in D minor** (*Anna Magdelena Notebook*)

# 10 Musical Ensembles

"Conductors must give unmistakable and suggestive signals to the orchestra—not choreography to the audience."

—George Szell

The great variety in musical instruments is matched by a wide assortment of ensembles, or performance groups. Some are homogeneous—for example, choral groups using only voices or perhaps only men's voices. Others are more heterogeneous—for example, the orchestra, which features instruments from the different families. Across the world, nearly any combination is possible.

## Choral Groups

Choral music is sung around the world, both for religious purposes (sacred music) and for nonspiritual (secular) occasions. Loosely defined, a *chorus* is a fairly large body of singers who perform together; their music is usually sung in several voice parts. Many groups include both men and women, but choruses can also be restricted to women's or men's voices only. A *choir* is traditionally a smaller group, often connected with a church or with the performance of sacred music. The standard voice parts in both chorus and choir correspond to the voice ranges described earlier: soprano, alto, tenor, and bass (abbreviated as *SATB*). In early times, choral music was often performed without accompaniment, a style of singing known as *a cappella* (meaning "in the chapel"). Smaller, specialized vocal ensembles include the *madrigal choir* and *chamber choir*.

SATB

A cappella

## Instrumental Chamber Ensembles

*Chamber music* is ensemble music for a group of two to about a dozen players, with only one player to a part—as distinct from orchestral music, in which a single

## STANDARD CHAMBER ENSEMBLES

| DUOS | QUARTETS | QUINTETS | Woodwind quintet |
|---|---|---|---|
| Solo instrument | String quartet | String quintet | Flute |
| Piano | Violin 1 | Violin 1 | Oboe |
| | Violin 2 | Violin 2 | Clarinet |
| | Viola | Viola 1 | Bassoon |
| **TRIOS** | Cello | Viola 2 | French horn (a |
| String trio | Piano quartet | Cello | brass instrument) |
| Violin 1 | Piano | Piano quintet | Brass quintet |
| Viola or Violin 2 | Violin | Piano | Trumpet 1 |
| Cello | Viola | String quartet | Trumpet 2 |
| Piano trio | Cello | (Violin 1, Violin 2, | French horn |
| Piano | | Viola, Cello) | Trombone |
| Violin | | | Tuba |
| Cello | | | |

instrumental part may be performed by as many as eighteen players or more. The essential trait of chamber music is its intimacy.

Many of the standard chamber music ensembles consist of string players. One well-known combination is the **string quartet**, made up of two violins, viola, and cello. Other popular combinations are the **duo sonata** (soloist with piano); the **piano trio**, **quartet**, and **quintet**, each made up of a piano and string instruments; the **string quintet**; as well as larger groups—the **sextet**, **septet**, and **octet**. Winds too form standard combinations, especially **woodwind** and **brass quintets**. Some of these ensembles are listed above.

*String quartet*

### Meet the Performers

#### The King's Singers

"It isn't really a surprise that one of the world's most popular vocal groups comes from England, for that country has long had an unsurpassed tradition of vocal music."

Meet the King's Singers, a highly acclaimed, *a cappella* vocal ensemble. This very popular, all-male British group began in 1968 with six choral students from King's College, Cambridge, who got together to record some "fun repertoire." Their reputation soared in Great Britain and the United States, where they appeared frequently on "The Tonight Show Starring Johnny Carson" in the 1980s; they were soon known and performing worldwide.

The key to the group's success is their showmanship, flawless harmonies, and ability to perform in many differing styles, from early music—where they made their start—to classical repertoire, as well as jazz, pop, folk, gospel, and world music. The King's Singers have worked with music greats such as opera stars Marilyn Horne and Plácido Domingo (one of the famous Three Tenors), songwriter/composer Paul McCartney, the revered Mormon Tabernacle

Choir, the deaf percussionist Evelyn Glennie (see p. 51), and the Boston Pops Orchestra, to name only a few.

The current singers in this esteemed ensemble are not the original ones who formed the group some forty years ago, but they are equally talented. The recent ensemble won a 2009 Grammy Award for their album *Simple Gifts*, which contains songs by Billy Joel, James Taylor, Paul Simon, and Randy Newman, as well as spirituals and hymns (including the joyous *'Tis the Gift to Be Simple*).

**Check out these recordings by the King's Singers:** *Fair Phyllis,* by John Farmer, on the album *Madrigal History Tour;* *'Tis the Gift to be Simple,* on the album *Simple Gifts*

**Meet the Performers**

**The Ying Quartet**

**"Commissioning and performing new compositions is the single most important activity that we can undertake as a quartet."**

Meet the Ying Quartet, an innovative ensemble whose members are pushing the boundaries of traditional chamber music. Founded in 1992 by four siblings, this quartet has toured internationally, playing in the most prestigious concerts halls—from New York's Carnegie Hall to the Sydney Opera House—and holding residencies at Harvard University and the Eastman School of Music in Rochester, New York, where they teach. Its members are also dedicated to making concert music a part of everyday life, giving performances at schools, businesses, and even youth prisons. They are known for rethinking traditional concert spaces, working with various actors, dancers, and electronics as well as a magician and a Chinese noodle chef in a series entitled "No Boundaries."

The Ying Quartet won a Grammy for the album *Four* *+ 4,* a collaboration with the popular Turtle Island Quartet; its most recent release, *Dim Sum*, features Chinese-American composers who combine Western classical music with traditional Chinese music. The group's ongoing project LifeMusic is dedicated to commissioning new works for string quartet from modern composers.

**Check out these recordings of the Ying Quartet:** *Song of the Ch'in*, by Zhou Long, on the album *Dim Sum*; *Variations on an Unoriginal Theme*, by Evan Price, on the album *Four + 4*

We will see that contemporary composers have experimented with new groupings that combine the voice with small groups of instruments and electronic elements with live performers. In some cultures, chamber groups mix what might seem to be unlikely timbres to the Western listener (see p. 57)—in India, for example, plucked strings and percussion are standard.

# The Orchestra

In its most general sense, the term "orchestra" may be applied to any performing body of diverse instruments—this would include the *gamelan* orchestras of Bali and Java, made up largely of gongs, xylophone-like instruments, and drums

## TYPICAL DISTRIBUTION OF ORCHESTRAL INSTRUMENTS

| | | |
|---|---|---|
| **STRINGS** | 16–18 first violins<br>16–18 second violins<br>12 violas | 10–12 cellos<br>8–10 double basses<br>1–2 harps, when needed |
| **WOODWINDS** | 2–3 flutes, 1 piccolo<br>2–3 oboes, 1 English horn | 3 clarinets, 1 bass clarinet<br>3 bassoons, 1 contrabassoon |
| **BRASS** | 4–6 French horns<br>4 trumpets | 3 trombones<br>1 tuba |
| **PERCUSSION** | 3–5 players | 1 timpani player (2–4 timpani) |

Cincinnati Symphony Orchestra, Paavo Järvi, Music Director, 2005.

A typical seating plan for an orchestra.

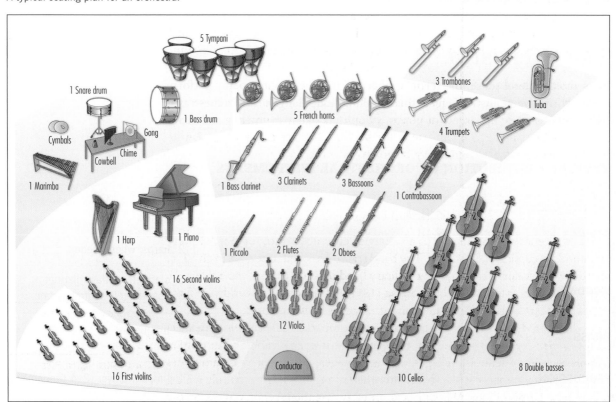

## Meet the Performers

### The Silk Road Ensemble

**"The music leapt across national boundaries in a strange and wonderful way. We were reminded that multi-culturalism has been a reality for many contemporary musicians for a very long time."**

Meet the Silk Road Ensemble, established by cellist Yo-Yo Ma in 2000 as part of the Silk Road Project—an artistic, cultural, and education organization with a vision of connecting the world's neighborhoods by bringing together artists and audiences around the globe. Now some sixty members strong, the ensemble includes not only musicians but also visual artists and storytellers from more than twenty countries along the ancient trade route that linked China with the West. The group, a part of the Silk Road Project, shares a unique perspective on the relationship between the traditional and the innovative in music, both Eastern and Western. In formal concerts and informal workshops given at universities and museums throughout the world, the ensemble promotes artistic exchange and cross-cultural awareness through music.

The ensemble performs on diverse traditional instruments, such as the Chinese pipa (a lute, see illustration of Wu Man on right), the Japanese shakuhachi (a bamboo flute), the Indian tabla (a pair of small hand drums), and the Galician, or Spanish bagpipe. The group has been actively commissioning new works from composers and arrangers to keep their musical traditions alive in the modern world. The group's most recent recording, *Traditions and Transformations: Sounds of Silk Road Chicago,* won a 2009 Grammy Award.

**Check out these recordings by the Silk Road Ensemble:** Pipa Concerto by Lou Harrison, from *Traditions and Transformations: Sounds of Silk Road Chicago* (Yo-Yo Ma, cello; Wu Man, pipa; Chicago Symphony Orchestra, Alan Gilbert and Miguel Harth-Bedoya, conductors)

---

(see illustration on p. 400). In the West, the term is now synonymous with *symphony orchestra,* an ensemble of strings coupled with an assortment of woodwinds, brass, and percussion instruments.

The symphony orchestra has varied in size and makeup throughout its history but has always featured string instruments as its core. From its origins as a small group, the orchestra has grown into an ensemble of more than a hundred musicians, approximately two-thirds of whom are string players. The list on page 61 shows the distribution of instruments typical of a large orchestra today.

The instruments of the orchestra are arranged to achieve the best balance of tone. Thus, most of the strings are near the front, as are the gentle woodwinds. The louder brass and percussion are at the back. A characteristic seating plan for the Cincinnati Symphony Orchestra is shown opposite.

# Concert, Jazz, and Rock Bands

"Band" is a generic name applied to a variety of ensembles, most of which feature winds and percussion at their core. The band is a much-loved American institution, whether it is a concert, marching, or military band or a jazz or rock ensemble. One American bandmaster, John Philip Sousa (1854–1932), achieved worldwide fame with his concert band and the repertory of marches he wrote for it.

In the United States today, the *concert band* (sometimes called a *wind ensemble*) ranges in size from forty to eighty or so players; it is an established institution in most secondary schools, colleges, and universities, and in many communities as well. Modern composers like to write for this ensemble, since it is usually willing to play new compositions. We will hear an early twentieth-century work by the

 **iMusic**

*Stars and Stripes Forever*

 **Video**

Sousa: *Washington Post*

The University of Wisconsin Marching Band.

American composer Charles Ives, arranged for band. The **marching band**, well known today in the United States and Canada, commonly entertains at sports events and parades. Besides its core of winds and percussion, this group often features remnants from its military origins, including a display of drum majors (or majorettes), flags, and rifles.

**Jazz and rock bands**      The precise instrumentation of **jazz bands** depends on the particular music being played but generally includes a reed section made up of saxophones of various sizes and an occasional clarinet, a brass section of trumpets and trombones, and a rhythm section of percussion, piano, double bass, and electric guitar. **Rock bands** typically feature amplified guitars, percussion, and synthesizers.

# The Role of the Conductor

Large ensembles, such as an orchestra, concert band, or chorus, generally need a conductor, who serves as the group's leader. Conductors beat time in standard metric patterns to help the performers keep the same tempo; many conductors use

**Baton**      a thin stick known as a **baton,** which is easy to see. These conducting patterns, shown in the diagrams below further emphasize the strong and weak beats of the measure. Beat 1, the strongest in any meter, is always given a downbeat, or a downward motion of the hand; a secondary accent is shown by a change of direction;

**BASIC CONDUCTIONG PATTERNS**                              ⊚ **iMaterials**

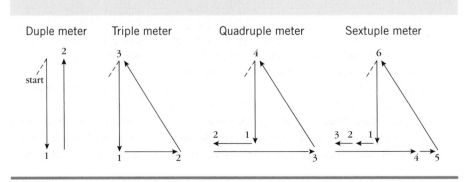

and the last beat of each measure, a weak beat, is always an upbeat or upward motion, thereby leaving the hand ready for the downbeat of the next measure.

Equally as important is the conductor's role in interpreting the music for the group. This includes deciding the precise tempo—how fast or slow—and the dynamics—how soft or loud—for each section of the piece. In most cases, the composer's markings are relative (how loud is *forte*?) and thus open to interpretive differences. Conductors also rehearse ensembles in practice sessions, helping the musicians to learn and interpret their individual parts. String players depend on the conductor, or sometimes the **concertmaster** (the first-chair violinist), to standardize their bowing strokes so that the musical emphasis, and therefore the interpretation, is uniform.

Below is the process that a musical work undergoes before you hear it.

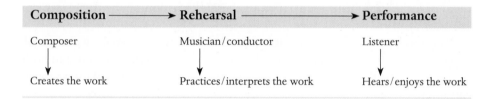

| Composition ──────► | Rehearsal ──────────► | Performance |
|---|---|---|
| Composer | Musician/conductor | Listener |
| ↓ | ↓ | ↓ |
| Creates the work | Practices/interprets the work | Hears/enjoys the work |

# The Orchestra in Action

A helpful introduction to the modern orchestra is Benjamin Britten's *Young Person's Guide to the Orchestra*, which was written expressly to illustrate the timbre of each instrument. The work, composed in 1946 and subtitled *Variations and Fugue on a Theme of Purcell*, is based on a dance tune by the great

## Meet the Performers

### Gustavo Dudamel

"My favorite game [as a child] was conducting my toys while playing recordings of the best orchestras. I was interested in what a conductor does, how he doesn't have an instrument, he doesn't make a sound."

Meet Gustavo Dudamel (born 1981), the new conductor of the Los Angeles Philharmonic Orchestra, appointed in 2009 at the incredible age of twenty-seven to head this venerable ensemble. Trained as a violinist, this talented young conductor is the son of two musicians and the product of the famous Venezuelan music education system, called *El Sistema*. He began winning conducting competitions at the age of fourteen, and his reputation soon spread. Newspapers all over the world began calling him "the hottest conductor around today." He is in constant demand as guest conductor of the world's finest orchestras.

In 1999, Dudamel took over as Musical Director of the Simón Bolívar Youth Orchestra, with whom he has toured extensively and whose performances have electrified audiences. With the Youth Orchestra, he has recorded several albums, including masterworks by Latin American composers. He has also recorded with the L.A. Philharmonic and conducted—and recorded—a birthday concert for Pope Benedict XVI. Dudamel has already been honored with several prestigious awards for his contributions to Latin cultural life. Los Angeles audiences have welcomed this talented musician, setting off a "Dudomania" frenzy.

**Check out these recordings by Gustavo Dudamel conducting the Simón Bolívar Orchestra of Venezuela:** *Mambo,* from *West Side Story,* by Leonard Bernstein on the album *Fiesta*; Symphony No. 7, IV, *Allegro con brio,* by Ludwig van Beethoven

Purcell: Rondeau

seventeenth-century English composer Henry Purcell (1659–1695). You can listen to Purcell's original dance tune—a rondeau in a broad triple meter, set in a minor key—at StudySpace.

In Britten's *Young Person's Guide*, the composer introduces the sound of the entire orchestra playing together, then the sonorities of each instrumental family as a group—woodwinds, brasses, strings, percussion—and finally repeats the statement by the full orchestra. Once the listener has the theme, or principal melody, well in mind, every instrument is featured in order from highest to lowest within each family. Next we encounter variations of the theme, each played by a new instrument with different accompanying instruments. (See Listening Guide 1 for the order of instruments.) The work closes with a grand fugue, a polyphonic form popular in the Baroque era (1600–1750), which is also based on Purcell's theme. The fugue, like the variations, presents its subject, or theme, in rapid order in each instrument. (For a general discussion of the fugue, see pp. 141–43.)

The modern orchestra, with its amplitude of tonal resources, its range of dynamics, and its infinite variety of color, offers a memorable experience to both the musician and the music lover. It is clearly one of the wonders of Western musical culture.

## Critical Thinking

**1.** What is the conductor's role in the interpretation of a musical work? What elements does he/she control?

**2.** What types of music do the various ensembles perform?

**3.** How does the makeup of instruments in these ensembles differ?

---

**LISTENING GUIDE 1**                                         ⊚ Playlist

# Britten: *The Young Person's Guide to the Orchestra*
## (*Variations and Fugue on a Theme of Purcell*)                 16:36

**DATE:**  1946

**BASIS:**  Dance (rondeau) from Henry Purcell's incidental music to the play *Abdelazar (The Moor's Revenge)*

At StudySpace, listen again to this orchestral work by Benjamin Britten—this time focusing on the listening elements noted here and on the individual instruments.

### WHAT TO LISTEN FOR:

| | | | | |
|---|---|---|---|---|
| Melody | Stately theme, based on tune by Baroque composer Henry Purcell | | Texture | Homophonic at beginning; closing fugue is polyphonic |
| Meter | Slow, triple meter for opening statement of theme, then changing to duple and compound | | Form | Theme with many variations |
| | | | Performing Forces | Full orchestra, statements by instrument families, then individual instruments |
| Harmony | Begins in minor tonality; shifts between major and minor | | | |

0:00   **I.  Theme:** 8 measures in D minor,
        stated 6 times to illustrate
        the orchestral families:

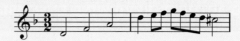

   1. Entire orchestra       4. Strings
   2. Woodwinds              5. Percussion
   3. Brass                  6. Entire orchestra

**II. Variations:** 13 short variations, each illustrating a different instrument.

| | VARIATION | FAMILY | SOLO INSTRUMENT | ACCOMPANYING INSTRUMENTS |
|---|---|---|---|---|
| 1:57 | 1 | Woodwinds: | flutes, piccolo | violins, harp, and triangle | |
| | 2 | | | oboes | strings and timpani |
| | 3 | | | clarinets | strings and tuba |
| | 4 | | | bassoons | strings and snare drum |
| 5:00 | 5 | Strings: | violins | brass and bass drum | |
| | 6 | | | violas | woodwinds and brass |
| | 7 | | | cellos | clarinets, violas, and harp |
| | 8 | | | double basses | woodwinds and tambourine |
| | 9 | | | harp | strings, gong, and cymbal |
| 9:34 | 10 | Brass: | French horns | strings, harp, and timpani | |
| | 11 | | | trumpets | strings and snare drum |
| | 12 | | | trombones, tuba | woodwinds and high brass |
| 11:53 | 13 | Percussion: | various | strings | |

(Order of introduction: timpani, bass drum, and cymbals; timpani, tambourine, and triangle; timpani, snare drum, and wood block; timpani, castanets, and gong; timpani and whip; whole percussion section)

13:47   **III.  Fugue:** Subject based on a fragment of the Purcell theme, played in imitation by each instrument of the orchestra in same order as variations:

Woodwinds:                    piccolo
(highest to lowest)           flutes
                              oboes
                              clarinets
                              bassoons

Strings:                      first violins
(highest to lowest)           second violins
                              violas
                              cellos
                              double basses
                              harp

Brass:                        French horns
(highest to lowest)           trumpets
                              trombones, tuba

Percussion:                   various

15:39   Full orchestra at the end with Purcell's theme heard over the fugue.

☺ **Now try the Listening Quiz.**

## LISTENING ACTIVITY: REVIEWING ENSEMBLES

At StudySpace (Chapter 10), listen to the works listed below, then complete the activity.

**Baroque Orchestra:** Alla Hornpipe, from *Water Music*, by Handel

   **1.** Check off the instrument families heard: __ strings __ woodwinds __ brass __ percussion

   **2.** Name two specific instruments you hear in this recording: _____

**Jazz Band:** *When the Saints Go Marching In* (traditional)

   **3.** Check off the instrument families heard: __ strings __ woodwinds __ brass __ percussion

   **4.** Name two specific instruments you hear in this recording: _____

**Woodwind Quintet**, Op. 88, No. 2, by Reicha

   **5.** Name all the instruments heard in this woodwind group: _____

Now let's compare two commonly heard ensembles—the orchestra and the concert band—to see if you can hear the differences in sonority.

     **a.** *Ride of the Valkyries* (Wagner)     **b.** *Stars and Stripes Forever* (Sousa)

____ **6.** Which work cited above is performed by an orchestra?

____ **7.** Which work features the percussion section?

____ **8.** Which instrument family is lacking from the concert band?
     **a.** brass   **b.** woodwinds   **c.** strings   **d.** percussion

____ **9.** Which instrument families are most prominent in the *Ride of the Valkyries*?
     **a.** woodwinds and percussion   **b.** strings and brass

In each of these examples below, select the two (2) instrument groups heard in the ensemble.

     **a.** aerophone   **b.** chordophone   **c.** idiophone   **d.** membranophone

____ and ____ **10.** *El Cihualteco* (Mexico)

____ and ____ **11.** *Tabuh Kenilu Sawik* (Indonesia)

---

### Understanding Ensembles (from iMusic):

#### Choral Groups:
Chamber choir: *Simple Gifts* (Shaker hymn)
Men's chorus: *El grillo* (Josquin)

#### Orchestra and Chamber Groups:
Baroque orchestra: **Alla hornpipe**, from
   *Water Music* (Handel)
Classical orchestra: **Surprise Symphony** (Haydn)
Romantic orchestra: **Ride of the Valkyries** (Wagner)
Contemporary orchestra: **Interlude**, from
   *Rappaccini's Daughter* (Catán)
String quartet: **Emperor Quartet, Op. 76, No. 3** (Haydn)

#### Brass quartet: **Contrapunctus I**, from
   *The Art of Fugue* (Bach)
Woodwind quintet: **Quintet, Op. 88, No. 2** (Reicha)

#### Other Western and World Music Ensembles:
Concert band: **Stars and Stripes Forever** (Sousa)
Jazz band: **When the Saints Go Marching In**
   (traditional, America)
Mexican mariachi: **El Cihualteco**
Chinese ensemble: **In a Mountain Place**
North Indian ensemble: **Bhimpalási**
Indonesian gamelan: **Tabuh Kenilu Sawik**

# 11 Style and Function of Music in Society

"A real musical culture should not be a museum culture based on music of past ages. . . . It should be the active embodiment in sound of the life of a community—of the everyday demands of people's work and play and of their deepest spiritual needs."

—Wilfrid Mellers

## KEY POINTS

**StudySpace** wwnorton.com/enjoy

- Music provides different functions—for religion, work, entertainment—in societies around the world.

- Most cultures have *sacred music*, for religious functions, and *secular music*, for nonreligious activities.

- There are many *genres*, or categories, of music; some works *cross over* categories, borrowing elements of one style for use in another.

- The *medium* is the specific group (e.g., orchestra, chorus) that performs a piece.

- Some music is not written down, but is known through *oral transmission*.

- The distinctive features of any artwork make up its *style*. A musical style is created through individual treatment of the basic musical elements.

- We organize styles of artworks into *historical periods*, each with its own characteristics.

In every culture, music is intricately interwoven with the lives and beliefs of its people. Music serves different functions in different societies, though some basic roles are universal. The social organization of any culture has much to do with its musical types and styles. In some cultures, such as in the Western classical tradition, only a few people are involved with the actual performance of music; in others, cooperative work is so much a part of society that the people sing as a group, with each person contributing a separate part to build a complex whole.

There is music for every conceivable occasion, but the specific occasions celebrated vary from one culture to another. Thus musical *genres*, or categories of repertory, do not necessarily transfer from one society to the next, though they may be similar. For example, Japanese *Noh* drama and Cantonese opera serve essentially the same social role as opera does in the Western world. And we can distinguish in most cultures between *sacred music*, for religious functions, and functions of *secular music*, for people outside a religious context.

It is important to differentiate between genre and form: a *genre* is a more general term that suggests something of the overall character of the work as well as its function. For example, the term *symphony* is a genre designation for a standard format—usually a four-movement orchestral work. As we will see later, each movement has a specific internal *form*, or structure. "Symphony" also implies the *medium*, or the specific group that performs the piece—in this case, an orchestra.

A Chinese performer singing Cantonese opera.

# The Role of Music in Society

The Americus Brass Band, a Civil War reenactment group, has been featured in numerous movies and TV series and is included in our iMusic recordings.

Music enhances many of our activities, including work, worship, and even warfare. Work songs, such as a sea shanty, can help synchronize group tasks like hoisting sails, hauling in nets, or raising the anchor. Blues and spirituals grew out of another type of work song—the field holler of slaves brought to the United States from West Africa. With emancipation, the tradition of singing at work continued on projects such as building the transcontinental railroad ("John Henry was a steel-driving man" and "I've been working on the railroad").

Music for worship can take many forms, but whether sung or played, this music shapes rituals and ceremonial acts. In the nineteenth century, African-American spirituals such as *Swing Low, Sweet Chariot* were sung at revival meetings as a comfort during hard times, and devotional hymns, like the Shaker song *Simple Gifts* ('Tis the gift to be simple"), were sung to remind parishioners of their purpose in life. Today, we can hear arrangements of spirituals in gospel and country music arrangements: the enduring Shaker hymn has served as the basis of the ballet *Appalachian Spring* by Aaron Copland (see p. 329), and the John Williams's work *Air and Simple Gifts*, written for

the 2009 inauguration of President Barack Obama.

The idea of a military band accompanying soldiers to war seems to have originated in India or the Middle East; the bagpipe (see illustration, p. 40), a popular folk instrument in various world cultures, spurred Scottish and Irish troops to battle from at least the sixteenth century; and in America, fife-and-drum corps, and later brass bands, accompanied Revolutionary and Civil War soldiers on the march with such rousing songs as *The Battle Hymn of the Republic* ("Mine eyes have seen the glory of the coming of the Lord . . . Glory, glory, hallelujah"). Wind instruments and percussion are still associated with military music; marches, such as John Philip Sousa's famous *Stars and Stripes Forever*, were written for military bands that include only brass, woodwind, and percussion instruments. Today, music spurs on military campaigns in new ways. You may recall that the popular comic strip *Doonesbury* has featured a relevant antiwar theme in

recent years. Here, political satirist and cartoonist Gary Trudeau has created Toogle, a soldier who, while serving in Iraq, offers to load soldiers' iPods with heavy metal music to get their adrenaline going as they head into danger.

---

ⓢ **iMusic**

*Riley* (work song: a sea shanty)
*Swing Low, Sweet Chariot* (African-American spiritual)
*Amazing Grace* (traditional hymn)
*Simple Gifts* (Shaker hymn)
*Battle Hymn of the Republic* (early American military song)
*Stars and Stripes Forever* (Sousa)

---

*In His Own Words*

Music is never stationary; successive forms and styles are only like so many resting places—like tents pitched and taken down again on the road to the ideal.

—*Franz Liszt*

Titles for musical compositions occasionally indicate the genre and key, such as Symphony No. 94 in G major, by Joseph Haydn. Another way works are identified is through a cataloguing system, often described by **opus number** (*opus* is Latin for "work"; an example is Nocturne, Opus 48, a piano work by Chopin). Other titles are more descriptive, such as *The Nutcracker* (a ballet by the Russian composer Tchaikovsky) and *The Trout* (a song by Schubert, an Austrian composer).

Just as the context for music—when, why, and by whom a piece is performed—varies from culture to culture, so do aesthetic judgments. For example, the Chinese consider a thin, tense vocal tone desirable in their operas, while the Italians prefer a full-throated, robust sound in theirs.

Not all music is written down. Music of most cultures of the world, including

## REVIEWING TERMS

**Title**: Symphony No. 5 in C minor, Op. 67
  (Op. = Opus = work number)
**Composer**: Ludwig van Beethoven
**Genre**: Symphony
**Form**: 4-movement work for orchestra
**Medium**: Symphony orchestra

**Title**: *Wiegenlied*, Op. 49, No. 4 (*Lullaby*)
**Composer**: Johannes Brahms
**Genre**: Romantic song (in German, *Lied*)
**Form**: Strophic (2 stanzas sung to same
  music)
**Medium**: Solo voice and piano

---

some styles of Western popular and traditional music, is transmitted by example or by imitation and is performed from memory. The preservation of music without the aid of written notation is referred to as *oral transmission*.

We will focus much of our study on Western art music—that is, the notated music of a cultivated society. We often label art music as "classical," or serious, for lack of better terms. However, the lines that distinguish art music from other kinds are often blurred. Popular and traditional musics are art forms in their own right, and both jazz and rock are considered by many to be new art forms, having already stood the test of time.

Note the stylistic differences between the paintings of similar subject matter: top, *The Guitar Player*, c. 1672, is by **Jan Vermeer** (1632–1675), and bottom, *The Old Guitar Player*, is by **Pablo Picasso** (1881–1973).

# The Concept of Style

*Style* may be defined as the characteristic way an artwork is presented. The word may also indicate the creator's personal manner of expression—the distinctive flavor that sets one artist apart from all others. Thus we speak of the literary style of Dickens or Shakespeare, the painting style of Picasso or Rembrandt, or the musical style of Bach or Mozart (see comparison of paintings on right).

What makes one musical work sound similar to or different from another? It is the individualized treatment of the elements of music. We have seen that Western music is largely a melody-oriented art based on a particular musical system from which the underlying harmonies are also built. Musics of other cultures may sound foreign to Western ears, because they are based on entirely different musical systems, and many do not involve harmony to any great extent. Complex rhythmic procedures and textures set some world musics apart from Western styles, while basic formal considerations—such as repetition, contrast, and variation—bring musics of disparate cultures closer. In short, a style is made up of pitch, time, timbre, and expression, creating a sound that each culture recognizes as its own.

# Musical Styles in History

The arts change from one age to the next, and each historical period has its own stylistic characteristics. Although the artists, writers, and composers of a particular era may vary in outlook, they have certain qualities in common. Because of this, we can tell at once that a work of art—whether music, poetry, painting, sculpture, or architecture—dates from the Middle Ages or the eighteenth century. The style of a period, then, is the total language of all its artists as they react to the artistic, political, economic, religious, and philosophical forces that shape their environment. We will find that a knowledge of historical styles will help us place a musical work within the context (time and place) in which it was created.

**Historical periods** The timeline below shows the generally accepted style periods in the history of Western music. Each represents a conception of form and technique, an ideal of beauty, a manner of expression and performance attuned to the cultural climate of the period—in a word, a style!

## Critical Thinking

**1.** What is the difference between the genre, the form, and the medium for a composition?

**2.** How does a composer create a unique musical style? Give an example.

## MUSICAL STYLES IN HISTORY

| 400 | 500 | 600 | 700 | 800 | 900 | 1000 | 1100 | 1200 | 1300 | 1400 | 1500 | 1600 | 1700 | 1800 | 1900 | 2000 |
|---|---|---|---|---|---|---|---|---|---|---|---|---|---|---|---|---|

Middle Ages (400–1450)

Early Christian period (400–600)

Gregorian chant (600–850)

Romanesque period—development of polyphony (850–1150)

Renaissance period (1450–1600)

Baroque period (1600–1750)

Classical period (1750–1825)

Romantic period (1820–1900)

Post-Romantic and Impressionist period (1890–1915)

Twentieth century and beyond (1900–present)

---

### Understanding Historical Style Periods (from ◉ iMusic):

Medieval: **Kyrie** (Hildegard)
Renaissance: ***Inviolata, integra et casta es Maria*** (Josquin)
Baroque: **Minuet in D** (*Anna Magdelena Notebook*) • **Concerto in C major for 2 Trumpets, I** (Vivaldi)
Classical: ***Surprise* Symphony No. 94** (Haydn) • ***Pathétique* Sonata, I** (Beethoven)
Romantic: *Åse's Death*, from *Peer Gynt Suite* (Grieg) • **Prelude in E minor, Op. 28, No. 4** (Chopin)
Early twentieth century: ***Jeux de vagues***, from *La mer* (Debussy) • *The Rite of Spring* (Stravinsky)
Later twentieth century: ***Lux aeterna*** (Ligeti)

### Understanding Categories of Music (from ◉ iMusic):

Sacred (religious) music: **"Hallelujah Chorus,"** from *Messiah* (Handel)
Secular (nonreligious) music: ***Moonlight* Sonata** (Beethoven)
Popular music: ***When the Saints Go Marching In*** (Jazz band) • ***If I Had a Hammer*** (Pete Seeger)
Crossover: ***Tonight***, from *West Side Story* (Bernstein)
Traditional music: ***Swing Low, Sweet Chariot*** (African-American spiritual) • *Los Jilicatas* (Peru)

## LISTENING ACTIVITY: COMPARING STYLES 1
## HISTORICAL PERIODS

**1.** At StudySpace (Chapter 11), listen to these two keyboard dances composed in different eras, then complete the activity below. You may answer both works, if appropriate.

      **a.** Minuet (*Anna Magdelena Notebook*)
      **b.** Joplin: *Pine Apple Rag*

| Melody | ___ built on major scale | Texture | ___ simple homophonic texture, focused on melody |
|---|---|---|---|
| | ___ built on minor scale | | ___ more complex texture, with emphasis on bass |
| Rhythm | ___ complex, syncopated rhythms | | |
| | ___ simple, "straight" rhythm | Performing Forces | ___ piano |
| Form | ___ simple binary (**A-A-B-B**) | | ___ harpsichord |
| | ___ longer, with more repeated sections | | |
| Meter | ___ duple meter | | |
| | ___ triple meter | | |

**2.** Now compare two orchestral works from divergent eras—the Classical period and the late twentieth century—to see if we can identify the elements that make them sound so different.

      **c.** *Military* Symphony (Haydn)
      **d.** *Interlude* from *Rappaccini's Daughter* (Catán)

| Melody | ___ melody prominent | Melody | ___ wide-ranging lines |
|---|---|---|---|
| | ___ melody sometimes obscured | | ___ moderate-ranging lines |
| Harmony | ___ highly dissonant | Meter | ___ regular, duple meter |
| | ___ predominantly consonant | | ___ irregular or mixed meter |
| Timbre | ___ consistent orchestral sound | Expression | ___ highly dramatic |
| | ___ changing instrumental timbres | | ___ moderately dramatic |

**3.** Listen to two non-Western works from different parts of the world and see what elements make up their style.

      **e.** *In a Mountain Path* (China)
      **f.** *Avaz of Bayate Esfahan* (Iran)

| Meter | ___ nonmetric and free | Timbre | ___ struck strings only |
|---|---|---|---|
| | ___ regular meter | | ___ bowed and struck strings |
| Melody | ___ tuneful focus on melody | Expression | ___ uses tremolo |
| | ___ short melodic ideas | | ___ uses sliding between pitches |

**4.** Listen to these two traditional works and answer the questions below.

      **g.** *Amazing Grace*
      **h.** *If I Had a Hammer*

| Rhythm | ___ highly regular movement | Function | ___ secular |
|---|---|---|---|
| | ___ free, improvised movement | | ___ sacred |
| Performing Forces | ___ voice and guitar | Special Effects | ___ heavy vibrato |
| | ___ voice and piano | | ___ call and response |
| Meter | ___ duple | | |
| | ___ triple | | |

# Medieval/Renaissance

## COMPOSERS AND WORKS

| | 500 | 600 | 700 | 800 | 900 | 1000 | 1100 | 1200 | 1300 | 1400 | 1420 | 1440 | 1460 | 1480 | 1500 | 1520 | 1540 | 1560 | 1580 | 1600 |

**(1098–1179)** Hildegard of Bingen (*Alleluia, O virga mediatrix*)

**(1100–1300)** Notre Dame School (Léonin, Pérotin)

**(c. 1250)** Anonymous (*Sumer canon*)

**(c. 1300–1377)** Guillaume de Machaut (*Puis qu'en oubli*)

**(c. 1450–1521)** Josquin des Prez (*Ave Maria . . . virgo serena*)

**(c. 1507–1568)** Jacques Arcadelt (*Il bianco e dolce cigno*)

**(c. 1515–c. 1571)** Tielman Susato (*Danseryie*)

**(c. 1525–1594)** Giovanni Pierluigi da Palestrina (*Pope Marcellus* Mass)

**(c. 1570–1603)** John Farmer (*Fair Phyllis*)

## EVENTS

| 500 | 600 | 700 | 800 | 900 | 1000 | 1100 | 1200 | 1300 | 1400 | 1420 | 1440 | 1460 | 1480 | 1500 | 1520 | 1540 | 1560 | 1580 | 1600 |

**476** Fall of the Roman Empire

**800** Charlemagne crowned first Holy Roman Emperor

**1271** Marco Polo to China

**1291** Last Crusade to the Holy Land

**1307** Dante Alighieri, Italian poet (*Divine Comedy*)

**1348** Black Death begins

**1456** Gutenberg Bible printed

**1492** Columbus discovers the New World

**1501** First music book printed in Italy

**1504** Michelangelo, Italian painter, sculptor (*David*)

**1545** Council of Trent begins

**1558** Elizabeth I crowned in England

**1601** Shakespeare's *Hamlet*

# Medieval and Renaissance Music

"Hearing," from *The Lady and the Unicorn* tapestry (late 15th century), Cluny Museum, Paris, France.

# The Culture of the Middle Ages and Renaissance

"Nothing exists without music, for the universe itself is said to have been framed by a kind of harmony of sounds, and the heaven itself revolves under the tone of that harmony."

**—Isidore of Seville**

## KEY POINTS

⊙ **StudySpace** wwnorton.com/enjoy

- The Middle Ages span nearly one thousand years (c. 476–1450).

- The early Christian church and the state were the centers of power during this time.

- Much surviving music from the Middle Ages is religious, or sacred, because of the sponsorship (**patronage**) of the church.

- The later Middle Ages saw the rise of cities, cathedrals, and great works of art and literature.

- The ideals of knighthood and the devotion to the Virgin Mary helped raise the status of women.

- The Renaissance saw exploration, scientific inquiry, artistic awakening, and secularization.

- Artists and writers found inspiration in the cultures of ancient Greece and Rome.

- Medieval and Renaissance musicians were employed in churches, cities, and courts or as instrument builders or music printers.

While we believe that many ancient civilizations enjoyed flourishing musical cultures, only a few fragments of their music survive today. We can not know what sounds echoed through the Greek amphitheatre or the Roman coliseum, but we do know that the ancient Mediterranean culture provided the foundation on which music of later ages was based. It is a fundamental part of the Western heritage.

*Early Middle Ages*

*Church and state*

The fall of the Roman Empire, commonly set in the year 476 C.E., marked the beginning of a one-thousand-year period known as the Middle Ages. The first half of this millennium, from around 500 to around 1000 and formerly referred to as the "Dark Ages," was not a period of decline but rather of ascent and development. During this era, all power flowed from the king, with the approval of the Roman Catholic Church and its bishops. The two centers of power, church and state, were bound to clash, and the struggle between them shaped the next chapter of European history. The modern concept of a strong, centralized government as the guardian of law and order is generally credited to Charlemagne (742–814), the legendary emperor of the Franks. A progressive monarch, who regretted until his dying day that he did not know how to write (he regarded writing as an inborn talent he simply did not possess), Charlemagne encouraged education and left behind him a magnificent library as well as a system of social justice that illuminated the perceived "darkness" of the early medieval world.

# The Medieval Church

The culture of this period was shaped in large part by the rise of monasteries. It was the members of these religious communities who preserved the learning of the ancient world and transmitted it, through their manuscripts, to later European scholars. Because music was an effective enhancement in the church service, the members of these religious communities supported it extensively, and because of their *patronage*, the art music of the Middle Ages was predominantly religious. Women as well as men played a role in preserving knowledge and cultivating music for the church, since nuns figured prominently in church society. One woman who stands out is Hildegard of Bingen, head of a monastery in a small town in western Germany. She is remembered today for her writings on natural history and medicine as well as for her poetry and music for special church services. We will study a religious chant by Hildegard in Chapter 12.

Reliquary of the emperor Charlemagne in the form of a portrait bust, c. 1350.

The late Middle Ages, from around 1000 to 1450, witnessed the construction of the great cathedrals, including Notre Dame in Paris (see illustration, p. 80), and the founding of universities throughout Europe. Cities emerged as centers of art and culture, and within them the townspeople played an ever-expanding role in civic life.

Trade flourished in the later Middle Ages when a merchant class arose outside of feudal society. Although travel was perilous—the roads plagued by robbers and the seas by pirates—each region of Europe exchanged its natural resources for those they lacked: the plentiful timber and furs of Scandinavia were traded for English wool and cloth manufactured in Flanders; England wanted German silver,

In this scene from the life of the Virgin, **Giotto di Bondone** (1267–1337) depicts the wedding procession of the Virgin accompanied by instruments. Detail from Scrovegni Chapel, Padua, Italy.

The writer Geoffrey Chaucer (c. 1343–1400), as depicted in a famous manuscript of his epic *Canterbury Tales* (c. 1410).

and above all, French and Italian wine; and European goods of all kinds flowed through the seaport of Venice to Constantinople in exchange for Eastern luxuries. This growing economic strength allowed medieval merchants a measure of freedom from local feudal landlords—a freedom that soon turned to a form of self-government through the growth of organized trade guilds.

Developing national literatures helped shape languages throughout Europe. Literary landmarks, such as the *Chanson de Roland* (c. 1100) in France, Dante's *Divine Comedy* (1307) in Italy, and Chaucer's *Canterbury Tales* (1386; see illustration at left) in England, find their counterparts in painting.

In an era of violence brought on by deep-set religious beliefs, knights embarked on holy—and bloody—Crusades to capture the Holy Land from the Muslims. Although feudal society was male-dominated and idealized the figure of the fearless warrior, the status of women was raised by the universal cult of Mary, mother of Christ (see illustration, p. 71), and by the concepts of chivalry that arose among the knights. In the songs of the court minstrels, women were adored with a fervor that laid the foundation for our concept of romantic love. This poetic attitude found its perfect symbol in the faithful knight who worshipped his lady from afar and was inspired by her to deeds of great daring and self-sacrifice.

The Middle Ages, in brief, encompassed a period of enormous turmoil and change. Out of this turbulent age emerged a profile of what we know today as Western civilization.

# The Arts in the Renaissance

"I am not pleased with the Courtier if he be not also a musician, and besides his understanding and cunning [in singing] upon the book, have skill in like manner on sundry instruments."

—*Baldassare Castiglione*

The Renaissance marks the passing of European society from a predominantly religious orientation to a more secular one, and from an age of unquestioning faith and mysticism to one of reason and scientific inquiry. The focus was on human fulfillment on earth rather than on the hereafter, and a new way of thinking centered on human issues and the individual. People gained confidence in their ability to solve their own problems and to order their world rationally, without relying exclusively on tradition or religion. This awakening—called humanism—was inspired by the ancient cultures of Greece and Rome, its writers and its artworks.

**Humanism**

A series of momentous circumstances helped to set off the new era from the old. The development of the compass made possible the voyages of discovery that opened up new worlds and demolished old superstitions. While the great European explorers of this age—Christopher Columbus, Amerigo Vespucci, and Ponce de León, among others—were in search of a new trade route to the riches of China and the Indies, they stumbled on North and South America. During the course of the sixteenth and seventeenth centuries, these new lands became increasingly important to European treasuries and society.

**New Worlds**

(Left) The Renaissance painter preferred realism to allegory and psychological characterizations to unnatural, stylized poses. *Mona Lisa*, by **Leonardo da Vinci** (1452–1519).

(Right) The human form, denied for centuries, was revealed in the Renaissance as an object of beauty. *David*, by **Michelangelo** (1475–1564).

**Invention of printing**

The revival of ancient writings mentioned earlier, spurred by the introduction of printing (c. 1455)—a development generally credited to the German goldsmith and inventor Johannes Gutenberg—had its counterpart in architecture, painting, and sculpture. Instead of the Gothic cathedrals and fortified castles of the medieval world, lavish Renaissance palaces and spacious villas were built according to the harmonious proportions of the classical style, which exemplified the ideals of order and balance. The strangely elongated saints and martyrs of medieval painting were replaced by the realism of Michelangelo's famous *David* statue and the gentle smiling Madonnas of Leonardo da Vinci. The nude human form, denied or covered for centuries, was revealed as a thing of beauty and used as an object of anatomical study. Nature entered painting as did a preoccupation with the laws of perspective and composition.

**Realism in art**

Medieval painting had presented life through symbolism; the Renaissance preferred realism. Medieval painters posed their figures impersonally, facing frontally; Renaissance artists developed portraiture and humanized their subjects. Medieval painting dealt in stylized portraits while the Renaissance was concerned with individuals. Space in medieval painting was organized in a succession of planes that the eye perceived as a series of episodes, but Renaissance painters made it possible to see the whole simultaneously. They discovered the landscape, created the illusion of distance, and focused on the physical loveliness of the world.

*In His Own Words*

I saw an angel in the marble and carved until I set him free.

—*Michelangelo*

The Renaissance first came to flower in Italy, the nation that stood closest to the classical Roman culture. As a result, the great names we associate with its painting and sculpture are predominantly Italian: Botticelli (1444–1510), Leonardo da Vinci (1452–1519), Michelangelo (1475–1564), and Titian (c. 1488–1576).

The colorful tapestry of Renaissance life presents a galaxy of great names. The list includes the German religious reformer Martin Luther (1483–1546), the Italian statesman Machiavelli (1469–1527), and his compatriot the scientist Galileo (1564–1642). This was an age of great writers as well: Rabelais (c. 1494–c. 1553) in France;

In *The Concert* (c. 1530–40), three ladies perform a French chanson with voice, flute, and lute. The Flemish artist is known only as the Master of the Female Half-Lengths.

Cervantes (1547–1616) in Spain; and, of course, Shakespeare (1564–1616) in England, to name but a few.

The Renaissance marks the birth of the modern European spirit and of Western society as we have come to know it. That turbulent time shaped the moral and cultural climate we live in today.

# Musicians in Medieval and Renaissance Society

Musicians were supported by the chief institutions of their society—the church, city, and state, as well as royal and aristocratic courts. Musicians found employment as choirmasters, singers, organists, instrumentalists, copyists, composers, teachers, instrument builders, and, by the sixteenth century, as music printers. There was a corresponding growth in a number of supporting musical institutions: church choirs and schools, music-publishing houses, civic wind bands. And there were increased opportunities for apprentices to study with master singers, players, and instrument builders. A few women can be identified as professional musicians in the Renaissance era, earning their living as court instrumentalists and singers.

The rise of the merchant class brought with it a new group of music patrons. This development was paralleled by the emergence, among the cultivated middle and upper classes, of the amateur musician. When the system for printing from movable type was successfully adapted to music in the early sixteenth century, printed music books became available and affordable. As a result, musical literacy spread dramatically.

### Critical Thinking

**1.** How did the Roman Catholic Church influence music in the Middle Ages?

**2.** What was the prevailing attitude toward women in the Middle Ages?

**3.** How did Renaissance thought differ from that of the Middle Ages?

**4.** How did the rise of urban centers and trade affect the development of music?

# 12 Sacred Music in the Middle Ages

"When God saw that many men were lazy, and gave themselves only with difficulty to spiritual reading, He wished to make it easy for them, and added the melody to the Prophet's words, that all being rejoiced by the charm of the music, should sing hymns to Him with gladness."

—St. John Chrysostom

StudySpace wwnorton.com/enjoy

## KEY POINTS

- The music of the early Christian church, called *Gregorian chant*, features monophonic, nonmetric melodies set in one of the church *modes*, or scales.

- Chant melodies fall into three categories (*syllabic*, *neumatic*, *melismatic*) based on how many notes are set to each syllable of text.

- The most solemn ritual of the Catholic church is the *Mass*, a daily service with two categories of prayers: the *Proper* (texts that vary according to the day) and the *Ordinary* (texts that remain the same for every Mass).

- Some chants are sung alternating a soloist and chorus in a *responsorial* performance.

- The Paris Cathedral of Notre Dame was a center for *organum*, the earliest type of *polyphony*, with two-, three-, or four-voice parts sung in fixed rhythmic patterns (*rhythmic modes*).

- Preexisting chants formed the basis for early polyphony, including organum and the *motet*.

The early music of the Christian church is testimony to the highly spiritual nature of the Middle Ages. These beautiful melodies, shaped in part by Greek, Hebrew, and Syrian influences, represent the starting point of artistic creativity in Western music. In time, it became necessary to assemble the ever-growing body of music into an organized liturgy. The *liturgy* refers to the set order of church services and to the structure of each service. The task extended over several generations, though tradition often credits Pope Gregory the Great (r. 590–604) with codifying these melodies, known today as Gregorian chant.

*Gregorian chant* (also known as *plainchant* or *plainsong*) consists of a single-line melody; it is monophonic in texture, and lacking harmony and counterpoint. Its freely flowing vocal line subtly follows the inflections of the Latin text and is generally free from regular accent.

The Gregorian melodies, numbering more than three thousand, form an immense body of music, nearly all of it anonymous. Gregorian chant avoids wide leaps, allowing its gentle contours to create a kind of musical speech. Free from regular phrase structure, the continuous, undulating vocal line is the musical counterpart to the lacy ornamentation typical of medieval art and architecture (see the Paris Cathedral of Notre Dame, p. 80).

Liturgy

Gregorian chant

## EXAMPLES OF TEXT-SETTING STYLES

From Handel's *Messiah*    DVD  CD 2 (23–28)  CD 1 (47–53)

**Syllabic:** 1 note set to each syllable of text, opening of "Hallelujah Chorus," CD 1 (51)

Hal - le - lu - jah,    Hal - le - lu - jah,    Hal - le - lu - jah,    Hal - le - lu - jah,

**Neumatic:** a few notes set to 1 syllable ("**reign**," "**ev**-er"), middle of "Hallelujah Chorus," CD 1 (53)

and he shall reign,_____ and he shall reign_____ for ev - er and ev - er,

**Melismatic:** many notes set to 1 syllable ("re-**joice**"), from aria "Rejoice greatly," CD 1 (48)

O daugh-ter of__ Zi - on, re - joice,_____ re - joice,_____

**Text settings**

Chant melodies fall into three main classes, according to the way they are set to the text: *syllabic*, with one note sung to each syllable of text; *neumatic*, generally with small groups of up to five or six notes sung to a syllable; and *melismatic*, with long groups of notes set to a single syllable of text. The melismatic style, which descended from the elaborate improvisations heard in Middle Eastern music, became an expressive feature of Gregorian chant and exerted a strong influence on subsequent Western music.

At first the chants were handed down through oral tradition from one generation to the next. But as the number of chants increased, singers needed help remembering the general shapes of the different melodies. Thus *neumes*, little ascending and descending symbols, were written above the words to suggest the contours of the melody. Neumes eventually developed into a musical notation consisting of square notes on a four-line staff (see opposite).

From Gregorian chant through Renaissance polyphony, Western music used a variety of scale patterns, or *modes*. These preceded major and minor modes, which possess a strong pull toward a tonic note; the earlier modes lacked this sense of attraction. The modes served as the basis for European art music for a thousand years. With the development of polyphony—music for several independent lines—a harmonic system evolved based on these scale patterns. The adjective *modal* thus refers to various melodic and harmonic types that prevailed in the medieval and early Renaissance eras. The term is frequently used in opposition to tonal, which refers to the harmony based on major-minor tonality that came later. In later chapters we will hear how the varied modes are used in some world musics as well.

Manuscript illumination of Pope Gregory the Great dictating to his scribe Peter. The dove, representing the Holy Spirit, is on his shoulder.

# The Mass

**Offices**

The services of the Roman Catholic Church can be divided into two categories: the daily *Offices*—a series of services celebrated at various hours of the day in monasteries and convents—and the Mass. A reenactment of the sacrifice of Christ, the *Mass* is the most solemn ritual of the Catholic church, and the one generally attended by public worshippers. Its name derives from the Latin words *ite, missa est* (go, it is the dismissal), recited at the end of the service by the priest. The collection of prayers that makes up the Mass (its liturgy) falls into two categories: the *Proper*, texts that vary from day to day throughout the church year, depending on the feast being celebrated; and the *Ordinary*, texts that remain the same in every Mass. (A chart showing the organization of the Mass with the individual movements of the Proper and Ordinary appears in Chapter 14, p. 92.) There are Gregorian melodies for each section of the ceremony. In this way, Gregorian chant has been central to the celebration of the Mass, which was and remains the primary service in the Catholic church.

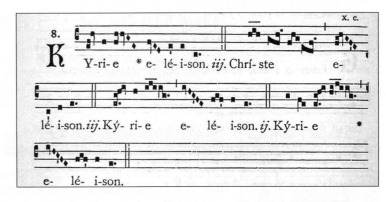

The opening of the Kyrie chant in Gregorian notation, from the *Liber usualis*.

Kyrie

Latin language

Aside from the *Kyrie*, which is a Greek text in a three-part form, the rest of the Mass texts are in *Latin*, the language of the ancient Romans and the language of learning throughout the Middle Ages and the Renaissance. You might be surprised to know that the Catholic church continued to celebrate the Mass in Latin until the middle of the twentieth century.

# Life in the Medieval Cloister

One vocation available to both men and women in the Middle Ages revolved around the Catholic church. Life in a cloister (a place for religious seclusion) allowed them to withdraw from secular society into the shelter of monasteries and convents, where they devoted themselves to prayer, scholarship, preaching, charity, or healing the sick, depending on the religious order they joined.

Parents might chose a religious life for a child if they had no further land holdings to give a son or no dowry for a daughter's wedding. Others might chose this spiritual path themselves as an adult, such as a widow who wished not to remarry or a young woman who longed for the education that cloistered life provided. A life devoted to the church was not an easy one. Some religious orders, such as the Franciscans, required vows of poverty; each new member discarded all worldly possessions upon joining. The discipline was arduous. A typical day began at 2:00 or 3:00 a.m. with the celebration of the first of the daily services (the Offices), the reading of lessons, and the singing of psalms. Each day in the church calendar had its own ritual and its own order of prayers. The members of the community interspersed their religious duties with work in the fields, in the library, or in the workshop. Some produced items that could be sold—wine, beer, or cheese, for example—thus bringing in revenue to the order.

In this 14th-century manuscript illumination, the monks sing during the celebration of Mass and an altar boy (left) pulls a bell rope.

Despite the grueling schedule, many men and women in religious life dedicated themselves to writing and preserving knowledge from earlier times. Such a person was Hildegard of Bingen, one of the most remarkable women of the Middle Ages, who was renowned in her day as a poet and prophet and who is popular today for her serenely beautiful music.

# The Music of Hildegard of Bingen

*"The words of the musical performance stand for the body, and the musical performance itself stands for the spirit. The celestial harmony announces the divinity, and the words truly uncover the humanity of the Word of God."*

The priest Volmar records Hildegard of Bingen's visions. The image, a miniature, is from her poetry collection *Scivias* (1141–51).

### Hildegard of Bingen (1098–1179)

**Hildegard of Bingen** was the daughter of a noble couple who promised her, as their tenth child, to the service of the church as a tithe (giving one tenth of what one owns). Raised by a religious recluse, she lived in a stone cell with one window and took her vows at the age of fourteen. From childhood, Hildegard experienced visions, which intensified in later life. She was reportedly able to foretell the future.

With the death of her teacher, Hildegard became the head of the religious community and, around the year 1150, founded a new convent in Rupertsberg, Germany. Her reported miracles and prophecies made her famous throughout Europe: popes, kings, and priests sought her advice on political and religious issues. Although never officially canonized, Hildegard is regarded as a saint by the church.

Her collected music forms a liturgical cycle for the different feasts throughout the church year. Her highly original style resembles Gregorian chant but is full of expressive leaps and melismas that clearly convey the meaning of the words.

**Major Works:** Poetry collection and visions entitled *Scivias* (*Know the Way*), one volume of religious poetry set to music (*Symphony of the Harmony of Celestial Revelations*), a sung morality play (*The Play of the Virtues*), and scientific and medical writings.

🎵 **iMusic:** Kyrie

## In Her Own Words

The words I speak come from no human mouth; I saw and heard them in visions sent to me. . . . I have no confidence in my own capacities—I reach out my hand to God that He may carry me along as a feather borne weightlessly by the wind.

# A Chant to the Virgin by Hildegard

Hildegard set many of her texts to music; her poetry is characterized by brilliant imagery and creative language. Some of her songs celebrate the lives of local saints such as Saint Rupert, the patron of her monastery, while many praise the Virgin Mary, comparing her to a blossoming flower or branch and celebrating her purity. Our example is an Alleluia (Listening Guide 2, p. 79), a movement from the Mass Proper, to be sung on a feast day for the Virgin. The chant is three-part, with the choral *Alleluia* framing the solo verse at the beginning and end. One of Hildegard's musical signatures can be heard here: an occasional upward leap of a fifth that gives the line a soaring feeling. It is the text that shapes the line, reaching its highest peaks on evocative words such as "holy womb," "flower," and "chastity." Hildegard elaborates some words with melismas, especially on the last syllables of *Alleluia* and in the last text line, describing the Virgin's purity or chastity.

# The Rise of Polyphony

*Polyphony*, or the combination of two or more simultaneous melodic lines, is the single most important development in the history of Western music. This style began to emerge toward the end of the Romanesque era (c. 850–1150). Once several melodic lines were sung at the same time, the flexible rhythms found in single-line music disappeared. Polyphony helped bring about the use of regular meters, which was necessary if the different voices were to keep together. Because this music had to be written down in a way that would indicate precise rhythm

**LISTENING GUIDE 2**                    ⊚ | DVD | CD 1 (11–13) | CD 1 (1–3)

# Hildegard of Bingen: *Alleluia, O virga mediatrix* (*Alleluia, O mediating branch*)

3:30

**DATE:** Late 12th century

**GENRE:** Alleluia plainchant, from the Proper of the Mass on feasts for the Virgin Mary

## WHAT TO LISTEN FOR:

| | | | |
|---|---|---|---|
| Melody | Unaccompanied, conjunct line with some expressive leaps and melismas | Expression | Dramatic leaps of a fifth; high range climaxes on important words |
| Rhythm | Free and nonmetric, following flow of words | Performing Forces | *A cappella* choir, alternating soloist and choir |
| Texture | Monophonic (single line) | Text | Prayer to the Virgin Mary, written by Hildegard |
| Form | 3-part structure (Alleluia-verse-Alleluia), performed responsorially | | |

| | | TEXT | TRANSLATION | PERFORMANCE |
|---|---|---|---|---|
| 1 | 0:00 | Alleluia. | Alleluia. | Solo intonation, then choral response; very melismatic. |
| 2 | 0:45 | O virga mediatrix | O mediating branch | Solo verse, with several melismas. |
| | | sancta viscera tua mortem superaverunt, | Your holy flesh has overcome death, | Higher range, neumatic text setting. |
| | | et venter tuus omnes creaturas illuminavit | and your womb has illuminated all creatures | |
| | | in pulchro flore de suavissima integritate | through the beautiful flower of your tender purity | |
| | | clausi pudoris tui orto. | that sprang from your chastity. | Melismatic at end. |
| 3 | 2:56 | Alleluia. | Alleluia. | Chorus; return to opening. |

Opening of solo chant, with melismatic setting on *Alleluia*:

Rising fifth and melisma on "mortem" (death):

⊚ **Now try the Listening Quiz.**

and pitch, a more exact notational system developed, not unlike the one in use today. (For an explanation of our modern notational system, see p. A-1.)

With the development of notation, music progressed from an art of improvisation and oral tradition to one that was carefully planned and preserved. During the Gothic era (c. 1150–1450), which saw the rise of cathedrals, the individual composer came to be recognized. Learned musicians, mostly clerics in religious communities, mastered the art of writing extended musical works in varied textures and forms.

### Did Women Sing Sacred Music?

In the earliest years of the Christian church, women, although excluded from the priesthood, did sing in services as members of the congregation and the choir. When the church's practices standardized in the fourth century, however, church leaders embraced St. Paul's admonition that women keep silent in church, and congregational singing gave way to professional choirs of men and boys. Women like Hildegard were the exception, entering all-female religious institutions, or convents. There, they could pursue music as self-expression to glorify the divine services. Nuns were trained in singing and even instrument playing, and they convened daily to celebrate the Offices and the Mass through song, just as their male counterparts did. One twelfth-century writer noted that "on feast days the nuns sit quietly in the cloister and practice reading and singing." In this secluded musical world, nuns also became composers of chant and eventually of polyphony. Modern scholarship has shown these practices were by no means isolated phenomena, and rich documentation continues to surface about the many musical communities of cloistered women across early modern Europe.

Façade of Cathedral of Notre Dame, Paris (1163–c. 1350). In both architecture and music, the Gothic period saw great advances in construction.

The earliest polyphonic music, called *organum*, grew out of the custom of adding a second voice to a Gregorian melody at the interval of a fifth or fourth. Soon a polyphonic art blossomed in which the individual voices moved with ever greater independence, not only in parallel but also in oblique and contrary motion (*oblique* implies that one voice is static while the other is moving, whereas *contrary motion* suggests that voices move in opposite directions). In the forefront of this evolution were the composers centered at the Cathedral of Notre Dame in Paris during the twelfth and thirteenth centuries. Their leader, Léonin (fl. 1150–c. 1201), is the first composer of polyphonic music whose name we know. He is credited with compiling the *Great Book of Organum* (*Magnus liber organi*), music for the entire church year, in this new musical style. His successor, Pérotin (fl. c. 1200), expanded the dimensions of organum by increasing the number of voice parts, first to three and then to four.

To the medieval mind, the new had to be founded on the old. Therefore composers of organum based their pieces on preexisting Gregorian chants. While the lower voice sang the fixed melody in extremely long notes, the upper voice sang a freely composed part that moved rapidly above it. In such a setting, the chant was no longer recognizable as a melody.

In the organum *Gaude Maria virgo* (Listening Guide 3), the opening polyphonic section features two voices singing in a *rhythmic mode*—a fixed pattern of long and short notes that is repeated or varied—over a sustained bottom voice that is drawn from the chant of the same name. The setting, in the style of Pérotin (and possibly by him), is highly melismatic, with many notes sung to each syllable of text, a prayer in praise of the Virgin Mary. The form of this organum is typical in that it alternates polyphony, sung by soloists, and monophonic chant, sung by the choir. What is remarkable about organum is that this was the genre in which composers first experimented with rhythmic ideas and also conceived a polyphonic style featuring open, hollow harmonies.

Toward the middle of the thirteenth century, musicians began writing new texts for the previously textless upper voices of organum. The addition of these texts resulted in the *motet* (from the French word *mot*, for word,) the most important form of early polyphonic music.

In the early motet, medieval composers based their own works on what had been handed down from the past. A composer selected a fragment of Gregorian chant for a particular voice part, and, keeping the pitches intact, gave them precise rhythmic values. This chant served as the structural skeleton of the piece, over which the composer added one, two, or three new melodies. In the medieval motet, a sacred text might be combined with one that was quite secular. We will see in the Renaissance era how composers developed the motet into the most innovative genre of sacred music.

### Critical Thinking

**1.** In what ways did composers of chant vary their melodies?

**2.** How did Hildegard of Bingen instill her music with emotional expression?

**3.** Why did composers of the earliest polyphony use chant as the basis for their works?

**LISTENING GUIDE 3**    ⓢ | DVD | **CD 1 (14–15)** | **CD 1 (4–5)**

# Notre Dame School: *Gaude Maria virgo* (*Rejoice Mary, virgin*)

1:26

**DATE:** Early 13th century
**GENRE:** Organum

**WHAT TO LISTEN FOR:**

| | | | |
|---|---|---|---|
| Melody | Short, repeated ideas exchanged between upper voices | Texture | 3-part polyphony, alternating with monophonic chant |
| Rhythm/ Meter | Simple pattern of long-short-long-short in upper voices over slow-moving bottom voice (tenor) | Expression | Opening words (*Gaude Maria*) drawn out in long melismatic setting |
| Harmony | Open, hollow-sounding cadences on intervals of fifths and octaves | Performing Forces | *A cappella*; soloists sing organum; choir sings chant |
| | | Text | Prayer in praise of Virgin Mary |

| | | TEXT | TRANSLATION | PERFORMANCE |
|---|---|---|---|---|
| 4 | 0:00 | Gaude Maria | Rejoice Mary, | Organum style; upper 2 voices moving rhythmically over sustained 3rd voice (tenor). |
| 5 | 1:07 | virgo cunctas hereses sola interemisti. | O virgin, you alone have destroyed all heresies. | Monophonic chant, melismatic, then continuing in neumatic setting. |

Opening of organum, with 2 rhythmic upper voices over long chant note:

ⓢ **Now try the Listening Quiz.**

**LISTENING ACTIVITY: COMPARING STYLES OF SACRED MUSIC**    ⓢ  🌐

Listen to these two examples of chant (StudySpace, Chapter 12), one from the Western tradition and one from the Islamic, then match these style traits with each piece.

    **a.** Hildegard: Kyrie    **b.** Call to Prayer (*Adhan*): *Blessings on the Prophet*

| | | |
|---|---|---|
| ____ small, 4-note range | ____ Arabic text | ____ solo vocal performance |
| ____ arched, flowing melody | ____ medium range, up to an octave | ____ long repeated sections |
| ____ responsorial performance | ____ static melody, focused around a single pitch | ____ Greek text |
| ____ short repeated sections | | |

# 13 Secular Music in the Middle Ages

"A verse without music is a mill without water."

**—Anonymous Troubadour**

## KEY POINTS

> **StudySpace** wwnorton.com/enjoy

- **Troubadours** and **trouvères** in France, and **Minnesingers** in Germany, performed secular music in courts; wandering minstrels performed in cities.

- Secular song texts focused on idealized love and the values of chivalry (code of behavior).

- Secular songs and dances were sung monophonically, with improvised instrumental accompaniment.

- Guillaume de Machaut was a poet-composer of the French **Ars nova** (new art) who wrote sacred music

- and polyphonic **chansons** (secular songs) set to fixed text forms (**rondeau**, **ballade**, **virelai**).

- Instrumental music was generally improvised, performed by ensembles of soft (**bas**) or loud (**haut**) instruments, categorized by their use.

- Religious wars (Crusades) and medieval explorations enabled the exchange of musical instruments and theoretical ideas about music with Middle Eastern and Far Eastern cultures (HTTN 2).

A longside the learned (or art) music of the cathedrals and choir schools grew a popular repertory of songs and dances that reflected every aspect of medieval life. The earliest secular songs that have been preserved were set to Latin texts, which suggests that they originated in university towns rather than in villages. These student songs—many with lewd texts—express the *carpe diem* ("seize the day") philosophy that has always inspired youthful poets. Both their poetry and their music immortalize the impermanence of love, the beauty of springtime, and the cruelty of fate. Seven hundred years later, the German composer Carl Orff admirably resurrected their spirit in *Carmina burana*, a popular choral work based on racy Latin texts (see p. 317).

*Latin secular songs*

## Medieval Minstrels

Minstrels emerged as a class of musicians who wandered among the courts and towns. Some were versatile entertainers who played instruments, sang and danced, juggled, presented tricks and animal acts, and performed plays. In an age that had no newspapers, they regaled their audience with gossip and news. These itinerant actor-singers lived on the fringes of society.

On a different social level were the poet-musicians who flourished at the various courts of Europe. Those who lived in the southern region of France known as Provence were called **troubadours** (women were called **trobairitz**), those living in northern France were called **trouvères**. Both terms mean the same thing—finders or inventors (in musical terms, composers). Some troubadours and trouvères were members of the aristocracy and some were even royalty. They either sang their music and poetry themselves or entrusted its performance to other musicians. In Germany, they were known as **Minnesingers**, or singers of courtly love.

Secular music supplied the necessary accompaniment for dancing, banquets, and after-dinner entertainment at medieval courts. It was central to court ceremonies, to tournaments, and to civic processions, while military music supported campaigns, inspired warriors departing on the Crusades, and welcomed them on their return.

The poems of the troubadour and trouvère repertory ranged from simple ballads to love songs, political and moral ditties, war songs, chronicles of the Crusades, laments, and dance songs. They praised the virtues of the age of chivalry: valor, honor, nobility of character, devotion to an ideal, and the quest for perfect love. Like so many of our popular songs today, many of the medieval lyrics dealt with the subject of unrequited—or unconsummated—passion. The object of the poet's desire was generally unattainable, either because of rank or because the beloved was already wed to another. This poetry dealt with love in its most idealized form. The subjects of poems by women were similar to those by men, ranging from the sorrow of being rejected by a lover to the joy of true love.

Illustrations from the *Cantigas de Santa María* (13th century) showing musicians playing pipes and tabors (top) and shawms (bottom).

## A Famous English Round

Alongside the haunting monophonic melodies of the troubadours, composers were already developing basic polyphonic textures. One of the earliest examples of polyphony comes from England, and is remarkable in its setting as a **round** (each voice enters in succession, with the same melody; see p. 28), resulting in as many as six voices singing at once. *Sumer is icumen in* (or *Summer is come*; see Listening Guide 4) was composed around 1250 and was probably performed by musicians at an abbey in Reading, England, where the manuscript of the work was found. The text, written in Middle English, celebrates the coming of summer, with the renewal of all living things. Because the manuscript was copied at a religious institution, it has a Latin sacred text as well: *Perspice Christicola*, a reflection on Christ's Crucifixion.

The catchy tune unfolds in a never-ending round over two tenor voices that serve as a scaffolding: these lower voices sing short repeated ideas that are exchanged back and forth (an **ostinato**, called the *pes*, or foot). The song can be sung by one, two, three, or four singers in a round, much like we heard earlier in *Row, Row, Row Your Boat* (◎ **iMusic** and p. 28). The simple rhythm of the melody (long-short-long-short) and the exchange of motive in the lower voices are both ideas we heard in organum, but in this work, set in major mode, the result is strikingly more modern.

The original notation of the canon *Sumer is icumen in* (c. 1250).

## LISTENING GUIDE 4

DVD | CD 1 (21–23) | CD 1 (6–8)

# Anonymous: *Sumer is icumen in (Summer is come)* 1:50

**DATE:** c. 1250

**GENRE:** Perpetual round

### WHAT TO LISTEN FOR:

| | | | |
|---|---|---|---|
| Melody | Lilting melody, set syllabically | Form | Sung 3 times over 2 insistent repeated bass parts: solo, then 2-voice round, then 4-voice round (on our recording) |
| Rhythm | Simple pattern of long-short-long-short throughout | | |
| Harmony | Modern sounding, with many 3rds and 6ths | Performing Forces | *A cappella;* 6 voices (male) |
| Texture | Imitative; up to 6-part polyphony | Text | Middle English, in praise of summer |

| | | |
|---|---|---|
| **6** | 0:00 | Bass patterns alone: "Sing cuccu." Solo voice enters over bass pattern. |
| **7** | 0:33 | 2 voices in imitation, bass patterns continue. |
| **8** | 1:06 | 4 voices in imitation over continuing bass patterns. Voices drop out one by one, leaving only the bass. |

Opening of 2-voice round over bass patterns:

Round voice 1: Su - mer is i - cu - men in,___ Lhu - de sing cuc - cu!

Round voice 2: Su - mer is i - cu - men in,___

Bass pattern 1: Sing cuc - cu nu;___ Sing cuc - cu!

Bass pattern 2: Sing cuc - cu! Sing cuc - cu nu;___

**MIDDLE ENGLISH**

Sumer is icumen in
Lhude sing cuccu!
Groweþ sed and bloweþ med
and springþ and wde nu.
Sing cuccu!

Awe bleteþ after lomb,
Lhouþ after calve cu.
Bulluc sterteþ
bucke verteþ
murie sing cuccu!
Cuccu, cuccu.
Wel singes þu cuccu,
Ne swik þu naver nu!

Sing cuccu nu; sing cuccu!

**MODERN ENGLISH**

Summer is come,
Sing loud, cuckoo!
The seed grows and the meadow blooms,
And now the woods turn green.
Sing, cuckoo!

The ewe bleats after the lamb,
The cow lows after the calf,
the bullock leaps,
the billy goat farts,
Sing merrily, cuckoo!
Cuckoo, cuckoo!
You sing well, cuckoo.
Don't ever stop now!

Sing, cuckoo, now; sing cuckoo!

**Now try the Listening Quiz.**

# The French *Ars nova*

"Music is a science that would have us laugh, sing, and dance."

The breakup of the feudal social structure inspired new concepts of life, art, and beauty. These changes were reflected in the musical style known as *Ars nova* (new art), which appeared at the beginning of the fourteenth century in France, and soon thereafter in Italy. The music of the French *Ars nova* is more refined and complex than music of the *Ars antiqua* (old art), which it displaced. Writers such as Petrarch, Boccaccio, and Chaucer were turning from otherworldly ideals to human subjects; painters soon discovered the beauty of nature and the attractiveness of the human form. Similarly, composers like the French master Guillaume de Machaut turned increasingly from religious to secular themes. The *Ars nova* ushered in developments in rhythm, meter, harmony, and counterpoint that transformed the art of music.

Manuscript illumination of the poet-musician Guillaume de Machaut.

## Guillaume de Machaut (c. 1300–1377)

**Guillaume de Machaut** was the foremost composer-poet of the *Ars nova* style. He took holy orders at an early age but worked much of his life at various French courts, including that of Charles, duke of Normandy, who subsequently became king of France.

Machaut's double career as cleric and courtier inspired him to write both religious and secular music. His own poetry embraces the ideals of medieval chivalry. One of his writings, a long autobiographical poem of more than nine thousand lines in rhymed couplets, tells the platonic love story of the aging Machaut and a young girl named Peronne. The two exchanged poems and letters, some of which the composer set to music. Machaut spent his old age as a canon at the Cathedral of Rheims, admired as the greatest musician and poet of the time.

**Major Works:** Motets, chansons (both monophonic and polyphonic), and a polyphonic Mass (*Messe de Notre Dame*), one of the earliest complete settings of the Ordinary of the Mass.

## A Chanson by Machaut

Machaut's music introduced a new freedom of rhythm characterized by gentle syncopations and the interplay of duple and triple meters. Machaut favored the chanson, which was generally set to French courtly love poems written in one of several fixed text forms. These poetic forms—the *rondeau*, *ballade*, and *virelai*—established the musical repetition scheme of the chansons. We will study his love song *Puis qu'en oubli*, a rondeau for three voices with a refrain echoing the pain of unrequited love ("Since I am forgotten by you, sweet friend, I bid farewell to a life of love and joy"; see Listening Guide 5, p. 86). In Machaut's elegant chanson, whose low melodic range makes it appropriate for three men's voices, the two musical sections alternate in a pattern dictated by the poetry. This may be the very work Machaut mentions in a letter to his beloved Peronne: "I am sending you a rondel with music of which I made the tune and the text some time ago, but I've newly made the tenor and contratenor [the two lower parts]; should you like to get to know it, it seems to me good." The influence of this last great poet-composer was far-reaching, his music and poetry admired long after his death.

A polyphonic chanson is performed with voice and lute in this miniature representing the Garden of Love, from a Flemish manuscript of *Le Roman de la Rose* (c. 1500).

**LISTENING GUIDE 5**  Ⓢ | DVD | CD 1 (24–28) | CD 1 (9–13)

# Machaut: *Puis qu'en oubli (Since I am forgotten)*  1:46

**DATE:**  Mid-14th century

**GENRE:**  Polyphonic chanson, setting of a French rondeau

## WHAT TO LISTEN FOR:

| | | | |
|---|---|---|---|
| Melody | Conjunct, low range; wavelike lines, with a few melismas | Form | 2 sections, **A** and **B,** repeated: **ABaAabAB** Capital letters = refrain (with repeated text and music); small letters = verse (new text) |
| Rhythm/ Meter | Slow triple meter, with subtle syncopations | Performing Forces | 3 male voices |
| Harmony | Open, hollow cadences at phrase endings | Text | Rondeau by the composer |
| Texture | 3-part polyphony | | |

Top-line melody of **A section**, with refrain text:

Puis  qu'en  ou - bli  sui  de  vous,  dous  a - mis,

Top-line melody of **B section**, with refrain text:

Vie  a - mou - reu - se  et  joie  a  Dieu  com - mant.

| | | | TEXT | MUSICAL FORM | TRANSLATION |
|---|---|---|---|---|---|
| 9 | 0:00 | Refrain | Puis qu'en oubli sui de vous, dous amis, Vie amoureuse et joie a Dieu commant. | A B | Since I am forgotten by you, sweet friend, I bid farewell to a life of love and joy. |
| 10 | 0:25 | Partial verse | Mar vi le jour que m'amour en vous mis; | a | Unlucky was the day I placed my love in you; |
| 11 | 0:38 | Partial refrain | Puis qu'en oubli sui de vous, dous amis. | A | Since I am forgotten by you, sweet friend. |
| 12 | 0:52 | Verse | Mais ce tenray que je vous ay promis: C'est que jamais n'aray nul autre amant. | a b | But what was promised you I will sustain: That I shall never have any other love. |
| 13 | 1:17 | Refrain | Puis qu'en oubli sui de vous, dous amis, Vie amoureuse et joie a Dieu commant. | A B | Since I am forgotten by you, sweet friend, I bid farewell to a life of love and joy. |

Ⓢ **Now try the Listening Quiz.**

# Early Instrumental Music

The fourteenth century witnessed a steady growth in the scope and importance of instrumental music. Though the central role in art music was still reserved for vocal works, instruments certainly played a supporting role in vocal literature,

**2    Here & There, Then & Now** 🌐

# Opening Doors to the East

In this miniature from the *Prayer Book* of Alfonso the Wise, King David is playing a rebec on his lap, in the manner of the Middle Eastern rabab.

Medieval minstrels of all social classes composed epics about chivalric love and great feats of knightly courage associated with the Crusades, the series of religious wars waged by Western Europeans to win back the Holy Land of Palestine from the Muslims. Extending over some two hundred years, from 1095 to 1291, the Crusades were at once among the most violent episodes in recorded history and one of the most influential forces on medieval Europe. The movement of vast armies across the European continent created increased trade along the routes, and allowed Westerners to gain a much broader knowledge of the world and other ways of life through their contact, albeit hostile, with Islam. Despite the pillaging and destruction, the interaction of distant cultures had positive results. The crusading knights learned from the expert military skills of the Turkish and Moorish warriors, and the advanced medical and scientific knowledge of the Arab world was imported to Europe. It was at this time too that the Arab number system was adopted in the West (until then, Europeans had used Roman numerals—I, II, III, IV, V rather than the Arabic numerals we use today—1, 2, 3, 4, 5).

Music benefited from this cultural interaction as well, since musicians often accompanied their noble lords to war. The troubadour Raimbaut de Vaqueiras, who died on the battlefield alongside his patron, left a colorful description of his adventures. These traveling minstrels brought music, theoretical ideas, and instruments of all types back to their homeland. For example, the medieval rebec, a small bowed string instrument that was a forerunner of the modern violin, derived from the Arab rabab (see illustration above), and the loud, double-reed shawm, the predecessor of the modern oboe, was a military instrument used by Turkish armies. We will see that many of our orchestral percussion instruments stem from Turkish models as well, including the cymbals, bells, and the bass drum. Crusaders heard the sounds of the Saracen military trumpets and drums and soon adopted these as their call to battle. The foundation of our Western system of early scales (modes) also came from Eastern theoretical systems.

Despite the long-standing intolerance these wars fostered between the Western and Islamic worlds, an aura of romance and mystery hovers over the Crusades. Composers have spun out the story of the First Crusade and the capture of Jerusalem in their operas, including, remarkably, the first opera by a woman composer, *The Liberation of Ruggiero* (1625) by Francesca Caccini, as well as works by the Baroque composers Gluck and Handel and the nineteenth-century Italian master Giuseppe Verdi. In these works, the exoticism of the Eastern world is evoked through sorcery and love potions. Today we revisit the fable, mystery, and brutality of these events through movies, such as the Indiana Jones films, one of which returns us to the knights of the First Crusade who are guarding the Holy Grail, and even popular video games that attempt to re-enact the fearsome deeds of crusading knights.

---

🄯 **iMusic**

Iranian (Persian) music: *Avaz of Bayate Esfahan* (played on the santur)
Haydn: Symphony No. 100 (*Military*), G major, II

---

doubling or accompanying the singers. Instrumental arrangements of vocal works grew increasingly popular. And instruments found their earliest prominence in dance music, where rhythm was the prime consideration.

Because instrumental music was largely an oral tradition, with much of what was played an improvisation, we must rely on surviving instruments in museums, artworks, and historical documents such as court payrolls to tell us about the instruments, their use, and playing techniques.

We can group medieval instruments into the same general families as modern ones—strings, woodwinds, brass, percussion, and keyboard—but they were

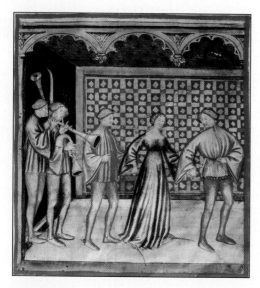

Medieval dancers are accompanied by shawm and bagpipe, in a miniature from a 14th-century handbook on wellness.

also divided into soft (**bas**), or indoor, and loud (**haut**), or outdoor, categories according to their use.

Among the most commonly used soft instruments were the **recorder,** an end-blown flute with a breathy tone, and its smaller cousin, the three-holed **pipe**; the **lute,** a plucked string instrument with a rounded back (of Middle Eastern origin); the **harp** and **psaltery,** plucked string instruments of biblical fame; the **hammered dulcimer** (derived from the santur of Persia); and the **rebec** and **vielle,** the two principal bowed string instruments of the Middle Ages (see illustration, p. 87).

The loud category of instruments, used mainly for outdoor occasions such as tournaments and processions, included the **shawm,** an ancestor of the oboe, with a loud, nasal tone; and the slide trumpet, which developed into the early trombone known as the **sackbut.** Some wind instruments that became increasingly popular in the late Middle Ages do not fit neatly into the categories of loud and soft. The **cornetto** developed from the traditional cow horn but was made of wood; it had a cup-shaped mouthpiece like a brass instrument's, with fingerholes like a woodwind's. We will hear some of these in our study of Renaissance dance music. Percussion instruments of the time included a large cylindrical drum called the **tabor** and small drums known as **nakers,** usually played in pairs. Several of these instruments had their origins in the Middle East, and nakers are mentioned in Marco Polo's account of his travels in Asia.

Several types and sizes of organ were already in use in the Middle Ages. There were large ones used in churches that required not only the performer but also someone to pump the giant bellows. At the other extreme were **portative** and **positive organs** (see illustration, p. 69)—smaller instruments with keyboards and a few ranks of pipes.

The revival of early music has grown in recent decades, as scholars and performers have worked to reconstruct some of the conditions under which the music was originally performed. Most of the ensembles that now specialize in this repertory boast players who have mastered the old instruments. Their concerts and recordings have made the public aware of the sound of these instruments to a degree that was undreamed of fifty years ago.

### Critical Thinking

**1.** What role did chivalry play in medieval court life? How was this reflected in the music?

**2.** How are medieval instruments similar to today's instruments? How are they different?

**3.** What ideas did Western European medieval society borrow from the Middle East?

# 14 Renaissance Sacred Music

"We know by experience that song has great force and vigor to move and inflame the hearts of men to invoke and praise God with a more vehement and ardent zeal."

—John Calvin

## KEY POINTS

> ⓢ **StudySpace** wwnorton.com/enjoy

- Renaissance sacred music was generally performed *a cappella* (for voices alone, without accompaniment) and features a fuller, more consonant sound (with thirds and sixths) than medieval music. Some works are built on a fixed, preexisting melody (*cantus firmus*).

- Josquin des Prez's *Ave Maria . . . virgo serena* is a *motet* to the Virgin Mary set in varied textural styles.

- Renaissance composers set texts from the *Ordinary of the Mass* (Kyrie, Gloria, Credo, Sanctus, Agnus Dei) for their polyphonic Masses.

- Giovanni Pierluigi da Palestrina's *Pope Marcellus* Mass met the **Council of Trent**'s demands for *a cappella* singing with clearly declaimed text.

Music played a prominent role in the ritual of the church during the Renaissance. In addition to the monophonic Gregorian chant, music for church services included polyphonic settings of the Mass, motets, and hymns. These were normally multivoiced and, especially in the early sixteenth century, based on preexisting music. Such works were sung by professional singers trained from childhood in the various cathedral choir schools.

The vocal forms of Renaissance music were marked by smoothly gliding melodies conceived especially for the voice. In fact, the sixteenth century has come to be regarded as the golden age of the *a cappella* style (the term refers to a vocal work without instrumental accompaniment). Polyphony in such works was based on the principle of **imitation**. In this procedure, which we heard in the *Sumer canon* (see Listening Guide 4, p. 84) the musical ideas are exchanged between vocal lines, the voices imitating one another so that the same phrase is heard in different registers. The result is a close-knit musical fabric capable of subtle and varied effects.

*A cappella* singing

Most church music was written for *a cappella* performance. In the matter of harmony, composers of the Renaissance leaned toward fuller chords. They turned away from the open fifths and octaves preferred in medieval times to the "sweeter" thirds and sixths. The use of dissonance in sacred music was carefully controlled.

Renaissance harmony

Polyphonic writing offered the composer many possibilities, such as the use of a fixed melody (*cantus firmus*) as the basis for elaborate ornamentation in the other voices. As we have seen, triple meter had been especially attractive to the medieval mind because it symbolized the perfection of the Trinity. The new era, much less preoccupied with religious symbolism, showed a greater interest in duple meter.

**Motet**    In the Renaissance, the **motet** became a sacred form with a single Latin text, for use in the Mass and other religious services. Motets in praise of the Virgin Mary were extremely popular because of the many religious groups all over Europe devoted to her worship. These works, written for three, four, or more voices, were sometimes based on a chant or other cantus firmus.

The preeminent composers of the early Renaissance (1450–1520) were from northern Europe and, in particular, present-day Belgium and northern France. Among these composers, we will consider Josquin des Prez (c. 1450–1521), one of the great masters of sacred music. In the late Renaissance (1520–1600), Italian composers rose to prominence, including Giovanni Pierluigi da Palestrina, whose famous *Pope Marcellus* Mass we will study. These musicians mark the transition from the shadowy figures of the late Gothic era to the highly individualized artists of the Renaissance.

# Josquin des Prez and the Motet

"He is the master of the notes. They have to do as he bids them; other composers have to do as the notes will."

—*Martin Luther*

IOSQVINVS PRATENSIS.

## Josquin des Prez (c. 1450–1521)

**Josquin** (as he is known) exerted a powerful influence on generations of composers to follow. After spending his youth in the north, his varied career led him to Italy, where he served at several courts—especially those of Cardinal Ascanio Sforza of Milan and Ercole d'Este, duke of Ferrara—and in the papal choir in Rome. During his stay in Italy, he absorbed the classical virtues of balance and moderation, the sense of harmonious proportion and clear form, visible in the paintings of the era. Toward the end of his life, Josquin returned to his native France, where he served as a provost at the collegiate church of Condé. He was buried in the choir of the church.

Josquin appeared at a time when the humanizing influences of the Renaissance were being felt throughout Europe. He was able to craft his work to the highest end: the expression of emotion. His music is rich in feeling, characterized by serenely beautiful melodies and expressive harmony.

**Major Works:** Over 100 motets, at least 17 Masses, as well as many French chansons and Italian secular songs.

◎ **iMusic:** *El grillo* (*The Cricket*)
       *Inviolata, integra et casta es Maria*

*Ave Maria . . . virgo serena* is a prime example of how Josquin used the motet to experiment with varied combinations of voices and textures (see Listening Guide 6). In this four-voice composition dedicated to the Virgin Mary, high voices engage

**Homorythmic texture**    in a dialogue with low ones and imitative textures alternate with **homorhythmic** settings (a texture in which all voices move together rhythmically). Josquin opens the piece with a musical reference to a chant for the Virgin, but soon drops this melody in favor of a freely composed form that is highly sensitive to the text. The final two lines of text, a personal plea to the Virgin ("O Mother of God, remember me"), is set in a simple texture that emphasizes the words, proclaiming the emotional and humanistic spirit of a new age.

**LISTENING GUIDE 6**                    DVD | **CD 1 (33–39)** | CD 1 (14–20)

# Josquin: *Ave Maria . . . virgo serena* (Hail Mary . . . gentle virgin)

4:38

**DATE:** 1480s?

**GENRE:** Latin motet

## WHAT TO LISTEN FOR:

| | |
|---|---|
| Melody | High vs. low voices, singing in pairs; opening phrase with rising 4th quotes chant |
| Rhythm/Meter | Duple, with shift to triple, then back |
| Harmony | Consonant; hollow-sounding cadences |
| Texture | Imitative polyphony, with moments of homorhythm |
| Form | Sectional according to strophes of poem (each begins "Ave") |
| Expression | Final personal plea from composer at end |
| Performing Forces | 4-voice choir; *a cappella* |
| Text | Rhymed, strophic prayer to the Virgin Mary |

| | | TEXT | TRANSLATION | DESCRIPTION |
|---|---|---|---|---|
| 14 | 0:00 | Ave Maria, gratia plena, Dominus tecum, virgo serena. | Hail Mary, full of grace, The Lord is with you, gentle Virgin. | 4 voices in imitation (SATB); chant used; duple meter. |
| 15 | 0:45 | Ave cujus conceptio Solemni plena gaudio Caelestia, terrestria, Nova replet laetitia. | Hail, whose conception, Full of solemn joy, Fills the heaven, the earth, With new rejoicing. | 2 and 3 voices, later 4 voices; more homorhythmic texture. |
| 16 | 1:21 | Ave cujus nativitas Nostra fuit solemnitas, Ut lucifer lux oriens, Verum solem praeveniens. | Hail, whose birth Was our festival, As our luminous rising light Coming before the true sun. | Voice pairs (SA/TB) in close imitation, then 4 voices in imitation. |
| 17 | 1:59 | Ave pia humilitas, Sine viro fecunditas, Cujus annuntiatio, Nostra fuit salvatio. | Hail, pious humility, Fertility without a man, Whose annunciation Was our salvation. | Voice pairs (SA/TB); a more homorhythmic texture. |
| 18 | 2:27 | Ave vera virginitas, Immaculata castitas, Cujus purificatio Nostra fuit purgatio. | Hail, true virginity, Unspotted chastity, Whose purification Was our cleansing. | Triple meter; clear text declamation; homorhythmic texture. |
| 19 | 3:04 | Ave praeclara omnibus Angelicis virtutibus, Cujus fuit assumptio Nostra glorificatio. | Hail, famous with all Angelic virtues, Whose assumption was Our glorification. | Imitative voice pairs; return to duple meter. |
| 20 | 3:59 | O Mater Dei, Memento mei. Amen. | O Mother of God, Remember me. Amen. | Completely homorhythmic; text declamation in long notes, separated by simultaneous rests. |

Rising melodic idea at opening:

A - ve   Ma - ri - a,

**Now try the Listening Quiz.**

## Musical Movements of the Mass

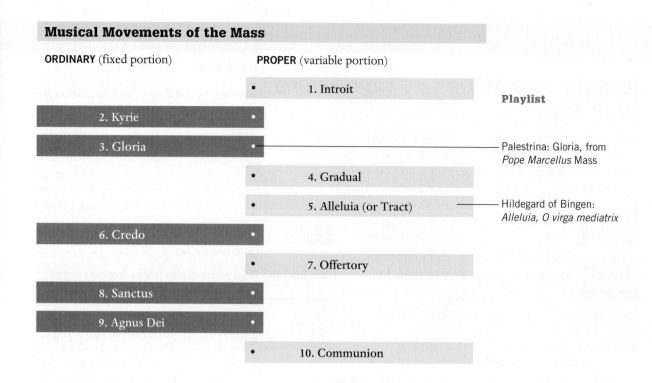

ORDINARY (fixed portion)  PROPER (variable portion)

- 1. Introit

Playlist

2. Kyrie

3. Gloria — Palestrina: Gloria, from *Pope Marcellus* Mass

- 4. Gradual

- 5. Alleluia (or Tract) — Hildegard of Bingen: *Alleluia, O virga mediatrix*

6. Credo

- 7. Offertory

8. Sanctus

9. Agnus Dei

- 10. Communion

# The Renaissance Mass

**Ordinary of the Mass**

With the rise of Renaissance polyphony, composers concentrated their musical settings on the Ordinary, the fixed portion of the Mass that was sung daily. Its five movements are the Kyrie, Gloria, Credo, Sanctus, and Agnus Dei. (Today, these sections of the Mass are recited or sung in the vernacular, that is, the language of the country, rather than in Latin.) The first section, the Kyrie, is a prayer for mercy that dates from the early centuries of Christianity, as its Greek text attests. As we mentioned on page 77, the Kyrie has an **A-B-A** form that consists of nine invocations: three of "Kyrie eleison" (Lord, have mercy), three of "Christe eleison" (Christ, have mercy), and again three of "Kyrie eleison." This movement is followed by the Gloria ("Glory be to God on high"), a joyful hymn of praise. The third movement, the Credo ("I believe in one God, the Father Almighty"), is the confession of faith and the longest of the Mass texts. Fourth is the Sanctus ("Holy, holy, holy"), a song of praise, which concludes with the "Hosanna" ("Hosanna in the highest"). The fifth and last part of the Ordinary, the Agnus Dei ("Lamb of God, Who takes away the sins of the world"), is sung three times, with a different text for its conclusion. The order of the Mass, with its Proper and Ordinary movements, appears above. (Remember that we studied an example of an Alleluia from the Proper of the Mass in Chapter 12.)

**Cantus firmus**

Early polyphonic settings of the Mass (such as medieval organum) were usually based on a fragment of Gregorian chant, which became the *cantus firmus* (fixed melody). The cantus firmus thus served as the foundation of the work, supporting the florid patterns that the other voices wove around it. Composers such as Guillaume Du Fay used a chant or sometimes a popular song as the basis for their Masses. This provided a fixed element that they could embellish, using all the resources of their artistry, and when set in all the movements, it helped unify the Mass.

# The Reformation and Counter-Reformation

Around the time of Josquin's death, major religious reforms were spreading across Northern Europe. In 1517, the Augustinian monk Martin Luther (1483–1546) began the Protestant movement known as the Reformation with his Ninety-Five Theses—a list of reforms he proposed to the practices of the Catholic church. Rather than adopt these new ideas, the church excommunicated Luther, and the rest is history. An admirer of Josquin, Luther sought to draw people to his new Protestant faith with music sung in the **vernacular**, the language of the people. The Catholic church eventually responded with its own reform movement focused on a return to Christian piety. Known as the **Counter-Reformation**, this movement strove to recapture the loyalty of its people with more accessible music. The Counter-Reformation, which extended from the 1530s to the end of the sixteenth century, witnessed sweeping changes in the church as religious orders increased their efforts to help the poor and combat heresy. The Catholic church organized what some view as the longest committee meeting in history: the **Council of Trent**, which met, with some interruptions, from 1545 to 1563.

In its desire to regulate every aspect of religious discipline, the Council of Trent took up the matter of church music. The attending cardinals noted the corruption of traditional chants by the singers, who added extravagant embellishments to the Gregorian melodies. The council members objected to the use of certain instruments in religious services, to the practice of incorporating popular songs in Masses, to the secular spirit that had invaded sacred music, and to the generally irreverent attitude of church musicians. In polyphonic settings of the Mass, the cardinals claimed, the sacred text was made unintelligible by the elaborate texture. Some advocated abolishing polyphony altogether and returning to Gregorian chant, but there were many music lovers among the cardinals who opposed so drastic a step.

The committee assigned to deal with the problem issued only general recommendations in favor of a pure vocal style that would respect the integrity of the sacred texts, avoid virtuosity, and encourage piety. We will hear some of these traits in the glorious polyphony by the Italian master Giovanni Pierluigi da Palestrina.

### By the way . . .

#### Did Palestrina Save Polyphony?

One frequently told story is that Palestrina single-handedly saved polyphonic music by writing his *Pope Marcellus* Mass to meet the Council's requirements of simplicity and clarity of text. This myth was apparently begun shortly after the composer's death in 1594 and perpetuated through an early twentieth-century opera entitled *Palestrina*. Recent scholarship has shown that Palestrina's Mass was probably written some years before the Council's recommendations on music, and that other, lesser-known composers more centrally influenced the Council's decision to allow polyphony. Furthermore, Palestrina did not fully abandon complex, imitative writing, nor did he avoid using secular music in his Masses—several are modeled on madrigals and chansons and two are notably based on a popular monophonic song *L'homme armé*. Still, there is no question that Palestrina's *Pope Marcellus* Mass is a masterwork of polyphonic clarity, which has served as a model for future composers of the Catholic Mass.

# Palestrina and the *Pope Marcellus* Mass

"I have held nothing more desirable than what is sung throughout the year, according to the season, should be more agreeable to the ear by virtue of its vocal beauty."

*In His Own Words*

Our wisest mortals have decided that music should give zest to divine worship. If people take great pains to compose beautiful music for secular songs, they should devote at least as much thought to sacred song.

Palestrina's *Pope Marcellus* Mass was once thought to have been written to satisfy the Council of Trent's recommendations for polyphonic church music, but this is probably not true (see Btw, above). Since the papal choir sang without instrumental accompaniment, the *Pope Marcellus* Mass was most likely performed *a cappella*. It was written for six voice parts—soprano, alto, two tenors, and two basses, a typical setting for the all-male church choirs of the era. The highest voice was sung by

## Giovanni Pierluigi da Palestrina (c. 1525–1594)

**Palestrina** (named for the town where he was born) worked as an organist and choirmaster at various Italian churches, including St. Peter's in Rome. He was appointed briefly to the Sistine Chapel Choir but, as a married man, was ineligible to serve there. Soon, however, he was appointed to another choir at St. Peter's where he spent the last twenty-three years of his life. He wrote largely sacred music—his output of Masses exceeds that of any other composer—and his music represents the pure *a cappella* style of vocal polyphony typical of the late Renaissance. He strove to make the words understood by properly accentuating them, thereby meeting the guidelines of the Catholic reform.

**Major Works:** Over 100 Masses (including the *Pope Marcellus* Mass) as well as madrigals and motets.

boy sopranos or male falsettists (singing in falsetto, or head voice), the alto part by male altos, or countertenors (tenors with very high voices), and the lower parts were distributed among the normal ranges of the male voice.

The Gloria from the *Pope Marcellus* Mass exhibits Palestrina's hallmark style—restrained, serene, and celestial. The opening line, "Gloria in excelsis Deo" (Glory be to God on high), is chanted by the officiating priest. Palestrina constructed a polyphonic setting for the remaining text, balancing the harmonic and polyphonic elements so that the words are audible, an effect that foreshadows the recommendations of the Council of Trent (see Listening Guide 7). Palestrina's music is representative of the pure *a cappella* style of vocal polyphony.

---

**LISTENING GUIDE 7**                    ⑤ | DVD | CD 1 (40–41) | CD 1 (21–22)

## Palestrina: *Pope Marcellus* Mass, Gloria                    5:50

**DATE:** Published 1567

**GENRE:** Gloria, from his setting of the Mass Ordinary

**WHAT TO LISTEN FOR:**

| | | | |
|---|---|---|---|
| Melody | Shifts between high- and low-range voices | Form | Through-composed (no major section repeated), with some short ideas exchanged between voices |
| Rhythm/ Meter | Slow duple, weak pulse | | |
| Harmony | Full, consonant harmony | Expression | Focus on the clarity of the words |
| Texture | Monophonic opening; then homorhythmic, with some polyphony; frequent changes in density of voices | Performing Forces | 6-part choir, *a cappella* |
| | | Text | Hymn of praise; second movement of Ordinary of the Mass |

First phrase of Gloria, sung monophonically, shown in chant notation:

G    Ló- ri- a in ex-cél-sis De-    o.

| | | TEXT | NO. OF VOICES | TRANSLATION |
|---|---|---|---|---|
| 21 | 0:00 | Gloria in excelsis Deo | 1 | Glory be to God on high, |
| | | et in terra pax hominibus | 4 | and on earth peace to men |
| | | bonae voluntatis. | 4 | of good will. |
| | | Laudamus te. Benedicimus te. | 4 | We praise Thee. We bless Thee. |
| | | Adoramus te. | 3 | We adore Thee. |
| | | Glorificamus te. | 4 | We glorify Thee. |
| | | Gratias agimus tibi propter | 5/4 | We give Thee thanks for |
| | | magnam gloriam tuam. | 3/4 | Thy great glory. |
| | | Domine Deus, Rex caelestis, | 4 | Lord God, heavenly King, |
| | | Deus Pater omnipotens. | 3 | God, the Father Almighty. |
| | | Domine Fili | 4 | O Lord, the only-begotten Son, |
| | | unigenite, Jesu Christe. | 6/5 | Jesus Christ. |
| | | Domine Deus, Agnus Dei, | 3/4 | Lord God, Lamb of God, |
| | | Filius Patris. | 6 | Son of the Father. |
| 22 | 2:44 | Qui tollis peccata mundi, | 4 | Thou that takest away the sins of the world, |
| | | miserere nobis. | 4 | have mercy on us. |
| | | Qui tollis peccata mundi, | 4/5 | Thou that takest away the sins of the world, |
| | | suscipe deprecationem nostram. | 6/4 | receive our prayer. |
| | | Qui sedes ad dexteram Patris, | 3 | Thou that sittest at the right hand of the Father, |
| | | miserere nobis. | 3 | have mercy on us. |
| | | Quoniam tu solus sanctus. | 4 | For Thou alone art holy. |
| | | Tu solus Dominus. | 4 | Thou only art the Lord. |
| | | Tu solus Altissimus. | 4 | Thou alone art most high. |
| | | Jesu Christe, cum Sancto Spiritu | 6/3/4 | Jesus Christ, along with the Holy Spirit |
| | | in gloria Dei Patris. | 4/5 | in the glory of God the Father. |
| | | Amen. | 6 | Amen. |

◎ **Now try the Listening Quiz.**

## Critical Thinking

**1.** How does the sound of Renaissance music differ from that of the Middle Ages?

**2.** What is the importance of Josquin des Prez to musical composition?

**3.** How did the Council of Trent influence the performance and style of sacred music?

# 15 Renaissance Secular Music

*"Come sing to me a bawdy song, make me merry."*

**—Falstaff, in William Shakespeare's *Henry IV, Part 1***

## KEY POINTS

⑤ **StudySpace** wwnorton.com/enjoy

- The Renaissance saw a rise in amateur music-making and in secular music (French *chansons* and Italian and English *madrigals*).

- The *madrigal* originated in Italy as a form of aristocratic entertainment.

- Jacques Arcadelt was an early master of the *Italian madrigal* and of expressive devices such

as *word painting*. The *English madrigal* was often simpler and lighter in style than its Italian counterpart.

- Professional and amateur musicians played instrumental *dance music*, often adding *embellishments*.

Musicians perform a polyphonic chanson with voice, flute, and lute. *The Prodigal Son among the Courtesans* (16th century, artist unknown).

## Music in Court and City Life

In the Renaissance, both professionals and amateurs took part in music-making. Professionals entertained noble guests at court and civic festivities, and with the rise of the merchant class, music-making in the home became increasingly popular. Secular music included both purely vocal works and those in which singers were supported by instruments. Solo instrumental music also became more popular; indeed, most prosperous homes had a lute (see left) or a keyboard instrument. The study of music was considered part of the proper upbringing for a young girl or, to a lesser degree, boy. Women began to have prominent roles in the performance of music both in the home and at court. During the later sixteenth century in Italy, a number of professional women singers achieved great fame.

From the union of poetry and music arose two important secular genres: the *chanson* (an outgrowth of the medieval version we heard by Machaut) and the *madrigal*. In both of these song forms, music was used to enhance the poetry. In turn, the intricate verse structures of French and Italian poetry helped to shape the musical forms. The expressive device of *word painting*—that is, making the music directly reflect the meaning of the words—was much favored in secular genres. An unexpected harsh dissonance might coincide with the word "death" or an ascending line might lead up to the word "heaven" or "stars." We will see how these so-called *madrigalisms* enhanced the emotional content of the music.

# The Italian Madrigal

*"By shallow rivers to whose falls
melodious birds sing madrigals."*

—*Christopher Marlowe*

A stylized 16th-century painting of four singers performing from music part books. The couple in back are beating time. *Concert in the Open Air*, Anonymous (Italian School).

The sixteenth-century *madrigal*—the most important secular genre of the era—was an aristocratic form of poetry and music that flourished at the Italian courts as a favorite diversion of cultivated amateurs. The text consisted of a short poem of lyric or reflective character, often including emotional words for weeping, sighing, trembling, and dying, which the Italian madrigalists set expressively. Love and unsatisfied desire were popular topics of the madrigal but by no means the only ones. Humor and satire, political themes, and scenes and incidents of city and country life were also portrayed; the Italian madrigal literature of the sixteenth century therefore presents a vivid panorama of Renaissance thought and feeling.

During the early period of the Renaissance madrigal (c. 1525–50) the composer's chief concern was to give pleasure to the performers, often amateurs, with little thought to virtuosic display. From the beginning, the madrigal became an art form in which words and music were clearly linked. We will hear one of the most beautiful madrigals of the early era, composed by Jacques Arcadelt.

The madrigal soon grew in complexity and expanded to five or six voices. The final phase of the Italian madrigal (1580–1620) extended beyond the late Renaissance into the world of the Baroque. The form became the direct expression of the composer's musical personality and feelings. Certain traits were carried to an extreme: rich chromatic harmony, dramatic declamation, vocal virtuosity, and vivid depiction of emotional words in music, all traits that lead us to the new Baroque style.

## Arcadelt and the Madrigal

Arcadelt's lovely madrigal *Il bianco e dolce cigno* (*The white and sweet swan*) was a huge hit in his lifetime and for some years to follow, perhaps because its intended audience was amateur performers. He delivers the words clearly, in a mostly homophonic setting, with subtle moments of word painting emphasizing certain words with melismas and others with chromaticism (see Listening Guide 8, p. 98). Madrigal texts typically offer various levels of meaning, and this one is no different. Literally, the text refers to swans singing—which according to ancient belief, they do only before they die. But references to death in madrigal poetry were usually understood as erotic—a conceit for sexual climax—which gives the text a whole new meaning. In this era, madrigals were sung as chamber music, with one singer on a line reading from part books (see illustration above).

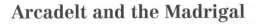

### Jacques Arcadelt (c. 1507–1568)

The northern composer **Jacques Arcadelt** was highly influential in the development of the Italian madrigal. He moved from present-day Belgium to Italy in the 1520s, working first in Florence—the birthplace of the madrigal—and later in Rome, as a singer in the Sistine Chapel choir. His earliest madrigal publications were issued during his years in Rome: his first book of madrigals (published in 1538 and including the famous *Il bianco e dolce cigno*) became the most widely reprinted collection of the time. In 1551, he moved north to take a post in France at the court of

*The Lute Player* by **Caravaggio** (1571–1610) performs an Arcadelt madrigal.

the Cardinal of Lorraine, where he continued to write and publish both sacred and secular music. His musical style is simpler and more lyrical than that of earlier composers, and he gives careful attention to the text. He set poems by many different writers, ranging from Petrarch to the Italian military commander Alfonso d'Avalos, who penned Arcadelt's most famous work.

**Major works:** Some 250 madrigals, mostly for 4 voices • About 125 French chansons, and sacred music, including Masses and motets.

---

**LISTENING GUIDE 8**                    ⑤ | DVD | **CD 1 (44–45)** | CD 1 (23–24)

# Arcadelt: *Il bianco e dolce cigno*
# (*The white and sweet swan*)                                     2:05

**DATE:** Published 1538

**GENRE:** Italian madrigal

## WHAT TO LISTEN FOR:

| | |
|---|---|
| Melody | Lyrical, conjunct; focus on top line |
| Rhythm/ Meter | Simple movement in duple meter |
| Harmony | Consonant full sound, with some dissonance and chromaticism for expression |
| Texture | Mostly homophonic; imitative entries on last line |

| | |
|---|---|
| Form | Through-composed until last line (many repetitions) |
| Expression | Emotional words set with dissonance, chromaticism, melisma, and repetition |
| Performing Forces | 4 voices, *a cappella* |
| Text | 10-line poem by Alfonso d'Avalos |

| | | TEXT | TRANSLATION |
|---|---|---|---|
| 23 | 0:00 | Il bianco e dolce cigno | The white and sweet swan |
| | | cantando more. Et io | dies singing. And I, |
| | | piangendo giung' al fin del viver mio. | weeping, come to the end of my life. |
| | | Stran' e diversa sorte, | Strange and different fate, |
| | | ch'ei more sconsolato, | that it dies disconsolate, |
| | | et io moro beato. | And I die happy— |
| | | Morte che nel morire, | a death that in dying |
| | | m'empie di gioia tutt'e di desire. | fills me fully with joy and desire. |
| | | Se nel morir' altro dolor non sento, | If when I die no other pain I feel, |
| 24 | 1:24 | di mille mort' il dì sarei contento. | with a thousand deaths a day I would be content. |

Last line repeated many times to emphasize *di mille morte* (a thousand deaths):

| Meter | 1 | 2 | 3 | 4 | 1 | 2 | 3 | 4 | 1 | 2 | 3 | 4 | 1 | 2 | 3 |
|---|---|---|---|---|---|---|---|---|---|---|---|---|---|---|---|
| **Soprano** | | | | | | | | | di mil- | le | mort'il | dì | | | |
| **Alto** | di mil- | le | mort'il dì, | di | mil- | | le | mort'il dì | | | | | | | |
| **Tenor** | | di | mil- | le mort' | il dì, | di | mil- | le | mort' il dì | | | | | | |
| **Bass** | | | di mil- | le mort' | il dì_____ | | | | | | | | | | |

⑤ **Now try the Listening Quiz.**

# The English Madrigal

"Since singing is so good a thing,
I wish that all men would learne to sing."

—*William Byrd*

Just as Shakespeare adapted the Italian sonnet, so the English composers developed the Italian madrigal into a native art form. The brilliance of the Elizabethan age is reflected in the school of madrigalists who flourished during the late sixteenth century and the reign of Elizabeth I (1558–1603).

In the first collection of Italian madrigals published in England, titled *Musica transalpina* (*Music from beyond the Alps*, 1588), the songs were "Englished"—that is, the texts were translated. In their own madrigals, some English composers followed the traditions of the late Italian madrigal, setting dramatic love poetry in serious, weighty works, while many others favored simpler texts in more accessible settings. New humorous madrigal types were cultivated, some with refrain syllables such as "fa la la." One of the most important English madrigal composers was John Farmer, whose delightful work *Fair Phyllis* we will study.

*Musica transalpina*

---

### John Farmer (c. 1570–1603)

The English composer **John Farmer** was active in Dublin, Ireland, as an organist and master of the choirboys at Christ Church. In 1599, he moved to London and published his only collection of four-voice madrigals. Farmer used clever word painting in these light-hearted works and helped shape the madrigal into a truly native art form.

**Major Works:** English songs and madrigals (for 4 and 6 voices).

A typical pastoral scene of a shepherd and sheperdess, by **Januarius Zick** (1730–1797).

---

## John Farmer's *Fair Phyllis*

The pastoral text, lively rhythms, and good humor of *Fair Phyllis* make it a perfect example of the English madrigal. The poem tells of a shepherdess (Phyllis) tending her sheep, when she is found and pursued by her lover Amyntas (their names are stock ones for such rustic characters). The narrative brings their story to a happy conclusion with their amorous love play. English composers adopted the Italian practice of word painting, allowing us to "hear" this charming story (see Listening Guide 9, p. 100). The Renaissance madrigal inspired composers to develop new techniques of combining music and poetry. In doing so, it prepared the way for one of the most influential forms of Western music—opera, which blossomed in the earliest years of the Baroque era.

# Instrumental Dance Music

The sixteenth century witnessed a blossoming of instrumental dance music. With the advent of music printing, books of dance music became readily available for solo instruments as well as for small ensembles. The dances were often fashioned from vocal works such as madrigals and chansons, which were published in simplified versions that were played instead of sung. These dance arrangements did not specify which instruments to use. As in medieval performances, outdoor concerts called for loud instruments such as the shawm and sackbut (medieval

## LISTENING GUIDE 9

# Farmer: *Fair Phyllis*

1:21

**DATE:**   Published 1599

**GENRE:**   English madrigal

**WHAT TO LISTEN FOR:**

| | | | |
|---|---|---|---|
| Melody | Dancelike, diatonic melody | Expression | Word painting on opening line ("all alone") and "up and down" |
| Rhythm/ Meter | Lively rhythms; begins in duple meter, shifts to triple and back | Performing Forces | 4 voices (SATB), *a cappella* |
| Texture | Varied: opens monophonically, some imitation, then homorhythmic for last line | Text | Light-hearted pastoral English poem |
| Form | Short, repeated sections | | |

**TEXT**

| | | |
|---|---|---|
| 25 | 0:00 | Fair Phyllis I saw sitting all alone, |
| | | Feeding her flock near to the mountain side. |
| | | The shepherds knew not whither she was gone, |
| | | But after her [her] lover Amyntas hied. |
| 26 | 0:24 | Up and down he wandered, whilst she was missing; |
| | | When he found her, oh, then they fell a-kissing. |
| | 0:48 | Up and down . . . |

**Examples of word painting:**

"Fair Phyllis I saw sitting all alone"—sung by soprano alone:

"Up and down"—descending line, repeated in all parts imitatively; shown in soprano and alto:

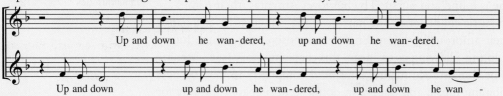

◉ **Now try the Listening Quiz.**

oboe and trombone); for intimate settings, soft instruments such as recorders and bowed strings were preferred. Although percussion parts were not written out in Renaissance music, evidence suggests that they were improvised.

A number of dance types became popular during the sixteenth century. The stately court dance known as the **pavane** often served as the first in a set that included one or more quicker dances, especially the Italian **saltarello** (jumping dance). Less courtly was the **ronde**, or round dance, a lively romp performed in a circle, usually in an outdoor setting.

**LISTENING GUIDE 10**                          ⑤ | DVD | CD 1 (48–51) | CD 1 (27–30)

# Susato: Three Dances                                          2:29

**DATE:** Published 1551

**GENRE:** Ronde (round dance)

## WHAT TO LISTEN FOR:

| | | | |
|---|---|---|---|
| Melody | Prominence of tune | Form | Each dance in binary (**A-A-B-B**) form; return to opening dance at end |
| Rhythm/ Meter | Duple meter, set in short phrases | Expression | Occasional improvised embellishments |
| Harmony | Consonant, full triads; Ronde 2 is modal | Performing Forces | 4-part instrumental ensemble; loud wind band (shawm, cornetto, sackbut, tabor, tambourine) |
| Texture | Mostly homophonic | | |

| SECTION | | INSTRUMENTS |
|---|---|---|
| | **Ronde 1** | |
| 27  0:00 | A | Solo shawm playing melody alone (4 measures). |
| 0:06 | A | Shawm with tabor. |
| 0:11 | B | Loud ensemble (shawm, trombones, tabor), 8 measures. |
| 0:22 | B | Repeat of **B**. |

Opening phrase (**A**) of Ronde 1:

| SECTION | | INSTRUMENTS |
|---|---|---|
| | **Ronde 2** | |
| 28  0:33 | C | Softer solo instrument (cornetto), with trombones, shawm, and tambourine, 4 measures; modal harmony. |
| 0:38 | C | Repeat of **C**. |
| 0:44 | D | New section, contrapuntal. |
| 0:55 | D | Repeat of **D**, embellished. |

Opening phrase (**C**) of Ronde 2:

| SECTION | | INSTRUMENTS |
|---|---|---|
| | **Transition: Ronde 1** | |
| 1:12 | A | Heard 4 times, each with melody played by a different instrument. |
| | **Ronde 3** | |
| 29  1:23 | E | Loud shawm, with full wind band and tabor, 8 measures. |
| 1:34 | E | Repeat of **E**. |
| 1:45 | F | New short section, 4 measures. |
| 1:51 | F | Repeat of **F**. |

Opening phrase (**E**) of Ronde 3:

| SECTION | | INSTRUMENTS |
|---|---|---|
| | **Repeat of Ronde 1** | |
| 30  1:57 | B | Played twice to round off set of dances. |
| 2:20 | | Final long bow chord. |

⑤ **Now try the Listening Quiz.**

One of the most popular dance collections of the century was published in Antwerp (in modern-day Belgium) in 1551 by Tielman Susato (c. 1515–c. 1571), a well-known printer, composer, and instrumentalist. His collection, called *Danserye*, includes a variety of popular dance types. Our selection is a set of three *rondes*. Although originally a country dance, the ronde became popular in the city and at the courts of the nobility. Our recording features

Tielman Susato

A city wind band. Detail from *Procession in honor of Our Lady of Sablon in Brussels,* by **Denis van Alsloot** (c. 1570–c. 1626), 1616.

the loud wind band (see illustration, left), which includes double reeds (*shawms* of various sizes), brass (*sackbut* and *cornetto*—a hybrid brass/woodwind instrument) and percussion (*tabor* and *tambourine*). (See Listening Guide 10.)

The repeated sections in the dances allow the musicians to improvise **embellishments**, or melodic decorations, as they see fit, and the sound is enriched and varied through different combinations of instruments. The dances flow from one to the next, closing with a brief return to the opening, thus rounding out the set. A final chord provides a cue for the dancers to make a sweeping bow. It was through such dance pieces that Renaissance composers began to explore the possibilities of purely instrumental forms.

## From the Renaissance to the Baroque

By the end of the sixteenth century, composers looked to new expressive means in their music, and in particular to find inventive ways to convey the text of vocal works through a single melody rather than several interweaving ones. This desire—a result of the humanistic spirit—created a variety of new genres,

### LISTENING ACTIVITY: COMPARING STYLES 2 MEDIEVAL, RENAISSANCE, AND BAROQUE

Listen to the three selections listed below (StudySpace, Chapter 15) to review the musical styles of the medieval, Renaissance, and Baroque eras. Then see if you can identify the characteristics that best fit each work by matching the letter to the descriptions below. Try to place each work with the trait that best suits its overall style. More than one work may fit the same style trait.

#### Examples

**a.** Hildegard: Kyrie (medieval)
**b.** Josquin: *El grillo* (*The Cricket*) (Renaissance)

**c.** Handel: "Hallelujah Chorus,"
from *Messiah* (Baroque)

#### Musical styles

**1.** _____ monophonic texture        _____ homorhythmic texture        _____ polyphonic texture

**2.** _____ duple meter        _____ triple meter        _____ nonmetric

**3.** _____ men's voices        _____ women's voices        _____ mixed voices

**4.** _____ secular music        _____ devotional music        _____ part of Mass liturgy

**5.** _____ music at court        _____ music at church        _____ public theater music

**6.** _____ syllabic text setting        _____ melismatic text setting

**7.** _____ *a cappella* performance        _____ concerted performance (with instruments)

including opera, the cantata, and the oratorio. Composers also explored the possibilities of pure instrumental music, and small forms such as the popular dances we just heard gave way to large soloistic genres of the Baroque such as the sonata and the concerto.

## Critical Thinking

**1.** How did Renaissance composers achieve a union of music and words?

**2.** Who performed secular songs and dances in the Renaissance? Where did these performances take place?

**3.** Which developments in Renaissance music lead directly to the new dramatic genres of the Baroque?

## A COMPARISON OF MEDIEVAL, RENAISSANCE, AND BAROQUE STYLES

| | MEDIEVAL (c. 400–1450) | RENAISSANCE (c. 1450–1600) | BAROQUE (c. 1600–1750) |
|---|---|---|---|
| **COMPOSERS** | Hildegard, Notre Dame composers, Machaut | Josquin des Prez, Palestrina, Arcadelt, Farmer, Susato | Monteverdi, Purcell, Strozzi, Bach, Mouret, Handel, Vivaldi |
| **MELODY** | Conjunct, small range | Arched, asymmetrical melodies | Lyrical and chromatic; continuous flow (late) |
| **RHYTHM/ METER** | Nonmetric (early); triple meter | Regular, gentle pulse; duple meter | Strongly rhythmic (late) |
| **HARMONY** | Modal | Modal, moving toward tonality | Major and minor tonality |
| **TEXTURE** | Monophonic (early); nonimitative polyphony (late) | Imitative polyphony | Mixed textures; polyphonic (late) |
| **MEDIUM** | *A cappella* vocal music | *A cappella* vocal music | Voices with instruments |
| **VOCAL GENRES** | Chant, organum, chanson, motet, Mass | Mass, motet, madrigal, chanson | Opera, cantata, oratorio |
| **INSTRUMENTAL GENRES** | Dance music | Dance music | Sonata, concerto, suite |
| **USE OF PRE-EXISTENT MUSIC** | Sacred music based on chant | Sacred music uses cantus firmus (early); move toward freely composed | Freely composed |
| **PERFORMANCE SITES** | Church, court | Church, court, home | Public theaters, court, church |

Ⓔ **Find an interactive version of this chart on StudySpace.**

# Baroque Era

1600 1610 1620 1630 1640 1650 1660 1670 1680 1690 1700 1710 1720 1730 1740 1750

## COMPOSERS AND WORKS

**(1567–1643)** Claudio Monteverdi (*The Coronation of Poppea*)

**(1619–c. 1677)** Barbara Strozzi (*Sleepyhead, Cupid!*)

**(1659–1695)** Henry Purcell (*Dido and Aeneas*)

**(1678–1741)** Antonio Vivaldi (*The Four Seasons*)

**(1682–1738)** Jean-Joseph Mouret (*Suite de symphonies*)

**(1685–1750)** Johann Sebastian Bach (*Sleepers, Awake*)

**(1685–1759)** George Frideric Handel (*Water Music Suite, Messiah*)

1600 1610 1620 1630 1640 1650 1660 1670 1680 1690 1700 1710 1720 1730 1740 1750

## EVENTS

**1603** Death of Elizabeth I

**1607** First settlement in Jamestown, Virginia

**1611** Bible: King James Version

**1628** Dr. William Harvey explains the circulatory system

**1643** Reign of Louis XIV begins

**1649** Period of Commonwealth begins in England

**1667** John Milton's *Paradise Lost*

**1684** Sir Isaac Newton's theory of gravitation

Reign of Louis XV begins **1715**

John Gay's *Beggar's Opera* performed **1728**

# The Baroque Era

**Judith Leyster** (1609–1660). *The Flute Player.*

# The Baroque Spirit

"These harmonic notes are the language of the soul
and the instruments of the heart."

**—Barbara Strozzi**

## KEY POINTS

- The Baroque era (1600–1750) was a time of turbulent changes in a society that saw religious wars (Protestants vs. Catholics) as well as exploration and colonization of the New World.

- The era also saw the rise of middle-class culture, with music-making centered in the home; art often portrayed scenes of middle-class life.

- The Baroque marks the introduction of *monody*, which featured solo song with instrumental accompaniment; its goal was to recreate the musical-dramatic art of ancient Greece.

- Harmony was notated with *figured bass*, a shorthand that allowed the performer to *improvise*

- the chords. The bass part, or *basso continuo*, was often played by two instruments (harpsichord and cello, for example).

- The *major-minor tonality* system was established in the Baroque era, as was the *equal temperament* tuning system.

- While early Baroque music moved more freely, later Baroque style is characterized by regular rhythms and continuous melodic expansion.

- As musical instruments developed technically, the level of virtuosity and playing techniques rose.

- The union of text and music was expressed in the Baroque *doctrine of the affections*.

The Baroque period stretched across a stormy century and a half of European history. Those years between 1600 and 1750 represent a period of change and adventure. The conquest of the New World stirred the imagination and filled the treasuries of Western Europe. The middle classes acquired wealth and power in their struggle against the aristocracy. Empires clashed for control of the globe. The era was characterized by appalling poverty and wasteful luxury, magnificent idealism and savage oppression. Baroque art—with its vigor, elaborate decoration, and grandeur—projected the pomp

**Baroque art**

and splendor of the era. Indeed, the eras's name *Baroque* means exaggerated, abnormal, or even bizarre.

The transition from the classically minded Renaissance to the Baroque was foreshadowed in the art of Michelangelo (1475–1564). His turbulent figures (see illustration opposite), their bodies twisted in struggle, reflect the Baroque love of the dramatic. In like fashion, the Venetian school of painters and northern masters such as Rubens studied and adopted their techniques, capturing the dynamic spirit of the new age and producing canvases ablaze in color and movement.

The Baroque was an era of absolute monarchy. Rulers throughout Europe modeled their courts on Versailles, a great palace on the outskirts of Paris. Louis

The bold and vigorous Baroque style was foreshadowed in this dramatic painting of *The Creation of Adam* by **Michelangelo** (1475–1564).

XIV's famous statement "I am the State" summed up a way of life in which all art and culture served the ruler. Courts large and small maintained elaborate musical establishments, including opera troupes, chapel choirs, and orchestras. Baroque opera, the favorite diversion of the aristocracy, told stories of gods and heroes of antiquity, in whom the nobility and courtiers saw flattering likenesses of themselves.

The middle classes, excluded from the salons of the aristocracy, created a culture of their own. Their music-making took place in the home. It was for the middle classes that the comic opera and the prose novel, both genres filled with keen and witty observations on life, came into being. For them, painting abandoned its grandiose themes and turned to intimate scenes of bourgeois life. The Dutch School, embodying the vitality of a new middle-class art, reached its high point with Rembrandt (1606–1669) and Vermeer (1632–1675, see illustration at right).

**Jan Vermeer** (1632–1675) is well known for his painting of bourgeois, or middle-class, women playing a keyboard instrument. *Young Woman at a Virginal.*

Under the leadership of wealthy merchants and financiers, the culture of the city came to rival that of the palace. These new art lovers vied with the court in their devotion to splendor. This aspect of the Baroque finds expression in the painting of Peter Paul Rubens (1577–1640; see illustration, p. 108), whose canvases exude a driving energy and a celebration of life. His voluptuous nudes established the seventeenth-century ideal of feminine beauty.

The Baroque was an age of discovery. The ideas of Galileo and Copernicus in physics and astronomy, of Descartes in mathematics, and of Spinoza in philosophy were milestones in the intellectual history of Europe. The English physician William Harvey explained the circulation of the blood, and Sir Isaac Newton formulated the theory of gravity.

The Baroque was also an intensely devout period, with religion a rallying cry on some of the bloodiest battlefields in history. Protestants were centered in England, Scandinavia, Holland, and northern Germany, all strongholds of the rising middle class. On the Catholic side were two powerful

The Flemish painter **Peter Paul Rubens** (1577–1640) instills his paintings with high energy and drama. *Diana and Her Nymphs.*

Religion

dynasties: the French Bourbons and the Austrian-Spanish Hapsburgs, who fought one another as fiercely as they did their Protestant foes. Religion was an equally important part of life in the New World as well, both in the colonies of Protestant refugees who settled on the East Coast and in the Spanish colonies (Mexico, Central America, and the Southwestern United States), all fervently Catholic.

Literature

England's John Milton (1608–1674) produced the poetic epic of Protestantism (*Paradise Lost*), just as Dante had expressed the Catholic point of view in *The Divine Comedy* three and a half centuries earlier. The Catholic world answered Martin Luther's call for reforms with the Counter-Reformation (see p. 93), whose rapturous mysticism found expression in the canvases of El Greco (1541–1614; see illustration opposite). These paintings were the creations of a visionary mind that distorted the real in its search for a reality beyond.

Creative artists played a variety of roles in Baroque society. Peter Paul Rubens was not only a famous painter but also an ambassador and friend of princes. The composer Antonio Vivaldi was also a priest, and George Frideric Handel an opera impresario. Artists usually functioned under royal or princely patronage, or, like Johann Sebastian Bach, they might be employed by a church or city administration. In all cases, artists were in direct contact with their public. Many musical works were created for specific occasions—an opera for a royal wedding, a dance suite for a court festivity, a cantata for a religious service—and for immediate use.

# Main Currents in Baroque Music

"The end of all good music is to affect the soul."

—*Claudio Monteverdi*

*In His Own Words*

I sought to imitate the ideas behind the words, trying to find those notes of greater or lesser affect based on the emotions of the text. . . .

—*Giulio Caccini*

The transition from Renaissance to Baroque brought with it a great musical change: interest shifted from a texture of several independent parts (polyphony) to one in which a single melody stood out (homophony). The new style, which originated in vocal music around the year 1600, was named **monody**. Literally "one song," monody is solo song with instrumental accompaniment (not to be confused with monophony, which is a single unaccompanied line; see p. 26).

Monody was first cultivated by a group of Florentine writers, artists, and musicians known as the **Camerata**, a name derived from the Italian word for "salon." The members of the Camerata were aristocratic humanists who aimed to resurrect the musical-dramatic art of ancient Greece. Although little was known of ancient music, the Camerata deduced that music must heighten the emotional power of the text. Thus the monodic style came into being, consisting of a melody that moved freely over a foundation of simple chords.

Camerata

The Camerata's members—including composer Giulio Caccini—engaged in excited discussions about "the new music," which they proudly named "the expressive style." The group soon realized that this style could be applied not only to a short poem but also to an entire drama. With this realization, they fostered the single most important achievement of Baroque music: the invention of opera.

Origins of opera

## New Harmonic Structures

The melody and chords of the new music were far removed from the complex interweaving of voices in the older Renaissance style, and a new kind of notation accommodated these changes. Since musicians were familiar with the basic harmonies, the composer put a numeral above or below the bass note, indicating the chord required (this kind of notation was called *figured bass*), and the performer filled in the necessary harmony. This system, known as **basso continuo**, often employed two instrumentalists for the accompaniment. One played the bass line on a cello or bassoon, and another filled in the harmonies on a chordal instrument (generally harpsichord, organ, or lute), thereby providing a foundation over which a vocal or instrumental melody could unfold.

This shift to a simpler style based on a single-line melody and less complex harmonies led to one of the most significant changes in all music history: the establishment of **major-minor tonality** (see Chapter 4). With this development, the thrust to the keynote, or tonic, became the most powerful force in music. Each chord could assume its function in relation to the key center, and the movement between keys, governed by tonality, helped shape musical structure. With this system, composers developed forms of instrumental music larger than had ever before been known.

The rapturous mysticism of the Counter-Reformation found expression in this eerie landscape of **El Greco** (1541–1614), *View of Toledo.*

This transition to major-minor tonality was marked by a significant technical advance: the establishment of a new tuning system that allowed instruments to play in any key. Called **equal temperament**, this tuning adjusted (or tempered) the mathematically "pure" intervals within the octave to equalize the distance between adjacent tones, making it possible to play in every major and minor key without experiencing unpleasant sounds. This development greatly increased the range of harmonic possibilities available to the composer.

Equal temperament

Johann Sebastian Bach demonstrated that he could write in every one of the twelve major and twelve minor keys. His *Well-Tempered Clavier* is a two-volume keyboard collection, each containing twenty-four preludes and fugues, or one in every possible key. Today, our ears are conditioned to the equal tempered system, since this is how pianos are now tuned.

*Well-Tempered Clavier*

The grand staircase of the Residenz, home of the prince-bishop of Würzburg, is a superb example of Baroque interior design, with its sculptural ornaments and elaborate decorations.

## Baroque Musical Style

During the Baroque era, the rhythmic freedom of the monodic style eventually gave way to a vigorous rhythm based on regular accent and carried by a moving bass part. Rhythm helped capture the drive and movement of this dynamic age. The elaborate scrollwork of Baroque architecture found its musical equivalent in the principle of continuous expansion of melody. A movement might start with a striking musical figure that spins out ceaselessly. In vocal music, wide leaps and chromatic tones helped create melodies that were highly expressive of the text.

Baroque musicians used dissonant chords more freely, for emotional intensity and color. In setting poetry, for example, a composer might use a dissonance to heighten the impact of a particularly expressive word.

The dynamic contrasts achieved in Renaissance music through varied imitative voicings gave way to a more nuanced treatment in the Baroque, which contributed to the expression of emotions, especially of the text. Dramatic *forte/piano* contrasts and echo effects were also typical of the era. By comparison with later eras, Baroque composers were sparing in their use of expression marks, leaving these interpretive decisions to performers.

## The Doctrine of the Affections

The Baroque inherited from the Renaissance an impressive technique of text painting, in which the music vividly mirrored the words. It was generally accepted that music ought to arouse the emotions, or affections—for example, joy, anger, love, or fear. By the late seventeenth century, an entire piece or movement was normally built on a single affection, applying what was known as the *doctrine of the affections*. The opening musical idea established the mood of the piece, which prevailed until the work's end. This procedure differs markedly from the practice of later eras, when music was based on two or more contrasting emotions.

# The Rise of the Virtuoso Musician

As the great musical instrument builders in Italy and Germany improved and refined their instruments, Baroque performers responded with more virtuosic playing. Composers in turn wrote works demanding even more advanced playing techniques. Out of these developments came the virtuosic violin works of Antonio Vivaldi (see p. 137).

The emergence of instrumental virtuosity had its counterpart in the vocal sphere. Women began to forge careers as professional singers (see HTTN 3), and the rise of opera saw the development of a phenomenal vocal technique, exemplified in the early eighteenth century by the *castrato,* a male singer who was castrated during boyhood in order to preserve the soprano or alto register of his voice for the rest of his life. What resulted, after years of training, was an incredibly agile voice of enormous range, powered by breath control unrivaled by most

Caricature of the famous castrato Farinelli, by **Pier Leone Ghezzi** (1674–1755).

# The Rise of the Professional Female Singer

Women had expanded opportunities to study and work as professional musicians in the early Baroque era. One important precedent was an exclusive group of women singers employed in the last decades of the sixteenth century by a small but wealthy court in northern Italy. Known as the *Concerto delle donne* (Ensemble of the Ladies), this group was highly praised by all those who were invited to hear them. One ambassador wrote in detail of their brilliant, florid singing, noting "The ladies vied with each other . . . in the design of exquisite passages. . . . They moderated their voices, loud and soft, heavy or light, according to the demands of the piece they were singing." The music they sang, all set in close, high-range harmony, expressed the new Baroque ideal of clarity of the text. Among the composers who wrote for this exclusive trio of women was Claudio Monteverdi (see p. 114), a master of early opera and of the madrigal.

Two early seventeenth-century women stand out for their talents as solo performers: Francesca Caccini (1587–after 1641), daughter of Giulio Caccini (one of the creators of the "new music," see p. 109), was deeply immersed in the musical culture of her time. She sang several important roles

in the earliest operas and was the first woman composer to write an opera. The other woman is Barbara Strozzi (see p. 118), whose access to the literary academies of Venice came both through her father (she was most likely his illegitimate daughter) and because she was probably a courtesan. She was a prolific composer of both secular and sacred music in the new monodic style (see p. 109).

With the establishment of opera houses throughout Europe, the opportunity for women to enter the ranks of professional performers greatly increased. Some women reached the level of superstars, such as the Italian sopranos Faustina Bordoni (see illustration above) and Francesca Cuzzoni, who engaged in a notoriously bitter rivalry in London as favored performers of Handel's operas. Bordoni reportedly had a brilliant, penetrating, and exceedingly agile voice, while Cuzzoni's high notes were unsurpassed in their clarity and sweetness, and her ability to sing ornaments reportedly "took possession of the soul of every auditor."

Consider the difference today for a woman aspiring to a professional singing career: for one, it is definitely easier to become an overnight sensation, thanks to the Internet, social network-

Singer Faustina Bordoni in a portrait by **Bartolomeo Nazari** (1699–1758).

ing, TV, and especially YouTube. Welsh soprano Charlotte Church (b. 1986) began her career performing classical music but soon branched out to popular styles with CDs and even her own television series. And who can forget the matronly Susan Boyle who took *Britain's Got Talent* by storm in early 2009 with her stirring rendition of *I Dreamed a Dream* from *Les Misérables*. Her second-place finish on the show seems not to have hurt her career at all—her first CD, issued in November 2009, made Amazon CD-sales history with the largest pre-order in the history of the retailer.

---

◉ **iMusic**

Monteverdi: *Lament of the Nymph*
Handel: "O thou that tellest good tidings," from *Messiah*

---

singers today. The castrato's voice combined the lung power of the male with the brilliance of the female upper register. Strange as it may seem to us, Baroque audiences associated this voice with heroic male roles. When castrato roles are performed today, they are usually sung in lower register by a tenor or baritone, or in the original register by a countertenor, or a woman singer in male costume.

Improvisation played a significant role in Baroque music. In addition to realizing the abbreviations of the figured bass, musicians added embellishments to what was written down (a custom found today in jazz and pop music). The practice was

Improvisation

A performance at the Teatro Argentina in Rome, 1729, as portrayed by **Giovanni Paolo Pannini** (1691–1765).

so widespread that Baroque music sounded quite different in performance from what was on the page.

**Internationalism**

The Baroque was a culturally international period in which there was free exchange among national cultures. The sensuous beauty of Italian melody, the pointed precision of French dance rhythm, the luxuriance of German polyphony, the freshness of English choral song—these nourished an all-European art that absorbed the best of each national style. We will see how George Frideric Handel, a German, wrote Italian opera for English audiences and gave England the oratorio.

**Exploration**

The Baroque era also saw great voyages of exploration open up unknown regions of the globe, sparking a vivid interest among Europeans in remote cultures and far-off locales. As a result, exoticism became a discernible element of Baroque music. A number of operas looked to faraway lands for their settings—Persia, India, Turkey, the Near East, Peru, and the Americas. These operas offered picturesque scenes, interesting local color, and dances that may not have been authentic but that delighted audiences through their appeal to the imagination. Thus an international spirit combined with an interest in the exotic to produce music that flowed easily across national boundaries.

### Critical Thinking

**1.** How did artists and composers bring drama to their Baroque works?

**2.** What is new about the so-called new music at the beginning of the Baroque?

**3.** How did women establish themselves as professional musicians in the Baroque era?

# 16 Baroque Opera and Its Components

"Opera is the delight of Princes."

—Marco da Gagliano

**KEY POINTS**

> ⓢ **StudySpace** wwnorton.com/enjoy

- The most important new genre of the Baroque era was **opera**, a large-scale music drama that combines poetry, acting, scenery, and costumes with singing and instrumental music.
- The principal components of opera include the orchestral **overture**, solo **arias** (lyrical songs) and **recitatives** (speechlike declamations of the text), and ensemble numbers, including **choruses.** The **librettist** writes the text of the opera.

- The early Baroque master Claudio Monteverdi wrote operas based on mythology and Roman history.
- Henry Purcell wrote *Dido and Aeneas,* based on *The Aeneid,* a Roman epic by Virgil.
- Barbara Strozzi was a noted singer and composer whose expressive solo arias foreshadow the three-part **da capo structure** that becomes standard by the late Baroque.

## The Components of Opera

An *opera* is a large-scale drama that is sung. It combines the resources of vocal and instrumental music—soloists, ensembles, chorus, orchestra, and sometimes ballet—with poetry and drama, acting and pantomime, scenery and costumes. To unify diverse elements is a challenge that has attracted some of the most creative minds in the history of music.

Recitative

In opera, the plot and action are generally advanced through a kind of musical declamation, or speech, known as *recitative.* This vocal style, which grew out of the earliest monodies of the Florentine Camerata, imitates the natural inflections of speech; its movement is shaped to the rhythm of the language. Rarely presenting a purely musical line, recitative is often characterized by a patter and "talky" repetition of the same note, as well as rapid question-and-answer dialogue that builds tension. In time, two styles of recitative became standard: *secco* (Italian for "dry"), which is accompanied only by continuo instruments and moves with great freedom, and *accompagnato,* which is accompanied by the orchestra and thus moves more evenly.

Aria

Recitative gives way at lyric moments to the *aria* (Italian for "air"), which releases through melody the emotional tension accumulated in the course of the action. The aria is a song, usually of a highly emotional nature. It is what audiences wait for, what they cheer, what they remember. An aria, because of its tunefulness, can be effective even when sung out of context—for example, in a concert or on a CD. One formal convention that developed early in the genre's history is the *da capo aria,* a ternary, or **A-B-A**, form that brings back the first section with

Da capo aria

**113**

**Ensemble**

embellishments improvised by the soloist. We will hear an early example of this aria structure by Barbara Strozzi (see p. 118).

An opera may contain ensemble numbers—duets, trios, quartets, and so on—in which the characters pour out their respective feelings. The chorus may be used to back up the solo voices or may function independently. Sometimes it comments and reflects on the action, as in the chorus of a Greek tragedy, or is integrated into the action.

**Overture**

The orchestra supports the action of the opera as well, setting the appropriate mood for the different scenes. The orchestra also performs the *overture*, an instrumental number heard at the beginning of most operas, which may introduce melodies from the arias. Each act of the opera normally opens with an orchestral introduction, and between scenes we may find interludes, or *sinfonias*, as they were called in Baroque opera.

**Libretto**

The opera composer works with a *librettist*, who writes the text of the work, using dramatic insight to create characters and the storyline, with its main threads and subplots. The *libretto*, the text or script of the opera, must be devised to give the composer an opportunity to write music for the diverse numbers—recitatives and arias, ensembles, choruses, interludes—that have become the traditional features of this art form.

## Early Opera in Italy

*In His Own Words*

I consider the principal passions or emotions of the soul to be three: namely, anger, serenity, and humility. The best philosophers affirm this; the very nature of our voice, with its high, low, and middle ranges, shows it; and the art of music clearly manifests it in these three terms: agitated, soft, and moderate.

—*Claudio Monteverdi*

An outgrowth of Renaissance theatrical traditions and the musical experiments of Florentine Camerata, early opera lent itself to the lavish spectacles and scenic displays that graced royal weddings and similar ceremonial occasions. Two such operas, *Orfeo* (1607) and *Arianna* (1608), were composed by the first great master of the new genre, Claudio Monteverdi (1567–1643). In Monteverdi's operas, the innovations of the Florentine Camerata reached artistic maturity, and the dramatic spirit of the Baroque found its true representative.

Although his earliest operas derived their plots from Greek mythology, for *The Coronation of Poppea* (1642), a late work from his Venetian period, Monteverdi turned to history. By this time, the first public opera houses had opened in Venice; opera was moving out of the palace and becoming a popular entertainment. In his early court operas, Monteverdi used an orchestra of diverse instruments. But in writing *Poppea* (his last opera) for a theater that would include works by other composers, he developed a more standardized ensemble with strings at its core.

Monteverdi's late operas have powerful emotions that find expression in recitatives, arias, and choruses. Because of him, Italian opera took on the basic shape it would maintain for the next several hundred years. The love duet, established in *The Coronation of Poppea*, became an essential operatic feature, and his powerful musical portrayal of human passions is echoed in the soaring melodies of Giuseppe Verdi's Romantic masterworks, as we will see later.

## The Spread of Opera

**French opera**

**Jean-Baptiste Lully**

By the turn of the eighteenth century, Italian opera had gained wide popularity in the rest of Western Europe. Only in France was the Italian genre rejected; here composers set out to fashion a French national style, drawn from their strong traditions of court ballet and classical tragedy. The most important composer of the French Baroque opera was Jean-Baptiste Lully (1632–1687), whose operas won him favor with the French royal court under King Louis XIV. Lully was the first to succeed in adapting recitative to the inflections of the French language. In a later chapter, we will hear a famous dance movement that typifies the splendor of the French royal court and its grand entertainments under King Louis XV.

## Opera in England

In England, in the early seventeenth century, the *masque,* a type of entertainment that combined vocal and instrumental music with poetry and dance, became popular among the aristocracy. Many masques were presented privately in the homes of the nobility. In the period of the Commonwealth that followed (1649–60), stage plays were forbidden because the Puritans regarded the theater as an invention of the devil. A play set to music, however, could be passed off as a "concert," as it was with the first great English opera, *Dido and Aeneas,* written by Henry Purcell during the late seventeenth century.

In this richly colored painting, *The Death of Dido* by **Giovanni Barbieri,** called **Guercino** (1591–1666), Dido has stabbed herself with Aeneas's sword and thrown herself on the funeral pyre. Her hand-maidens look on in horror; in the background, Aeneas's ships leave the harbor.

## Purcell's *Dido and Aeneas*

Purcell's *Dido and Aeneas,* first performed at the girls' school in Chelsea where he taught, is based on an episode in Virgil's *Aeneid,* the ancient Roman epic that traces the adventures of the hero Aeneas after the fall of Troy. Since Baroque audiences knew this Virgil classic, librettist Nahum Tate could compress the plot and suggest rather than fill in the details. Aeneas and his men are shipwrecked at Carthage on the northern shore of Africa. Dido, the Carthaginian queen, falls in love with him, and he returns her affection. But Aeneas cannot forget that the gods have commanded him to continue his journey until he reaches Italy, since he is destined to be the founder of Rome. Much as he hates to hurt the queen, he knows that he must depart.

### Henry Purcell (1659–1695)

**Purcell**'s standing as a composer gave England a leading position in the world of Baroque music. His career began at the court of Charles II (r. 1660–85) and extended through the turbulent reign of James II (r. 1685–88)—both Stuart kings—and into the period of William and Mary (r. 1689–1702). At these courts, Purcell held various posts as singer, organist, and composer. He wrote masques and operas for several venues; his famous stage work, *Dido and Aeneas,* was written for a girls' boarding school in Chelsea where he taught. His incidental music for plays includes *Abdelazar (The Moor's Revenge),* from which Benjamin Britten borrowed a dance as the basis for his *Young Person's Guide to the Orchestra* (see p. 60).

A truly international figure, Purcell wrote in many genres, assimilating the Italian operatic style with the majesty of French music, all while adding his own lyrical gift for setting the English language to music.

**Major Works:** Dramatic music, including *Dido and Aeneas* (1689), *The Fairy Queen* (1692), and incidental music for plays (including *Abdelazar,* or *The Moor's Revenge,* 1695) • Sacred and secular vocal music • Instrumental music, including fantasias, suites, and overtures.

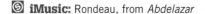

 **iMusic:** Rondeau, from *Abdelazar*

# Purcell: *Dido and Aeneas,* Act III, excerpts          5:32

**DATE:** 1689

**GENRE:** Opera, English

**BASIS:** Roman epic *The Aeneid,* by Virgil

**CHARACTERS:** Dido, queen of Carthage (soprano)
Aeneas, adventuring hero (baritone)
Belinda, Dido's serving maid (soprano)
Sorceress, Spirit, Witches

---

**Act III, Opening**          1:32

**WHAT TO LISTEN FOR:**

Prelude, Solo verse, and Chorus

| | | | | |
|---|---|---|---|---|
| Melody | Jaunty, playful tune | | Form | Strophic form, with instruments, solo voice, then chorus |
| Rhythm/ Meter | Sprightly tempo, in triple meter; use of Scotch snap dotted figures | | Performing Forces | String orchestra, with solo voice and men's chorus |
| Harmony | Major key, with chromatic foreshadowing of lament | | | |

Opening of hornpipe as solo verse:

|  | 0:00 | **Orchestral Prelude** |
|---|---|---|
| 31 | | |
| 32 | 0:32 | **Solo verse:** First Sailor |

Come away fellow sailors, come away,
Your anchors be weighing;
Time and tide will admit no delaying;
Take a boosey short leave of your nymphs on the shore,
And silence their mourning with vows of returning,
Tho' never intending to visit them more.

| 33 | 1:02 | **Chorus:** repeated |
|---|---|---|

---

**Recitative: "Thy hand, Belinda," sung by Dido**          0:57

**WHAT TO LISTEN FOR:**

Recitative and Dido's Lament

| | | | | |
|---|---|---|---|---|
| Melody | Recitative with half-step movement; aria more lyrical | | Form | Aria in 2 sections, each repeated (**A-A-B-B**), over ground bass |
| Rhythm/ Meter | Free recitative followed by slow aria in triple meter | | Performing Forces | Baroque-period instruments with solo voice |
| Harmony | Based on repeated chromatic ground bass, stated 11 times | | | |

Recitative introduces lament aria; accompanied by continuo only.

|  |  | **TEXT** |
|---|---|---|
| 34 | 0:00 | Thy hand, Belinda; darkness shades me. |
|  |  | On thy bosom let me rest; |
|  |  | More I would, but Death invades me; |
|  |  | Death is now a welcome guest. |

**Aria: "When I am laid in earth," Dido's Lament**                                   3:03

*Basis:* Ground bass, 5-measure pattern in slow triple meter, descending chromatic scale, repeated 11 times.

Opening of aria, with 2 statements of the ground bass (first statement shaded):

| | | **TEXT** | | **GROUND BASS STATEMENT NO.** |
|---|---|---|---|---|
| 35 | 0:00 | Instrumental introduction | | 1 |
| | 0:12 | When I am laid in earth, may my wrongs create | **A** | 2 |
| | | no trouble in thy breast. | | 3 |
| | | When I am laid . . . | **A** | 4 |
| | | no trouble . . . | | 5 |
| 36 | 1:19 | Remember me, remember me, but ah, forget | **B** | 6 |
| | | my fate, remember me, but ah, forget my fate. | | 7 |
| | | Remember me . . . | **B** | 8 |
| | | forget my fate . . . | | 9 |
| | | Instrumental closing | | 10 |
| | | Instrumental closing | | 11 |

◎ **Now try the Listening Quiz.**

Purcell begins the last act of his opera with a sprightly tune in the style of a ***hornpipe*** (see p. 132), a dance form often associated with sailors. Frequently heard in English stage works, the hornpipe is characterized by a reversed dotted figure called a ***Scotch snap*** (short-long rhythm).

The crew is ready to leave Carthage, although Aeneas has not yet told Dido of his imminent departure. This lively tune, introduced by the orchestra, is sung responsorially: one sailor presents the verse, answered by the male chorus. Despite their festive mood, the growing chromaticism of the bass line foreshadows Dido's Lament.

In her grief, upon hearing of Aeneas's mission, Dido decides her fate—death—in the moving recitative "Thy hand, Belinda," and the heartrending lament that is the culminating point of the opera, "When I am laid in earth." (For the text, see Listening Guide 11, p. 116.) In Virgil's poem, Dido mounts the funeral pyre, whose flames light the way for Aeneas's ships as they sail out of the harbor. Dido's Lament

**Ground bass**

unfolds over a five-measure *ground bass*, a repeated phrase that descends along the chromatic scale, always symbolic of grief in Baroque music. Despite the success of *Dido and Aeneas,* this masterpiece did not inspire similar efforts in England until two centuries later.

*In Her Own Words*

Since I am no more held back by feminine weakness than by any allowance made for my sex, I fly in lightest leaves in devotion to make my bow.

# Barbara Strozzi and the Baroque Aria

"Had she been born in another era she would certainly
  have usurped or enlarged the place of the muses."
                                          —*G. F. Loredano, of Barbara Strozzi*

Barbara Strozzi was certainly one of the more intriguing figures of her time. She made her mark as a composer of high-quality and masterful music, and as a singer. Strozzi was a professional musician in a day when few women could claim that title.

Our selection, the lighthearted aria *Amor dormiglione* (*Sleepyhead, Cupid!* see Listening Guide 12)—an invocation to the God of Love—exemplifies her careful sensitivity to the text. Notice how she uses the melody, shooting straight upward, to depict Cupid's weapons of love (arrows). And when he does not awake easily, she writes a static melodic line to emphasize his laziness. Her arias, some of which have partial or full refrains of the opening, foreshadow the **A-B-A** structure (called *da capo*) that soon became standard in opera.

### Barbara Strozzi (1619–c. 1677)

**Barbara Strozzi** is a unique figure in the early Baroque era. She was the adopted (and probably illegitimate) daughter of the Venetian poet and playwright Giulio Strozzi; her mother, Isabella Garzoni, was his servant. Giulio oversaw Barbara's education and introduction to the intellectual elite of Venice through an academy (not unlike the Florentine Camerata) where she performed as a singer, as a participant in debates, and as a hostess or mistress of ceremonies—all highly unusual, since the meetings of such academies were generally open to men only.

It has been suggested that Barbara Strozzi was a courtesan, and while it is true she possessed the artistic skills of this profession—singing, playing the lute, and writing poetry—this remains a theory. The provocative portrait to the left (by Bernardo Strozzi) is generally believed to be of Barbara. Her musical talents were praised by her contemporaries, one noting her "bold and graceful singing," and another comparing her voice to the harmonies of the spheres. Although Barbara did not hold any official musical posts at court, in churches, or at the theater, she did publish many of her compositions.

**Major Works:** 8 books of vocal music, including madrigals, arias, cantatas, and motets.

### Critical Thinking

**1.** What was Monteverdi's role in establishing opera as a major musical genre?

**2.** How does each component of opera (recitative, aria, chorus, instrumental numbers) contribute to the drama?

## LISTENING GUIDE 12

DVD | **CD 1 (67–69)** | CD 1 (37–39)

# Strozzi: *Amor dormiglione (Sleepyhead, Cupid!)*    2:16

**DATE:**  Published 1651

**GENRE:**  Da capo aria

### WHAT TO LISTEN FOR:

| | |
|---|---|
| Melody | Rising opening melody; lines shaped to express the text |
| Rhythm/Meter | Lilting triple meter; brief switch to duple at beginning of 2nd section |
| Harmony | Consonant, with some chromaticism |
| Texture | Monody (accompanied solo song) |

| | |
|---|---|
| Form | Da capo aria (3 parts: **A-B-A**) |
| Performing Forces | Solo soprano with harpsichord or bass lute |
| Text | Anonymous Italian poem |

| | | TEXT | TRANSLATION |
|---|---|---|---|
| | | **A section** | |
| 37 | 0:00 | Amor, non dormir più! | Cupid, stop sleeping! |
| | | Sù, sù svegliati oh mai, | Get up, wake up now, |
| | | ché mentre dormi tu | for while you sleep |
| | | dormon le gioie mie, vegliano i guai! | my joys sleep too and my pains are awake! |
| | | Non esser, Amor dappoco! | Cupid, don't be a good-for-nothing! |
| | | Strali, strali, foco, foco! | Arrows, arrows, fire, fire! |
| | | Sù, sù non dormir più! | Get up, stop sleeping! |
| | | Amor, svegliati, su su! | Cupid, wake up, get up now! |
| | | **B section** | |
| 38 | 1:01 | Oh pigro, oh tardo, | O lazy, o idle one, |
| | | tu non hai senso, | You feel nothing, |
| | | Amor melenso, | foolish Cupid, |
| | | Amor codardo! | cowardly Cupid! |
| | | Ahi, quale io resto, | Alas, while I stay here |
| | | che nel mio ardore | consumed with ardor, |
| | | tu dorma Amore: | you are sleeping, Cupid: |
| | | mancava questo! | this is more than I can stand! |
| | | **A section** repeated | |
| 39 | 1:37 | Amor, non dormir più! . . . | |

Examples of word painting—rising line at opening paints the idea of getting Cupid up:

Quick, descending line to depict "arrows" and "fire":

**Now try the Listening Quiz.**

# The Baroque Cantata and Oratorio

"I wish to make German psalms for the people, that is to say sacred hymns, so that the word of God may dwell among the people also by means of song."

—Martin Luther

- The church *cantatas* of north German composer Johann Sebastian Bach were mostly written for the Lutheran church service; they are multimovement works with solo arias, recitatives, and choruses, all with orchestral accompaniment.

- Lutheran cantatas are generally unified by a *chorale,* or hymn tune, sung in four-part harmony.

- Bach's cantata *Wachet auf* (*Sleepers, Awake*) is based on a well-known Protestant chorale tune.

- The *oratorio* is a large-scale dramatic genre with a sacred text performed by solo voices, chorus, and orchestra; it is not staged or costumed.

- George Frideric Handel was known for his Italian operas and, later in life, his English-texted oratorios (including *Messiah*).

The Baroque era inherited the great vocal polyphonic traditions of the Renaissance, while, at the same time, composers pursued a new interest in monody—solo song in dramatic declamation accompanied by instruments. In addition to opera, which we have already considered, two new large-scale genres of religious music were also born from this fusion of styles: the *church cantata* (from the Italian *cantare*, to sing) served the thriving Lutheran Church while the *oratorio* was best suited for performance in a church or concert hall. We will hear masterworks in these genres by the two greatest composers of the late Baroque era—Johann Sebastian Bach's famous cantata *Sleepers, Awake* and George Frideric Handel's well-known oratorio *Messiah*.

## Bach and the Church Cantata

In the Lutheran tradition, to which Bach belonged, the *cantata* was an integral part of the church service, related, along with the sermon and prayers that followed it, to the Gospel reading for the day. Most Sundays of the church year required their own cantata. Extra works for holidays and special occasions brought the annual cycle to about sixty cantatas. Bach composed four or five such cycles, from which only about two hundred works survive.

By the second quarter of the eighteenth century, the German cantata had absorbed the varied style of recitative, the aria, and duet of the opera; the pomp of the French operatic overture; and the dynamic instrumental style of the Italians. These elements were unified by the anchoring presence of the Lutheran chorale.

A *chorale* is a hymn tune specifically associated with German Protestantism. For one of his reforms, Martin Luther required that the congregation participate in the service. To this end, he inaugurated services in German rather than Latin, and allotted an important role to congregational singing. Luther and his fellow reformers created the first chorales by adapting melodies from Gregorian chant, secular art music, and even popular tunes. Originally sung in unison, these hymns soon were written in four-part harmony and sung by the choir. The melody was put in the soprano, where all could hear it and join in the singing. In this way, the chorales greatly strengthened the trend toward clear-cut melody supported by chords (homophonic texture).

An 18th-century engraving of Leipzig's St. Thomas's Church and choir school where Bach worked from 1723 until he died, in 1750.

In the elaborate cantatas that were sung in the Protestant church service, the chorale served as a unifying thread. When at the close of an extended work the chorale sounded in simple four-part harmony, its strength reflected the faith of a nation. The chorale nourished centuries of German music and came to full flower in the art of Bach.

Bach's cantatas typically have five to eight movements, of which the first, last, and usually one middle movement are choral numbers—normally fashioned from a chorale tune—ranging from simple hymnlike settings to intricate choral fugues. Interspersed with the choruses are solo arias and recitatives, some of which may also be based on a chorale melody or its text.

Bach's lyricism found its purest expression in his arias, elaborate movements with ornate vocal lines. The expressive instrumental accompaniments abound in striking motives that combine contrapuntally with the vocal line to create the proper mood for the text and illustrate its meaning. In many cases, the aria is conceived as a kind of duet between the voice and a solo instrument, so that a single instrumental color prevails throughout the piece.

## Bach's Cantata *Wachet auf (Sleepers, Awake)*

An evening outdoor concert in 1744 by the Collegium Musicum of Jena, Germany, featuring an orchestra of strings, woodwinds, trumpets, and drums gathered around a harpsichord.

Bach wrote his cantata *Wachet auf (Sleepers, Awake)* in 1731, for the end of the church year. The reading of the Gospel for this church feast is the parable of the Wise and Foolish Virgins (see illustration, p. 125), in which the watchmen sound a call on the city wall above Jerusalem to the wise virgins to meet the arriving bridegroom (Christ). The biblical text (Matthew 25:1–3) clearly suggests to all Lutherans to prepare themselves spiritually for the coming of Christ at Christmas.

Bach chose the chorale *Wachet auf* by Philipp Nicolai (1599) as the basis for his work, using this tune's inexhaustible possibilities in three of the cantata's seven movements. The chorale is in a standard three-part structure known as **bar form** (**A-A-B**), in which the first section is repeated with new words and the second section is rounded off with the same closing phrase as the first

## Johann Sebastian Bach (1685–1750)

**Johann Sebastian Bach** was heir to the polyphonic art of the past. He is the culminating figure of the Baroque style and one of the giants in the history of music.

Born at Eisenach, Germany, he followed the family vocation of organist. At the age of twenty-three, he was appointed to his first important position: court organist and chamber musician to the duke of Weimar. During his Weimar period (1708–17), Bach's fame as organ virtuoso spread; he also wrote many of his most important works for that instrument.

In 1717, Bach accepted an offer from the prince of Anhalt-Cöthen. In his five years at Cöthen (1717–23), Bach produced suites, concertos, sonatas for various instruments, and a wealth of keyboard music; he also composed the six concerti grossi dedicated to the margrave of Brandenburg. His wife had died in 1720, and in late 1721, he married Anna Magdalena Wilcke, a young singer at court. Bach's two marriages produced at least nineteen offspring, many of whom did not survive infancy, but four of his sons became leading composers of the next generation.

Bach was thirty-eight when he was appointed to one of the most important music positions in Germany, that of cantor at St. Thomas's Church in Leipzig. His duties at St. Thomas's were formidable (see quote at left). He supervised the music for the city's four main churches, selected and trained their choristers, and wrote music for the daily church services. He also served as director of the **collegium musicum**, a group of university students and musicians that gave regular concerts. In the midst of all this activity, Bach managed to produce truly magnificent works during his twenty-seven years in Leipzig (1723–50).

The two hundred or so church cantatas form the centerpiece of Bach's religious music, constituting a personal document of spirituality. His epic Mass in B minor, which occupied him for much of his Leipzig period, is too long for the Catholic service, but is often performed in a concert setting.

Best known in his lifetime as an organist, Bach wrote many organ compositions, including free, improvisatory works and strict forms. His most important keyboard works are contained in *The Well-Tempered Clavier,* which encompasses forty-eight preludes and fugues in two volumes, and his last masterwork, *The Art of Fugue*, at which point he had reached the height of his contrapuntal wizardry (see Chapter 20).

His orchestral music includes four suites of dance movements and the often-performed *Brandenburg Concertos*, which present various unique instrumental combinations pitted one against the other (see Chapter 19). Bach raised existing forms to the highest level rather than originating new forms. His mastery of contrapuntal composition, especially fugal writing, has never been equaled.

**Major Works:** Sacred vocal music (over 200 church cantatas, 4 Passions, and the Mass in B minor, 1749) • Orchestral music (4 suites) • Concertos (including 6 *Brandenburg Concertos*) • Solo sonatas and keyboard music (*Well-Tempered Clavier*, *The Art of Fugue*, English and French suites, and many organ works, including Toccata and Fugue in D minor).

### ◎ iMusic:

| | |
|---|---|
| *The Art of Fugue,* Contrapunctus I | Sarabande, from Cello Suite No. 2 |
| *Brandenburg Concerto* No. 1, I | Toccata in D minor |
| *Jesu, Joy of Man's Desiring* | "Endlich, endlich wird mein Joch" from Cantata 56 |

### *In His Own Words*

Whereas the Honorable and Most Wise Council of this Town of Leipzig have engaged me as Cantor of the St. Thomas School . . .
I shall set the boys a shining example. . . , serve the school industriously, . . . bring the music in both the principal churches of this town into good estate, . . . faithfully instruct the boys not only in vocal but also in instrumental music . . . arrange the music so that it shall not last too long, and shall . . . not make an operatic impression, but rather incite the listeners to devotion.

(see tune in Listening Guide 13). This structure determines the form of the three choral movements that feature Nicolai's tune.

This seven-movement cantata is carefully structured symmetrically in a near palindrome (something that is the same backwards or forwards), with recitatives and arias based on biblical passages framing the central fourth-movement chorus (see Listening Guide 13). The first movement is a grand chorale fantasia that begins with a majestic, marchlike motive signaling the arrival of Christ. This energetic instrumental idea, a *ritornello,* unifies the movement, recurring several times

# Bach: Cantata No. 140, *Wachet auf* (*Sleepers, Awake*), I and IV

10:19

**DATE:**  1731, performed in Leipzig

**BASIS:**  Chorale (3 stanzas) by Philipp Nicolai, in movements 1, 4, and 7

**OVERVIEW:**  **1. Chorale fantasia** (stanza 1 of chorale), E-flat major
2. Tenor recitative (freely composed), C minor
3. Aria: Soprano/Bass duet (freely composed), C minor
**4. Unison chorale** (stanza 2 of chorale), E-flat major
5. Bass recitative (freely composed), E-flat to B-flat major
6. Aria: Soprano/Bass duet (freely composed), B-flat major
7. Chorale (stanza 3 of chorale), E-flat major

Chorale tune
(**A-A-B**)

1
Wa-chet auf, ruft uns die Stim - me
Mit - ter - nacht heißt die - se Stun - de;

2
der Wäch-ter sehr_ hoch auf der
sie ru - fen uns_ mit hel-lem

3
Zin - ne, wach auf, du Stadt Je - ru - sa - lem!
Mun - de: wo seid ihr klu-gen Jung-frau - en?

4
Wohl auf, der

5
Bräut 'gam kommt, steht auf, die Lam-pen nehmt!

6
Al - le - lu - ja!

7
Macht euch be - reit zu_ der Hoch-zeit, Ihr

8 (3)
müs-set ihm ent - ge - gen-gehn!

---

**1. Chorale fantasia** (chorus and orchestra)  6:06

**WHAT TO LISTEN FOR:**

| | |
|---|---|
| Melody | Sopranos have slow-moving chorale melody; opening rising line = watchmen's motive; long melisma on "alleluia" |
| Rhythm | Insistent dotted rhythm in orchestra, begun in ritornello 1 |
| Harmony | Uplifting major key (E flat) |
| Form | 3-part bar-form (**A-A-B**) based on chorale tune structure, separated by instrumental ritornellos |
| Texture | Alternation between instrument groups; complex, imitative polyphony in lower voices |
| Performing Forces | 4-part choir (SATB), with strings, double reeds, corno (horn), bassoon, organ, violino piccolo |
| Text | Music depicts the text (watchmen, wake-up call) |

---

**40**  0:00  Ritornello 1: march-like dotted rhythm, alternating between violins and oboes:

Violins  Oboe  Violins
Oboe  Violins  Oboe

*Continued on following page*

**A section**

| | | TEXT | TRANSLATION |
|---|---|---|---|
| 41 | 0:29 | Wachet auf, ruft uns die Stimme<br>der Wächter sehr hoch auf der Zinne,<br>auf der Zinne,<br>wach auf, du Stadt Jerusalem! | Awake! The voice of the<br>watchmen calls us from high<br>on the tower,<br>Awake, you town Jerusalem! |
| | 1:32 | Ritornello 2 | |

**A section** repeated (new text)

| | | | |
|---|---|---|---|
| 42 | 2:00 | Mitternacht heisst diese Stunde,<br>sie rufen uns mit hellem Munde:<br>Wo seid ihr klugen Jungfrauen? | Midnight is this very hour;<br>they call to us with bright voices:<br>where are you, wise virgins? |
| | 3:04 | Ritornello 3 | |

**B section**

| | | | |
|---|---|---|---|
| 43 | 3:24 | Wohl auf, der Bräut'gam kommt,<br>steht auf, die Lampen nehmt!<br>Alleluja!<br>Macht euch bereit,<br>zu der Hochzeit,<br>Ihr müsset ihm entgegengehn! | Take cheer, the Bridegroom comes,<br>Arise, take up your lamps!<br>Alleluia!<br>Prepare yourselves<br>for the wedding,<br>You must go forth to meet him. |
| | 5:32 | Ritornello 4 | |

---

**4. Unison chorale**                                            4:13

**WHAT TO LISTEN FOR:**

| Melody | Tenors sing chorale melody in unison, set against moving countermelody in strings | Form | 3-part bar-form (**A-A-B**), with instrument ritornellos between vocal sections |
|---|---|---|---|
| Harmony | Bright, major key (E flat) | Texture | 3-line counterpoint, with slow-moving vocal lines; faster strings and walking bass line |

| | | | |
|---|---|---|---|
| 44 | 0:00 | Ritornello 1 | |
| 45 | 0:41 | **A section** | |
| | | Zion hört die Wächter singen,<br>das Herz tut ihr vor Freuden springen,<br>sie wachet und steht eilend auf. | Zion hears the watchmen singing,<br>for joy her very heart is springing,<br>she wakes and rises hastily. |
| | 1:11 | Ritornello 2 | |
| 46 | 1:50 | **A section** (new text) | |
| | | Ihr Freund kommt vom Himmel prächtig,<br>von Gnaden stark, von Wahrheit mächtig,<br>ihr Licht wird hell, ihr Stern geht auf. | From resplendent heaven comes her friend,<br>strong in grace, mighty in truth,<br>her light shines bright, her star ascends. |
| | 2:20 | Ritornello 3 | |
| 47 | 2:47 | **B section** | |
| | | Nun komm du werte Kron,<br>Herr Jesu, Gottes Sohn.<br>Hosiana! | Now come, you worthy crown,<br>Lord Jesus, God's own son.<br>Hosanna! |
| | 3:08 | Ritornello 4 (in minor) | |

3:29    **B section** continues

| | |
|---|---|
| Wir folgen all | We follow all |
| zum Freudensaal | to the joyful hall |
| und halten mit das Abendmahl. | and share the Lord's supper. |

Chorale tune in tenors set against countermelody in strings:

*Zi - on   hört   die   Wäch - ter   sin - gen,*

◎ **Now try the Listening Quiz.**

between the vocal statements of the chorale. The chorus enters with the sopranos sounding the ascending chorale melody in slow note-values that suggest the watchmen's fanfare. Bach's contrapuntal mastery is evident in the lower voices, which take part in a complex web of imitative polyphony unrelated to the chorale tune. The orchestral timbres heard include a horn (*corno da caccia*, or hunting horn), the watchmen's signal instrument, and various sized oboes that play in alternation with the strings.

This opening chorus is followed by a brief narrative recitative (*Er kommt, er kommt*), sparse in style, that introduces a love duet between the Soul (a soprano) and Christ the bridegroom (sung by a bass) set in **da capo aria** form (**A-B-A′**). Neither of these two solo movements refers to the chorale tune, but the cantata's central fourth movement—a unison chorale sung by the tenors—sounds the second stanza of Nicolai's text against a memorable orchestral countermelody representing the song of the watchmen. This movement's mystical aura has spawned many arrangements, including one by Bach for organ. This work reveals Bach's deep-rooted faith and his ability to communicate dramatically a meaningful spiritual message onto a vast and complex musical canvas.

Dutch painter **Godfried Schalcken** (1643–1706) captures the biblical story of the *Five Wise and Five Foolish Virgins* described musically in Bach's Cantata *Wachet auf.*

# Handel and the Oratorio

"What the English like is something they can beat time to, something that hits them straight on the drum of the ear."

*In His Own Words*

Whether I was in my body or out of my body as I wrote it [the "Hallelujah Chorus"], I know not. God knows.

The **oratorio**, one of the great Baroque vocal forms, descended from the religious play-with-music of the Counter-Reformation. It took its name from the Italian word for "a place of prayer." A large-scale musical work for solo voices, chorus,

George Frideric Handel holding a score of *Messiah* (c. 1749).

*In His Own Words*

What the English like is something they can beat time to, something that hits them straight on the drum of the ear.

A German cantata performance with orchestra and organ, as depicted in **J. G. Walther's** *Dictionary* (1732).

## George Frideric Handel (1685–1759)

If Bach represents the spirituality of the late Baroque, **Handel** embodies its worldliness. Though born in the same year, the two giants of the age never met.

Handel was born in Halle, Germany and attended the University of Halle. The ambitious youth then moved to Hamburg, where he entered the opera house orchestra as a second violinist and absorbed the Italian operatic style popular at the time. He spent the next three years in Italy, where his operas were enthusiastically received and where he wrote his first oratorio, *La Resurrezione* (*The Resurrection*).

At the age of twenty-five, he was appointed conductor to the elector of Hanover. A visit to London in 1710 brought him to the city that became his home for nearly fifty years. His opera *Rinaldo* (1711) conquered the English public with its fresh, tender melodies. A year later, Handel returned to London, this time for good.

His great opportunity came in 1720 with the founding of the Royal Academy of Music, launched for the purpose of presenting Italian opera. For the next eight years, he was active in producing and directing his operas as well as writing them. To this period belongs *Julius Caesar,* perhaps his most famous **opera seria** (serious Italian opera). Despite Handel's productivity, the Royal Academy failed. The final blow came in 1728 with the sensational success of John Gay's *The Beggar's Opera.* Sung in English and with tunes familiar to the audience, this humorous **ballad**, or **dialogue, opera** was the answer of middle-class England to the gods and heroes of the aristocratic *opera seria*.

Rather than accept failure, Handel turned from opera to oratorio, quickly realizing the advantages offered by a genre that dispensed with costly foreign singers and lavish scenery. Among his greatest achievements in this new genre were *Messiah* and *Judas Maccabaeus*. The British public could not help but respond to the imagery of the Old Testament as set forth in Handel's heroic music.

In 1759, shortly after his seventy-fourth birthday, Handel began his usual oratorio season; his most famous oratorio, *Messiah,* closed the series. He collapsed in the theater at the end of the performance and died some days later. The nation he had served for half a century accorded him its highest honor: a burial at Westminster Abbey.

Handel's rhythm has the powerful drive of the late Baroque. He leaned toward diatonic harmony, with melodies rich in expression that rise and fall in great majestic arches. And with his roots in the world of the theater, Handel knew how to use tone color for atmosphere and dramatic expression.

Handel's more than forty operas tell stories of heroes and adventurers, in ingenious musical settings. His arias run the gamut from brilliant virtuosic displays to poignant love songs. He was prolific as well in composing instrumental music; his most important works are his concertos and his two memorable orchestral suites, the *Water Music* (1717) and *Music for the Royal Fireworks* (1749). (We will consider a movement from the *Water Music* in Chapter 18).

**Major Works:** Over 40 Italian operas (including *Rinaldo* and *Julius Caesar*) • English oratorios (including *Israel in Egypt, Judas Maccabeus*, and *Messiah*) • Other vocal music • Orchestral suites, including *Music for the Royal Fireworks* and *Water Music* • Keyboard and chamber music.

**iMusic:** Alla hornpipe, from *Water Music*
"Hallelujah Chorus," from *Messiah*
"Oh thou that tellest good tidings," from *Messiah*

and orchestra, the oratorio was generally based on a biblical story and performed in a church or hall without scenery, costumes, or acting. The action was usually depicted with the help of a narrator, in a series of recitatives and arias, ensemble numbers such as duets and trios, and choruses. The role of the chorus was often emphasized. George Frideric Handel (1885–1759) became the consummate master of this vocal form.

# *Messiah*

In the spring of 1742, the city of Dublin witnessed the premiere of one of the world's best-loved works, Handel's *Messiah*. Writing down the oratorio in only twenty-four days, the composer worked as if possessed. His servant found him, after the completion of the "Hallelujah Chorus," with tears in his eyes. "I did think I did see all Heaven before me, and the Great God Himself!" Handel said.

The libretto is a compilation of biblical verses from the Old and New Testaments, set in three parts. The first part (the Christmas section) relates the prophecy of the coming of Christ and his birth; the second (the Easter section), his suffering, death, and the spread of his doctrine; and the third, the redemption of the world through faith.

Handel's orchestration of *Messiah* features mainly strings and continuo; oboes and bassoons strengthen the choral parts and trumpets and drums were reserved for special numbers. The Overture opens the Christmas section with a solemn, slow section in which the strings project an intense drama followed by a sturdy fugue in three instrumental voices. The first part of the oratorio proceeds with a series of arias, recitatives, and choruses, including the jubilant "Glory to God," which illustrates the pomp and majesty of Handel's music.

The lovely da capo soprano aria "Rejoice greatly, O daughter of Zion" is in three-part, or **A-B-A'** form (see Listening Guide 14). In this type of aria, the composer usually did not write out the third part, since it duplicated the first, with added ornamentation. For "Rejoice greatly," Handel did write out the last section, varying it considerably from the first.

At the beginning of this aria, violins introduce an energetic figure that will soon be taken up by the voice. Notable are the melismatic passages on the word "rejoice." Throughout, the instruments exchange motives with the voice and help provide an element of unity with the ritornellos, or instrumental refrains, that brings back certain passages.

The climax of *Messiah* comes at the close of the second part, the Easter section, with the familiar "Hallelujah Chorus." In this movement, we hear shifting textures in which the voices and text overlap and then come together to clearly declaim the text. The musical emphasis given the key word "Hallelujah" is one of those strokes of genius that resound through the ages.

## Critical Thinking

1. What are the various ways Bach used the chorale to unify his cantata?

2. How does an oratorio differ from an opera? How is it similar?

3. What do you think accounts for the continued popularity of Handel's *Messiah* today?

A performance of Handel's *Messiah* in 1784, from an 18th-century engraving.

### By the way ...

**Why Do People Stand for the "Hallelujah Chorus"?**

This tradition dates back to the first London performance of *Messiah* on March 23, 1743, nearly a year after the work's premiere in Dublin. The venue was Covent Garden, now the Royal Opera House. King George II was in attendance, and he reputedly rose to his feet during the "Hallelujah Chorus" (at the words "For the Lord God omnipotent reigneth") and remained standing throughout the chorus. Of course, when the king stands, the audience follows his lead. But why he stood at that moment is debatable: was it in reverence for the sentiment expressed in Handel's chorus, or was he was snoozing and jarred awake by the loud opening, or was his gout acting up and he needed to stretch his legs? A spectacular *Messiah* performance was put on at London's Crystal Palace in 1883 with 4,000 singers: imagine the sight of an audience of 87,769 all rising together for the chorus! Today, there are mixed views about this tradition—while the late conductor Robert Shaw asked audiences to remain seated during the chorus, Nicholas McGegan, who recently conducted *Messiah* in London, suggested that the audience stand immediately upon hearing the first chord, to avoid ruining the first thirty seconds with rustling programs and crashing chairs.

# Handel: *Messiah,* Nos. 18 and 44                    7:48

**DATE:**  1742

**GENRE:**  Oratorio, in 3 parts

**PARTS:**  I—Christmas section
II—Easter section
III—Redemption section

## Part I: Christmas Section

### 18. Soprano aria (A-B-A')                                    4:15

**WHAT TO LISTEN FOR:**

| Melody | Lyrical lines, with long melisma on "re-joice"; slower second part in minor key | Form | 3 part (da capo, **A-B-A**), with shortened last section; instrumental introduction (ritornello) |
|---|---|---|---|

| 48 | 0:00 | Instrumental ritornello | Vocal theme presented in violins in B-flat major. |
|---|---|---|---|
| | | **A** | |
| | 0:16 | Rejoice greatly, O daughter of Zion shout, O daughter of Jerusalem, behold, thy King cometh unto thee. | Disjunct rising line, melismas on "rejoice"; melody exchanged between soprano and violin. Syncopated, choppy melody, ends in F major. Instrumental ritornello. |
| | | **B** | |
| 49 | 1:30 | He is the righteous Saviour and he shall speak peace unto the heathen. | Begins in G minor, slower and lyrical; modulates to B-flat major. |
| | | **A'** | |
| 50 | 2:33 | Rejoice greatly . . . | Abridged instrumental ritornello; new melodic elaborations; longer melismas on "rejoice." |

Extended melisma on "rejoice" from last section:

re-joice_____

great - ly,

## Part II: Easter Section

### 44. Chorus                                                    3:33

**WHAT TO LISTEN FOR:**

| Texture | Varies from homorhythmic (all voices together) to imitative polyphony; fugal treatment, with overlapping voices | Expression | Varied dynamics for dramatic effect |
|---|---|---|---|
| | | Performing Forces | SATB chorus, with voices in alternation, accompanied by orchestra |

| | TEXT | DESCRIPTION |
|---|---|---|
| **51** 0:00 | | Short instrumental introduction. |
| | Hallelujah! | 4 voices, homorhythmic at opening. |
| **52** 0:24 | For the Lord God omnipotent reigneth. | Textural reductions, leading to imitation and overlapping of text, builds in complexity, imitative entries. |
| 1:12 | The kingdom of this world is become the Kingdom of our Lord and of His Christ; | Homorhythmic treatment, simple accompaniment. |
| **53** 1:29 | and He shall reign for ever and ever. | Imitative polyphony, voices build from lowest to highest. |
| 1:51 | King of Kings and Lord of Lords. Hallelujah! | Women's voices introduce the text, punctuated by "Hallelujah"; closes in homo-rhythmic setting with trumpets and timpani. |

Opening of chorus, in homorhythmic style:

⊚ **Now try the Listening Quiz.**

## LISTENING ACTIVITY: REVIEWING BAROQUE VOCAL GENRES

Listen to the following examples (StudySpace, Chapter 17) and match traits below to the selections:

**a.** Monteverdi: *Lament of the Nymph*
**b.** Bach: "Endlich, endlich wird mein Joch," from Cantata 56
**c.** Handel: "O thou that tellest good tidings," from *Messiah*

**1.** Solo voice part:      soprano _____      alto _____      baritone _____

**2.** Language:      English _____      German _____      Italian _____

**3.** Use of instruments:      full orchestra _____      Baroque woodwinds _____      basso continuo only _____

**4.** Genre:      oratorio _____      Lutheran cantata _____      Secular song _____

**5.** Performance at:      court _____      church _____

# 18 Baroque Instruments and the Suite

"If music be the food of love, play on."

—**William Shakespeare, _Twelfth Night_**

## KEY POINTS

⑤ **StudySpace** wwnorton.com/enjoy

- In the Baroque era, instruments were improved and featured in several large-scale genres, including the **suite** (a collection of dances).

- The Baroque **suite** is a group of dances, usually in the same key, with each piece in binary form (**A-A-B-B**) or ternary form (**A-B-A**). The standard dances are the **allemande, courante, sarabande**, and **gigue**.

- Handel's best-known orchestral suites are _Water Music_ and _Music for the Royal Fireworks_.

- The French love for dancing and spectacular staged entertainments contributed to the development of the orchestra.

- Jean-Joseph Mouret's ensemble suites were probably meant for outdoor festivals at the French Royal Court.

## The Rise of Instrumental Music

During the Baroque era, instrumental music became as important as vocal music for the first time in history. New instruments were developed while old ones were vastly improved. Great virtuosos such as Bach and Handel at the organ, and Vivaldi on the violin (see Chapters 19 and 20), raised the technique of playing to new heights.

On the whole, composers still thought in terms of line rather than instrumental color, which meant that the same line of music might be played on a string, a woodwind, or a brass instrument. But the late Baroque composers began to choose specific instruments according to their timbre, and they wrote more idiomatically for particular instruments, asking them to do what they could do best. As instrument designations became more precise, the art of orchestration was born.

Detail of the orchestra for a 1740 concert in the Turin Teatro Regio, painted by **Pietro Domenico Oliviero** (1679–1755).

# Baroque Instruments

The seventeenth century saw a dramatic improvement in the construction of string instruments. Some of the finest violins ever built came from the workshops of Stradivarius, Guarneri, and Amati. The best of these now fetch sums unimagined even a generation ago.

The strings of Baroque instruments were made of gut rather than the steel used today. Gut, produced from animal intestines, yielded a softer yet more penetrating sound. In general, the string instruments of the Baroque resemble their modern descendants except for certain details of construction. Playing techniques, though, have changed somewhat, especially bowing.

In *A Concert* by **Leonello Spada** (1576–1622), musicians play theorbo (a long-necked lute) and Baroque violin. A guitar sits on the table.

In the late Baroque, composers used woodwind instruments increasingly for color. The penetrating timbres of the recorder, flute, and oboe, all made of wood at the time, were especially effective in suggesting pastoral scenes, while the bassoon cast a somber tone.

The trumpet developed from an instrument used for military signals to one with a solo role in the orchestra. It was still a "natural instrument"—that is, without the valves that would enable it to play in all keys—demanding real virtuosity on the part of the player. Trumpets contributed a bright sonority to the orchestral palette, to which the French horns, also natural instruments, added their mellow, huntlike sound. Timpani were occasionally added to the orchestra, furnishing a bass to the trumpets.

In recent years, a new drive for authenticity has made the sounds of eighteenth-century instruments familiar to us. Recorders and wooden flutes, restored violins with gut strings, and mellow-toned, valveless brass instruments are being played again, so that the Baroque orchestra has recovered not only its smaller scale but also its transparent tone quality.

# The Baroque Suite

One of the most important instrumental genres of the Baroque was the suite, which presented a group of short dances performed by the diverse array of instruments just described. It was a natural outgrowth of earlier traditions, which had paired dances of contrasting tempos and character. The Baroque suite was made up of an international galaxy of dance types, all in the same key: the German *allemande*, in quadruple meter at a moderate tempo; the French *courante*, in triple meter at a moderate tempo; the Spanish *sarabande*, a stately dance in triple meter; and the English *jig* (*gigue*), in a lively 6/8 or 6/4. These began as popular dances, but by the late Baroque had left the ballroom far behind and become abstract types of art music. Between the slow sarabande and fast gigue, composers could insert a variety of optional dances—the **minuet**, the

## By the way . . .

### Why Are Stradivarius Violins So Special?

String players long to own, or play, an instrument built by Antonio Stradivari (c. 1644–1737). His legendary masterworks are viewed as the finest string instruments ever created; of the more than 1,000 he built, about 650 survive today. Stradivari (the Italian version of his name) opened his shop in the small Italian town of Cremona, long famous for musical instrument manufacturing. What is special about a Strad is the glorious sound each instrument produces, thought to be the result of an elaborate formula for the dimensions, woods, and varnish. Despite many tests, modern researchers have not fully explained what elements produce the unique sound of Stradivari instruments, which today can fetch over 3 million dollars apiece. A few fortunate—and wealthy—musicians own Strads, including cellist Yo-Yo Ma (see p. 45) and violinist Itzhak Perlman. Each surviving instrument has a name—the "Swan" was appropriately the last one he built before his death—and they can be seen and sometimes heard today at a variety of museums, including The Library of Congress in Washington, DC, and at the University of South Dakota's National Music Museum.

A royal sortie on the Thames River in London, as depicted by **Giovanni Antonio Canal (Canaletto)** (1697–1768).

*gavotte,* the lively ***bourrée,*** the ***passepied,*** the jaunty ***hornpipe;*** some were of peasant origin and thus introduced a refreshing earthiness to their more formal surroundings. The suite sometimes opened with an ***overture,*** and might include other brief pieces with descriptive titles.

Each piece in the Baroque suite was set either in binary structure, consisting of two sections of approximately equal length, each rounded off by a cadence and each repeated (**A-A-B-B**), or in ternary form (**A-B-A**), which we will hear in the selection from Handel's *Water Music.* In both structures, the **A** part usually moves from the home key (tonic) to a contrasting key (dominant), while the **B** part makes the corresponding move back. The two sections often use closely related melodic material. The form is easy to hear because of the modulation and the full stop at the end of each part.

Orchestral suites

 **Video**

*Tafelmusik*

The principle of combining dances into a suite could be applied to solo instrumental music, notably for harpsichord or solo violin, to chamber ensembles (see Chapter 20) as well as to orchestral forces. Notable examples of the orchestral suite include over 125 by the German composer Georg Philip Telemann (1681–1767), Bach's four orchestral suites (No. 3 contains his famous "Air"), and two large-scale works by Handel (see Composer box, p. 126), one of which we will consider.

# Handel and the Orchestral Suite

The two orchestral suites by Handel, the *Water Music* and *Music for the Royal Fireworks,* are memorable contributions to the genre. The *Water Music* was surely played (although probably not first composed) for a royal party on the Thames River in London on July 17, 1717. Two days later, the *Daily Courant* reported:

> On Wednesday Evening, at about 8, the King took Water at Whitehall in an open Barge, . . . and went up the River towards Chelsea. Many other Barges with Persons of Quality attended, and so great a Number of Boats, that the whole River in a manner was cover'd; a City Company's Barge was employ'd for the Musick, wherein were 50 Instruments of all sorts, who play'd all the Way from Lambeth (while the Barges drove with the Tide without Rowing, as far as Chelsea) the finest Symphonies, compos'd express for this Occasion, by Mr. Handel; which his Majesty liked so well, that he caus'd it to be plaid over three times in going and returning.

The twenty-two numbers of the *Water Music* were performed without continuo instruments, since it was not possible to bring a harpsichord aboard the barge.

 **iMusic**

Bach: Sarabande, from Cello Suite No. 2

Minuet in D minor (*Anna Magdalena Notebook*)

Handel: Alla hornpipe, from *Water Music*

## STANDARD ORDER OF THE BAROQUE DANCE SUITE

1. Overture (optional)
2. Allemande
3. Courante
4. Sarabande
5. Other dances (optional, e.g., hornpipe, minuet)
6. Gigue (jig)

The conditions of an outdoor performance, in which the music would have to contend with the breeze on the river, birdcalls, and similar noises, prompted Handel to create music that was marked by lively rhythms and catchy melodies.

The *Water Music* opens with an overture and includes a variety of dance numbers (not in the standard order of the suite), among them minuets in graceful 3/4 time, bourrées in fast 4/4, and hornpipes (an English country dance) in lively triple meter. In these varied numbers, Handel combined the Italian string style with the songfulness of Purcell and the rhythmic vivacity of French music to produce a style that was uniquely his own and was perfectly suited to the taste of an English audience.

The Suite in D major opens with a majestic three-part Allegro that sounds a fanfare in the trumpets, answered by the French horns and strings. One of the most recognized dances from the *Water Music* is the hornpipe from the Suite. Its catchy

---

**LISTENING GUIDE 15**                    ⓢ | DVD | CD 2 (29–34) | CD 1 (54–56)

# Handel: *Water Music,* Suite in D major, Alla hornpipe    2:50

**DATE:** 1717 (first performance)

**GENRE:** Dance suite

**MOVEMENTS:**  Allegro              Lentement
               **Alla hornpipe**    Bourrée
               Minuet

**Second Movement: Alla hornpipe, D major**                    2:50

**WHAT TO LISTEN FOR:**

| Melody | Ascending line with leaps and trills; second section has descending minor-scale melody | Form | 3-part (**A-B-A**) |
|---|---|---|---|
| Rhythm/ Meter | Triple meter in spritely tempo | Timbre | Instrument groups exchange motivic ideas |

---

**54**   0:00   **A section**—disjunct theme in strings and double reeds, with trills, later answered by trumpets and French horns; in D major, at a moderate, spritely tempo:

Continued alternation of motives between brass and strings.

**55**   0:55   **B section**—strings and woodwinds only (no brass); fast-moving string part with syncopated winds; in B minor:

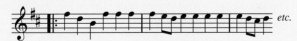

**56**   1:46   **A section**—repeat of entire first section; ends at close of section in D major.

ⓢ **Now try the Listening Quiz.**

The architectural plan of Chambord, a French castle in the Loire Valley, evokes a seven-part form related to a rondo (**A-B-A-C-A-B-A**).

opening theme features decorative trills in the strings and woodwinds, answered by majestic brass and timpani; this is followed by a more reflective **B** section set in a minor key. The return of **A** completes the ternary form that is typical of many Baroque dances. (See Listening Guide 15.)

More than two and a half centuries after it was written, Handel's *Water Music* is still a favorite with the public, indoors or out. We need to hear only a few measures of the work to understand why.

# Music at the French Royal Court

*"To enjoy the effects of music fully, we must completely lose ourselves in it."*

—*Jean-Philippe Rameau*

Few cultural centers could equal the splendor of the courts of Louis XIV (r. 1643–1715) and Louis XV (1715–1774). The opulence of the palace of Versailles, just outside Paris, was echoed in the grand entertainments celebrated at court. Jean-Baptiste Lully, court composer to Louis XIV, was central to the development of French stage works, including comedy-ballets and tragic operas. He also served as director of the instrumental groups at court, including the famous 24 Violons du Roy; this string ensemble was an important precursor to the modern orchestra. Among the musicians who worked in this rich cultural milieu was Jean-Joseph Mouret (1682–1738).

We will hear a movement from a collection by Mouret entitled *Suite de symphonies*, written in 1729. Scored for trumpets, oboes, bassoons, timpani, and strings, this suite was most likely intended for an outdoor festival. You may recognize our selection: it is the theme for *Masterpiece Theatre*, a PBS program that has been coming into our homes since 1971 (or you may also recognize it as the theme for *Sesame Street's Monsterpiece Theater*, a parody of the acclaimed PBS series).

Mouret's familiar fanfare is a ***rondeau***, a French form that led directly to the ***rondo*** (the words are cognates), frequently employed by later eighteenth-century composers. The five-part structure is unified by the repetitions of the opening

### Jean-Joseph Mouret (1682–1738)

A native of Avignon, in southern France, **Mouret** came to Paris to serve the duke of Maine, a son of Louis XIV. The success of his first opera won Mouret several prestigious musical appointments, including with the Académie Royale de Musique and as conductor of the Paris Opéra. These positions afforded him an affluent lifestyle. Although a popular composer of theatrical works in his day, Mouret's good fortune ended late in life, and he died penniless and insane, living out his days in a charitable asylum.

**Major Works:** Dramatic stage works, including opera-ballets and *divertissements* (entertainments) to accompany plays • Vocal music, including solo motets and cantatas • Instrumental ensemble suites, (including *Suite de symphonies*, 1729).

ⓘ **iMusic:** Rondeau, from *Suite de symphonies*

**LISTENING GUIDE 16**    ⊚ | DVD | CD 2 (35–37) | CD 1 (57–59)

# Mouret: Rondeau, from *Suite de symphonies*    1:47

**DATE:**  1729

**GENRE:**  Rondeau, from dance suite

## WHAT TO LISTEN FOR:

| Melody | Fanfare-like opening in regular phrases (4 and 8 measures); frequent trills in melody |
|---|---|
| Rhythm/Meter | Regular rhythms in duple meter, punctuated by timpani |
| Form | 5-part structure (**A-B-A-C-A**), with **A** serving as a ritornello |

| Expression | Varied dynamics and instrumentation |
|---|---|
| Performing Forces | Orchestra of trumpets, oboes, bassoons, violins, double bass, timpani, and continuo |

| | | SECTION | DESCRIPTION |
|---|---|---|---|
| 57 | 0:00 | A | Opening fanfare theme, heard twice in full orchestra; trumpets and timpani prominent (16 measures). |
| 58 | 0:24 | B | Short, quiet contrasting section (8 measures) featuring oboes and violins. |
| | 0:35 | A | Return of opening theme, played once (8 measures). |
| 59 | 0:47 | C | Longer, contrasting section (20 measures). |
| | 1:17 | A | Repeat of opening (16 measures). |

Opening martial melody, **A section**, in high range:

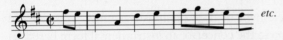

*etc.*

**B section** melody, with oboes and violins, set in lower range:

*etc.*

⊚ **Now try the Listening Quiz.**

---

*ritornello* (a recurring theme) set against several contrasting sections. Mouret varies the mood through changes in dynamics and instrumentation. The main theme is majestic, stated twice by the full orchestra in which the clear, high trumpet is predominant (see Listening Guide 16). This music conjures up the grandeur of the sumptuous banquets, elegant ballets, and spectacular pageants that dominated life at the French Royal Court.

Ritornello

## Critical Thinking

**1.** How would you describe the sound of Baroque-era instruments compared with modern ones?

**2.** How is the suite an international musical genre?

# 19 The Baroque Concerto

"'Tis God gives skill,
But not without men's hands:
He could not make Antonio Stradivari's violins
Without Antonio."

**—George Eliot**

## KEY POINTS

**StudySpace** wwnorton.com/enjoy

- Two types of concertos were popular during the Baroque: the **solo concerto**, with one instrument set against the orchestra; and the **concerto grosso**, with a small group of soloists and orchestra.

- Antonio Vivaldi, a virtuoso violinist, composed *The Four Seasons*, a well-known set of solo violin concertos representing **program music.**

- J. S. Bach's 6 *Brandenburg Concertos* are excellent examples of the concerto grosso.

Contrast was as basic an element of Baroque music as unity. This twofold principle found expression in the concerto, an instrumental form based on the opposition between two dissimilar bodies of sound. (The Latin verb *concertare* means "to contend with," or "to vie with.")

Baroque composers produced two types of concerti: the **solo concerto** and the *concerto grosso*. The first type, a concerto for solo instrument and an accompanying instrumental group, lent itself to experiments in sonority and virtuoso playing, especially in the hands of the Italian master Antonio Vivaldi. The violin was the instrument featured most frequently in the solo concerto, which usually consisted of three movements, in the sequence Allegro–Adagio–Allegro. This flexible form prepared the way for the solo concerto of the Classical and Romantic periods.

The *concerto grosso* was based on the opposition between a small group of instruments, the *concertino*, and a larger group, the **tutti**, or **ripieno** (Italian for "full"). Several Italian composers contributed significantly to the development of the concerto, establishing a three-movement structure, as well as unifying **ritornellos** in individual movements. Bach captured the spirit of the concerto grosso in his six *Brandenburg Concertos,* written for presentation to the Margrave Christian of Brandenburg. Each features a unique instrumentation in the solo group. Concerto No. 2 of this set has long been a favorite because of its brilliant trumpet part.

The concerto embodied what one writer of the time called "the fire and fury of the Italian style." This Italian style spread all over Europe and strongly influenced the German masters Bach and Handel, among others. Of the many Italian concerto composers, Vivaldi was the most famous and the most prolific.

**Solo concerto**

**Concerto grosso**

## Antonio Vivaldi (1678–1741)

The son of a violinist, **Vivaldi** grew up in his native Venice. He was ordained in the church while in his twenties and became known as "the red priest," a reference to the color of his hair. For the greater part of his career, Vivaldi was *maestro de' concerti,* or music master, at the most important of the four music schools for which Venice was famous, the Conservatorio dell'Ospedale della Pietà. These schools were attached to charitable institutions established for the upbringing of orphaned children—mostly girls—and played a vital role in the musical life of Venetians. Much of Vivaldi's output was written for concerts at the school, which attracted visitors from all over Europe (see illustration, p. 139)

One of the most prolific composers of his era, he also wrote much chamber music and numerous operas, as well as cantatas, an oratorio, and an extended setting of the Gloria, which is today one of his most performed works. His life came to a mysterious end: a contemporary Venetian account notes that the composer, who had once earned 50,000 ducats in his day (about 4 million dollars today), died in poverty as a result of his extravagance.

**Major Works:** Over 230 violin concertos, including *Le quattro stagioni* (*The Four Seasons*, Op. 8, Nos. 1–4, c. 1725) • Other solo concertos (bassoon, cello, flute, recorder) • Multiple concertos • Sinfonias • Vocal music, including operas and oratorios, Mass movements, and Magnificat.

◉ **iMusic:** Concerto in C major for 2 trumpets, I

# Antonio Vivaldi and the Solo Concerto

Vivaldi, one of the most prolific composers of his era, is best remembered for his more than 500 concertos—some 230 of which are for solo violin. Many of these have descriptive titles, such as *The Four Seasons,* a group of violin concertos (see Listening Guide 17, p. 138). He was active during a period that was crucially important to the exploration of a new style in which instruments were liberated from their earlier dependence on vocal music. His novel use of rapid scale passages, extended arpeggios, and contrasting registers contributed decisively to the development of violin style and technique. And he played a leading part in the history of the concerto, effectively exploiting the contrast in sonority between large and small groups of players.

## *The Four Seasons*

Vivaldi's best-known work is *Spring,* from *The Four Seasons,* a group of four solo violin concertos. We have observed the fondness for word painting in Baroque vocal works, where the music is meant to portray the action and emotion described by the words. In *The Four Seasons,* Vivaldi applies this principle to instrumental music. Each concerto is accompanied by a poem, describing the joys of that particular season. Each line of the poem is printed above a certain passage in the score; the music at that point mirrors graphically the action described; this literary link is called *program music.*

### By the way . . .

#### Who Were Vivaldi's Students?

In 1703, Vivaldi joined the staff of the Pietà as a teacher of violin and viola, but he soon was named director of the orchestra and house-composer. While most girls at the Pietà were orphans, some aristocratic families placed their daughters there, paying well for them to receive an excellent music education. Girls could not leave the Pietà unless given permission to marry or to join a convent, and many stayed on at the school to teach. One of the most talented of Vivaldi's students was Anna Maria della Pietà—her lack of a surname reflects her status as a foundling. Abandoned in the revolving drawer where people placed babies they could not care for, she was branded on the bottom of her foot with the letter P, designating her as one of the Pietà. Anna Maria studied voice and violin, and, under Vivaldi's tutelage, became a noted soloist with the orchestra. Her playing was highly praised by visitors, who claimed she had few peers among male violinists. Vivaldi dedicated some thirty of his concertos to her, and when he left to pursue his performance career, Anna Maria took over as *maestra* of the orchestra and violin teacher, instructing several girls who achieved careers as professional violinists.

**LISTENING GUIDE 17** ⓢ | DVD | CD 2 (38–45) | CD 1 (60–65)

# Vivaldi: *Spring,* from *The Four Seasons* (*La primavera,* from *Le quattro stagioni*), Op. 8, No. 1, I    3:33

**DATE:** Published 1725

**GENRE:** Programmatic concerto for solo violin, Op. 8 (*The Contest Between Harmony and Inspiration*), Nos. 1–4, each based on an Italian sonnet:

| | |
|---|---|
| **No. 1: *Spring (La primavera)*** | No. 2: *Summer (L'estate)* |
| **Allegro** | No. 3: *Autumn (L'autunno)* |
| Largo | No. 4: *Winter (L'inverno)* |
| Allegro | |

I. Allegro

Joyful spring has arrived,
the birds greet it with their cheerful song,
and the brooks in the gentle breezes
flow with a sweet murmur.

The sky is covered with a black mantle,
and thunder and lightning announce a storm.
When they fall silent, the little birds
take up again their melodious song.

II. Largo

And in the pleasant, flowery meadow,
to the gentle murmur of bushes and trees,
the goatherd sleeps, his faithful dog at his side.

III. Allegro
(Rustic Dance)

To the festive sounds of a rustic bagpipe
nymphs and shepherds dance in their favorite spot
when spring appears in its brilliance.

---

**First Movement: Allegro, E major**

**WHAT TO LISTEN FOR:**

| | |
|---|---|
| **Melody** | Flashy solo violin line; fast-running scales and trills |
| **Form** | Ritornello as unifying theme; alternates with contrasting epidoes |
| **Timbre** | Distinctive sound of Baroque-era string instruments |

| | |
|---|---|
| **Performing Forces** | Solo violin with string orchestra and basso continuo (keyboard) |
| **Expression** | Musical pictorialization of images from poem (spring, birds, brooks, gentle breeze, thunderstorm) |

Ritornello theme:

| | **DESCRIPTION** | **PROGRAM** |
|---|---|---|
| **60** 0:00 | Ritornello 1, in E major. | Spring |
| 0:32 | Episode 1; solo violin with birdlike trills and high running scales, accompanied by violins. | Birds |
| **61** 1:07 | Ritornello 2. | Spring |
| **62** 1:15 | Episode 2; whispering figures like water flowing, played by orchestra. | Murmuring brooks |

|  | 1:39 | Ritornello 3. | Spring |
| **63** | 1:47 | Episode 3 modulates; solo violin with repeated notes, fast ascending minor-key scales, accompanied by orchestra. | Thunder, lightning |
|  | 2:15 | Ritornello 4, in relative minor (C sharp). | Spring |
| **64** | 2:24 | Episode 4; trills and repeated notes in solo violin. | Birds |
|  | 2:43 | Ritornello 5, returns to E major; brief solo passage interrupts. |  |
| **65** | 3:12 | Closing tutti. |  |

◎ **Now try the Listening Quiz.**

In *Spring (La primavera),* the mood and atmosphere of the poem are literally evoked. The poem is a sonnet whose first two quatrains (making eight lines of text) are distributed throughout the first movement, an Allegro in E major. (See Listening Guide 17 for the text.)

Both poem and music evoke the birds' joyous welcome to spring and the gentle murmur of streams, followed by thunder and lightning. The image of birdcalls takes shape in staccato notes, trills, and running scales; the storm is portrayed by agitated repeated notes answered by quickly ascending minor-key scales. Throughout, an orchestral **ritornello,** or refrain, returns again and again (representing the general mood of spring) in alternation with the episodes, which often feature the solo violin. Ultimately, "the little birds take up again their melodious song" as we return to the home key. A florid passage for the violin soloist leads to the final ritornello.

In *Concert in a Girls' School,* **Francesco Guardi** (1712–1793) depicts a Venetian concert by an orchestra of young women (upper left) similar to the one directed by Vivaldi.

In the second movement, a Largo in 3/4, Vivaldi evokes an image from the poem of the goatherd who sleeps "in a pleasant, flowery meadow" with his faithful dog by his side. Over the bass line played by the violas, which sound an ostinato rhythm, he wrote, "The dog who barks." In the finale, an Allegro marked "Rustic Dance," we can visualize nymphs and shepherds cavorting in the fields as the music suggests the drone of bagpipes. Ritornellos and solo passages alternate in bringing the work to a happy conclusion.

Like Bach, Vivaldi was renowned in his day as a performer rather than a composer. Today, he is recognized both as the "father of the concerto," having established ritornello form as its basic procedure, and as a herald of musical Romanticism in his use of pictorial imagery.

### Critical Thinking

**1.** How did composers achieve both unity and contrast in the concerto?

**2.** What musical techniques did Vivaldi employ in *La Primavera* to depict the imagery of spring?

# 20 Other Baroque Instrumental Music

> "He, who possessed the most profound knowledge of all the contrapuntal arts, understood how to make art subservient to beauty."
>
> —C. P. E Bach, about his father, J. S Bach

## KEY POINTS

> **StudySpace** wwnorton.com/enjoy

- The **organ, harpsichord,** and **clavichord** were the main keyboard instruments of the Baroque era.

- J. S. Bach's keyboard music includes **chorale preludes** (short organ works elaborating on a chorale melody) and **preludes and fugues** (free-form pieces followed by strict imitative pieces).

- Bach's *Well-Tempered Clavier* is his most famous collection of preludes and fugues, and *The Art of Fugue* is his last and most comprehensive example of contrapuntal writing.

- Baroque instrumental music was often set in forms built on a repeating bass line (**ground bass**).

- The French Rococo and the German "sentimental" styles ushered in the new Classical era.

## Baroque Keyboard Instruments

This two-manual harpsichord was built by the Flemish maker **Jan Couchet** (c. 1650).

Beginning in the Baroque era, keyboard instruments played a central role in chamber music, taking an equal role in small ensembles to melody instruments. They also were the most popular solo instruments for both home music-making and professional performers. The three most important keyboard instruments of the Baroque were the organ, the harpsichord, and the clavichord. In ensemble music, these provided the continuo (continuous bass). The Baroque *organ*, used both in church (see p. 141) and in the home, had a pure, transparent timbre. The colors produced by the various sets of pipes contrasted sharply, so that the ear could pick out the separate lines of counterpoint. And the use of multiple keyboards made it possible to achieve terraced levels of soft and loud.

The *harpsichord* differed from the modern piano in two important ways. First, its strings were plucked by quills rather than struck with hammers, and its tone could not be sustained like that of the piano, a product of the early Classical era. Second, the pressure of the fingers on the keys produced subtle dynamic nuances but not the piano's extremes of loud and soft. Rather, in order to obtain different sonorities and levels of sound on the harpsichord, makers often added another set or two of strings, usually with a second keyboard.

# Keyboard Forms

Keyboard forms of the Baroque fall generally into two categories: those built on harmony, with a strong element of improvisation; and those based on strict forms of counterpoint, such as the fugue. Bach is a master in all these forms. Among the first type of works are the passacaglia and chaconne: a *passacaglia* is structured on a repeating bass line, or ground bass (as we heard in Dido's Lament, from Purcell's opera), over which continuous variations are created; and a *chaconne* is built on a succession of harmonic progressions repeated over and over, as in the famous Pachelbel Canon in D (🔘 **iMusic**). Both these constructs exemplify the Baroque urge toward abundant variation and embellishment, and they are not exclusive to keyboard music. (Bach's solo violin and cellos suites make use of these forms as well.)

Other forms based on improvisation include the *prelude*, a short study based on the continuous expansion of a melodic or rhythmic figure. First conceived as a solo improvisatory pieces, by the late Baroque the prelude often introduced a group of dance pieces or a fugue. Since its texture was mostly homophonic, it made an effective contrast with the contrapuntal texture of the fugue that followed. The *toccata* was another such free, often highly virtuosic, form—you may know Bach's famous Toccata and Fugue in D Minor (🔘 **iMusic**), which was the opening music for Disney's *Fantasia* and has been used in many films since.

A spectacular Baroque organ (1738) in St. Bavo's Cathedral, Haarlem, The Netherlands.

# The Fugue and Its Devices

A *fugue* is a contrapuntal composition in which a single theme pervades the entire fabric, entering in one voice (or instrumental line) and then in another. The fugue, then, is based on the principle of imitation. Its main theme, the *subject*, constitutes the unifying idea, the focal point of interest in the contrapuntal web.

We have already encountered the fugue or fugal style in a number of works: at the beginning of the book, in *The Young Person's Guide to the Orchestra (Variations and Fugue on a Theme of Purcell)* by Britten; in Handel's "Hallelujah Chorus" in *Messiah;* and in the opening movement of Bach's cantata *Wachet auf (Sleepers, Awake).* Thus a fugue may be written for a group of instruments, for a full chorus, or, as we shall see, for a solo keyboard instrument.

The *subject*, or main theme of the fugue, is stated alone at the beginning in one of the voices—referred to by the range in which it sounds: soprano, alto, tenor, or

**Subject and answer**

In **Josef Alber**'s (1888–1976) *Fugue* (1925), the interlocking and parallel lines resemble the polyphonic textures of the fugue.

## CONTRAPUNTAL DEVICES

Subject and Answer (begins 5 notes higher, intervals changed), from *The Art of Fugue*.

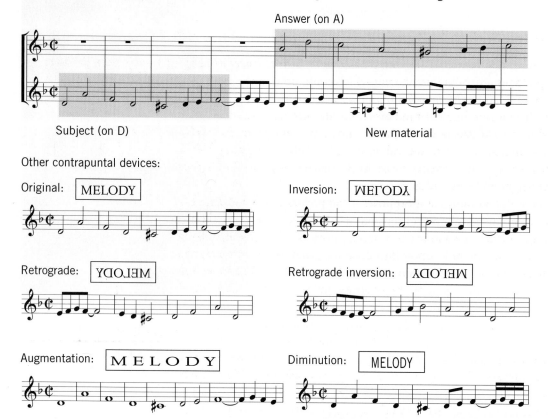

Other contrapuntal devices:

bass. It is then imitated in another voice—this is the ***answer***—while the first can continue with a countertheme or new material.

**Fugue, exposition, and episode**    When the theme has been presented in each voice once, the first section of the fugue, the ***exposition***, is at an end. From then on, the fugue alternates between sections that feature entrances of the subject and ***episodes***—interludes that serve as areas of relaxation—until it reaches its home key.

The subject of the fugue is stated in the home key, the tonic, while the answer is given in a related key, the dominant, which lies five tones above the tonic. There may be modulation to foreign keys in the course of the fugue, which builds up tension before the return home. The Baroque fugue thus embodies the opposition between home and contrasting keys, which was one of the basic principles of the new major-minor system.

**Contrapuntal devices**    Contrapuntal writing is marked by a number of devices used since the earliest days of polyphony. A melody can be presented in longer time values, often twice as slow as the original, using ***augmentation***, or in shorter time values that go by faster, called ***diminution***. The pitches can be stated backwards (starting from the last note and preceding to the first), in ***retrograde***, or turned upside down (in mirror image), moving by the same intervals but in the opposite direction, a technique called ***inversion*** (see "Contrapuntal Devices," above). Overlapping statements of the subject, called ***stretto***, heighten the tension.

The Baroque fugue, then, was a form based on imitative counterpoint that combined the composer's technical skill with imagination, feeling, and exuberant ornamentation to produce one of the supreme achievements of the era.

# Bach's Keyboard Fugues

Bach is undisputedly the greatest master of fugal writing. His *Well-Tempered Clavier*, a collection of preludes and fugues issued in two volumes and demonstrating the new system of equal temperament for tuning keyboard instruments, is a testament to his skill. The first volume of the collection, completed in 1722 during the years Bach worked in Cöthen, contains a prelude and fugue in each of the twelve major and twelve minor keys. The second volume, also containing twenty-four preludes and fugues, appeared twenty years later. The whole collection is thus made up of forty-eight preludes and fugues.

*Well-Tempered Clavier*

Bach's last demonstration of contrapuntal mastery was *The Art of Fugue*, a collection of fourteen fugues and four canons that systematically explores all the wizardry of fugal devices. Because it is unclear which instrument(s) Bach intended this work, it has been recorded by orchestras, chamber ensembles, and even brass groups—among them the well-known Canadian Brass. The collection is viewed today as keyboard music, probably meant for organ or harpsichord.

## Bach's Contrapunctus I, from *The Art of Fugue*

🎬 Video

We will consider the opening fugue, called Contrapunctus I. Its four voices introduce the subject successively in the order alto-soprano-bass-tenor. This constitutes the **exposition**. (The soprano and tenor have the answer form of the subject, set in the key of the dominant; see Listening Guide 18, p. 144.) At this point, the first **episode** distracts our attention from the subject, and for the extended middle section of the fugue, we wait with anticipation for other statements of the familiar tune that alternate with episodes. Bach tricks the ear with several false entries that anticipate a full statement of the theme, and in one case, he overlaps the subjects, beginning one before the previous statement is completed (in **stretto**). The tonic (D minor) is reestablished by a bold statement in the bass, heard on the organ pedals, and we feel solidly in the home key with the sustained pedal note on D. The final chord—a major triad—jolts us from the contemplative minor-key setting.

Although this fugue does not exploit all the compositional devices described, Bach increases the complexity of the counterpoint with each fugue in this collection, which is the climax of Bach's fugal art.

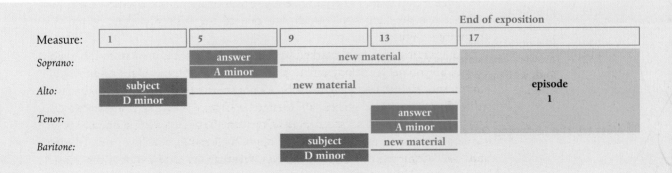

## LISTENING GUIDE 18

Ⓢ Video | Ⓢ | DVD | CD 2 (56–59) | CD 1 (66–69)

# Bach: Contrapunctus 1, from *The Art of Fugue*                    3:12

**DATE:**   1749, published 1751

**GENRE:**   Fugue (from collection of canons and fugues on a single theme)

**WHAT TO LISTEN FOR:**

| | |
|---|---|
| Melody | Tune (called *subject*) outlines minor chord |
| Harmony | Minor throughout, but closes on a major chord; last fugue statement over sustained pitch (pedal point) |
| Texture | Imitative entries of same melody: subject (on D) alternates with answer (on A) |

| | |
|---|---|
| Form | 4-voice fugue, with exposition, middle, and closing sections; episodes separate fugue statements |
| Performing Forces | Solo keyboard (organ or harpsichord) |

**EXPOSITION** (see chart on p. 143)

4 entries of subject (answer) in alternation:

| 66 | 0:00 | alto (subject) |
|---|---|---|
| | 0:10 | soprano (answer) |
| | 0:19 | bass (subject) |
| | 0:28 | tenor (answer) |
| 67 | 0:38 | Episode 1 (6 measures)—ends exposition. |

**MIDDLE ENTRIES**

Subject stated 2 times:

| 68 | 0:52 | alto |
|---|---|---|
| | 1:05 | soprano (transposed to A) |
| | 1:12 | Answer in bass (overlaps soprano in stretto). |
| | 1:21 | Episode 2 (4 measures). |
| | 1:30 | Answer in tenor. |
| | 1:40 | Episode 3 (5 measures). |
| | 1:52 | Answer heard; anticipated in alto, then full statement in soprano. |

**CLOSING SECTION**

| 69 | 2:10 | Subject in bass (but anticipated in soprano). |
|---|---|---|
| | 2:19 | Episode 4. |
| | 2:26 | Pedal point in bass. |
| | 2:44 | Rhetorical pauses. |
| | 2:52 | Answer—final statement over sustained pedal on tonic. Ends with major chord. |

Ⓢ **Now try the Listening Quiz.**

# Looking Ahead to the Classical Era

*"A musician cannot move others unless he too is moved. He must feel all the emotions that he hopes to arouse in his audience."*

—*C. P. E. Bach*

By the mid-eighteenth century, a new social attitude had surfaced that was manifested in a simpler artistic expression. The so-called Rococo era took shape as a reaction against the grandiose gestures of the late Baroque. The word Rococo derives from the French *rocaille*, "a shell," suggesting the decorative scroll- and shellwork typical of the style. The greatest painter of the French Rococo was Jean-Antoine Watteau (1684–172; see illustration below), whose canvases with intimate and pastoral scenes projected a world of love and gallantry that reflected the shift in French society. The musical counterpart to Watteau was François Couperin (1668–1733), who was considered the greatest composer of the French keyboard school.

**Rococo**

This period witnessed a profound change in taste; composers embraced a new ideal of beauty. Elaborate polyphonic textures yielded to a single melody line with a simple chordal accompaniment (homophony), in much the same way that the contrapuntal complexities of late Renaissance music gave way to the early Baroque ideal of monody. This era desired its music to be, above all, simple and to express natural feelings. Thus was born the Germanic "sensitive," or "sentimental," style that marked the first stirrings of a direct and natural expression that flowered fully with Romanticism.

**Jean-Antoine Watteau** (1684–1721), with his dream world of love and gallantry, was the artistic counterpart of François Couperin. *La gamme d'amour (The Gamut of Love).*

The vast social changes taking shape in the eighteenth century were bound to be reflected in the lyric theater. Grandiose Baroque opera, geared to an era of absolute monarchy, had no place in the shifting societal structure. Increasingly its pretensions were satirized all over Europe. In 1728, *The Beggar's Opera*, by John Gay (1685–1732), a satirical play with folk songs and popular tunes arranged by Johann Christoph Pepusch (1667–1752), sounded the death knell of *opera seria* (serious Italian-texted opera with heroic or tragic subjects) in England, and ushered in a vogue of racy pieces with popular songs and dances.

A new, realistic style of Italian comic opera—called *opera buffa*—developed throughout Europe. We will see how this dramatic genre reached new heights in popularity and mastery in the hands of Mozart.

## Critical Thinking

1. How does contrast provide the basis for Baroque keyboard works (e.g., Prelude and Fugue, Toccata and Fugue)?
2. What are some of the devices used in the fugue to vary the main melody?
3. How do early keyboard instruments differ from modern ones?

## A COMPARISON OF BAROQUE AND CLASSICAL STYLES

| | BAROQUE (c. 1600–1750) | CLASSICAL (c. 1750–1825) |
|---|---|---|
| **COMPOSERS** | Monteverdi, Purcell, Barbara Strozzi, Vivaldi, Handel, Mouret, Bach | Haydn, Mozart, Beethoven, Schubert |
| **MELODY** | Speechlike melody in monody; continuous melody with wide leaps, chromatic tones for emotional effect | Symmetrical melody in balanced phrases and cadences; tuneful, diatonic, with narrow leaps |
| **RHYTHM** | Single rhythm predominant; steady, energetic pulse; freer in vocal music | Dance rhythms favored; regularly recurring accents |
| **HARMONY** | Chromatic harmony for expressive effect; major-minor system established with brief excursions to other keys | Diatonic harmony favored; tonic-dominant relationship expanded, becomes basis for large-scale form |
| **TEXTURE** | Monodic texture (early Baroque); polyphonic texture (late Baroque); linear-horizontal dimension | Homophonic texture; chordal-vertical dimension |
| **INSTRUMENTAL GENRES** | Trio sonata, concerto grosso, suite, prelude, fugue, chaconne, passacaglia | Symphony, solo concerto, solo sonata, string quartet, other chamber music genres |
| **VOCAL GENRES** | Opera, Mass, oratorio, cantata | Opera, Mass, oratorio |
| **FORM** | Binary and ternary forms predominant | Larger forms, including sonata-allegro form, developed |
| **DYNAMICS** | Subtle dynamic nuances; *forte/piano* contrasts; echo effects | Continuously changing dynamics through *crescendo* and *decrescendo* |
| **TIMBRE** | Continuous tone color throughout one movement | Changing tone colors between sections of works |
| **PERFORMING FORCES** | String orchestra, with added woodwinds; organ and harpsichord in use | Orchestra standardized into four families; introduction of clarinet, trombone; rise of piano to prominence |
| **IMPROVISATION** | Improvisation expected; harmonies realized from figured bass | Improvisation largely limited to cadenzas in concertos |
| **EMOTION** | Single affection; emotional exuberance and theatricality | Emotional balance and restraint |

Ⓢ **Find an interactive version of this chart on StudySpace.**

## LISTENING ACTIVITY: COMPARING STYLES 3 BAROQUE TO CLASSICAL

### Keyboard Instruments

Listen to these three keyboard works (StudySpace, Chapter 20). Match each of them to an instrument and to an era.

| Instrument | Era |
|---|---|
| **a.** harpsichord | **d.** Baroque era |
| **b.** piano | **e.** Classical era |
| **c.** organ | |

| | Instrument | Era |
|---|---|---|
| **1.** Bach: *Jesu, Joy of Man's Desiring* | _____ | _____ |
| **2.** Minuet in D minor | _____ | _____ |
| **3.** Mozart: *Ah! vous dirai-je, maman* | _____ | _____ |

### Melody/Rhythm and Texture

Listen to the two works below to decide the prevailing melodic/rhythmic traits, the texture, and the era that best suits this description.

| Melody/Rhythm | Texture | Era |
|---|---|---|
| **f.** continuous line with energetic rhythm | **h.** homophonic | **j.** Baroque era |
| **g.** symmetrical phrases with regularly accented meter | **i.** polyphonic | **k.** Classical era |

**4.** Bach: *Brandenburg Concerto* No. 1, I

Melody/Rhythm _____     Texture _____     Era _____

**5.** Haydn: *Emperor* Quartet, II

Melody/Rhythm _____     Texture _____     Era _____

### Genres

Note the specific genre that best suits each of the examples below and note the era in which it was composed.

| Genre | Era |
|---|---|
| **l.** solo concerto | **p.** Baroque era |
| **m.** concerto grosso | **q.** Classical era |
| **n.** suite | |
| **o.** symphony | |

| | Genre | Era |
|---|---|---|
| **6.** Handel: Alla hornpipe, from *Water Music* | _____ | _____ |
| **7.** Mozart: Clarinet Concerto, II | _____ | _____ |
| **8.** Bach: *Brandenburg Concerto*, I | _____ | _____ |
| **9.** Mouret: Rondeau, from *Suite de symphonies* | _____ | _____ |

# Classical Era

1700  1710  1720  1730  1740  1750  1760  1770  1780  1790  1800  1810  1820  1830  1840  1850

## COMPOSERS AND WORKS

**(1732–1809)** Joseph Haydn

Symphony No. 100, *Military*
*The Creation*

**(1756–1791)** Wolfgang Amadeus Mozart

Piano Concerto, G major, K. 453
*Don Giovanni*
*Eine kleine Nachtmusik*
Requiem

**(1770–1827)** Ludwig van Beethoven

*Moonlight* Sonata
Symphony No. 5

**(1797–1828)** Franz Schubert

*Elfking*
*The Trout*

1700  1710  1720  1730  1740  1750  1760  1770  1780  1790  1800  1810  1820  1830  1840  1850

## EVENTS

**1715** Reign of Louis XV begins

**1732** George Washington born

**1752** Benjamin Franklin's electricity discoveries

**1762** Catherine II crowned empress of Russia

**1771** First edition of *Encyclopaedia Britannica*

**1775** American Revolution begins

**1785** Schiller writes *Ode to Joy*

**1789** French Revolution begins

**1796** Jenner discovers vaccination
for smallpox

**1804** Coronation of Napoleon

**1815** Defeat of Napoleon at
Battle of Waterloo

# Eighteenth-Century Classicism

**Jean-Marc Nattier** (1685–1766). *Henriette of France.*

# 4 Classicism in the Arts

"Music [is] the favorite passion of my soul."

**—Thomas Jefferson**

## KEY POINTS

⑤ **StudySpace** wwnorton.com/enjoy

- The Classical era (1750–1825) is characterized by order, objectivity, and harmonious proportion. This is reflected in the art and architecture of the time, modeled on ancient Greek and Roman styles.

- The American Revolution (1775–83) and the French Revolution (1789–99) profoundly changed political systems and social order.

- The era saw significant advances in science and ideas, and the Industrial Revolution made mass production possible.

- German writers like Goethe and Schiller expressed the emerging romantic view of the world.

- Haydn, Mozart, Beethoven, Schubert—all members of the Viennese school—composed in large-scale forms (symphony, concerto, sonata).

- Classical music is characterized by a singable, lyrical melody; diatonic harmony; regular rhythms and meters; homophonic texture; and frequent use of folk elements.

- Music-making revolved around the court, with composers (especially Haydn) employed under the patronage system. Women also held court positions as musicians and teachers.

Historians observe that style in art moves between two extremes, the classical and the romantic. Both the classicist and the romanticist strive to express emotions within artistic forms. Where they differ is in their point of view. Classicists seek order, reason, and serenity while the romantics long for strangeness, wonder, and ecstasy. Classicists are more objective in their approach; they try to view life rationally and "to see it whole." Romanticists, on the other hand, view the world in terms of their personal feelings. Throughout history, Classical and Romantic ideals have alternated and even existed side by side, for they correspond to two basic impulses in human nature: the need for moderation and the desire for uninhibited emotional expression.

Classicism vs. Romanticism

The "Classical" and "Romantic" labels are also attached to two important stylistic periods in European art. The Classical era encompasses the last half of the eighteenth century and the early decades of the nineteenth, when literature and art of the ancient Greeks and Romans were considered models of excellence to be emulated. We have come to associate the qualities of order, stability, and harmonious proportion with the Classical style.

The rule of strong aristocratic sovereigns continued throughout Europe. Louis XV presided over extravagant celebrations in Versailles, and Frederick the Great ruled in Prussia, Maria Theresa in Austria, and Catherine the Great in Russia. In such societies, the ruling class enjoyed its power through hereditary right.

Near the end of the eighteenth century, Europe was convulsed by the French Revolution (1789–99). This social upheaval transferred power from the aristocracy to the middle class, whose wealth was based on a rapidly expanding capitalism. Such a drastic shift was made possible by the Industrial Revolution, which gathered momentum in the mid–eighteenth century through a series of important inventions, from James Watt's improved steam engine and James Hargreaves's spinning jenny in the 1760s to Eli Whitney's cotton gin in the 1790s.

These decades saw significant advances in science as well. Benjamin Franklin harnessed electricity, Joseph Priestley discovered oxygen, and Edward Jenner perfected vaccination. There were important events in intellectual life too, such as the publication of the French *Encyclopédie* (1751–52) and the first edition of the *Encyclopaedia Britannica* (1771).

The Parthenon, Athens (447–432 B.C.E.). The architecture of ancient Greece embodied the ideals of order and harmonious proportions.

The American Revolution (1775–83) broke out more than fourteen years before the French. Its immediate cause was the anger of the colonists at the economic injustices imposed on them by English king George III. Beyond that, however, was the larger issue of human equality and freedom. Thomas Jefferson, principal author of the Declaration of Independence, wrote that all people have the right to life, liberty, and the pursuit of happiness. These words remain fundamental to the principles of democracy.

The eighteenth century has been called the Age of Reason and the Enlightenment. Philosophers such as Voltaire and Rousseau considered social and political issues with reason and science, but they were also advocates for the rising middle class. They therefore became prophets of the approaching social upheaval. The intellectual climate of the Classical era, then, was nourished by two opposing streams. While Classical art captured the exquisite refinement of a way of life that

**The Enlightenment**

Thomas Jefferson's design for the Rotunda of the University of Virginia at Charlottesville, completed in 1826, reflects his admiration for classical architecture.

**Jacques-Louis David** (1748–1825). *Napoleon Crossing the Great Saint Bernard Pass, May 20, 1800.*

Romanticism in literature

was drawing to a close, it also caught the first wave of a new social structure.

Just as eighteenth-century thinkers idealized the civilization of the Greeks and Romans, artists revered the unity and proportions of ancient architecture and fine arts. Strangely enough, a favorite subject of the foremost painter of revolutionary France, Jacques-Louis David, was the French general Napoleon Bonaparte, whose military compaign was, he claimed, to liberate the peoples of Europe. In this spirit too, Thomas Jefferson patterned the nation's Capitol, the University of Virginia (see p. 151), and his home at Monticello after Greek and Roman temples. His example spurred on a classical revival in the United States, which made Ionic, Doric, and Corinthian columns indispensable features of public buildings well into the twentieth century.

By the 1760s, though, a romantic point of view was emerging in literature. The French philosopher Jean-Jacques Rousseau (1712–1778), sometimes called the "father of Romanticism," produced some of his most significant writings during this time. His celebrated declaration "Man is born free, and everywhere he is in chains" epitomizes the temper of the time. The first manifestation of the Romantic spirit in Germany was a literary movement known as *Sturm und Drang* (storm and stress). Two characteristic works appeared in the 1770s by the era's most significant young writers: the *Sorrows of Young Werther*, by Johann Wolfgang von Goethe, and *The Robbers*, by Friedrich von Schiller. The famous *Ode to Joy*, a hymn set by Beethoven in his Ninth Symphony, was Schiller's proclamation of universal brotherhood; and as we will see, Goethe became the favorite lyric poet of the Romantic composers. By the end of the century, the atmosphere had completely changed. The old world of the aristocracy was beginning to give way to a new society of the people and to an era that produced some of the greatest artworks of Western culture.

# Classicism in Music

The Viennese School

The Classical period in music (c. 1750–1825) is characterized best by the masters of the so-called Viennese School—Haydn, Mozart, Beethoven, and their successor Franz Schubert. These composers worked in an age of great musical experimentation and discovery, when musicians took on new challenges: first, to explore fully the possibilities offered by the major-minor system; and second, to perfect a large-scale form of instrumental music—what we will learn as sonata form—that exploited those possibilities to the fullest degree. Having found this ideal structure, composers then developed it into the solo and duo sonata, the trio and quartet (especially the string quartet), the concerto, and the symphony.

"Classicism" did not imply a strict adherence to traditional forms; as we will see, the composers of the Viennese School experimented boldly and ceaselessly with the materials at their disposal. And it should not surprise us to find that Romantic elements appear as well in the music of Haydn, Mozart, and Beethoven, especially their late works. These composers dealt with musical challenges so brilliantly that their works have remained unsurpassed models for all who followed.

# Elements of Classical Style

The music of the Viennese masters is notable for its elegant, lyrical melodies. Classical melodies "sing," even those intended for instruments. These melodies are usually based on symmetrical four-bar phrases marked by clear-cut cadences, and they often move stepwise or by small leaps within a narrow range. Clarity is further provided by repetition and the frequent use of sequence (the repetition of a pattern at a higher or lower pitch). These devices make for balanced structures that are readily accessible to the listener.

**Lyrical melody**

The harmonies that sustain these melodies are equally clear. The chords are built from the seven tones of the major or minor scale (meaning they are *diatonic*) and therefore are firmly rooted in the key. The chords underline the balanced symmetry of phrases and cadences, and they form vertical columns of sound over which the melody unfolds freely and easily, generally in a *homophonic* texture (a melody with accompanying harmony). Note that this is related to the *homorhythmic* textures we heard in earlier eras, in which all voices moved together.

**Diatonic structure**

**Homophonic texture**

Melody and harmony are powered by strong rhythms that move at a steady tempo. Much of the music is in one of the four basic meters—2/4, 3/4, 4/4, or 6/8. If a piece or movement begins in a certain meter, it is apt to stay there until the end. Classical rhythm works closely with melody and harmony to make clear the symmetrical phrase-and-cadence structure of the piece. Clearly shaped sections establish the home key, move to contrasting but closely related keys, and return to the home key. The result is the beautifully molded architectural forms of the Classical style, fulfilling the listener's need for both unity and variety.

**Rhythmic regularity**

Despite its aristocratic elegance, music of the Classical era absorbed a variety of folk and popular elements. This influence made itself felt not only in the German dances and waltzes of the Viennese masters but also in their songs, symphonies, concertos, string quartets, and sonatas.

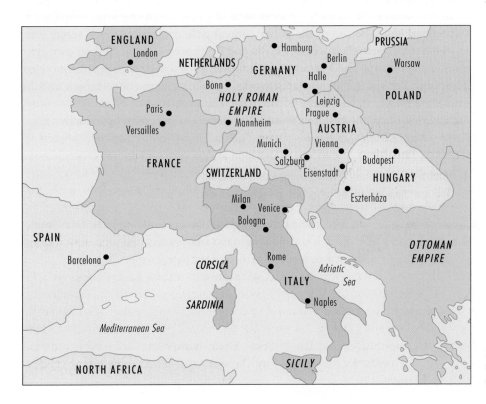

Map of Europe, 1763–1789, showing major musical centers.

An aristocratic concert. Oil and wood panel, attributed to **Jean-Honoré Fragonard** (1732–1806).

*In His Own Words*

The master of music, Mr. Haydn, is reminded to apply himself more assiduously to composition than he has done so far . . . and, to show his zeal, he will hand in the first piece of every composition in a clean, tidy copy.

*—Prince Esterházy*

# The Patronage System

The culture of the eighteenth century thrived under the patronage, or sponsorship, of an aristocracy that viewed the arts as a necessary adornment of life. Music was part of the elaborate lifestyle of the nobility, and the center of musical life was the palace.

The social events at court created a steady demand for new works from composers, who had to supply whatever their patrons wanted. Although musicians ranked little better than servants, their situation was not quite as depressing as it sounds. The patronage system actually gave musicians economic security and provided a social framework within which they could function. It offered important advantages to the great masters who successfully adjusted to its requirements, as the career of Haydn clearly shows. On the other hand, Mozart's tragic end illustrates how heavy the penalty could be for those unable to make that adjustment (see Chapter 22).

While aristocratic women like Princess Henriette of France, sister of King Louis XV (see illustration, p. 149) continued their avid music studies, middle-class women also found a place as musicians under the patronage system. In Italy and France, professional female singers achieved prominence in opera and in court ballets. Others found a place within aristocratic circles as court instrumentalists and music teachers, offering private lessons to members of the nobility. As we will see, a number of women pianists and violinists also made their mark as solo performers. With the growth of the music trades, especially music printing and publishing, women found more professional opportunities open to them. And as more amateurs participated in music-making, women of the middle as well as upper classes found an outlet for their talents.

At this time, musical performances were beginning to move from the palace to the concert hall. The rise of the public concert gave composers a new venue (site) in which to perform their works. Haydn and Beethoven conducted their own symphonies at concerts, and Mozart and Beethoven played their own piano concertos. The public flocked to hear the latest works—unlike modern concertgoers who are interested mainly in the music of the past. The eagerness of eighteenth-century audiences for new music surely stimulated composers to greater productivity.

### Critical Thinking

**1.** What are the primary characteristics of Classicism?

**2.** How are Classical ideas reflected in eighteenth-century music?

# 21 The Development of Classical Forms

> "I alter some things, eliminate and try again until I am satisfied. Then begins the mental working out of this material in its breadth, its narrowness, its height and depth."
>
> —Ludwig van Beethoven

**KEY POINTS**

⑤ **StudySpace** wwnorton.com/enjoy

- Melodic ideas, or *themes*, are used as building blocks in a composition; these melodies are made up of short melodic or rhythmic fragments known as *motives*.

- Themes can be expanded by varying the melody, rhythm, or harmony through *thematic development*; this usually happens in large-scale works.

- Development and variation are processes found in all styles of music.

- Repeated short patterns, or *ostinatos*, can also be used to build compositions.

- Form is the most important organizing element in *absolute music*, which has no specific pictorial or literary program.

- The Classical-era symphony, sonata, string quartet, and concerto are in standard *multimovement cycles* of three of four movements.

- The first movement of the cycle is usually in a fast tempo and in *sonata-allegro form*, with three main sections: *exposition, development*, and *recapitulation*.

- The second movement is usually slow and can be in various forms, including *theme and variations* or *ternary* (**A-B-A**) form.

- The third movement is a triple-meter dance— either a *minuet and trio* or a *scherzo and trio*.

- The fourth movement is fast and lively, often in *rondo* or *sonata-allegro* form.

Thinking, whether in words or music, demands continuity. Every thought should flow from the one before and lead logically into the next, thereby creating steady progress toward a goal. Uniting the first phrase of one melody and the second phrase of a different one would not make any more sense than joining the beginning of one sentence to the end of another.

## Expanding Musical Ideas

As noted in our study of form, a musical idea that is used as a building block in the construction of a composition is called a *theme*. The expansion of a theme, achieved by varying its melodic outline, rhythm, or harmony, is considered *thematic development*. This is one of the most important techniques in musical composition and requires both imagination and craft on the part of the creator. In addition to its capacity for growth, a theme can be fragmented by dividing it into

*Theme and thematic development*

British optical artist **Bridget Riley** (b. 1931) explores the large-scale development of a motive through subtle variations in size, shape, and position. *Evoë 3* (2003).

Pachelbel: Canon in D

Thematic development

Absolute music

Multimovement cycle

its constituent motives, a ***motive*** being its smallest melodic or rhythmic unit. A motive can grow into an expansive melody, or it can be treated in ***sequence***, that is, repeated at a higher or lower level. A short, repeated musical pattern—called an ***ostinato***—can also be an important organizing feature of a work. One well-known work that uses this technique is the Pachelbel Canon in D, in which rich string lines unfold very gradually over an ever-present bass pattern.

The use of thematic development is generally too complex for short pieces, where a simple contrast between sections and modest expansion of material usually supply the necessary continuity. But thematic development is necessary in larger forms of music, where it provides clarity, coherence, and logic.

The development of thematic material—through extension, contraction, and repetition—occurs in music from all corners of the world. We have already seen that some music is improvised, or created spontaneously, by performers. Although it might seem that structure and logic would be alien to this process, this is rarely the case. In jazz, for example, musicians organize their improvised melodies within a highly structured, pre-established harmonic pattern, time frame, and melodic outline that is understood by all the performers. In many parts of Asia, improvisation is a refined and classical art, where the seemingly free and rhapsodic spinning out of the music is tied to a prescribed musical process that results in a lacework of variations.

# Classical Forms

Every musical work has a form; it is sometimes simple, other times complex. In ***absolute music,*** form is especially important because there is no prescribed story or text to hold the music together. The story is the music itself, so its shape is of primary concern for the composer, the performer, and the listener. Large-scale works have an overall form that determines the relationships between the movements and their tempos. In addition, each movement has an internal form that binds its different sections into one artistic whole. We have already learned two of the simplest forms: two-part, or binary (**A-B**), and three-part, or ternary (**A-B-A**).

Now let's examine an important structural procedure in Western instrumental music—the standard ***multimovement cycle*** that was used from around 1750 through the Romantic era. This cycle generally consists of three or four

## LISTENING ACTIVITY: THEMATIC DEVELOPMENT

Let's compare the way themes are developed in music from two different cultures, using these examples (StudySpace, Chapter 21).

*In a Mountain Path* (Chinese song): Answer these true/false questions.

___ **1.** The work starts with a brief introduction.

___ **2.** We hear a short melodic motive with the pattern long-short-short-long-long.

___ **3.** The main melodic idea is heard starting on the same pitch each time.

___ **4.** The melodic idea is expanded as the work progresses.

___ **5.** This example is based on a 7-note major scale.

Beethoven, Symphony No. 5, I: Answer these true/false questions.

___ **6.** The work begins with a short melodic idea or motive (short-short-short-long).

___ **7.** The motive is heard in sequence, starting on other pitches.

___ **8.** The motive does not change or expand and never becomes any longer.

___ **9.** The same instruments play the main motive throughout.

___ **10.** The opening is not heard again, once the piece progresses to a contrasting section.

**Understanding the Development of Musical Ideas** (from ⊚ **iMusic**):

Thematic development (variation): Symphony No. 94, II (Haydn)
Improvisation: *Avaz of Bayate Esfahan*
Ostinato: Canon in D (Pachelbel)

movements in prescribed forms and tempos and is employed in various genres, including the symphony, the sonata, the string quartet (and many other chamber works as well), and the concerto.

# The First Movement

The most highly organized and often the longest movement in this cycle is the opening one, which is usually in a fast tempo such as Allegro and is written in *sonata-allegro form* (also known as *sonata form*). A movement in sonata-allegro form establishes a home key, then moves or modulates to another key, and ultimately returns to the home key. We may therefore regard sonata-allegro form as a drama between two contrasting key areas. In most cases, each key area is associated with a theme, which has the potential for development (such as the short, incisive opening to Beethoven's Symphony No. 5; see Listening Activity above). The themes are stated, or "exposed," in the first section; developed in the second; and restated, or "recapitulated," in the third.

   The opening section of sonata-allegro form—the *exposition*, or statement—generally presents the two opposing keys and their respective themes. (In some cases, a theme may consist of several related ideas, in which case we speak of a *theme group*.) The first theme and its expansion establish the home key, or tonic.

Sonata-allegro form

 **iMusic**

Symphony No. 5

Exposition

In *Convex and Concave* (1955), Dutch graphic artist **M. C. Escher** (1898–1972) stimulates the brain to recognize patterns and to perceive how the action draws the eye toward the center, much like the pull of the tonic in a large-scale musical form.

**Bridge**

A ***bridge***, or transitional passage, leads into a contrasting key; in other words, the function of the bridge is to modulate. The second theme and its expansion establish the contrasting key. A closing section—sometimes with a new closing theme—rounds off the exposition in the contrasting key. In eighteenth-century sonata-allegro form, the exposition is repeated to establish the themes.

**Development**

Conflict and action, the essence of drama, characterize the ***development***. This section may wander further through a series of foreign keys, building up tension against the inevitable return home. The frequent modulations contribute to a sense of activity and restlessness. Here, the composer reveals the potential of the themes by varying, expanding, or contracting them, breaking them into their component motives, or combining them with other motives or with new material.

When the development has run its course, the tension lets up and a bridge passage leads back to the key of the tonic. The beginning of the third section, the

**Recapitulation**

***recapitulation***, or restatement, is the psychological climax of sonata-allegro form. The return of the first theme in the tonic satisfies the listener's need for unity. Like the exposition, the recapitulation restates the first and second themes more or less in their original form, and in the home key, but with new and varied twists. One important difference from the exposition is that the recapitulation remains in the tonic, thereby asserting the dominance of the home key. The movement often

**Coda**

ends with a ***coda***, an extension of the closing idea that leads us to the final cadence in the home key.

The features of sonata-allegro form, summed up in the chart opposite (which is color-coded to show keys), are present in one shape or another in many movements, yet no two pieces are exactly alike. Thus what might at first appear to be a fixed plan provides a supple framework for infinite variety in the hands of the composer.

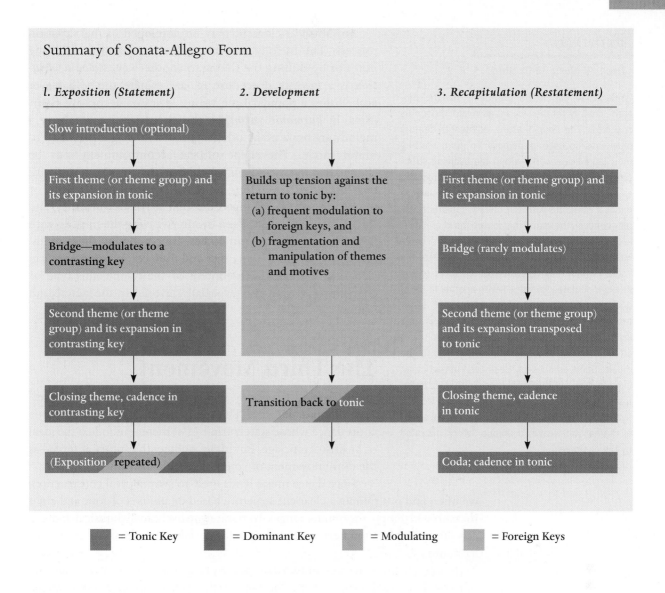

## Summary of Sonata-Allegro Form

**l. Exposition (Statement)**      **2. Development**      **3. Recapitulation (Restatement)**

| Exposition | Development | Recapitulation |
|---|---|---|
| Slow introduction (optional) | | |
| First theme (or theme group) and its expansion in tonic | Builds up tension against the return to tonic by:<br>(a) frequent modulation to foreign keys, and<br>(b) fragmentation and manipulation of themes and motives | First theme (or theme group) and its expansion in tonic |
| Bridge—modulates to a contrasting key | | Bridge (rarely modulates) |
| Second theme (or theme group) and its expansion in contrasting key | | Second theme (or theme group) and its expansion transposed to tonic |
| Closing theme, cadence in contrasting key | Transition back to tonic | Closing theme, cadence in tonic |
| (Exposition repeated) | | Coda; cadence in tonic |

■ = Tonic Key    ■ = Dominant Key    ■ = Modulating    ■ = Foreign Keys

# The Second Movement

The second is usually the slow movement of the cycle, offering a contrast to the Allegro that preceded it, and characterized by lyrical, songful melodies. Typically, it is an Andante or Adagio in **A-B-A** form, a shortened sonata form, or a theme-and-variations forms.

We have already noted that variation is an important procedure in music, but in one form—***theme and variations***—it is the ruling principle. There, the theme is clearly stated at the outset and serves as the point of departure. The melody may be newly invented or borrowed (like the theme in Britten's *Young Person's Guide to the Orchestra*; see Listening Guide 1, p. 60). The theme is likely to be a small two- or three-part idea, simple in character to allow room for elaboration. The statement of the theme is followed by a series of structured variations in which certain features of the original idea are retained while others are altered. Each variation sets forth the idea with some new modification— one might say in a new disguise—through which the listener glimpses something of the original theme.

**Theme and variations**

### Does All Music Tell a Story?

While some composers provide a specific program, or story, for their works, as Vivaldi did for his concertos *The Four Seasons*, eighteenth-century musicians focused principally on form, setting their large-scale works within the evolving structures of the era. Even in absolute music focused on form, however, we can equate elements of a musical structure with the literary construct of a play or novel: the varied themes are the characters, each of which is developed as the work proceeds. Moments of conflict and tension characterize the "plot," which may take unexpected turns as the music modulates from one key to another or introduces a new idea that is not anticipated. Inevitably there will be one or more climaxes of high drama, after which we feel a sense of resolution, often returning us to something familiar in the music. Some composers, Beethoven in particular, liked to draw out the conclusion, so that we anticipate it with baited breath. Each musical work or individual movement can be understood as a kind of drama that weaves a unique "story" narrated by the composer.

Any musical element may be developed in the variation process. The melody may be varied by adding or omitting notes or by shifting the theme to another key. *Melodic variation* is a favorite procedure in jazz, where the solo player embellishes a popular tune with a series of decorative flourishes. In *harmonic variation*, the chords that accompany a melody are replaced by others, perhaps shifting from major to minor mode. The shape of the accompaniment may be changed, or the melody may be shifted to a lower register with new harmonies sounding above it. Note lengths, meter, or tempo can also be changed through *rhythmic variation*, and the texture may be enriched by interweaving the melody with new themes or countermelodies. By combining these methods with changes in dynamics and tone color, composers can also alter the expressive content of the theme; this type of character variation was especially favored in the nineteenth century.

# The Third Movement

In the Classical symphony, the third movement is almost invariably a *minuet and trio*. The minuet was originally a Baroque court dance whose stately triple (3/4) meter embodied the ideal of an aristocratic age. But in the eighteenth century, it served as the third movement of some large-scale instrumental works.

Since dance music lends itself to symmetrical construction, we often find in a minuet a clear-cut structure based on phrases of four and eight measures. In tempo, the minuet ranges from stately to lively and whimsical. Indeed, certain of Haydn's minuets are closer in spirit to folk dance than to the palace ballroom.

It was customary to present two dances as a group, the first repeated at the end of the second (resulting in **A-B-A**). The dance in the middle was originally arranged for only three instruments, hence the name "trio," which persisted even after the customary setting for three had long been abandoned. At the end of the trio, we

**Da capo**    find the words *da capo* ("from the beginning"), signifying that the first section is to be played over again (as it was in the Baroque aria; see p. 113).

Minuet-trio-minuet is a symmetrical three-part structure in which each part in turn subdivides into two-part, or binary, form (**a-a-b-b**). The second (**b**) section of

**Rounded binary form**    the minuet or trio may bring back the opening theme, making a *rounded binary form* (see chart below). The composer indicates the repetition of the subsections

## MINUET AND TRIO

 iMusic iMaterials

|  | Minuet (**A**) | Trio (**B**) | Minuet (**A**) |
|---|---|---|---|
| Binary | ‖: **a** :‖: **b** :‖ | ‖: **c** :‖: **d** :‖ | **a-b** |
|  | or | or | or |
| Rounded binary | ‖: **a** :‖: **b-a** :‖ | ‖: **c** :‖: **d-c** :‖ | **a-b-a** |

within repeat signs ( ‖ : : ‖ ). However, when the minuet returns after the trio, it is customarily played straight through, without repeats.

In the early nineteenth century, the minuet was replaced by the *scherzo*, a quick-paced dance in triple meter with the same overall three-part structure (scherzo-trio-scherzo). The scherzo—Italian for "jest"—is marked by abrupt changes of mood, from humorous or whimsical to mysterious and even demonic. In Beethoven's hands, the scherzo displayed great rhythmic drive.

Scherzo

# The Fourth Movement

The Classical sonata and symphony often ended with another sonata-allegro form or a spirited *rondo*. The latter form is based on the recurrence of a musical idea—the rondo theme, or refrain—in alternation with contrasting episodes, much like the ritornello procedure of the Baroque era. Its symmetrical sections create a balanced architecture that is satisfying aesthetically and easy to hear. In its simplest form, **A-B-A-C-A**, the rondo is an extension of three-part form. We saw a version of this form in the French rondeau by Mouret (see p. 135). As developed by the Classical masters, the rondo was more ambitious in scope, often taking a longer, arched form (**A-B-A-C-A-B-A**; see illustration, p. 134). As the last movement, it featured a catchy, dancelike theme that lent itself to being heard over and over again.

Rondo

# The Multimovement Cycle as a Whole

The multimovement cycle of the Classical masters, as found in their symphonies, sonatas, string quartets, concertos, and other types of chamber music, became the vehicle for their most important instrumental music. The outline below sums up the common practice of the Classical-Romantic era. The outline will be helpful provided you remember that it is no more than a general scheme.

## MULTIMOVEMENT CYCLE: GENERAL SCHEME

| MOVEMENT | CHARACTER / TEMPO | FORM/KEY | PLAYLIST |
|---|---|---|---|
| **FIRST** | Long, dramatic<br>Allegro | Sonata-allegro<br>Tonic Key | Mozart: *Eine kleine Nachtmusik*, I<br>Beethoven: Symphony No. 5, I |
| **SECOND** | Slow, lyrical<br>Andante, Adagio | Theme and variations<br>(or **A-B-A**) or modified<br>sonata-allegro<br>Related Key | Haydn: *Emperor* Quartet, II<br>Haydn: Symphony No. 100 (*Military*), II |
| **THIRD**<br>(optional) | Dancelike<br>Allegro, Allegretto | Minuet and Trio (18th c.)<br>Scherzo and Trio (19th c.)<br>Tonic Key | Mozart: *Eine kleine Nachtmusik*, III<br>Beethoven: Symphony No. 5, III |
| **FOURTH**<br>(last) | Lively, spirited<br>Allegro, Vivace | Rondo (or sonata-rondo,<br>sonata-allegro)<br>Tonic Key | Beethoven: Symphony No.5, .IV |

This large-scale structure satisfied composers' need for an extended instrumental work of an abstract nature, and showcased the contrasts of key and mode inherent in the major-minor system. With its fusion of emotional and intellectual elements, its intermingling of lyricism and action, the multimovement cycle may justly claim to be one of the most ingenious art forms ever devised.

### Critical Thinking

1. What are some ways that composers unify their compositions?
2. How can music structures from this era be compared to a play or novel?
3. How can musical elements be modified to achieve variation? How is this different from using new musical elements to create contrast in a composition?

## LISTENING ACTIVITY: HEARING LARGER FORMS

Let's consider two works (StudySpace, Chapter 21) with which we can practice hearing larger forms.

> Mouret: Rondeau
> Mozart: Symphony No. 40, III

Review first the Baroque Rondeau (p. 134) by the French court composer Jean-Joseph Mouret that we studied.

____ 1. How many sections do you hear (when the music or style changes)?
   **a.** two
   **b.** five
   **c.** eight

____ 2. Which theme do you hear come back?
   **a.** the first theme
   **b.** the second theme

____ 3. How many times do you hear this theme (separated by other music)?
   **a.** two times

   **b.** three times
   **c.** five times

____ 4. In which meter is this dance?
   **a.** duple
   **b.** triple
   **c.** sextuple

____ 5. Which of these forms best suits this dance?
   **a.** minuet and trio
   **b.** sonata-allegro
   **c.** rondo

Now let's try a Classical-era dance movement (a movement from Mozart Symphony No. 40) and see what differences we can hear.

____ 6. In which meter is this dance?
   **a.** duple
   **b.** triple
   **c.** sextuple

____ 7. There are two main musical sections. Which is longer?
   **a.** first theme
   **b.** second theme

____ 8. Which of these best outlines the form of the dance that you heard?
   **a.** a-b-a-b
   **b.** a-a-b-b
   **c.** a-b-c-d

____ 9. Which of these forms do we expect as the third movement of a symphony?
   **a.** sonata-allegro
   **b.** theme and variations
   **c.** minuet and trio

____ 10. This symphony by Mozart was referred to as the "Romantic." Which of these traits makes it seem more expressive?
   **a.** minor key
   **b.** dancelike character
   **c.** size of the orchestra

# 22 Classical Chamber Music

"The free arts and the beautiful science of composition will not tolerate technical chains. The mind and soul must be free."

—Joseph Haydn

- The Classical era is the golden age of **chamber music** (ensemble music for two to about ten performers, with one player per part).

- The **string quartet** (made up of 2 violins, viola, and cello) was the most important chamber music genre of the era; duos, trios, quintets, serenades, and divertimentos were also popular.

- Joseph Haydn worked under the patronage of the Esterházy court.

- Haydn's *Emperor* Quartet has a famous set of variations on a hymn he wrote for the Austrian emperor.

- Wolfgang Amadeus Mozart was a child prodigy who started to write music before the age of five.

- Mozart contributed to nearly all musical genres, including the symphony, sonata, concerto, chamber music, sacred music, and various types of opera.

- Mozart's music is notable for its lyrical melodies, colorful orchestration, and dramatic content. One of Mozart's best-known works is *Eine kleine Nachtmusik* (*A Little Night Music*), a serenade for strings.

**C**hamber music, as we have seen, is music for a small ensemble—two to about ten players—with one player to a part. In this intimate genre, each instrument is expected to assert itself fully, but function as part of a team rather than as a soloist.

The Classical era was the golden age of chamber music. Haydn and Mozart, Beethoven and Schubert established the true chamber music style, a friendly conversation among equals. The central position in Classical chamber music was held by the **string quartet**, which consists of two violins (a first and a second), a viola, and a cello. Other favored combinations were the **duo sonata**—violin and piano, or cello and piano; the **piano trio**—violin, cello, and piano; and the **quintet**, usually a combination of string or wind instruments, or a string quartet and solo instrument such as the piano or clarinet. (See chart on p. 54.) Composers of the era also produced some memorable examples of chamber music for larger groups, including sextets, septets, and octets, as well as some popular genres of social music. We will consider both the string quartet, with an example by Haydn, and a serenade, written for a larger chamber group, by Mozart.

String quartet

*In His Own Words*

You listen to four sensible persons conversing, you profit from their discourse, and you get to know their several instruments.

—*Johann Wolfgang von Goethe, writing about quartets*

## The String Quartet

The string quartet soon became the most influential chamber music genre of the Classical period. Its structure follows the four-movement scheme of the

## Joseph Haydn (1732–1809)

**Joseph Haydn** was one of the most prolific composers of the Classical period. Born in the small Austrian village of Rohrau, he absorbed the folk songs and dances of his homeland. The beauty of his voice secured him a place as a choirboy at St. Stephen's Cathedral in Vienna, where he remained until he was sixteen. Haydn then settled in Vienna, where he made his living by teaching and accompanying.

Before long, Haydn attracted the notice of the music-loving aristocracy of Vienna. In 1761, when he was twenty-nine, he entered the service of the Esterházys, a family of enormously wealthy Hungarian princes famous for their patronage of the arts. He remained with this family for almost thirty years, the greater part of his creative career. The family palace of Eszterháza was one of the most splendid in Europe (see illustration, p. 167), and music played a central role in the constant round of festivities there—the court even boasted its own opera house. The musical establishment under Haydn's direction included an orchestra, an opera company, a marionette theater, and a chapel. His life exemplifies the patronage system at its best.

By the time Haydn reached middle age, his music had brought him much fame. After the prince's death, he made two visits to England (1791–92 and 1794–95), where he conducted his works with phenomenal success. He died in 1809, revered by his countrymen and acknowledged throughout Europe as the premier musician of his time.

It was Haydn's historic role to help perfect the new instrumental music of the late eighteenth century. Significant too was his expansion of the orchestra's size and resources in his late symphonies through greater emphasis on the brass, clarinets (new to the orchestra), and percussion. His expressive harmony, structural logic, and endlessly varied moods expressed the mature Classical style.

The string quartet occupied a central position in Haydn's output, as did the symphonies—over a hundred in number—which extend across Haydn's entire career. Among the most popular symphonies are the twelve written in the 1790s for his appearances in England.

**Major Works:** Chamber music, including 68 string quartets (*Emperor*, Op. 76, No. 3) • Over 100 symphonies (including the 12 *London* symphonies, Nos. 93-104) • Concertos for violin, cello, harpsichord, and trumpet • Sacred vocal music (Masses, motets, and 2 oratorios, including *The Creation*) • 14 operas • Keyboard music (including 40 sonatas).

**iMusic:** *Emperor* Quartet, Op. 76, No. 3, II    Symphony No.100 (*Military*), II
Symphony No. 94 (*Surprise*), II

This anonymous watercolor depicts a performance of a string quartet, the most influential chamber music genre of the era.

standard multimovement cycle described in Chapter 21. The first movement is usually an Allegro in sonata-allegro form. The second is a slow, lyrical movement, often in **A-B-A** or theme and variations form. Third is a moderate dance in minuet and trio form, and the fourth is a fast movement in either sonata-allegro or rondo form.

Because the string quartet was intended as salon music, to be enjoyed by a small group of cultivated music lovers, composers did not need expansive gestures here. They could present their most private thoughts, and indeed, the final string quartets of Haydn, Mozart, and Beethoven contain some of their most profound expressions.

Joseph Haydn, with his sixty-eight string quartets, played a central role in the evolution of this genre. These works are among his best loved and most frequently performed in the repertory today.

# Haydn's *Emperor Quartet*

Haydn wrote most of his string quartets in sets of six, and his Op. 76 quartets are no exception. The quartets in this set owe much to the style of Mozart, who so esteemed the older composer that he dedicated a set of six quartets to him in the mid-1780s, now called the "Haydn" quartets.

The third in the set is known as the *Emperor* because the second movement is based on a hymn Haydn wrote for the Austrian emperor Franz Joseph. The invasion of Vienna by Napoleonic armies in 1796 raised a spirit of patriotism across Austria, to which Haydn responded with a musical tribute that became the country's national anthem, *Gott erhalte Franz den Kaiser* (*God Keep Franz the Emperor*). The hymn was sung in all the theaters of Vienna for the emperor's birthday on February 12, 1797; thanks to Haydn, Austria now had a moving anthem comparable to those of England (*God Save the King*) and France (*La Marseillaise*).

In summer 1797, Haydn wrote his Op. 76, No. 3 quartet, using the imperial hymn tune as a basis for a majestic theme and variations in the slow movement (see Listening Guide 19). Here, Haydn demonstrates his ability to produce a full, almost orchestral sound with only four instruments, all of which he treats equally. After the tune is introduced by the first violin in a simple setting, each instrument takes its turn with a variation: the second violin, with an embroidered accompanying line from its violin partner; the cello, with its deep and dignified tone; then the dark viola—Haydn's own instrument—with rich chromatic color. The fourth and final variation is a kind of recapitulation that brings back the tune in a more complex polyphonic texture.

This lyrical tune, a favorite of Haydn's throughout his lifetime and reportedly the last music he played before his death on May 26, 1809, remained the national anthem of Austria until 1947, when for political reasons the country chose another. The hymn had been adopted in 1922 by Germany, with new words (*Deutschland über alles*), which took on propagandist meanings associated with the Nazi regime. Today, Germany claims the hymn as its national song, but sings only the third stanza, celebrating "unity and justice and freedom" (*Einigkeit und Recht und Freiheit*).

### In His Own Words

My Prince was always satisfied with my works. I not only had the encouragement of constant approval but as conductor of an orchestra I could make experiments, observe what produced an effect and what weakened it, and . . . improve, alter, make additions, or omissions, and be as bold as I pleased.

---

**LISTENING GUIDE 19**                                    DVD | CD 2 (60–64) | CD 1 (70–74)

# Haydn: String Quartet, Op. 76, No. 3 (*Emperor*), II        6:46

**DATE:** 1797

| | |
|---|---|
| **MOVEMENTS:** | I. Allegro; sonata-allegro form |
| | **II. Poco adagio, cantabile; theme & variations** |
| | III. Menuetto, Allegro; minuet and trio form |
| | IV. Finale, Presto; sonata-allegro form |

**WHAT TO LISTEN FOR:**

| | | | | |
|---|---|---|---|---|
| Melody | Lyrical melody in 5 phrases of 4 measures each, several of which are repeated: **a-a-b-c-c** | Texture | Homophonic opening; becomes more polyphonic |
| Rhythm/ Meter | Simple rhythms in quadruple meter; some syncopation in later variations | Form | Theme (**a-a-b-c-c**) and 4 variations, each in same structure; closing 4-measure coda |
| Harmony | In G major, some chromaticism in variation 3 | Expression | Tempo = rather slowly, in a singing style; subtle and contrasting dynamics |
| | | Performing Forces | 2 violins, viola, and cello |

*Continued on following page*

Structure of the theme:

Phrase **a** (repeated):

Phrase **b**:

Phrase **c** (repeated):

| | | |
|---|---|---|
| **70** | 0:00 | **Theme**: played by the first violin, with a simple chordal accompaniment. |
| **71** | 1:19 | **Variation 1**: theme played by the second violin in a duet with high-range decorative figurations in the first violin. |
| **72** | 2:28 | **Variation 2**: theme played by the cello, accompanied by other instruments; grows more polyphonic. |
| **73** | 3:46 | **Variation 3**: theme played by the viola; syncopated accompaniment in first violin; some chromaticism. |
| **74** | 5:04 | **Variation 4**: theme returns to violin 1, set in a polyphonic texture. |
| | 6:18 | **Coda**—short closing with sustained cello note, over which instruments fade out softly. |

ⓢ **Now try the Listening Quiz.**

# Mozart and Chamber Music

> "People make a mistake who think that my art has come easily to me. Nobody has devoted so much time and thought to composition as I. There is not a famous master whose music I have not studied over and over."

**Serenade**

Some types of composition stood midway between chamber music and the symphony, their chief purpose being entertainment. Most popular among those were the **divertimento** and the **serenade**. Both are lighter genres that were performed in the evening or at social functions. Mozart wrote a large quantity of social music—divertimentos and serenades of great variety, the most famous of which is *Eine kleine Nachtmusik* (1787).

## *Eine kleine Nachtmusik*

Mozartean elegance is embodied in *Eine kleine Nachtmusik,* a serenade for strings whose title means literally *A Little Night Music*. The work was most likely written for a string quartet supported by a double bass and was meant for public entertainment, in outdoor performance. The four movements of the version we know (originally there were five) are compact, intimate, and beautifully proportioned.

**Rocket theme**

The first movement is a perfect and concise introduction to sonata-allegro form. It opens with a strong, marchlike theme that rapidly ascends to its peak (this is sometimes called a **rocket theme**), then turns downward at the same rate. Mozart

A modern-day photograph of the Eszterháza Palace in Fertöd, Hungary, where Haydn was employed.

balances this idea with an elegant descending second theme. The closing theme exudes a high energy level, moving the work into its short development; the third section recaps the themes, ending with a vigorous coda. (See Listening Guide 20, p. 168, for a detailed view of the work's themes and structure.)

The second movement is the Romanza, an eighteenth-century Andante that maintains the balance between lyricism and restraint. In this movement, symmetrical sections are arranged in a rondo-like structure.

**Third movement**

The minuet and trio is marked by regular four-bar phrases set in rounded binary form (see chart, p. 160). The minuet opens brightly and decisively. The trio, with its polished soaring melody, presents a lyrical contrast. The opening music then returns, satisfying the Classical desire for balance and symmetry.

**Fourth movement**

The last movement is a sprightly Allegro in the home key of G, a bright, jovial finale stamped with an aristocratic refinement. This work is Mozartean from its first note to its last, and is a perfect introduction to the master's astonishing creative talents.

## Wolfgang Amadeus Mozart (1756–1791)

Something miraculous hovers above the music of Mozart. His elegant writing and his rich instrumental colors sound effortless. This deceptive simplicity is the secret of his art.

**Mozart** was born in Salzburg, Austria, the son of Leopold Mozart, an esteemed composer-violinist at the court of the Archbishop of Salzburg. The most extraordinarily gifted child in the history of music, he started to compose before he was five, and, with his talented sister Nannerl, performed at the court of Empress Maria Theresa at the age of six. By age thirteen, the boy had written sonatas, concertos, symphonies, religious works, and several operas.

The high-spirited young artist rebelled against the social restrictions imposed by the patronage system and at twenty-five established himself in Vienna as a struggling freelance musician. In 1782, he married Constanze Weber, against his domineering father's wishes.

He reached the peak of his career in the late 1780s with his three comic operas (*The Marriage of Figaro, Don Giovanni,* and *Così fan tutte*) on librettos by Lorenzo da Ponte. Although in poor health, Mozart continued to produce masterpieces for the Viennese public, including his Clarinet Concerto (he was one of the first to compose for this new instrument) and his final opera, *The Magic Flute* (1791). With a kind of fevered desperation, he then turned to the Requiem Mass, which had been commissioned by a music-loving count. There are indications that Mozart became obsessed with the notion that this Mass for the Dead was intended for himself and that he would not live to finish it. He died on December 4, 1791, shortly before his thirty-sixth birthday.

Mozart is revered for the inexhaustible wealth of elegant and songful melodies. His instrumental music combines a sense of drama with contrasts of mood ranging from lively and playful to solemn and tragic. His orchestration is colorful, and his development sections full of chromatic harmonies. His symphonic masterpieces are the six written in the final decade of his life. In chamber music, Mozart, like Haydn, favored the string quartet. His last ten quartets are some of the finest in the literature, among them a set of six dedicated to Haydn.

*In His Own Words*

I learned from Haydn how to write quartets. No one else can do everything—be flirtatious and be unsettling, move to laughter and move to tears—as well as Joseph Haydn.

—*Wolfgang Amadeus Mozart*

One of the outstanding pianists of his time, he also wrote many works for his own instrument. His piano concertos (including the G major Concerto, K. 453, which we will study) elevated this genre to one of prime importance in the Classical era. (Note that the K. refers to the catalogue number in Mozart's output, determined by Ludwig Köchel.)

But the genre most central to Mozart's art was opera. He wrote in three dramatic styles: **opera buffa**, or Italian comic opera (including *Don Giovanni*, which we will study*); **opera seria**, or Italian serious opera and **Singspiel**, a lighter form of German opera with spoken dialogue.

**Major Works:** Chamber music, including 23 string quartets • Divertimentos and serenades (*Eine kleine Nachtmusik*, K. 525) • Keyboard music, including 17 piano sonatas • Sets of variations (*Ah! vous dirai-je maman*) • Orchestral music, including some 40 symphonies • Concertos, including 27 for piano, 5 for violin, others for solo wind instruments (clarinet, oboe, French horn, and bassoon) • Comic (buffa) operas, including *Le nozze di Figaro* (*The Marriage of Figaro*, 1786) and *Don Giovanni* (1787) • Serious (seria) operas, including *Idomeneo* (1791) • German Singspiel, including *Die Zauberflöte* (*The Magic Flute*, 1791) • Sacred choral music, including Requiem (incomplete, 1791).

ⓢ **iMusic:** *Eine kleine Nachtmusik*, I, III     Variations on *Ah! vous dirai-je, maman*
                Clarinet Concerto, II                 *Tuba mirum,* from Requiem
                Symphony No. 40, III              Horn Concerto, III
                                                  Piano Concerto, K. 467, II

---

## LISTENING GUIDE 20

ⓢ Video | ⓢ | DVD | CD 3 (1–20) | CD 2 (1–8)

# Mozart: *Eine kleine Nachtmusik* (*A Little Night Music*), K. 525, I and III

7:39

**DATE:** 1787

**MOVEMENTS:**
    **I.** **Allegro; sonata-allegro form, G major**
    II. Romanza, Andante; sectional rondo form, C major
    **III.** **Allegretto; minuet and trio form, G major**
    IV. Allegro; sonata-rondo form, G major

---

**First Movement: Allegro**

5:30

**WHAT TO LISTEN FOR:**

| | | | |
|---|---|---|---|
| Melody | Marchlike; disjunct, ascending (rocket) theme; then graceful descending tune | Texture | Homophonic |
| Rhythm/ Meter | Quick duple meter | Form | Sonata-allegro form (3 themes) in 3 sections: Exposition-Development-Recapitulation |
| Harmony | Consonant, in G major (tonic key) | Performing Forces | String quartet with double bass (or string orchestra) |

**EXPOSITION**

| 1 | 0:00 | Theme 1—aggressive, ascending "rocket" theme, symmetrical phrasing, in G major: |

Transitional passage, modulating.

**2** | 0:46 | Theme 2—graceful, contrasting theme, less hurried, in key of dominant, D major:

0:58 | Closing theme—insistent, repetitive, ends in D major:

Repeat of exposition.

**DEVELOPMENT**

**3** | 3:07 | Short, begins in D major, manipulates theme 1 and closing theme; modulates, and prepares for recapitulation in G major.

**RECAPITULATION**

**4** | 3:40 | Theme 1—in G major.

**5** | 4:22 | Theme 2—in G major.

4:34 | Closing theme—in G major.

5:05 | Coda—extends closing, in G major.

---

**Third Movement: Allegretto** 2:09

**WHAT TO LISTEN FOR:**

| | | | |
|---|---|---|---|
| Melody | Decisive minuet melody in regular phrases; conjunct and expressive trio | Harmony | Consonant, in G major (tonic key) |
| | | Texture | Homophonic |
| Rhythm/ Meter | Strongly rhythmic dance, in triple meter | Form | 2 dances (minuet-trio), with minuet returning; each dance is binary |

**6** | 0:00 | Minuet theme—in accented triple meter, decisive character, in 2 sections (8 measures each), both repeated:

**7** | 0:44 | Trio theme—more lyrical and connected, in 2 sections (8 + 12 measures), both repeated:

**8** | 1:41 | Minuet returns, without repeats.

◎ **Now try the Listening Quiz.**

## Critical Thinking

**1.** How did the careers of Haydn and Mozart differ under the patronage system?

**2.** How does Mozart's serenade *Eine kleine Nachtmusik* fit the model for multimovement instrumental works in this era?

# 23 The Classical Symphony

"I frequently compare a symphony with a novel in which the themes are characters. After we have made their acquaintance, we follow their evolution, the unfolding of their psychology."

—Arthur Honegger

## KEY POINTS

- The symphony was one of the principal instrumental forms of the Classical era.

- Quickly ascending **rocket themes** and **steamroller effects** (drawn-out *crescendos*) became standard in the Classical symphony.

- The heart of the Classical orchestra (about thirty to forty players) was the strings, assisted by woodwinds, brass, and percussion.

- Mozart's Symphony No. 40 in G minor, subtitled the *Romantic*, mingles Classical and Romantic elements.

- Joseph Haydn wrote over 100 symphonies; among these, his last twelve—the so-called *London* symphonies, including the *Military* Symphony (No. 100)—are his masterpieces in the genre.

- Ludwig van Beethoven's music straddles the Classical and Romantic eras. Of his nine monumental symphonies intended for the concert hall, best known is his Fifth, built on a famous four-note motive that permeates all four movements.

## Historical Background

The symphony, which held the central place in Classical instrumental music, grew in dimension and significance throughout the era. With the final works of Mozart and Haydn and the nine monumental symphonies by Beethoven, it became the most important type of absolute music.

The symphony had its roots in the Italian opera overture of the early eighteenth century, an orchestral piece in three sections: fast-slow-fast. First played to introduce an opera, these sections eventually became separate movements, to which the early German symphonists added a number of effects that were later taken over by the classical masters. One innovation was the use of a quick, aggressively rhythmic theme rising from low to high register with such speed that it became known as a **rocket theme** (as in Mozart's *Eine kleine Nachtmusik*). Equally important was the use of drawn-out *crescendos* (sometimes referred to as a **steamroller effect**) slowly gathering force as they rose to a climax. Both effects are generally credited to composers active at Mannheim, a German city along the Rhine River. With the addition of the minuet and trio, also a Mannheim contribution, the symphony paralleled the string quartet in following the four-movement multimovement cycle.

Rocket theme

Mannheim School

**THE CLASSICAL ORCHESTRA (30–40 PLAYERS)**    ◎ iMusic

| | HAYDN'S ORCHESTRA | BEETHOVEN'S ORCHESTRA |
|---|---|---|
| | *(Symphony No. 94, 1792)* | *(Symphony No. 5, 1807–08)* |
| **STRINGS** | Violins 1<br>Violins 2<br>Violas<br>Cellos and Double basses | Violins 1<br>Violins 2<br>Violas<br>Cellos<br>Double basses |
| **WOODWINDS** | 2 Flutes<br>2 Flutes<br>2 Oboes | 1 Piccolo (4th movement only)<br>2 Flutes<br>2 Oboes<br>2 Clarinets<br>2 Bassoons<br>1 Contrabassoon (4th movement only) |
| **BRASS** | 2 French horns<br>2 Trumpets | 2 French horns<br>2 Trumpets<br>3 Trombones (4th movement only) |
| **PERCUSSION** | Timpani | Timpani |

# The Classical Orchestra

The Classical masters established the orchestra as we know it today: as an ensemble of the four instrumental families. The heart of the orchestra was the string family. Woodwinds provided varying colors and assisted the strings, often doubling them. The brass sustained the harmonies and contributed body to the sound mass, while the timpani supplied rhythmic life and vitality. The eighteenth-century orchestra numbered from thirty to forty players (see chart above); thus the volume of sound was still more appropriate for the salon than the concert hall. (We will hear a movement from Haydn's Symphony No. 100 on eighteenth-century period instruments.)

Natural horns (without valves) and woodwinds are seen in this painting of a small orchestra performing in an 18th-century Venetian palace.

Classical composers created a dynamic style of orchestral writing in which all the instruments participated actively and each timbre could be heard. The interchange and imitation of themes among the various instrumental groups assumed the excitement of a witty conversation.

# The Movements of the Symphony

The first movement of a Classical symphony is an Allegro in sonata-allegro form, sometimes preceded by a slow introduction (especially in the symphonies of Haydn). Sonata-allegro form, as we saw in Chapter 21 (p. 161), is based on the

**First movement**

opposition of two keys, made clearly audible by the contrast between two themes. Haydn, however, sometimes based a sonata-allegro movement on a single theme, which was first heard in the tonic key and then in the contrasting key. Such a movement is referred to as **monothematic.** Mozart, on the other hand, preferred two themes with maximum contrast, which he achieved in his Symphony No. 40 through varied instrumentation, with the first theme introduced by the strings, and the second by the woodwinds. We will see that Beethoven took the art of thematic development to new levels in his Symphony No. 5, creating a unified masterpiece from a small motivic idea.

**Second movement**

The slow movement of a symphony is often a three-part form (**A-B-A**)—as we will see in Haydn's Symphony No. 100. Other typical forms include a theme and variations, or a **modified sonata-allegro** (without a development section). Generally a Largo, Adagio, or Andante, this movement is in a key other than the tonic, with colorful orchestration that often emphasizes the woodwinds. The mood is lyrical, and there is less development of themes here than in the first movement.

**Third movement**

**Ⓢ iMusic**

Mozart: Symphony No. 40, III

Third is the minuet and trio in triple meter, a graceful **A-B-A** form in the tonic key; as in the string quartet, its tempo is moderate. The trio is gentler in mood, with a moderately flowing melody and a prominent wind timbre. Beethoven's **scherzo** (a replacement for the minuet and trio), also in 3/4 time, is taken at a swifter pace, as we will hear in his famous Fifth Symphony.

**Fourth movement**

The fourth movement (the finale), normally a vivacious Allegro molto or Presto in rondo or sonata-allegro form, is not only faster but also lighter than the first movement and brings the cycle to a spirited ending. We will see that with Beethoven's Fifth Symphony how the fourth movement was transformed into a triumphant finale in sonata-allegro form.

# Haydn and the Symphony

*"Can you see the notes behave like waves? Up and down they go! Look, you can also see the mountains. You have to amuse yourself sometimes after being serious so long."*

Haydn contributed well over one hundred symphonies to the genre, thereby establishing the four-movement structure and earning himself the nickname "Father of the Symphony." His masterworks in the genre are his last set of twelve works, the so-called *London* Symphonies, commissioned for a concert series in London. These late works abound in expressive effects, including syncopation, sudden *crescendos* and accents, dramatic contrasts of soft and loud, daring modulations, and an imaginative plan in which each family of instruments plays its own part.

## Haydn's Symphony No. 100

Haydn's Symphony No. 100, the *Military*, was first presented in 1794 during his second London visit and was received enthusiastically by the British public. The symphony's nickname comes from the composer's use of percussion instruments associated with Turkish military music—namely triangle, cymbals, bass drum, and bell tree. The work also features a solo trumpet fanfare, another colorful military effect. Haydn, as well as Mozart and Beethoven, knew of these new instruments from the **Turkish Janissary bands** that performed in Vienna; after many centuries of wars between the Austrian Hapsburg Empire and the powerful

**Turkish Janissary bands**

# Haydn: Symphony No. 100 in G major (*Military*), II    5:33

**DATE:** 1794

**MOVEMENTS:**
    I.  Adagio-Allegro; sonata-allegro form, G major
    **I.  Allegretto; A-B-A′ form, C major**
   III.  Moderato; minuet and trio form, G major
   IV.  Presto; sonata-allegro form, G major

**Second movement: Allegretto**

**WHAT TO LISTEN FOR:**

| | |
|---|---|
| **Melody** | Simple, graceful theme, in regular phrases |
| **Rhythm/ Meter** | Marchlike, regular duple meter |
| **Harmony** | Change from C major to C minor, then back to C major |
| **Texture** | Homophonic |

| | |
|---|---|
| **Form** | 3-part form, with varied return (**A-B-A′**); **A** in binary form |
| **Expression** | Sudden dynamic contrasts |
| **Performing Forces** | Large orchestra, including woodwinds, trumpets, French horns, and many percussion instruments |

---

**75**   0:00   **A section**—C major, rounded binary form ‖: a :‖: b a :‖

    **a** = elegant, arched theme with grace notes; 8 measures, with string and flute:

    Repeated with oboes, clarinets, and bassoons.

**76**   0:29   **b** = 8+-measure theme developed from **a,** with strings and flute.
    **b** + **a** phrases repeated with oboes, clarinets, and bassoons:

**77**   1:40   **B section**—C minor, "military" sound, with added percussion (triangle, cymbals, bass drum); begins with loud, C-minor statement of **a;** mixes **a** and **b** themes with sudden dynamic changes:

**78**   2:45   **A section**—returns to C major, later adds percussion section; varied statements featuring different instruments.

**79**   4:33   **Coda**—solo trumpet fanfare, followed by drum roll, leads to *fortissimo* chord in A-flat major; motive from theme **a** repeated until full orchestra closing.

⊚ **Now try the Listening Quiz.**

The hall in the Eszteráza Palace where Haydn presented his symphonies.

Ottoman Empire, cultural exchanges between these political domains allowed Western Europeans the opportunity to hear—and adopt—these exotic sounds.

Haydn's *Military* symphony follows the multimovement pattern, and features a memorable second movement that combines the concept of variations with a simple three-part, or ternary, structure (see Listening Guide 21, p. 173). The graceful opening theme is heard in various guises that alter the timbre and harmony throughout. We are startled by the sudden change to minor mode in the middle section, and also struck by the trumpet fanfare and drum roll that introduce the closing coda. The works ends with a victorious *fortissimo* climax.

# Beethoven and the Symphony in Transition

"Freedom above all"

The symphony provided Beethoven with the ideal medium through which to address his public. The first two symphonies are closest in style to the two Classical masters who preceded him, but with his Third Symphony, the *Eroica,* Beethoven achieved his own mature approach. The Fifth Symphony, which we consider here, is popularly viewed as the model of the genre. The finale of the Ninth, or *Choral* Symphony, in which vocal soloists and chorus join the orchestra, is a setting of Schiller's *Ode to Joy,* a ringing prophecy of the time when "all people will be brothers" (for more on the Ninth, see HTTN 4, p. 181).

## Ludwig van Beethoven (1770–1827)

**Ludwig van Beethoven** was born in Bonn, Germany, into a troubled family situation. From age eleven, he supported his mother and two younger brothers by performing as an organist and harpsichordist. At seventeen, during a visit to Vienna, he played for Mozart; the youth improvised so brilliantly that Mozart remarked to his friends, "Keep an eye on him—he will make a noise in the world some day."

Although he was not attached to the court of a prince, the music-loving aristocrats of Vienna helped Beethoven in various ways—by paying him handsomely for lessons or presenting him with gifts. He was also aided by the emergence of a middle-class public and the growth of concert life and music publishing. Then fate struck in a vulnerable spot: Beethoven began to lose his hearing. His helplessness in the face of this affliction dealt a shattering blow to his pride: ". . . how could I possibly admit an infirmity in the one sense that should have been more perfect in me than in others." As deafness closed in on him—the first symptoms appeared when he was in his late twenties—it brought a sense of isolation from the world. He retired in

1802 to Heiligenstadt, outside Vienna, where he wrote his famous Heiligenstadt Testament, a letter penned to his brother that exposed how he was torn between the destructive forces in his soul and his desire to live and create.

Although he never regained his hearing, he fought his way back to health, and the remainder of his career was spent in ceaseless effort to achieve his artistic goals. A ride in an open carriage during severe weather brought on, however, an attack of edema that proved fatal. Beethoven died at age fifty-seven, famous and revered.

Beethoven is the supreme architect in music. His genius found expression in the structural type of thinking required in large-scale forms like the sonata and the symphony. The sketchbooks in which he worked out his ideas show how his pieces gradually reached their final shape.

Beethoven's compositional activity fell into three periods. The first reflected the Classical elements he inherited from Haydn and Mozart. The middle period saw the appearance of characteristics more closely associated with the nineteenth century: strong dynamic contrasts, explosive accents, and longer movements. In his third period, Beethoven used more chromatic harmonies and developed a skeletal language from which all nonessentials were rigidly pared away. It was a language that transcended his time.

Beethoven's nine symphonies are conceived on a scale too large for the aristocratic salon; they demand the concert hall. His highly virtuosic piano concertos coincided with and encouraged the popularity of this new instrument (see Btw, p. 188). The thirty-two piano sonatas are indispensable to the instrument's repertory, often considered the performer's New Testament. Of his chamber music, the string quartet was closest to his heart, and, like his sonatas, they span his entire compositional career. In the realm of vocal music, his one opera, *Fidelio*, and his *Missa solemnis* both rank among his masterpieces.

*In His Own Words*

I carry my thoughts about with me for a long time . . . before writing them down. I change many things, discard others, and try again and again until I am satisfied; . . . I turn my ideas into tones that resound, roar, and rage until at last they stand before me in the form of notes.

**Major Works:** Orchestral music, including 9 symphonies (*Ode to Joy*, from Symphony No. 9), overtures • Concertos, including 5 for piano and 1 for violin • Chamber music, including string quartets, piano trios, sonatas for violin, cello, wind chamber music • 32 piano sonatas, including Op. 13 (*Pathétique*) and Op. 27, No. 2 (*Moonlight*) • Other piano music (*Für Elise*) • 1 opera (*Fidelio*) • Choral music, including *Missa solemnis* • Songs and 1 song cycle.

◎ **iMusic:** *Für Elise*         Symphony No. 5, I
        *Moonlight* Sonata, I    *Ode to Joy*, from Symphony No. 9
        *Pathétique* Sonata, I

## The Fifth Symphony

Perhaps the best-known of all symphonies, Beethoven's Symphony No. 5 progresses from conflict and struggle to victorious ending. The first movement, in a sonata-allegro form marked Allegro con brio (lively, with vigor), springs out of the rhythmic idea of "three shorts and a long" that dominates the entire symphony. This idea, perhaps the most commanding gesture in the whole symphonic literature, is pursued with an almost terrifying single-mindedness in this dramatic movement. In an extended coda, the basic rhythm reveals a new fount of explosive energy. Beethoven described the motive as "Fate knocks at the door."(See Listening Guide 22.)

The second movement is a serene theme and variations, with two melodic ideas. In this movement, Beethoven exploits his two themes with all the procedures of variation—changes in melodic outline, harmony, rhythm, tempo, dynamics, register, key, mode, and timbre. The familiar four-note rhythm (short-short-short-long) is sounded in the second theme, providing unity to the symphony.

Third in the cycle of movements is the scherzo, which opens with a rocket theme introduced by cellos and double basses. After the gruff, humorous trio in C major, the scherzo returns in a modified version, followed by a transitional passage to the final movement in which the timpani sound the memorable four-note motive.

**LISTENING GUIDE 22**   ⓥ Video | ⓓ | DVD | CD 3 (31–55) | CD 2 (9–33)

# Beethoven: Symphony No. 5 in C minor, Op. 67   31:34

**DATE:** 1807–8

**MOVEMENTS:**  I. Allegro con brio; sonata-allegro form, C minor
II. Andante con moto; theme and variations form (2 themes), A-flat major
III. Allegro; scherzo and trio form, C minor
IV. Allegro; sonata-allegro form, C major

---

**First Movement: Allegro con brio**   7:31

**WHAT TO LISTEN FOR:**

| | | | |
|---|---|---|---|
| **Melody** | Fiery 4-note motive is basis for thematic development; contrasting, lyrical second theme | **Texture** | Mostly homophonic |
| **Rhythm/ Meter** | 4-note rhythmic idea (short-short-short-long) shapes work | **Form** | Concise sonata-allegro form, with extended coda; repetition, sequence, and variation techniques |
| **Harmony** | C minor, with dramatic shifts between minor and major tonality | **Expression** | Wide dynamic contrasts; forceful, energetic tempo |

**EXPOSITION**

[9]  0:00  Theme 1—based on famous 4-note motive (short-short-short-long), in C minor:

0:06  Motive expanded sequentially:

0:43  Expansion from 4-note motive; horns modulate to key of second theme.

[10]  0:46  Theme 2—Lyrical, in woodwinds, in E-flat major; heard against relentless rhythm of 4-note motive:

*basic rhythm*

1:07  Closing theme—rousing melody in descending staccato passage, then 4-note motive.
1:26  Repeat of exposition.

**DEVELOPMENT**

[11]  2:54  Beginning of development, announced by horn call.

3:05     Manipulation of 4-note motive through a descending sequence:

3:16     Melodic variation, interval filled in and inverted:

4:12     Expansion through repetition leads into recapitulation; music saturated with 4-note motive.

**RECAPITULATION**

| 12 | 4:18 | Theme 1—explosive statement in C minor begins recapitulation, |
|    | 4:38 | followed by brief oboe cadenza. |
| 13 | 5:15 | Theme 2—returns in C major, not in expected key of C minor. |
|    | 5:41 | Closing theme. |
| 14 | 5:58 | Coda—extended treatment of 4-note motive; ends in C minor. |

---

**Second Movement: Andante con moto**          10:01

**WHAT TO LISTEN FOR:**

| **Melody** | 2 contrasting themes: smooth first theme; rising second theme built on 4-note idea | **Texture** | Mostly homophonic |
| **Rhythm/ Meter** | Flowing triple meter | **Form** | Variations, with 2 themes; varied rhythms, melodies, harmony (major and minor) |
| **Harmony** | Related key: A-flat major | **Timbre** | Orchestra sections featured in groups: warm strings, brilliant woodwinds, powerful brass |

| 15 | 0:00 | Theme 1—broad, flowing melody, heard in low strings: |

| 16 | 0:52 | Theme 2—upward-thrusting 4-note (short-short-short-long) motive heard first in clarinets: |

Brass fanfare follows.

**Examples of variations on theme 1**

| 17 | 1:57 | Embellished with running sixteenth notes, low strings: |

Continued on following page

| 18 | 3:52 | Embellished with faster (thirty-second) notes in violas and cellos: |

| 19 | 5:04 | Melody exchanged between woodwind instruments (fragments of theme 1): |

| 20 | 6:36 | Melody shifted to minor, played staccato (detached version of theme 1): |

| 21 | 8:10 | Coda—*Più mosso* (faster), in bassoon. |

---

**Third Movement: Scherzo, Allegro**                                      **5:30**

**WHAT TO LISTEN FOR:**

| Melody | Wide-ranging, ascending scherzo theme; more conjunct, quick trio theme | Form | **A-B-A'** (scherzo-trio-scherzo); added link to final movement |
|---|---|---|---|
| Rhythm/ Meter | Quick triple meter throughout; insistent focus on 4-note rhythm | Expression | Wide-ranging dynamic contrasts; fast tempo |
| Harmony | Dramatic C-minor scherzo; trio in C major | Timbre | Low strings featured with themes; plucked (pizzicato) strings at return of scherzo; timpani in transition to last movement |
| Texture | Homophonic; some fugal treatment in trio | | |

| 22 | 0:00 | Scherzo theme—a rising, rocket theme in low strings, sounds hushed and mysterious: |

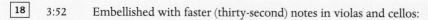

|  | 0:19 | Rhythmic motive (from movement I) explodes in horns, *fortissimo*: |

| 23 | 1:59 | Trio theme—in C major, in double basses, set fugally, played twice; contrast with C-minor scherzo: |

|  | 2:30 | Trio theme is broken up and expanded through sequences. |
| 24 | 3:29 | Scherzo returns, with varied orchestration, including pizzicato strings. |

| 25 | 4:46 | Transition to next movement with timpani rhythm from opening 4-note motive: |

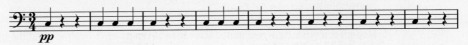

Tension mounts, orchestra swells to heroic opening of fourth movement.

**Fourth Movement: Allegro (without pause from movement III)**　　　　　　8:32

**WHAT TO LISTEN FOR:**

| Melody | Triumphant theme outlining C-major triad; energetic second theme |
| Rhythm/ Meter | Very fast, duple meter; 4-note rhythmic idea |
| Harmony | C major; remains in major throughout |
| Texture | Mostly homophonic |

| Form | Sonata-allegro form, with long coda; cyclic (return of material from earlier movements) |
| Expression | Forceful dynamics; *fp* (*forte/piano*) effects; intense and spirited |
| Performing Forces | Added instruments (piccolo, contrabassoon, trombones) |

**EXPOSITION**

| 26 | 0:00 | Theme 1—in C major, a powerful melody whose opening outlines triumphant C-major chord: |

| 27 | 0:33 | Lyrical transition theme in French horns, modulating from C to G major: |

| 28 | 0:59 | Theme 2—in G major, vigorous melody with rhythm from 4-note motive, in triplets: |

|  | 1:25 | Closing theme—featuring clarinet and violas, decisive. |

**DEVELOPMENT**

| 29 | 1:50 | Much modulation and free rhythmic treatment; brings back 4-note motive (short-short-short-long) from first movement. |
| 30 | 3:34 | Brief recurrence, like a whisper, of scherzo. |

**RECAPITULATION**

| 31 | 4:09 | Theme 1—in C major; full orchestra, *fortissimo.* |
| 32 | 5:13 | Theme 2—in C major, played by strings. |
|  | 5:40 | Closing theme, played by woodwind. |
| 33 | 6:08 | Coda—long extension; tension resolved over and over again until final, emphatic tonic. |

ⓢ **Now try the Listening Quiz.**

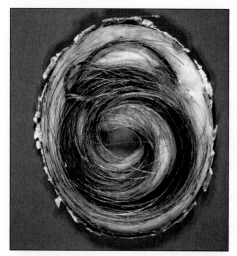

The Guevara lock of Beethoven's hair, from the Ira F. Brilliant Center for Beethoven Studies, San Jose State University, might help determine the cause of the composer's death (see Btw).

The monumental fourth movement bursts forward without pause, once again bringing back the unifying rhythmic motive. This unification makes the symphony an early example of *cyclical form* (in which a theme or musical idea from one movement returns in a later movement). Here, Beethoven unleashes not only a new energy and passion but also new instruments not yet part of the standard orchestra. These include the piccolo, contrabassoon, and trombones, all of which expand the ensemble's range and intensity. This last movement, in sonata-allegro form with an extended coda, closes with the tonic chord proclaimed triumphantly by the orchestra again and again.

Beethoven's career bridged the transition from the old society to the new. His commanding musical voice and an all-conquering will forged a link to the coming Romantic age.

## Critical Thinking

1. How did Classical composers vary the standard structure of the symphony?
2. What contributions did Haydn make to the genre of the symphony?
3. Which Romantic qualities are heard in Beethoven's symphonies? Which are Classical-era traits?

Beethoven's hearing aid, an ear trumpet, resting on a copy of his Third Symphony, the *Eroica.*

**4    Here & There, Then & Now**

# Beethoven and the Politics of Music

Composers have produced some of their most powerful music in response to the political climate in which they lived. This is especially true of Ludwig van Beethoven, who was born in Germany but adopted Austria as his homeland during a time of great tumult and change.

An advocate for democracy and the underprivileged, Beethoven watched the French general Napoleon Bonaparte rise to power after the French Revolution (1789–99). At first, he greatly admired Napoleon, idealizing him in his only opera, *Fidelio*. The composer's Third Symphony (*Eroica*) was to have celebrated Napoleon as well (he originally called it *Bonaparte*), but when the ruler declared himself emperor in 1804, Beethoven tore up the title page bearing the dedication. "So he too is nothing more than an ordinary man," Beethoven wrote. "Now he also will trample on all human rights and indulge only his own ambition. He will place himself above everyone and become a tyrant." After the French forces invaded his beloved Vienna, Beethoven's dislike of the French intensified.

Besides Austria, Beethoven also claimed a kinship with Great Britain—for both the people and their democratic parliamentary system. These heartfelt nationalistic sentiments found expression in his *Battle Symphony* (1813), also known as *Wellington's Victory*. This patriotic work celebrated the British victory at the Battle of Vitoria (1813), when the Allied Forces, led by the British duke of Wellington, demolished the Napoleonic army in Spain. First written for a strange mechanical organ known as the panharmonicon, *Wellington's Victory* was premiered in 1813 at a benefit concert for Austrian troops wounded in the war. Beethoven soon scored the work for orchestra, which included a large battery of percussion replete with muskets and cannons. Not strictly a symphony, *Wellington's Victory* is programmatic in its vivid retelling of the battle through fanfares and patriotic tunes associated with both the French (*Marlborough s'en va-t-en guerre*, or *Marlborough, he's gone to war*) and the British (*Rule, Britannia* and *God Save the King*). Today, *Wellington's Victory* is heard most frequently at Fourth of July celebrations in the United States to accompany fireworks and ceremonial pageantry.

One of Beethoven's most famous works is the last movement of his Symphony No. 9, which includes *Ode to Joy*, on a poem by Friedrich von Schiller. The text is an expression of universal brotherhood inspired by the powerful social forces behind the French Revolution. Beethoven's sympathies were in line with Schiller's and with the French people's call for "Liberty, Equality, Fraternity." This great symphony, written between 1822 and 1824, has become a rallying cry for widely divergent philosophies ever since. The German dictator Adolf Hitler demanded that Beethoven's work be played for his birthday in 1941; it was then the most performed symphony in Germany. The hymn is now played on official occasions of both the Council of Europe and the European Union; and in 1989, it was selected to celebrate the fall of the Berlin Wall. The ideology behind this work is valued outside of Western culture as well: in 1971, it was named the national anthem of Rhodesia (now Zimbabwe) in Africa; in 1989, student protestors at China's Tiananmen Square revolt chose the *Ode to Joy* as their freedom statement; and each year, the work is performed in Japan with a colossal choir to ring in the New Year.

More recently, Beethoven's music took on yet another political role: to help build a musical bridge between North and South Korea. The New York Philharmonic's 2008 concert in Seoul closed with the uplifting strains of Beethoven's Symphony No. 5 while the composer's *Ode to Joy* was chosen for the swearing-in ceremony of South Korean President Lee Myung-Bak.

---

◉ **iMusic**

*America* (*God Save the King*)
*Ode to Joy*, from Symphony No. 9

German crowds at the official opening of the Berlin Wall in November 1989.

# 24 The Classical Concerto

"Give me the best instrument in Europe, but listeners who understand nothing or do not wish to understand and who do not feel with me in what I am playing, and all my pleasure is spoilt."

—W. A. Mozart

StudySpace wwnorton.com/enjoy

## KEY POINTS

- The Classical concerto form has three movements, alternating fast-slow-fast.
- The first movement is the longest and most complex, combining elements of Baroque ritornello procedure and *sonata-allegro form*, resulting in *first-movement concerto form*.
- Mozart's Piano Concerto in G major, K. 453—with its graceful melodies, brilliant piano passagework, and virtuosic *cadenzas* (improvised solo passages)—is a notable example of the genre.

## The Movements of the Concerto

Mozart's fortepiano, now in the Mozarteum in Salzburg. Notice how the colors of the white and black keys are the reverse of today's piano.

During the Baroque era, the word "concerto" implied a mixing together of contrasting forces and could refer to a solo group and orchestra or to a solo instrument and orchestra. The Classical era shifted the emphasis to the latter combination, with the piano the most common solo instrument. We will consider Mozart's approach to the piano concerto—his own instrument—in one of his most appealing works.

The three movements of the Classical concerto follow the fast-slow-fast pattern established by Vivaldi. One unique feature of the solo concerto is the *cadenza*, a fanciful solo passage in the manner of an improvisation that, toward the end, interrupts the movement. In the solo concerto, the cadenza has a dramatic effect: the orchestra falls silent, and the soloist launches into a free play of fantasy on one or more themes of the movement.

The Classical concerto begins with a first-movement form that adapts the principles of the Baroque concerto's ritornello procedure (based on a recurring theme) to those of sonata-allegro form. *First-movement concerto form* is sometimes described as a sonata-allegro form with a double exposition. The movement usually opens with an orchestral exposition, or ritornello, in the tonic key, often presenting several themes. A second exposition, for the solo instrument and orchestra, then makes the necessary key change to the dominant (or to the relative major). The soloist plays elaborated versions of the themes first heard in the orchestra, and often has new material as well. The development section offers ample opportunity for solo virtuosic display, in dialogue with the orchestra. In the recapitulation, the soloist and orchestra bring back the themes in the tonic. The solo cadenza, a brilliant improvisation, appears near the end of the movement, and a coda brings the movement to a close with a strong affirmation of the home key.

The slow and lyrical second movement, generally an Andante, Adagio, or Largo, features songlike melodies. This movement is often composed in a key closely related to the home key. Thus, if the first movement is in C major, the second might be in F major (the subdominant), four steps above.

A typical finale is an Allegro molto or Presto (very fast) that is shorter than the first movement and in rondo form, which could be modified to adopt some developmental features of sonata-allegro form. This movement may contain its own cadenza that calls for virtuoso playing and brings the piece to an exciting end.

## A Piano Concerto by Mozart

Mozart played a crucial role in the development of the piano concerto. His twenty-seven concertos, written primarily as display pieces for his own public performances, abound in the brilliant flourishes and elegant gestures characteristic of eighteenth-century music.

In 1784, Mozart wrote five of his most impressive piano concertos. Of these, he noted they were "compositions which I keep for myself or for a small circle of music-lovers or connoisseurs." He wrote his G major Concerto, K. 453, for his young student Babette (Barbara) von Ployer (see p. 185). This work beautifully illustrates the richness of Mozart's creativity and formal clarity in this genre. In the first movement, the orchestral exposition sets up the main themes, after which the soloist weaves figurations around these melodies—including a new, lighthearted one as well—in its exposition. An orchestral tutti leads to the development section, which refers again to this added "piano" theme and makes virtuosic demands on the soloist. This concerto, notable for its graceful writing for piano and woodwinds, is usually performed today with a cadenza that Mozart wrote for this work. (For analysis, see Listening Guide 23, p. 184.)

The lyrical slow movement features a kind of double exposition format that is more typical of concerto first movements. The closing movement, an Allegretto in 2/2, or cut time, is in theme and variations form featuring a graceful, dancelike tune (Mozart was so fond of the tune that he taught it to his pet starling, who consistently missed one note and got the rhythm wrong).

## Famous Women Virtuosos

Because eighteenth-century society deemed it proper for noble and upper-middle-class women to study music, many became highly skilled amateurs. Some women were able to make a living as music teachers, and a few became professional performers. Three women in particular—all associated with Mozart—stand out as impressive keyboard players of the late eighteenth century. Maria Anna Mozart (1751–1829), known as Nannerl, was an accomplished pianist who as a child toured extensively with her brother Wolfgang, performing concertos and four-hand piano works). Her father noted that Nannerl, at age twelve, was "one of the most skillful players in Europe," able to perform the most difficult works with "incredible precision," and that she played "so beautifully that everyone is talking about her and admiring her execution." Later, when she had retired from professional life to raise a family, her brother wrote several works for her and sent his piano cadenzas for her to try out.

The career of the blind musician Maria Theresia von Paradis (1759–1824) parallels that of her friend Mozart. An excellent pianist and organist, she was renowned for her remarkable musical memory, which retained some sixty different concertos that she prepared for an extended European tour (1783–86).

*In His Own Words*

The pianoforte is the most important of all musical instruments; its invention was to music what the invention of printing was to poetry.

—*George Bernard Shaw*

Leopold Mozart with his two young children, Nannerl and Wolfgang, performing in Paris (1763–64), after a watercolor by **Louis de Carmontelle** (1717–1806).

# Mozart: Piano Concerto in G major, K. 453, I

11:29

**DATE:** 1784

**MOVEMENTS:**
    I.  **Allegro; first-movement concerto form, G major**
    II.  Andante; first-movement concerto form, C major
    III.  Allegretto, Presto; theme and variations form, G major

**First Movement: Allegro**

**WHAT TO LISTEN FOR:**

| | | | |
|---|---|---|---|
| Melody | Lilting 1st theme; quiet and lyrical 2nd theme; new, graceful piano theme in 2nd exposition; decorative piano writing | Texture | Mostly homophonic |
| Rhythm/ Meter | Lively, marchlike rhythm and tempo | Form | First-movement concerto form, with orchestral and solo expositions, then development, recapitulation, and coda |
| Harmony | Major key; shift to key of dominant (D) in piano exposition | Expression | Elegant and graceful, with decorative turns |
| | | Performing Forces | Solo piano and orchestra (pairs of woodwinds, horns, and strings) |

**ORCHESTRAL RITORNELLO (EXPOSITION), in G major**

| 34 | 0:00 | Theme 1—refined theme in violins, with woodwind figurations: |

| | 0:27 | Transitional theme—forceful, in full orchestra. |
| 35 | 1:01 | Theme 2—gently undulating theme in violins, answered in woodwinds: |

| | 1:40 | Closing theme—stated quietly in orchestra. |

**SOLO EXPOSITION**

| 36 | 2:10 | Theme 1—piano enters with sweep into main theme, decorated, in G major; woodwind accompaniment; scales and arpeggio figurations in piano. |
| | 2:45 | Transitional theme—orchestral ritornello; piano with decorative part; modulates to key of dominant. |
| 37 | 3:11 | Piano theme—introduced by piano alone in D major, then presented in woodwinds: |

| 38 | 4:01 | Theme 2—in piano, with string accompaniment. |
| | 4:55 | Closing—decisive, in D major. |

**DEVELOPMENT**

| 39 | 5:16 | Virtuosic piano part, references to piano theme, runs and arpeggios against woodwinds; various modulations, leading back to tonic. |

**RECAPITULATION**

| 40 | 6:34 | Theme 1—returns in strings, with woodwind accompaniment; piano plays decorated version of theme. |
| | 7:01 | Transition theme—forceful, in full orchestra. |
| 41 | 7:32 | Piano theme, solo, in G major, more decorated, with light orchestral accompaniment. |
| 42 | 8:23 | Theme 2—in piano, then in woodwinds, now in G major. |
| 43 | 9:28 | Cadenza—solo piano, variations on earlier themes; ends on dominant. |
| 44 | 10:44 | Closing—final ritornello, in G major. |

Ⓢ **Now try the Listening Quiz.**

Paradis was a composer herself, but many of her works, including two concertos, a piano trio, and a number of sonatas, have been lost.

Another gifted pianist was Barbara von Ployer, a young student of Mozart's for whom he wrote two concertos, including the G-major work we just studied. Mozart was so proud of his talented student that he invited the composer Giovanni Paisiello (1740–1816) to the premiere of the concerto. He wrote to his father, "I am fetching Paisiello in my carriage, as I want him to hear both my pupil and my compositions."

The public prominence achieved by these women performers was unusual for the era. However, the many engravings and paintings of the time illustrating music-making scenes make it clear that women participated frequently in performances at home, in aristocratic salons, and at court.

Engraving of a concerto performance (1777), with woman soloist, by **Johann Rudolf Holzhalb** (1723–1806).

### Critical Thinking

**1.** How is the Classical-era concerto like the Baroque concerto? How does it differ?

**2.** How is the virtuosic ability of the performer displayed in the Classical concerto?

---

**LISTENING ACTIVITY: MOZART AND THE CONCERTO**                                    Ⓢ

Listen to these three examples from Mozart solo concertos (StudySpace, Chapter 24) and match these works to the traits below (you can match more than one concerto to a trait, if appropriate):

   **a.** Horn Concerto, K. 447, III   **b.** Piano Concerto, K. 467, II   **c.** Clarinet Concerto, K. 662, II

| **1.** Melody | ____ conjunct | ____ somewhat disjunct | ____ very disjunct |
| **2.** Meter | ____ duple | ____ triple | ____ sextuple (compound) |
| **3.** Tempo | ____ Adagio | ____ Andante | ____ Allegro |
| **4.** Orchestral Accompaniment | | ____ pizzicato strings | ____ bowed strings |

**5.** Solo Instrument: Which solo features the widest range?
     ____ horn     ____ piano     ____ clarinet

# 25

# The Sonata in the Classical Era

"The sonatas of Mozart are unique; they are too easy for children, and too difficult for artists."

—**Artur Schnabel**

## KEY POINTS

**StudySpace** wwnorton.com/enjoy

- Classical **sonatas** were set either for one solo instrument (the **fortepiano**, an early piano) or for duos (violin and piano, for example).
- The solo piano sonatas of Mozart and especially

Beethoven are the most significant in the keyboard literature.

- The *Moonlight* Sonata, Beethoven's best-known piano work, evokes the new Romantic style.

## The Movements of the Sonata

Haydn, Mozart, and their successors understood the term "sonata" as an instrumental work for one or two instruments, consisting of three or four contrasting movements. The movements followed the basic multimovement cycle described earlier in the discussions of string quartet, symphony, and concerto.

In the Classical era, the sonata—for piano solo or for two instruments (violin or cello and piano)—became an important genre for amateurs in the home, as well as for composers like Mozart and Beethoven performing their own music at concerts. Beethoven's thirty-two piano sonatas, which span his entire compositional output, are among his most important works. His so-called *Moonlight* Sonata dates from his formative years but looks forward to the emotional expressiveness of the Romantic era.

An 18th-century engraving dated 1773 and showing a typical violin-piano duo.

### Beethoven's *Moonlight* Sonata

Shortly after Beethoven's death, the *Moonlight* Sonata was given its title by the poet Ludwig Rellstab, who likened the work to the moonlit scenery along Lake Lucerne in Switzerland. When Beethoven composed the sonata in 1801 (at the end of his first style period), he was already enamored of his young pupil, Countess Giuletta Guicciardi. The sonata is dedicated to her, but since this dedication seems to have been a last-minute decision, the work is probably not a programmatic statement of his love. The Countess was, however, once thought to be the mystery woman in the composer's life—his "Immortal Beloved"—and the recipient of the 1812 letter in which Beethoven bared his soul. This sonata, one of a set

**LISTENING GUIDE 24**

⊚ | DVD | CD 4 (32–45) | CD 2 (45–48)

# Beethoven: Piano Sonata in C-sharp minor, Op. 27, No 2 (*Moonlight*), I

5:45

**DATE:** 1801

**MOVEMENTS:** **I. Adagio sostenuto; modified song form, C-sharp minor**
II. Allegretto; scherzo and trio, D-flat major
III. Presto agitato; sonata-allegro form, C-sharp minor

**First Movement: Adagio sostenuto**

**WHAT TO LISTEN FOR:**

| | | | |
|---|---|---|---|
| Melody | Delicate, singing melody, moves slowly; heard in various ranges; then short ideas passed between hands | Texture | Homophonic, with active accompaniment; then contrapuntal |
| Rhythm/ Meter | Continuous triplet pattern of accompaniment under slow, duple melody | Form | Modified song form; strophic with 2 strophes separated by developmental section |
| Harmony | Expressive minor key; modulations | Expression | Ethereal mood; soft dynamic |

**INTRODUCTION**

45 | 0:00 | Four-measure arpeggiated chords.

**STROPHE 1**

0:23 | Melody in right hand (shaded), with dotted figure on repeated note accompanied by left-hand arpeggios, C-sharp minor; 4-measure phrases:

0:48 | Melody in new key, expands and modulates.

1:12 | New 3-note idea in dialogue between two hands:

1:51 | Melody returns set in higher range.

*Continued on following page*

**MIDDLE SECTION**

46    2:14    Motivic development of dialogue, exchanged between hands.
Pedal on dominant (G sharp) under arpeggiated chords.

**STROPHE 2**

47    3:20    Returns to opening melody and key center (C-sharp minor), followed by short dialogue idea.

**CODA**

48    4:52    Closes with melody stated in bass on repeated pitch (left hand).
Resolution on tonic cadence with arpeggios and chords.

Now try the Listening Quiz.

Countess Giulietta Guicciardi, the dedicatee of the *Moonlight* Sonata.

from Op. 27, breaks the formal molds—he called it a fantasy sonata (sonata *quasi una fantasia*), although he retains the typical three-movement format. In the dreamy first movement, perhaps the most famous of any of his works, the melody sings continuously, moving through various keys and registers. A short contrasting idea intervenes between two statements of the melody. While the form of this movement has elements of development and recapitulation, it does not present the opposition of themes nor keys typical of a first movement. Instead it looks ahead to the modified strophic song forms favored by Romantic composers (see Listening Guide 24).

The second movement, a gentle scherzo and trio set in a major key, provides necessary psychological relief between the emotionally charged opening movement and the stormy finale. The full force of Beethoven's dramatic writing is reserved for this closing movement, which he finally sets in a full-blown sonata-allegro form. Although Beethoven was not particularly won over by this sonata—he argued, "Surely I have written better things"—it was an immediate success with audiences and remains one of the most beloved works in the Classical repertory.

### Critical Thinking

**1.** What are the types of sonata composed in the Classical era?

**2.** What is unusual about the form of Beethoven's *Moonlight* Sonata?

---

### By the way . . .

#### Who Invented the Piano?

Most credit the Italian harpsichord builder Bartolomeo Cristofori (1655–1731). Working under the patronage of the powerful Medici family in Florence, Cristofori developed a new instrument around the year 1700 described as a harpsichord "that plays both soft and loud." This gave the instrument its original name: pianoforte. Cristofori's innovative technology featured hammers that struck the strings and then released, dampers to soften the sound, two keyboards, and a range extending four octaves. Despite the new instrument's possibilities, Bach showed little interest. Indeed, many late Baroque composers found its sound too soft and dull. It was not until the next generation of composers—including Mozart and Beethoven—that the pianoforte caught on, and Vienna became one of the main centers for its construction and for performance. You can admire one of Cristofori's earliest instruments today at the spectacular collection in New York's Metropolitan Museum of Art.

# 26 Classical Choral Music and Opera

"Praise ye the Lord. . . .
Praise him with the sound of the trumpet: praise him with
the psaltery and harp.
Praise him with the timbrel and dance: praise him with
stringed instruments and organ.
Praise him upon the loud cymbals: praise him upon the
high-sounding cymbals."

**—Psalm 150**

## KEY POINTS

StudySpace wwnorton.com/enjoy

- The **Mass, Requiem Mass**, and **oratorio** were the dominant choral forms of the Classical era.

- Mozart's Requiem Mass (Mass for the Dead) is one of the masterworks of the Classical era; the composer died before completing it.

- Haydn wrote two oratorios, including *The Creation*, based on the book of Genesis and on John Milton's *Paradise Lost*. Like Handel's *Messiah*, *The Creation* consists of solo arias, recitatives, ensembles, and choruses.

- In the Classical era, two types of Italian opera prevailed: **opera buffa** (comic opera) and **opera seria** (serious opera).

- In opera, each **aria** allows for emotional expression, while **recitative** moves the action forward.

- Mozart's three comic operas based on librettos by Lorenzo da Ponte—*The Marriage of Figaro, Don Giovanni,* and *Così fan tutte*—are among the greatest masterworks in the genre.

## Mass, Requiem, and Oratorio

The late eighteenth century inherited a rich tradition of choral music from the Baroque. Among the principal genres were the Mass, the Requiem Mass, and the oratorio. A **Mass,** you will recall, is a musical setting of the most solemn service of the Roman Catholic Church, and a **Requiem** is a musical setting of the Mass for the Dead. The third category is the **oratorio**, which you recall from our study of Handel's *Messiah* is generally focused on a biblical story. All these genres were originally intended to be performed in church, but by the nineteenth century, they had found a much larger audience in the concert hall. The blending of many voices in a large space such as a church or cathedral could not fail to be an uplifting experience. For this reason, both the Catholic and Protestant churches were patrons of choral music throughout the ages.

Haydn, Mozart, and Beethoven all made significant contributions to the Mass repertory; in particular, Mozart's Requiem, his last composition, is viewed as a masterpiece of the Classical Viennese School.

The oratorio was another important genre, made popular buy Handel in such works as *Messiah*. Haydn wrote two oratorios—*The Creation* and *The Seasons*—which attained enormous popularity and are often performed today.

# Classical Opera

"I like an aria to fit a singer as perfectly as a well-tailored suit of clothes."

—*W. A. Mozart*

Opera had become the branch of musical entertainment that reached the widest public, and the opera house was now a center of experimentation. The opera of the early eighteenth century accurately reflected the society from which it sprang. The prevalent form was *opera seria*, "serious," or tragic, Italian opera, a highly formalized genre inherited from the Baroque consisting mainly of recitatives and arias specifically designed to display the virtuosity of star singers to the aristocracy. Its rigid conventions were shaped largely by the poet Pietro Metastasio (1698–1782), whose librettos, featuring stories of kings and heroes drawn from classical antiquity, were set again and again throughout the century.

**Opera seria**

Increasingly, however, the need was felt for simplicity and naturalness, for a style that reflected human emotions more realistically. One impulse toward reform came from the operas of Christoph Willibald Gluck (1714–1787), a German-born and Italian-trained composer who was able to liberate serious opera from its outmoded conventions. In his fusion of choral and dance scenes, animated ensembles, a vigorous instrumental style and broad, singable vocal lines, Gluck created a new, highly expressive music drama that had much audience appeal. Another reform gave rise to the popular comic opera that flourished in every country of Europe. Known in England as *ballad*, or *dialogue, opera*, in Germany as *Singspiel*, in France as *opéra comique*, and in Italy as *opera buffa*, this lighter genre was the rising middle class's response to the aristocratic form that was inevitably supplanted.

Comic opera differed from opera seria in several basic ways. It was generally in the language of the audience (the vernacular), although Italian opera buffa was popular throughout much of Europe. It presented lively, down-to-earth plots rather than the remote concerns of gods and mythological heroes. It featured an exciting ensemble at the end of each act in which all the characters participated, instead of the succession of solo arias heard in the older style. And it abounded in farcical situations, humorous dialogue, popular tunes, and the impertinent remarks of the *buffo*, the traditional character derived from the theater of buffoons, who spoke to the audience in a bass voice, with a wink and a nod. This was a new sound in theaters previously dominated by the artificial soprano voice of the castrato.

As the Age of Revolution approached, comic opera became an important social force whose lively wit delighted even the aristocrats it satirized. Classical opera buffa spread quickly, steadily expanding its scope until it culminated in the works of Mozart, the greatest dramatist of the eighteenth century.

## By the way . . .

### How Did Mozart Die?

For more than two centuries, there has been speculation about what led to Mozart's sudden death at the age of thirty-five. The theory that he was poisoned by his rival Salieri—either medically or psychologically—was the main theme of the controversial play *Amadeus* (1979) by Peter Schaffer, adapted in 1984 into an Academy Award–winning movie. Other popular theories include malpractice on the part of his physician, rheumatic fever, heart disease, and even trichinosis from eating undercooked pork chops. Not long ago, DNA specialists thought they had found Mozart's skull. Unfortunately, there was no DNA match between this relic and that of his close relatives, which made it impossible to make any definitive analysis of the cause of his death. Medical specialists suggest that Mozart may have died of a more common problem: a streptococcal infection, possibly a bad case of strep throat that led to edema (a swelling in parts of the body) and kidney failure. According to historical records, there was a spike in such cases in Vienna among young men in the months surrounding Mozart's death. We may never know for sure, since no remains of the composer are extant for modern forensic testing.

Vienna, Burgtheater, where *The Marriage of Figaro* was first performed.

## Mozart's Opera *Don Giovanni*

 **Video**

Mozart's *Don Giovanni* is a work of genius that combines elements of comic *opera buffa* with those of more complex *opera seria*. Set to a libretto by Lorenzo da Ponte, with whom Mozart worked on his other comic masterworks, *Don Giovanni* recounts the tale of the aristocratic Don Juan, an amoral womanizer who has seduced and abandoned women across Europe, and who, in the end, is doomed to hell by the ghost of a man he has murdered. It is ironic that the most notorious Don Juan—the Venetian nobleman Giacomo Casanova —attended the 1787 premiere of the opera in Prague and, as a friend of da Ponte, even contributed to the libretto.

Costume design for *Don Giovanni* as sung by Adolphe Nourrit (1802–1839).

The opera begins with an overture in full sonata-allegro form, its themes easily associated with the characters to come. In Act I, the servant Leporello (whose name means "Little Rabbit" and who is the buffo, or comic, character in the opera) is keeping guard impatiently outside the house of Donna Anna (Lady Anna) while his master, Don Giovanni (Don Juan), is inside trying to seduce her. But something goes awry and the masked culprit rushes out of the house (and onto the stage) with Donna Anna in pursuit, intent not only on catching the offender but also in learning his true identity. Donna Anna's cries for help awake her father, the Commendatore (the commandant), who rushes out to protect his daughter but is killed in a duel with Don Giovanni. Grief stricken, Donna Anna makes her fiancé, Don Ottavio, swear to avenge his death. Both Anna and the Commendatore are characters suited to opera seria, as is the opening murder scene.

In the next scene, which we will hear, we meet another woman, Donna Elvira, who is in a rage over a man who has abandoned her—again, Don Giovanni. In her aria "Ah chi mi dice mai" (Ah, who can tell me where that cruel one is), Donna Elvira recounts with sweeping lines, accompanied by bold orchestral gestures, how she was spurned by the man she loved and now vows to rip his heart out (see Listening Guide 25).

**5   Here & There, Then & Now**

# Mozart and the World of Opera

Vienna, in the time of Haydn, Mozart, and Beethoven, was Europe's leading musical center, the art well supported by the city's music-loving aristocracy. Emperor Joseph II (Holy Roman Emperor from 1765–1790) was an avid patron of opera, commissioning works from Mozart and employing in his court two of the most important librettists: Pietro Metastasio and Lorenzo da Ponte. In *opera seria*, Mozart looked to Metastasio, both in his first masterpiece, *Idomeneo, King of Crete* (1781), and in *The Clemency of Titus* (1791), set to a Metastasio libretto. But Mozart's most famous works are his three comic operas on librettos by Lorenzo da Ponte: *The Marriage of Figaro, Don Giovanni*, and *Così fan tutte* (roughly translated as *Women Are Like That*). The latter opera may have been written at the suggestion of the emperor himself.

*The Marriage of Figaro* was based on a controversial play by Pierre Beaumarchais that was banned in Vienna because it poked fun at the aristocracy. Yet Mozart's opera was successfully premiered there in 1786, with nine performances at the emperor's Burgtheater (see illustration, p. 191). According to a Vienna newspaper, "what is not permitted to be spoken in these times is now sung"; some think the emperor allowed the production of *Figaro* in order to keep the rebellious nobility—who despised the emperor—in their place. Always one to exert control over all aspects of his empire, Joseph found the performances too long and proclaimed that the solo arias should not be repeated, thus taking away the show-stopping encores that furthered the fame and egos of the leading ladies and men. In Mozart's day, singers wangled deals for virtuosic solo arias and duets that showed off their respective talents.

The operatic term *prima donna*, meaning leading lady, is still used to refer to a difficult woman.

Joseph II was interested in all aspects of opera, and he wanted to develop the genre of *Singspiel*—German-texted lighter opera with spoken dialogue—into a national art form. Accordingly he commissioned Mozart to write the exotic *Abduction from the Seraglio* (1782) set in a Turkish harem. Once again, the emperor had something to say about Mozart and his opera: one tale recounts that Joseph thought the work too complicated, suggesting "there are too many notes," to which Mozart replied "There are just as many as there should be." Mozart's *Magic Flute*, composed the year he died, is his greatest masterpiece in this more popular genre.

Today, opera directors create new interpretations of these masterworks, hoping to make them more relevant to modern and younger audiences, often creating controversy in doing so. American director Peter Sellars produced *The Marriage of Figaro* in 1987, setting it in the luxurious Trump Towers in New York City, and *Don Giovanni*, set in Spanish Harlem with Don Giovanni and Donna Anna as heroin addicts. A more recent storm arose over a 2003 production in Berlin of *Idomeneo*, in which the lead character enters with the decapitated head of Neptune (as per the original libretto) and also with those of Jesus, Buddha, and Muhammad. These innovative, if contentious, productions are not unusual in the modern world of opera performances, many of which are featured on TV and, more recently, in inexpensive live HD broadcasts in movie theaters (from the Metropolitan Opera in New York). You might be surprised how engaging you would find a Mozart opera today!

The final scene of *Don Giovanni* from the macabre production directed by Peter Sellars. Here, the closing sextet is sung from hell by ghosts of the "surviving" characters (including Donna Anna, Donna Elvira, Zerlina, Don Ottavio, Masetto, and Leporello).

**LISTENING GUIDE 25**                    ⊙ Video | ⑤ | DVD | CD 4 (57–64) | CD 2 (49–56)

# Mozart, *Don Giovanni,* Act I, Scene 2                    11:54

**DATE:** 1787
**GENRE:** Opera buffa
**LIBRETTIST:** Lorenzo da Ponte
**CHARACTERS:** Don Giovanni, a licentious young nobleman (baritone)
Leporello, Giovanni's servant (bass)
Donna Anna, a noblewoman (soprano)
Commendatore, the commandant; father of Donna Anna (bass)
Don Ottavio, fincae of Donna Anna (tenor)
Donna Elvira, a lady from Burgos, Spain, deserted by Giovanni (soprano)
Zerlina, a peasant girl (soprano)
Masetto, a peasant, fiancé to Zerlina (bass)

**Aria (Donna Elvira, with Don Giovanni and Leporello)**                    3:34

**WHAT TO LISTEN FOR:**

| Melody | Short orchestral introduction, then disjunct aria outlining triads, with many leaps; wide-ranging cadenza near end | Performing Forces | Short orchestral introduction, then alternates between soprano aria, orchestra, and interjections from Don Giovanni and Leporello |
|---|---|---|---|
| Rhythm/ Meter | Accented duple meter | Expression | Anger emphasized by sudden dynamic shifts, quick tempo, and wide range changes |
| Form | Two main sections, each repeated with variation (**A-B-A'-B'**) | | |

**DONNA ELVIRA**

**A section**

| 49 | 0:00 | **Orchestral introduction** | |
|---|---|---|---|
| | 0:22 | A chi mi dice mai, | Ah, who can tell me |
| | | quel barbaro dov'è? | where that cruel one is? |
| | | Che per mio scorno amai, | I loved him, to my shame, |
| | | che mi mancò di fè. | and he broke his pledge to me. |

**B section**

| 50 | 0:42 | Ah, se ritrovo l'empio, | Ah, if I find that evil one, |
|---|---|---|---|
| | | e a me non torna ancor, | and he doesn't return to me, |
| | 0:54 | vo' farne orrendo scempio, | I'll make a horrible scene, |
| | | gli vo' cavar il cor! | I'll rip his heart out! |

**DON GIOVANNI (to LEPORELLO)**

| | 1:06 | Udisti? Qualche bella del vago | You hear? A lovely one |
|---|---|---|---|
| | | abbononata. Poverina! Poverina! | abandoned by her lover. Poor girl! |
| | | Cerchiam di consolare il suo tormento. | Let's try to ease her pain. |

**LEPORELLO**

| | | Così ne consolò mille e ottocento. | Just as he consoled 1,800 of them. |
|---|---|---|---|

**A section** repeated, with variations

| 51 | 1:44 | A chi mi dice mai . . . | Ah, who can tell me . . . |
|---|---|---|---|

*Continued on following page*

**B section** repeated, with variations

2:06   Ah, se ritrovo l'empio . . .                    Ah, if I find that evil one,

DON GIOVANNI

Signorina!                                             Signorina!

Donna Elvira's anger, shown with wide-ranging, disjunct line (**B section**):

Consoling interjection of "poverina" (poor girl) by Don Giovanni:

---

**Recitative (Donna Elvira, Don Giovanni, Leporello)**                              **2:47**

**WHAT TO LISTEN FOR:**

| Melody | More static lines, speechlike | Performing Forces | Accompanied by continuo instrument only |
| --- | --- | --- | --- |
| Rhythm | Quick notes, delivered freely | | |

DONNA ELVIRA

52   0:00   Chi è là?                                   Who's there?

DON GIOVANNI

Stelle! che vedo?                                      What the devil! Who do I see?

LEPORELLO (aside)

Oh bella! Donna Elvira!                                Oh, lovely! Donna Elvira!

DONNA ELVIRA

Don Giovani! Sei qui? Mostro, fellon,                 Don Giovanni! You're here? Monster,
nido d'inganni!                                        criminal, con man!

LEPORELLO (aside)

Che titoli cruscanti! Manco male che                  What charming epithets! She knows
conosce bene.                                          him well.

DON GIOVANNI

Via, cara Donna Elvira, calmate quella                Now, now, dear Donna Elvira, calm that
collera—sentite—lasciatemi parlar!                     rage. Listen, let me speak!

DONNA ELVIRA

0:23   Cosa puoi dire dopo azion sì nera?              What can you have to say after so black a deed?
In casa mia entra furtivamente, a forza               You stole into my house, and with lies,
d'arte, di giuramenti e di lusinghe arrivi            promises, and endearments
a sedurre il cor mio! M'innamori, o                   you seduced my heart! You made me fall in
crudele!                                              in love with you, oh cruel one.

Mi dichiari tua sposa, e poi—                          You called me your wife and then, betraying
mancando della terra e del ciel al santo              all the sacred laws of heaven and earth—
dritto—con enorme delitto, dopo tre dì da             oh, enormous crime—you left Burgos after
Burgos t'allontani. M'abbandoni, mi                    three days. You abandoned me and fled

fuggi—e lasci in preda al rimorso ed al pianto per pena forse che t'amai cotanto!

from me, leaving me prey to remorse and tears, as a punishment for loving you so much.

**LEPORELLO (aside)**

1:09  Pare un libro stampato!

As if she recited it from a book! [or, I've heard all this many times before!]

**DON GIOVANNI**

Oh, in quanto a questo ebbi le mie ragioni. (a Leporello) E vero?

Oh, as to that, I had my reasons. (to Leporello) Isn't that so?

**LEPORELLO**

E vero. (ironicamente) E che ragioni forti!

That's so. (ironically) And what compelling reasons!

**DONNA ELVIRA**

E quali sono, se non la tua perfidia, la legerezza tua? Ma il giusto cielo vuole, ch'io ti trovassi per far le sue, le mie vendette.

And what would those be, if not your own wickedness and shallowness? But God in heaven wanted me to find you to take his revenge and mine.

**DON GIOVANNI**

1:30  Via, cara Donna Elvira, siate più ragionevole! (a parte) Mi pone a cimento costei. (forte) Se non credete al labbro mio, credete a questo galantuomo.

Come, dear Donna Elvira, be reasonable! (aside) This woman will drive me round the bend. (aloud) If you won't believe it from my lips, believe it from this gentleman.

**LEPORELLO**

Salvo il vero.

It's the truth.

**DON GIOVANNI**

Via; dille un poco.

Go on, tell her.

**LEPORELLO (quietly)**

E cosa devo dirle?

And what should I tell her?

**DON GIOVANNI (aloud)**

Sì. sì, dille pur tutto.

Yes, yes, tell her the whole thing.

**DONNA ELVIRA (to Leporello)**

Ebben, fa presto.

Well, hurry up then.

**LEPORELLO**

53  1:47  Madama—veramente—in questo mondo conciosia cosa quando fosse che il quadro non è tondo—

Madame—truly—since in this world the square cannot be round—

**Don Giovanni Exits.**

**DONNA ELVIRA**

Sciagurato! Così del mio dolor gioco ti prendi! Ah voi—Stelle! l'iniquo fuggi! Misera me! Dov'è? In qual parte?

Wicked one! You laugh at my grief! And as for you—Heavens! The wicked one has fled! Poor me! Where is he, where did he go?

**LEPORELLO**

2:11  Eh, lasciate che vada! Egli non merita ch'a lui voi più pensiate.

Oh, let him go! He's not worth your thinking about at all.

*Continued on following page*

**DONNA ELVIRA**

| | |
|---|---|
| Il scelerato m'ingannò, mi tradì! | The scoundrel tricked me, he betrayed me! |

**LEPORELLO**

| | | |
|---|---|---|
| 2:20 | Eh consolatevi! Non siete voi, non foste, e non sarete né la prima, né l'ultima. Guardate questo non piccolo libro: è tutto pieno dei nomi di sue belle. Ogni villa, ogni borgo, ogni paese è testimone di sue donnesche imprese. | Well, console yourself! You are not, were not, and will not be the first or the last. Look! This hefty book is full of the names of his conquests. Every village, every town, every country is a testimony to his amorous triumphs. |

---

**Catalog Aria (Leporello)**                                                                 5:37

**WHAT TO LISTEN FOR:**

| Melody | Opening section, fast and patter quality (syllabic text setting); second section more lyrical | Rhythm/ Meter | Opening Allegro in duple meter; then slower minuetlike Andante in 3/4 |
|---|---|---|---|
| | | Form | 2 main sections (Allegro, Andante), some repeated text with varied music |

**A section: Allegro**

| | | | |
|---|---|---|---|
| 54 | 0:00 | Madamina! Il catalogo è questo, delle belle, che amò il padron mio! Un catalogo egli è ch'ho fatto io: osservate, leggete con me! | My dear lady, this is the catalogue of the beauties my master made love to! It's a catalogue I made myself: look at it, read it with me! |
| | 0:23 | In Italia, sei cento e quaranta; In Alemagna, due cento trent'una; Cento in Francia, in Turchia novant'una; ma, ma in Ispagna, son già mille e tre! | In Italy, six hundred and forty In Germany, two hundred and thirty-one; A hundred in France, in Turkey ninety-one; but—but, in Spain there are already a thousand and three! |
| | 0:54 | V'han fra queste contadine, cameriere, cittadine; v'han Contesse, Baronesse, Marchesane, Principesse, e v'han donne d'ogi grado, d'ogni forma d'ogni età. | Among these are country girls, chambermaids and city girls; there are countesses, baronesses, marchionesses, princesses, there are women of every class, of every form and every age. |
| | 1:11 | In Italia, sei cento e quaranta . . . | [repeated text, varied music] |

**B section: Andante con moto**

| | | | |
|---|---|---|---|
| 55 | 2:04 | Nella bionda, egli ha l'usanza di lodar la gentilezza; nella bruna la costanza, nella bianca la dolcezza! | With blondes, he likes to praise their charm; with brunettes, their constancy, with the white haired [or, the old ones], their sweetness! |
| | 2:47 | Vuol d'inverno la grassotta, vuol d'estate la magrotta; E la grande, maestosa; la piccina, ognor vezzosa. | In the winter he prefers the plump ones, in the summer, the thin ones; and the large ones, the majestic ones, the small ones, are always welcome. |

**B section: music repeated with variations**

| | | | |
|---|---|---|---|
| 56 | 3:40 | Delle vecchie fa conquista per piacer di porle in lista. Sua passion predominante | He seduces the old ones just for the pleasure of adding them to the list. But his main passion is for |

è la giovin principiante.
Non si picca, se sia ricca,
se sia brutta, se sia bella;
4:26    purché porti la gonella,
voi sapete quel che fa.

the young beginners.
He doesn't mind whether she's rich,
whether she's ugly, whether she's pretty;
as long as she wears a skirt,
you know what he does.

Syllabic, patter-quality in **A section** of Catalog aria:

In   I - ta - li-a, sei cen-to e qua-ran - ta

Soothing, lyrical quality in **B section** of Catalog aria, in lilting 3/4:

Nel - la bion - da    e - gli ha l'u-san - za

◎ **Now try the Listening Quiz.**

Giovanni and Leporello overhear her, and, as he has done so many times before, with so many women, Giovanni wishes to "console" her. But when she raises her veil, he suddenly recognizes her, as she does him. In a lengthy recitative, he dodges the situation and runs away, but not before insisting that Leporello tell her all.

The famous Catalog aria follows, in which Leporello—first in a rapid, speech-like patter and then in comforting, lyrical tones—regales Elvira with a list of Giovanni's conquests: 640 in Italy, 230 in Germany, 100 in France, 91 in Turkey, but in Spain, 1003! In a lilting minuet, he comically describes the various types of women—blondes, brunettes, plump ones, thin ones, old ones, and young ones.

A wedding scene follows in which the peasants Zerlina and Maseppo are about to marry. Attracted to the bride, Giovanni begins his seduction by flattering Zerlina with his own marriage proposal in the lovely duet "Là ci darem la mano" (There we will be, hand in hand). Although not sung between lovers, this is the main love duet in the opera.

Throughout the opera, Giovanni maintains his pursuit of numerous women, claiming he needs them "as much as the food I eat and the air I breathe." Even knowing that Giovanni is a murderer, Elvira continues her pathetic pleas for Giovanni to accept her love. In his final nocturnal adventure, Don Giovanni escapes trouble by leaping over a wall into a graveyard and, face-to-face with the statue of the Commendatore—when killed—demands that the cowering Leporello invite him to dinner.

Baritone Bryn Terfel as Leporello, singing the famous Catalogue aria, with soprano Carol Vaness as Donna Elvira in Mozart's *Don Giovanni* on stage at the Metropolitan Opera in New York.

The Irish landscape painter **Joseph Wright** captures a serene fishing scene in *Outlet of Wyburn Lake* (1796), demonstrating the early Romantic artist's love of nature.

Amazingly, the statue talks and accepts the invitation, only to drag the evil-doer to his death when he arrives for dinner.

*Don Giovanni* was downright scandalous in its negative portrayal of the aristocracy as lacking any moral fiber. This striking commentary on the waning of aristocratic society makes the satire in his earlier opera, *The Marriage of Figaro,* seem innocuous indeed (see HTTN 5, p. 192).

# From Classicism to Romanticism

"I am in the world only for the purpose of composing.
What I feel in my heart, I give to the world."

—*Franz Schubert*

**Viennese School**

We have studied the music of the three great Classical masters—Haydn, Mozart, and Beethoven. Together, they are often referred to as the *Viennese School*, since the careers of all three culminated in Vienna, Europe's leading musical center, where they were supported by the city's music-loving aristocracy. We have noted too that the music of all three composers showed traits that foreshadowed the Romantic period. Examples include Mozart's Symphony No. 40, sometimes called "the Romantic" for its deeply emotional character, minor mode, and dramatic themes and modulations, as well as Haydn's forward-looking use of new instruments, sudden dynamic contrasts, and daring modulations in his late symphonies. Beethoven's music pushes us yet closer to Romanticism, with his striking dynamic contrasts and explosive accents, his expansion of Classical forms and hymnlike slow movements, and the overall dramatic intensity of his music.

Nineteenth-century Vienna continued as a major arts center, attracting in the later years of the century many of music history's giants including Johannes Brahms (see p. 246). But the city's native son, Franz Schubert (1797–1828), whose life coincided with the first upsurge of Romanticism, reveals himself as the true heir of the Classical tradition. In his symphonies and chamber music, he carried on the traditions of Haydn, Mozart, and Beethoven in his choice of formal structures.

**By the way . . .**

**Does Listening to Mozart Make You Smarter?**

The "Mozart effect" is a widely discussed phenomenon in the scientific community that has been much hyped in the popular media. Studies have suggested that participants show improved spatial-temporal skills after listening to music by Mozart, thereby increasing one's performance on certain mental tasks, including solving math problems. Scientists at the MIND (Music Intelligence Neural Development) Institute at Irvine, California, have been examining how we hear and process music; they have demonstrated how the brain recognizes symmetries in the language of music and then looks for similar patterns in reasoning out other tasks. Encouraging experiments with young children have suggested that studying music can produce enhanced reasoning skills that last for days. Try this for yourself: listen carefully to a Mozart work before doing your math homework.

But we will see that in his songs, he adopts some of the prime interests of the new era, including a focus on folklore and on nature. One pair of works demonstrates this dichotomy of interests. His song *The Trout* (*Die Forelle*), which relates a fishing tale of a trout that is sought and finally caught, displays the composer's supreme gift for melody in this simple tale of nature. He used this same song as the basis for a movement in a chamber work—a quintet for piano and strings, also subtitled *Forelle*—that is set in a typical Classical variations structure much like we heard in Haydn's *Emperor* String Quartet. We will further explore Schubert's Romantic approach to song in the next chapter through his dramatic setting of the narrative ballad *Elfking*, which draws on both folklore and on the mysteries of the unknown.

 **iMusic**

Schubert: *The Trout*

## Critical Thinking

**1.** What are the major choral genres of the Classical era and how do they differ from one another?

**2.** What are the three prevailing types of opera in the Classical era and how do these differ from one another?

**3.** Is the subject matter of Mozart's opera *Don Giovanni* timeless? In what ways?

## A COMPARISON OF CLASSICAL AND ROMANTIC STYLES

|  | CLASSICAL (c. 1750–1825) | ROMANTIC (c. 1820–1900) |
| --- | --- | --- |
| **COMPOSERS** | Haydn, Mozart, Beethoven, Schubert | Beethoven, Schubert, Fanny Mendelssohn Hensel, Felix Mendelssohn, Clara Schumann, Robert Schumann, Chopin, Liszt, Berlioz, Brahms, Tchaikovsky, Verdi, Wagner |
| **MELODY** | Symmetrical melody in balanced phrases and cadences; tuneful; diatonic, with narrow leaps | Expansive, singing melodies; wide ranging; more varied, with chromatic inflections |
| **RHYTHM** | Clear rhythmically, with regularly recurring accents; dance rhythms favored | Rhythmic diversity and elasticity; tempo rubato |
| **HARMONY** | Diatonic harmony favored; tonic-dominant relationships expanded, became basis for large-scale forms | Increasing chromaticism; expanded concepts of tonality |
| **TEXTURE** | Homophonic textures; chordal-vertical perspective | Homophony, turning to increased polyphony in later years of era |
| **INSTRUMENTAL GENRES** | Symphony, solo concerto, solo sonata, string quartet, other chamber music genres | Same large genres, adding one-movement symphonic poem; solo piano works |
| **VOCAL GENRES** | Opera, Mass, oratorio | Same vocal forms, adding works for solo voice and piano/orchestra |
| **FORM** | Ternary form predominant; sonata-allegro form developed; absolute forms preferred | Expansion of forms and interest in continuous as well as miniature programmatic forms |
| **AUDIENCE** | Secular music predominant; aristocratic audience | Secular music predominant; middle-class audience |
| **DYNAMICS** | Continuously changing dynamics through *crescendo* and *decrescendo* | Widely ranging dynamics for expressive purposes |
| **TIMBRE** | Changing tone colors between sections of works | Continual change and blend of tone colors; experiments with new instruments and unusual ranges |
| **PERFORMING FORCES** | String orchestra with woodwinds and some brass; 30-to-40-member orchestra; rise of piano to prominence | Introduction of new instruments (tuba, English horn, valved brass, harp, piccolo); much larger orchestras; piano predominant as solo instrument |
| **VIRTUOSITY** | Improvisation largely limited to cadenzas in concertos | Increased virtuosity; composers specified more in scores |
| **EXPRESSION** | Emotional balance and restraint | Emotions, mood, atmosphere emphasized; interest in the bizarre and macabre |

◎ **Find an interactive version of this chart on StudySpace.**

## LISTENING ACTIVITY: COMPARING STYLES 4 CLASSICAL TO ROMANTIC

Listen to these two examples and match each with the traits that best fit it. Then compare these two examples from famous Requiem Masses (StudySpace, Chapter 26) and answer the questions below.

    **a.** Grieg: *Åse's Death*, from *Peer Gynt*
    **b.** Mozart: Symphony No. 35, II

**1.** Melody        _____ graceful, courtly melody      _____ expressive, mournful melody

**2.** Rhythm/Tempo    _____ Adagio, with little movement      _____ Andante, with steady pulse

**3.** Harmony       _____ major scale      _____ minor scale

**4.** Performing Forces    _____ strings only      _____ strings and winds

Compare these two examples of choral music and match each with the traits that best fit it.

    **c.** Mozart: *Confutatis,* from Requiem
    **d.** Verdi: *Dies irae*, from Requiem

**5.** Rhythm        _____ strongly accented, changing to veiled accents

                       _____ strongly accented throughout

**6.** Texture        _____ voices sing together, while instruments have independent parts

                       _____ voices in imitation of each other, with orchestral accompaniment

**7.** Expression      _____ consistent dramatic mood      _____ alternating dramatic with serene mood

**8.** Performing Forces    _____ begins with men's voices and orchestra

                       _____ begins with huge orchestra and full SATB choir

Finally, let's compare these two piano works and match the traits that best suit each.

    **e.** Chopin: Prelude, Op. 28, No. 2
    **f.** Beethoven: Sonata No. 13 (*Pathétique*), II

**9.** Melody        _____ lyrical, singing in long phrases      _____ marked melody in shorter motives

**10.** Harmony      _____ consonant      _____ dissonant

**11.** Key          _____ minor key      _____ major key

**12.** Expression     _____ dark mood, in low range      _____ gentle mood, in middle range

# Romantic Era

## COMPOSERS AND WORKS

**(1797–1828)** Franz Schubert (*Elfking*)

**(1803–1869)** Hector Berlioz (*Symphonie fantastique*)

**(1805–1847)** Fanny Mendelssohn Hensel (*The Year*)

**(1809–1847)** Felix Mendelssohn (Violin Concerto)

**(1810–1849)** Frédéric François Chopin (Mazurka, Op. 24, No. 4)

**(1810–1856)** Robert Schumann (*A Poet's Love*)

**(1813–1901)** Giuseppe Verdi (*Rigoletto* and Requiem Mass)

**(1813–1883)** Richard Wagner (*Die Walküre*)

**(1824–1884)** Bedřich Smetana (*The Moldau*)

**(1826–1864)** Stephen Collins Foster (*Jeanie with the Light Brown Hair*)

**(1833–1897)** Johannes Brahms (Symphony No. 3)

**(1838–1875)** Georges Bizet (*Carmen*)

**(1840–1893)** Peter Ilyich Tchaikovsky (*The Nutcracker*)

**(1843–1904)** Antonín Dvořák (Symphony No. 9)

**(1858–1924)** Giacomo Puccini (*Madame Butterfly*)

| 1780 | 1790 | 1800 | 1810 | 1820 | 1830 | 1840 | 1850 | 1860 | 1870 | 1880 | 1890 | 1900 | 1910 | 1920 | 1930 |

## EVENTS

**1803** Louisiana Purchase

**1815** Defeat of Napoleon at Waterloo

**1830** Tuba first used in major orchestral work

**1840** Saxophone developed by Adolphe Sax

**1847** Emily Brontë's novel *Wuthering Heights*

**1859** Darwin's *Origin of Species*

**1861** American Civil War begins

**1862** Victor Hugo's novel *Les Misérables*

**1877** Cylinder phonograph invented

# PART
# 5

# The Nineteenth Century

Portrait of Giuseppina Strepponi (1815–1897), Italian soprano and wife of Giuseppe Verdi.

# The Spirit of Romanticism

"Music, of all the liberal arts, has the greatest
influence over the passions."

—**Napoleon Bonaparte**

- The French Revolution fostered the rise of a middle-class, or bourgeois, society.

- Romantic poets and artists turned to passionate and fanciful subjects; novels explored deep human conflicts and exotic settings and subjects.

- The Industrial Revolution spurred many technical advances in musical instruments, making them more flexible and affordable.

- Educational opportunities broadened as music conservatories appeared across Europe and the Americas.

- The orchestra grew in size and sound when new and improved instruments were introduced; in response, composers demanded new levels of expression.

- Romantic composers used nationalistic, folkloric, and exotic subjects.

- Romantic music is characterized by memorable melodies, richly expressive harmony, and broad, expanded forms.

- Women musicians excelled as performers, teachers, composers, and music patrons.

## French Revolution

The Romantic era grew out of the social and political upheavals that followed the French Revolution and came into full bloom during the second quarter of the nineteenth century. The Revolution itself was a consequence of the inevitable clash between the old political and social order and the new one, and signaled the transfer of power from a hereditary landholding aristocracy to the middle class. This change was firmly rooted in urban commerce and industry, which emerged from the Industrial Revolution that brought millions of people from the country into the cities. This new society, based on free enterprise, celebrated the individual as never before. The slogan of the French Revolution—"Liberty, Equality, Fraternity"—inspired hopes and visions to which artists responded with zeal. Sympathy for the oppressed, interest in peasants, workers, and children, faith in humankind and its destiny, all formed part of the increasingly democratic character of the Romantic period.

*In His Own Words*

Our sweetest songs are those that tell of saddest thoughts.

—*"To a Skylark,"*
*Percy Byssche Shelley*

## Romantic Writers and Artists

The spirit of the nineteenth century was rooted in a reaction against the rational ideals of the eighteenth. Romantic poets and artists rebelled against the conventional concerns of their Classical predecessors and were drawn instead to the fanci-

The spirit of the French Revolution is captured in *Liberty Leading the People,* by **Eugène Delacroix** (1798–1863).

ful, the picturesque, and the passionate. These men and women emphasized intense emotional expression and were highly aware of themselves as individuals apart from all others. "I am different from all the men I have seen," proclaimed Jean Jacques Rousseau. "If I am not better, at least I am different." In Germany, a group of young writers created a new kind of lyric poetry that culminated in the art of Heinrich Heine, who became a favorite poet of Romantic composers. A similar movement in France was led by Victor Hugo, the country's greatest prose writer, and Alphonse de Lamartine, its greatest poet. In England, the revolt against the formalism of the Classical age produced an outpouring of emotional lyric poetry that reached its peak in the works of Byron, Shelley, and Keats.

**Individualism**

The newly won freedom of the artist proved to be a mixed blessing. Confronted by a world indifferent to artistic and cultural values, artists felt more and more cut off from society. A new type of artist emerged—the bohemian, a rejected dreamer who starved in an attic and who shocked the establishment through peculiarities of dress and behavior. Eternal longing, regret for the lost happiness of childhood, an indefinable discontent that gnawed at the soul—these were the ingredients of the Romantic mood. Yet the artist's pessimism was based in reality. It became apparent that the high hopes fostered by the Revolution were not to be realized overnight. Despite the brave slogans, all people were not yet equal or free. The new optimism gave way to doubt and disenchantment, a state of mind that was reflected in the arts and in literature.

Sympathy for the oppressed underscored the dramatic character of the Romantic movement. **Honoré Daumier** (1808–1879), *The Burden*.

The nineteenth-century novel found one of its great themes in the conflict between the individual and society. Hugo dedicated *Les Misérables* "to the unhappy ones of the earth." Among the era's memorable discontented are Jean Valjean, the hero of Hugo's novel (well-known from the 1985 musical *Les Misérables*); Heathcliff in Emily Brontë's *Wuthering Heights*; and Tolstoy's Anna Karenina, in the novel of the same name.

Some writers sought escape by glamorizing the past, as Sir Walter Scott did in *Ivanhoe* and Alexandre Dumas *père* in

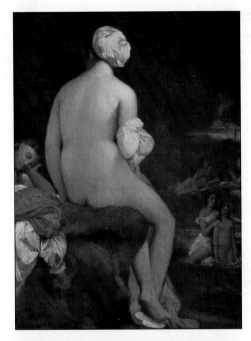

(Top) In *The Small Bather*, the artist taunts the viewer with unattainable desire in this Romanticized glimpse inside a harem. **Jean-Auguste Dominique Ingres** (1780–1867)

(Bottom) The trombone multipavilions was one of the many new, and unusual, instruments created by the Belgian instrument maker **Adolphe Sax**, inventor of the saxophone.

*The Three Musketeers.* A longing for far-off lands inspired the exotic scenes that glow on the canvases of Jean-Auguste Dominique Ingres (see left) and Eugène Delacroix. The Romantic world was one of "strangeness and wonder": the eerie landscape we meet in Samuel Taylor Coleridge's poem *Kubla Khan,* the isolation we feel in Nathaniel Hawthorne's novel *The Scarlet Letter,* and the supernatural atmosphere we encounter in Edgar Allen Poe's poem *The Raven.*

Romanticism dominated the artistic output of the nineteenth century. It gave its name to a movement and an era and created a multitude of colorful works that still hold millions in thrall. Many of the forces that characterized painting and literature also influenced the world of music.

# Romanticism in Music

The Industrial Revolution brought with it the means to create more affordable and responsive musical instruments, as well as the technical improvements that strongly influenced the sound of Romantic music. For example, valves made brass instruments much more maneuverable so that composers like Wagner and Tchaikovsky could write horn and trumpet melodies that would have been unplayable in earlier eras. Several new wind instruments were developed as well, including the tuba and the saxophone. Improved manufacturing techniques provided the piano with a cast-iron frame and thicker strings, giving it a deeper and more brilliant tone. We will hear that a piano work by Chopin sounds different from one by Mozart, not only because the Romantic era demanded a different kind of expression but also because composers were writing for a piano capable of effects that were never before possible.

The gradual democratization of an industrialized society broadened educational opportunities. The chief cities of Europe established new conservatories to train more and better musicians, and as a result nineteenth-century composers could count on performers whose skills were considerably more advanced.

As music moved from palace and church to the public concert hall, orchestras increased in size, giving composers more varied and colorful means of expression. Naturally, this directly influenced the sound. New instruments such as the piccolo, English horn, and contrabassoon added varied timbres and extended the extreme high and low ranges of the orchestra (see Table on p. 208). The dynamic range also expanded—sweeping contrasts of very loud (*fff*) and very soft (*ppp*) now lent new drama to the music of the Romantics. And as orchestral music developed, so did the technique of writing for instruments—individually and together. **Orchestration** became an art in itself. Composers now had a palette as broad as those of painters, and they used it to create mood and atmosphere and to evoke profound emotional responses. With all these developments, it was no longer feasible to direct an orchestra from the keyboard or the first violin desk, as had been the tradition in the eighteenth century, and thus a central figure—the conductor—was needed to guide the performance.

In order to communicate their intentions as precisely as possible, composers developed a vocabulary of highly expressive terms. Among the directions frequently encountered in nineteenth-century musical scores are *dolce* (sweetly), *cantabile* (songful), *dolente* (sorrowful), *maestoso* (majestic), *gioioso* (joyous), and *con amore* (with love, tenderly). These and similar terms suggest not only the character of the music but also the frame of mind of the composers.

**Use of folklore**

A new interest in folklore and a rising tide of nationalism inspired Romantic composers to make increased use of the folk songs and dances from their native lands. As a result, a number of national idioms—Hungarian, Polish, Russian, Bohemian, Scandinavian, and eventually American—flourished, greatly enriching the melodic, harmonic, and rhythmic language of music. We will hear the diversity of these nationalistic expressions in the piano music of Polish-born Frédéric Chopin, as well as in the orchestral music of the Eastern European musician Bedřich Smetana and the Norwegian composer Edvard Grieg.

**Exoticism**

Nineteenth-century exoticism appeared first in the northern nations' longing for the warmth and color of the south, and then in the West's interest in the fairy-tale splendors of Asia and the Far East. The first impulse found expression in the works of Russian, German, and French composers who turned for inspiration to Italy and Spain. The long list of such works includes Tchaikovsky's *Capriccio italien*, Mendelssohn's *Italian* Symphony, Ravel's *Spanish Rhapsody*, and Bizet's *Carmen*.

The glamour of the East was brought to international attention by the Russian national school, whose music recalls the fairy-tale background of Asia. Rimsky-Korsakov's orchestrally resplendent *Sheherazade*, as well as several dances from Tchaikovsky's famous *Nutcracker* ballet (see p. 271) are among the many Eastern-inspired works that found favor with Western audiences. A number of French and Italian opera composers also drew on exotic themes: notably Verdi in *Aida*, set in Egypt; and Puccini in his Japanese-inspired opera *Madame Butterfly* (see p. 275) and his *Turandot*, drawn from an ancient Persian fable and set in China.

*In His Own Words*

We have learned to express the more delicate nuances of feeling by penetrating more deeply into the mysteries of harmony.

—*Robert Schumann*

# Romantic Style Traits

Above all, nineteenth-century musicians tried to make their instruments "sing." Romantic melody was marked by a lyricism that gave it an immediate appeal, and it is no accident that themes from Romantic symphonies, concertos, and other instrumental works have been transformed into popular songs. Tunes by composers such as Chopin, Verdi, and Tchaikovsky have enjoyed an enduring popularity among the general public.

Nineteenth-century writers created emotionally charged and highly expressive harmony. Composers employed combinations of pitches that were more chromatic and dissonant than those of their predecessors. Romantic composers expanded the instrumental forms they had inherited from the Classical masters to give their ideas more time to play out. A symphony by Haydn or Mozart takes about twenty minutes to perform; one by Tchaikovsky, Brahms, or Dvořák lasts at least twice that long. Nineteenth-century composers approached the writing of a symphony with greater deliberation than their predecessors did.

The Royal Pavilion at Brighton, England (1815–1818), with its Islamic domes, minarets, and screens, reflects the 19th-century fascination with Eastern culture. Designed by **John Nash** (1752–1835).

## THE ROMANTIC ORCHESTRA

| BERLIOZ'S ORCHESTRA | BRAHMS'S ORCHESTRA | TCHAIKOVSKY'S ORCHESTRA |
|---|---|---|
| (*Symphonie fantastique*, 1830) | (*Symphony No. 3*, 1883) | (*The Nutcracker*, 1892) |
| **STRINGS**<br>Violins 1<br>Violins 2<br>Violas<br>Cellos<br>Double basses<br>2 Harps | **STRINGS**<br>Violins 1<br>Violins 2<br>Violas<br>Cellos<br>Double basses | **STRINGS**<br>Violins 1<br>Violins 2<br>Violas<br>Cellos<br>Double basses<br>2 Harps |
| **WOODWINDS**<br>2 Flutes (1 on Piccolo)<br>2 Oboes<br>2 Clarinets (1 on E-flat Clarinet)<br>English horn<br>4 Bassoons | **WOODWINDS**<br>2 Flutes<br>2 Oboes<br>2 Clarinets<br>2 Bassoons, Contrabassoon | **WOODWINDS**<br>2 Flutes and Piccolo<br>2 Oboes, 1 English horn<br>2 Clarinets, Bass clarinet<br>2 Bassoons |
| **BRASS**<br>4 French horns<br>2 Cornets, 2 Trumpets<br>3 Trombones (1 Bass trombone)<br>2 Ophicleides | **BRASS**<br>4 French horns<br>2 Trumpets<br>3 Trombones | **BRASS**<br>4 French horns<br>2 Trumpets<br>2 Trombones, Bass trombone<br>Tuba |
| **PERCUSSION**<br>Timpani<br>Cymbals<br>Snare drum<br>Bass drum<br>Tubular bells (chimes) | **PERCUSSION**<br>Timpani | **PERCUSSION**<br>Timpani<br>Cymbals, gong, triangle<br>Tambourine, castanets<br>Bass drum<br>Tubular bells (chimes)<br>Other special effects (including toy instruments)<br>Keyboard<br>Celesta |

*In His Own Words*

Music is the vapor of art. It is to poetry what reverie is to thought . . . what the ocean of clouds is to the ocean of waves.

—*Victor Hugo*

Where Haydn wrote more than a hundred symphonies and Mozart more than forty, Schubert and Dvořák (following the example of Beethoven) wrote nine, and Robert Schumann and Brahms four each. New orchestral forms emerged as well, including the one-movement symphonic poem, the choral symphony, and works for solo voice with orchestra.

Music in the nineteenth century drew steadily closer to literature and painting. The connection with Romantic poetry and drama is most obvious in the case of music with words. However, even in their purely orchestral music, many Romantic composers responded to the mood of the time and captured with remarkable vividness the emotional atmosphere that surrounded nineteenth-century poetry and painting. Franz Liszt's symphonic poem *Faust* captures the drama of Goethe's tragedy just as Felix Mendelssohn's *Fingal's Cave* Overture depicts the energy of Turner's painting.

Nineteenth-century music was linked to dreams and passions—to profound meditations on life and death, human destiny, God and nature, pride in one's country, desire for freedom, the political struggles of the age, and the ultimate triumph

The Hungarian pianist and composer Franz Liszt conducting one of his oratorios in Budapest (1811).

of good over evil. These intellectual and emotional associations, nurtured by the Romantic movement, brought music into a commanding position as a link between the artist's most personal thoughts and the realities of the outside world.

# The Musician in Society

The newly democratic society liberated composers and performers. Musical life reached the general populace, since performances were now in the public concert hall as well as in the salons of the aristocracy. Where eighteenth-century musicians had relied on aristocratic patronage and the favor of royal courts, nineteenth-century musicians were supported by the new middle-class audience and could make a living in their profession. Musicians of the eighteenth century belonged to a glorified servant class; in the nineteenth century, musicians met their audiences as equals. Indeed, as solo performers began to dominate the concert hall, whether as pianists, violinists (such as Niccolò Paganini, right), or conductors, they became "stars" who were idolized by the public.

With this expansion of musical life, composers and performing artists were called on to assume new roles as educators. Felix Mendelssohn, active as a composer, pianist, and conductor, founded the Leipzig Conservatory, whose curriculum became a model for music schools all over Europe and America. Composer and conductor Robert Schumann became a widely read music critic. Franz Liszt, considered to be the greatest pianist of his time, taught extensively and trained a generation of great concert pianists. And opera composer Richard Wagner contructed his own theater at Bayreuth, thus helping the newly interested public understand his music dramas.

Niccolò Paganini with his violin, painted in 1830 by **Eugène Delacroix** (1798–1863).

# Women in Music

We have already observed several women who were recognized in their day as virtuoso performers (see HTTN 3, p. 111). Nineteenth-century society saw women make great strides in establishing careers as professional musicians. This path was now possible through the broadening of educational opportunities: in public conservatories, women could receive training as singers, instrumentalists, and even composers. Likewise, the rise of the piano as the favored chamber instrument—both solo and with voice or other instruments—provided women of the middle and upper classes with a performance outlet that was socially acceptable.

A salon concert, c. 1855, hosted by the Berlin composer Bettina von Arnim, who is seated in the black dress. Watercolor by **Carl Johann Arnold** (1829–1916).

Although composition remained largely a man's province, some women broke away from tradition and overcame social stereotypes to become successful composers. Among them were Fanny Mendelssohn Hensel, known for her songs, piano music, and chamber works; and Clara Schumann, a talented performer and composer of piano, vocal, and chamber music.

Women also exerted a significant influence as patrons of music or through their friendships with composers. Novelist George Sand played an important role in Chopin's career, as did Princess Carolyne Sayn-Wittgenstein in that of Liszt. Nadezhda von Meck is remembered as the mysterious woman who supported Tchaikovsky in the early years of his career and made it financially possible for him to compose. Several women of the upper class presided over musical salons where composers could gather to perform and discuss their music. One such musical center was the home of the Mendelssohn family, where Fanny Mendelssohn organized concerts that featured works by her more famous brother, Felix.

All in all, women musicians made steady strides toward professional equality throughout the nineteenth century and thereby laid the foundation for even greater achievements in the twentieth and twenty-first centuries.

The Romantic period was a time of experimentation and challenge for both men and women. Artists across the board rejected the role of "artistic servant," wrote and created what pleased them, and dared the public to follow them—a public that was yearning for new sensations.

### Critical Thinking

**1.** What are the principal ideas of Romanticism? How are these reflected in art and literature?

**2.** How did the rise of the virtuoso performer affect the development of Romantic music?

**3.** How did the opportunities for women in music change in the Romantic era?

# 27 Song in the Romantic Era

"Out of my great sorrows I make my little songs."
—Heinrich Heine

- Typical Romantic song structures include *strophic* and *through-composed* forms; some songs fall between the two, into a *modified strophic* form.
- The German art song, or *Lied*—for solo voice and piano—was a favored Romantic genre.
- Composers wrote *song cycles* that unified a group of songs by poem or theme.
- The poetry of the Lied used themes of love and nature; the favored poets were Goethe and Heine.

- Franz Schubert created more than six hundred Lieder and several famous song cycles.
- *Elfking*—a through-composed Lied based on a German legend set in a dramatic poem by Goethe—is one of his most famous songs.
- Robert Schumann is known for his symphonies, piano music, chamber music, and Lieder.
- Many of Schumann's Lieder were inspired by his fiancée, the pianist and composer Clara Wieck. These include *A Poet's Love,* a song cycle set to the poetry of Heinrich Heine.

The art song met the nineteenth-century need for intimate personal expression. The form came into prominence in the early decades of the century and emerged as a favored example of the new lyricism.

## Types of Song Structure

In the nineteenth century, two main song-structures prevailed. One already familiar is *strophic form,* in which the same melody is repeated with every stanza, or strophe, of the poem—hymns, carols, as well as most folk and popular songs are strophic. This form sets up a general atmosphere that accommodates all the stanzas of the text. The first may tell of a lover's expectancy, the second of his joy at seeing his beloved, the third of her father's harshness in separating them, and the fourth of her sad death, all sung to the same tune.

Strophic form

The other song type, *through-composed,* proceeds from beginning to end, without repetitions of whole sections. Here the music follows the story line, changing according to the text. This makes it possible for the composer to mirror every shade of meaning in the words.

Through-composed form

There is also an intermediate type that combines features of the other two. The same melody may be repeated for two or three stanzas, with new material introduced when the poem requires it, generally at the climax. This is considered a *modified strophic form,* similar to what we heard in the lovely slow movement of Beethoven's *Moonlight* Sonata. One song that follows this form is Schubert's well-known *The Trout (Die Forelle).*

**iMusic**

Schubert: *The Trout*

The immense popularity of the Romantic art song was due in part to the emergence of the piano as the universal household instrument. A lithograph by **Achille Devéria** (1800–1857), *In the Salon*.

# The Lied

Though songs have existed throughout the ages, the art song as we know it today was a product of the Romantic era. The *Lied* (plural, *Lieder*), as the new genre was called, is a German-texted solo vocal song, generally with piano accompaniment. Among the great Romantic masters of this form of art song are Franz Schubert, Robert Schumann, and Johannes Brahms as well as Fanny Mendelssohn Hensel and Clara Schumann. Some composers wrote groups of Lieder that were unified by a narrative thread or descriptive theme. Such a group is known as a ***song cycle***; an example is Robert Schumann's *A Poet's Love*, which we will study.

The rise of the Lied was fueled by the outpouring of lyric poetry that marked German Romanticism. Johann Wolfgang von Goethe (1749–1832) and Heinrich Heine (1797–1856) were the two leading figures among a group of poets who, like Wordsworth, Byron, Shelley, and Keats in English literature, favored short, personal, lyric poems. The texts of the Lied range from tender sentiment to dramatic balladry; its universal themes are love, longing, and the beauty of nature.

Another circumstance that popularized the Romantic art song was the emergence of the piano as the preferred household instrument of the nineteenth century. The piano accompaniment to a song translated its poetic images into music. Voice and piano together infused the short lyric form with feeling and made it suitable for amateurs and artists alike, in both the home and the concert hall.

We will hear two of the most poignant songs from the era: Franz Schubert's narrative ballad *Elfking*, with a text by Goethe, and "In the lovely month of May" from Robert Schumann's song cycle *A Poet's Love*, set to texts by Heinrich Heine. These songs present highly personal approaches to the genre, ranging from intensely dramatic to longingly sentimental.

# Schubert and the Lied

"When I wished to sing of love, it turned to sorrow. And when I wished to sing of sorrow, it was transformed for me into love."

Franz Schubert's life has become a romantic symbol of the artist's fate. He was not properly appreciated during his lifetime, and he died very young, leaving the world a musical legacy of some nine hundred works. As we will see, his life was centered in the home, in salon concerts, and amid a select circle of friends and acquaintances.

## *Elfking*

This masterpiece of Schubert's youth captures the Romantic "strangeness and wonder" of Goethe's celebrated ballad. *Elfking* is based on a legend that whoever is touched by the king of the elves must die.

## Franz Schubert (1797–1828)

**Franz Schubert** was born outside Vienna and educated at the Imperial Chapel, where he served as one of the famous Vienna Choir Boys. His teachers marveled at his innate musicality, one noting that Franz "had learned everything from God." Although his family hoped he would pursue a career in teaching, Schubert fell in with a small group of writers, artists, and fellow musicians who organized a series of concerts, called Schubertiads, where the young composer's newest works could be heard. One of his friends noted the spontaneity of his writing, claiming "Everything he touched turned to song." Indeed he wrote his song *Elfking* when he was still a teenager. This work won him swift public recognition; still, he had difficulty finding a publisher for his later works and he was often pressed for money, selling his music for much less than it was worth. Schubert suffered deeply during his later years, largely from the progressive debilitation associated with the advanced stages of syphilis. His later works, including his song cycle *Winter's Journey*, sound a somber lyricism that reflects his struggle with life. Schubert's life has become a symbol of the Romantic artist's fate. His dying wish was to be buried near the master he worshipped—Beethoven. He died at age thirty-one, and his wish was granted.

Schubert's music marks the confluence of the Classical and Romantic eras. His symphonies and chamber music are classical in their clear forms: his *Trout* Quintet shows he was the direct descendant of Haydn and Mozart. In his short piano works, he makes the instrument sing, a central element of the Romantic spirit. In his songs, he was wholly the Romantic, writing melodies with a tender, longing quality that matches the tone of the poetry he set. Many of his songs—over six hundred of them—were written at breakneck speed, with descriptive piano accompaniments such as that in the *Elfking*. To his earlier masterpieces he added, in the final year of his life, a group of profound works that includes the Mass in E flat, the String Quintet in C, three piano sonatas (published posthumously), and thirteen of his finest songs.

**Major Works:** More than 600 Lieder, including *Erlkönig* (*Elfking*, 1815), *Die Forelle* (*The Trout*, 1817), and 3 song cycles, including *Die schöne Müllerin* (*The Lovely Maid of the Mill*, 1823) and *Winterreise* (*Winter's Journey*, 1827) • 9 symphonies, including the *Unfinished* (No. 8, 1822) • Chamber music, including *The Trout* Quintet, string quartets, piano trios, and piano sonatas • 7 Masses • Other choral music • Operas and incidental music.

◎ **iMusic:** *The Trout* (song) and *Trout* Quintet, IV
*The Miller and the Brook*, from *The Lovely Maid of the Mill*

### In His Own Words

No one understands another's grief, no one understands another's joy. . . . My music is the product of my talent and my misery. And that which I have written in my greatest distress is what the world seems to like best.

The Legend of *The Elfking* (c. 1860), as portrayed by **Moritz von Schwind** (1804–1871).

# Schubert: *Elfking (Erlkönig)*                                    4:00

**DATE:**  1815

**GENRE:**  Lied

## WHAT TO LISTEN FOR:

| | |
|---|---|
| Melody | Wide-ranging; each character sings in a different range:<br>**Narrator:** middle register, minor key<br>**Father:** low register, minor key<br>**Son:** high register, minor<br>**Elfking:** middle register, major |
| Rhythm/<br>Meter | Constant triplets in piano until last line; duple meter; more lilting feel for Elfking |
| Harmony | Shifts from minor to major (for Elfking); dissonance to project boy's terror |

| | |
|---|---|
| Form | Through-composed |
| Expression | Fast, with mood of urgency in piano accompaniment and dramatic dialogue |
| Performing<br>Forces | Solo voice and piano |
| Text | Narrative poem by Johann Wolfgang von Goethe |

---

| | | |
|---|---|---|
| **1** | 0:00 | Piano introduction—minor key and rapid repeated octaves in triplets set mood, simulating horse's hooves: |

| TEXT | TRANSLATION |
|---|---|
| **NARRATOR (minor mode, middle range)** | |

|   |   | | |
|---|---|---|---|
| | 0:23 | Wer reitet so spät durch Nacht und Wind?<br>Es ist der Vater mit seinem Kind;<br>er hat den Knaben wohl in dem Arm,<br>er fasst ihn sicher, er hält ihn warm. | Who rides so late through night and wind?<br>It is the father with his child;<br>he has the boy close in his arm,<br>he holds him safely, he keeps him warm. |

| **FATHER (low range)** | |
|---|---|
| "Mein Sohn, was birgst du so bang dein Gesicht?" | "My son, why do you hide your face in fear?" |

| **SON (high range)** | |
|---|---|
| "Siehst, Vater, du den Erlkönig nicht?<br>Den Erlenkönig mit Kron' und Schweif?" | "Father, don't you see the Elfking?<br>The Elfking with his crown and train?" |

| **FATHER (low range)** | |
|---|---|
| "Mein Sohn, es ist ein Nebelstreif." | "My son, it is a streak of mist." |

| **ELFKING (major mode, melodic)** | |
|---|---|

|   |   | | |
|---|---|---|---|
| **2** | 1:29 | "Du liebes Kind, komm, geh mit mir!<br>Gar schöne Spiele spiel' ich mit dir;<br>manch' bunte Blumen sind an dem Strand;<br>meine Mutter hat manch' gülden Gewand." | "You dear child, come with me!<br>I'll play very lovely games with you.<br>There are lots of colorful flowers by the shore;<br>my mother has some golden robes." |

**SON (high range, frightened)**

| 3 | 1:51 | "Mein Vater, mein Vater, und hörest du nicht, was Erlenkönig mir leise verspricht?" | "My father, my father, don't you hear the Elfking whispering promises to me?" |

**FATHER (low range, calming)**

"Sei ruhig, bleibe ruhig, mein Kind;
in dürren Blättern säuselt der Wind."

"Be still, stay calm, my child;
it's the wind rustling in the dry leaves."

**ELFKING (major mode, cajoling)**

| 4 | 2:13 | "Willst, feiner Knabe, du mit mir geh'n? Meine Töchter sollen dich warten schön; meine Töchter führen den nächtlichen Reih'n und wiegen und tanzen und singen dich ein." | "My fine lad, do you want to come with me? My daughters will take care of you; my daughters lead the nightly dance, and they'll rock and dance and sing you to sleep." |

**SON (high range, dissonant outcry)**

| 5 | 2:31 | "Mein Vater, mein Vater, und siehst du nicht dort, Erlkönigs Töchter am düstern Ort?" | "My father, my father, don't you see the Elfking's daughters over there in the shadows?" |

**FATHER (low range, reassuring)**

"Mein Sohn, mein Sohn, ich seh' es genau,
es scheinen die alten Weiden so grau."

"My son, my son, I see it clearly,
it's the gray sheen of the old willows."

**ELFKING (loving, then insistent)**

| 6 | 3:00 | "Ich liebe dich, mich reizt deine schöne Gestalt, und bist du nicht willig, so brauch' ich Gewalt." | "I love you, your beautiful form delights me! And if you're not willing, then I'll use force." |

**SON (high range, terrified)**

| 7 | 3:12 | "Mein Vater, mein Vater, jetzt fasst er mich an! Erlkönig hat mir ein Leids gethan!" | "My father, my father, now he's touching me! The Elfking has done me harm!" |

**NARRATOR (middle register, speechlike)**

| 8 | 3:26 | Dem Vater grauset's, er reitet geschwind, er hält in Armen das ächzende Kind, erreicht den Hof mit Müh und Noth: in seinen Armen das Kind war todt. | The father shudders, he rides swiftly, he holds the moaning child in his arms; with effort and urgency he reaches the courtyard: in his arms the child was dead. |

Melody of son's dissonant outcry
on "My father, my father":

Mein Va - ter, mein Va - ter,

Ⓢ **Now try the Listening Quiz.**

The eerie atmosphere of the poem is first established by the piano. Galloping triplets are heard against a rumbling figure in the bass. This motive, suggesting a horse's pounding hooves, pervades the song, helping to unify it. The poem's four characters—the narrator, the father, the child, and the seductive elf—are all presented by one soloist but vividly differentiated through changes in the melody, register, harmony, rhythm, and accompaniment. The child's terror is suggested by clashing dissonance and a high vocal range. The father calms his son's fears with a more rounded vocal line, sung in a low register. And the Elfking cajoles the child in suavely melodious phrases set in a major key.

The song is through-composed; the music follows the action of the story with a steady rise in tension—and pitch—that builds almost to the end. The obsessive triplet rhythm slows down as the horse and rider reach home, then drops out altogether on the last line: "In his arms the child"—a dramatic pause precedes the two final words—"was dead." The work of an eighteen-year-old, *Elfking* was a milestone in the history of Romanticism (see Listening Guide 26, p. 214).

The German word "Erlkönig" translates as "Elfking," a forest creature derived from Norse mythology who carried people off to their deaths. There are many such characters in European folklore: for example, the sirens who lure ship captains to crash onto the rocks (in Germany, the Lorelei) or other kinds of dangerous water spirits that take human form. The poet Goethe was familiar with a German ballad about the Elfking that tells of Sir Oluf, who, while riding through the forest to meet his bride-to be, is waylaid by the music of the elves. The Elfkings's daughter wishes to dance with him, but he spurns her offer and goes on his way, only to be found dead on the day of his wedding. In Goethe's interpretation of the fantasy, the protagonist preys on children rather than on those of the opposite sex. We will see later how a fascination with Nordic folklore culminated in the Romantic era with Richard Wagner's immense operatic cycle *The Ring of the Nibelung*. Today, you are likely to know about elves and evil dwarves from the writings of J. R. R. Tolkien (*The Lord of the Rings*), based on the same myth as the Wagner operas, as well as from video games (*World of Warcraft*) and Viking metal lyrics inspired by Norse folklore.

# Robert Schumann and the Song Cycle

*"Music is to me the perfect expression of the soul."*

The turbulence of German Romanticism, its fantasy and subjective emotion, found its voice in Robert Schumann. His music is German to the core yet transcends national styles. Like Schubert, Robert Schumann showed his lyric gifts in his songs, many of which appear in unified song cycles with texts from a single poet.

## Robert Schumann [1810–1856]

**Robert Schumann** was born in Zwickau, Germany, and studied law at the University of Leipzig and at Heidelberg. But he soon surrendered to his passion for music—it was his ambition to become a pianist and to study with Friedrich Wieck, one of the foremost teachers of his day. An injury to his right hand dashed his dream of being a pianist, and he turned his efforts to composition. In a burst of energy, he created, while still in his twenties, many of his most important piano works. His literary talent found expression through a publication he established, *Neue Zeitschrift für Musik* (*The New Journal of Music*); this soon became the leading journal of music criticism in Europe. Throughout the 1830s, Robert carried on an intense courtship with the gifted pianist and composer Clara Wieck, daughter of his former teacher. Friedrich viewed his daughter as his supreme achievement, and he refused to allow them to marry. The two finally wed in 1840, when Clara was twenty-one and Robert thirty. Robert and Clara settled in Leipzig, pursuing their careers side by side. Clara furthered Robert's music as the foremost interpreter of his piano works, but her devotion could not ward off Robert's increasing withdrawal from the world. He began to complain of "unnatural noises" in his head—these auditory hallucinations led to his final breakdown. After he threw himself into the Rhine River, Clara was forced to place him in an asylum, where his psychotic behavior gave way to advanced dementia, the result of syphilis. He died in 1856, at the age of forty-six.

Schumann's music is imbued with impassioned melodies, novel changes of harmonies, and driving rhythms that reveal him as a true Romantic. His four symphonies exude a lyric freshness and Romantic approach to harmony. He often attached literary meanings to his piano music and was fond of cycles of short pieces connected by a literary theme or musical motto. In his songs, he stands alongside Schubert. A common theme in his works was love, particularly from a woman's point of view. Just as Schubert had an affinity for the poetry of Goethe, Schumann favored the texts of Heine, whose poems he set in his song cycle *A Poet's Love* (*Dichterliebe*).

**Major Works:** More than 100 Lieder • Song cycles, including *Dichterliebe* (*A Poet's Love*, 1840) • Orchestral music, including 4 symphonies and 1 piano concerto • Chamber music, including string quartets, piano trios, 1 piano quintet, and 1 piano quartet • Piano music, including sonatas and numerous miniatures • 1 opera • Choral music • Incidental music.

◉ **iMusic:** "In the lovely month of May," from *A Poet's Love*

*In His Own Words*

The singing voice is hardly sufficient in itself; it cannot carry the whole task of interpretation unaided. In addition to its overall expression, the finer shadings of the poem must be represented as well—provided that the melody does not suffer in the process.

—Robert Schumann

## Schumann's Song Cycle: *A Poet's Love*

Schumann wrote his great song cycle *A Poet's Love* (*Dichterliebe*) in 1840, his "year of song," at lightning-fast speed. For the texts, he chose sixteen poems by Heinrich Heine, who wrote some of the Romantic era's most poignant works. Heine's poetry often presents ironic or cynical remarks that reflect disillusioned hopes, but the tone of Schumann's music for this cycle is more neutral. The songs tell no real story; rather, they follow a psychological progression that spirals downward from the freshness of love through a growing disappointment to complete despair.

We will consider the first song in the cycle, "In the lovely month of May." The piano's introduction to the first strophe sets a wistful rather than joyous mood. Schumann's setting evokes the fragility of a new love through its harmonic meandering between two key centers and by its lack of a final resolution—we are left suspended, knowing there is much more to this story in the songs that follow. The meandering lines paint the text, as the end of the first verse rises to a climax on the words "did love rise up." The two text strophes are framed by the piano's introduction, interlude and postlude, which provide a circular shape to the song. We might wonder if this Lied is really about a new relationship, or rather the longing and desire of a lost or unrequited love. Clearly, Schumann was able to achieve the desired unity of expression in this perfect fusion of dramatic and lyric elements (see Listening Guide 27).

**Clara Schumann** at age 31, with Robert. Anonymous lithograph (1850).

### Critical Thinking

**1.** What are the respective roles of the singer and the piano in performing a Lied?

**2.** How do Schubert and Schumann portray the mood of a poem musically?

**3.** What is Romantic about the songs of Schubert and Schumann?

# Robert Schumann: "In the lovely month of May," from *A Poet's Love* (*Dichterliebe*), No. 1   1:38

**DATE:**  1840

**GENRE:**  Lied, from a song cycle

## WHAT TO LISTEN FOR:

| | |
|---|---|
| Melody | Winding melodic line, set syllabically; each verse rises to a climax |
| Rhythm/Meter | Low; piano moving somewhat freely in rising lines |
| Harmony | Meandering; lack of resolution to tonic |

| | |
|---|---|
| Form | Strophic (2 verses); piano prelude, interlude, and postlude |
| Expression | Melancholic mood portrays unrequited love |
| Performing Forces | Solo voice and piano |
| Text | Heinrich Heine poem; text painting |

| | | TEXT | TRANSLATION |
|---|---|---|---|
| 9 | 0:00 | Piano introduction. | |
| | | **Strophe 1** | |
| | 0:13 | Im wunderschönen Monat Mai<br>als alle Knospen sprangen,<br>da ist in meinem Herzen<br>die Liebe aufgegangen. | In the lovely month of May,<br>as all the buds were blossoming,<br>then in my heart<br>did love rise up. |
| 10 | 0:45 | Piano interlude. | |
| | | **Strophe 2** | |
| | 0:52 | Im wunderschönen Monat Mai<br>als alle Vögel sangen,<br>da hab ich ihr gestanden<br>mein Sehnen und Verlangen. | In the lovely month of May,<br>as all the birds were singing,<br>then did I confess to her<br>my longing and desire. |
| | 1:18 | Piano postlude. | |

Opening of vocal line, suggesting minor key (F sharp):

Im wun - der-schö-nen Mo - nat Mai,

Piano postlude, ending on dissonance with no final resolution of harmony.

⊚ **Now try the Listening Quiz.**

# 28 Romantic Piano Music

*"I have called my piano pieces after the names of my favorite haunts . . . they will form a delightful souvenir, a kind of second diary."*

**—Fanny Mendelssohn Hensel**

## KEY POINTS

**StudySpace** wwnorton.com/enjoy

- Technical improvements to the nineteenth-century piano led to the development of the modern concert grand piano.
- The short lyric piano piece, often with a fanciful title, was a favorite Romantic genre.
- Frédéric Chopin dedicated his entire compositional output to the piano; he is said to have originated the modern piano style. His output includes *études*—highly virtuosic and technical study

pieces—meditative *nocturnes*, preludes, and dances (including Polish *mazurkas* and *polonaises*), as well as sonatas and concertos for piano.

- Fanny Mendelssohn Hensel, sister of Felix Mendelssohn, was a talented pianist and composer, remembered today for her Lieder and piano music, including the autobiographical cycle, *The Year* (*Das Jahr*).

The rise in popularity of the piano helped shape the musical culture of the Romantic era. All over Europe and America, the instrument became a mainstay of music in the home and salon (see HTTN 6, p. 221). It proved especially attractive to amateurs because, unlike the string and wind instruments, melody and harmony could be performed on one instrument together. The piano thus played a crucial role in the taste and experience of the new mass public.

Hardly less important was the rise of the virtuoso pianist. At first the performer was also the composer; Mozart and Beethoven introduced their own piano concertos to the public, and Franz Liszt was the first to present his *Hungarian Rhapsodies*. With the developing concert industry, however, a class of virtuoso performers arose whose only function was to dazzle audiences by playing music composed by others.

The nineteenth century saw a series of crucial technical improvements that led to the development of the modern concert grand piano. Romantic composers' quest for greater power and dynamic range mandated increased string diameter and tension, which in turn required more bracing within the wooden piano case. Piano manufacturing eventually moved from the craft shop to the factory, allowing a huge increase in production at a significantly reduced cost. A standardized instrument was developed that had a metal frame supporting the increased string tension, as well as an improved mechanical action and extended range of notes—from five octaves to

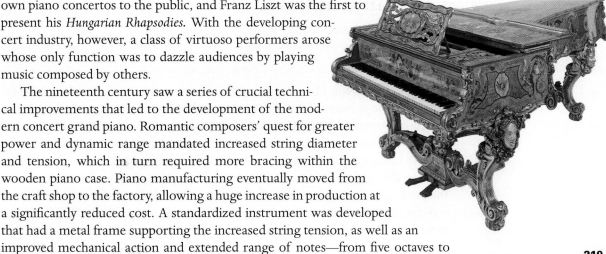

This beautiful, ornate grand piano was made by Erard, c. 1840, for the Baroness of Kidderminster.

German artist **Ludwig Richter** (1803–1884) portrays a typical family music-making scene in his woodcut *Hausmusik* (1851).

seven or more. At the Paris Exhibition of 1867, two American manufacturers took the top awards, among them Steinway, maker of some of today's finest pianos. By the early twentieth century, the piano had become a universal fixture in the homes of many middle-class and upper-class families.

# The Short Lyric Piano Piece

With its ability to project melodious and dramatic moods within a compact form, the short lyric piano piece was the equivalent to the song. Composers adopted new and sometimes fanciful terms for such works. Some titles—"Prelude," "Intermezzo" (interlude), "Impromptu" (on the spur of the moment), and "Nocturne" (a night piece), for example—suggest free, almost improvisational forms. Many composers turned to dance music and produced keyboard versions of the Polish mazurka and polonaise, the Viennese waltz, and the lively scherzo. Composers sometimes chose more descriptive titles, such as *Wild Hunt, The Little Bell,* and *Forest Murmurs* (all by Franz Liszt).

The nineteenth-century masters of the short piano piece—Schubert, Chopin, Liszt, Felix Mendelssohn, Fanny Mendelssohn Hensel, Robert and Clara Schumann, and Brahms—showed inexhaustible ingenuity in exploring the technical resources of the instrument and its potential for expression. We will consider music by Frédéric Chopin, often called the "poet of the piano," and Fanny Mendelssohn Hensel, whose piano works epitomize the Romantic concept of "songs without words."

# Chopin and Piano Music

"My life [is] an episode without a beginning and with a sad end."

Frédéric François Chopin's music, rooted in the heart of Romanticism, made this era the piano's golden age. His style was entirely his own—there is no mistaking it for any other—and he remains one of the most original artists of the nineteenth century.

Chopin was the only master of the first rank whose entire creative life revolved around the piano, and he is credited with originating the modern piano style. The delicate ornaments in his melodies—trills, grace notes, runs—seem magically to prolong the single tones, and widely spaced chords in the bass line, sustained by the pedal, set up masses of tone that encircle the melody. All this generally lies so well for the trained hand that the music seems almost to play itself. "Everything must be made to sing," he told his pupils.

**6** **Here & There, Then & Now**

# Chopin and the Salon

Although Chopin's music is central to the modern concert pianist's repertory—and thus a mainstay of today's concert hall performance—he composed for the more intimate atmosphere of the salon, or drawing room (the word derives from the French *salle*, or room). Like the Italian academies of earlier centuries (see p. 113), the Parisian salon was conceived as a gathering of musicians, artists, and intellectuals who shared similar interests and tastes, and was hosted by a wealthy aristocrat, often a woman.

A Parisian salon concert depicted by **James Tissot** (1836–1902).

It was also a place where professional performers and artists could mingle freely with amateurs. But Chopin, who arrived in Paris with "but one ducat in my pocket," found that although the wealthy clientele were eager to be entertained by him—and receive lessons from him as well—they were less inclined to accept him as an equal. He soon won over the hearts and purses of cosmopolitan Parisian circles with his music. It was at one of these events—a party hosted by the Countess d'Agoult, the mistress of the composer Franz Liszt—that Chopin met his future mistress, the author George Sand; see p. 222).

As in the European salon, the piano became a focal point in gatherings of friends and families in nineteenth-century America. Statistics show that the manufacturing of pianos soared in the United States: in 1830, some 2,500 pianos were built, while in 1860, 21,000 instruments were produced—which was one piano for every 1,500 persons! An English writer noted that "in cities and villages, from one extremity of the union to the other, wherever there is a good house . . . the ringing of pianos is almost as universal a sound as the domestic hum of life within." He swore that there were "ten pianofortes for every American town or village to one in England."

Americans were huge consumers of published sheet music as well, craving songs and piano music of limited to moderate difficulty playable by amateurs. Chopin's music was a natural answer to this demand. His dances, especially waltzes and marches, were relatively uncomplicated and technically fairly easy. (You may know the so-called *Minute* Waltz by Chopin—a brilliant work that, ironically, takes nearly two minutes to play.) His mazurkas, full of nostalgic longing for his native Poland, were considered "gems for the parlor" and his impromptus suitable for "refined salon conversation." First introduced to American audiences in 1839, Chopin's waltzes and marches were published in collections in Boston and Philadelphia by the 1840s, and by the 1850s his music had appeared in method books.

In imitation of the great salons of Europe, American socialites opened their homes to musical and artistic gatherings. In Boston alone, there were five famous salons—all hosted by prominent women. These included the poet Amy Lowell; the painter Sara Choate Sears; two composers—Clara Kathleen Rogers and Amy Beach—and the patroness Isabella Stewart Gardner.

Chopin's fame spread quickly in the Americas; women's music clubs arose in towns and cities across the United States as the principal venue for concert life, and especially piano performances.

Today, solo piano recitals and chamber music are still the most popular forms of classical music performed in private homes or salons. This kind of venue is preferred for intimate events, often for fund-raising purposes, sponsored by women's clubs and arts organizations. But in the world of popular music, some superstars regularly give private VIP concerts for fan clubs or highly elite—and often wealthy—audiences. Madonna performed for three private fêtes—in New York, Paris, and London—to promote her 2008 hip-hop-inspired album, *Hard Candy*, which went on to top the charts in Europe. One avid fan reputedly flew to Paris from Thailand for this promotional event. Mariah Carey landed a very high-paying gig in Turkey in May 2009, when she received $1.5 million for a single performance to open the Mardan Palace in Antalya, one of the most expensive luxury resorts ever built. On top of this extraordinary pay, she was showered with valuable gems including a five-carat diamond cut to resemble her signature butterfly shape.

---

ⓘ **iMusic**

Prelude in E minor, Op. 28/4
Prelude in B-flat minor, Op. 28/ 16

*In Her Own Words*

His creative power was spontaneous, miraculous. It came to him without effort or warning. . . . But then began the most heartrending labor I have ever witnessed.

—*George Sand*

## Frédéric François Chopin (1810–1849)

**Chopin** was born to a French father and a Polish mother. He studied at the newly founded Conservatory of Warsaw, but soon left for Paris, where he spent the remainder of his career. Paris in the 1830s was the center of the new Romanticism. The circle in which Chopin moved included the most famous composers, writers, and artists in France, as well as the German poet Heinrich Heine. A man ruled by his emotions, Chopin was profoundly influenced by these leading intellectuals.

Through the virtuoso pianist Liszt, Chopin met Aurore Dudevant, known to the world as the novelist George Sand. Madame Sand was brilliant and domineering; her need to dominate complemented Chopin's need to be ruled. She left a memorable account of the composer at work (see quote at left). For eight years, Chopin spent his summers at Sand's estate in Nohant, where she entertained many of France's prominent artists and writers. These were productive years for the composer, although his health grew progressively worse and his relationship with Sand ran its course from love to conflict, jealousy, and hostility. They finally parted in bitterness. The lonely despair of the Romantic artist pervades Chopin's last letters. "What has become of my art?. . . And my heart, where have I wasted it?"

Chopin died of tuberculosis in Paris at the age of thirty-nine. The artistic world bid its farewell to the strains of the composer's own funeral march, from his Piano Sonata in B-flat minor.

Chopin's works are central to the pianist's standard repertory, including the four ballades—epic works of spacious proportions—the thoroughly romantic Sonatas in B minor and B-flat minor, and the two piano concertos. The nocturnes—night songs, as the name implies—are melancholic and meditative. The preludes are visionary fragments, and in the études, which crown the literature of the study piece, Chopin's piano technique is transformed into poetry. The impromptus are fanciful and capricious, and the waltzes capture the brilliance and coquetry of the salon. The mazurkas, derived from a Polish peasant dance, evoke the idealized landscape of his youth, and polonaises revive the stately processional dance in which Poland's nobles hailed their kings.

**Major Works:** Pieces for piano and orchestra, including 2 piano concertos • Piano music, including 4 ballades, 3 sonatas, preludes, études, mazurkas, polonaises, scherzos, waltzes, impromptus, and nocturnes • Chamber music, all with piano • Songs.

Ⓒ **iMusic:** Prelude in E minor, Op. 28, No. 4    Prelude in B-flat minor, Op. 28, No. 16

Portrait of George Sand (Aurore Dupin, Baroness Dudevant, 1804–1876), famous novelist and Chopin's lover.

# A Mazurka By Chopin

Much of Chopin's piano music looks back to his Polish roots, including his polonaises and mazurkas, both native dance forms. The *mazurka* originated in Mazovia, Chopin's home district in Poland, as a lively triple-meter dance with accents on the second or third beat of the measure. In his hands, the genre was transformed from a heroic folk dance to a true art form. His Mazurka in B-flat minor, Op. 24, No. 4, one of a set of four written in 1833, is an exquisite musical poem. We are drawn into the sinuous melody that is rich in chromaticism and elusive in mood. While most mazurkas have a simple ternary (**A-B-A**) form, this one is longer, with clearly defined sections, each colored with new emotional content (see Listening Guide 28). Chopin's music calls for use of *rubato*, or robbed time, in which certain liberties are taken with the rhythm without upsetting the basic beat. Chopin taught his students that the left hand should remain steady while the right-hand melody might hesitate a little here and hurry forward there, catching up before the end of a phrase. The subtle harmonic shifts between major, minor, and modal scales typical of folk music, the spirited rhythms as well as the large-scale structure make this one of Chopin's most ambitious works. Robert Schumann praised the expressive depth of Chopin's music, suggesting he was a "poet."

**LISTENING GUIDE 28**　　　　　　　　Ⓢ | DVD | CD 5 (11–16) | CD 3 (11–16)

# Chopin: Mazurka in B-flat minor, Op. 24, No. 4　　5:06

**DATE:** 1833

**GENRE:** Mazurka for solo piano

**WHAT TO LISTEN FOR:**

| | | | |
|---|---|---|---|
| Melody | Chromatic lines, wide-ranging, disjunct | Texture | Largely homophonic, with regular left-hand accompaniment in quarter notes |
| Rhythm/Meter | Moderate triple meter; dancelike dotted and double-dotted rhythms; frequent accents on 3rd beat, later on 2nd beat | Form | **A-B-A-C-D-A,** with some sections repeated; long coda |
| Harmony | Shifts between major and minor; modal harmonies; much chromaticism | Expression | Much rubato; many accents |

**Introduction**

11 — 0:00 — Melodic octave, decreases chromatically in Introduction:

**A section**

0:09 — Short syncopated, dotted-note idea, rises sequentially, accompanied by "om-pah-pah" bass; beat 3 accented in alternate measures:

**B section**

12 — 0:35 — More disjunct, with rising line, answered by falling double-dotted pattern; accents now on 3rd beat of each measure:

0:57 — Section closes with a reminiscence of **A.**

1:21 — **B section** repeated.

**C section**

13 — 2:10 — Simpler texture in octaves, more lyrical; start octaves at opening of **C section**, answered by block chords:

*Continued on following page*

|  |  |  |
|---|---|---|
| | 2:22 | **C section** repeated. |
| | | **D section** |
| 14 | 2:33 | Triplet pattern in melody; animated with accents now on 2nd beat of each measure: |

|  |  |  |
|---|---|---|
| 15 | 3:24 | **A section** returns, introduced by falling chromatic intervals reminiscent of **B section**. |
| | | **Coda** |
| 16 | 3:50 | Simpler, more static melody; accented on 2nd beat; slows into final cadence on F; accompaniment drops out for lingering last melodic idea. |

Now try the Listening Quiz.

# Fanny Mendelssohn Hensel and the Piano Miniature

*"I want to admit how terribly uppity I've been and announce that six 4-part Lieder . . . are coming out next . . . My choir has enjoyed singing them . . . and I've made every effort to make them as good as possible."*

***In Her Own Words***

I'm beginning to publish . . . and if I've done it of my own free will . . . I hope I shall not disgrace you all, for I am no *femme libre* . . . If people like the pieces and I receive further offers, I know it will be a great stimulus to me, which I have always needed in order to create. If not, I shall be at the same point where I have always been.

The music of Fanny Mendelssohn Hensel has been neglected until recent years, when she was lifted from the shadow of her famous brother, Felix, to reveal her genuine talents. Well-educated in music and recognized in her lifetime as a gifted composer, she remained reluctant to make her compositions public. Her story enhances our modern-day understanding of the challenges faced by Romantic-era women musicians.

## A Piano Cycle: *The Year*

Fanny Mendelssohn Hensel's cycle of piano works entitled *The Year* (*Das Jahr*) shows her at the pinnacle of her artistry. This set of twelve pieces, each named for a month of the year, and one postlude, was once thought to be a kind of travel diary, documenting her year-long trip to Italy in 1839–40. But with the discovery of a lost manuscript in her hand—missing for nearly 150 years—scholars have found a deeper meaning in the works. The manuscript, uncovered in 1989, features different colored paper for each month, and each miniature work is prefaced by a poetic epigram and a painting done by her husband, Wilhelm Hensel. The poems and the artwork seem to suggest the passage of time or the seasons of one's life, perhaps her own. The cycle of miniatures is unified musically through recurring motives, tonal schemes, and references to the works of other composers, including her brother, Felix.

We will consider the movement entitled *September: At the River* (see Listening Guide 29, p. 226), which is accompanied by a drawing of a bare-footed woman by the stream and several poetic lines from Goethe: "Flow, flow, dear river, Never

## Fanny Mendelssohn Hensel (1805–1847)

**Fanny Mendelssohn** was born into a highly cultured family (her grandfather, Moses Mendelssohn, was a leading Jewish scholar/philosopher). She was especially close throughout her life with her younger brother, Felix, a renowned composer and conductor.

Raised in Berlin, Fanny received her earliest piano instruction from her mother. She later studied theory and composition with the well-known composer and conductor Carl Friedrich Zelter. Because of her gender, however, Fanny was actively discouraged from pursuing music as a career. Her father cautioned her to focus on "the only calling for a young woman—that of a housewife," and Felix echoed the sentiment. But Felix finally approved of her publishing her own music, writing "may the public only send you roses and never sand; may the printer's ink never seem black and oppressive to you."

In 1829, Fanny Mendelssohn married the court artist Wilhelm Hensel, with whom she had a son, Sebastian. She remained active during the following years as a composer, pianist, and participant in the regular salon concerts held each Sunday at the Mendelssohn residence. Shortly after a year-long trip to Italy (1839–40), her mother died and Fanny took over the organization of the famous Sunday concerts. Fanny died suddenly of an apoplectic stroke on May 13, 1847, while preparing to conduct a cantata written by her brother. Having lost his dearest companion, Felix died just six months later after a series of strokes.

Although she wrote several large-scale works, including a piano trio and a string quartet, Fanny's output was dominated by Lieder, choral part songs, and piano music, notably *The Year* (*Das Jahr*), a set of twelve character pieces. Most of her compositions were intended for performance at the family's Sunday musical gatherings. Her solo vocal music is highly lyrical, displaying a wide range of tonal, harmonic, and formal procedures. Her choice of German Romantic poets and her complex piano writing place her in the mainstream of the Lieder tradition. Her piano music is well crafted, reflecting her strong interest in Bach's contrapuntal procedures.

**Major Works:** Instrumental music, including 1 orchestral overture, a string quartet, and a piano trio • Over 125 piano works, including sonatas, preludes and fugues, and character pieces, including *Das Jahr* (*The Year*, 1841) • Vocal music, including 4 cantatas and part songs for chorus, and over 250 Lieder.

---

will I be happy." This melancholic idea is captured in the haunting, meandering melody, sounded below a stream of notes signifying the flowing river. The movement takes us on a daring journey through distant key centers, unfolding in a typical three-part form of Statement—Departure—Return, framed by a brief introduction and coda. This cycle of works was never published in its entirety; indeed, only this movement was included in her collection of piano works and without its literary and visual details. The musical and extra-musical links in this set make it a significant large-scale venture for the composer, who reached a new level of achievement that even her brother had not yet attained in his piano works.

### Critical Thinking

**1.** What types of piano compositions were new to the Romantic period? Which continue from the Classical era?

**2.** Why is Chopin considered "the poet of the piano"?

**3.** What difficulties did a woman composer face in this era?

LISTENING GUIDE 29     ⓢ | DVD | CD 5 (27–31) | CD 2 (57–61)

# Fanny Mendelssohn Hensel: *September: At the River*, from *The Year (Das Jahr)*     3:02

**DATE:** 1841

**GENRE:** Character piece, from a programmatic cycle of 12

**WHAT TO LISTEN FOR:**

| | |
|---|---|
| **Melody** | Slow-paced melody in middle range of piano, set against fast-moving, churning notes; much chromaticism |
| **Rhythm/Meter** | Lilting 6/8 meter; constant running sixteenth notes; some *rubato* |
| **Harmony** | Begins and ends in B minor; modulates through various distant keys in middle; very chromatic |
| **Texture** | Polyphonic, with slow-moving melodies accompanied by fast-moving lines and chords |
| **Form** | Ternary (**A-B-A′**) with short introduction and coda |
| **Expression** | Free push and pull of beat (*rubato*); swelling and *decrescendo* in dynamics; movement evokes the flow of the river |

**Introduction**

`57`  0:00  Gentle, flowing sixteenth notes, punctuated by chords and octaves; slows before next section.

**A section**

`58`  0:12  Wistful, slow-moving melody in the middle register, accompanied by constantly flowing fast notes and bass chords. Opening of **A section** (melody notes circled), in B minor:

More movement in main melody; grows chromatic and modulates; slows into next section, growing louder.

**B section**

`59`  1:23  Melody moving quicker, with more emphasis under churning accompaniment.

**B section** in new key, with more emphasized melody (circled):

Grows louder and more chromatic with high-range octaves exchanging 3-note idea with main melody; builds in swirling crescendo.

**A′ section**

`60`  1:56  Return to main melody, in B minor, but more chromaticism; octave chords make long descent to tonic.

**Coda**

`61`  2:38  Introduction returns; fast-moving notes with chords; dies away *pianissimo*.

ⓢ **Now try the Listening Quiz.**

# 29 Music in Nineteenth-Century America

"Weep no more my lady,
Oh! Weep no more today;
We will sing one song for the
old Kentucky home,
For the old Kentucky home far away."

—Stephen Foster

**KEY POINTS**  ⑤ **StudySpace** wwnorton.com/enjoy

- Music publications in early America were largely devotional, some written in the **shape-note** system designed for easy reading.

- The parlor and minstrel songs of Stephen Foster (including *Jeanie with the Light Brown Hair*) were very popular during his lifetime and remain so today.

Music in eighteenth- and early-nineteenth-century American life was largely imported from Europe. Early Protestant settlers had brought their devotional psalms with them, printing the first American psalm book as early as 1640. Because many people were not musically literate at the time, publishers reached out to a wider public by issuing books of folk hymns and so-called white spirituals with music printed in *shape-note notation*, a new, easy system. The melodies of the shape-note hymns, which resemble those of ballads and fiddle tunes of the era, are set in simple four-part harmonizations. Publications such as *The Easy Instructor* and *The Sacred Harp* disseminated this repertory from New England, where the presses were located, to rural and urban audiences in the South and Midwest, where the hymns were used in singing schools, churches, and social gatherings. As a result, the body of hymns and anthems has been preserved not only in devotional music books but through a continued oral tradition: some of these works remain popular even today in gospel and contemporary Christian music arrangements.

Although the composers and lyricists of nineteenth-century America are mostly forgotten today, several prophets of American music can be named, including Louis Moreau Gottschalk, one of America's most original spirits and the country's first great classical pianist, and Stephen Foster, known for his lyrical parlor ballads, minstrel show tunes, and poignant plantation songs.

Shape-note notation

 iMusic

*Amazing Grace*

# Stephen Foster and American Popular Music

Stephen Foster is often considered America's first great songwriter. His music is distinctly American, and his classic songs, including *Oh, Susanna!*, *Beautiful Dreamer*, and *Jeanie with the Light Brown Hair*, are universally known and loved.

## Stephen Foster (1826–1864)

**Stephen Foster** grew up outside Pittsburgh, where he spent much of his life, and attended Jefferson College (now Washington & Jefferson College). Rather than completing his degree, he moved to Cincinnati where he wrote his first hit song, *Oh, Susanna!* Many of Foster's early songs were for blackface minstrel shows that were popular during this era. Even these, although culturally insensitive by today's standards, conveyed the deep-felt emotions and sufferings of African slaves. From 1847 on, Foster was under contract with the Christy Minstrels, who specialized in performing blackface shows. For them, he wrote some of his most enduring songs, including *Camptown Races* and *Old Folks at Home* ("Way down upon the Swanee River"). Later he turned to ballads and love songs, like *Jeanie with the Light Brown Hair*, which was inspired by his wife Jane Denny McDowell. These songs, evoking themes of lost youth and happiness, reflect his desire to write more serious music. Although Foster did not spend much time in the South, it is thought that his famous work *My Old Kentucky Home*, today the state song of Kentucky, was inspired by Harriet Beecher Stowe's anti-slavery novel *Uncle Tom's Cabin*.

Foster is perhaps the first American to make a living as a professional songwriter, but in this era, composers made little profit off their publications. After he and his wife separated, Foster moved to New York, where he wrote his most famous song, *Beautiful Dreamer*, conceived in the style of an Italian air. He died there at the age of thirty-seven, a penniless alcoholic, victim to a fall in a cheap New York hotel room. Today, Foster's songs are much better known than he is.

 **iMusic:** *Camptown Races*     *Oh, Susannah!*

## A Song by Stephen Foster

Foster's classic ballad *Jeanie with the Light Brown Hair* was written in 1853–54, just after he separated from his wife. In his sketchbook, the original title was not "Jeanie" but "Jennie," drawn from Jane Denny McDowell's name. The tone is bittersweet, wishing for days gone by. The song, like most of Foster's, is strophic and set for solo voice and piano, thereby meeting the growing need for parlor music appropriate for amateurs. The internal structure of each strophe foreshadows song forms we will see in later works, and the brief cadenza in each strophe marks a moment of free interpretation for the performer (see Listening Guide 30). Although *Jeanie with the Light Brown Hair* was not a huge success during Foster's lifetime, it reached millions nearly a century later when, in 1941, a dispute over licensing fees forced radio broadcasters to air music in public domain. The alternate title for the song, *I Dream of Jeannie*, inspired the well-known 1960s sitcom of the same name.

The title page to Stephen Foster's song *Jeanie with the Light Brown Hair* (1854).

### Critical Thinking

1. What makes the lyrics and music of Stephen Foster universal today?
2. Do you think the works of Stephen Foster were viewed as popular or as classical music in their day?

**LISTENING GUIDE 30**

DVD | CD 5 (32–33) | CD 2 (62–63)

# Foster: *Jeanie with the Light Brown Hair* 3:03

**DATE:** 1854

**GENRE:** Parlor song

**WHAT TO LISTEN FOR:**

| | |
|---|---|
| **Melody** | Wavelike (descending, then ascending); syllabic setting |
| **Rhythm/ Meter** | Moderate tempo in broad quadruple meter; free ascending cadenza in each verse |
| **Harmony** | Major key, simple block- and broken-chord accompaniment |
| **Texture** | Homophonic (some polyphony in duet) |

| | |
|---|---|
| **Form** | Strophic; with each verse in **A-A'-B-A** song form |
| **Performing Forces** | 2 soprano voices in alternation and duet; accompanied by hammer dulcimer |
| **Text** | 2-verse poem by Stephen Foster |

| 62 | 0:00 | **Introduction** | |
|---|---|---|---|
| | 0:16 | **Verse 1** | |

| | |
|---|---|
| I dream of Jeanie with the light brown hair, Borne, like a vapor, on the summer air! | **A section** |
| I see her tripping where the bright streams play, Happy as the daisies that dance on her way. | **A' section** (varied). |
| Many were the wild notes her merry voice would pour, Many were the blithe birds that warbled them o'er; | **B section** Slows down, ascending cadenza. |
| Oh! I dream of Jeanie with the light brown hair, Floating like a vapor, on the soft summer air. | **A section** returns. |

| | 1:28 | **Interlude** | |
|---|---|---|---|
| 63 | 1:37 | **Verse 2** (alternating singers and in a duet) | |

| | |
|---|---|
| I long for Jeanie with the daydawn smile, Radiant in gladness, warm with winning guile; | **A section** |
| I hear her melodies, like joys gone by, Sighing round my heart o'er the fond hopes that die; | **A' section** (varied). Sung as duet. |
| Sighing like the night wind and sobbing like the rain, Wailing for the lost one that comes not again; | **B section** Slows down, ascending cadenza. |
| Oh! I long for Jeanine, and my heart bows low Never more to find her where the bright waters flow. | **A section** returns (unison). Sung as duet. |

| | 2:50 | Brief postlude |
|---|---|---|

Opening of Verse 1, with descending melodic line:

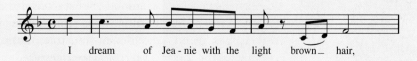

B section, with wavelike line:

**Now try the Listening Quiz.**

# 30 Romantic Program Music

> "The painter turns a poem into a painting;
> the musician sets a picture to music."
>
> —**Robert Schumann**

## KEY POINTS

> **StudySpace** wwnorton.com/enjoy

- Many Romantic composers cultivated *program music*—instrumental music with a literary or pictorial association supplied by the composer—over *absolute music*.

- The four main types of program music include the *concert overture*, *incidental music* to a play, the *program symphony* (a multimovement work), and the *symphonic poem* (a one-movement work).

- Hector Berlioz's *Symphonie fantastique* is a five-movement program symphony unified by a recurring theme (*idée fixe*) that represents his beloved.

- Political unrest throughout Europe stimulated schools of nationalistic composers in Russia, Scandinavia, Spain, England, and Bohemia.

- Edvard Grieg looked to the folklore of his native Norway in many of his works; his incidental music for *Peer Gynt* was written to accompany a play by Henrik Ibsen about this folk legend.

- Bedřich Smetana wrote about his Bohemian homeland in a set of six symphonic poems entitled *My Country*; the most famous of these is *The Moldau*.

Shakespeare's play *A Midsummer Night's Dream* inspired this fanciful canvas by **Henry Fuseli** (1741–1825), *Titania and Bottom* (c. 1790).

Music often evokes specific visual images or ideas. Sometimes these are the products of the listener's imagination, but other times they are intended by the composer. Robert Schumann's quote above aptly suggests how a composer might think when creating a work. This genre of evoking images and ideas became known as *program music,* or instrumental music that has literary or pictorial associations. The program is supplied by the composer, either in the title or in an explanatory note. A title such as *King Lear* (by Berlioz), for example, suggests specific characters and events, while the title *Pièces fugitives* (*Fleeting Pieces,* by Clara Schumann) merely labels the mood or character of the work. Program music is distinguished from *absolute,* or pure, music, which consists of musical patterns that have no literary or pictorial meanings.

Program music was especially important during the nineteenth century, when musicians became sharply conscious of the connection between their art and the world around them. Adding a programmatic title brought music closer to poetry and painting, and helped composers relate their own work to the moral and political issues of their time.

# Varieties of Program Music

One type of program music came out of the opera house, where the overture was a rousing orchestral piece in one movement designed to serve as an introduction to an opera (or a play). Many operatic overtures became popular as separate concert pieces which, in turn, pointed the way to a new type of overture not associated with an opera: a single-movement concert piece for orchestra based on a literary idea, such as Tchaikovsky's *Romeo and Juliet*. This **concert overture** might evoke a land- or seascape or embody a literary or patriotic idea.

*The concert overture*

Another type of program music, **incidental music**, usually consists of an overture and a series of pieces performed between the acts of a play and during important scenes. The most successful pieces of incidental music were arranged into suites (such as Mendelssohn's music for Shakespeare's *A Midsummer Night's Dream* and Edvard Grieg's *Peer Gynt*, see p. 240). Incidental music is still important today, in the form of film music and background music for television.

*Incidental music*

The passion for program music was so strong that it invaded even the most revered form of absolute music, the symphony. Thus the **program symphony**, a multimovement orchestral work came into being. Important examples are the program symphonies of Berlioz—including *Symphonie fantastique* (see p. 232)—and Liszt's *Faust* and *Dante* Symphonies.

*Program symphony and symphonic poem*

Eventually, composers felt the need for a large form of orchestral music that would serve the Romantic era as the symphony had served the Classical. Franz Liszt created the symphonic poem (he first used the term in 1848), the nineteenth century's most original contribution to large forms. Liszt's *Les préludes* is among the best-known examples of this genre. A **symphonic poem** is program music for orchestra, in one movement, with contrasting sections to develop a poetic idea, suggest a scene, or create a mood. It differs from the concert overture, which usually retains one of the traditional Classical forms, by having a much freer structure. The symphonic poem (also called **tone poem**) gave composers the flexibility they needed for a big single-movement form. It became the most widely used type of orchestral program music through the second half of the century. We will study two examples: *The Moldau* by the Bohemian composer Bedřich Smetana, and *Prelude to "The Afternoon of a Faun"* by Claude Debussy.

Program music is one of the most striking manifestations of nineteenth-century Romanticism. This new, descriptive genre impelled composers to express specific feelings; it proclaimed the direct relationship between music and life.

The Faust legend was a popular theme in art, literature, and music. *Mephistopheles in Faust's Study* by **Eugène Delacroix** (1798–1863).

# Berlioz and the Program Symphony

"To render my works properly requires a combination of extreme precision and irresistible verve, a regulated vehemence, a dreamy tenderness, and an almost morbid melancholy."

The flamboyance of Victor Hugo's poetry and the dramatic intensity of Eugène Delacroix's painting (see above) found their musical counterpart in the works of Hector Berlioz, whose music is intense, bold, and passionate. He was the first great proponent of musical Romanticism in France.

## Hector Berlioz (1803–1869)

**Hector Berlioz** was born in France in a small town near Grenoble. His father, a well-to-do physician, expected the boy to follow in his footsteps, but he made a decision that horrified his upper-middle-class family: he gave up medicine for music.

The Romantic revolution was brewing in Paris, and Berlioz, along with Victor Hugo and Eugène Delacroix, found himself in the camp of "young France." He became a huge fan of Beethoven and of Shakespeare, to whose plays he was introduced by a visiting English troupe. Berlioz fell madly in love with an actress in this troupe, whose portrayals of Ophelia and Juliet excited the admiration of the Parisians. In his *Memoirs,* he describes his infatuation with Harriet Smithson: "I became obsessed by an intense, overpowering sense of sadness. I could not sleep, I could not work, and I spent my time wandering aimlessly about Paris and its environs."

In 1830, Berlioz won the coveted Prix de Rome, which gave him an opportunity to live and work in Italy. That same year he composed the *Symphonie fantastique,* his most celebrated work. After returning from Rome, he began a hectic courtship with Harriet Smithson. Although they married, Berlioz realized it was Shakespeare he had loved rather than Harriet. All the same, the first years of his marriage were the most productive of his life. By age forty, he had produced many of his most famous works.

Berlioz's works show the favorite literary influences of the Romantic period, drawing on Goethe, the English poet Lord Byron, and especially Shakespeare, the source for his overture *King Lear,* his opera *Béatrice et Bénédict*, and his dramatic symphony *Romeo and Juliet.* His most important opera, *The Trojans,* on his own libretto after the ancient Roman poet Virgil, has been successfully revived in recent years.

It was in the domain of orchestration that Berlioz's genius asserted itself most fully. His daring originality in handling the instruments opened up a new world of Romantic sound. His scores, calling for the largest orchestra that had ever been used (see Table on p. 208), abound in novel effects and discoveries.

Berlioz was one of the boldest innovators of the nineteenth century. His approach to music was wholly individual, his sense of sound unique. From the start, he had an affinity in his orchestral music for the vividly dramatic or pictorial program.

*In His Own Words*

Generally speaking, my style is very bold . . . the prevailing characteristics of my music are passionate expression, intense ardor, rhythmical animations, and unexpected turns.

**Major Works:** Orchestral music, including overtures (*King Lear*) and program symphonies (*Symphonie fantastique* and *Romeo et Juliette*) • Choral music, including a Requiem Mass • 3 operas, including *Les Troyens* (*The Trojans*) • 9 works for solo voice and orchestra • Writings about music, including an orchestration treatise.

Berlioz's *idée fixe* was inspired by the Shakespearean actress Harriet Smithson.

## *Symphonie fantastique*

Berlioz wrote his best-known program symphony when he was twenty-seven years old, drawing its story from his personal life. His score describes "a young musician of morbid sensibility and ardent imagination, in . . . lovesick despair, [who] has poisoned himself with opium. The drug, too weak to kill, plunges him into a heavy sleep accompanied by strange visions. . . . The beloved one herself becomes for him a melody, a recurrent theme that haunts him everywhere."

The symphony's recurrent theme, called an ***idée fixe*** (fixed idea), symbolizes the beloved; it becomes a musical thread unifying the five diverse movements, though its appearances are varied in harmony, rhythm, meter, tempo, dynamics, register, and instrumental color. (See Listening Guide 31 for theme and analysis.) This type of unification, called **thematic transformation** and developed by Franz Liszt in his symphonic poems, serves the huge, expansive form of Berlioz's program symphony. These transformations take on literary as well as musical significance, as the description by Berlioz shows (see pp. 234–35).

**LISTENING GUIDE 31**   Ⓢ | DVD | CD 5 (41–53) | CD 3 (17–22)

# Berlioz: *Symphonie fantastique*, IV   4:37

**DATE:** 1830

**GENRE:** Program symphony with 5 movements

**PROGRAM:** A lovesick artist in an opium trance is haunted by a vision of his beloved, which becomes an *idée fixe* (fixed idea).

**MOVEMENTS:**   I. *Reveries, Passions*: Largo, Allegro agitato e appassionato assai (Lively, agitated, and impassioned)
II. *A Ball*: Valse, Allegro non troppo (waltz, not too fast)
III. *Scene in the Fields*: Adagio
**IV. *March to the Scaffold*: Allegretto non troppo**
V. *Dream of a Witches' Sabbath*: Larghetto, Allegro assai

### I. *Reveries, Passions*

First movement introduces the main theme, the fixed idea:

Ⓢ **iMusic**

*Symphonie fantastique*, I (*idée fixe*)

### IV. *March to the Scaffold*

**WHAT TO LISTEN FOR:**

| | | | | |
|---|---|---|---|---|
| Melody | 2 main march themes (**A** and **B**), both strongly accented | | Form | Sonata-like, with 2 themes introduced, developed, then recapped. |
| Rhythm/ Meter | Duple meter march | | Expression | Diabolical mood; sudden dynamic changes, idea of beloved at end as clarinet solo, then sudden chord (beheading) |
| Harmony | Set in minor mode | | Timbre | Prominent timpani; instruments in unusual ranges |

| | | | |
|---|---|---|---|
| **17** | 0:00 | Opening motive: muted horns, timpani, and pizzicato low strings, forecasts syncopated rhythm of march (theme **B**): |  |
| **18** | 0:24 | Theme A—an energetic, downward minor scale, played by low strings, then violins (with bassoon obbligato): |  |
| **19** | 1:31 | Theme **B**—diabolical march tune, played, by brass and woodwinds: |  |

*Continued on following page*

| 20 | 1:56 | Developmental section:<br>Theme **B**—in brass, accompanied by strings and woodwinds.<br>Theme **A**—soft, with pizzicato strings.<br>Theme **B**—brass, with woodwinds added.<br>Theme **A**—soft, pizzicato strings, then loud in brass. |
| --- | --- | --- |
| 21 | 3:02 | Theme **A**—full orchestra statement in original form, then inverted (now an ascending scale). |
| 22 | 4:05 | *Idée fixe* (fixed idea) melody in clarinet ("a last thought of love"), marked "dolce assai e appassionato" (as sweetly and passionately as possible), followed by loud chord that cuts off melody ("the fall of the blade"): |

Loud forceful chords close movement, depicting the head falling into a basket.

◎ **Now try the Listening Quiz.**

**The program**

I. *Reveries, Passions.* "[The musician] remembers the weariness of soul, the indefinable yearning he knew before meeting his beloved. Then, the volcanic love with which she at once inspired him, his delirious suffering . . . his religious consolation." The Allegro section introduces a soaring melody—the fixed idea.

II. *A Ball.* "Amid the tumult and excitement of a brilliant ball he glimpses the loved one again." This dance movement is in ternary, or three-part, form. In the middle section, the fixed idea reappears in waltz time.

III. *Scene in the Fields.* "On a summer evening in the country he hears two shepherds piping. The pastoral duet, the quiet surroundings . . . all unite to fill his heart with a long-absent feeling of calm. But she appears again [*idée fixe*]. His heart contracts. Painful forebodings fill his soul." The composer said that his aim in this pastoral movement was to establish a mood "of sorrowful loneliness."

IV. *March to the Scaffold.* "He dreams that he has killed his beloved, that he has been condemned to die and is being led to the scaffold. . . . At the very end the fixed idea reappears for an instant, like a last thought of love interrupted by the fall of the blade."

**Francisco Goya** (1746–1828) anticipated the passionate intensity of Berlioz's music in this painting of the *Witches' Sabbath,* c. 1819–23.

V. *Dream of a Witches' Sabbath.* "He sees himself at a witches' sabbath surrounded by a host of fearsome spirits who have gathered for his funeral. Unearthly sounds, groans, shrieks of laughter. The melody of his beloved is heard, but it has

lost its noble and reserved character. It has become a vulgar tune, trivial and grotesque. It is she who comes to the infernal orgy. A howl of joy greets her arrival. She joins the diabolical dance. Bells toll for the dead. A burlesque of the *Dies irae*. Dance of the witches. The dance and the *Dies irae* combined."

The last two movements of *Symphony fantastique* are perfect examples of the Romantic era's preoccupation with the grotesque and the supernatural. The fourth movement, a diabolical march in minor, exemplifies the nineteenth-century love of the fantastic. The theme of the beloved appears at the very end, in the clarinet, and is cut off by a grim *fortissimo* chord. In this vivid portrayal of the story, we clearly hear the final blow of the guillotine blade, the head rolling, and the resounding cheers of the crowd.

*Fourth movement*

In the final movement, Berlioz sounds an infernal spirit that nourished a century of satanic operas, ballets, and symphonic poems. The mood is heightened by the introduction of the traditional religious chant *Dies irae* (Day of Wrath) from the ancient Mass for the Dead, scored for the bassoons and tubas.

*Dies irae*

Berlioz's music has grandeur of line and gesture, and an abundance of vitality and invention. A larger-than-life figure who did everything on a grand scale—both personal and musical—he is one of the major prophets of his era.

# Musical Nationalism

"I grew up in a quiet spot and was saturated from earliest childhood with the wonderful beauty of Russian popular song. I am therefore passionately devoted to every expression of the Russian spirit. In short, I am a Russian through and through!"

—*Peter Ilyich Tchaikovsky*

In nineteenth-century Europe, political conditions encouraged the growth of nationalism to such a degree that it became a decisive force within the Romantic movement. The pride of conquering nations and the struggle for freedom of suppressed ones gave rise to strong emotions that inspired the works of many creative artists.

The Romantic composers expressed their nationalism in a variety of ways. Some based their music on the songs and dances of their people, others wrote dramatic works based on folklore or peasant life—for example, the Russian fairy-tale operas and ballets of Tchaikovsky (see HTTN 7, p. 236) and Edvard Grieg's *Peer Gynt* (see p. 240). And some wrote symphonic poems and operas celebrating the exploits of a national hero, a historic event, or the scenic beauty of their country, such as Smetana's *The Moldau*, which we will consider.

In associating music with the love of homeland, composers were able to give expression to the hopes and dreams of millions of people. The political implications of this musical nationalism were not lost on the authorities. Many of Verdi's operas, for example, had to be altered again and again to suit the Austrian censor (his plots often portrayed rulers as unjust or suggested "dangerous" ideas). Finnish composer Jean Sibelius's orchestral hymn *Finlandia*, written for a national pageant in 1899, was banned in 1917 because the hymn promoted national identity for Finland, which was then a part of the mighty Russian empire. During the Second World War, the Nazis outlawed the playing of Chopin's polonaises in Warsaw and Smetana's descriptive symphonic poems in Prague because of the powerful symbolism behind these two works. We will consider one of these inspiring compositions—Smetana's *The Moldau*, today a beloved standard in the entire orchestral repertory.

*In His Own Words*

Music expresses that which cannot be said and on which it is impossible to be silent.

—*Victor Hugo*

**7** ▶ **Here & There, Then & Now**

# Music, Folklore, and Nationalism

Prince Ivan with the magical firebird in a Russian folktale depicted by **Ivan Bilibin** (1876–1942).

Composers throughout the ages have looked to the folklore of their native lands for inspiration. We will see that Bedřich Smetana was moved—in his case, through deeply felt patriotism—to write a cycle of six symphonic poems entitled *My Country* that presents not only images of the scenery and history but also the folk legends of his beloved Bohemia. One work from the cycle, entitled *Šárka,* tells the Central European folktale about a warrior princess who, spurned by her lover, joins a group of other warrior-women to punish men.

Each culture has a value system that lies at the heart of its folklore: children often learn right from wrong and prepare for adulthood through folktales, which are transmitted, like folk music, through oral tradition. The characters we find in these folk legends are often rascals whose wrongdoings prove the moral of the story. We will meet Peer Gynt, a peasant figure from Norwegian history whose adventures are recounted musically by Edvard Grieg in his much-loved incidental music to the drama by Henrik Ibsen. Another famous musical rogue, this one from medieval German legend, is portrayed in Richard Strauss's popular tone poem *Till Eulenspiegel's Merry Pranks* (1895). Till's adventures include riding through a marketplace and upsetting all the goods, disguising himself as a priest, mocking a group of professors, and finally paying the penalty for his pranks: he is tried and hanged, though his spirit cannot be suppressed.

Folk material inspired the Russian composer Igor Stravinsky in his ballet suite *The Firebird,* based on the tale of a mythical, glowing bird that was both a blessing and a curse to its captor. Magi-cal birds abound in folklore and in music: perhaps the most famous is the phoenix, an Egyptian mythical bird that rises out of the ashes as a sign of hope and rebirth (you may remember the phoenix Fawkes, who was Dumbledore's pet in the *Harry Potter* books).

Folk legends often transcend national boundaries. For example, both Russian and German folklore feature a witch who lures children to her hut in the woods, where she eats them. This story is captured by the Russian composer Modest Mussorgsky in his *Hut on Fowl's Legs,* part of his programmatic suite *Pictures at an Exhibition,* and, in the version told by Jakob and Wilhelm Grimm, in the opera *Hansel and Gretel* by Engelbert Humperdinck.

The well-known French tales "Sleeping Beauty" and "Cinderella" (both from the 1697 collection by Charles Perrault) were set as Russian ballets (*The Sleeping Beauty* by Tchaikovsky in 1890 and *Cinderella* by Prokofiev in 1945); and a fanciful story by the German writer E. T. A. Hoffmann, in an expanded version by French writer Alexandre Dumas, served as the basis for Tchaikovsky's most famous ballet, *The Nutcracker* (1892), which we will study.

Today, favorite stories such as Perrault's "Sleeping Beauty," the Grimms' "Beauty and the Beast," and "The Princess and the Frog," a fairy tale common to many countries, are well known through Disney animated films. But some folktales are much more recent. The symphonic fairy tale of *Peter and the Wolf* (1936) by Russian composer Sergei Prokofiev is a twentieth-century story created by the composer. And you undoubtedly know the stories of *The Lord of the Rings* by J. R. R. Tolkien (loosely drawn from the same Norse mythology that is the basis for Wagner's operatic cycle *The Ring*) and *The Chronicles of Narnia* by C. S. Lewis (which develops ideas from Greek and Roman mythology as well as from English and Irish fairy tales). These contemporary fantasies have inspired classical music settings as well as film soundtracks, and are now firmly established in our modern literary heritage.

---

◉ **iMusic**

Grieg: *Åse's Death,* from *Peer Gynt*
Tchaikovsky: *Waltz of the Flowers,* from *The Nutcracker*
Wagner: *Ride of the Valkyries,* from *Die Walküre* (see p. 262)

# A Czech Nationalist: Bedřich Smetana

*"My compositions do not belong to the realm of absolute music,
  where one can get along well enough with musical signs and a metronome."*

Bedřich Smetana was the first Bohemian composer to rise to prominence. While many of his works project his strong nationalistic feelings, Smetana's cycle of six symphonic poems, entitled *My Country* (*Má vlast*), vividly portray the beauty of Bohemia's countryside, the rhythm of its folk songs and dances, and the pomp and pageantry of its legends.

## Bedřich Smetana (1824–1884)

**Smetana** was born in a small village in eastern Bohemia (now the Czech Republic). In his teens, he was sent to school in Prague, where his love for music was kindled by the city's active cultural life. Smetana's career, like those of other nationalist composers, played out against a background of political agitation. Bohemia was caught up in a surge of nationalist fervor that culminated in a series of uprisings against Austrian rule in 1848. The young Smetana joined the patriotic cause. After the revolution was crushed, the atmosphere in Prague was oppressive for those suspected of sympathy with the nationalists, so in 1856, he accepted a conducting position in Sweden.

On his return to Prague several years later, Smetana resumed his musical career by writing operas for the National Theater, where performances were given in his native tongue. Of his eight operas, *The Bartered Bride* won him worldwide fame. Through these works he attempted to create a uniquely Czech operatic genre. Today he is best known for *My Country* (*Má vlast*), a expansive cycle of six symphonic poems whose composition occupied his time from 1874 to 1879. While writing the cycle, Smetana's health declined as a result of advanced syphilis, and, like Beethoven, he grew deaf. His diary reveals his deep suffering: "If my illness is incurable," he wrote, "then I should prefer to be delivered from this miserable existence."

**Major Works:** 8 operas, including *The Bartered Bride* • Orchestral music, including *Má vlast* (*My Country*), cycle of 6 symphonic poems including *Vltava* (*The Moldau*) • Chamber music and keyboard works, choral music, and songs.

### In His Own Words

I am no enemy of old forms in old music, but I am against imitating them today. I came to the conclusion myself . . . that hitherto existing forms are finished.

## The Moldau

In *The Moldau*, the second of the programmatic poems from *My Country*, the Bohemian river Moldau becomes a poetic symbol of Smetana's beloved homeland. (For the text of the composer's program, see Listening Guide 32.)

The Moldau River flows in majestic peace through the Czech Republic capital city of Prague.

# Smetana: *The Moldau*                                           11:36

**DATE:** 1874–79

**GENRE:** Symphonic poem, from cycle *My Country (Má vlast)*

## WHAT TO LISTEN FOR:

| | | | |
|---|---|---|---|
| Melody | Wide-ranging river theme, heard throughout | Timbre | Varied instrumentation for each scene: |

Melody | Wide-ranging river theme, heard throughout

Rhythm/Meter | Begins in flowing 6/8; shifts to duple for peasant dance, then back to 6/8

Harmony | Shifts between minor and major mode

Expression | Depicts scenes along the river Moldau

Timbre | Varied instrumentation for each scene:
Flutes for bubbling spring
French horns for the hunt
Staccato strings for peasant dance
Double reeds for nymphs in moonlight
Brass for ancient castle

**Smetana's program:** "Two springs pour forth in the shade of the Bohemian forest, one warm and gushing, the other cold and peaceful. Coming through Bohemia's valleys, they grow into a mighty stream. Through the thick woods it flows as the merry sounds of a hunt and the notes of the hunter's horn are heard ever closer. It flows through grass-grown pastures and lowlands where a wedding feast is being celebrated with song and dance. At night, wood and water nymphs revel in its sparkling waves. Reflected on its surface are fortresses and castles—witnesses of bygone days of knightly splendor and the vanished glory of martial times. The Moldau swirls through the St. John Rapids, finally flowing on in majestic peace toward Prague to be welcomed by historic Vyšehrad. Then it vanishes far beyond the poet's gaze."

| | | PROGRAM | DESCRIPTION |
|---|---|---|---|
| 23 | 0:00 | Source of river, two springs | Rippling figures in flute, then added clarinets; plucked string accompaniment. |
| | | Stream broadens | Rippling figure moves to low strings. |
| 24 | 1:06 | River theme | Stepwise melody in violins, minor mode, rippling in low strings; repeated: |

| | | | |
|---|---|---|---|
| 25 | 3:01 | Hunting scene | Fanfare in French horns and trumpets: |

Rippling continues (in strings); dies down to gently rocking motion.

| | | | |
|---|---|---|---|
| 26 | 3:58 | Peasant dance | Repeated notes in strings lead to rustic folk tune, staccato in strings and woodwinds: |

Closes with repeated single note in strings.

| | | | |
|---|---|---|---|
| **27** | 5:39 | Nymphs in moonlight | Mysterious, long notes in double reeds and higher strings, with harp: |

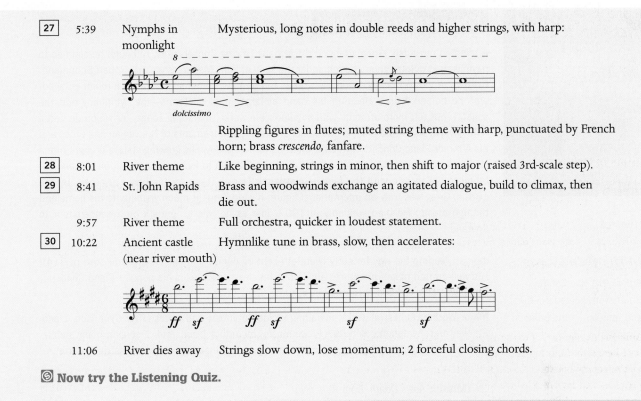

*dolcissimo*

Rippling figures in flutes; muted string theme with harp, punctuated by French horn; brass *crescendo,* fanfare.

| | | | |
|---|---|---|---|
| **28** | 8:01 | River theme | Like beginning, strings in minor, then shift to major (raised 3rd-scale step). |
| **29** | 8:41 | St. John Rapids | Brass and woodwinds exchange an agitated dialogue, build to climax, then die out. |
| | 9:57 | River theme | Full orchestra, quicker in loudest statement. |
| **30** | 10:22 | Ancient castle (near river mouth) | Hymnlike tune in brass, slow, then accelerates: |

*ff    sf        ff    sf            sf            sf*

| | | | |
|---|---|---|---|
| | 11:06 | River dies away | Strings slow down, lose momentum; 2 forceful closing chords. |

**Now try the Listening Quiz.**

The music suggests first the rippling streams that flow through the forest to form the mighty river. Smetana then evokes a hunting scene by using French horns and trumpets, followed by a peasant wedding in a lilting folk dance. The mood changes to enchantment as nymphs emerge from their fairy-tale haunts to hold their nightly revels under the moonlight; here, the melody is heard in muted strings over a bubbling accompaniment. The portrayal of the St. John Rapids musters all the brass and percussion, which announce the broad river theme now transformed and in major mode. Finally, as the Moldau approaches the capital city of Prague, it flows past castles and fortresses that remind the composer of his country's proud history. The river then flows out to sea, as the music fades to a *pianissimo,* closing a work that has captured the imagination of listeners for more than a century.

# A Scandinavian Nationalist: Edvard Grieg

"I dipped into the rich treasures of native folk song and sought to create a national art out of this hitherto unexploited expression of the folk soul of Norway."

Among the nationalist composers of the nineteenth century, the Norwegian master Edvard Grieg stands out for his ability to capture the essence of his country's folklore and dance through music. It was his goal to create an art that was accessible to the public.

## Edvard Grieg (1843–1907)

A talented musician, **Grieg** attended the famous Leipzig Conservatory. Although he claimed to have learned nothing there, he fell under the spell of Felix Mendelssohn and Robert Schumann. Grieg returned to Norway, where he worked to promote Scandinavian music through an academy he helped found. He tried his hand at larger musical forms—the symphony and the sonata—but felt more at home with smaller-scale works, including songs, for which he had a lyric gift. He also wrote many piano works, including arrangements of Norwegian folk tunes and his A minor Piano Concerto, which is often performed today. His growing stature brought him a stipend from the Norwegian government that allowed him to focus on composition and an invitation to collaborate with the famous playwright Henrik Ibsen for his play *Peer Gynt*. By the 1880s, Grieg was truly an international figure, having brought much visibility to his homeland through music. He died suddenly in 1907, just as he was to embark on a concert tour to England.

Grieg's music is notable for its lyricism and for his nationalistic use of folk music and dances, leading the way for early twentieth-century composers like Béla Bartók (see p. 314). His well-crafted piano miniatures are among his best works, as is his popular Piano Concerto, which was admired and performed by virtuoso Franz Liszt.

**Major Works:** Orchestral works, including incidental music and suites (*Peer Gynt,* Nos. 1 and 2), overtures, symphonic dances • Piano music, including 1 concerto, 1 sonata, many small-scale pieces, including dances • Chamber music, including violin sonatas, 1 string quartet • Songs.

ⓢ **iMusic:** *Åse's Death*, from *Peer Gynt*

*In His Own Words*

Artists like Bach and Beethoven erected churches and temples in the heights. I wanted . . . to build dwellings for men in which they might feel at home and happy.

# *Peer Gynt* Suite

Henrick Ibsen's play *Peer Gynt*, based on a Norwegian folk tale, premiered in Christiana, Norway, in 1876. Like most folktales, the story presents a strong moral message.

Peer is a lazy and boastful youth; his mother Åse reprimands him for his laziness, which caused him to lose his bride-to-be, Ingrid, to another. At her wedding, however, Peer abducts Ingrid, only to abandon her later. Peer runs away to a forest, where he meets—and seduces—another young girl who turns out to be a daughter of the Mountain King, ruler of the trolls. When her sisters find out she is pregnant, they vow to revenge her rape, but Peer manages to escape them. Now an outlaw, he builds a cottage in the woods where Solveig, a girl he once loved, comes to live with him. Life seems safe for a while, but when Peer's mother dies, he sets off on a series of fantastical adventures, including to the shores of North Africa, where he cavorts with the Arabian girl Anitra, who does a sultry dance for him. Peer finally returns home many years later to find Solveig, now a middle-aged woman, still faithful to him.

At Ibsen's invitation, Edvard Grieg composed some twenty-two pieces, including preludes, interacts, and dances, as incidental music for the play. Not altogether happy with the result, Grieg extracted eight of the movements and combined them—in a different order than they fall in the play—into two orchestral suites, each of four movements.

Two of the most endearing and popular pieces—*Morning Mood* and *In the Hall of the Mountain King*—are from Grieg's first suite,

*The King of the Trolls*, from Ibsen's *Peer Gynt* as illustrated by **Arthur Rackham** (1867–1939).

## LISTENING GUIDE 33

◎ | DVD | CD 5 (62–67) | CD 3 (31–36)

# Grieg: *Peer Gynt,* Suite No. 1, Op. 46, excerpts    6:21

**DATE:** 1874–75; published 1888

**GENRE:** Incidental music to a play by Henrik Ibsen

**MOVEMENTS:** *Morning Mood*
*Åse's Death*
*Anitra's Dance*
**In the Hall of the Mountain King**

### WHAT TO LISTEN FOR:

*Morning Mood*

| | |
|---|---|
| Melody | Dreamy melody, inverted arch shape with decorative grace notes |
| Rhythm/ Meter | Lilting 6/8 meter |
| Harmony | E major, with many harmonic inflections; static chords |
| Texture | Homophonic |
| Form | 3-part (**A-B-A′**) |
| Expression | Grows to loud climax; swells in dynamics, then dies away |
| Performing Forces | Pastoral instruments (flute, oboe, horn) prominent |

*In the Hall of the Mountain King*

| | |
|---|---|
| Melody | 2-phrase ghostly melody, rising line and accented |
| Rhythm/ Meter | Duple meter march; short, staccato notes and offbeat accents |
| Harmony | Set in B minor |
| Texture | Homophonic |
| Form | Single theme repeated over and over; closing coda |
| Expression | Huge crescendo and accelerando to dramatic ending |
| Performing Forces | Pizzicato strings and staccato woodwinds effects; offbeats in brass and percussion |

---

*Morning Mood*    3:50

**A section**

**31** | 0:00 | Flowing melody exchanged between flute and oboe, with sustained string chords; builds in *crescendo:*

| 0:49 | Full orchestra statement, marked *forte;* continues to build, then dies down; cello motive leads to new *crescendo.*

**B section**

**32** | 1:29 | Reaches climax, then cellos alternate with higher strings in sudden dynamic changes; builds in *crescendo* and *decrescendo;* brief shift to minor.

**A′ section**

**33** | 1:59 | French horn with main theme, accompanied by wavering woodwinds.
| 2:12 | Louder statement in low strings and woodwinds.
| 2:32 | Horn introduces slower statement of theme in violins, answered by clarinet.

*Continued on following page*

**Coda**

2:45    Quiet mood, with trills in woodwinds; solo French horn.

3:17    Flute with theme, slowing, then bassoon; tranquil chords in strings; closing chords in full orchestra with soft timpani roll.

---

*In the Hall of the Mountain King*                                                              2:31

**34**  0:00    Eerie theme heard 6 times, played softly in low pizzicato strings and bassoons:

0:55    Theme continues in violins, answered by woodwinds, strong offbeat accents.

1:11    Pizzicato theme moves to higher range in violins, grows louder and a little faster; answered by oboes and clarinets.

1:26    Louder statement accompanied by bowed spinning figure.

**35**  1:40    Full orchestra at *fortissimo*, with strong accents.

1:52    Brass prominent as music speeds up and is more accented.

**Coda**

**36**  2:12    Sudden chords, alternating with running passages; timpani roll leads to final chord.

◎ **Now try the Listening Quiz.**

---

which also includes *Åse's Death* and *Anitra's Dance. Morning Mood* opens the suite (it was originally the prelude to the last act of the play) and is an atmospheric depiction of the sunrise. The work features a lyrical theme that is passed between instruments, building to a long climax (see Listening Guide 33). Grieg skillfully captures the stillness of the new dawn, writing "I imagine the sun breaking through the clouds at the first forte."

*In the Hall of the Mountain King* was conceived as grotesque ballet music—a march for the wild daughters of the Mountain King. The girls taunt and threaten Peer for seducing one of them, with the insistent theme growing louder and faster as they chase him, shouting "slay him, slay him!" The crashing final chords signify the collapse of the mountain on top of the trolls.

A Polovetsian maiden and a Russian warrior. **Ivan Bilibin**'s (1876–1942) costume designs for Borodin's opera *Prince Igor*.

# Other Nationalists

In addition to the Czech national school, represented by Smetena, and the Scandanavian School, which included Edvard Grieg (Norway) and Jean Sibelius (Finland), many other regions throughout Europe gave rise to a national voice through music. In particular, the Russian school produced a circle of young musicians called "The Mighty Five" (or "The Mighty Handful") that included Modest Musorgsky and Nikolai

## SCHOOLS OF MUSICAL NATIONALISM

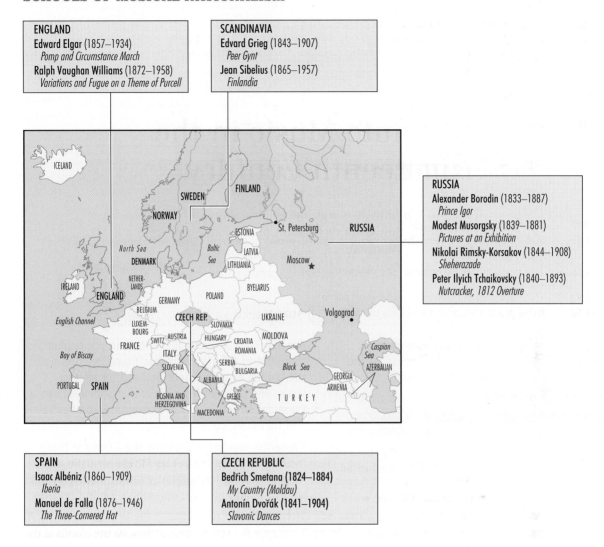

**ENGLAND**
Edward Elgar (1857–1934)
*Pomp and Circumstance March*
Ralph Vaughan Williams (1872–1958)
*Variations and Fugue on a Theme of Purcell*

**SCANDINAVIA**
Edvard Grieg (1843–1907)
*Peer Gynt*
Jean Sibelius (1865–1957)
*Finlandia*

**RUSSIA**
Alexander Borodin (1833–1887)
*Prince Igor*
Modest Musorgsky (1839–1881)
*Pictures at an Exhibition*
Nikolai Rimsky-Korsakov (1844–1908)
*Sheherazade*
Peter Ilyich Tchaikovsky (1840–1893)
*Nutcracker, 1812 Overture*

**SPAIN**
Isaac Albéniz (1860–1909)
*Iberia*
Manuel de Falla (1876–1946)
*The Three-Cornered Hat*

**CZECH REPUBLIC**
Bedřich Smetana (1824–1884)
*My Country (Moldau)*
Antonín Dvořák (1841–1904)
*Slavonic Dances*

Rimsky-Korsakov; its members sought to free themselves from the older sounds of the German symphony, French ballet, and Italian opera. In doing so, the group expressed a true Russian spirit. England and Spain produced nationalistic composers as well whose music echoed the souls of their countries (see map above).

## Critical Thinking

**1.** What is Romantic about the program and music of Berlioz's *Symphonie fantastique*?

**2.** What are some ways that nationalism is reflected in nineteenth-century music?

# 31 Absolute Music in the Nineteenth Century

"A great symhony is a man-made Mississippi down which we irresistibly flow from the instant of our leave-taking to a long foreseen destination."

—Aaron Copland

**KEY POINTS**

⑤ **StudySpace** wwnorton.com/enjoy

- Composers continued writing *absolute music* throughout the nineteenth century, including the symphony, concerto, and chamber music.

- Romantic symphonies were characterized by lyrical themes, colorful harmonies, expanded proportions, and larger orchestras featuring new instruments.

- The first movement of a symphony usually remains in sonata-allegro form, and the third is most often a spirited scherzo.

- Johannes Brahms continued the Classical traditions of the Viennese masters in his four symphonies. His Third Symphony is Classical in structure but Romantic in tone.

- Antonín Dvořák found inspiration in nationalist themes and traditional music from Bohemia and the United States, where he lived for several years. His popular *New World* Symphony retains a Classical structure but is Romantic in orchestral and harmonic color.

- Romantic concertos preserve the Classical three-movement structure but use these forms more freely, allowing for brilliant virtuoso display by the soloist, as in Felix Mendelssohn's Violin Concerto in E minor.

**Absence of program**

In addition to the new programmatic genres we have considered—such as the symphonic poem, program symphony, and incidental music—Romantic composers continued writing in the multimovement absolute genres established in the Classical era, which included the symphony, the concerto, and chamber music (string quartets and quintets, piano trios, and quartets). You will remember that the most important organizing element in absolute music is form, since there is no prescribed story or extramusical literary program provided by the composer. While the basic components of the three- or four-movement cycle we considered in Chapter 21 are retained, nineteenth-century composers took new freedoms with the structures. We will consider in this chapter the Romantic symphony—specifically the Third Symphony of Johannes Brahms and, more briefly, the *New World* Symphony by Antonín Dvořák—as well as the Romantic concerto. In both genres, we can identify Classical elements in the formal structures along with Romantic traits, such as colorful harmonies and orchestral color, expressive "singing" melodies, and expansive proportions that do not always follow the "traditional rules."

# The Romantic Symphony

During the Classical period, the symphony became the most exalted form of absolute orchestral music. The three Viennese masters—Haydn, Mozart, and Beethoven—carried it to its highest level of formal beauty and status. They passed on to composers of the Romantic era a flexible art form that could be adapted to meet the emotional needs of the new age.

In the course of its development, the symphony gained weight and importance. Nineteenth-century composers found the symphony a suitable framework for their lyrical themes, harmonic experiments, and individual expressions. By the Romantic era, music had moved from palace to public concert hall, the orchestra had vastly increased in size (see Table on p. 208), and the symphonic structure was growing steadily longer and more expansive. As noted earlier, the nineteenth-century symphonists were not as prolific as their predecessors had been. Felix Mendelssohn, Robert Schumann, Brahms, and Tchaikovsky each wrote fewer than seven symphonies. These were in the domain of absolute music, while Liszt and Berlioz cultivated the program symphony.

Some Romantic works, like the *New World* Symphony by Bohemian composer Antonín Dvořák, straddle both these symphonic genres. The overall structure of this symphony, for example, follows the Classical multimovement cycle and includes several sonata-allegro movements; but its middle movements have a literary link to Henry Wadsworth Longfellow's poem *Son of Hiawatha,* and the general character of the work, written while the composer was teaching in New York City, evokes the American landscape as well as African-American spirituals (see HTTN 8, p. 250).

*In His Own Words*

A symphony must be like the world; it must embrace everything.

—*Gustav Mahler*

# The Expanded Symphonic Form

In the hands of Romantic composers, the standard four-movement Classical symphony took on new dimensions. For example, the usual number and tempo scheme of the movements was not religiously followed; Tchaikovsky closed his *Pathétique* Symphony with a long, expressive slow movement, and Beethoven pushed the cycle to five movements in his *Pastoral* Symphony (No. 6).

The first movement, the most dramatic of the Romantic symphony, generally retains the basic elements of sonata-allegro form. It might draw out the slow introduction, and it often features a long and expressive development section that ventures into distant keys and transforms themes into something the ear perceives as entirely new.

The second movement may retain its slow and lyrical nature but can also range in mood from whimsical and playful to tragic and passionate. This movement frequently takes a loose three-part form.

Third in the cycle is a strongly rhythmic dance, with overtones of humor, surprise, caprice, or folk dance. Its mood can be anything from elfin lightness or melancholy to demonic energy. The tempo marking—usually Allegro, Allegro molto, or Vivace—

The 19th-century orchestra offered the composer new instruments and a larger ensemble. Engraving of an orchestral concert at the Covent Garden Theatre, London, 1846.

## A TYPICAL ROMANTIC SYMPHONY

| | | |
|---|---|---|
| **FIRST MOVEMENT** | **Sonata-allegro form** **Home key** Slow Introduction Exposition —Theme 1 (home key) —Theme 2 (contrasting key) —Closing theme (same contrasting key) Development (free modulation) Recapitulation —Theme 1 (home key) —Theme 2 (home key) —Closing theme (home key) | **Allegro** Optional Rhythmic character Lyrical character Fragmentation or expansion of themes; introduction of new material; distant keys |
| **SECOND MOVEMENT** | **Sonata-allegro form, A-B-A form, or theme and variations** **Different key** | **Slow, lyrical; varied moods** ⎤ ⎥ sometimes inverted |
| **THIRD MOVEMENT** | **Scherzo and trio, A-B-A** **Home Key** Scherzo, 2 sections Trio, 2 sections Scherzo returns | **Triple meter, fast-paced** Sections repeated ⎦ |
| **FOURTH MOVEMENT** | **Sonata-allegro form, rondo form, or some other form** **Home Key** | **Allegro or Presto** Shorter and lighter than first movement |

indicates a lively pace. Scherzo form generally follows the **A-B-A** structure of the minuet and trio. In some symphonies, such as Beethoven's Ninth, the scherzo is second in the cycle. We will see that Johannes Brahms wrote a melancholy waltz for the third movement of his Symphony No. 3.

Fourth movement      The fourth and final movement of the Romantic symphony has a dimension and character designed to balance the first. Often, this movement is a spirited Allegro in sonata-allegro form and may close the symphony on a note of triumph or pathos. The chart above reviews the standard form of the symphony.

# Brahms and the Late Romantic Symphony

"It is not hard to compose, but it is wonderfully hard to let the superfluous notes fall under the table."

Johannes Brahms created a Romantic art in the purest Classical style. His veneration of the past and his mastery of musical architecture brought him closer to the spirit of Beethoven than any of his contemporaries.

## Johannes Brahms (1833–1897)

Born in Hamburg, **Brahms** gave his first performance on piano at age ten. He soon developed a lifelong affection for folk music, collecting songs and folk sayings throughout his life. Brahms was fortunate to study with Robert Schumann at Düsseldorf, who recognized in Brahms a future leader of the circle dedicated to absolute music. Robert and his wife Clara took the young musician into their home, and their friendship opened up new horizons for him. But then came the tragedy of Schumann's mental collapse (see p. 216). With tenderness and strength, Brahms supported Clara through the ordeal of Robert's illness.

The death of Brahms's mother in 1865 inspired him to write his *German Requiem* in her memory. He ultimately settled in Vienna where, at age forty, he finally began writing his great symphonic works, beginning with his *Variations on a Theme by Haydn,* followed soon thereafter by his first two symphonies. During these years, he became enormously successful, the acknowledged heir of the Viennese masters.

Although he complained of loneliness, he was unable to accept the responsibility of a sustained relationship. In 1896, Clara Schumann's declining health gave rise to his *Four Serious Songs.* Her death deeply affected the composer, already ill with cancer. He died ten months later and was buried in Vienna, near Beethoven and Schubert.

Brahms's four symphonies are unsurpassed in the late Romantic period for their breadth of conception and design, yet their forms draw upon those of earlier eras. In his two piano concertos and his violin concerto, the solo instrument is integrated into a full-scale symphonic structure.

Brahms also captured the intimacy of chamber-music style. He is an important figure in piano music as well, writing two beloved variation sets and many short lyric piano pieces. As a song writer, Brahms stands in the direct succession from Schubert and Robert Schumann. His output includes about two hundred solo songs on love, nature, and death. His *German Requiem,* written to biblical texts that he selected himself, made him famous during his lifetime.

**Major Works:** Orchestral music, including 4 symphonies, variations, overtures • 4 concertos (2 for piano, 1 for violin, 1 double concerto for piano/violin • Chamber music, including string quartets and quintets • Duo sonatas • Piano music, including sonatas, character pieces, dances, variations • Choral music, including a Requiem and part songs • Lieder, including *Wiegenlied* (*Lullaby*).

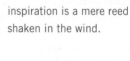

*In His Own Words*

Without craftsmanship, inspiration is a mere reed shaken in the wind.

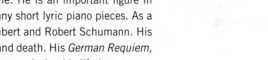

◎ **iMusic:** *Lullaby*                    Symphony No. 4, IV

# Symphony No. 3 in F Major

Brahms was a traditionalist; his aim was to show that new and important things could still be said in the tradition of the Classical masters. The Third Symphony, written in 1883 when Brahms was fifty years old, is the shortest of his four symphonies and the most Romantic in tone. In form, however, the work looks back to the Classical structures of the eighteenth century. The first movement, a conventional sonata-allegro, opens with a dramatic figure: a three-note motive (F-A♭-F) that is often related to the composer's personal motto; this idea permeates the entire symphony. The slow movement, a haunting Andante in sonata-allegro form, evokes the peacefulness of nature with its simple, hymnlike theme in the woodwinds.

Rather than following with a scherzo, Brahms writes a melancholy waltz in C minor, set in ternary form (see Listening Guide 34). The opening theme, a poignant cello melody, is heard throughout this impassioned orchestral "song without words," accompanied by restless string figures. First the violins, then the woodwinds take up the melody, whose arched rise and fall suggests a huge orchestral sigh. The middle section, now in a major key, presents two themes set against an expressive, chromatic accompaniment. The return of the opening theme is

**Third movement**

## LISTENING GUIDE 34

DVD | CD 6 (1–3) | CD 3 (37–39)

# Brahms: Symphony No. 3 in F major, Third Movement   6:24

**DATE:** 1883

**GENRE:** Symphony

**MOVEMENTS:**   I. Allegro con brio; sonata-allegro, F major
II. Andante; modified sonata form, C major
**III. Poco allegretto; A-B-A' form, C minor**
IV. Allegro; sonata-allegro; F major

---

**Third movement: Poco allegretto**                                         6:24

**WHAT TO LISTEN FOR:**

| | |
|---|---|
| **Melody** | Lyrical melancholic melody with waltzlike feeling; arched, regular phrases |
| **Rhythm/ Meter** | Moderate triple meter; rhythmic complexity with 3-against-2 patterns (contrasting rhythms sounded together) and syncopation |

| | |
|---|---|
| **Harmony** | Alternates minor-major-minor keys; chromatic in middle section |
| **Form** | 3-part structure (**A-B-A'**) |
| **Expression** | Arched dynamics and subtle rubato |
| **Timbre** | Woodwinds featured in middle section; French horns bring return to **A** |

---

**37**   0:00   **A section**—yearning cello melody, accompanied by rustling string figures; symmetrical phrasing:

0:27   Violins repeat the cello theme, extending the range and dynamics.
0:52   Theme 2, played by violins, "leans" over the barline over moving cello line; violins and cellos in duet:

1:27   Return of opening theme in flutes and oboes, with broader accompaniment.

**38**   1:57   **B section**—connected 3-note figure in woodwinds, in A-flat major, accompanied by offbeat sixteenth notes in the cellos:

3:27   Woodwinds hint at return to main theme, accompanied by sustained strings.

**39**   3:46   **A' section**—French horns announce the opening theme in C minor, with richer orchestration.
4:14   Oboes take up the haunting melody as accompaniment builds.
4:41   Theme 2, now heard in the clarinets and bassoons.
5:17   Violins and cellos take up the main theme, played in octaves for greater intensity; generally thicker and more contrapuntal accompaniment.
5:44   **Brief coda**; reminiscent of **B section**; last chord is punctuated by pizzicato strings.

Now try the **Listening Quiz**.

newly orchestrated, then closes with an emotional statement by the violins and cellos playing in octaves. A short coda brings back the mood of the middle section, closing with two soft pizzicato chords.

The finale, a dramatic sonata-allegro, features concise themes and abrupt changes of mood. Throughout, the listener is challenged by shifting moods, timbres, and melodies that affirm the technical command and the creative invention of a great Romantic master.

**Fourth movement**

# The Romantic Concerto

The origins of the Romantic concerto reach back to the late eighteenth century. Mozart and Beethoven, both formidable pianists, performed their concertos in public, delighting and dazzling their audiences. This element of virtuosic display, combined with appealing melodies, helped make the concerto one of the most widely appreciated types of concert music. As the concert industry developed, technical brilliance became a more and more important element of concerto style. We have noted that nineteenth-century composer-performers such as Paganini and Liszt carried virtuosity to new heights. This development kept pace with the increase in the size and resources of the symphony orchestra. The Romantic concerto became one of the most favored genres of the age. Felix Mendelssohn, Chopin, Liszt, Robert and Clara Schumann, Brahms, Tchaikovsky, and Dvořák all contributed to its literature. Unlike Mozart's day, when composers wrote concertos to showcase their own talent as performers, Romantic composers often wrote with a particular artist in mind.

*In His Own Words*

People often complain that music is too ambiguous, that what they should be thinking as they hear it is unclear, whereas everyone understands words. With me, it is exactly the reverse. . . . [Words] seem to me . . . so vague, so easily misunderstood in comparison to genuine music which fills the soul with a thousand things better than words.

—*Felix Mendelssohn*

## The Romantic Concerto Form

The Romantic concerto retains the Classical three-movement form, opening with a dramatic Allegro, usually in sonata form, which is followed by a lyrical slow movement and a brilliant finale. The first movement, though, is usually freer than

## A TYPICAL ROMANTIC CONCERTO

| FIRST MOVEMENT | Concerto form (double exposition) | Allegro |
| --- | --- | --- |
| | **Home key** | |
| | Orchestral exposition (optional) | Solo instrument may play at opening |
| | —Several themes | |
| | Solo exposition | |
| | —Same themes and others | |
| | Development | |
| | Recapitulation | |
| | Cadenza (solo instrument alone) | Cadenza may occur earlier |
| | Coda, or closing | |
| **SECOND MOVEMENT** | **A-B-A form** | **Andante or Adagio** |
| | **Contrasting key** | Slow, lyrical, songful |
| **THIRD MOVEMENT** | **Rondo form or sonata-allegro form** | **Allegro or Presto** |
| | **Home key** | Possible cadenza |

**8** ▶ **Here & There, Then & Now**

# Dvořák, the Symphony, and African-American Music

The Bohemian composer Antonín Dvořák presents a fascinating case of cultural assimilation. While living in the U.S., Dvořák absorbed some of America's unique musical traditions—African-American spirituals, Creole songs and dances, and what he perceived as Native American music. His best-known works from these years are written in absolute forms—the symphony (*From the New World*), the Cello Concerto, and the *American* String Quartet—and infused with American elements. People claim to hear the "open prairie," pentatonic scales drawn from Native American music (although Czech folk songs are also pentatonic), as well as hints of spirituals and a literary reference to Longfellow's poem *Song of Hiawatha* in these works. Dvořák himself suggested he would "never have written these works 'just so' if I hadn't seen America."

But Dvořák gave much more back to American music than he took. As a respected teacher, he issued a challenge to American composers to reject the domination of European music and to forge paths of their own, using the "beautiful and varied themes . . . the folk songs of America." Several of Dvořák's African-American students followed his suggestion. Henry T. Burleigh (1866–1949), who had fostered Dvořák's interest in spirituals, published a landmark collection of spirituals arranged as art-music (*Jubilee Songs of the U.S.A.*, 1916); his goal was to bring this genre to the concert stage. Will Marian Cook (1869–1944), another

student of Dvořák's, began writing an opera on *Uncle Tom's Cabin* (a novel about slavery) but turned his efforts to musical theater.

Dvořák's *New World* Symphony clearly inspired several African-American composers: Florence Price (1888–1953), the first American black woman recognized as a distinguished composer, wrote her Symphony in E minor (the same key as Dvořák's symphony) drawing on African-American melodic and rhythmic ideas. But the composer who best rose to Dvořák's challenge was William Grant Still (1895–1978), whose output spans all major art-music genres and evokes African-American work songs, spirituals, ragtime, blues, and jazz. Paramount among his works are his *Afro-American* Symphony (1930) and his jazzy Suite for Violin and Piano (see p. 326).

Today, the lines between art and traditional music are less defined than ever, and the African-American spiritual—so influential to Dvořák, Price, and Still in their symphonies—has taken on a new life as an art music genre. We can credit several singers with historic breaks in the concert tradition: Paul Robeson, a renowned bass-baritone and avid political activist, brought spirituals to the Broadway stage and radio in the 1920s; and Marian Anderson, the leading operatic contralto of the twentieth century, upset the concert world by ending her 1935 Salzburg recital with a set of spirituals. Modern singers like Leontyne Price (see p. 361) and Jessye Norman

have provided new interpretations of these moving songs in concerts and recordings, allowing us to appreciate this music within a new social context. Dvořák certainly would have been pleased!

◎ **iMusic**

*Swing Low, Sweet Chariot* (spiritual)
*Pine Apple Rag,* by Scott Joplin

Singer Jessye Norman performed spirituals at this June 2009 concert in Munich, Germany.

its Classical counterpart: the solo instrument may not wait for the orchestral exposition to make its first statement, and the cadenza, normally played at the close of the recapitulation and before the coda, may occur earlier, as part of the development. The second movement continues to present songful melodies, often in a loosely structured three-part form. And the finale, which brings the dramatic tension between soloist and orchestra to a head, often features another cadenza, leading the work to an exciting close.

One work that epitomizes the Romantic treatment of the genre is Felix Mendelssohn's famous Violin Concerto in E minor. Mendelssohn was dedicated to preserving the traditions of Classical form, setting his concerto in the standard three-movement structure. But Romantic elements are equally notable: these movements are to be played without pause, and later movements bring back the first movement's themes. Mendelssohn also does away with the customary orchestral introduction, bringing in the solo violin almost immediately, with a dramatic and an expansive melody. The work gives the soloist much opportunity for brilliant virtuosic display, another Romantic trait. The tender sentiment of the work is balanced by a Classical moderation that characterizes Mendelssohn's music.

Joseph Joachim, premier violinist of the 19th century, and pianist Clara Schumann (1854). Pastel on paper by **Adolph von Menzel** (1815–1905).

## Critical Thinking

1. What remains "classical" about the treatment of absolute music in the Romantic era? What is "romantic" about these structures?
2. How would you describe the expressive devices (melody and harmony, for example) of Romantic composers of the symphony and concerto?

---

## LISTENING ACTIVITY: ROMANTIC-ERA ORCHESTRAL MUSIC

Let's compare two examples representing Romantic symphonies (StudySpace, Chapter 31), one from the early part of the era and the other from the last decades of the nineteenth century. Match each work with the appropriate traits you hear. (Coincidentally, both are last movements from the fourth symphony in the composer's output.)

    **a.** Mendelssohn: Symphony No. 4, IV (*Italian*)
    **b.** Brahms: Symphony No. 4, IV

| 1. Melody/Rhythm | ____ quick-paced, dancelike theme | ____ slow moving theme in triple meter |
|---|---|---|
| 2. Harmony/Expression | ____ somber mood, in minor key | ____ bright mood, in major key |
| 3. Performing Forces | ____ small orchestra, featuring woodwinds and strings | |
| | ____ larger orchestra, featuring brass, percussion, woodwinds, and strings | |
| 4. Era | ____ early Romantic era (c. 1830) | ____ late-Romantic composition (c. 1885) |

Now let's consider two selections that are both examples of Romantic program music.

    **c.** Tchaikovsky: *Waltz of the Flowers*, from *Nutcracker* (ballet)
    **d.** Musorgsky: *Great Gates of Kiev* (from suite)

| 5. Rhythm/Meter | ____ broad, majestic quadruple meter | ____ flowing triple meter, then free |
|---|---|---|
| 6. Performing Forces | ____ features woodwinds and plucked strings | ____ features brass and percussion |
| 7. Expression | ____ hymnlike mood | ____ dreamy mood |

# 32 National Schools of Romantic Opera

"Opera is free from any servile imitation of nature. By the power of music it attunes the soul to a beautiful receptiveness."

—**Friedrich von Schiller**

**StudySpace** wwnorton.com/enjoy

## KEY POINTS

- Romantic opera developed distinct national styles in Italy, Germany, and France, and women singers excelled in all styles.

- Both **opera seria** (serious opera) and **opera buffa** (comic opera) were favored in Italy; they marked the peak of the **bel canto** (beautiful singing) style.

- Giuseppe Verdi is best known for his operas, which embody the spirit of Romantic drama and passion. His *Rigoletto*, based on a play by Victor Hugo, is one of the most performed works today.

- In Germany, the genre **Singspiel** (light, comic drama with spoken dialogue) gave way to more serious works, including Richard Wagner's **music drama**, which integrated all elements of opera.

- Wagner's **music dramas** are not sectional (in arias, ensembles, and the like) but are continuous, unified by **leitmotifs**, or recurring themes, that represent a person, place, or idea. His most famous work is his four-opera cycle, *The Ring of the Nibelung*.

- The opera *Carmen,* by French composer Georges Bizet, exemplifies a trend toward exoticism by romanticizing Gypsy culture in Spain.

As one of the most important and best-loved theatrical genres of the nineteenth century, opera fostered different national styles in three European countries known for their music—Italy, Germany, and France. We will hear a masterpiece representing several national operatic styles. First, however, we will take a brief look at the women who excelled as singers during this golden age.

## Women in Opera

*In His Own Words*

I have never encountered anything more false and foolish than the effort to get truth into opera. In opera everything is based upon the untrue.

*—Peter Ilyich Tchaikovsky*

Opera was one medium that allowed women musicians a good deal of visibility. Only a few tried their hand at composing full-scale operas, but those who did were able to see a number of their works produced. But women opera singers were among the most prominent performers of their day, idolized and in demand throughout Europe and the Americas. One international star was Jenny Lind, known as the "Swedish nightingale" and famous for her roles in operas by the Italians Donizetti and Bellini, among others. A concert artist as well, Lind made her American debut in 1850 in a tour managed with immense hoopla by circus impresario P. T. Barnum.

Professional singing was often a family tradition: the celebrated Spanish tenor Manuel García provide a case in point. A brilliant teacher, García coached two of

A portrait of Swedish soprano Jenny Lind (1820–1887).

The Margrave's Opera House in Bayreuth, 1879. A painting by **Gustav Bauernfeind** (1848–1904).

his daughters to stardom. His eldest, Maria Malibran (1808–1836), became renowned as an interpreter of Rossini, until a riding accident brought her successful career to a tragic close. Her youngest sister, Pauline Viardot (1821–1910), was a highly acclaimed singer who performed the premieres of vocal works by Brahms, Robert Schumann, and Berlioz, among others. A composer herself, Viardot's intellectual approach to her art did much to raise the status of women singers.

# Verdi and Italian Opera

*"Success is impossible for me if I cannot write as my heart dictates!"*

Italy in the nineteenth century still recognized the opposing genres of *opera seria* (serious opera) and *opera buffa* (the Italian version of comic opera), legacies of an earlier period. One of the most important composers of this era was Gioachino Rossini (1792–1868), whose masterpieces include *Il barbiere di Siviglia* (*The Barber of Seville*, 1816) and *Guillaume Tell* (*William Tell*, 1829). These operas marked the high point of a *bel canto* (beautiful singing) style, characterized by florid melodic lines delivered by voices of great agility and purity of tone.

 **iMusic**

*William Tell Overture*

**Bel canto style**

The consummate master of nineteenth-century Italian opera was Giuseppe Verdi, who sought to develop a uniquely national style. In his case, time, place, and personality were happily merged. He inherited a rich musical tradition, his capacity for growth was matched by extraordinary energy, and he was granted a long life in which to engage fully his creative gifts.

## Verdi's *Rigoletto*

 **Video**

The epitome of Romantic drama and passion, Verdi's music communicates each dramatic situation with profound emotion. The writer Victor Hugo, an acknowledged leader of French Romanticism, was Verdi's source of inspiration for *Rigoletto*. Hugo's play *Le roi s'amuse* (*The King Is Amused*, 1832) was banned in France but achieved universal popularity through its adaptation in Verdi's opera.

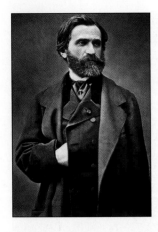

## Giuseppe Verdi (1813–1901)

Born in a small town in northern Italy, **Giuseppe Verdi**, because of his musical talent, soon had commissions to write operas for Milan's La Scala opera house. At the time, he faced a string of crises in his life: the deaths of his daughter, his baby son, and his young wife. The distraught composer wrote no music for months. Then one night he met the director of La Scala, who insisted he take home a libretto about Nebuchadnezzar, king of Babylon. Verdi returned to work, and the resulting opera, *Nabucco,* launched him on a spectacular career.

Italy at the time was liberating itself from Austrian Hapsburg rule. Verdi identified himself with the national cause from the beginning. In this charged atmosphere, his works took on special meaning for his compatriots. The chorus of exiled Jews from *Nabucco* became an Italian patriotic song that is still sung today. Although he became a world-renowned figure, Verdi returned to Busseto, the town where he ws born.

Despite his busy public life, Verdi was somehow able to produce one masterpiece after another. He was fifty-seven when he wrote *Aida.* At seventy-three, he completed *Otello,* his greatest lyric tragedy. And in 1893, on the threshold of eighty, he astonished the world with *Falstaff.* In all, he wrote twenty-eight operas.

Verdi's favorite literary source was Shakespeare, whose works he drew upon in *Macbeth*—his first operatic success—as well as *Otello* and *Falstaff,* a comic opera based on *The Merry Wives of Windsor.* His operas also drew on favorite novels and plays of his day, including *La traviata* (from *La dame aux camellias* by Alexandre Dumas) and *Il trovatore* (on a fanciful Spanish play). His operas from the 1860s—including *The Masked Ball* and *Don Carlos*—were on a larger scale, drawing from the traditions of French grand opera. He carried these goals even further in *Aida,* a monumental work commissioned in 1870 by the ruler of Egypt to mark the opening of the Suez Canal and premiered in Cairo. In 1874, Verdi completed his magnificent Requiem Mass (see p. 268)—dedicated to Alessandro Manzoni, a novelist and patriot whom Verdi revered.

**Major Works:** 28 operas, including *Macbeth* (1847), *Rigoletto* (1851), *Il trovatore* (*The Troubadour,* 1853), *La traviata* (*The Lost One,* 1853), *Un ballo in maschera* (*The Masked Ball,* 1859), *Don Carlos* (1867), *Aida* (1871), *Otello* (1887), and *Falstaff* (1893) • Vocal music, including a Requiem Mass.

◎ **iMusic:** *Dies irae,* from Requiem

### In His Own Words

It seems to me that the best material I have yet put to music is *Rigoletto.* It has the most powerful situations, it has variety, vitality, pathos; all the dramatic developments result from the frivolous, licentious character of the Duke. Hence Rigoletto's fears, Gilda's passion, etc., which give rise to many dramatic situations, including the scene of the quartet.

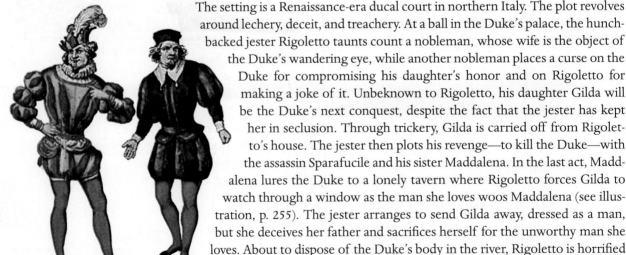

Costumes for the first production of Verdi's *Rigoletto* at Teatro la Fenice, Venice, March 11, 1851.

The setting is a Renaissance-era ducal court in northern Italy. The plot revolves around lechery, deceit, and treachery. At a ball in the Duke's palace, the hunchbacked jester Rigoletto taunts count a nobleman, whose wife is the object of the Duke's wandering eye, while another nobleman places a curse on the Duke for compromising his daughter's honor and on Rigoletto for making a joke of it. Unbeknown to Rigoletto, his daughter Gilda will be the Duke's next conquest, despite the fact that the jester has kept her in seclusion. Through trickery, Gilda is carried off from Rigoletto's house. The jester then plots his revenge—to kill the Duke—with the assassin Sparafucile and his sister Maddalena. In the last act, Maddalena lures the Duke to a lonely tavern where Rigoletto forces Gilda to watch through a window as the man she loves woos Maddalena (see illustration, p. 255). The jester arranges to send Gilda away, dressed as a man, but she deceives her father and sacrifices herself for the unworthy man she loves. About to dispose of the Duke's body in the river, Rigoletto is horrified to find Gilda in the sack instead of the nobleman. He recalls the curse one last time, as Gilda dies in his arms.

Two of the most popular operatic moments of all time occur in Act III. The Duke sings the best known of Verdi's tunes, "La donna è mobile" (Woman is fickle), a simple but rousing song accompanied by a guitarlike orchestral strumming. The

## By the way . . .

### Did Women Compose Operas?

The high costs of mounting an opera production in a large public theater, along with the elite status of the art, made it difficult for women composers to compete with men during the nineteenth century. The French musician Louise Bertin (1805–1877) broke through these barriers to compose four operas, two of which were produced in major Parisian venues. Bertin came from a wealthy family—her father owned the most influential newspaper in Paris—and was broadly trained in the arts. Like many composers of the time, she turned to literature for her opera plots, drawing on popular novels. *Esmeralda*, based on Victor Hugo's *Hunchback of Notre Dame*, was produced at the Paris Opéra, with the assistance of Hector Berlioz. This opera focuses on the Gypsy girl Esmeralda, who, when accused of being a witch, is given sanctuary inside the Cathedral by the hunchback Quasimodo. Bertin preferred "dark" plots, setting the Faust legend (in *Fausto*), based on Goethe's drama, and writing a one-act comic opera about a werewolf (*Le loup-garou*). Despite her active career, Bertin had to contend with prejudice against her gender and her own deformity—paralysis that she suffered from birth; indeed, she sometimes concealed her identity as a composer. It took nearly another century for the world of opera to welcome women composers and their artistic creations.

The quartet scene from Verdi's *Rigoletto* in the London premiere (1853) at Covent Garden. Rigoletto and his daughter, Gilda (on the right), are watching the Duke and Maddalena inside the tavern.

orchestra previews the catchy melody, which is heard numerous times as a ritornello in a strophic setting that brings back the opening text as a refrain.

The quartet that follows shortly is a masterpiece of operatic ensemble writing, as Verdi himself noted in the quote on p. 254. Each of the four characters presents a different point of view: the Duke woos Maddalena in a lovely bel canto–style melody; Maddalena answers with a laughing line in short notes; Gilda, watching from outside, is heartbroken as she laments her lost love; and Rigoletto hushes her, swearing vengeance for such treatment of his beloved daughter (see Listening Guide 35 for text and form). These two show-stopping numbers ensured the immediate success of *Rigoletto*. It remains one of the most frequently performed operas of the international repertory.

## LISTENING GUIDE 35

◎ Video | ◎ | DVD | **CD 6 (13–18)** | CD 3 (40–45)

# Verdi: *Rigoletto*, Act III, excerpts                        8:13

**FIRST PERFORMANCE:**  1851, Venice

**LIBRETTIST:**  Francesco Maria Piave

**BASIS:**  *Le roi s'amuse*, a play by Victor Hugo

**MAJOR CHARACTERS:**  The Duke of Mantua (tenor)
Rigoletto, the Duke's jester, a hunchback (baritone)
Gilda, Rigoletto's daughter (soprano)
Sparafucile, an assassin (bass)
Maddalena, Sparafucile's sister (contralto)

*Continued on following page*

Aria: "La donna è mobile" (Duke)                                        2:44

**WHAT TO LISTEN FOR:**

| Aria | | Quartet | |
|---|---|---|---|
| Melody | Soaring tenor line, with accented notes | Melody | Dialogue between characters; then simpler, square melody (*Bella figlia*) |
| Rhythm/Meter | Lilting triple-meter, "um-pah-pah" accompaniment; some rubato | Rhythm/Meter | Allegro, with agitated movement |
| Form | 2 strophes in aria, framed by orchestral ritornello that unifies aria | Expression | Each character reveals his/her emotion |
| Expression | Stirring music, with broadly contrasting dynamics | Performing Forces | Quartet (Duke, Maddalena, Gilda, Rigoletto) |

**40**    0:00    Orchestral ritornello previews the Duke's solo; opening melody of aria:

La don-na è   mo-bi-le   qual pium-a al   ven-to,   mut-a d'ac-cen-to

*The Duke, in a simple cavalry officer's uniform, sings in the inn;*
*Sparafucile, Gilda, and Rigoletto listen outside.*

| | TEXT | TRANSLATION |
|---|---|---|
| | **DUKE** | |
| 0:12 | La donna è mobile | Woman is fickle |
| | qual piuma al vento, | like a feather in the wind, |
| | muta d'accento, | she changes her words |
| | e di pensiero. | and her thoughts. |
| | sempre un amabile | Always lovable, |
| | leggiadro viso, | and a lovely face, |
| | in pianto o in riso, | weeping or laughing, |
| | è menzognero. | is lying. |
| | La donna è mobile, etc. | Woman is fickle, etc. |
| 1:10 | Orchestral ritornello | |
| **41**  1:21 | È sempre misero | The man's always wretched |
| | chi a le s'affida, | who believes in her, |
| | chi lei confida | who recklessly entrusts |
| | mal cauto il core! | his heart to her! |
| | pur mai non sentesi | And yet one who never |
| | felice appieno | drinks love on that breast |
| | chi su quel seno | never feels |
| | non liba amore! | entirely happy! |
| | La donna è mobile, etc. | Woman is fickle, etc. |

*Sparafucile comes back in with a bottle of wine and two glasses, which he sets on the table; then he*
*strikes the ceiling twice with the hilt of his long sword. At this signal, a laughing young woman in gypsy*
*dress leaps down the stairs: the Duke runs to embrace her, but she escapes him. Meanwhile Sparafucile*
*has gone into the street, where he speaks softly to Rigoletto.*

| | **SPARAFUCILE** | |
|---|---|---|
| | È là il vostr'uomo . . . | Your man is there . . . |
| | Viver dee o morire? | Must he live or die? |

**RIGOLETTO**

Più tardi tornerò l'opra a compire.      I'll return later to complete the deed.

*Sparafucile goes off behind the house toward the river. Gilda and Rigoletto remain in the street,*
*the Duke and Maddalena on the ground floor.*

---

**Quartet: "Un dì" (Duke, Maddalena, Gilda, Rigoletto)**      5:29

**DUKE**

| | |
|---|---|
| 42   2:44 | |

Un dì, se ben rammentomi,      One day, if I remember right,
o bella, t'incontrai . . .      I met you, O beauty . . .
Mi piacque di te chiedere,      I was pleased to ask about you,
e intesi che qui stai.      and I learned that you live here.
Or sappi, che d'allora      Know then, that since that time
sol te quest'alma adora!      my soul adores only you!

**GILDA**

Iniquo!      Villain!

**MADDALENA**

Ah, ah! . . . e vent'altre appresso      Ha, ha! . . . And perhaps now
le scorda forse adesso?      twenty others are forgotten?
Ha un'aria il signorino      The young gentleman looks like
da vero libertino . . .      a true libertine . . .

**DUKE** (starting to embrace her)

Sí . . . un mostro son . . .      Yes . . . I'm a monster . . .

**GILDA**

Ah padre mio!      Ah, Father!

**MADDALENA**

Lasciatemi, stordito.      Let me go, foolish man!

**DUKE**

Ih che fracasso!      Ah, what a fuss!

**MADDALENA**

Stia saggio.      Be good.

**DUKE**

E tu sii docile,      And you, be yielding,
non fare tanto chiasso.      don't make so much noise.
Ogni saggezza chiudesi      All wisdom concludes
nel gaudio e nell'amore.      in pleasure and in love.

(He takes her hand.)

La bella mano candida!      What a lovely, white hand!

**MADDALENA**

Scherzate voi, signore.      You're joking, sir.

**DUKE**

No, no.      No, no.

**MADDALENA**

Son brutta.      I'm ugly.

*Continued on following page*

|  |  |
|---|---|
| **DUKE** | |
| Abbracciami. | Embrace me. |
| **GILDA** | |
| Iniquo! | Villain! |
| **MADDALENA** | |
| Ebro! | You're drunk! |
| **DUKE** | |
| D'amor ardente. | With ardent love. |
| **MADDALENA** | |
| Signor l'indifferente, | My indifferent sir, |
| vi piace canzonar? | would you like to sing? |
| **DUKE** | |
| No, no, ti vo' sposar. | No, no, I want to marry you. |
| **MADDALENA** | |
| Ne voglio la parola. | I want your word. |
| **DUKE** (ironic) | |
| Amabile figliuola! | Lovable maiden! |
| **RIGOLETTO** (to Gilda, who has seen and heard all) | |
| È non ti basta ancor? | Isn't that enough for you yet? |
| **GILDA** | |
| Iniquo traditor! | Villainous betrayer! |
| **MADDALENA** | |
| Ne voglio la parola. | I want your word. |
| **DUKE** | |
| Amabile figliuola! | Lovable maiden! |
| **RIGOLETTO** | |
| È non ti basta ancor? | Isn't that enough for you yet? |

**Quartet (2nd part): "Bella figlia" (Duke, Maddalena, Gilda, Rigoletto)**

*Overall form:* **A-B-A'-C**

Diagram showing how characters interact in the ensemble and how they fit into the musical structure:

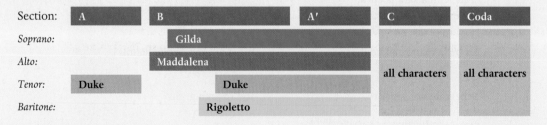

Opening melody of "Bella figlia," sung by Duke:

|  |  | **DUKE** |  | **Section** |
|---|---|---|---|---|
| **43** | 4:15 | Bella figlia dell'amore, | Beautiful daughter of love, | **A** |
|  |  | schiavo son de' vezzi tuoi; | I am the slave of your charms; |  |
|  |  | con un detto sol tu puoi | with a single word you can |  |
|  |  | le mie pene consolar. | console my sufferings. |  |
|  |  | Vieni, e senti del mio core | Come, and feel the quick beating |  |
|  |  | il frequente palpitar . . . | of my heart . . . |  |
|  |  | Con un detto sol tuo puoi | With a single word you can |  |
|  |  | le mie pene consolar. | console my sufferings. |  |

(Many text lines repeated)

**MADDALENA**

|  |  |  |  |  |
|---|---|---|---|---|
| **44** | 5:19 | Ah! ah! rido ben di core, | Ha! Ha! I laugh heartily, | **B** |
|  |  | chè tai baie costan poco. | for such tales cost little. |  |

**GILDA**

Ah! cosí parlar d'amore . . .   Ah! To speak thus of love . . .

**MADDALENA**

Quanto valga il vostro gioco,   Believe me, I can judge
mel credete, sò apprezzar.   how much your game is worth.

**GILDA**

. . . a me pur l'infame ho udito!   . . . I too have heard the villain so!

**RIGOLETTO (to Gilda)**

Taci, il piangere non vale.   Hush, weeping is of no avail.

**GILDA**

Infelice cor tradito,   Unhappy, betrayed heart,
per angoscia non scoppiar. No, no!   do not burst with anguish. Ah, no!

**MADDALENA**

Son avvezza, bel signore,   I'm accustomed, handsome sir,
ad un simile scherzare.   to similar joking.
Mio bel signor!   My handsome sir!

**DUKE**

|  |  |  |  |  |
|---|---|---|---|---|
| **45** | 6:01 | Bella figlia dell'amore, etc. | Beautiful daughter of love, etc. | **A'** |
|  |  | Vieni! | Come! |  |

**RIGOLETTO**

Ch'ei mentiva sei sicura.   You are sure that he was lying.
Taci, e mia sarà la cura   Hush, and I will take care
la vendetta d'affrettar.   to hasten vengeance.
sì, pronta fia, sarà fatale,   Yes, it will be swift and fatal,
io saprollo fulminar.   I will know how to strike him down.
taci, taci . . .   Hush, hush . . .

**ALL CHARACTERS**

|  |  |  |  |
|---|---|---|---|
|  | Repeated text from above. |  | **C** |
|  | 7:27 | Coda, featuring all characters. | **Coda** |

Ⓢ **Now try the Listening Quiz.**

# Wagner and the Music Drama in Germany

*"How strange! Only when I compose do I fully understand the essential meaning of my works. Everywhere I discover secrets which hitherto had remained hidden to my eyes."*

Nineteenth-century Germany had no long-established opera tradition, as Italy and France did. The immediate predecessor of German Romantic opera was the ***Singspiel,*** a light or comic drama with spoken dialogue. Mozart's *Die Zauberflöte* (*The Magic Flute*) is a typical example of this style.

*Singspiel*

The greatest figure in German opera—and one of the most significant in the history of the Romantic era—was Richard Wagner, who created the ***music drama,*** a genre that attempted to integrate theater and music and did away with the concept of separate arias, duets, ensembles, and choruses. He looms as the single most important phenomenon in the artistic life of the later nineteenth century. Historians often divide the period into "before" and "after Wagner." The course of post-Romantic music is unimaginable without the impact of this complex and fascinating figure. We will consider his music drama *Die Walküre* (which includes the famous *Ride of the Valkyries*), a part of his cycle *The Ring of the Nibelung* (see below).

Music drama

## *Die Walküre*

 **Video**

Wagner did away with the concept of separate arias, duets, ensembles, choruses, and ballets, developing an "endless melody" that was molded to the natural inflections of the German language, more melodious than the traditional recitative, but more flexible and free than the traditional aria. He conceived opera as a total artwork (in German, ***Gesamtkunstwerk***) in which the arts of music, poetry, drama, and visual spectacle were fused together. The orchestra became its focal point and unifying element, fashioned out of concise themes, the ***leitmotifs,*** or "leading motives"—Wagner called them basic themes—that recur throughout a work, undergoing variation and development as do the themes and motives of a symphony. The leitmotifs carry specific meanings, suggesting in a few notes a person, an emotion, an idea, an object. Through a process of continual transformation, the leitmotifs trace the course of the drama, the changes in the characters, their experiences and memories, and their thoughts and hidden desires.

Gesamtkunstwerk

Leitmotifs

Wagner based his musical language on chromatic harmony, which he pushed to its then farthermost limits. Chromatic dissonance gives Wagner's music its restless, intensely emotional quality. Never before had unstable pitch combinations been used so eloquently to portray states of the soul.

*Ring of the Nibelung*

The story of *The Ring of the Nibelung* centers on the treasure of gold that lies hidden in the depths of the Rhine River and is guarded by three Rhine Maidens. Alberich the Nibelung, who comes from a hideous race of dwarfs that inhabit the dark regions below the earth, tries to make love to the maidens. When they repulse him, he renounces love, steals the treasure, and makes it into a ring that will bring unlimited power to its owner. Wotan, father of the gods (for whom our Wednesday, or Wotan's Day, is named), obtains the ring through trickery, whereupon Alberich pronounces a terrible curse: may the ring destroy the peace of mind of all who gain possession of it, may it bring them misfortune and death.

*In His Own Words*

The whole [Ring] will then become—out with it! I am not ashamed to say so—the greatest work of poetry ever written.

Thus begins the cycle of four dramas that ends only when the curse-bearing

## Richard Wagner (1813–1883)

**Richard Wagner** was born in Leipzig, Germany. At twenty, he abandoned his academic studies at the University of Leipzig and over the next six years gained practical experience conducting in provincial theaters. He married the actress Minna Planer when he was twenty-three and produced his first operas at this time. He wrote the librettos himself, as he did for all his later works. In this way, he was able to unify music and drama more than anyone had before.

Wagner's early opera, *Rienzi*, won a huge success in Dresden. With his next three works, *The Flying Dutchman, Tannhäuser,* and *Lohengrin,* Wagner took an important step by shifting his focus from the drama of historical intrigue to the idealized folk legend. He chose subjects derived from medieval German epics, displayed a profound feeling for nature, employed the supernatural as an element of the drama, and glorified the German land and people.

When a revolution broke out in Dresden in 1849, Wagner was sympathetic to the revolutionaries. When the revolt failed, he fled to Switzerland, where he commenced the most productive period of his career, including the creation of his important literary works, which set forth his theories of the ***music drama***, the name he gave his concept of opera that integrated theater and music completely. He next proceeded to put theory into practice in the cycle of four music dramas called *The Ring of the Nibelung*, and two more—*Tristan and Isolde* and *Die Meistersinger von Nürnberg*.

Wagner's musical scores accumulated without hope of performance; Europe contained neither singers nor a theater capable of presenting them. But he soon found support and admiration of the young monarch Ludwig II of Bavaria, who commissioned Wagner to complete the *Ring,* and Wagner picked up where he had left off a number of years earlier.

A theater was planned specifically for the presentation of Wagner's music dramas, which ultimately became the Festival Theater at Bayreuth (see illustration, p. 253). And he found a woman he considered his equal in will and courage—Cosima, the daughter of his old friend Liszt. She left her husband and children in order to join Wagner

The Wagnerian gospel spread across Europe as a new art-religion. The *Ring* cycle was completed in 1874, and the four dramas were presented to worshipful audiences at the first Bayreuth Festival two years later. At age seventy, Wagner undertook *Parsifal* (1877–82), a drama based on the legend of the Holy Grail. Wagner died shortly thereafter and was buried at Bayreuth.

**Major Works:** 13 operas (music dramas), including *Rienzi* (1842), *Der fliegende Holländer* (*The Flying Dutchman,* 1843), *Tannhäuser* (1845), *Lohengrin* (1850), *Tristan und Isolde* (1865), *Die Meistersinger von Nürnberg* (*The Mastersingers of Nuremberg,* 1868), and *Parsifal* (1882) • Cycle of music dramas: *Der Ring des Nibelung* (*The Ring of the Nibelung*), consisting of *Das Rheingold* (*The Rhine Gold,* 1869), *Die Walküre* (*The Valkyrie,* 1870), *Siegfried* (1876), and *Götterdämmerung* (*The Twilight of the Gods,* 1876) • Orchestral music • Piano music • Vocal and choral music • Writings: *Art and Revolution; The Art Work of the Future.*

◉ **iMusic:** *Ride of the Valkyries*

*In His Own Words*

True drama can be conceived only as resulting from the collective impulse of all the arts to communicate in the most immediate way with a collective public. . . . Thus the art of tone . . . will realize in the collective artwork its richest potential. . . . For in its isolation music has formed itself an organ capable of the most immeasurable expression—the orchestra.

ring is returned to the Rhine Maidens. Gods and heroes, mortals and Nibelungs, intermingle freely in this tale of betrayed love, broken promises, magic spells, and general corruption brought on by the lust for power. Wagner freely adapted the story from the myths of the Norse sagas and the legends associated with a medieval German epic poem, the *Nibelungenlied*. (Norse mythology and Wagner's *Ring of the Nibelung* were also the inspiration for J. R. R. Tolkien's epic *Lord of the Rings* and for the three popular movies of that literary work.)

**Tolkien's *Lord of the Rings***

Wagner wrote the four librettos in reverse order. First came his poem on the death of the hero Siegfried. This became the final opera, *Götterdämmerung,* in the course of which Siegfried, now possessor of the ring, betrays Brünnhilde, to whom

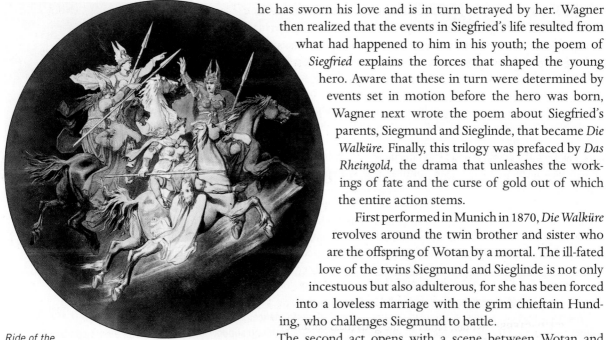

*Ride of the Valkyries,* from Wagner's opera *Die Walküre,* in a design by **Carl Emil Doepler** (c. 1876).

he has sworn his love and is in turn betrayed by her. Wagner then realized that the events in Siegfried's life resulted from what had happened to him in his youth; the poem of *Siegfried* explains the forces that shaped the young hero. Aware that these in turn were determined by events set in motion before the hero was born, Wagner next wrote the poem about Siegfried's parents, Siegmund and Sieglinde, that became *Die Walküre.* Finally, this trilogy was prefaced by *Das Rheingold,* the drama that unleashes the workings of fate and the curse of gold out of which the entire action stems.

First performed in Munich in 1870, *Die Walküre* revolves around the twin brother and sister who are the offspring of Wotan by a mortal. The ill-fated love of the twins Siegmund and Sieglinde is not only incestuous but also adulterous, for she has been forced into a loveless marriage with the grim chieftain Hunding, who challenges Siegmund to battle.

The second act opens with a scene between Wotan and Brünnhilde. She is one of the Valkyries, the nine daughters of Wotan, whose perpetual task is to circle the battlefield on their winged horses and swoop down to gather up the fallen heroes, whom they bear away to Valhalla, where they will sit forever feasting with the gods. At the insistence of Wotan's wife, Fricka (the goddess of marriage), Wotan realizes that Siegmund has violated the holiest law of the universe and that he must die in combat with Hunding. Wotan sadly realizes that even he must obey the law. Brünnhilde decides to disobey her father by shielding Siegmund. Wotan appears and holds out his spear, upon which Siegmund's sword is shattered. Hunding then buries his own spear in Siegmund's breast. Wotan, overcome by his son's death, turns a ferocious look upon Hunding, who falls dead. Then the god hurries off in pursuit of the daughter who dared to defy his command.

**Ride of the Valkyries**

Act III opens with the famous *Ride of the Valkyries,* a vivid orchestral picture of these nine warrior maidens who are on their way from the battlefield back to Valhalla, carrying fallen heroes slung across the saddles of their winged horses. They meet on a summit, calling to one another with the fearsome cry, "Hojotoho! Heiaha!" This prelude features some of Wagner's most brilliant scoring. The rustling strings and woodwinds give way to the memorable "Ride" theme (familiar from many movie sound tracks and even from the *What's Opera, Doc?* Warner Brothers cartoon), which is sounded repeatedly by a huge and varied brass section through a dense orchestral texture that builds to several climaxes beneath the warriors' voices (see Listening Guide 36). The Valkyries gather on a rocky peak to await Brünnhilde; she is the last to arrive, carrying Sieglinde and several fragments of Siegmund's sword. Sieglinde wants to die, but Brünnhilde tells her she must live to bear his son, who will become the world's mightiest hero. Brünnhilde remains to face her father's wrath. Her punishment is severe: she is to be deprived of her godhood, Wotan tells her, to become a mortal. He will put her to sleep on a rock, and she will fall prey to the first mortal who finds her. Brünnhilde begs him to soften her punishment: let him at least surround the rock with flames so that only a fearless hero will be able to penetrate the wall of fire. Wotan relents and grants her request. He kisses her on both eyes, which close at once.

 **iMusic**

*Ride of the Valkyries*

Striking the rock three times, he invokes Loge, the god of Fire. Flames spring up around the rock, and the "magic fire" leitmotif is heard, followed by the "magic sleep" and "slumber" motives. "Whosoever fears the tip of my spear shall never pass through the fire," he sings, as the orchestra announces the theme of Siegfried, the fearless hero who in the next music drama will force his way through the flames and awaken Brünnhilde with a kiss. The curtain falls on a version of the Sleeping Beauty legend as poetic as any artist ever created.

**Famous leitmotifs**

---

**LISTENING GUIDE 36**     ◉ Video | ◉ | DVD | CD 6 (19–29) | CD 3 (46–51)

# Wagner: *Die Walküre* (The Valkyrie), Act III, Opening

**5:36**

**DATE:** 1856; first performed 1870, Munich

**GENRE:** Music drama: second in cycle of 4 (*The Ring of the Nibelung*)

**CHARACTERS:** Wotan, father of the gods (bass-baritone)
Valkyries, the 9 daughters of Wotan
  Brünnhilde, favorite daughter (soprano), Ortlinde (soprano)
  Gerhilde (soprano), Helmwige (soprano)
  Schwertleite (alto), Waltraute (alto), Siegrune (alto)
  Rossweisse (alto), Grimgerde (alto)

---

**Act III, Scene 1: *Ride of the Valkyries***

**WHAT TO LISTEN FOR:**

| | |
|---|---|
| Melody | Swirling strings and woodwinds, then famous "Ride" leitmotif ascends, repeated many times; battle cries from soloists in call and response; continual melody |
| Rhythm/ Meter | Lively dotted rhythm in 9/8 for "Ride" leitmotif |
| Harmony | Leitmotif heard in minor and major |
| Texture | Polyphonic, combines main theme and swirling idea |

| | |
|---|---|
| Expression | Excited mood; huge dynamic contrasts; evokes battle cries and flying warriors |
| Performing Forces | Huge orchestra featuring many brass (including 8 French horns, bass trumpet, various sized trombones, Wagner tubas and contrabass tuba); woodwinds (including piccolos, English horn, and bass clarinet); large percussion section (including cymbals, triangle, glockenspiel, gong) and many string players (including 6 harps) |

---

| 46 | 0:00 | Orchestral prelude, marked *Lebhaft* (Lively), in 9/8 meter. |
| | | Rushing string figure alternates with fast wavering in woodwinds, then |
| | 0:08 | insistent dotted figure begins in horns and low strings. |
| | | Swirling string and woodwind lines, accompanied by dotted figure. |
| 47 | 0:23 | Famous "Ride" motive, heard first in minor key in horns: |

| | 0:35 | "Ride" motive, now heard in major key in trumpets. |
| | | 4-note dotted motive exchanged between low and high brass instruments, heard above swirling idea. |

*Continued on following page*

|48| 1:06    "Ride" motive heard *fortissimo*, as curtain opens.

*(Four Valkyries, in full armor, have settled on the highest peak above a cave.)*

**TEXT**                                                                    **TRANSLATION**

GERHILDE (calling from the highest peak)

|49| 1:20    Hojotoho! Hojotoho! Heiaha! Heiaha!                            Hoyotoho! Hoyotoho! Heiaha! Heiaha!
             Helmwige! Hier! Hieher mit dem Ross!                          Helmwige, here! Bring your horse here!

Gerhilde's disjunct battle cry, which is echoed by her sisters:

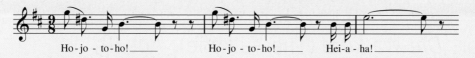

Ho - jo - to - ho!_____    Ho - jo - to - ho!_____    Hei - a - ha!_____

HELMWIGE (answering in the distance)

Hojotoho! Hojotoho! Heiaha!                                                Hoyotoho! Hoyotoho! Heiaha!

1:45    "Ride" motive heard in low brass, first in minor, then major; ideas exchanged in brass.
        Climax with timpani and cymbals on following cry, then *decrescendo*.

GERHILDE, WALTRAUTE, SCHWERTLEITE (calling out to Brünnhilde, who approaches)

Heiaha! Heiaha!                                                            Heiaha! Heiaha!

ORTLINDE

|50| 2:23    Zu Ortlinde's Stute stell' deinen Hengst,                     Put your stallion next to Ortlinde's mare:
             Mit meiner Grauen gras't gern dein Brauner!                   Your bay will like grazing with my grey.

WALTRAUTE

Wer hängt dir im Sattel?                                                   Who hangs from your saddle?

HELMWIGE

Sintolt, der Hegeling!                                                     Sintolt the Hegeling!

SCHWERTLEITE

Führ deinen Braunen fort von der Grauen:                                   Take your bay away from my grey.
Ortlindes Märes trägt Wittig, den Irming!                                  Ortlinde's mare carries Wittig the Irming.

GERHILDE

Als Feinde nur sah ich Sintolt und Wittig!                                 I only saw them as enemies, Sintolt and Wittig.

ORTLINDE

Heiaha! Die Stute stösst mir der Hengst!                                   Heiaha! The mare is being shoved by the stallion!

GERHILDE (laughing)

Ha ha ha ha ha ha ha ha!                                                   Ha ha ha ha ha ha ha ha!
Der Recken Zwist entzweit noch die Rosse!                                  The warriors' dispute upsets even the steeds!

HELMWIGE

Ruhig, Brauner! Brich nicht den Frieden.                                   Be still, my bay! Do not disturb the peace!

WALTRAUTE

Hoioho! Hoioho! Siegrune, hier!                                            Hoyoho! Hoyoho! Siegrune, here!
Wo säumst du so lang?                                                      Where were you dallying so long?

3:06    "Ride" motive heard as Siegrune arrives.

**SIEGRUNE**

| | |
|---|---|
| Arbeit gab's! | There was work to be done! |
| Sind die and'ren schon da? | Are the others already here? |

**SCHWERTLEITE, WALTRAUTE**

| | |
|---|---|
| Hojotoho! Hojotoho! Heiaha! | Hoyotoho! Hoyotoho! Heiaha! |

**GERHILDE**

| | |
|---|---|
| Heiaha! | Heiaha! |

**GRIMGERDE, ROSSWEISSE (appear illuminated by flash of lighting)**

| | |
|---|---|
| Hojotoho! Hojotoho! Heiaha! | Hoyotoho! Hoyotoho! Heiha! |

**WALTRAUTE**

| | |
|---|---|
| Grimgerd' und Rossweisse! | Grimgerde and Rossweisse! |

**GERHILDE**

| | |
|---|---|
| Sie reiten zu zwei. | They are riding abreast. |

[51]   3:43   Ride motive heard *fortissimo*, at change to major key, in full orchestra with cymbals and triangle.

**HELMWIGE, ORTLINDE, SIEGRUNE**

| | |
|---|---|
| Gegrüsst, ihr Reisige! Rossweiss' | Greetings, riders! Rossweisse |
| und Grimgerde! | and Grimgerde! |

**ROSSWEISSE, GRIMGERD**

| | |
|---|---|
| Hojotoho! Hojotoho! Heiaha! | Hoyotoho! Hoyotoho! Heiha! |

**THE OTHER 6 VALKYRIES**

4:14   Hojotoho! Hojotoho! Heiaha! Heiaha!   Hoyotoho! Hoyotoho! Heiaha! Heiaha!

Gradual *decrescendo* in orchestra.

**GERHILDE**

4:54   In'Wald mit den Rossen zu Rast und Weid'!   Into the woods with the steeds to rest and graze.

**ORTLINDE**

| | |
|---|---|
| Führet die Mähren fern von einander, | Place the mares far from each other, |
| Bis unsrer Helden Hass sich gelegt! | Until our heroes' hatred is abated! |

**VALKYRIES (laughing)**

| | |
|---|---|
| Ha ha ha ha ha ha ha ha! | Ha ha ha ha ha ha ha ha! |

**HELMWIGE**

| | |
|---|---|
| Der Helden Grimm büsste schon die Graue! | The heroes' anger made even the grey suffer! |

**VALKYRIES (laughing)**

| | |
|---|---|
| Ha ha ha ha ha ha ha ha! | Ha ha ha ha ha ha ha ha! |

**ROSSWEISSE, GRIMGERDE**

| | |
|---|---|
| Hojotoho! Hojotoho! | Hoyotoho! Hoyotoho! |

**THE OTHER 6 VALKYRIES**

| | |
|---|---|
| Wilkommen! Wilkommen! | Welcome! Welcome! |

ⓔ **Now try the Listening Quiz.**

Italian singer Gabriella Besanzoni (1888–1962) as a colorful Carmen.

# Exoticism in Opera

We have seen that a yearning for far-off lands was an important component of the Romantic imagination. The urge found a perfect outlet in opera, which could be set anywhere in the world. A prime example is Verdi's *Aida,* which manages within the traditional idiom of Italian opera to evoke ancient Egypt under the pharaohs. The turn-of-the-century Italian master Giacomo Puccini (1858–1924) produced two well-known operas with Asian settings: *Turandot,* based on a legend of ancient China, and *Madame Butterfly* (see p. 275), a romantic drama set in late-nineteenth-century Japan.

French composers have always been fascinated by Spain. Thus a number of French orchestral classics describe the colorful peninsula, as Bizet does in his alluring opera *Carmen.* His brilliant orchestration and rhythmic vitality evoke the warmth and color of the southern country (iMusic, *Toreador Song,* from *Carmen*). This opera remains one of the great examples of nineteenth-century exoticism, its picturesque atmosphere inescapably romantic.

## Critical Thinking

**1.** What innovations did Wagner bring to the world of opera?

**2.** What famous literary works became the basis for Romantic operas?

**3.** Why was opera a good vehicle for nationalism? For exoticism?

# 33

# Late Romantic and Post-Romantic Music

"I would be willing to set even a newspaper or a letter . . . to music, but in the theater the public will stand for anything except boredom."

–Giuseppe Verdi

**KEY POINTS**

> **StudySpace** wwnorton.com/enjoy

- Choral music grew in popularity during the Romantic era, and favored genres include *part songs* (unaccompanied secular songs in three or four parts), the oratorio, the Mass, and the **Requiem Mass**. Verdi's Requiem is one of the masterworks of late Romantic choral repertory.

- *Ballet* became an independent dramatic form in the eighteenth century, particularly in France and Russia. The three ballets of Russian composer Peter Ilyich Tchaikovsky—*Swan Lake, Sleeping Beauty,* and *The Nutcracker*—remain favorites today.

- Two important movements surfaced at the turn of the twentieth century: *post-Romanticism*, in Germany, Austria, and Italy; and *Impressionism*, in France.

- The post-Romantic composer Giacomo Puccini wrote some of the best-loved operas of all time, including *Madame Butterfly*, which combines two end-of-the-century trends: *verismo* (realism) and *exoticism* (Japanese culture and music).

I n the last decades of the nineteenth century, composers took different paths in their musical expression, some choosing to steer a traditional course, retaining the musical language of the late Romantic era, while others, as we shall see in later chapters, struck out in entirely new directions. In this chapter, we will investigate three dramatic masterworks representing very different genres. All fell under, and some reacted against, the momentous influence of Wagner's new musical language, rich in chromaticism and emotive power. Verdi's powerful Requiem Mass will allow us to view how choral music became a major outlet for Romantic composers; the world-famous ballet *Nutcracke*r, by Russian composer Peter Ilyich Tchaikovsky, demonstrates how this genre became one of the most important vehicles for dramatic expression; and Giacomo Puccini's opera *Madame Butterfly* shows us a new, more realistic approach to opera that also evokes new ideals of exoticism.

*In His Own Words*

The oldest, truest, most beautiful organ of music, the origin to which our music owes its being, is the human voice.

—*Richard Wagner*

## Romantic Choral Music

The nineteenth century witnessed a spreading of the democratic ideal and an enormous expansion of the audience for music. This climate was uniquely favorable to choral singing, a group activity enjoyed by increasing numbers of amateur music

Verdi conducting a performance of his Requiem Mass at the Paris Opéra-Comique in 1874.

lovers that played an important role in the musical life of the Romantic era.

Choral music offered the masses an outlet for their artistic energies. The repertory centered on the great choral heritage of the past. Nevertheless, if choral music was to remain a vital force, its literature had to be enriched by new works that would reflect the spirit of the time. The list of composers active in this area includes some of the most important names of the nineteenth century: Schubert, Berlioz, Felix and Fanny Mendelssohn, Clara and Robert Schumann, Liszt, Verdi, Brahms, and Dvořák. These composers produced a body of choral music that represents some of the best creative efforts of the Romantic period.

In addition to a vast repertory of secular choral pieces known as ***part songs*** (written for three or four parts), large-scale genres of choral music in the nineteenth century were also cultivated, including the Mass, the Requiem Mass, and the oratorio. We have seen that all three were originally intended to be performed in church, but by the nineteenth century they had found a wider audience in the concert hall. This is certainly the case with Verdi's monumental Requiem Mass.

## Verdi's Requiem

### *In His Own Words*

No one understands the meaning of life better than Verdi, no one expressed it better than he did. He was a man among men: this was a risk he wanted to take. If he had been offered the chance to be a god, he would have turned it down, because he wanted to feel a human being and a victor in the fiery circle of our earthly ordeal.

*—Arrigo Boito*

Verdi's Requiem sets the Roman Catholic Mass for the Dead text but the proportions of this monumental composition make it more appropriate for the stage than as a liturgical work for the church. Verdi first conceived writing a Requiem Mass in 1868, on the death of composer Gioachino Rossini, inviting a number of composers to collaborate on a collective tribute and setting the Requiem text *Libera me* as his contribution. This project never came to pass, but with the death of the famous Italian poet and humanist Alessandro Manzoni, a man whom Verdi admired greatly, the composer wrote the whole work himself. His Requiem Mass was first performed in May 1874 to commemorate the first anniversary of Manzoni's death. Although some complained that the Mass was too theatrical—calling for a large chorus, orchestra, and soloists—the Mass quickly won acclaim across Europe.

The most powerful part of the Requiem Mass is the *Dies irae*, a text which deals with the last judgment, reminding the listener of the transience of life on earth. Here we will consider the *Libera me* (Deliver me, O Lord) section of the Mass, which reprises some of the earlier texts, including the *Dies irae* (Day of wrath) and also the *Requiem aeternam* (Grant them eternal rest), using the same themes (see Listening Guide 37). In a funeral Mass, the *Libera me* is a prayer recited over the coffin, asking for mercy upon the deceased at the Last Judgment. We hear first in this movement a recap of the terrifying strains of *Dies irae*, proclaiming the day of judgment with the full force of the chorus and orchestra. The dramatic mood rekindles again as the soprano soloist begs for deliverance from the judgment of the world by fire. The emotional tension lets up as the *Dies irae* text is sounded from the depths of the choir's bass section, followed by an ethereal, angelic call by the solo soprano for eternal rest and perpetual light, accompanied

# Verdi and the Power of Music

Verdi's stirring Requiem Mass was first performed in 1874, to commemorate the one-year anniversary of the death of Italian writer Alessandro Manzoni. Its premiere, in Manzoni's hometown of Milan, was a huge success and was followed by performances at the La Scala opera house and in Paris at the Opéra-Comique. The fiery music for the *Dies irae* brings to mind the apocalyptic destruction of the world and the Day of Judgment, just as Michelangelo's dramatic *Last Judgment* fresco in the Sistine Chapel does (see illustration at right), an artwork that Verdi most certainly knew and admired.

Today, Verdi's Requiem is one of the most widely performed choral masterworks, though no performance could match the emotional impact of those given in 1943–44 by a pickup choir of about 150. These performances were given in the notorious Nazi concentration camp Terezín in the former Czechoslovakia by Jewish prisoners condemned to die. The project was organized by conductor Raphael Schaechter, an inmate in the prison who, understanding the power of music to lift one's spirits and knowing this was their only means of defiance toward the Nazis, recruited singers and instrumentalists. In fact, he had to reorganize the choir several times as people were shipped off to the death camps. Some members of the camp's Council of Jewish Elders opposed Schaechter's plan, since Verdi's work is a Catholic Mass. But many others found emotional strength in the music, allowing it to bolster their faltering spirits in the face of death. And Schaechter's mantra—"We can sing to them what we cannot say to them" —maintained a certain determination. The section we heard from the Requiem, the haunting *Libera me* ("Set me free"), was especially telling for those imprisoned. Terezín was different from other death camps: it was the Nazi's "showcase" prison, where inmates were allowed to take part in cultural and artistic activities, but only so that the visiting Red Cross teams would find the conditions acceptable. Out of the more than 150,000 Jews sent there, about 17,000 survived.

Recently, conductor Murry Sidlin resurrected this historical event in a series of multimedia presentations that includes a performance of the Requiem accompanied by images of Terezín and narratives from survivors of the concentration camp. This drama—*Defiant Requiem*—premiered on PBS on Holocaust Remembrance Day, 2004, and is a powerful account of this very dark period in history. One survivor summed up her experience in the interview: "God sent us Verdi— God sent us the music—God sent us Rafael Schaechter—God sent us the way to live."

---

**iMusic**

Verdi: *Dies irae,* from Requiem Mass

Trumpet-playing angels herald the Day of Judgment, in this detail from the *Last Judgment* by **Michelangelo** (1475–1564).

very softly by an *a cappella* choir. This sinuous expressive section closes with the soprano's octave leap toward the heavens, sung at an impossible *pppp* dynamic level. Verdi's Requiem Mass is indeed a fitting tribute to the great man who inspired it; the intensity and emotional depth Verdi instilled in the work are almost without parallel (see HTTN 9).

# Verdi: Requiem, *Libera me*, excerpt                     5:46

**DATE:** 1874

**GENRE:** Requiem Mass

## WHAT TO LISTEN FOR:

### *Libera me: Dies irae*

| | |
|---|---|
| Melody | Choral declamation of theme; answered by rushing strings (descending, then ascending) |
| Rhythm/ Meter | Agitated allegro with accented chords and offbeats (timpani) |
| Harmony | Pounding chords in minor key |
| Expression | Very loud and forceful, then mood shifts to soft and mysterious |
| Performing Forces | Soprano solo, chorus, and large orchestra; strong percussion and brass |
| Text | Responsory from Catholic funeral Mass |

### *Libera me: Requiem aeternam*

| | |
|---|---|
| Melody | Soaring soprano solo; expressive lines and leaps |
| Rhythm/ Meter | Slow-paced duple meter |
| Harmony | Begins in minor, then shifts to major; very chromatic |
| Texture | Homophonic, chantlike treatment; text carefully declaimed |
| Expression | Soft dynamics with careful shaping; peaceful mood (marked *dolcissimo*, sweetly) |
| Performing Forces | Solo soprano and *a cappella* chorus |

---

| 52 | 0:00 | Forceful chords in the orchestra. | |
| | 0:05 | *Dies irae, dies illa* (text repeats) | The day of wrath, that day of |
| | 0:43 | *calamitatis et miseriae, dies magna et amara valde.* | calamity and misery, a great day of bitterness. |

| 53 | 1:10 | *Dies irae, dies illa* | The day of wrath, that day of |
| | | *calamitatis et miseriae, dies magna et amara valde.* | calamity and misery, a great day of bitterness, |
| | 1:44 | *Dum veneris judicare saeculum per ignem.* | when thou shalt come to judge the world by fire. |

| 54 | 2:23 | *Requiem aeternam dona eis, Domine,* | Grant them eternal rest, O Lord, |
| | 3:00 | *et lux perpetua luceat eis.* | and may perpetual light shine upon them. |

(Soprano solo *ppp* — Re - qui - em æ - - ter - nam)

🎧 **Now try the Listening Quiz.**

# Tchaikovsky and the Ballet

"Dance is the hidden language of the soul."

—*Martha Graham*

*In His Own Words*

O body swayed to music,
O brightening glance,
How can we know the
dancer from the dance?

—*W. B. Yeats*

Ballet has been an adornment of European culture for centuries. Ever since the Renaissance it has been central to lavish festivals and theatrical entertainments presented at the courts of kings and dukes. Royal weddings and similar celebrations were accompanied by spectacles with scenery, costumes, and staged dancing. Louis XIV himself, as the Sun King, took part in one. Elaborate ballets were also featured in the operas of Lully and Rameau and in the *divertissements* by French court composer Mouret (see p. 134).

The eighteenth century saw the rise of ballet as an independent art form. French and Russian ballet achieved preeminence in the nineteenth century. And in 1847, the great choreographer Marius Petipa created the dances for more than a hundred works, invented the structure of the classic *pas de deux* (dance for two), and brought the art of staging ballets to unprecedented heights.

The history of early-twentieth-century ballet is closely identified with the career of the impresario Serge Diaghilev (1872–1929), whose Paris-based dance company, the Ballets Russes, opened up a new chapter in the cultural life of Europe. He surrounded his dancers—the greatest were Vaslav Nijinsky and Tamara Karsavina—with productions worthy of their talents. He invited artists such as Picasso and Braque to paint the scenery, and commissioned the three ballets—*The Firebird, Petrushka,* and *The Rite of Spring*—that catapulted the composer Igor Stravinsky to fame. (We will study Stravinsky's ballet *The Rite of Spring* in Chapter 36.) Diaghilev's ballets have served as models for the composers and choreographers who followed.

Few composers typify the end-of-the-century mood as does Peter Ilyich Tchaikovsky, who belonged to a generation that saw its truths crumbling and found none to replace them. This composer expressed, above all, the pessimism that engulfed the late Romantic movement.

## The Nutcracker

Tchaikovsky had a natural affinity for the ballet. His three ballets—*Swan Lake, The Sleeping Beauty,* and *The Nutcracker*—were soon established as basic works of the Russian repertory.

*The Nutcracker* was based on a fanciful story by E. T. A. Hoffmann. An expanded version by Alexandre Dumas *père* served as the basis for choreographer Petipa's scenario. Act I takes place at a Christmas party during which two children, Clara and Fritz, receive a nutcracker from their godfather. The children go to bed but

A traditional Russian nutcracker—a toy soldier who comes alive in Tchaikovsky's ballet.

### Peter Ilyich Tchaikovsky (1840–1893)

The son of a Russian government official, Tchaikovsky had initially planned a career in the government, but at the age of twenty-three, he entered the newly founded Conservatory of St. Petersburg. He was immediately recommended by Anton Rubinstein, director of the school, for a teaching post in the new Moscow Conservatory. His twelve years in Moscow saw the production of some of his most successful works.

Extremely sensitive by nature, Tchaikovsky was subject to attacks of depression. The social issues associated with being a homosexual may have led him to marry a student at the conservatory, Antonina Milyukova, but they soon separated. Good fortune followed when Nadezhda von Meck, the wealthy widow of an industrialist, sent Tchaikovsky money to go abroad, and launched him on the most productive period of his career. Von Meck's passion was music, especially Tchaikovsky's but bound by the rigid conventions of her time and her class, she had to be certain that her enthusiasm was for the artist, not the man; hence she stipulated that she never meet the recipient of her patronage.

Tchaikovsky's fame spread quickly. He was the first Russian whose music appealed to Western tastes—his music was performed in Vienna, Berlin, and Paris—and in 1891 he was invited to participate in the ceremonies for the opening of Carnegie Hall in New York.

In 1893, he conducted his *Pathétique* Symphony in St. Petersburg, where the work met with a lukewarm reception. He died within several weeks, at the age of fifty-three, and the tragic tone of his last work led to rumors that he had committed suicide. More likely he contracted cholera from tainted water.

To Russians, Tchaikovsky is a national artist. He himself declared, "I am Russian through and through!" At the same time, Tchaikovsky came under the spell of Italian opera, French ballet, and German symphony and song. These he joined to the strain of folk melody that was his heritage as a Russian, imposing on this mixture his sharply defined personality.

**Major Works:** Stage works—8 operas and 3 ballets: *Swan Lake* (1877), *The Sleeping Beauty* (1890), and *The Nutcracker* (1892) • Orchestral music, including 7 symphonies (1 unfinished), 3 piano concertos, 1 violin concerto, symphonic poems (*Romeo and Juliet*), and overtures (*1812 Overture*) • Chamber and keyboard music • Choral music • Songs.

ⓢ **iMusic:** *March,* from *The Nutcracker*
*Waltz of the Flowers*, from *The Nutcracker*

ⓢ **Video:** Symphony No. 5, III

Clara returns to gaze at her gift, falls asleep, and begins to dream. First, she is terrified to see mice scampering around the tree. Then the dolls she has received come alive and fight a battle with the mice, which reaches a climax in the combat between the Nutcracker, now a handsome prince, and the Mouse King. Clara helps her beloved Nutcracker by throwing a slipper at the Mouse King, who is vanquished. The Nutcracker then becomes the Prince, who takes Clara away with him.

A performance of *Trepak* from Tchaikovsky's ballet *The Nutcracker*, by the Royal Ballet at Covent Garden, London, in 2008.

**LISTENING GUIDE 38**                    ⑤ | DVD | CD 6 (40–48) | CD 3 (55–60)

# Tchaikovsky: *The Nutcracker*, Two Dances                    2:56

**DATE:** 1892

**GENRE:** Ballet (from which an orchestral suite was made)

**BASIS:** E. T. A. Hoffmann story, expanded by Alexandre Dumas *père*

**CHOREOGRAPHER:** Marius Petipa

| **SEQUENCE OF DANCES:** | *March* | *Chinese Dance* |
|---|---|---|
| | ***Dance of the Sugar Plum Fairy*** | *Dance of the Toy Flutes* |
| | ***Trepak*** | *Waltz of the Flowers* |
| | *Arab Dance* | |

---

*Dance of the Sugar Plum Fairy*: Andante non troppo                    1:44

**WHAT TO LISTEN FOR:**

| Melody | Staccato melody, somewhat chromatic | Expression | Quiet and mysterious mood |
|---|---|---|---|
| Rhythm/ Meter | Bouncy duple meter | Performing Forces | Bell-like timbre of celesta, accompanied by bass clarinet and pizzicato strings |
| Form | 3-part (**A-B-A**) | | |

---

| 55 | 0:00 | **A section** <br> Short introduction (4 measures) of pizzicato strings. |
|---|---|---|

|  | 0:08 | Main theme introduced by celesta, staccato in high range (heard in dialogue with bass clarinet): |
|---|---|---|

| 56 | 0:39 | **B section** <br> Brief section with arched lines in woodwinds and celesta, answered by strings. |
|---|---|---|

| 57 | 1:11 | **A section** <br> Solo celesta leads back to main theme, accompanied by plucked strings. Closes with loud pizzicato chord. |
|---|---|---|

---

*Trepak* (Russian Dance): Tempo di trepak, molto vivace (very lively)                    1:12

**WHAT TO LISTEN FOR:**

| Melody | Short, staccato note melody, descending, with *sfz* (sforzandos) | Form | 3-part (**A-B-A**) |
|---|---|---|---|
| Rhythm/ Meter | Lively peasant dance, heavy accents; accelerando | Expression | Vivacious mood; builds to frenzy at end |
| Texture | Homophonic; contrapuntal **B** section | Performing Forces | Tambourine featured with strings and woodwinds; trumpet fanfare |

*Continued on following page*

| 58 | 0:00 | **A section**<br>Lively dance tune in strings, repeated in full orchestra: |  |
|----|------|---------------------------------------------------------|---|
| 59 | 0:27 | **B section**<br>Brief diversion in same rhythmic style, melody in low strings. | |
| 60 | 0:47 | **A section**<br>Return of dance tune, quickens at end, with trumpet fanfare and syncopations. | |

◎ **Now try the Listening Quiz.**

Act II takes place in Confiturembourg, the land of sweets, which is ruled by the Sugar Plum Fairy. The Prince presents Clara to his family, and a celebration follows, with a series of dances that reveal all the attractions of this magic realm.

◎ **iMusic**

*March*, from *Nutcracker*

The energetic *March* from Act I is played as the guests arrive for the party. "I have discovered a new instrument in Paris," Tchaikovsky wrote to his publisher, "something between a piano and a glockenspiel, with a divinely beautiful tone, and I want to introduce it into the ballet." The instrument was the *celesta,* whose timbre perfectly suits the Sugar Plum Fairy's dance with her veils. In the *Trepak* (Russian

◎ **iMusic**

*Waltz of the Flowers*

Dance, with the famous Cossack squat-kick; see illustration, p. 272), the orchestral sound is enlivened by a tambourine. Other exotic dances follow, from Arabia and China, climaxing with the *Waltz of the Flowers*. This engaging work conjures up everything we have come to associate with the Romantic ballet.

## Meet the Performers

### Mikhail Baryshnikov

**"Dancing is my obsession—my life."**

Meet Mikhail Baryshnikov, perhaps the greatest living dancer. Born in Latvia in 1948, Baryshnikov trained from a young age in Riga, Latvia, and then in Leningrad, where he was accepted into Russia's most important ballet school. There he studied with the legendary dance master Alexander Pushkin, after which he won a starring role with the prestigious Kirov Ballet company. On a tour to Canada in 1974, Baryshnikov finished his performance of *Don Quixote* in Toronto and then defected by jumping into a "getaway" car, disappearing into the Canadian wilderness. Much admired in the West, Baryshnikov soon won a lead with the American Ballet Theater in New York City, partnering with Natalia Makarova, who had defected earlier.

His dance style has frequently been compared with legendary dancers Vaslav Nijinsky (who premiered Debussy's *Afternoon of a Faun*) and Rudolf Nureyev, also a Pushkin pupil and who defected from the Kirov Ballet, moving on to international stardom. Baryshnikov also danced with the New York City Ballet, where he expanded his arsenal of styles and techniques working with choreographer George Balanchine. He made his film premiere in *The*

*Turning Point* (1977), for which he received an Oscar nomination, and he starred in the Academy Award–nominated film *White Nights* (1985). In 1980, he was appointed artistic director of the American Ballet Theater, and later founded his own, more progressive company—White Oak

Mikhail Baryshnikov in a New York City Ballet production of *The Nutcracker.*

Dance Project, which he co-founded with dancer Mark Morris—to bring modern dance to the masses. You may remember him from the last season of *Sex and the City*, where he played a famous Russian artist and Carrie's (Sarah Jessica Parker's) love interest.

**Check out these DVDs of Mikhail Baryshnikov:** His classic *Nutcracker*, with the American Ballet Theater (1977), and the film *White Nights* (1985).

# The Post-Romantic Era

*"God touched me with His little finger and said, 'Write for the theater,
only for the theater.' And I obeyed the supreme command."*

—*Giacomo Puccini*

It became apparent toward the end of the nineteenth century that the Romantic impulse had run its course. In the period from about 1890 to 1910, composers took several divergent paths. **Impressionism**, embraced by French composers Claude Debussy and Maurice Ravel, heralded the modernist age with its wholly new sense of timbre and movement (we will consider the music of these composers in a later chapter). The other path—**post-Romanticism**—was highly influenced by Wagner's chromatic language, pushing it to its limits.

The late Romantic ideals were carried into the post-Romantic era through the Italian operatic tradition—in particular, with Giacomo Puccini—and in the works of German composers such as Richard Strauss (1864–1949) and Gustav Mahler (1860–1911), both remembered for inspired orchestral writing infused with sensuous lyricism. We will consider one champion of post-Romanticism: Puccini. His much-loved opera *Madame Butterfly* radiates an *exoticism* that was gaining popularity in the arts at the time (see p. 207).

# Puccini and Verismo Opera

Giacomo Puccini was the main voice among a group of opera composers associated with a movement known as *verismo* (realism). The advocates of this trend tried to bring into the theater the naturalness of writers such as Emile Zola and Henrik Ibsen. Instead of choosing historical or mythological themes, they picked subjects from everyday life and treated them in down-to-earth fashion. The most famous operas in this tradition include *La bohème* (*Bohemian Life*, 1896) and *Tosca* (1900), both by Puccini, and *I Pagliacci* (The Clowns, 1892) by Ruggero Leoncavallo. Although it was a short-lived movement, verismo had counterparts in Germany and France and produced some of the best-loved works in the operatic repertory, including Puccini's *Madame Butterfly*.

*La Japonaise* (1876), by **Claude Monet** (1840–1926), depicting the 19th-century Paris fad for all things Japanese.

## *Madame Butterfly*

 **Video**

Puccini's style emphasizes soaring melodies and a rich manipulation of orchestral timbres and colors, as well as elements borrowed from Wagner, notably his use of leitmotifs, or recurring melodies. Puccini's style is deceivingly simple, yet his operas are complex mechanisms built out of many different influences.

Puccini's inspiration for the opera *Madame Butterfly* came in 1900 during a visit to London, where he attended a performance of David Belasco's play *Madame Butterfly,* a dramatization of a short story by John Luther Long, which was in turn taken from Pierre Loti's tale *Madame Chrysanthème*. The libretto was by Ilica and Giacosa.

Like his other operas, Puccini's *Madame Butterfly* tells the story of a tragic-heroic female protagonist—here, a young geisha named Cio-Cio-San (Madame Butterfly) from Nagasaki who renounces her profession and religion in order to marry an American naval officer named Pinkerton. (A *geisha* is most closely equivalent to a courtesan in Western culture; see Btw, p. 278.) The two, who have never met before, get married in a house promised to the couple by the marriage broker. Pinkerton departs soon thereafter. When he returns several years later—with his new American wife in tow—Pinkerton learns that Butterfly has given birth to their son and decides to take the child to America. Butterfly

## Giacomo Puccini (1858–1924)

**Giacomo Puccini** was born in Lucca, Italy, the son of a church organist. He found himself attracted to the theater, especially opera, and in 1880 he traveled to Milan, where he studied at the Conservatory. For *Manon Lescaut*, his first success, he teamed up with librettists Luigi Illica and Giuseppe Giacosa, both of whom also collaborated with him on the three most successful operas of the early twentieth century: *La bohème* (1896), *Tosca* (1900), and *Madame Butterfly* (1904).

His travels to oversee the international premieres of several of his works were demanding. In 1903, a serious car crash left him bedridden for six months, and in 1908 his infidelity to his wife caused a public scandal. "I am always falling in love," he once declared. "When I no longer am, make my funeral." In 1910, his *The Girl of the Golden West* received its world premiere at the Metropolitan Opera House in New York; this was followed by a trio of three one-act works that included *Gianni Schicchi* (1918), one of his best-loved masterpieces.

Puccini's last opera, *Turandot,* is based on a Chinese fairy tale about a beautiful but cruel princess. Sick with cancer, Puccini pushed on to complete the project, but he died in 1924 before finishing the final scene. His friend Franco Alfano completed the opera, using Puccini's sketches. The first performance occurred in 1926 at La Scala, and was conducted by Arturo Toscanini, Puccini's greatest interpreter. The opera ended as Puccini had requested, without the final scene—Toscanini laid down his baton during the lament over the body of Li, turned to the audience and said in a choking voice, "Here ends the master's work."

**Major Works:** 12 operas, including *Manon Lescaut* (1893), *La bohème* (1896), *Madame Butterfly* (1904), *La fanciulla del west* (*The Girl of the Golden West,* 1910), *Turandot* (1926), and *Gianni Schicchi* (1918) • Choral works • Solo songs • Orchestral, chamber, and solo piano works.

### In His Own Words

I have had a visit today from Mme. Ohyama, wife of the Japanese ambassador. . . . She has promised to send me native Japanese music. I sketched the story of the libretto for her, and she liked it, especially as just such a story as Butterfly's is known to her as having happened in real life.

The geisha Cio-Cio-San on the cover of the earliest English vocal score of *Madame Butterfly,* published by Ricordi. Design by **Leopold Metlicovitz** (1868–1944).

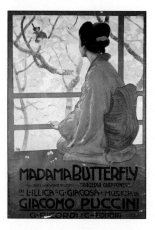

accepts his decision with dignity, but rather than return to her life as a geisha, she commits suicide (the samurai warrior's ritual *seppuku,* also known as *hara-kiri*). Despite its elements of *verismo,* Butterfly herself is not a believable character—yet it is her naivety and vulnerability that makes her a beloved heroine.

*Madame Butterfly* marks a turn-of-the-century interest in exoticism. The entire score is tinged with Japanese color: traditional Japanese melodies are juxtaposed with pentatonic and whole-tone passages, and instrument combinations evoking the timbres of a Japanese ***gagaku*** orchestra (with harp, flute and piccolo, and bells) are heard. Simple moments in the score—a single, unaccompanied melody, for example—have their visual equivalents in the clear lines of Japanese prints. Here too Puccini captures the ritualistic aspect of Japanese life. Another exotic touch is heard in the opening of Act I, when Puccini makes a brief reference to *The Star-Spangled Banner.*

Our selection is from Act II, set three years after the marriage. Butterfly has heard nothing from her husband, which leads her maid Suzuki to doubt that Pinkerton will ever return. She is quickly rebuked, however, in Butterfly's soaring aria, "Un bel dì" (One beautiful day), in which the young bride pictures their happy reunion and recalls Pinkerton's promise to return "when the robins build their nests" (see Listening Guide 39).

The aria "Un bel dì" is one of the most memorable in all opera literature. At first, Butterfly sings with a distant, ethereal quality, accompanied by solo violin, while she dreams of Pinkerton's return. The intensity rises when she envisons seeing his ship in the harbor. She relates the vision and her reaction in a speechlike melody that peaks on the word "morire" (die), as she explains how she will playfully hide from him at first in order not to die at their reunion. The emotional level builds—along with the dynamics—as Butterfly swears that "all this will happen." Her final soaring line climaxes on "l'aspetto" (I will wait for him), with the orchestra now playing the heartrending music at *fff.*

**LISTENING GUIDE 39**    ⓥ Video | ⓓ DVD | **CD 6 (49–50)** | CD 3 (61–62)

# Puccini: "Un bel dì," from *Madame Butterfly*, Act II    4:35

| | |
|---|---|
| **DATE:** | 1904 |
| **LIBRETTISTS:** | Giuseppe Giacosa and Luigi Ilica |
| **BASIS:** | Play by David Belasco, from short story by John Luther Long, derived from Pierre Loti's tale *Madame Chrysanthème* |
| **SETTING:** | Nagasaki, Japan, at the beginning of the 20th century |
| **PRINCIPAL CHARACTERS:** | Cio-Cio-San, or Madame Butterfly (soprano) |
| | Suzuki, her maid (mezzo-soprano) |
| | B. F. Pinkerton, lieutenant in the U.S. Navy (tenor) |
| | Sharpless, U.S. consul at Nagasaki (baritone) |
| | Goro, marriage broker (tenor) |
| | Prince Yamadori (tenor) |
| | Kate Pinkerton, American wife of Pinkerton (mezzo-soprano) |
| | Relatives and friends of Cio-Cio-San |

**WHAT TO LISTEN FOR:**

| | | | |
|---|---|---|---|
| Melody | Soaring line, alternates with speechlike section; reaches several climaxes | Expression | Dreamlike, then passionate and emotional; rising dynamic lines |
| Rhythm/ Meter | Slow and dreamy, then more agitated rhythmically | Performing Forces | Sparse accompaniment at opening by solo violin |
| Harmony | Rich accompaniment; some unison writing | | |

Opening, ethereal vocal line:

Un___ bel di, ve - dre - mo    le - var - si un fil di fu - mo

Final climactic moment on "l'aspetto" (I am waiting for him):

Tien - ti    la tua    pa - u - ra, io con si - cu - ra    fe - de    l'a - spet - to.

| | | **TEXT** | **TRANSLATION** |
|---|---|---|---|
| 61 | 0:00 | Un bel dì, vedremo | One lovely day we'll see |
| | | levarsi un fil di fumo | a thread of smoke rise |
| | | sull'estremo confin del mare. | at the distant edge of the sea. |
| | | E poi la nave appare— | And then the ship appears— |
| | | poi la nave bianca entra nel porto, | then the white ship enters the harbor, |
| | | romba il suo saluto. | thunders its salute. |
| | | Vedi? E venuto! | You see? He's come! |
| | | Io non gli scendo incontro. Io no. | I don't go down to meet him. Not I. |
| | | Mi metto là sul cieglio del colle | I place myself at the brow of the hill |
| | | e aspetto gran tempo e non mi pesa, | and wait a long time, but the long |
| | | la lunga attesa. | wait doesn't oppress me. |

*Continued on following page*

|  |  | E uscito dalla folla cittadina | And coming out of the city's crowd |
|  |  | un uomo, un picciol punto | a man, a tiny speck |
|  |  | s'avvia per la collina. | starts toward the hill. |
| **62** | 2:14 | Chi sarà? Chi sarà? | Who will it be? Who? |
|  |  | E come sarà giunto | And when he arrives |
|  |  | che dirà? Che dirà? | what will he say? What? |
|  |  | Chiamerà Butterfly dalla lontana. | He'll call Butterfly from the distance. |
|  |  | Io senza dar risposta me ne starò nascosta | I'll stay hidden, partly to tease him |
|  |  | un po' per celia | and partly not to die |
|  |  | e un po' per non morire al primo incontro, | at our first meeting, |
|  |  | ed egli alquanto in pena chiamerà: | and a little worried he'll call |
|  |  | piccina mogliettina olezzo di verbena, | little wife, verbena blossom, |
|  |  | i nomi che mi dava al suo venire | the names he gave me when he came here. |
|  |  | tutto questo avverrà, te lo prometto. | All this will happen, I promise you. |
|  |  | Tienti la tua paura, | Keep your fear to yourself, |
|  |  | io con sicura fede l'aspetto. | with certain faith I am waiting for him. |

◉ **Now try the Listening Quiz.**

**By the way. . . .**

**Are There Still Geisha Today?**

Geisha are traditional Japanese entertainers who are highly trained in such arts as classical music, dancing, and poetry. The tradition emerged during the 1600s in the so-called "pleasure quarters" of Japan. Actually the first geishas were men, but by the 1800s, geisha were women who entertained men with their singing and playing on **shamisen** (a three-string, long-necked lute) or **koto** (a long, wooden zither); engaged them in stimulating or flattering conversation; or challenged them to *go*, an ancient board game of strategy and skill. The geisha is easily recognizable by her elaborate hairdo (piled high in black lacquered coils with decorative pins), distinctive makeup (white-painted face and crimson lips), ornate silk kimono and obi (a wide, stiff sash), and high, wooden clogs. In the 1920s there were as many as 80,000 geisha in Japan; today, however, there are only a few thousand who entertain VIPs visiting the cities of Tokyo and Kyoto. This Japanese tradition has intrigued Westerners for centuries, prompting the publication of Arthur Golden's book *Memoirs of a Geisha* (1997, and made into an art film in 2005) and inspiring anthropologist Liza Dalby to infiltrate this exotic community of women to better understand and describe geisha culture.

Japanese geisha were trained to perform on various instruments. Here they play (from left to right) shamisen, koto, and traditional bamboo flute (c. 1880).

# Looking Ahead to Modernist Trends

We have seen how late-nineteenth-century masters like Puccini and Tchaikovsky exploited the tonal system to its fullest while looking to world cultures for new timbres and musical systems. In the early twentieth century, musicians reexamined the traditions handed to them, suppressing Romanticism in their music to create works based on innovative structures and soundscapes. Some composers were influenced by the new trends of popular music—including blues, ragtime, jazz, and film music—while others devised novel systems of organizing pitch, leading to atonality and twelve-tone music. Composers could not ignore the profound changes taking place in art and literature in the years prior to World War I; we will hear their response to these diverse styles in the works of the early modernists, beginning with Impressionism and the music of Claude Debussy.

## LISTENING ACTIVITY: OPERA IN CHINA AND THE WEST

Operatic-like genres exist around the world, and notably in China, where two styles developed side by side: Peking (or Beijing) opera, popular in the capital city as well as in Shanghai; and Cantonese opera, from the southern region of China. These musical theater works combine a dramatized story with stylized gestures and movements, acrobatics, and elaborate makeup and costumes appropriate to each role, each of whom represents a stock character (see illustration, p. 63). The plots focus on popular legends, historical events, or sometimes a literary source. Chinese sung drama has many of the same musical elements as Western opera, including arias—some lyrical, some dramatic—speechlike recitation, and instrumental music. The "orchestra" for Chinese opera is usually made up of various string and percussion instruments, some of which are melodic while others provide more rhythmic and dramatic accompaniment.

*The Kiss* (1907–08), by **Gustav Klimt** (1862–1918), reflects how turn-of-the-century artists responded to the vogue for Eastern effects.

Let's consider an example from the Cantonese opera *Ngoh wai heng kong* (*I'm mad for you*), written in 1939, about a young man who travels to the capital city to take a difficult examination required for a government job. While there, he visits a brothel where the girls entertain and sing for him. He immediately falls in love with one of the girls and wants to marry her, but she is "owned" by a powerful woman who sells her to a wealthy merchant. Here is the opening text for his poignant aria:

*In the warm season, the willow tree has long leaves,*
*Its flowers are very fragrant.*
*The bed is the color of roses.*
*I always think of her, and am very sad.*
*I wish to drink, but when the wine reaches my belly,*
*I am even sadder.*

Now let's compare this short example with the aria *Un bel dì*, from Puccini's *Madame Butterfly* (StudySpace, Chapter 33), comparing styles and elements. For each style trait, select which work best suits the description.

    **a.** *Ngoh wai heng kong* (Cantonese opera)
    **b.** *Un bel dì* (Puccini)

| | | | |
|---|---|---|---|
| **1.** Melody | _____ lyrical, soaring line | _____ choppy line, feels disjunct |
| **2.** Scale | _____ pentatonic with microtonal inflections | _____ diatonic/chromatic |
| **3.** Rhythm | _____ clear, accented beat | _____ floating quality, not accented |
| **4.** Meter | _____ flowing triple meter | _____ duple meter |
| **5.** Texture | _____ heterophonic, with instruments weaving around vocal line | _____ homophonic, with instruments moving with voice |
| **6.** Performing Force | _____ large orchestra | _____ string instruments (bowed and plucked) |
| **7.** Vocal Quality | _____ nasal, pinched quality | _____ open sound, with wide vibrato |

## A COMPARISON OF ROMANTIC, IMPRESSIONIST, AND EARLY-TWENTIETH-CENTURY STYLES

| | ROMANTIC (c. 1820–1900) | IMPRESSIONIST (c. 1890–1915) | EARLY 20TH CENTURY (c. 1900–1940) |
|---|---|---|---|
| **REPRESENTATIVE COMPOSERS** *Early Romantic* *Later Romantic* | Schubert, Chopin, Berlioz, Fanny Mendelssohn Verdi, Smetana, Tchaikovsky, Brahms, Puccini | Debussy, Ravel | Stravinsky, Schoenberg, Berg, Copland, Still, Revueltas |
| **MELODY** | Expansive, singing melodies; wide-ranging; many chromatic inflections and dramatic leaps | Built on chromatic, whole-tone, and non-Western scales | Instrumental conception; disjunct, wide-ranging; interest in folk tunes |
| **HARMONY** | Increasing chromaticism, expanded concepts of tonality | Weak tonal center; free treatment of dissonance | Atonality; polychords and polyharmony; based on tone rows; extremes in dissonance |
| **RHYTHM** | Rhythmic diversity, tempo rubato | Floating rhythm; obscured pulse; no sense of meter | Changing meter favored; polyrhythm, syncopation |
| **TEXTURE** | Homophonic (early); increasingly polyphonic in later years | Homophonic; chords moving in parallel motion | Contrapuntal, linear movement |
| **INSTRUMENTAL GENRES** | Symphonic poem, program symphony, symphony, concerto, ballet; also miniatures | Programmatic genres, symphonic poem, preludes | Neoclassical genres (symphony, concerto), ballet suites |
| **VOCAL GENRES** | Lied (solo), part song, Mass, opera | Solo song with orchestra, opera | Solo song with chamber ensemble, opera |
| **FORM** | Expansion of forms; interest in continuous as well as miniature programmatic forms | Short, lyric forms | Succinct, tight forms; revived older forms |
| **AUDIENCE** | Secular music predominant; middle class and aristocratic salons | Public theaters | Public concerts, radio broadcasts |
| **TIMBRE** | Continual change, blend of true colors; experiments with new instruments | Veiled blending of timbres, muted instruments, shimmering colors | Bright, lean sound; piano part of orchestra; winds and percussion favored |
| **PERFORMING FORCES** | New instruments, including English horn, tuba, valved brass, harp, piccolo; larger orchestra; piano is predominant solo instrument | Adds 1 or 2 harps; bell-like percussion | Diverse percussion instruments; non-Western added; unusual combinations and ranges of instruments |

ⓢ **Find an interactive version of this chart on StudySpace.**

## LISTENING ACTIVITY: COMPARING STYLES 5
## ROMANTIC TO TWENTIETH CENTURY

We can hear the profound changes in musical style between the 19th and 20th centuries using several different genres. We'll begin with the art song: listen to the two examples below (StudySpace, Chapter 33) and then select the work(s) that match each characteristic.

>    **a.** Schumann: "In the lovely month of May"
>    **b.** Schoenberg: *The Moonfleck*, from *Pierrot lunaire*

____ **1.** solo song with piano accompaniment (Lied)

____ **2.** solo song accompanied by chamber ensemble

____ **3.** disjunct, unlyrical singing style

____ **4.** chromaticism; vague sense of final cadence on tonic

____ **5.** atonal; abandonment of tonality

____ **6.** contrapuntal; independent lines

____ **7.** homophonic texture; focused on voice

Now let's compare two orchestral works composed just two decades apart, and see how drastically musical style changed in those transitional years. For each trait below, select the work(s) that best reflect it.

>    **c.** Debussy: *Jeux de vagues*, from *La mer*
>    **d.** Stravinsky: *The Rite of Spring*, Introduction

____ **8.** strong, shifting accents; frequent meter changes

____ **9.** free-flowing rhythm; little sense of meter

____ **10.** lyrical, chromatic melodic line

____ **11.** dissonant blocks of chords; polyharmony

____ **12.** vague sense of tonality; free treatment of dissonance

____ **13.** focus on instrumental color; one instrument featured at a time

____ **14.** huge orchestral forces; constantly changing timbres

____ **15.** contrapuntal texture; many lines at once

____ **16.** homophonic texture; with parallel movement of lines

## Critical Thinking

**1** Why did choral music experience an increased popularity in the nineteenth century?

**2.** How can Verdi's Requiem Mass be viewed both as operatic and ecclesiastical?

**3.** How does Tchaikovsky's ballet *The Nutcracker* embrace and depart from musical nationalism and exoticism?

**4.** How does Puccini evoke exoticism in his Italian opera *Madame Butterfly*?

# Impressionism and Early 20th Century

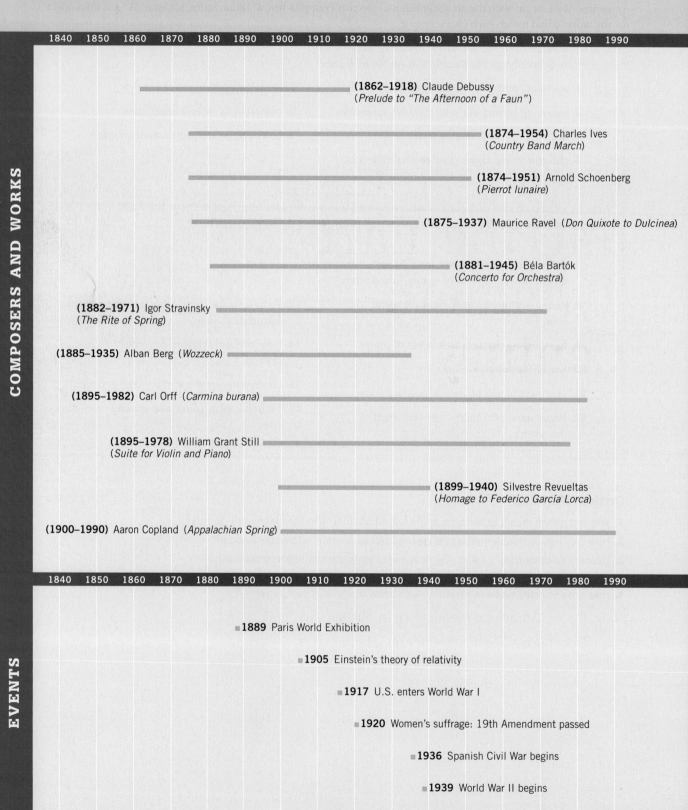

**COMPOSERS AND WORKS**

1840 1850 1860 1870 1880 1890 1900 1910 1920 1930 1940 1950 1960 1970 1980 1990

**(1862–1918)** Claude Debussy
(*Prelude to "The Afternoon of a Faun"*)

**(1874–1954)** Charles Ives
(*Country Band March*)

**(1874–1951)** Arnold Schoenberg
(*Pierrot lunaire*)

**(1875–1937)** Maurice Ravel (*Don Quixote to Dulcinea*)

**(1881–1945)** Béla Bartók
(*Concerto for Orchestra*)

**(1882–1971)** Igor Stravinsky
(*The Rite of Spring*)

**(1885–1935)** Alban Berg (*Wozzeck*)

**(1895–1982)** Carl Orff (*Carmina burana*)

**(1895–1978)** William Grant Still
(*Suite for Violin and Piano*)

**(1899–1940)** Silvestre Revueltas
(*Homage to Federico García Lorca*)

**(1900–1990)** Aaron Copland (*Appalachian Spring*)

1840 1850 1860 1870 1880 1890 1900 1910 1920 1930 1940 1950 1960 1970 1980 1990

**EVENTS**

**1889** Paris World Exhibition

**1905** Einstein's theory of relativity

**1917** U.S. enters World War I

**1920** Women's suffrage: 19th Amendment passed

**1936** Spanish Civil War begins

**1939** World War II begins

# PART 6

# Impressionism and the Early Twentieth Century

**Juan Gris** (1887–1927). *Harlequin with Guitar* (1919).

# Modernism in the Arts

*"The entire history of modern music may be said to be a history of the gradual pull-away from the German musical tradition of the past century."*

—**Aaron Copland**

- **Impressionism** was a French movement developed by painters who tried to capture their "first impression" of a subject through varied treatments of light and color.

- The literary response to Impressionism was **Symbolism**, in which writings are suggestive of images and ideas rather than literally descriptive.

- The diverse artistic trends of the early twentieth century were a reaction against Romanticism.

- Early-twentieth-century artistic trends explored simplicity and abstraction (interest in non-Western

arts, **Dadaism**, **Cubism**) and the world of dreams and the inner soul (**Surrealism**, Expressionism).

- **Expressionism** was the international counterpart to French Impressionism; in music, composers such as Schoenberg and Webern explored new harmonic systems and the extreme registers of instruments.

- The **Neoclassical movement** sought to revive balance and objectivity in the arts by returning to formal structures of the past.

J ust as European and American societies saw great changes in the era from 1890 to 1940, so did the arts witness a profound upheaval. The earliest harbingers of modernism were French artists and writers, who abandoned the grandiose subjects and expressions of Romanticism. Impressionist artists wished to capture on canvas the freshness of their first impressions and were fascinated with the continuous change in the appearance of their subjects through varied treatment of light and color. Claude Monet's painting, *Impression: Sun Rising*, completed in 1867, was rebuffed by the academic salons of Paris (see illustration opposite), and **"Impressionism"** quickly became a term of derision. However, Monet's hazy, luminous painting style was embraced by Parisian artists such as Camille Pissarro (1830–1903), Edouard Manet (1832–1883), Edgar Degas (1834–1917), and August Renoir (1841–1919). We will see how composers like Claude Debussy tried to emulate the use of color and iridescence that characterize this new style.

Impressionism

A parallel development in poetry was similarly influential to French composers: the **Symbolist** movement sought to evoke poetic images through suggestion rather than description, through symbol rather than statement. This literary revolt against tradition gained prominence in the works of French writers Charles Baudelaire (1821–1867), Stéphane Mallarmé (1842–1898), and Paul Verlaine (1844–1896), all of whom were strongly influenced by the American poet Edgar

Symbolism

The Impressionists took painting out of the studio and into the open air; their subject was light. **Claude Monet** (1840–1926), *Impression: Sun Rising.*

Allan Poe (1809–1849). Through their experiments in free verse forms, the Symbolists were able to achieve in language an abstract quality that had once belonged to music alone.

# The Reaction against Romanticism

Other styles soon arose as early-twentieth-century composers severed their ties with their Romantic pasts. These new attitudes took hold just before the advent of the First World War (1914–1918), when European arts tried to break away from overrefinement and to capture the spontaneity and the freedom from inhibition that was associated with primitive life. Artists were inspired by the abstraction of African sculpture, and painters Paul Gauguin and Henri Rousseau created exotic works of monumental simplicity. Likewise, some composers turned to the vigorous energy of non-Western rhythm, seeking fresh concepts in the musics of Africa, Asia, and eastern Europe. Out of the unspoiled, traditional music in these areas came powerful rhythms of an elemental fury, as reflected in Bartók's *Allegro barbaro* (1911) and Stravinsky's *Rite of Spring* (1913), which we will study.

The powerful abstraction of African sculpture strongly influenced European art.

In those years surrounding the First World War, two influential arts movements arose: ***Futurism***, whose manifesto of 1909 declared its alienation from established institutions and its focus on the dynamism of twentieth-century life; and ***Dadaism***, founded in Switzerland after 1918. The Dadaists, principally writers and artists who reacted to the horrors of the war's bloodbath that had engulfed Europe, rejected the concept of art as something to be reverently admired. To make their point, they produced works of absolute absurdity. They also reacted against the excessive complexity of Western art by trying to recapture the simplicity of a child's world-

Parisian painter **Paul Gauguin** (1848–1903) was drawn to the simplicity of Tahitian life and the emotional directness of his native subjects. *Nave, Nave Moe* (*Miraculous Source,* 1894).

view. Following their example, the French composer Erik Satie led the way toward a simple, "everyday" music, and exerted an important influence—along with the writer Jean Cocteau—on the group called *Les Six* (The Six; see Chapter 37).

**Surrealism and Cubism**

The Dada group, with artists such as Hans Arp and Marcel Duchamp, merged into the school of *Surrealism*, which included Salvador Dali and Joan Miró (see illustration), both of whom explored the world of dreams. Other styles of modern art included *Cubism*, the Paris-based style of painting embodied in the works of Pablo Picasso, Georges Braque, and Juan Gris (see p. 283), which encouraged the painter to construct a visual world in terms of geometric patterns; and Expressionism, which we will see had a significant impact on music of the early twentieth century.

Spanish artist **Joan Miró** (1893–1983) explores the surrealist world of dreams through the distortion of shapes. *Dutch Interior I.*

# Expressionism

Expressionism was the international counterpart to French Impressionism. While the French explored radiant impressions of the outer world, the Germanic temperament preferred digging down to the depths of the psyche. As with Impressionism, the impulse for the Expressionist movement came from painting. Wassily Kandinsky (1866–1944), Paul Klee (1879–1940), Oskar Kokoschka (1886–1980; see illustration opposite), and Edvard Munch (1863–1944)—famous for *The Scream*—influenced the composer Arnold Schoenberg (see p. 306) and his followers just as the Impressionist painters influenced Debussy. Expressionism is reflected not only through the paintings of Kandinsky, Kokoschka, and Munch, but also in the writings of Franz Kafka (1883–1924). Expressionism in music triumphed first in central Europe, especially Germany, and reached its full tide in the dramatic works of the *Second Viennese School* (a term referring to Arnold Schoenberg and his disciples Alban Berg and Anton Webern).

The Austrian Expressionist painter **Oskar Kokoschka** (1886–1980) reveals his terror of war in *Knight Errant* (1915).

The musical language of Expressionism favored hyperexpressive harmonies, extraordinarily wide leaps in the melody, and the use of instruments in their extreme registers. Expressionist music soon reached the boundaries of what was possible within the major-minor system. Inevitably, it had to push beyond.

# Neoclassicism

One way of rejecting the nineteenth century was to return to earlier eras. Instead of revering Beethoven and Wagner, as the Romantics had done, composers began to emulate the great musicians of the early eighteenth century—Bach, Handel, and Vivaldi—and the detached, objective style that is often associated with their music.

Neoclassicism tried to rid music of the story-and-picture meanings favored in the nineteenth century. Neoclassical composers turned away from the symphonic poem and the Romantic attempt to bring music closer to poetry and painting. They preferred absolute to program music, and they focused attention on crafts- manship and balance, a positive affirmation of the Classical virtues of objectivity and control.

**Absolute music**

As in previous movements, Modernism was both a reaction against the past and a distillation of it. It was in part an investigation into why the past needed to change and in part an attempt to make the arts more relevant—more "modern"—while still challenging conventional perceptions. The movement transformed a culture and allowed for endless experimentation. It was to have far-reaching consequences in all fields, including the arts, literature, the sciences, philosophy, and religion.

**Modernism**

Let us now consider two key composers from the first modern generation in France: the Impressionist composer Claude Debussy and the post-Impressionist/ Neoclassicist Maurice Ravel.

## Critical Thinking

**1.** How do the artistic movements of Impressionism and Expressionism differ? Do they share any similarities?

**2.** How are the major artistic trends of the early twentieth century a reaction against earlier styles?

**3.** What appealed to artists about non-Western art and music?

# 34 Impressionism and Post-Impressionism

"For we desire above all—nuance,
Not color but half-shades!
Ah! nuance alone unites
Dream with dream and flute with horn."

—**Paul Verlaine**

## KEY POINTS

> ⓢ **StudySpace** wwnorton.com/enjoy

- Impressionism in music is characterized by modal and exotic scales (*chromatic*, *whole tone*, and *pentatonic*), unresolved dissonances, parallel chords, rich orchestral color, and free rhythm, all generally cast in small-scale programmatic forms.
- The most important French Impressionist composer was Claude Debussy. His orchestral

work, *Prelude to "The Afternoon of a Faun,"* was inspired by a Symbolist poem.

- Debussy and Maurice Ravel were highly influenced by new sounds of non-Western and traditional music styles heard at the Paris World Exhibition of 1889 (see HTTN 10).

I mpressionism surfaced in France at a crucial time in European music history. Just as post-Romantic composers like Puccini were attracted to new, exotic scales, Claude Debussy and Maurice Ravel were attracted to scales from around the world and also to the church modes of medieval music, which gave their music an archaic sound.

They began to emphasize the primary intervals—octaves, fourths, fifths—and the parallel movement of chords in the manner of medieval organum. Impressionists responded especially to non-Western music: the Moorish strain in the songs and dances of Spain, and the Javanese and Chinese orchestras that performed in Paris during the World Exposition of 1889. Here they found rhythms, scales, and colors that offered a bewitching contrast to the more familiar sounds of Western music

The major-minor system, as we saw, is based on the pull of the active tones to the tonic, or rest tone. Impressionist composers regarded this as a formula that had become too obvious. In their works, we do not hear the triumphal final cadence of the Classical-Romantic period, in which the dominant chord is resolved to the tonic with the greatest possible emphasis. Instead, more subtle harmonic relationships came into play. Rather than viewing dissonance as a momentary disturbance, composers began to use dissonance for itself, freeing it from the need to resolve. They taught their contemporaries to accept tone combinations that had formerly been regarded as inadmissible, just like the Impressionist painters taught people to see colors in sky, grass, and water that they had never seen there before.

Impressionist composers made use of the entire spectrum in the **chromatic scale**, and also explored the **whole-tone scale**, derived from various non-Western musics. A whole-tone scale is built entirely of whole-tone intervals (without half steps): for example, C-D-E-F♯-G♯-A♯-C. The result is a fluid sequence of pitches that lacks the pull toward a tonic (see chart on p. 290).

Impressionist composers also explored the use of parallel, or "gliding," chords. Such motion was truly groundbreaking. Free from a strong tonal center and rigid harmonic guidelines, composers experimented with new tone combinations such as the ninth chord, a set of five notes in which the interval between the lowest and highest tones was a ninth. The effect was one of hovering between tonalities, creating elusive effects that evoke the misty outlines of Impressionist painting.

These floating harmonies demanded the most subtle colors, and here composers learned new techniques of blending timbres from their counterparts in art. Painters juxtaposed brush strokes of pure color on the canvas, leaving it to the eye of the viewer to do the mixing. An iridescent sheen bathes each painting. Debussy replaced the lush, full sonority of the Romantic orchestra with veiled sounds: flutes and clarinets in their dark velvety registers, violins in their lustrous upper range, trumpets and horns discreetly muted; and over the whole, a shimmering gossamer of harp, celesta, triangle, glockenspiel, muffled drum, and brushed cymbal. One instrumental color flows into another close by, as from oboe to clarinet to flute, in the same way that Impressionist painting moves from one color to another in the spectrum, as from yellow to green to blue.

This music scene is typical of the everyday activities captured by Impressionists. *Young Girls at the Piano* (1892), by **Pierre-Auguste Renoir** (1841–1919).

Impressionist rhythm too shows the influence of non-Western music. The metrical patterns of the Classical-Romantic era gave way to a new dreamlike style, where the music glides in a floating rhythm that obscures the pulse.

Impressionism continued the fundamental tendencies of the Romantic movement in its emphasis on program music, tone painting, and nature worship; addiction to lyricism; attempt to unite music, painting, and poetry; and emphasis on mood and atmosphere. The abstraction of their musical expression had its counterpart in Symbolist poetry, as we will see in Debussy's tone poem *Prelude to "The Afternoon of a Faun,"* inspired by the evocative poetry of Paul Verlaine.

In *The Boating Party*, by the American painter **Mary Cassatt** (1844–1926), the eye is drawn toward the relaxed mother and child figures. This work features the strong lines and dramatic colors of second-generation Impressionists.

Impressionist artists abandoned the drama-packed themes that inspired centuries of European art in favor of everyday scenes of middle-class life: music lessons, dancing girls, boating and café scenes, and nature in all its beauty. Accordingly, composers turned away from large forms such as symphonies and concertos. They preferred short lyric forms—preludes, nocturnes, arabesques—whose titles suggested intimate themes of nature such as Debussy's *Clair de lune (Moonlight)* and *Nuages (Clouds)*. In effect, the Impressionists substituted a thoroughly French conception of Romanticism.

## CHARACTERISTICS OF MUSICAL IMPRESSIONISM

1. Whole-tone scale (beginning on C):

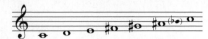

2. Example from Debussy's opera *Pelléas and Mélisande*, illustrating use of whole-tone scales:

3. Parallel movement (octaves and open fifths) in example of early organum:

4. Parallel movement of chords (fifths and octaves) from Debussy's *Sunken Cathedral*:

## *Prelude to "The Afternoon of a Faun"*

The great Russian dancer Vaslav Nijinsky as the Faun in the 1912 ballet version of *L'après-midi d'un faune.* Design by **Léon Bakst** (1866–1924).

Debussy's best-known orchestral work is a symphonic poem that was inspired by a pastoral poem by Symbolist writer Stéphane Mallarmé. The text evokes a landscape of antiquity, describing the faun, a mythological creature of the forest that is half man, half goat. This "simple sensuous passionate being" awakes in the woods and tries to remember: was he visited by three lovely nymphs, or was this but a dream? He will never know. The sun is warm, the earth fragrant. He curls himself up and falls into a wine-drugged sleep.

Debussy's handling of the orchestra is thoroughly French, allowing individual instruments to stand out against the ensemble. In his scores, the melodic lines are widely spaced, the texture light and airy.

The work follows the familiar pattern of statement-departure-return (**A-B-A'**), yet the movement is fluid and rhapsodic. The relaxed rhythm flows across the bar line in a continuous stream. By weakening the accent, Debussy achieved that dreamlike fluidity that is a prime trait of Impressionist music.

We first hear a flute solo in the velvety lower register. The melody glides along the chromatic scale, narrow in range and languorous. (See Listening Guide 40). Glissandos on the harp usher in a brief dialogue in the horns, a mixture of colors never heard before.

Next, a more decisive motive emerges, marked *en animant* (growing lively). This is followed by a third theme—an impassioned melody that carries the composition to an emotional climax. The first theme then returns in an altered guise. At the close, antique cymbals play *pianissimo.* (*Antique cymbals* are small disks of brass; the rims are struck

## Claude Debussy (1862–1918)

The most important French composer of the early twentieth century, **Claude Debussy** was born near Paris in the town of St. Germain-en-Laye. He entered the Paris Conservatory when he was eleven. Within a few years, he shocked his professors with bizarre harmonies that defied the rules. He was only twenty-two when his cantata *The Prodigal Son* won the coveted Prix de Rome. By this time, he had already realized his future style.

The 1890s, the most productive decade of Debussy's career, culminated in the opera *Pelléas and Mélisande*, based on the symbolist drama by the Belgian poet Maurice Maeterlinck. The premiere took place at the Opéra-Comique on April 30, 1902. At first, *Pelléas* was attacked as being decadent and lacking in melody, form, and substance, but this opera made Debussy famous, and he began appearing in the capitals of Europe to conduct his works.

His energies sapped by the ravages of cancer, Debussy continued to work with remarkable fortitude. He died in March 1918, during the bombardment of Paris. The funeral procession made its way through deserted streets while the shells of the German guns ripped into his beloved city just eight months before victory was celebrated in France.

Like the artist Monet and the writer Verlaine, Debussy considered art to be a sensuous experience. The grandiose themes of Romanticism offended his temperament as both a man and an artist. "French music," he declared, "is clearness, elegance, simple and natural declamation. French music aims first of all to give pleasure." Debussy turned against sonata-allegro form, regarding it an outmoded formula. At first a Wagner fan, he soon found Wagner's *Ring* cycle ponderous and tedious. In the end, however, he paid moving tribute to the master, calling him "a beautiful sunset that was mistaken for a dawn."

Debussy's fame rests on a comparatively small output; *Pelléas and Mélisande* is viewed by many as his greatest achievement. Among his orchestral compositions, the *Prelude to "The Afternoon of a Faun"* became a favorite with the public early on, as did the three nocturnes *(Clouds, Festivals, Sirens)* and *The Sea (La mer)*.

Debussy's distinctive new style of writing for the piano exploited the instrument's resources and wide range with finesse. Many of his piano pieces demonstrate an interest in non-Western scales and instruments, which he first heard at the Paris Exhibition in 1889 (see HTTN 10). Debussy also helped establish the French song as a national art form. His settings of the French Symbolist poets Baudelaire, Verlaine, and Mallarmé are exquisite and refined.

*In His Own Words*

I love music passionately. And because I love it, I try to free it from barren traditions that stifle it. It is a free art gushing forth, an open-air art boundless as the elements, the wind, the sky, the sea. It must never be shut in and become an academic art.

**Major Works:** Orchestral music, including *Prélude à L'après midi d'un faune* (*Prelude to "The Afternoon of a Faun,"* 1894), Nocturnes (1899), *La mer* (*The Sea*, 1905) • Dramatic works, including the opera *Pelléas et Mélisande* (1902) and a ballet • Chamber music, including a string quartet and various sonatas • Piano music, including 2 books of preludes (1909–10, 1912–13) • Songs, choral music, and cantatas.

◎ **iMusic:** *Jeux de vagues*, from *La mer*

together gently and allowed to vibrate.) "Blue" chords (with lowered thirds and sevenths) are heard on the muted horns and violins, sounding infinitely remote. The work dissolves into silence, leaving us, and the faun, in a dreamlike state.

Debussy's symphonic poem was later choreographed for the Ballets Russes (Russian Ballet) and was first performed in 1912 with Vaslav Nijinsky dancing the role of the faun (see illustration, opposite), who cavorts among the nymphs. This work is often viewed as a turning point in modern ballet, although the sensuous nature of the dancing caused a scandal in Paris. The Ballets Russes, under the directorship of Sergei Diaghilev, sought to combine new music, dance, and art. Diaghilev looked not only to Debussy's work for their innovative productions, but also to the music of Igor Stravinsky, whose revolutionary ballet *The Rite of Spring* (1913) we will consider in a later chapter.

**LISTENING GUIDE 40** DVD | CD 6 (55–59) | CD 4 (1–5)

# Debussy: *Prelude to "The Afternoon of a Faun" (Prélude à L'après-midi d'un faune)* 9:45

**DATE:** 1894

**GENRE:** Symphonic poem

**WHAT TO LISTEN FOR:**

| | |
|---|---|
| Melody | Lyrical, sinuous melody; chromatic at opening and closing |
| Rhythm/Meter | Free-flowing rhythms; sense of floating; lacks pulse; middle section more animated |
| Harmony | Use of "blue" chords, with lowered thirds |
| Texture | Homophonic; light and airy |
| Form | Loose **A-B-A′** structure |
| Expression | Evocative mood; sensual |
| Timbre | Rich colors; especially woodwinds |
| Performing Forces | Strings (with 2 harps), woodwinds, French horns, and antique cymbals |

**Opening of poem:**

| TEXT | TRANSLATION |
|---|---|
| Ces nymphes, je les veux perpétuer. | These nymphs I would perpetuate. |
| Si clair | So light |
| Leur incarnat léger, qu'il voltige dans l'air | their gossamer embodiment, floating on the air |
| Assoupi de sommeils touffus. | inert with heavy slumber. |
| Amais-je un rêve? | Was it a dream I loved? |

**A section**

1 0:00 Opening chromatic melody in flute; passes from one instrument to another, accompanied by muted strings and vague sense of pulse:

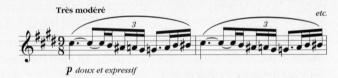

**B section**

2 2:48 Clarinet introduces more animated idea, answered by rhythmic figure in cellos.

3 3:16 New theme, more animated rhythmically in solo oboe, builds in *crescendo:*

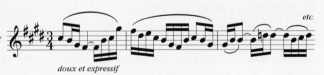

4 4:34 Contrasting theme in woodwinds, then strings, with syncopated rhythms, builds to climax:

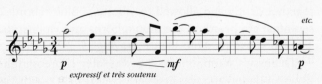

**A′ section**

5 6:22 Abridged return, in varied setting.

Now try the Listening Quiz.

# The Paris World Exhibition of 1889: A Cultural Awakening

In 1889, France hosted a World Exhibition marking the centenary of the French Revolution. The Eiffel Tower was the French showcase for this world's fair. Musicians from around the world performed for a receptive European public. One of the most popular exhibits, from the Indonesian island of Java, featured dancers and *gamelan*. (A gamelan is an ensemble of mainly percussion instruments—including gongs, chimes, and drums; see p. 400.) Many classical composers, including Claude Debussy and Maurice Ravel, heard this gamelan for the first time. Debussy wrote of its unique sound to a friend: "Do you not remember the Javanese music able to express every nuance of meaning, even unmentionable shades, and which makes our tonic and dominant seem like empty phantoms?" He attempted to capture something of this sound—its pentatonic scale and unusual timbre in a number of his compositions, including the famous symphonic poem *La mer* (*The Sea*, 1905), and also several piano preludes. Twentieth-century composers continued to explore the unique timbre of the gamelan, including the bold innovator John Cage (see p. 397).

Other events sparked the imagination of visitors to the Paris Exhibition.

This watercolor of a *Cambodian Dancer* (1906), by the French artist **Auguste Rodin** (1840–1917), reflects the artistic interest in exotic subjects.

Evening festivities included a parade of musicians representing various African and Asian nations. Performances included belly dancers and whirling dervishes from the Middle East; African-American cakewalk dancers and dancing women from Cambodia (see illustration). It was there too that Debussy was introduced to the music of Hungarian and Spanish Gypsies,

and he attempted to capture the strumming style of flamenco guitars in several of his piano works (*The Interrupted Serenade* and *Evening in Granada*).

The French composer Maurice Ravel was even more profoundly influenced by this new world of music. Born in the Basque region of France (where the Pyrénées separate France from Spain), Ravel imbued his *Spanish Rhapsody* and his hypnotic *Boléro* with rich Iberian color, his violin work *Tzigane* (*Gypsy*, 1924) with showy, exotic effects, and his orchestral song cycle *Sheherazade* (1903) was inspired by the Arabian folktales of *The Thousand and One Nights*.

Today, we do not need to attend a world exposition to experience music from around the world. We have only to tune in a PBS (Public Broadcasting System) station or surf the Internet to find music and dancing that stimulates our eyes, ears, and imagination.

---

**◎ iMusic**

*Jeux de vagues*, from *La mer* (Debussy)

*Boléro* (Ravel)

*Tabu Kenilu Sawik*: Indonesian gamelan orchestra

*Gota* (Ghana)

*In a Mountain Path* (China)

## Critical Thinking

**1.** How does the innovative use of color in Impressionist painting translate into sound?

**2.** How did non-Western musical ideas affect Impressionist composers?

**3.** How do the literary devices of Symbolism relate to Impressionism in music?

## LISTENING ACTIVITY: MUSIC AT THE 1889 WORLD'S FAIR

In this Listening Activity, we will explore elements of certain world musics—scales, metric ideas, and instruments—similar to those heard at the 1889 Paris World Exhibition (see HTTN 10). We know that the music at the fair represented all corners of the world, including the Far East, the Middle East, Eastern Europe, and Africa. Try to hear the different style traits in each of these examples (StudySpace, Chapter 34).

### New Scale Types:

Match these world music excerpts with the scale type on which each is built:

____ **1.** *In a Mountain Path* (China)          **a.** tritonic (3-note) scale

____ **2.** *Gota* (Ghana)                        **b.** pentatonic (5-note) scale

____ **3.** *Avaz of Bayate Esfahan* (Iran)       **c.** 6-note scale with microtonal inflections

### New Concepts of Rhythm/Meter:

Match these examples with new ideas in rhythm/meter:

____ **4.** *Gankino horo* (Bulgaria)             **d.** rhapsodic, free meter

____ **5.** *Avaz of Bayate Esfahan* (Iran)       **e.** dancelike, shifting meter

____ **6.** *Gota* (Ghana)                        **f.** polymetric (multiple simultaneous patterns)

### New Timbres:

Match these examples with new instrumental and vocal timbres heard at the Exhibition:

____ **7.** *Tabuh Kenilu Sawik* (Indonesia)      **g.** nasal male operatic voice

____ **8.** *In a Mountain Path* (China)          **h.** metallophones and membranophones

____ **9.** *Los Jilicatas* (Peru)                **i.** chordophones, both bowed and struck

____ **10.** *Ngoh wai heng kong* (China)         **j.** folklike aerophones

Now let's listen to two examples by composers who heard world and traditional music at the Exhibition and were influenced by these new sounds. Match the Debussy and Ravel work with the traits that fit each.

**a.** Debussy: *Jeux de vagues*, from *La mer*
**b.** Ravel: *Boléro*

____ **11.** weaving chromatic lines              ____ **15.** evocative of waves in the sea

____ **12.** floating movement with vague meter   ____ **16.** regular triple meter

____ **13.** snare drum evokes Spanish dancer's castanets    ____ **17.** focus on a solo wind instrument

____ **14.** colorful orchestration with many timbres

# 35 Early Modern Musical Style

"To study music, we must learn the rules.
To create music, we must break them."

—Nadia Boulanger

## KEY POINTS

▣ StudySpace   wwnorton.com/enjoy

- Early-twentieth-century composers revitalized rhythm by increasing its complexity—using, for example, *polyrhythms* and *changing meters*.

- Melody was no longer the focus of a composition; it was often more "instrumental" in character.

- New concepts of harmony (*polychords, polytonality, atonality*) pressed music beyond the traditional systems of tonality.

- The *twelve-tone method* (or *serialism*) devised by Arnold Schoenberg was an important and influential compositional technique.

- Linear movement replaced vertical, chordal conceptions, and extreme dissonance became part of the sound palette.

- The early-twentieth-century orchestra grew smaller and focused on the penetrating timbres of winds, percussion, and piano rather than on strings.

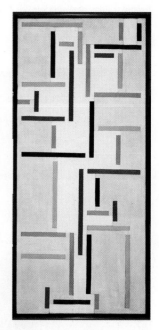

**Theo van Doesburg** (1883–1931) explores changing patterns in *Rhythm of a Russian Dancer* (1918).

## The New Rhythmic Complexity

Twentieth-century music enriched the standard rhythmic patterns of duple, triple, and quadruple meter, now exploring the possibilities of nonsymmetrical patterns based on odd numbers: five, seven, eleven, or thirteen beats to the measure. In nineteenth-century music, a single meter customarily prevailed through an entire movement or section. Now the metrical flow shifted constantly (*changing meter*), sometimes with each measure. Formerly, one rhythmic pattern was used at a time. Now composers turned to *polyrhythm*—the simultaneous use of several rhythmic patterns. As a result of these innovations, Western music achieved something of the complexity and suppleness of Asian and African rhythms.

The new generation of composers preferred rhythms of the highest flexibility that gave their works an almost physical power and drive. This revitalization of rhythm is one of the major achievements of early-twentieth-century music.

Composers also enlivened their music with materials drawn from popular styles. Ragtime, with its elaborate syncopations, traveled across the Atlantic to Europe. The rhythmic freedom of jazz captured the ears of many composers, who strove to achieve something of the spontaneity that distinguished popular style.

# The New Melody

Rhythm was not the only element in which symmetrical structure was abandoned; melody was affected, too. Twentieth-century composers rejected the neatly balanced phrase repetitions of earlier music. Their ideal was a direct, forward-driving melody from which all nonessentials had been cut away.

Nineteenth-century melody is fundamentally vocal in character—composers tried to make the instruments "sing." In contrast, early-twentieth-century melody is not conceived in relation to the voice but is more instrumental, abounding in wide leaps and dissonant intervals. Melody is often not even a primary element. Twentieth-century composers have greatly expanded our notion of what a melody is, creating tunes and patterns that would have been inconceivable a century ago.

# The New Harmony

*Polychords and polyharmony*

No single factor sets off early-twentieth-century music from that of the past more decisively than the new conceptions of harmony. The triads of traditional harmony, we saw, were formed by combining three tones, on every other degree of the scale, or in thirds: 1-3-5 (for example, C-E-G), 2-4-6 (D-F-A), and so on. Traditional harmony also employed four-note combinations, with another third piled on top of the triad, known as seventh chords (1-3-5-7), and (in music of the Impressionists) five-note combinations known as ninth chords (1-3-5-7-9). Twentieth-century composers added more "stories" to such chords, forming highly dissonant **polychords** of six and seven notes. The emergence of these complex "skyscraper" chords brought increased tension and dissonance to music and allowed the composer to play two or more streams of harmony against each other, creating **polyharmony**.

## New Conceptions of Tonality

The new sounds of twentieth-century music burst the confines of traditional tonality and called for new means of organization, extending or replacing the major-minor system. These approaches, in general, followed four principal paths— expanded tonality, polytonality, atonality, and twelve-tone music.

The widespread use of chromatic harmony in the late nineteenth century led, in the early twentieth, to the free use of all twelve tones around a center. Although this approach retained the basic principle of traditional tonality—gravitation to the tonic—it wiped out the distinction between diatonic and chromatic and between major and minor modes.

From the development of polyharmony, a further step followed logically: heightening the contrast of two keys by presenting them simultaneously, which resulted in **polytonality**. Confronting the ear with two keys at the same time meant a radical departure from the basic principle of traditional harmony: centering on a

Irregular lines and sudden leaps characterize this vista from Arches National Park in Utah.

single key. Polytonality came into prominence with the music of Stravinsky, in such works as *The Rite of Spring* (see p. 302).

Atonality

The idea of abandoning tonality altogether is associated with the composer Arnold Schoenberg, who advocated doing away with the tonic by giving the twelve tones of the chromatic scale equal importance—thus creating *atonal* music. (We will study an example of atonality in Schoenberg's song cycle *Pierrot lunaire.*) Atonality entirely rejected the framework of key. Consonance, according to Schoenberg, was no longer capable of making an impression; atonal music moved from one level of dissonance to another, functioning always at maximum tension, without areas of relaxation.

## The Twelve-Tone Method

Having accepted the necessity of moving beyond the existing tonal system, Schoenberg sought a unifying principle that would take its place. He found this in a strict technique, worked out by the early 1920s, that he called "the method of composing with twelve tones"—that is, with twelve equal tones. Each composition that uses Schoenberg's method, also known as *serialism,* is based on a particular arrangement of the twelve chromatic tones called a **tone row.** The term *dodecaphonic,* the Greek equivalent of *twelve-tone,* is sometimes also used for Schoenberg's method.) This row is the unifying idea for a composition and the source for all the melodic and harmonic events that take place in it.

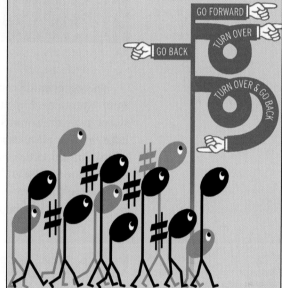

This *New Yorker* cartoon helps visualize the concept of a tone row and its permutations.

Once established, a tone row is the basis from which a composer builds themes, harmonies, and musical patterns. Schoenberg provided flexibility and variety in this seemingly confining system through alternative forms of the tone row. A *transposed row* keeps the same pattern of intervals but begins on a different pitch. In *inversion,* the movement of the notes is in the opposite direction, up instead of down and vice versa, so that the row appears upside down. *Retrograde* is an arrangement of the pitches in reverse order, so that the row comes out backward, and *retrograde inversion* turns the row upside down and backward. (You will remember that the same techniques were used in the Baroque fugue; see diagram on p. 142.)

## The Emancipation of Dissonance

As we have discovered, the history of music has been the history of a steadily increasing tolerance on the part of listeners. Throughout this long evolution, one factor remained constant: a clear distinction was drawn between dissonance—the element of tension—and consonance—the element of rest. Consonance was the norm, dissonance the temporary disturbance. In many twentieth-century works, however, tension became the norm. Therefore, a dissonance can serve even as a final cadence, provided it is less dissonant than the chord that came before; in relation to the greater dissonance, it is judged to be consonant. Twentieth-century composers emancipated dissonance by freeing it from the obligation to resolve to consonance. Their music taught listeners to accept tone combinations whose like had never been heard before.

*In His Own Words*

Every dissonance doesn't have to resolve if it doesn't happen to feel like it, any more than every horse should have its tail bobbed just because it's the prevailing fashion.

—*George Ives, to his son Charles*

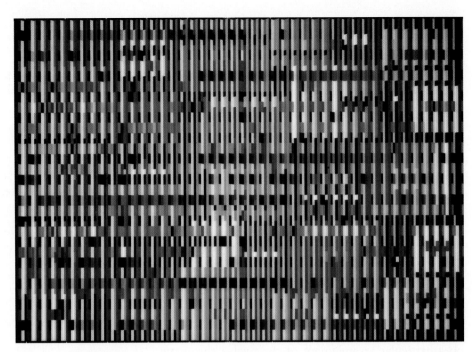

*Double Metamorphosis III* (*Counterpoint and Sequence*, 1968–69) by **Yaacov Agam** (b. 1928) focuses on the jarring effect of interlocking lines and colors.

The nineteenth century was preoccupied with opulent, lush harmony; the early twentieth emphasized linear movement, or counterpoint. The new style swept away the sounds of both the Romantic cloudburst and the Impressionistic haze. In their place came a sparse linear texture that fit the New Classical ideal of craftsmanship, order, and objectivity. Composers began to use dissonance to set off one line against another. Instead of basing their counterpoint on the agreeable intervals of the third and sixth, they turned to astringent seconds and sevenths, and heightened the independence of the voices by putting them in different keys.

# Orchestration

Romanian sculptor **Constantin Brancusi** (1876–1957) revolutionized the movement to abstraction and reductive formalism in *The Kiss* (1908).

The rich sonorities of nineteenth-century orchestration gave way to a leaner sound, one that was hard and bright, played by a smaller orchestra. The decisive factor in the handling of the orchestra was the change to a linear texture. Color came to be used in the new music not so much for atmosphere as for bringing out the lines of counterpoint and of form. The string section lost its traditional role as the heart of the orchestra; its tone was felt to be too warm. Attention was focused on the more penetrating winds. Composers favored darker instruments—viola, bassoon, trombone. The emphasis on rhythm brought the percussion group into greater prominence and the piano, which in the Romantic era was preeminently a solo instrument, found a place in the orchestral ensemble.

# New Conceptions of Form

The first quarter of the century saw the final expansion of traditional forms in the gigantic symphonies and symphonic poems of Mahler and Strauss. What had been a concise, twenty-five-minute structure in the hands of Haydn and Mozart now could take over an hour and a half to play. As music could hardly go further in this direction, composers returned to the Classical ideals of tight organization

## LISTENING ACTIVITY: PREVIEWING EARLY-20TH-CENTURY STYLES

We can preview some of these new early-twentieth-century musical ideas in the examples below (StudySpace, Chapter 35). For each musical element, match the description to the musical example. We will consider all three composers and several of these works in detail in the next chapter.

### Stravinsky: *Rite of Spring*, Introduction

**1.** ___ Melody
  **a.** clear but angular melody line
  **b.** static, with little sense of melody

**2.** ___ Rhythm/Meter
  **a.** shifting accents, no clear meter
  **b.** gentle meter shifts from duple to triple

**3.** ___ Harmony
  **a.** harsh, dissonant block chords
  **b.** rich, lush, post-Romantic harmonies

**4.** ___ Texture
  **a.** complex polyphony with simultaneous lines
  **b.** focus on single line, largely homophonic

### Berg: *Wozzeck*, Act I, Scene 1

**5.** ___ Melody
  **a.** lyrical, singeable vocal line
  **b.** disjunct, speechlike vocal line

**6.** ___ Harmony
  **a.** harshly dissonant, pounding harmonies
  **b.** gently dissonant harmonies

**7.** ___ Texture
  **a.** simple, homophonic texture focused on voice
  **b.** complex polyphonic texture

### Webern: *Variations for Orchestra*, Op. 30

**8.** ___ Melody
  **a.** disjunct, wide-ranging line
  **b.** static melody, with no sense of line

**9.** ___ Rhythm/Meter
  **a.** changing tempo throughout
  **b.** steady beat and tempo

**10.** ___ Harmony
  **a.** clearly rooted in tonality
  **b.** no feeling of tonic or tonality

**11.** ___ Texture
  **a.** many simultaneous lines
  **b.** one or two main horizontal lines

**12.** ___ Timbre
  **a.** quickly changing instrument color
  **b.** main focus on string instrument timbres

and succinctness. In addition, they revived a number of older forms such as toccata, fugue, concerto grosso, and suite, while retaining the traditional symphony, sonata, and concerto. They valued the formal above the expressive, a principle known as *formalism*. The New Classicism, like the old, strove for purity of line and proportion. We will consider how these new ideas took shape in the works of Modernist composers writing in the first decades of the twentieth century.

Formalism

### Critical Thinking

**1.** How did the traditional system of tonality break down in the early twentieth century and what replaced it?

**2.** How did composers change their approach to the orchestra in early-twentieth-century music? How did they approach form?

# 36

# Music of the Early Modernists

"I hold that it was a mistake to consider me a revolutionary. If one only need break habit in order to be labeled a revolutionary, then every artist who has something to say and who in order to say it steps outside the bounds of established convention could be considered revolutionary."

—**Igor Stravinsky**

## KEY POINTS       Ⓢ **StudySpace** wwnorton.com/enjoy

- Russian composer Igor Stravinsky experimented with rhythm, new instrumental combinations, the percussive use of dissonance, as well as **polyrhythmic** and **polytonal** writing.

- Stravinsky's early works, including his ballets *The Firebird, Petrushka,* and *The Rite of Spring,* are strongly nationalistic; the last of these re-creates rites of ancient Russia.

- Arnold Schoenberg, along with his students Alban Berg and Anton Webern, comprise the **Second Viennese School.**

- Schoenberg was highly influential in German Expressionism: his song cycle *Pierrot lunaire* represents his atonal-Expressionist period. He also experimented with abandoning the tonal system, creating a **twelve-tone,** or **serial,** method that revolutionized twentieth-century composition.

- Alban Berg's music is rooted in the post-Romantic tradition, but he also drew on the twelve-tone system devised by his teacher, Schoenberg.

- Berg's most famous work is *Wozzeck,* an opera based on the Expressionist play about a disturbed man who moves between reality and hallucination.

I n this chapter, we will see how three early modern composers exploited the innovative compositional techniques of the early twentieth century (described in Chapter 35) to create radical levels of complexity in rhythm and texture, new angular melodies that could only be played on instruments, and a fresh sound-world that allowed both unprecedented types of dissonance and a different kind of organizational freedom. We will hear how Igor Stravinsky revolutionized rhythm and unleashed a harmonic language so dissonant that his ballet *The Rite of Spring* shocked and enraged audiences; how Arnold Schoenberg, in his song cycle *Pierrot lunaire,* dared to discard the established harmonic system used for some three hundred years while introducing a singing style that was the antithesis of lyrical; and how Alban Berg evokes both traditional and post-tonal harmonic idioms in his darkly Expressionist opera *Wozzeck.*

# Stravinsky and the Revitalization of Rhythm

Certain artists embody the most significant impulses of their time and affect the cultural life in a singularly powerful fashion. One such artist was Igor Stravinsky, the Russian composer who for half a century reflected the main currents in twentieth-century music.

## Igor Stravinsky (1882–1971)

**Igor Stravinsky** was born in Oranienbaum, not far from St. Petersburg, and grew up in a musical environment: his father was the leading bass singer at the Imperial Opera. His parents wanted him to study law; but while enrolled at the University of St. Petersburg, he continued his musical studies.

Success came early to Stravinsky. His music attracted the notice of Serge Diaghilev, the legendary impresario of the Paris-based Ballets Russes, who commissioned Stravinsky to write a score for *The Firebird.* Diaghilev pointed him out to the ballerina Tamara Karsavina with the words "Mark him well—he is a man on the eve of fame." *The Firebird* was followed a year later by the ballet *Petrushka,* which secured Stravinsky's position in the forefront of the modern movement. The spring of 1913 saw the staging of the third and most spectacular of the ballets Stravinsky wrote for Diaghilev, *The Rite of Spring.* On opening night, the revolutionary score touched off a near riot (see Btw, p. 302). However, when the work was presented a year later, it was received with enthusiasm and established itself as a masterpiece.

With the outbreak of war in 1914, Stravinsky and his family took refuge in Switzerland, their home for the next six years, where he wrote Neoclassical works more intimate in spirit and modest in dimension. In 1920, he settled in France and remained there until 1939. During these years, Stravinsky concertized extensively throughout Europe, performing his own music as pianist and conductor. When the Second World War broke out, he settled in California, outside Los Angeles, and in 1945, he became an American citizen. Stravinsky's later concert tours around the world made him the most celebrated figure in twentieth-century music. He died in New York on April 6, 1971, at the age of eighty-nine.

Stravinsky's style evolved continuously throughout his career—from the post-Impressionism of *The Firebird* and the primitivism of *The Rite of Spring* to the controlled classicism of his mature style and, finally, to the serialism of his late works.

Nationalism predominates in such early works as *The Firebird, Petrushka,* and *The Rite of Spring,* the last of which re-creates sacrificial rites of ancient Russia. In the decade of the First World War, the composer turned to a more economical style, writing *The Soldier's Tale,* a dance-drama for four characters and seven-piece band, and culminating in *Oedipus Rex,* an "opera-oratorio" based on a Greek tragedy by Sophocles. The *Symphony of Psalms,* for chorus and orchestra, is regarded by many as the chief work of Stravinsky's maturity.

Late in life, Stravinsky showed an increasing receptiveness to the twelve-tone style. The technique reveals itself in works from the middle 1950s; the most important are the ballet *Agon* and the choral work *Threni: Lamentations of the Prophet Jeremiah.*

**Major Works:** Orchestral music, including Symphonies of Wind Instruments (1920) and Symphony in Three Movements (1945) • Ballets, including *L'oiseau de feu* (*The Firebird,* 1910), *Petrushka* (1911), *Le sacre du printemps* (*The Rite of Spring,* 1913) • Operas, including *Oedipus Rex* (1927) • Other theater works, including *L'histoire du soldat* (*The Soldier's Tale,* 1918) • Choral music, including *Symphony of Psalms* (1930) and *Threni: Lamentations of the Prophet Jeremiah* (1958) • Chamber music • Piano music • Songs.

◉ **iMusic:** *Rite of Spring,* Introduction

# The Rite of Spring

First through his ballets, Stravinsky was a leader in the revitalization of rhythm in European art music; his rhythms were unparalleled in their dynamic power. He is also considered one of the great orchestrators, his music's sonority marked by a polished brightness and a clear texture. *The Rite of Spring,* subtitled *Scenes of Pagan Russia,* not only embodies the cult of primitivism that so startled its first-night audience, but also sets forth a new musical language characterized by the percussive use of dissonance, as well as polyrhythms and polytonality.

In Part I of the ballet, celebrations for the arrival of spring include a lustful abduction of women, a rivalry between two tribes, and a round dance. At the climax of these activities, the oldest and wisest man of the village is brought out for the ritual kissing of the earth, and the tribes respond joyfully and energetically.

Part II is more solemn. The women of the tribe, conducting a mysterious game, select a young maiden whom they will sacrifice in order to save the fertility of the earth. The Chosen One begins her fatal dance in front of the elders, and her limp body is eventually carried off to the Sun God Yarilo. The plot is vague, the anthropology is dubious, but the visions are effectively theatrical.

As a ballet, *The Rite of Spring* had a brief life, but the music survived independently as a concert piece. Today, it stands as one of the landmarks in twentieth-century symphonic literature. The size of the orchestra is monumental, even by the standards of late Romanticism. Stravinsky often uses the full force of the brass and percussion to create a barbaric, primeval sound and gives the strings percussive material such as pizzicato and successive down-bow strokes. The overall impact of the orchestration is harsh and loud, with constantly changing colors.

Stravinsky's treatment of melody and harmony creates a static quality. The melodies are modeled after Russian folk-songs—in fact, a number of authentic tunes are quoted—and the remaining melodic material, often presented in short fragments, uses limited ranges and extended repetition in a folk-song-like manner. The harmonies are derived from an eclectic language, including whole-tone and octatonic (eight-tone) scales, polytonality, and dissonance. Within each scene, Stravinsky minimizes harmonic changes through the use of ostinatos, pedal points, and melodic repetition.

The energetic interaction between rhythm and meter is the most innovative and influential element of *The Rite of Spring.* In some scenes, a steady pulse is set up, only to serve as a backdrop for unpredictable accents or melodic entrances. In other passages, the concept of a regular metric pulse is totally abandoned as downbeats occur seemingly at random. With *The Rite of Spring,* Stravinsky freed Western music from the traditional constraints of metric regularity.

In the Introduction to Part I, *Adoration of the Earth,* a writhing bassoon melody set in its uppermost range depicts the awakening of the Earth in spring. We hear the melody recur at the conclusion of the Introduction. Quietly, the

## By the way . . .

### How Could Stravinsky's Ballet Have Caused a Riot?

Audience members at the premiere of Stravinsky's *Rite of Spring*, held on May 29, 1913, at the swanky Parisian Théâtre des Champs-Elysées, knew they were witnessing music history in the making. The much anticipated ballet was the product of four great minds: the noted impresario and founder of the Ballets Russes, Serge Diaghilev; choreographer and legendary dancer Vaslav Nijinsky; designer and folklorist Nicholas Roerich; and Igor Stravinsky. No amount of publicity could have prepared the audience for the unballetic, flat-footed dancing; the complex, hallucinating rhythms; and the torturous melodies and dissonance levels. How could images of spring, a time of renewal in nature, be so frightful? And how could a rite—frequently a solemn or religious event—equal horrendous cult practices like human sacrifice? Indeed, reaction to the ballet was immediate that first night: mild protests at the opening, even before the curtain was raised, soon turned to an uproar. Cries of "Shut up" were heard around the theater, and one critic barked obscenities at the elegantly dressed ladies who found the work offensive. Stravinsky left in a rage: he loved the music and could not comprehend why people protested before hearing the entire ballet. When the dust settled, the reactions ranged from "magnifique" to "abominable." Composer Giacomo Puccini declared the choreography "ridiculous" and the music "sheer cacophony . . . the work of a madman." Still, Stravinsky believed in his creation, knowing that one day he would "witness triumph." Today we recognize that Igor Stravinsky—at the young age of thirty-one—revolutionized music with *The Rite of Spring* and catapulted him to stardom amid a frenzy of media attention. Perhaps you will hear this work now with new ears and a fascination with its rowdy history!

strings follow with a four-note motive played pizzicato. This motive signals the end of the Introduction and establishes the duple pulse necessary for the ensuing rhythmic conflict.

*The Dance of the Youths and Maidens* erupts with a series of violent and percussive chords that sound on unpredictable accents reinforced by the power of eight French horns, creating an intense conflict with the established meter. The harsh dissonance is fashioned from the combination of two traditional harmonies, resulting in a massive eight-note chord.

This opening section forms a block of sound that alternates with other sound masses and folk-like melodies during *The Dance of the Youths and Maidens*. Unifying these diverse passages are the unchanging harmonies and a constant eighth-note motion that maintains the duple pulse. The ideas recur like an ostinato, as the level of activity increases. The dense texture and loud dynamics build to a climax at the end of the section.

The opening of *Game of Abduction* provides a brief respite from the dense activity. A new folk melody is subjected to a similar ostinato-like treatment. The level of activity quickly rises again, complete with brash horn calls. Adding to the frenzy are loud accents that sound randomly, with no established pulse. The overall effect is primitive and lusty. The scenes that follow continue the pubescent rites, using modal harmonies to create a primitive atmosphere. Part I closes with the *Dance of the Earth*, which requires the utmost physicality from the players.

In Part II, Stravinsky continues his primitive rhythmic treatment, eerie orchestration, and bitingly dissonant tonalities. The work culminates in the *Sacrificial Dance,* during which the young girl dances herself to death in a frenzied climax.

The rhythmic arrangement of line and color in *The Dance* (1909–10), by **Henri Matisse** (1869–1954), is suggestive of the *Dance of the Youths and Maidens*, from Stravinsky's *Rite of Spring.*

---

**LISTENING GUIDE 41**   Ⓢ | DVD | **CD 7 (7–13)** | CD 3 (63–69)

# Stravinsky: *The Rite of Spring (Le sacre du printemps)*, Part I, excerpts

4:34

| | |
|---|---|
| **DATE:** | 1913 |
| **GENRE:** | Ballet (often performed as a concert piece for orchestra) |
| **BASIS:** | Scenes of pagan Russia |
| **SCENARIO:** | Nikolai Roerich and Igor Stravinsky |
| **CHOREOGRAPHY:** | Vaslav Nijinsky |

**SECTIONS:**

Part I: *Adoration of the Earth*
**Introduction**
**Dance of the Youths and Maidens**
**Game of Abduction**
*Spring Rounds*
*Games of the Rival Tribes*
*Procession of the Sage*
*Dance of the Earth*

Part II: *The Sacrifice*
*Introduction*
*Mystic Circle of the Adolescents*
*Glorification of the Chosen One*
*Evocation of the Ancestors*
*Ritual Action of the Ancestors*
*Sacrificial Dance*

*Continued on following page*

*Introduction*, closing measures

**WHAT TO LISTEN FOR:**

| | | | |
|---|---|---|---|
| Melody | Disjunct, floating folk-song melody | Expression | Haunting mood, represents awakening of earth; very slow tempo (*Lento*) |
| Rhythm/Meter | Free shifting meter, the 4-note rhythmic idea establishes duple pulse | Timbre | High-range bassoon with solo clarinets, pizzicato strings |

**63**   0:00   Folk tune played by the bassoon, from opening:

0:12   Pizzicato rhythmic figure in violins:

0:19   Clarinet flourish, followed by sustained string chord.
0:22   Violin figure returns to establish meter for next section.

*Dance of the Youths and Maidens*

**WHAT TO LISTEN FOR:**

| | | | |
|---|---|---|---|
| Melody | Russian folk-song melodies alternate with nonmelodic sound blocks | Form | Sectional, with opening section recurring several times (**A-B-A'-C-A-D-E-F-G-A″-F'**) |
| Rhythm/Meter | Basic duple pulse with irregular accents; constant 8th-note motion | Expression | Forceful, with high energy and changing dynamics |
| Harmony | Dissonant chord (polytonal) repeated over and over; sound blocks | Timbre | Changing instrumental colors throughout |
| Texture | Dense, complex polyphony | Performing Forces | Huge orchestra with expanded brass, woodwind, and percussion sections |

**64**   0:30   Strings play harsh, percussive chords (**A**), reinforced by 8 horns, with unpredictable accents:

0:37   English horn (**B**) plays the pizzicato motive from *Introduction*.
0:42   Brief return of opening accented chords (**A'**).
0:45   Motives combine with new ideas (**C**). Strings continue chords; English horn repeats its 4-note motive; loud brass interruptions and a descending melodic fragment.
1:02   Return of opening accented chords (**A**).

**65**   1:10   Bassoon plays syncopated folk melody (**D**), over accented string chords:

| | | |
|---|---|---|
| | 1:38 | Steady eighth-note pulse (**E**); 4-note motive alternates between the English horn and trumpet; scurrying motives in the winds and strings, and sustained trills. |
| | 1:50 | 4-note motive (English horn, then violins) and sustained trills; low strings hit strings with the wood of their bows (*col legno*). |
| 66 | 1:57 | French horn and flute introduce a folklike melody (**F**); texture thickens with activity: |

| | | |
|---|---|---|
| | 2:23 | Flutes repeat theme (from **F**). |
| 67 | 2:28 | New melody (**G**) appears in trumpets with parallel chords: |

| | | |
|---|---|---|
| | 2:42 | Texture abruptly reduced; accents of the opening section (**A″**) return; frenetic activity continues. |
| | 2:50 | Melody (**F′**) in piccolo, then in lutes and strings; unpredictable accents, scurrying activity, and an expanding texture leads to climax. |

### Game of Abduction

**WHAT TO LISTEN FOR:**

| | | | | |
|---|---|---|---|---|
| Melody | Scurrying melodic figures and horn calls, brief folk tune | | Texture | Dense, with shifting activity |
| | | | Expression | Frenetic and primitive mood |
| Rhythm/ Meter | Fast tempo, meter not established; unpredictable accents | | Timbre | Quickly shifting instrumental colors |
| Harmony | Harshly dissonant, crashing chords | | | |

| | | |
|---|---|---|
| 68 | 3:16 | Sustained chords, hurrying string sounds, and syncopated accents. |
| | 3:20 | Woodwinds and piccolo trumpet introduce folk theme; texture dense with constantly changing activity and timbres: |

| | | |
|---|---|---|
| | 3:29 | Horns introduce new motive, alternating interval of a fourth: |

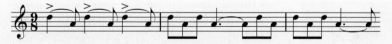

| | | |
|---|---|---|
| 69 | 3:48 | New thematic idea, in homorhythmic texture and changing meters: |

| | | |
|---|---|---|
| | 3:56 | Horn motive returns. |
| | 4:07 | Timpani and full orchestra alternate strong beats; irregular accents. |
| | 4:24 | Series of loud chords and sustained trill end movement. |

🎧 **Now try the Listening Quiz.**

# Schoenberg and the Second Viennese School

*"I personally hate to be called a revolutionist, which I am not. What I did was neither revolution nor anarchy."*

(Top) **Arnold Schoenberg**'s Expressionist painting, *The Red Gaze* (1910), is highly reminiscent of Edvard Munch's *The Scream*.

(Botttom) French Expressionist artist **Georges Rouault** (1871–1958) painted many images of the Pierrot character. *Blue Pierrots*, c. 1943.

The Expressionist movement manifested itself in the music of Arnold Schoenberg and his followers. Schoenberg's pioneering efforts in the breakdown of the traditional tonal system and his development of the twelve-tone method, described earlier, revolutionized musical composition. His innovations were taken further by his most gifted students, Alban Berg (whom we will consider; see p. 309) and by Anton Webern, who employed Schoenberg's twelve-tone method with unprecedented strictness, moving toward complete, or total serialism. These three composers are often referred to as the ***Second Viennese School*** (the first school being Haydn, Mozart, and Beethoven).

## Pierrot lunaire

For his song cycle *Pierrot lunaire,* Schoenberg drew on the stock characters of the Italian *commedia dell'arte* (improvised comedy), a comic theatrical entertainment that originated in the mid-sixteenth century. One of the most parodied characters is the clown Pierrot (Pagliaccio in Italian; Petrushka in Russian), who has been the model for pantomime for centuries.

Schoenberg chose the texts for his song cycle from a collection of poems by the Belgian writer Albert Giraud, a disciple of the Symbolists. Giraud's Pierrot was the poet-rascal-clown whose chalk-white face, passing abruptly from laughter to tears, enlivened every puppet show and pantomime in Europe. The poems were liberally spiced with elements of the macabre and the bizarre that suited the end-of-century taste for decadence; with their abrupt changes of mood from guilt and depression to atonement and playfulness, they fired Schoenberg's imagination. He picked twenty-one texts and set them for a female reciter and a chamber music ensemble of five players using eight instruments. Despite the small ensemble, no song in the cycle uses the same instrumentation. The work, he explained, was conceived "in a light, ironical, satirical tone."

One of Schoenberg's goals was to bring spoken word and music as close together as possible; he achieved this aim through **Sprechstimme** (spoken voice), a new style in which the vocal melody is spoken rather than sung on exact pitches and in strict rhythm. The result is a weird but strangely effective vocal line brought to perfection in *Pierrot lunaire.*

Giraud's short poems enabled Schoenberg to create a series of miniatures balanced by the utmost variety in structure, texture—from dense to sparse—and instrumentation from one piece to the next. Schoenberg also experimented with what he called **Klangfarbenmelodie** (tone-color melody), in which each

## Arnold Schoenberg (1874–1951)

**Arnold Schoenberg** was born in Vienna. Having decided to devote his life to music, he took lessons in counterpoint with a young musician, Alexander von Zemlinsky. This was the only musical instruction he ever had. Through Zemlinsky, young Schoenberg was introduced to the advanced musical circles of Vienna, which at that time were under the spell of Wagner's operas. In 1899, when he was twenty-five, Schoenberg wrote the string sextet *Transfigured Night*.

Schoenberg became active as a teacher and soon gathered about him a band of students that included Alban Berg and Anton Webern. With each new work, Schoenberg moved closer to taking as bold a step as any composer has ever taken—the rejection of tonality. The First World War interrupted his creative activity. He was called for military service, followed by a compositional silence of eight years (1915–23), during which he evolved a set of structural procedures to replace tonality. His "method of composing with twelve tones" firmly established him as a leader of contemporary musical thought.

He taught composition in Berlin until Hitler came to power in 1933, when Schoenberg emigrated to America and joined the faculty of the University of Southern California; he was later appointed professor of composition at the University of California, Los Angeles. Like Stravinsky, he became an American citizen in 1940, taught until his retirement at the age of seventy, and continued his musical activities until his death seven years later.

Schoenberg's early works exemplify post-Wagnerian Romanticism; they still used key signatures and remained within the boundaries of tonality. In Schoenberg's second period, the atonal-Expressionist abolished the distinction between consonance and dissonance and any sense of a home key. We will hear these traits, along with extreme chromaticism, in *Pierrot lunaire*. In Schoenberg's third style period, he exploited the twelve-tone method, and in the last part of his career—the American phase—he carried the twelve-tone technique to further stages of refinement. Several of the late works present the twelve-tone style in a manner markedly more accessible than earlier pieces, often with tonal implications, as in his cantata *A Survivor from Warsaw*.

**Major Works:** Orchestral music, including Five Pieces for Orchestra, Variations for Orchestra, and 2 concertos (violin, piano) • Operas • Choral music, including the cantata *A Survivor from Warsaw* (1947) • Chamber music, including 4 string quartets and string sextet *Verklärte Nacht* (*Transfigured Night*, 1899) • Piano music.

### In His Own Words

Whether one calls oneself conservative or revolutionary, whether one composes in a conventional or progressive manner, whether one tries to imitate old styles or is destined to express new ideas . . . one must be convinced of the infallibility of one's own fantasy and one must believe in one's own inspiration.

---

## LISTENING GUIDE 42

⊚ | DVD | CD 7 (14–17) | CD 4 (6–7)

# Schoenberg: *Pierrot lunaire*, No. 18     0:51

**DATE:** 1912

**GENRE:** Song cycle (21 songs in 3 parts)

*Part I*  Pierrot, a sad clown figure, is obsessed with the moon, having drunk moonwine; his loves, fantasies, and frenzies are exposed.

*Part II:*  Pierrot becomes ridden with guilt and wants to make atonement.

*Part III:*  Pierrot climbs from the depths of depression to a more playful mood, but with fleeting thoughts of guilt; then he becomes sober.

1. *Moondrunk*
2. *Columbine*
3. *The Dandy*
4. *Pale Washerwoman*
5. *Valse de Chopin*
6. *Madonna*
7. *The Sick Moon*

8. *Night*
9. *Prayer to Pierrot*
10. *Theft*
11. *Red Mass*
12. *Gallows Ditty*
13. *Beheading*
14. *The Crosses*

15. *Homesickness*
16. *Vulgar Horseplay*
17. *Parody*
18. **The Moonfleck**
19. *Serenade*
20. *Homeward Journey*
21. *O Scent of Fabled Yesteryear*

*Continued on following page*

## 18. *The Moonfleck (Der Mondfleck)*

### WHAT TO LISTEN FOR:

| | | | |
|---|---|---|---|
| **Melody** | Disjunct line, quasi-speechlike (Sprechstimme) | **Form** | Rondeau text with poetic/musical refrain |
| **Rhythm/ Meter** | Very fast, sounds free-flowing | **Timbre** | Pointillistic, flickering instrumental effects |
| **Harmony** | Harshly dissonant | **Performing Forces** | Voice with 5 instruments (piccolo, clarinet, violin, cello, piano) |
| **Texture** | Complex counterpoint with canonic (strict imitative) treatment | **Text** | 21 poems from Albert Giraud's *Pierrot lunaire,* all in rondeau form |

| | TEXT | TRANSLATION |
|---|---|---|
| **6**  0:00 | *Einen weissen Fleck des hellen Mondes*<br>*Auf dem Rücken seines schwarzen Rockes.*<br>So spaziert Pierrot im lauen Abend,<br>Aufzusuchen Glück und Abenteuer. | *With a fleck of white—from*<br>*the bright moon—on the back of his black jacket.*<br>Pierrot strolls about in the<br>mild evening seeking his fortune and adventure. |
| | Plötzlich stört ihn was an seinem Anzug,<br>Er beschaut sich rings und findet richtig— | Suddenly something strikes<br>him as wrong, he checks his<br>clothes and sure enough finds |
| **7**  0:23 | *Einen weissen Fleck des hellen Mondes*<br>*Auf dem Rücken seines schwarzen Rockes.* | *a fleck of white—from the*<br>*bright moon—on the back of his black jacket.* |
| | Warte! denkt er: das ist so ein Gipsfleck!<br>Wischt und wischt, doch—bringt ihn<br>nicht herunter!<br>Und so geht er, giftgeschwollen, weiter,<br>Reibt und reibt bis an den frühen Morgen—<br>*Einen weissen Fleck des hellen Mondes.* | Damn! he thinks: that's a<br>spot of plaster! Wipes and<br>wipes, but—he can't get it<br>off. And so goes on his way,<br>his pleasure poisoned, rubs<br>and rubs till the early morning—<br>*a fleck of white from the bright moon.* |

Opening of vocal line

○ **Now try the Listening Quiz.**

note of a melody is played by a different instrument, creating a shifting effect that evokes the moonbeams mentioned in the poems.

We will focus on one of the songs from the last group in the cycle. In No. 18, *The Moonfleck (Der Mondfleck;* see Listening Guide 42 for the text), Pierrot, out to have fun, is disturbed by a white spot—a patch of moonlight—on the collar of his jet-black jacket. He rubs and rubs but cannot get rid of it. The piano introduces a three-voice fugue, while the other instruments unfold devices such as strict canons in diminution (smaller note values) and retrograde (backward). Schoenberg was obviously fascinated by such constructions, which recall the wizardry of the Renaissance and Baroque contrapuntists.

# Berg and Early-Twentieth-Century Opera

"Boredom . . . is the last thing one should experience in the theater."

Alban Berg brought great lyrical imagination to the abstract procedures of the Schoenbergian technique. In his operas, he was drawn to Expressionist themes focusing on human foibles and depravity, and on characters who were utterly powerless to control the world around them.

## Alban Berg (1885–1935)

**Berg** was born in Vienna into a well-to-do family and grew up in an environment that fostered his artistic interests. At nineteen, he began studying with Arnold Schoenberg, an exacting master and mentor who shaped Berg's outlook on art.

At the outbreak of war in 1914, Berg was called up for military service despite his uncertain health (he suffered from asthma and a nerve ailment). With the premiere of his opera *Wozzeck* at the Berlin State Opera in 1925, Berg rose from obscurity to international fame.

During his mature years, he was active as a teacher and also wrote about music, propagandizing tirelessly on behalf of Schoenberg and his school. With the coming to power of Hitler, the works of the twelve-tone composers were banned in Germany as alien to the spirit of the Third Reich.

Exhausted and ailing after the completion of his Violin Concerto, Berg went to the country for a short rest before resuming work on his second opera *Lulu*. An insect bite brought on an abscess, then infection, and finally blood poisoning on his return to Vienna. He died on Christmas Eve 1935, seven weeks before his fifty-first birthday.

Besides the opera *Wozzeck*, Berg's most widely known composition is the *Lyric Suite*, a work in six movements, the first and last of which strictly follow the twelve-tone method. Berg spent the last seven years of his life working on the opera *Lulu*, which is based on a single twelve-tone row. The opera remained unfinished at his death until the orchestration was completed by the Austrian composer Friedrich Cerha, and now *Lulu* has taken its place alongside *Wozzeck* as one of the more challenging works of the modern lyric theater. Alban Berg is probably the most widely admired master of the twelve-tone school. His premature death at the age of fifty robbed contemporary music of a major figure.

**Major Works:** 2 operas: *Wozzeck* (1917–22) and *Lulu* (unfinished, 1935) • Orchestral music, including Three Orchestral Pieces, Op. 6 (1915) and the Violin Concerto (1935) • Chamber music, including *Lyric Suite* (1926) • Piano music • Songs.

◉ **iMusic:** *Wozzeck*, Act 1, Scene 1

*In His Own Words*

When I decided to write an opera, my only intentions . . . were to give the theater what belongs to the theater. . . . The music was to be so formed as consciously to fulfill its duty of serving the action at every moment.

## Berg's *Wozzeck*

Berg's style was rooted in German Romanticism and formal procedures of the past, even after he had adopted the twelve-tone style. An Expressionist play by Georg Büchner (1813–1837) inspired Berg to write his opera *Wozzeck*. The play is based on gruesome, real-life events. In the title character of Wozzeck, Büchner created an archetype of "the insulted and injured" inhabitants of the earth. The action centers on Wozzeck's unhappy love for Marie, by whom he has fathered an illegitimate child. Wozzeck, a common soldier, is the victim of the sadistic Captain and the coldly scientific Doctor, who uses Wozzeck for his experiments.

# Berg: *Wozzeck*, Act III, Scene 4

4:44

**DATE:** 1922

**GENRE:** Opera, in 3 acts

**BASIS:** Expressionist play by Georg Büchner

**CHARACTERS:** Wozzeck, a soldier (baritone      Captain (tenor))
Marie, his common-law wife (soprano)      Doctor (bass)
Marie's son (treble)      Doctor (bass)

## Act III, Scene 4: By the pond

**WHAT TO LISTEN FOR:**

| | | | |
|---|---|---|---|
| Melody | Use of Sprechstimme (speechlike melody); disjunct line | Expression | Intensely emotional vocal line, supported by dissonance and surging dynamics |
| Rhythm | Movement alternates between metric and free-flowing | Timbre | Eerie mood created by celeste and unusual instrument combinations; colorful orchestral effects |
| Harmony | Both tonal and atonal language; dissonant and chromatic | | |

**WOZZECK**

| 8 | 0:00 | Das Messer? Wo ist das Messer? Ich hab's dagelassen. Näher, noch näher. Mir graut's . . . da regt sich was. Still! Alles still und tot. | The knife? Where is the knife? I left it there. Around here somewhere. I'm terrified . . . something's moving. Silence. Everything silent and dead. |
|---|---|---|---|

*(shouting)*

Mörder! Mörder!      Murderer! Murderer!

*(whispering again)*

Ha! Da ruft's. Nein, ich selbst.      Ah! Someone called. No, it was only me.

*(Still looking, he staggers a few steps further and stumbles against the corpse.)*

Marie! Marie! Was hast du für eine rote Schnur um den Hals? Hast dir das rote Halsband verdient, wie die Ohrringlein, mit deiner Sünde! Was hängen dir die schwarzen Haare so wild? Mörder! Mörder! Sie werden nach mir suchen. Das Messer verrät mich!      Marie! Marie! What's that red cord around your neck? Was the red necklace payment for you sins, like the earrings? Why's your dark hair so wild about you? Murderer! Murderer! They will come and look for me. The knife will betray me!

*(looks for it in a frenzy)*

Da, da ist's.      Here! Here it is!

*(at the pond)*

So! Da hinunter!      There! Sink to the bottom!

*(throws knife into the pond)*

Es taucht ins dunkle Wasser wie ein Stein.      It plunges into the dark water like a stone.

*(The moon appears, blood-red, from behind the clouds. Wozzeck looks up.)*

Aber der Mond verrät mich, der Mond ist blutig. Will denn die ganze Welt es      But the moon will betray me: the moon is bloodstained. Is the whole world going to

| | |
|---|---|
| ausplaudern! Das Messer, es liegt zu weit vorn, sie finden's beim Baden oder wenn sie nach Muscheln tauchen. | incriminate me? The knife is too near the edge: they'll find it when they're swimming or diving for snails. |

*(wades into the pond)*

| | |
|---|---|
| Ich find's nicht. Aber ich muss mich waschen. Ich bin blutig. Da ein Fleck— und noch einer. Weh! Weh! Ich wasche mich mit Blut— das Wasser ist Blut . . . Blut . . . | I can't find it. But I must wash myself. There's blood on me. There's a spot here— and another. Oh, God! I am washing myself in blood— the water is blood . . . blood . . . |

*(drowns)*

Wozzeck's last words before drowning, accompanied by very soft ascending chromatic scales in strings:

*(The Doctor appears, followed by the Captain.)*

**CAPTAIN**

| | |
|---|---|
| 9   3:03   Halt! | Wait! |

**DOCTOR** *(stops)*

| | |
|---|---|
| Hören Sie? Dort! | Can you hear? There! |

**CAPTAIN** *(stops as well)*

| | |
|---|---|
| Jesus! Das war ein Ton! | Jesus! What a ghastly sound! |

**DOCTOR** *(pointing to the pond)*

| | |
|---|---|
| Ja, dort! | Yes, there! |

**CAPTAIN**

| | |
|---|---|
| Es ist das Wasser im Teich. Das Wasser ruft. Es ist schon lange niemand ertrunken. Kommen Sie, Doktor! Es ist nicht gut zu hören. | It's the water in the pond. The water is calling. It's been a long time since anyone drowned Come away, Doctor. It's not good for us to be hearing it. |

*(tries to drag the Doctor away)*

**DOCTOR** *(resisting and continuing to listen)*

| | |
|---|---|
| Das stöhnt, als stürbe ein Mensch. Da ertrinkt Jemand! | There's a groan, as though someone were dying. Somebody's drowning! |

**CAPTAIN**

| | |
|---|---|
| Unheimlich! Der Mond rot, und die Nebel grau. Hören Sie? . . . Jetzt wieder das Ächzen. | It's eerie! The moon is red, and the mist is gray. Can you hear? . . . That moaning again. |

**DOCTOR**

| | |
|---|---|
| Stiller,... jetzt ganz still. | It's getting quieter . . . now it's stopped altogether. |

**CAPTAIN**

| | |
|---|---|
| Kommen Sie! Kommen Sie schnell! | Come! Come quickly! |

*(He rushes off, pulling the Doctor along with him.)*

Ⓢ **Now try the Listening Quiz.**

Singers Georg Nigl and Angela Denoke perform during a dress rehearsal of Berg's opera *Wozzeck* at Vienna's Theater an der Wien in 2010.

Marie is hopelessly infatuated with the handsome Drum Major. Wozzeck slowly realizes that she has been unfaithful to him. Ultimately he cuts her throat, then, driven back to the death scene by guilt and remorse, he drowns himself.

Harmonically, the greater part of the opera is cast in an atonal-Expressionist idiom. Berg anticipates certain twelve-tone procedures; he also looks back to the tonal tradition, writing a number of passages in major and minor keys and using leitmotifs in the Wagnerian manner. Throughout we hear moments of passionate lyricism that alternate with speechlike vocal lines (Sprechstimme).

**Act III, Scene 4**      We will consider one of the final scenes in the opera. In Scene 4 of Act III, Wozzeck returns to the path near the pond where he has killed Marie, and stumbles against her body. He asks, "Marie, what's that red cord around your neck?" (See Listening Guide 43 for the text.) He finds the knife with which he committed the murder, throws it into the pond, and, driven by his delusions, follows it into the water. His last words as he drowns—"I am washing myself in blood—the water is blood . . . blood!" The Doctor appears, followed by the Captain. We see the haunted scene through their eyes as, terrified, they run away.

**Act III, Scene 5**      After a passionate symphonic interlude, the final scene takes place in the morning in front of Marie's house, where children are playing. Marie's little boy rides a hobbyhorse. Other children rush in with news of the murder, but Marie's son does not understand. The children run off as he continues to ride and sing. Then, noticing that he has been left alone, he calls "Hop, hop" and rides off on his hobbyhorse. This closing scene—with the curtain closing on an empty stage—is utterly heartbreaking.

*Wozzeck* envelops the listener in a hallucinated world that could only have come from central Europe in the 1920s. But its characters reach out beyond time and place to become eternal symbols of the human condition.

### Critical Thinking

**1.** What elements made Stravinsky's *Rite of Spring* shocking to its first audiences? Is it still shocking today?

**2.** What effect does Schoenberg's use of atonality (in *Pierrot lunaire*) have on the listener?

**3.** What is Expressionistic about Schoenberg's *Pierrrot lunaire* and Berg's *Wozzeck*?

# 37 European National Schools

"Folk songs bind the nation, bind all nations and all people
with one spirit, one happiness, one paradise.

—Leoš Janáček

## KEY POINTS

> **StudySpace** wwnorton.com/enjoy

- Twentieth-century composers used more authentic folk and traditional elements in their nationalistic music than nineteenth-century composers did.

- National "schools" of composition developed across Europe in France, Russia, England, Germany, Spain, Scandinavia, and in various Eastern European countries.

- Hungarian composer Béla Bartók collected traditional songs and dances from his native land and incorporated elements from them into his compositions.

- Bartók's music displays new scales and rhythmic ideas and a modern, polytonal harmonic language, all set in Classical forms. His *Concerto for Orchestra* is a programmatic work that uses the whole ensemble as the "soloist."

- German composer Carl Orff set racy medieval lyrics of wandering monks in his well-known cantata *Carmina burana*. The most famous section is the stirring opening and closing chorus that evokes Fortuna, the goddess of luck.

Twentieth-century nationalism differed from its nineteenth-century counterpart in one important respect: composers approached traditional music with a scientific spirit, prizing the ancient tunes precisely because they departed from the conventional mold. By this time, the phonograph had been invented. The new students of folklore (*ethnomusicologists*, who study music in its cultural and global context) took recording equipment into the field to preserve the songs exactly as the village folk sang them. And composers who were inspired by these folk elements tried to retain the traditional flavor of the original songs and dances in their works.

Ethnomusicologists

We presented an overview of schools of musical nationalism in the Romantic era (see p. 235), and many of these continued into the twentieth century. The modern English school for example, is best represented by Benjamin Britten (1913–1976), known for his operas, including *Peter Grimes* (1945), about an English fishing village, and *Billy Budd* (1951), based on a Herman Melville story. You will recall that Britten's *Variations and Fugue on a Theme of Purcell* (*The Young Person's Guide to the Orchestra*) was discussed earlier (Chapter 10). The Russian school continued with two important figures as well: Sergei Prokofiev (1891–1953), known for his symphonies, operas, and piano concertos, as well as the popular, narrated *Peter and the Wolf* and his film score to *Lieutenant Kijé;* and Dmitri Shostakovich, whose symphonies and operas established his international reputation during the era of the Soviet Union (1917–91). French composers in the generation after Debussy and Ravel tried to recapture the wit and spirit that were part of their national heritage. One

Inspired by the German bombing of the Basque town of Guernica on April 26, 1937, this nationalistic painting was produced by **Pablo Picasso**.

group in particular, called *Les Six* (The Six), promoted new concepts of harmony while looking back to Neoclassical ideals. Darius Milhaud (1892–1974) is remembered for his jazzy ballet *The Creation of the World* (1923) and for his role in developing polytonality. Francis Poulenc (1899–1963) is perhaps the most known member of Les Six, recognized for his songs and his opera, especially *Dialogue of the Carmelites* (1957). Among the composers who came into prominence in the years after the First World War, Paul Hindemith (1895–1963) was the most important. He left Germany when Hitler came to power—his music was banned by the Third Reich as "cultural Bolshevism"—and spent two decades in the United States, where he taught at Yale University.

We will consider here the music of two composers who strongly evoke the folk traditions of their homelands: Béla Bartók, a major proponent of Hungarian nationalism and an avid collector of folk songs; and Carl Orff, who was inspired by both historical poetry and traditional folk music of his native Germany.

# Béla Bartók and the Eastern European Tradition

Béla Bartók reconciled the traditional songs of his native Hungary with the main currents of European music, thus creating an entirely personal language. His search for the authentic folk music led him to collect, with his colleague Zoltán Kodály, more than 2,000 songs and dances representing various Eastern European cultures.

## *Concerto for Orchestra*

Bartók rejected the late Romantic orchestral sound for a palette of colors all his own. His orchestration ranges from brilliant mixtures to threads of pure color that bring out the intertwining melody lines. In the summer of 1943, two years before his death, Bartók was commissioned to write the *Concerto for Orchestra*. The work, set in five movements, is called a concerto because he treated "the single orchestral instruments in a concertante or soloistic manner." Here, the virtuoso is the entire orchestra.

*Interrupted Intermezzo*    We will consider the fourth movement, titled *Interrupted Intermezzo,* which opens with a plaintive tune in the oboe and flute; its pentatonic structure evokes a Hungarian folk song. The nonsymmetrical rhythm, alternating between 2/4 and 5/8 meter, gives the movement an unpredictable charm. A memorable broad theme is then heard in the strings, but the mood is interrupted by a harsh clarinet melody borrowed from the Russian composer Dmitri Shostakovich's Symphony No. 7, a musical portrayal of the Nazi invasion of Russia in 1942. Bartók made an autobiographical statement in this movement: "The artist declares his love for his native land in a serenade, which is suddenly interrupted in a crude and violent manner; he is seized by rough, booted men who even break his instrument." The two opening themes eventually return in a sentimental declaration of the composer's love for his homeland.

## Béla Bartók (1881–1945)

A native Hungarian, **Bartók** studied at the Royal Academy in Budapest. His interest in the nationalist movement and folklore led him to realize that what passed for Hungarian in the eyes of the world was really the music of Roma, or Gypsies. With his fellow composer Zoltán Kodály, he toured the remote villages of the country, determined to collect the native songs before they died out forever (see illustration, p. 317).

Although Bartók became a leading figure in his country's musical life, he was troubled by the alliance between the Hungarian government and Nazi Germany on the eve of the Second World War. He therefore moved to the United States in 1940, settling in New York City.

Suffering from leukemia in his final years, Bartók received a series of commissions from various sources that spurred him to compose his last works, which rank among his finest. He died in New York City at the age of sixty-four.

Bartók discovered that Eastern European traditional music was based on ancient modes, unfamiliar scales, and nonsymmetrical rhythms. His study of this music brought him to new concepts of melody, harmony, and rhythm—his harmony can be bitingly dissonant, and polytonality abounds in his work.

He is also one of the great rhythmic innovators of modern times. Like Stravinsky, Bartók frequently used pounding, stabbing rhythms, syncopation, changing meters, and repeated patterns (ostinatos). In his middle years, he turned from thinking harmonically to thinking linearly. The resulting complex texture is a masterly example of modern dissonant counterpoint. But again, like Stravinsky, he carefully disclaimed the role of revolutionary. Despite the newness of his musical language, he adhered to the logic and beauty of Classical form.

A virtuoso pianist himself, Bartók was one of the masters of modern piano writing; his works typify the twentieth-century use of the piano as an instrument of percussion and rhythm. His six string quartets rank among the finest achievements of the twentieth century. He is best known to the public for the major works of his last period: the *Music for Strings, Percussion, and Celesta,* regarded by many as his masterpiece, and the *Concerto for Orchestra,* a favorite with American audiences (and the work we will study).

**Major Works:** Orchestral music, including *Music for Strings, Percussion, and Celesta* (1936) • *Concerto for Orchestra* (1943) • Concertos (2 for violin; 3 for piano) • Stage works, including 1 opera (*Bluebeard's Castle,* 1918) and 2 ballets • Chamber music, including 6 string quartets, sonatas, duos • Piano music, including *Allegro barbaro* (1911) and *Mikrokosmos* (6 books, 1926–39) • Choral music • Folk song arrangements for solo voice and for choir.

### In His Own Words

To handle folk tunes is one of the most difficult tasks. If we keep in mind that borrowing a tune means being bound by its individual peculiarity, we shall understand one part of the difficulty. Another is created by the special character of folk tune. We must penetrate it, feel it, and bring out its sharp contours by the appropriate setting.

---

## LISTENING GUIDE 44

DVD | **CD 7 (25–31)** | CD 3 (70–76)

# Bartók: *Interrupted Intermezzo,*
# from *Concerto for Orchestra*

4:20

**DATE:** 1943

**GENRE:** Orchestral concerto

**MOVEMENTS:** 1. Introduction, Allegro non troppo / Allegro vivace; sonata-allegro form
2. *Game of Pairs,* Allegretto scherzando; **A-B-A′** form
3. Elegia, Andante non troppo; in 3 episodes
4. **Interrupted Intermezzo, Allegretto; rondo-like form**
5. Pesante / Presto; sonata-allegro form

*Continued on following page*

**Fourth Movement:** *Interrupted Intermezzo*

**WHAT TO LISTEN FOR:**

| | | | |
|---|---|---|---|
| Melody | 3 contrasting themes:<br>　1) folklike and pentatonic (**A**)<br>　2) broad and lyrical (**B**)<br>　3) harsh descending line in clarinet (**C**) | Harmony | Polytonal and atonal harmonies; dissonant |
| | | Form | Rondo-like structure (**A-B-A′-C′-B′-A″**) |
| | | Expression | Nostalgic and sentimental; violent interruption at idea of Nazi invasion |
| Rhythm/<br>Meter | Shifting meters (2/4, 5/8, 3/4, 5/8) and irregular rhythms | Timbre | Solo woodwinds featured (oboe, clarinet, flute); darkly colored (violas) |

70　0:00　　Dramatic 4-note introduction, unison in strings.

　　0:05　　**A section**—plaintive, folklike tune, played by oboe in changing meter with asymmetrical rhythms:

Theme heard in flute and clarinets; dialogue continues in woodwinds and French horn.

71　1:00　　**B section**—sweeping lyrical melody in violas, in shifting meter:

Violins take up lyrical theme an octave higher, with countermelody in violas; marked "calmo" (calm).

72　1:44　　**A′ section**—dissonant woodwinds lead to varied statement of opening theme; more chromatic.

73　2:04　　**C section**—tempo picks up; clarinet introduces new theme (from Shostakovich symphony):

　　2:17　　Dissonant punctuations in brass and woodwinds.

　　2:31　　Theme parodied in violins.

74　2:44　　Theme of **C section** introduced by tubas with theme in its original form, then heard in inversion in strings:

75　2:57　　**B′ section**—flowing B section theme returns in muted strings.

76　3:31　　**A″ section**—woodwinds with fragments of open theme; flute cadenza; leads into gentle closing.

ⓢ **Now try the Listening Quiz.**

## Bartók—A Folk-Song Collector

Béla Bartók recording Slovakian folk songs on an acoustic cylinder machine in the Hungarian village of Zobordarázs, in 1907.

Béla Bartók, along with fellow composer Zoltán Kodály (1882–1967), searched out the national musics of various Eastern European cultures. The two took on this project not as composers but as folklorists who wanted to study traditional music scientifically. (The comparative study of musics of the world, focusing on the cultural context of performance, is known as ***ethnomusicology***.) Their fieldwork, in the villages and countrysides of Eastern Europe, centered on the music of numerous distinct groups: Slovak, Romanian, Bulgarian, Serbian, Croatian, Hungarian, as well as Roma, or Gypsy, and Arab. The many thousands of songs they collected reflect the very essence of these peoples—their social rituals and their religious ceremonies.

Bartók drew extensively in his compositions from the melodies, rhythms, and poetic structures of this rich body of traditional music. He was partial to modal scales, but rhythm was the primary attraction of this body of folk music and dance. Bartók tried at times to imitate the vocal style of Hungarian music, which is based on free speech-rhythms and follows the natural inflection of the language. At other times, he used the irregular folk dance rhythms typical of Bulgarian music. These propelling rhythms were driven by additive meters built from unit groups of 2, 3, or 4. We can hear an example of this in the Bulgarian folk dance *Gankino horo*, a line dance with intricate footwork. This dance, played in our iMusic example on folk accor-dion, is written in an asymmetrical meter of 11/16 that subdivides as 2 + 2 + 3 + 2 + 2. (On additive meter, see pp. 14–15.) By adopting this folk legacy, Bartók fashioned a unique musical style that places him, alongside Stravinsky, as a major innovator in the revitalization of rhythm, infusing it with earthy vitality and tension.

---

🔘 **iMusic**
*Gankino horo* (Bulgaria)

# The German Composer Carl Orff

*"Melody and speech belong together. I reject the idea of a pure music."*

---

Carl Orff (1895–1982) was one of the few composers who remained active during the Nazi regime in Germany and won success around the world. His musical voice is very much his own, looking simultaneously to early music and German folklore while remaining veiled in a religious mysticism.

## Orff's *Carmina burana*

Orff's starting point in his famous cantata was a collection of medieval poems that was discovered in 1803 at the monastery of Benedikbeuren, in southern Germany. (Orff's title means simply "songs of Beuren.") The manuscript includes poems written by wandering scholar/monks on a variety of topics, including moralizing and satirical themes, vagabond songs on the joys of gambling, drinking and the free life, as well as earthy, even erotic, love songs.

Medieval poetry

Premiered in 1937 in Frankfurt-am-Main, Orff's *Carmina burana* saw performances in many of Europe's most prestigious opera houses during the next decade. Orff intended that his cantata be a dramatic presentation, accompanied by dance and mime. *Carmina burana* is eclectic in its brutally percussive effects, blaring

## Carl Orff (1895–1982)

**Orff** began studying piano and cello at a very young age and soon became enthralled with the contradictory sound worlds of Debussy and Schoenberg. In 1924, he founded, along with pedagogue Dorothee Günther, a school for music and dance based on gymnastics and movement. Although this school was closed by the Nazis in 1944, his famous Schulwerk program grew out of this collaboration. The program, which gained international popularity, linked music and gesture, and provided a hands-on method of learning for children, using percussion instruments and recordings.

In the 1930s, Orff took over the direction of a concert series in Munich, but he resigned that post with the coming of national socialism. He has come under criticism for his continued musical activity in Germany during the Nazi era. His interest in early music led him to edit some excerpts from Monteverdi operas and to explore medieval Latin lyrics. Inspired by the educated medieval mind, he wrote *Carmina burana* (1937), which marked his first success. His dual interest in the theatrical and the archaic led to two more cantatas—*Catulli carmina* and *Trionfo di Afrodite*—which, with *Carmina burana*, he shaped into a trilogy. In his later works, Orff continued his focus on antiquity, writing on the dramas of *Antigone*, *Oedipus*, and *Prometheus*. Orff served as a composition professor at the music conservatory of Munich. Today, Orff is most remembered for his pedagogical Schulwerk program for children.

Orff's music exudes the folklike nature of German folk song steeped in a vigorous rhythmic style void of complex harmonies or textures. His dissonant treatment is harsh but largely tonal. His goal of mass audience appeal was gained through primitive simplicity and his works' dynamism.

*In His Own Words*

Everything I have so far written . . . must be pulped! My collected works begin with *Carmina burana.*

**Major Works:** Stage works, including *Antigone* (1949), *Oedipus der Tyrann* (1959), *Prometheus* (1969), and his trilogy of cantatas: *Carmina burana* (1937), *Catulli carmina* (1941–43), and *Trionfo di Afrodite* (1953) • Orchestral music • Lieder • Pedagogical materials, including *Orff-Schulwerk* (1931–34) and *Musik für Kinder* (*Music for Children*, 1950–54).

A 2009 theatrical performance of Orff's *Carmina burana* in London's O2 arena.

dissonances, and hypnotic ostinatos combined with lyricism and simplicity of idea. Its appeal is both sensuous and primitive, not unlike that of Stravinsky's *Rite of Spring*. The cantata's movements are in five scenes that are link to the concept of the whirling wheel of fortune, which can turn hope to heartache, happiness to sorrow. In *O fortuna*, Orff gives center stage to the chorus, which is accompanied by a huge orchestra rich in percussion. The chorus sings—in syllabic declamation—a persistent motive that feels asymmetrical because of its offset accents set over an unceasing pedal point. The dramatic opening presents this idea in slow motion, sung *fortissimo,* after which it shifts to a quick tempo, hushed at first and then forceful with a strong, primeval rhythmic drive throughout (see Listening Guide 45). With its archaic texts and modal-tinged harmonies that evoke a much earlier era, *Carmina burana* is new music that feels old.

### Critical Thinking

1. Who are some of the major nationalist composers of the early twentieth century and which national schools do they represent?

2. How does Bartók evoke nationalistic ideas in his music?

3. How does Orff's music present old and new musical ideas in *Carmina burana*?

# Orff: *O fortuna*, from *Carmina burana*    2:30

**DATE:** 1936

**GENRE:** Secular cantata

## WHAT TO LISTEN FOR:

| | |
|---|---|
| Melody | Choral recitation with syllabic text declamation |
| Rhythm/Meter | 3/2 meter, with choral entrances on the second beat of phrases; insistent pulsations with accented downbeats and continuous offbeats |
| Harmony | Harshly dissonant; tonal but evoking archaic music; sustained low pitch (pedal point) |
| Texture | Simple, homorhythmic texture with underlying urgent accompaniment |
| Form | 3 large strophes, each subdividing into four 4-measure phrases; highly repetitive, first slow, then fast for many statements |
| Expression | Forceful accents give primeval effect; changing tempos and dynamics for drama |
| Performing Forces | Chorus, soloists and large orchestra, with 5 percussionists |
| Timbre | Percussion prominent (timpani, cymbals, gong, bass drum) |
| Text | Medieval Latin poem |

| | | TEXT | TRANSLATION | DESCRIPTION |
|---|---|---|---|---|
| | | **Strophe 1** | | |
| 10 | 0:00 | O fortuna, velut Luna statu variabilis, | O Fortune like the moon you are always changeable, | *Fortissimo* opening, weighty and slow; timpani and cymbals prominent; harsh choir chords, enters on second beat. |
| 11 | 0:25 | semper crescis aut decrescis; vita detestabilis | ever waxing and waning; hateful life | *Pianissimo;* faster and urgent, with continuous rhythmic pulsations in lower strings and bassoon; choir declaiming text in repeated phrases. |
| | 0:35 | nunc obdurat et tunc curat ludo mentis aciem, | now oppressive and then soothing as fancy takes it; | |
| | 0:45 | egestatem potestatem dissolvit ut glaciem. | poverty, power, it melts them like ice. | Choir pitch moves up a 3rd; continues repeated phrases; gong and timpani, with woodwind pulsations. |
| | | **Strophe 2** | | |
| 12 | 0:56 | Sors immanis et inanis, rota tu volubilis, status malus, vanus salus semper dissolubilis, | Fate, monstrous and empty, you ever-turning wheel, are malevolent; well-being is in vain and always fades to nothing, | Choir returns to original pitch level; insistent, repetitive phrasing in declamation. |
| | 1:15 | obumbrata et velata michi quoque niteris; nunc per ludum dorsum nudum fero tui sceleris. | shadowed and veiled you plague me too; now through the game my back is bared to your villanry. | Choir pitch moves up a 3rd, unrelenting repetitive phrases. |

*Continued on following page*

**Strophe 3**

13

| 1:33 | Sors salutis | Fate, in health | Loud (*forte*), with high-range choral recita- |
|  | et virtutis | and virtue, | tion up an octave; heavily accented; punc- |
|  | Michi nunc contraria, | is against me, | tuated by bass drum and timpani; full |
|  | est affectus | driven on | orchestra in urgent rhythmic pulsations. |
|  | et defectus | and weighted down, | |
|  | imper in angaria. | Always enslaved. | |
| 1:53 | Hac in hora | So at this hour | *Fortissimo*, with choir chords divided in |
|  | sine mora | without delay | high octave; loud percussion accents; |
|  | cordum pulsum tangite; | pluck the vibrating strings; | repeated rhythmic motive; increased |
|  | quod per sortem | since Fate | dissonance. |
|  | sternit fortem, | strikes down the strong, | |
| 2:07 | mecum omnes plangite! | everyone weep with me! | Choral melisma on "omnes" (everyone); |
|  |  |  | *crescendos* into final triple *fff* chord; speed |
|  |  |  | increases as orchestra (brass) drive to the |
|  |  |  | final chord. |

Dramatic choral opening:

Insistent rhythmic idea
heard throughout
(percussion on downbeat;
pulsations in bassoon):

◎ **Now try the Listening Quiz.**

# 38 American Modernism in Music

> "Armies of men . . . have turned to a better life by first hearing the sounds of a Salvation Army band. The next time you hear a Salvation Army band, no matter how humble, take off your hat."
>
> —**John Philip Sousa**

## KEY POINTS

**StudySpace** wwnorton.com/enjoy

- The great bandmaster and composer John Philip Sousa fostered the American wind band tradition, an outgrowth of the British military band.

- Charles Ives was one of the most innovative and original composers of his time, but his music was not recognized until very late in his life.

- Ives drew on the music of his New England childhood—hymns, patriotic songs, brass band marches, and dance tunes—which he set in a very modern style, using *polytonality* and *polyrhythms*.

We have explored several early representatives of American music, noting the growing popularity throughout the nineteenth century of piano music and song, especially the parlor ballads of Stephen Foster. America's vernacular traditions also included music for brass bands. An outgrowth of the British military band, wind groups thrived throughout the United States, first serving as regimental bands for colonial militia during the Revolutionary War (1775–83) and continuing after the war. The most famous eighteenth-century band was the U.S. Marine Band, originally a small group of woodwinds, French horns, and percussion (see Meet the Performers, p. 322). The refinement of rotary-valved brass instruments by various makers, including the Belgian Adolphe Sax (inventor of the saxophone and many brass instruments; see p. 206), revolutionized the makeup of civic bands. Thus, by the Civil War era (1861–65), both Northern and Southern regiments marched to the sounds of brass bands. After the war, many bands reorganized as concert and dance ensembles; such was the case with the Union Army group under the direction of virtuoso cornet player and bandmaster Patrick S. Gilmore, who wrote the lyrics for the rousing *When Johnny Comes Marching Home* to welcome back soldiers from North and South alike.

America's most famous bandmaster was John Philip Sousa (1854–1932), who conducted the U.S. Marine Band from 1880 to 1892, after which he formed his own band. Known as "The March King," Sousa wrote over 130 marches for band, as well as dance music and operettas. He toured North America and Europe extensively with his group, delighting audiences with his *Semper Fidelis* (1897), *Washington Post* (1889), and his ever-popular *Stars and Stripes Forever* (1897), as well as band arrangements of ragtime, the newest rage (see p. 346).

**Bands in America**

**iMusic**

Sousa: *Stars and Stripes Forever*

**Video**

Sousa: *Washington Post*

**The United States Marine Band**

The U.S. Marine Band, with its director, **John Philip Sousa**, playing cornet (in right front).

"Strike up the band!"

The United States Marine Band has a long and illustrious history dating back to its establishment in 1798 by an act of Congress. The close link to the White House began shortly thereafter, when, in 1801, President John Adams invited the band to perform there for New Year's Day celebrations. The group also played for the March 1801 inauguration of President Thomas Jefferson—an avid music lover and accomplished musician; he even gave the band its current title of "The President's Own." From 1880 to 1892, the great bandmaster John Philip Sousa conducted this renowned group, leading official ceremonies under five presidents. In modern times, the U.S. Marine Band plays for many public and official events, including presidential inaugurations, state and military funerals, as well as ceremonies for visiting dignitaries. Although exempt from training and combat missions, these corps members meet their national duty through a staggering calendar of performances at which they represent America's finest military units. The Marine Band plays a diverse repertory of works for wind band, including national songs like *The Star-Spangled Banner*, the *Marine's Hymn* ("From the halls of Montezuma") and the band's official march, *Semper Fidelis* by John Philip Sousa. This work, written

in 1889, refers to the motto of the Marine Corps, meaning "always faithful." As the premier wind ensemble in the country, they perform not only the requisite patriotic works mentioned above, but also perform, record, and commission some of the most important new wind works and arrangements.

**Check out these recordings from the United States Marine Band:** *The Star-Spangled Banner*, *El Capitan*, and *Washington Post*, on *Stars and Stripes: America's Greatest Hits* (1997), and *Variations on America* and *Country Band March*, from *Charles Ives's America* (2008).

Sousa created, nearly single-handedly, a national music for America that continues to resonate in its concert halls, on its streets, in its sports stadiums, and in the hearts of its people.

One New England musician born into this rich environment of patriotic songs and brass bands was Charles Ives. Since his father was a Civil War bandmaster, Ives was thoroughly steeped in the vernacular heritage of his country. His compositional voice, however, followed very modernist tendencies, making him one of the most innovative, yet misunderstood, composers of the early twentieth century.

# The Modernist Charles Ives and New England Culture

Charles Edward Ives had to wait many years for recognition. Today he stands as the first great American composer of the twentieth century, and one of the most original spirits of his time.

## Ives's *Country Band March*

Ives's tonal imagery was drawn from his childhood—hymns, patriotic songs, marches, parlor ballads, and fiddling songs. Growing up in a small town, he was accustomed to hearing the pungent clash of dissonance when two bands in a parade, each playing a

## Charles Ives (1874–1954)

Ives was born in Danbury, Connecticut, the son of a U.S. Army band leader in the Civil War. At thirteen, he held a job as church organist, and at twenty, he entered Yale, where he studied composition with Horatio Parker. Ives's talent for music was evident throughout his four years at Yale, yet he decided against a professional life in music, suspecting that society would not pay him for the kind of music he wanted to compose. He was right.

Ives entered the business world, and two decades later, he was head of the largest insurance agency in the country. He composed at night, on weekends, and during vacations, working in isolation, concerned only to set down the sounds he heard in his head. The few conductors and performers he tried to interest in his compositions pronounced them unplayable, so he hired a few musicians to play his works in order to hear them. When well-meaning friends suggested that he try to write music people would like, he could only respond, "I can't do it—I hear something else!"

Ives's double life as a business executive by day and composer by night finally took its toll. In 1918, when he was forty-four, he suffered a physical breakdown that left his heart damaged. Although he lived almost forty years longer, he produced very little music.

When Ives recovered, he privately printed his Second Piano Sonata (*Concord*)—and the *Essays Before a Sonata,* a kind of elaborate program note that formulated his views on life and art. These were followed by the *114 Songs.* The three volumes, which were distributed free to libraries, music critics, and whoever else asked for them, but they gained Ives the support of other experimental composers who were also struggling to make their way in an indifferent music world. Beginning with a performance in 1939 of his *Concord* Sonata in New York City, Ives was finally "discovered" by the general public and proclaimed as the "grand old man" of American music. In 1947, his Third Symphony was performed and won a Pulitzer Prize. Ives awoke at seventy-three to find himself famous. He died in New York City at the age of eighty.

The central position in Ives's orchestral music is held by the four symphonies. Among his other orchestral works are *Three Places in New England, The Unanswered Question,* and *A Symphony: New England Holidays,* a cycle of four symphonic poems. The Sonata No. 2 for piano—"Concord, Mass., 1840–1860"—which occupied him from 1909 to 1915, reflects various aspects of New England's culture. Ives was a master songwriter as well, penning over 100 songs, some of which are highly nostalgic because of his use of familiar tunes—some patriotic, some religious, some from the popular tradition—tinged with bittersweet harmonies.

**Major Works:** Orchestral music, including 4 symphonies, *Three Places in New England* (1914, including *Putnam's Camp*), *The Unanswered Question* (1908), and *A Symphony: New England Holidays* (1913) • Chamber music, including string quartets and violin sonatas • Piano music, including sonatas (No. 2, *Concord,* 1915) • Choral music and many songs.

### In His Own Words

Beauty in music is too often confused with something that lets the ear lie back in an easy chair. . . . Analytical and impersonal tests will show that when a new or unfamiliar work is accepted as beautiful on its first hearing, its fundamental quality is one that tends to put the mind to sleep.

*American Gothic,* by **Grant Wood** (1891–1942), is an example of regionalism, celebrating rural life in the United States.

different tune in a different key, came close enough together to overlap. He was also familiar with the effect of **quarter tones** (an interval half the size of a half step) when fiddlers at country dances veered a bit off pitch. These dissonances, Ives realized, were not exceptions but rather the norm of American musical life. Thus he found his way to such concepts as polytonality, polyharmony, and polyrhythm.

Ives took bold steps in his *Country Band March,* an early work written around 1903, just after he graduated from Yale. Here he set his compositional path for the future by using many well-known musical quotations—from children's songs, patriotic tunes, hymns, and even two marches by John Philip Sousa (see p. 321). The main march theme we hear is most likely by Ives himself, but he weaves a highly complex mesh of other tunes into the march, creating all manner of chaos. We hear polytonality and polyrhythms as tunes collide and overlap. The many songs cited are nostalgic ones for Ives,

**Florine Stettheimer's** (1871–1944) patriotic *Cathedrals of Wall Street* celebrates the 150th anniversary of the inauguration of George Washington.

from his Protestant New England upbringing, but we hear also the playful side of the composer who simulates in his *Country Band March* the realism of an amateur band's performance skills with musicians playing out-of-tune, making bad entrances, and hitting wrong notes. You will recognize some of the tunes quoted: *London Bridge* and *Yankee Doodle*; *Massa's in de Cold Cold Ground* and *My Old Kentucky Home* (both by Stephen Foster, see p. 228); and the Sousa marches *Semper Fidelis* and *Washington Post* (see p. 321). The work is not actually in a march form (which resembles a rag, see p. 321) but rather a five-part sectional one that brings back the opening march theme in various guises (see Listening Guide 46).

Ives reused much of the music from *Country Band March* in his more famous *Putnam's Camp*, from the orchestral work *Three Places in New England*—in that movement, he evokes a Fourth of July picnic and parade (with competing bands) at the historic Revolutionary War landmark known as Putnam's Camp in Connecticut. He also quoted part of the march in his *Concord* Sonata, in which the movements are all associated with nineteenth-century American writers known for protests against the general state of society and culture (called Transcendentalists). Ives rarely heard his own music performed—he wrote *Country Band March* for a small chamber orchestra that he could afford to hire. Ives did, however, write music for bands, and this version of *Country Band March* works perfectly for such a wind group.

### Critical Thinking

**1.** What elements make the music of Ives so experimental and modernist?

**2.** What older traditions does Ives draw on in his music?

---

**LISTENING GUIDE 46**                    Ⓢ | DVD | **CD 7 (41–47)** | **CD 4 (14–20)**

# Ives: *Country Band March*                                   4:20

**DATE:** c. 1903

**GENRE:** March, arranged for band

**WHAT TO LISTEN FOR:**

| | |
|---|---|
| Melody | Forceful march theme, over which many well-known tunes occur; main march returns throughout |
| Rhythm/ Meter | Mostly duple, but with syncopation and triplets that disguise meter |
| Harmony | Harshly dissonant, polytonal |
| Form | Sectional (**A-B-A-B'-A'**) |

| | |
|---|---|
| Expression | Humorous; realism of amateur bands; nostalgic American tunes |
| Performing Forces | Large wind ensemble, including woodwinds (piccolo, flutes, oboes, various clarinets, bassoons, various saxophones), brass (cornets, trumpets, French horns, trombones, baritones, tubas), and percussion (drums, cymbals, bells, triangle, xylophone) |

**A section**

| 14 | 0:00 | Short introduction, with marked descending line in full ensemble, chromatic, and syncopated and shifting meters; repeated-note transition. |
|---|---|---|

0:11    Main march tune, regular duple meter, with onbeat and offbeat accents; various other tunes:

0:27    Fleeting reference to *London Bridge* in trumpets and oboe, answered immediately by *The Girl I Left Behind Me*, in piccolo and flute:

15   0:33    Slower passage in woodwinds and saxophones, followed by repeated-note transition.

0:45    *Arkansas Traveler* tune heard in trumpets and cornets, slightly offset rhythmically:

0:55    *Semper fidelis* march by Sousa (trio), as cornet solo:

**B section**

16   1:05    Quieter, more lyrical oboe solo, intervals drawn from *Marching through Georgia*:

17   1:28    Clear statement *of London Bridge*:

1:44    *My Old Kentucky Home,* in slow triplets:

**A section** repeated

18   1:51    Introduction

2:03    March tune

2:38    *Arkansas Traveler*

2:47    *Semper fidelis*

**B′ section,** with new closing section

19   2:58    Oboe solo leads to new material.

3:05    Rhythmic, syncopated idea.

**A′ section,** with variations

20   3:19    March tune in new key.

3:29    *British Grenadiers* march stated:

3:42    Brief transition.

3:46    March theme returns.

◎ **Now try the Listening Quiz.**

# 39 Nationalism in the Americas

"A nation creates music—the composer only arranges it."

—**Mikhail Glinka**

## KEY POINTS

StudySpace wwnorton.com/enjoy

- African-American composer William Grant Still broke numerous racial barriers, earning many firsts in Classical music. His Suite for Violin and Piano looks to three black visual artists for inspiration.

- American composer Aaron Copland used the early American song *Simple Gifts* in his famous ballet *Appalachian Spring*, commissioned by the great choreographer/dancer Martha Graham.

- The music of Mexican composer Silvestre Revueltas is expressively nationalistic, with folkloric rhythms and melodies set in a dissonant idiom.

- Revueltas' orchestral work *Homage to Federico García Lorca* honors the Spanish writer executed in 1936 during the Spanish Civil War.

- Both Copland and especially Revueltas were influenced by the Mexican *mariachi ensemble*, a popular, traditional music group.

I n this chapter, we will consider three unique voices of nationalism in the Americas. William Grant Still, a representative of the Harlem Renaissance movement, incorporated black music idioms in his works as a means to promote the position of African Americans in the United States. Aaron Copland, one of the most prolific composers of the twentieth century, was able to capture the spirit of the American experience through accessible musical language and imagery. And Mexican composer Silvestre Revueltas, a representative of the "mestizo realism" movement, drew inspiration from the popular contemporary culture and music of his homeland.

# William Grant Still: African-American Composer

African-American composer William Grant Still was the most important musical voice in the early-twentieth-century movement known as the Harlem (or "New Negro") Renaissance, which celebrated African-American culture and arts. His music is infused with elements of spirituals, blues, and jazz—all truly American genres.

## Still's Suite for Violin and Piano

In his Suite for Violin and Piano, Still based each movemnt on a different art work by African-American artists. The spirited first movement was inspired by the sculpture *African Dancer* by Richmond Barthe, a noted Harlem Renaissance artist. The

## William Grant Still (1895–1978)

**Still** grew up in Little Rock, Arkansas. His parents, both educators, encouraged his early music studies on violin. He left college to work as a professional musician and was hired in 1916 to play in, and write arrangements for, W. C. Handy's bands in Memphis and later in New York. His reputation as an arranger for radio and musical theater grew quickly, but he continued his classical music studies as well, training with French-born composer Edgard Varèse, who guided Still's writing toward lyricism and an expansive freedom. Still deliberately moved away from the avant-garde, however, to find his original voice in the music of his black cultural heritage.

His first symphony, the *Afro-American*, was premiered in 1931 by the Rochester Philharmonic Orchestra. This represented a landmark in black history: Still's was the first symphony by an African-American composer to be performed by a major American orchestra. The symphony brought him numerous commissions from major orchestras, including the New York Philharmonic. In 1934, he won a Guggenheim Fellowship for composition and left New York for Los Angeles, where he wrote film and television scores. He soon turned his energies toward art music, and his opera *Troubled Island* was produced by New York's City Opera in 1949, marking another first for an African-American composer.

In 1939, Still was divorced from his first wife and then married Verna Arvey, with whom he collaborated in his operas. His later works were viewed as stylistically conservative and therefore were not favorably received; however, he was recognized with many honorary degrees during his last years and wrote theme music for such popular TV series as *Gunsmoke* and *Perry Mason*. William Grant Still remained in Los Angeles until his death in 1978.

His approximately 150 compositions span most genres of his day, and his stylistic development can be divided into three distinct periods. The first comprises his student works written during his studies with Edgard Varèse, from 1923–25; these connect him with the growing momentum of the Harlem Renaissance.

The works from his second period, ranging from 1926–34, all stem from his time in Harlem. Of these years, his most important works include the African ballet *Sahdji* (1930), based on a play by a young Harlem writer, and the *Afro-American Symphony* (1930).

In the works from his third period, Still continued to look to writers and artists of the Harlem Renaissance for inspiration, including the renowned African-American poet Langston Hughes, whose libretto he set in his opera *Troubled Island*, on the struggles of the Haitian people. For his bluesy Suite for Violin and Piano, which we will consider, Still was inspired by black visual artists.

**Major Works:** Orchestral music, including 4 symphonies (No. 1, *Afro-American Symphony*, 1930) • Orchestral suites • Film scores • Stage works, including 4 ballets (*La Guiablesse*, 1927, *Sahdji*, 1930) • 8 operas, including *Troubled Island* (1937–49) • Chamber music, including Suite for Violin and Piano (1943) • Vocal music, including *Songs of Separation* (1949) and spiritual arrangements • Piano music • Choral music.

### In His Own Words

What are the qualities which must be inherent in the person who aspires to write music? First, and most important, is the ability to induce the flow of inspiration, that indefinable element which transforms lifeless intervals into throbbing, vital, and heartwarming music.

second movement evokes the expressive mood of *Mother and Child* by Sargent Johnson, one of the first Californian African-American artists to achieve fame. The rhythmically charged closing movement draws on the impish humor of a sculpture entitled *Gamin* by Augusta Savage, the most prominent African-American woman artist of her day. The sculpture (see right) captures the confident image of a street-smart kid in Harlem (gamin suggests a street urchin); indeed, the artist used her own nephew as the model for this work, completed in 1929.

The movements of the suite are all bluesy in flavor, with modal harmonies and melodies featuring lowered thirds and sevenths, typical of the blues (see p. 347). Throughout his compositional career, Still favored blues as source material for his music, explaining that "they, unlike spirituals, do not exhibit the influence of Caucasian music." The last movement of the suite zips along with a flashy and syncopated violin line accompanied by an insistent bass that resembles the jazz piano

*Gamin,* a sculpture by **Augusta Savage** (1892–1962), an important Harlem Renaissance artist.

style known as *stride*. Sometimes called Harlem stride piano, this style evolved from ragtime (see p. 346) and features a regular four-beat pulse with offbeat chords on the second and fourth beats. The movement unfolds in sections, sometimes engaging the piano and violin in a call-and-response exchange, but it keeps returning to the opening exuberant idea that is varied with ornamentation and dazzling glissandos in the violin (see Listening Guide 47). The Suite for Violin and Piano was completed in 1943 and first performed in Boston the next year by the well-known American violinist Louis Kaufman and his pianist/wife Annette.

---

**LISTENING GUIDE 47**                    ⓢ | DVD | CD 7 (51–54) | CD 3 (77–80)

# Still: Suite for Violin and Piano, Third movement                    2:07

**DATE:**   1943

**GENRE:**   Suite for violin and piano

**MOVEMENTS:**   I. Majestically and vigorously (based on Richmond's Barthe's *African Dancer*)
II. Slowly and expressively (based on Sargent Johnson's *Mother and Child*)
**III. Rhythmically and humorously (based on Augusta Savage's *Gamin*)**

## WHAT TO LISTEN FOR:

| | | | |
|---|---|---|---|
| Melody | Bluesy, short, syncopated ideas, with flatted 3rd and 7th scale tones; ideas exchanged between violin and piano | Texture | Mostly homophonic |
| | | Form | Sectional form, with 4- and 8-measure ideas; opening returns frequently |
| Rhythm/ Meter | Quick 2/4 meter; rhythmic and highly syncopated with chords played on offbeats | Timbre | Violin trills, glissandos, and double stops |
| Harmony | Modal with blues chords; stride bass; use of ostinatos | Expression | Playful and humorous; evokes image of cocky street kid depicted by sculpture |

---

**77**   0:00   4-measure introduction in piano, with ostinato bass and offbeat chords.

0:05   Violin enters with syncopated line, 4-measure idea in fragments, with stride piano accompaniment:

0:26   Rising line to new syncopated violin idea, accompanied by syncopated, more active piano part.

0:35   Low-range repeated-note idea in violin, against moving piano line.

**78**   0:45   Piano takes over low-range melody, with violin playing double stops:

| | 0:56 | Opening motive returns, varied, in violin; piano more syncopated. |
| **79** | 1:06 | Humorous repeated-note exchange between piano and violin. |
| | 1:17 | Opening motive returns in violin, includes glissando and more active piano accompaniment. |
| | 1:27 | Repeated-note idea developed in violin. |
| **80** | 1:38 | Recapitulation of opening, including brief piano introduction. |
| | 1:59 | Coda, with rising violin line, trios, then triumphant double-stop chords and glissando to last chord. |

◉ **Now try the Listening Quiz.**

---

### By the way . . .

#### What Was the Harlem Renaissance?

Sometimes referred to as "the New Negro Movement," the Harlem Renaissance was a literary, artistic, and sociological movement that highlighted African-American intellectual life in the 1920s and '30s (see p. 326). The most important literary figure associated with the Harlem Renaissance was Langston Hughes, a well-educated African-American poet and novelist whose works, depicting the struggles of working-class blacks, radiated black pride. A frequent visitor to the Harlem jazz clubs, he wrote verse that imitated the rhythms and flow of jazz, thus creating a new kind of jazz poetry. Most jazz musicians, including Duke Ellington and Billie Holiday (see pp. 353 and 349), gained early recognition performing in Harlem jazz clubs as well, including the famous Cotton Club. A composer and a performer, Ellington considered his works to be "tone parallels" to the lives of blacks. African-American musicians uniformly rejected the stereotyped images that had been popular in minstrel shows and worked to break down the long-standing racial prejudice against black musicians and artists. Among these crusaders was William Grant Still, whose creative efforts merged art and traditional genres.

# Aaron Copland: American Nationalist

> "I no longer feel the need of seeking out conscious Americanism. Because we live here and work here, we can be certain that when our music is mature it will also be American in quality."

Aaron Copland is one of America's greatest contemporary composers. Few have been able to capture the spirit of this country so successfully—his well-crafted and classically proportioned works have an immediate appeal. His ballet suites are quintessentially American in his portrayal of rural life (*Appalachian Spring*) and the Far West (*Rodeo* and *Billy the Kid*).

## Copland's *Appalachian Spring*

Among Copland's ballets, *Appalachian Spring* is perhaps his best known. He collaborated with the celebrated choreographer Martha Graham (see Meet the Performers, p. 333), who also danced the lead in the ballet. Copland noted that when he wrote the music, he considered Graham's unique choreographic style: "She's unquestionably very American: there's something prim and restrained, simple yet strong, about her, which one tends to think of as American." The ballet portrays "a pioneer celebration in spring around a newly-built farmhouse in the Pennsylvania hills in the early part of the nineteenth century. The bride-to-be and the young farmer-husband enact the emotions, joyful and apprehensive, their

## Aaron Copland (1900–1990)

**Copland** was born in Brooklyn, New York, and during his early twenties studied in Paris with the famous teacher Nadia Boulanger. He was her first full-time American pupil.

In his growth as a composer, Copland mirrored the dominant trends of his time. After his return from Paris, he turned to the jazz idiom, a phase that culminated in his brilliant Piano Concerto. He then experimented with Neoclassicism, producing the Piano Variations, *Short Symphony,* and *Statements for Orchestra.* But he felt alienated from his public. He realized that a new public for contemporary music was being created by the radio, phonograph, and film scores. "It made no sense to ignore them [the audience] and to continue writing as if they did not exist.

The 1930s and 1940s saw the creation of works that established Copland's popularity. *El Salón México* (1936) is an orchestral piece based on Mexican melodies and rhythms. His three ballets—*Billy the Kid, Rodeo,* and *Appalachian Spring,* continue to delight international audiences. Copland was drawn to the film industry, which promised large audiences and high pay. Among his film scores are two on novels by John Steinbeck and *The Heiress,* which brought him an Academy Award. He wrote two important works during wartime: *A Lincoln Portrait,* for speaker and chorus, with texts drawn from Lincoln's own speeches, and the Third Symphony. Despite his nationalism, Copland was investigated in the 1950s as a supporter of the Communist party, and in 1953, he was removed from the inaugural ceremonies of President Eisenhower as a result of his leftist politics and the McCarthyism of the 1950s. In the 1960s, Copland demonstrated that he could also handle twelve-tone techniques when he wrote his powerful *Connotations for Orchestra.*

**Major Works:** Orchestral music, including 3 symphonies, a piano concerto, *El Salón México* (1936), *A Lincoln Portrait* (1942), *Fanfare for the Common Man* (1942) • Ballets, including *Billy the Kid* (1938), *Rodeo* (1942), and *Appalachian Spring* (1944) • Operas, including *The Tender Land,* (1954) • Film scores, including *Of Mice and Men* (1939), *Our Town* (1940), *The Red Pony* (1948), and *The Heiress* (1948) • Piano music • Chamber music • Choral music • Songs.

🅢 **iMusic:** *Simple Gifts*

### In His Own Words

I would say that a composer writes music to express and communicate. . . . The resultant work of art should speak to men and women . . . with a directness and immediacy of communicative power that no previous art expression can give.

---

🅢 **iMusic**

*Simple Gifts*

Members of the Protestant Shaker sect in a dance. Lithograph by **Nathaniel Currier** (1813–1888).

new partnership invites." The ballet, which premiered in 1944 in Washington, DC, was the basis for his popular 1945 orchestral suite, set in seven sections.

The opening section of the suite introduces the characters in the ballet with a serene, ascending motive that evokes the first hint of daybreak over the vast horizon. In the most famous part of *Appalachian Spring,* we hear the well-known early American song *Simple Gifts* ('Tis the Gift to Be Simple), a tune associated with the Shaker religious sect, known for its spiritual rituals that included spinning and dancing. This simple, folklike tune provides a quintessential American sound; Copland sets the modal melody in a clearcut theme and variations that presents colorful orchestration tinged with gentle dissonance. The flowing tune takes on several guises, shaded by changing timbres, keys, and tempos. You may recall the quartet arrangement of this tune by John Williams entitled *Air and Simple Gifts* that premiered in January 2009 at President Barack Obama's inauguration ceremony. Williams's work also explored variations on the Shaker melody.

## LISTENING GUIDE 48

⑥ | DVD | CD 7 (55–62) | CD 4 (21–28)

# Copland: *Appalachian Spring*, excerpts

**5:45**

**DATE:** 1945

**GENRE:** Ballet suite in 7 sections

**WHAT TO LISTEN FOR:**

Section 1

| | |
|---|---|
| Melody | Rising motive quietly unfolds; outlines a triad |
| Rhythm/Meter | Very slow, tranquil; changing meter is imperceptible |
| Harmony | Overlapping of chords (polychordal) produces gentle dissonance |
| Timbre | Individual instruments featured |
| Expression | Introduces the characters; evokes broad landscape at daybreak |

Section 7

| | |
|---|---|
| Melody | Theme with 4 phrases (**a-a'-b-a''**); later variations use only first part of tune |
| Rhythm/Meter | Flowing duple meter, then tune in augmentation (slower) |
| Harmony | Moves between various keys |
| Form | Theme and 4 variations, on a traditional Shaker hymn |
| Timbre | Each variation changes tone colors, individual instruments featured |
| Expression | Calm and flowing; majestic closing |

---

**Section I: Very slowly**    **2:42**

**21**  0:00   Low string sustained pitch; solo clarinet, then flute with rising motive:

0:16   Violin and flutes alternate rising figure; harp punctuates; other instruments enter, creating dissonance.

**22**  0:52   Violin in high range, with more movement, rising figure heard in various instruments.

1:25   Solos in various woodwinds and trumpet.

1:54   Solo oboe, then bassoon; descending motive.

2:31   Clarinet with closing triad, over sustained harmony.

---

**Section 7: Theme (*Simple Gifts*) and 5 variations**    **3:03**

**Theme**

**23**  0:00   Solo clarinet with tune in 4 phrases (**a-a'-b-a''**), accompanied by harp (playing harmonics) and flute:

*Continued on following page*

0: 28   Brief transition.

**Variation 1**

[24]   0:34   Oboe and bassoon present tune; growing dissonant, with *sforzando* on 3rd phrase featuring all woodwinds.

0:56   Short, rhythmic transition.

**Variation 2**

[25]   0:59   Tune in violas in augmentation (steady rhythmic accompaniment continues); violins (in octaves) enter in 2nd phrase of tune in canon with the violas (dissonance on the last note shown):

1:35   Transition.

**Variation 3**

[26]   1: 45   Trumpets and trombones, with swirling strings; loud brass section; then quieter in woodwinds.

**Variation 4**

[27]   2:10   Woodwinds with slower version of tune.

**Variation 5**

[28]   2:30   Full orchestra with majestic, homophonic statement; somewhat dissonant; *fortissimo,* then dies out.

◎ **Now try the Listening Quiz.**

# Art Music Traditions in Mexico

"From an early age I learned to love [the music of] Bach and Beethoven. . . .
I can tolerate some of the classics and even some of my own works, but I
prefer the music of my people that is heard in the provinces."

—*Silvestre Revueltas*

The modern musical traditions of Mexico are rich and varied, drawing from the indigenous Amerindian cultures as well as from the country's Hispanic culture. Mexico's ties to Spain began in 1519, when Spanish soldiers colonized the country, and continued until 1821, when Mexico achieved its independence.

By the late nineteenth century, nationalistic stirrings lured musicians and artists alike to Amerindian and mestizo cultures. (*Mestizos* are people of mixed Spanish and Amerindian ancestry; today they are the majority in Latin American countries.) The Mexican Revolution of 1910 further changed the artistic life of the country, conjuring strong feelings of patriotism. In the post–Revolutionary period—sometimes called the "Aztec Renaissance"—composers did not wish to

## Meet the Performers

### Martha Graham

*"Great dancers are not great because of their technique; they are great because of their passion."*

Meet Martha Graham (1894–1991), a pioneer in the field of modern dance who pushed her art to new limits. Graham started dancing later than most—she was past twenty when she performed her first solo recital in New York—but her innovative, abstract style, which featured precise, angular moves coupled with an intense emotional and spiritual expression, brought her much acclaim. She was the first dancer to perform at the White House—in 1937 for President Franklin Roosevelt, and then for seven more presidents throughout her lifetime. She received many awards, including the U.S. Medal of Freedom, the highest civilian award in the country. Graham devoted much of her energy to teaching in her own dance school in New York City. In 1929, she formed The Martha Graham Dance Company, the oldest continuing dance company in the United States. In addition to her teaching and performing, Graham choreographed more than 180 ballets, including *Appalachian Spring*, with music by Aaron Copland; this American-themed work looks back to Graham's roots in Allegheny, Pennsylvania. She collaborated in ballets with many other famous composers. One of her notable late works is a new choreography for Stravinsky's *Rite of Spring* (you recall this was originally a ballet), with an updated story about big-city crime and the violent death of a young girl. Martha Graham's devotion to modern dance and to teaching has produced new generations of dancers and choreographers who press their bodies and their art yet further.

recreate the traditional music but only to evoke, or suggest, the character of this native music. The works of Carlos Chávez (1899–1978)—including seven symphonies and two Aztec ballets—are rich in Amerindian flavor. Chávez was one of the most decisive influences on Mexican musical culture (see HTTN 12, p. 337), along with Silvestre Revueltas, whom we will consider.

# Silvestre Revueltas: Mexican Nationalist

Silvestre Revueltas, a Mexican nationalist composer, is considered a representative of "mestizo realism," a movement that drew on elements of the traditional culture of contemporary Mexico. His music is highly flavored with Mexican folk elements, especially mariachi band traditions.

## Homage to Federico García Lorca

Revueltas responded to one of the early tragedies of the Civil War: the execution in 1936 of the poet Federico García Lorca by a Fascist firing squad. The openly homosexual García Lorca had made anti-Fascist statements and had provoked the Spanish dictator Franco with his politically controversial plays. Revueltas's moving composition *Homenaje a Federico García Lorca (Homage to Federico García Lorca)* premiered in Madrid in 1937 during a Fascist bombing of the city. The review in the *Heraldo de Madrid* accorded Revueltas's music a "revolutionary status." Another profound artistic expression of war-torn Spain is Pablo Picasso's painting *Guernica,* depicting the German bombing of the Basque town with the same name (see p. 314).

With *Homage to Federico García Lorca,* Revueltas erases the boundaries between

## Silvestre Revueltas (1899–1940)

Born in the mountain state of Durango, **Silvestre Revueltas** was a child prodigy on violin and later studied composition at the Conservatorio Nacional de Música in Mexico City. He continued his studies in the United States until 1929, when he was called home by his friend Carlos Chávez to serve as assistant conductor of the Orquesta Sinfónica de Mexico.

With the onset of the Spanish Civil War in the late 1930s, the intensely political Revueltas went to Spain, where he participated in the cultural activities of the Loyalist government. Upon his return home in late 1937, his life began to fall apart. Despite his acute alcoholism, for which he was institutionalized on several occasions, Revueltas continued to produce masterworks, including his best-known orchestral piece, *Sensemayá* (1938), a work inspired by the verses of Afro-Cuban poet Nicolás Guillén—another anti-Fascist—that imitates onomatopoetically the sounds and rhythm of Afro-Cuban music and speak against colonial imperialism. In 1939, Revueltas wrote the film score for *La Noche de los Mayas,* which projects a modern primitivism not unlike Stravinsky's *Rite of Spring.* The composer died at age forty of alcohol-induced pneumonia.

Revueltas instills his music with colorful, folkloric elements. His love for Mexican provincial music is immediately obvious, voiced through lyrical, direct melodies that are driven by complex rhythms utilizing techniques such as polyrhythms and ostinatos. Despite a very modern harmonic language rich in dissonance and chromaticism, Revueltas's music is deeply emotional and Romantic in its inspiration. His skillful handling of the orchestral palette—often with unusual instrumental combinations—evokes the picturesque *orquestas típicas*—the traditional orchestras—of Mexico.

**Major Works:** Orchestral music, including *Semsemayá* (1938) • 7 film scores, including *La noche de los Mayas* (1939) • Chamber music, including *Homenaje a Federico García Lorca* (*Homage to Federico García Lorca*, 1937) • 2 ballets • Songs, including 7 *Canciones* (1938, on texts by García Lorca).

*In His Own Words*

There is in me a particular interpretation of nature. Everything is rhythm. . . . Everybody understands or feels it. . . . My rhythms are dynamic, sensual, vital; I think in images that meet in melodic lines, always moving dynamically.

The murals of the Mexican painter **Diego Rivera** (1886–1957) glorify his native culture and people in an elegant social and historical narrative. *Flower Festival* (1925).

popular and classical music. The work is for a chamber ensemble, heavily balanced toward winds—the string section has only two violins and one bass—and includes piano. The first movement, *Baile* (Dance), features bitingly dissonant tunes over a frenzied ostinato. The second movement, *Duelo* (Sorrow), also makes use of an ostinato—this time a rocking accompaniment in pianos and strings—against a soulful melody.

The title of the last movement, *Son*, refers to a type of traditional Mexican dance. Although there are regional differences in the dance steps and the performing ensembles, *sones* (plural of *son*) are characterized by shifting meter, frequently moving between simple triple (3/4) and compound duple (6/8) meter. Revueltas's writing here is highly evocative of a Mexican **mariachi ensemble**, one of the most common groups that performs *sones*. The typical mariachi consists of several trumpets, violins, and guitars (see p. 336). Revueltas maintains the distinctive mariachi sound of paired trumpets and violins, while enriching the highest and lowest registers with woodwinds, brass, and bass, and replacing the guitars with piano.

This movement, in a rondo-like form, begins explosively, tossing about fragmentary ideas with unrestrained energy. The strings and piano then establish a steady 6/8 pulse, over which the muted trumpet sounds a narrow-ranged theme built from whole tones (see Listening Guide 49). Complex rhythms and percussive accents lead to the principal theme—a syncopated Mexican dance tune (the *son*) in the trumpets and violins, played in parallel thirds

**LISTENING GUIDE 49**

DVD | **CD 7 (63–68)** | CD 4 (29–34)

# Revueltas: *Homage to Federico García Lorca,* Third Movement, *Son*

2:55

**DATE:** 1937

**GENRE:** Chamber orchestra suite

**MOVEMENTS:** I. *Baile* (Dance)
II. *Duello* (Sorrow)
**III. *Son***

**WHAT TO LISTEN FOR:**

| | | | |
|---|---|---|---|
| **Melody** | 3 themes, syncopated; colorful and folklike ideas | **Expression** | Evokes a mariachi ensemble |
| **Rhythm/ Meter** | Strongly rhythmic and syncopated; shifting meters; percussive accents; use of ostinatos | **Timbre** | Unusual instrumentation, focused on winds; trumpets and violins in pairs; piano prominent |
| **Harmony** | Dissonant, with mariachi-like idea played in thirds (**C section**) | **Performing Forces** | Chamber orchestra (including piccolo, E-flat clarinet, 2 trumpets, trombone, tuba, piano, percussion, 2 violins and bass) |
| **Texture** | Polyphonic and complex | | |
| **Form** | Sectional, rondo-like (**A-B-A-C-A-C-B-A-C-Coda**) | | |

**29** 0:00 **A section**—rhythmic and highly syncopated, in shifting meter; 7-note melodic turns in piano and violins, with glissandos in violins (Violin I shown):

**30** 0:15 **B section**—piano and string ostinato introduces chromatic solo trumpet melody (accompanied by trombone):

0:29 **A section**—rhythmic punctuations, as in introduction.

**31** 0:35 **C section**—Mexican dance theme *(son)* in alternating meter (6/8 and 2/4 = sesquialtera); muted trumpets playing in parallel thirds:

Trumpets answered by violins and woodwinds.

*Continued on following page*

| | 0:58 | Development of rhythmic figure from above, in low brass (tuba), answered by woodwinds, then trumpets. |
| | 1:08 | Brief return of **A**. |
| **32** | 1:21 | Return of Mexican tune (**C section**), in full orchestra. |
| | 1:37 | Rhythmic figure from **C** developed. |
| **33** | 1:55 | **B section**—return of slow trumpet melody, with trombone countermelody. |
| | 2:05 | **A section**—return of opening section. |
| **34** | 2:16 | **C section**—mariachi melody in violins, trumpet offbeats. Grows dissonant. |
| | 2:34 | **Coda**—cluster chord in piano, then fast, loud, frenetic. |

◎ **Now try the Listening Quiz.**

The Mariachi Regio Internacional (violins, trumpets, guitarrón, and guitar) performing in Plaza Garibaldi, home to many of Mexico City's mariachi bands.

typical of mariachi style. A rhythmic idea from this theme is then developed by various instruments, after which the mariachi tune returns in a full orchestral statement, set in a new key. A final frenetic coda is unleashed after two dissonant cluster chords in the piano.

This carefree movement may seem like a strange homage to the slain poet. But the traditional Mexican view of life (and death) is to experience each day to the fullest. In Mexico, the Day of the Dead is celebrated joyfully—houses are decorated with colorful skulls made from sugar, and tables are adorned with breads shaped like bones. The poet Rafael Alberti praised *Homage to Federico García Lorca*, noting that "what Manuel de Falla did with . . . Spanish music . . . Silvestre Revueltas achieves with the accent of his own country—and in magisterial style."

# Music from the Mariachi Tradition

One strong voice of growing Mexican nationalism in the early 1900s was the traditional mariachi ensemble. The group originated in the mid-nineteenth century near Guadalajara, in the Jalisco region of western Mexico, as a string orchestra

# Preserving Mexico's Musical Traditions

American composer Aaron Copland's interest in Latin American music stretches back to his friendship with Mexican composer/conductor Carlos Chávez during the 1920s. Paralleling the lead of artists in Mexico who had already begun a nationalist school of painting (including Diego Rivera; see p. 334), Chávez instigated a government-sponsored program to move toward a national voice in music.

Copland accepted Chávez's invitation to visit Mexico City in the fall of 1932 and became captivated by the country's traditional music. These visits resulted in Copland's delightful orchestral work *El Salón México*, named after a popular dance hall. Chávez premiered his friend's work in 1937 with the Mexico City Orchestra, to great success.

While in Mexico, Copland also befriended Mexican composer Silvestre Revueltas (see p. 333) whose colorful orchestral tone poems conjured up "the bustling life of a typical Mexican fiesta." These two Mexican composers—Chávez and Revueltas—are at the core of the modernist school of Mexican art music. Both,

like Copland, expressed their nationalism through the distinctly European genre of ballet.

Daniel Catán (b. 1949), today's pre-eminent Mexican composer, continues this cultural integration by writing stage works that celebrate his Latin American roots. His ballet *Ausencia de flores* honors the centennial of the Mexican muralist José Clemente Orozco (1883–1949; see below), and his operas draw on Nobel Prize–winning Latin American writers: Mexican author Octavio Paz, on whose poem Catán's

*Rappaccini's Daughter* (1994) is based; and Colombian novelist Gabriel García Márquez, whose famous novel *Love in the Time of Cholera* loosely inspired Catán's *Florencia en el Amazonas*. Here, Latin American dance rhythms are merged with soaring Puccini-like lines in a postmodern dissonant language.

---

🔘 **iMusic**

Catán opera: *Rappaccini's Daughter*
Traditional Mexican music (mariachi ensembles): *El Cihualteco*

Muralist **José Clemente Orozco** (1883–1949) captures the spirit of the revolutionary movement in *Zapatistas* (1931).

with both bowed and plucked instruments: violins, guitars (including a large acoustic bass guitar known as the **guitarrón**), and **vihuelas** (rounded-back folk guitars). In the 1930s, the mariachi ensemble took on a distinctly urban sound, adding trumpets and other instruments.

**Guitarrón and vihuela**

The mariachi ensembles heard today were standardized during the 1950s. Modern players often wear the costumes of the *charros*—Mexican cowboys with wide-brimmed sombreros—or other, more regional dress. Typical instrumentation consists of a melody group, with violins and trumpets; and a rhythm section of vihuelas, guitar, guitarrón, and occasionally harp. Their repertory is largely

## LISTENING ACTIVITY: THE SOUNDS OF THE MARIACHI TRADITION

Listen to *El Cihualteco* (*The Man from Cihuatlán*), a famous dance piece in the mariachi tradition (StudySpace, Chapter 39). *El Cihualteco* is associated with the Spanish flamenco-style dance known as the *zapateado* and is characterized by strongly syncopated rhythms against which dancers drive their boots into the floor. This selection falls into the standard verse/chorus structure, with witty four-line verses, alternating with the chorus (*Ay, sí, sí; ay, no, no*). Listen how the melodic lines are sounded in parallel thirds by the violins and trumpets, and how shifting rhythmic accents disguise the meter of this dance.

| | TEXT | TRANSLATION |
|---|---|---|
| **Verse 1** | Arriba de Cihuatlán | Above Cihualtlán, |
| | le nombran "la água escondida" | they call it "hidden waters," |
| | donde se van a bañar | where the dear Cihualtecan girls |
| | Cihualtecas de mi vida. | go to bathe. |
| **Chorus** | Ay, sí, sí; ay, no, no. | Ay, yes, yes; ay, no, no. |
| | Ay, sí, sí; ay, no, no. | Ay, yes, yes; ay, no, no. |
| | Ay, sí; ay, no. | Ay, yes; ay, no. |
| | Ay, sí; ay, no. | Ay, yes; ay, no. |
| | De veras sí, de veras no. | Surely yes, surely no. |
| | Lo que te dije se te olvidó | You forgot what I told you |
| | y al cabo sí, y al cabo no. | and finally yes, and finally no. |
| **Verse 2** | Cihualteco de mi vida, | Dear Cihualteco, |
| | dime quién te bautizó. | tell me who baptized you. |
| | ¿Quien te puse "Cihualteco" | Who named "El Cihualteco" |
| | para que te cante yo? | so that I can sing to you? |

Chorus repeated with slightly changed text.

Select the trait that best fits each section of the mariachi song *El Cihualteco*:

**Instrumental introduction**

_____ **1.** Rhythm/Meter
     **a.** clear triple meter, or      **b.** highly syncopated rhythms

_____ **2.** Melody
     **c.** instruments playing in 3rds, or      **d.** solo instruments featured

**Verse**

_____ **3.** Melody
     **e.** countermelody in violins, or      **f.** countermelody in trumpets

_____ **4.** Accompaniment
     **g.** bass played by tuba, or      **h.** bass played by large guitar

**Chorus**

_____ **5.** Melody
     **i.** long, arched phrases, or      **j.** short, repeated motives

_____ **6.** Texture
     **k.** homophonic texture, or      **l.** polyphonic texture

**7.** Which of the following traits did you hear in *Son* from *Homage to Federico García Lorca*, by Revueltas?

_____ **m.** clear metric treatment       _____ **p.** instruments playing in 3rds

_____ **n.** complex, polyphonic texture       _____ **q.** verse/chorus structure

_____ **o.** guitarrón on bass line       _____ **r.** highly syncopated rhythms

## LISTENING ACTIVITY: COMPARING STYLES 6
## EARLY TO LATER TWENTIETH CENTURY

Listen to these two orchestral examples (StudySpace, Chapter 39) and compare the treatment of the orchestra and musical elements. Match the work that best fits the description.

   **a.** Debussy: *Jeux de vagues* (*Play of the Waves*), from *La mer* (*The Sea*)
   **b.** Messiaen: *Turangilîla-symphonie*, excerpt

| | | |
|---|---|---|
| **1.** Melody | _____ wide-ranging, disjunct lines | _____ chromatic, winding lines |
| **2.** Rhythm | _____ floating sense of rhythm | _____ driving rhythmic movement |
| **3.** Harmony | _____ highly dissonant idiom | _____ chromatic and gently dissonant |
| **4.** Timbre | _____ brass and percussion prominent | _____ features woodwinds and strings, with harp |
| **5.** Expression | _____ eerie, sliding effects | _____ arpeggios, glissandos, and trills |

Listen to these two vocal examples and compare the treatment of the voices and musical elements. Match the work that best fits the description.

   **c.** Orff: *Carmina burana, O fortuna*
   **d.** Ligeti: *Lux aeterna*, excerpt

| | | |
|---|---|---|
| **6.** Melody | _____ no sense of melodic line | _____ small-ranged melodic line |
| **7.** Rhythm | _____ steady accented beat | _____ no rhythmic pulse |
| **8.** Harmony | _____ slowly unfolding, highly dissonant | _____ repeated harmonies, somewhat dissonant chords |
| **9.** Timbre | _____ pure vocal timbres | _____ voices with instruments |
| **10.** Expression | _____ supernatural mood | _____ sense of urgency |

traditional dances, many set in triple meter but with shifting accents and strong syncopations. One of the most famous dance pieces is *Jarabe tapatío*, known in the United States as the *Mexican Hat Dance*. The *son*, a mixture of native, Spanish, and African traditions, is a standard form of the mariachi. We will consider an example of a **son jalisciense** (from the Jalisco region) in the accompanying Listening Activ-   *Son* ity, which compares the sounds of this traditional music style with the art music of a composer who emulated it.

   Today, mariachi groups play all types of dance music—mambo, danzón, chachacha, salsa, cumbia, and popular music as well. Festivals are held in the western and southwestern United States, and some universities sponsor mariachi ensembles as part of their music programs.

## Critical Thinking

**1.** How does the music of William Grant Still fit the ideals of the Harlem Renaissance movement?

**2.** What qualities in the music of Aaron Copland are particularly American?

**3.** How does Silvestre Revueltas merge classical and art music traditions?

**4.** What elements are distinctive in mariachi music, and how did composers emulate these in their compositions?

# Music beyond the Concert Hall

## COMPOSERS AND WORKS

| 1860 | 1870 | 1880 | 1890 | 1900 | 1910 | 1920 | 1930 | 1940 | 1950 | 1960 | 1970 | 1980 | 1990 | 2000 | 2010 |

**(1898–1937)** George Gershwin (*Porgy and Bess*)

**(1915–1967)** Billy Strayhorn
(*Take the A Train*)

**(1915–1959)** Billie Holiday (*Billie's Blues*)

**(1918–1990)** Leonard Bernstein
(*West Side Story*)

**(b. 1932)** John Williams (*Raiders of the Lost Ark*)

**(b. 1941)** Bob Dylan (*Mr. Tambourine Man*)

## EVENTS

| 1860 | 1870 | 1880 | 1890 | 1900 | 1910 | 1920 | 1930 | 1940 | 1950 | 1960 | 1970 | 1980 | 1990 | 2000 | 2010 |

**1917** U.S. enters World War I

**1920** Prohibition begins in the U.S.
19th Amendment passed, granting women the vote

**1929** Great Depression begins

**1939** World War II begins

**1946** First Fender electric guitar

**1958** First stereo recordings released

**1965** First Rolling Stones hit

**1969** Woodstock Festival

**1991** Soviet Union dissolved

**1994** Kurt Cobain of Nirvana dies

**2001** iTunes media player introduced

# Music beyond the Concert Hall

**Romare Bearden** (1911–1988). *Trombone Solo* (1984).

# 7

# The Rise of American Popular Styles

"They teach you there's a boundary line to music.
But man, there's no boundary line to art. "

— **Charlie Parker**

⑤ **StudySpace** wwnorton.com/enjoy

- By the turn of the twentieth century, New York City had become the cultural center of America, witnessing the rise of the *Broadway musical* and the sheet-music business by *Tin Pan Alley* composers.

- The U.S. involvement in World War I gave rise to a patriotic voice in music, and facilitated the dissemination of American popular styles of *ragtime* and *jazz* throughout Europe.

- The advent of radio and "talkie" films promoted music and the "roaring 20s" dance craze.

- *Big band jazz* and dance clubs provided a brief escape from the difficulties of the Great Depression of the 1930s and the trials of World War II in the early 1940s.

- Throughout the twentieth century, songwriters have focused on important political events and sociological trends as fodder for their music.

- The 1950s and early 1960s witnessed a repressive political environment in which many Americans—composers and performers alike— were under scrutiny for their potentially leftist views.

- The era of the Vietnam War saw many causes voiced through music, including an antiwar stance, civil rights and feminist issues, protests against political corruption, and a new view of personal and sexual freedoms. Today, political issues and social causes continue to stir musicians and film-makers toward inspired creative efforts.

**Broadway musicals**

Although theatrical productions were not allowed in the earliest years of the American colonies—they were banned in most of the colonies on religious and moral grounds—this restriction was soon lifted, and many immigrant musicians came to the United States in the later eighteenth century to perform, often in New York, which was considered the cultural center of the country. Works like John Gay's *The Beggar's Opera* and later Gilbert and Sullivan operettas (*The Mikado* and *H.M.S. Pinafore*, for example) were performed in New York, and entrepreneurs like P. T. Barnum brought traveling shows to various New York venues. The heart of the theater district soon moved to midtown Manhattan, with theaters lining Broadway, a wide street that runs the length of Manhattan. Throughout the country, minstrel shows, popular in the late nineteenth century, soon gave way to *vaudeville*, a type of comedic musical sketch, many written by immigrant composers.

By the late nineteenth century, New York City was the center of music publishing as well. The term *Tin Pan Alley* refers to the writers and publishers of popular music, many of whom set up business in Manhattan. George Gershwin first broke into the music business as a "song plugger" who demonstrated and sold sheet music in New York. Perhaps the most successful Tin Pan Alley composer was Irving Berlin, whose first hit song, *Alexander's Ragtime Band*, set off a ragtime craze worldwide; he followed this with the timeless songs *White Christmas* and *Easter Parade*, among many others.

In 1917, the United States officially entered World War I, an act that spurred the composition of many patriotic songs, marches, and love ballads. Songwriter George M. Cohan's inspirational *Over There* (see illustration), announcing that "the Yanks are coming," resounded across oceans and eventually won him the Congressional Gold Medal of Honor. The war facilitated the dissemination of American music abroad, in part through the efforts of James Reese Europe, an African-American musician and U.S. army band leader who introduced ragtime and early jazz styles to France. Upon his return home in 1919, he stated, "I have come from France more firmly convinced than ever that Negros should write Negro music. We have our own racial feeling and if we try to copy whites, we will make bad copies."

America came out of "The Great War" a changed country. The next decade, known as the "roaring 20s," witnessed the growth of radio—in 1920, a Detroit station aired the first news broadcast. The film industry gained popularity in the 1920s as well, with the advent of the "talkie" (as opposed to a silent film).

The 1920s were relatively prosperous and brought on many social changes, including prohibition, which banned the manufacture and sale of alcohol; the ratification of the Nineteenth Amendment, granting women the right to vote; the Harlem Renaissance (see p. 329), celebrating African-American literary and artistic culture; and the jazz age, which furthered the ballroom culture across the United States (the seductive tango and the "kicky" Charleston were "all the rage") as well as "flapper" fashions for women that discarded Victorian modes of dress in favor of shapeless straight shifts that stopped at the knees.

In 1929, the booming world economy suffered a huge setback with the Wall Street crash, and the country settled into a decade-long Great Depression, viewed as the most serious economic collapse in the history of the United States. Tin Pan Alley faded, and the jazz club scene, as well as films and Broadway musical theater, allowed a brief escape from the difficulties of the era. Among the popular entertainments from the Depression was Gershwin's musical *Girl Crazy* (1930), featuring the very popular *I Got Rhythm*. Big band jazz dominated popular music, promoted by the dance craze, radio, and live concerts. One of the most well-known bands was the Duke Ellington Orchestra, which we will hear playing this group's signature tune, *Take the A Train*.

The Second World War (1939–1945), like the First, had a dramatic impact on American society. The big band phenomenon continued through World War II, during which time many musicians toured with the USO, performing for the soldiers serving their country. By this time, radio had reached many corners of the world, including the American troops abroad via Armed Forces Radio. Once again, songwriters capitalized on the patriotic spirit with such tunes as *Boogie Woogie Bugle Boy (of Company B)* and Irving Berlin's *God Bless America*, written earlier but revived by

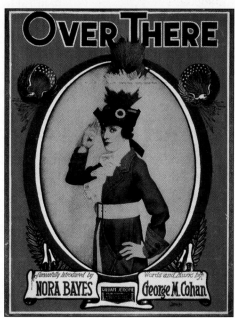

(Top) A vaudeville show from 1917. Watercolor by **Charles Demuth** (1883–1935).

(Bottom) The cover to the sheet music of George M. Cohan's famous World War I song *Over There* (1917).

**Otto Dix** (1891–1969) captures the energy of the Charleston dance craze, in *Big Town* (1927–28).

singer Kate Smith in a famous and moving 1938 radio broadcast.

Recordings became more readily available in the postwar era of the 1950s, both LP (long-playing 33-rpm) and 45-rpm records. Accordingly, many consumers purchased hi fi's (high fidelity music systems), as well as the newest invention—television—for their homes. Music-focused TV shows introduced the newest acts to the public, including early rock-and-roll performers. Among these shows were *Your Hit Parade*, which aired from 1950–59 and *Dick Clark's American Bandstand* (on the air in various versions from 1952 until 1989). The cultural icon Elvis Presley took TV audiences by storm with his appearance on several family programs, including the *Ed Sullivan Show*, where he premiered his hit ballad *Love Me Tender* and was paid an unprecedented $50,000. The prosperous economy of the 1950s also supported a huge growth in the musical theater business—it was in this era that some of our most enduring musicals were first produced, including Lerner and Loewe's *My Fair Lady*, Rodgers and Hammerstein's *Oklahoma!*, and Bernstein's *West Side Story*, which we will consider.

Political issues have also been hugely influential to music and musicians. The "red scare" of communism during the McCarthy era (the 1950s and early 1960s) saw the blacklisting of many creative Americans, including composers Aaron Copland (who wrote the very American *Appalachian Spring*, p. 329) and Leonard Bernstein (composer of the musical *West Side Story*, p. 361), clarinetist Artie Shaw (who performed with Billie Holiday, p. 349), folksinger Pete Seeger, as well as Langston Hughes (Harlem Renaissance writer, see p. 329) and W. E. B. Du Bois (librettist for *Porgy and Bess*, see p. 358). Even the physicist J. Robert Oppenheimer, the "father of the atomic bomb" and subject of the John Adams opera *Doctor Atomic*, was not exempt (see p. 423).

U.S. troops disembarking on the beaches of Normandy, France, during World War II (June 6, 1944).

Protest songs are a long-standing American tradition, and the last decades of the twentieth century provided many causes that inspired musicians' creativity. Folksinger Bob Dylan's voice was clearly heard with landmark protest songs (*Blowin' in the Wind* and *The Times They Are A-Changin'*) during the civil rights movement of the 1960s (see p. 375), and Pete Seeger's *If I Had a Hammer* became, along with *We Shall Overcome*, anthems for civil rights causes. America's involvement in the Vietnam War provided more ammunition for musical protests, many of which were heard at the original Woodstock Festival (see p. 378). New musical styles that developed in the 1980s—punk rock and rap, in particular— were strong voices of protest against discrimination, poverty, corruption, and government policies (as in Public Enemy's *Don't Believe the Hype*, 1988), while other pop singers, like Michael Jackson, worked to help the disastrous famine in Africa (*We are the World*, 1985). The intense drug culture and sexual revolution of the 1960s was reflected in songs of many rock groups, including the Rolling Stones and in the ground-breaking, antiwar musical *Hair* (1967, revived 2008). Musical feminism took many forms as well, from the folksy protest songs of Joan Baez (see illustration) to the "in-your-face" music of the Dixie Chicks. Other significant social issues include environmental causes and public acceptance of the atrocities of war, notably the Holocaust (portrayed in the 1993 film *Schindler's List,* with a soundtrack by John Williams). Iraq has fueled a revival of musical commentaries, as have recent political campaigns. Obama's 2008 campaign for the presidency attracted the talents of Black Eyed Peas' member will.i.am, who wrote the now famous collage-style video *Yes We Can.*

**Protest songs**

In the next chapters, we will explore various types of music that are most often heard outside the concert hall setting, beginning with the development of early jazz styles and musical theater songs, and continuing with music scores for films and a brief survey of rock. All these genres have had enormous social impact, supporting some of the most significant causes of our time, and they remain vibrant and relevant today.

(Top) Before the advent of TV in the early 1950s, families gathered around the radio for home entertainment.

(Bottom) American folksinger Joan Baez performs at an anti-Vietnam War rally in London's Trafalgar Square in May 1965.

## Critical Thinking

**1.** How did the United States move past the domination by European music in the nineteenth century toward its own musical voice in the early twentieth century?

**2.** How did music inspire wartime causes throughout the twentieth century? How did antiwar sentiments find a musical voice?

**3.** What contemporary causes have attracted musicians and inspired them toward new works?

# 40 Ragtime, Blues, and Jazz

"All riddles are blues,
And all blues are sad,
And I'm only mentioning
Some blues I've had."

—**Maya Angelou**

## KEY POINTS

> **StudySpace** wwnorton.com/enjoy

- **Jazz** drew elements from African traditions and Western popular and art music. Its roots are in West African music and nineteenth-century African-American ceremonial and work songs.

- **Ragtime** developed from an African-American piano style characterized by syncopated rhythms and sectional forms, and made famous by Scott Joplin, the "King of Ragtime."

- **Blues** is an American genre of folk music based on a repetitive, poetic-musical form with three-line strophes set to a repeating harmonic pattern. Billie Holiday was a leading blues and jazz singer.

- Louis Armstrong (trumpet) was associated with **New Orleans-style jazz**, characterized by a small ensemble improvising simultaneously.

- The 1930s saw the advent of the **swing era** (or **big band era**) and the brilliantly composed jazz of Duke Ellington.

- In the late 1940s, big band jazz gave way to smaller group styles, including **bebop**, **cool jazz**, and **West Coast jazz**.

- Later jazz styles include **third stream jazz**, which borrowed elements of art music, as well as **fusion**, **Neoclassical style**, **free jazz**, and **new-age jazz**.

Ragtime, blues, and jazz are part of the great American identity. *Jazz* refers to a music created mainly by African Americans around the turn of the twentieth century as they blended elements drawn from African musics with the popular and art traditions of the West. One of the most influential precursors of jazz was *ragtime*, originally an African-American piano style that gained popularity in instrumental ensemble arrangements by Scott Joplin. Known as the "King of Ragtime," he was one of the first black Americans to gain importance as a composer.

## Scott Joplin and Ragtime

Scott Joplin is best remembered today for his piano rags, which reflect Joplin's preoccupation with classical forms. They exhibit balanced phrasing and key structures, combined with imaginative and highly syncopated melodies. Like earlier dance forms, they are built in clear-cut sections, their patterns of repetition reminiscent of those heard in the marches of John Philip Sousa, whose own band frequently played arrangements of Joplin rags.

## Scott Joplin (1868–1917)

**Joplin** was born in Texarkana, Texas, to a musical family. His father, a former slave, played violin, and his mother sang and played banjo. He began musical instruction on the guitar and bugle but soon showed such a gift that he was given free piano lessons. He left home when he was only fourteen and traveled throughout the Mississippi Valley playing in honky-tonks and piano bars. He arrived in St. Louis in 1885, the center of a growing ragtime movement.

Joplin helped ragtime gain public notice when he and his small orchestra performed at the 1893 World Exposition in Chicago. Around this time, he also sought more formal musical training at the George R. Smith College in Sedalia, Missouri. It was at a club in Sedalia that Joplin, surrounded by a circle of black entertainers, introduced his *Maple Leaf Rag*. Fame came to the composer in 1899 when the sheet music of the piece sold a million copies. He eventually moved to New York, where he was active as a teacher, composer, and performer.

Scott Joplin strove to elevate ragtime from a purely improvised style to a more serious art form that could stand on a level with European art music. Realizing that he must lead the way in this merger of styles, he began work on his opera *Treemonisha*, which he finished in 1911. But the opera was not well received, and Joplin fell into a severe depression from which he never fully recovered; he died in New York City on April 1, 1917. *Treemonisha* remained unknown until its successful revival in 1972 by the Houston Grand Opera. In 1976, nearly sixty years after his death, Joplin was awarded a Pulitzer Prize for his masterpiece.

**Major Works:** Stage works, including 2 operas (*Treemonisha*, 1911) • Piano rags, including *Maple Leaf Rag* (1899) and *Pine Apple Rag* (1908) • Piano music • Songs.

**iMusic:** *Pine Apple Rag*

---

The *Maple Leaf Rag*, perhaps the best-known rag ever composed, is typical in its regular, sectional form. Quite simply, the dance presents a series of sixteen-measure phrases, called **strains**, in a moderate duple meter; each strain is repeated before the next one begins. The *Maple Leaf Rag* established the form, with four strains (see Listening Guide 50, p. 348). As in most rags, the listener's interest is focused throughout on the syncopated rhythms of the melodies, played by the right hand, which are supported by an easy, steady, duple-rhythm accompaniment in the left hand. Joplin's sophisticated piano rags brought him worldwide recognition.

Title page of *Maple Leaf Rag* (1899), by Scott Joplin.

# Blues and New Orleans Jazz

*Blues* is an American form of folk music based on a simple, repetitive, poetic-musical structure. The term refers to a mood as well as a harmonic progression, which is usually twelve (or occasionally sixteen) bars in length. Characteristic is the **blue note**, a slight drop in pitch on the third, fifth, or seventh tone of the scale. A blues text typically consists of a three-line stanza of which the first two lines are identical. Its style derives from the work songs of Southern blacks.

Blues is a fundamental form in jazz. The music we call jazz was born in New Orleans through the fusion of African-American elements such as ragtime and blues with other traditional styles—spirituals, work songs, and shouts. (For more on the roots of jazz, see HTTN 13.) In all of these styles, the art of improvisation was crucially important. Performers made up their parts as they went along, often with several musicians improvising at the same time (see Btw, p. 355).

**LISTENING GUIDE 50**

DVD | **CD 7 (74–78)** | CD 4 (35–39)

# Joplin: *Maple Leaf Rag*

3:21

DATE: Published 1899

GENRE: Piano rag

## WHAT TO LISTEN FOR:

| | |
|---|---|
| Melody | Catchy syncopated melodies; disjunct |
| Rhythm/ Meter | Marchlike duple meter; syncopated in right hand; steady beat in bass |
| Harmony | Major key; shifts to new key in C section (the trio); decorative rolled chords |
| Texture | Homophonic; chordal accompaniment to melody |

| | |
|---|---|
| Form | Sectional dance form, 4 sections (strains), each 16 measures with repeats: **A-A-B-B-A-C-C-D-D** |
| Performing Forces | Joplin plays on a 1910 Steinway piano roll |

---

| 35 | 0:00 | **A**—strain 1—syncopated middle-range ascending melody, accompanied by steady bass; begins with upbeat in bass; in A-flat major; performer adds ornamental flourishes in left hand: |
|---|---|---|

| | 0:22 | **A**—strain 1 repeated. |
|---|---|---|

| 36 | 0:44 | **B**—strain 2—similar syncopated pattern in melody; begins in higher range and descends; steady bass accompaniment; in A-flat major: |
|---|---|---|

| | 1:06 | **B**—strain 2 repeated. |
|---|---|---|

| 37 | 1:28 | **A**—return to strain 1. |
|---|---|---|

| 38 | 1:50 | **C**—strain 3, also called trio—in D-flat major; more static melody; new rhythmic pattern with right hand playing on downbeats; bass accompaniment more disjunct: |
|---|---|---|

| | 2:12 | **C**—strain 3 repeated. |
|---|---|---|

| 39 | 2:34 | **D**—strain 4—return to A-flat major, with contrasting theme; syncopated pattern related to strain 1: |
|---|---|---|

| | | **D**—strain 4 repeated. |
|---|---|---|

Now try the **Listening Quiz.**

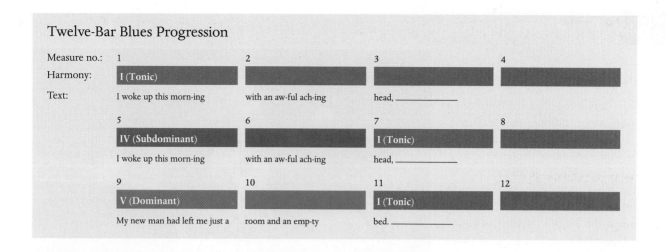

Twelve-Bar Blues Progression

| Measure no.: | 1 | 2 | 3 | 4 |
|---|---|---|---|---|
| Harmony: | I (Tonic) | | | |
| Text: | I woke up this morn-ing | with an aw-ful ach-ing | head, _____ | |
| | 5 | 6 | 7 | 8 |
| | IV (Subdominant) | | I (Tonic) | |
| | I woke up this morn-ing | with an aw-ful ach-ing | head, _____ | |
| | 9 | 10 | 11 | 12 |
| | V (Dominant) | | I (Tonic) | |
| | My new man had left me just a | room and an emp-ty | bed. _____ | |

*New Orleans jazz* depended on the players' multiple improvisation to create a polyphonic texture. The trumpet or cornet played the melody or an embellished version of it; the clarinet was often featured in a countermelody above the main tune; the trombone improvised below the trumpet and signaled the chord changes; and the rhythm section—consisting of string bass or tuba, guitar and banjo, or piano and drums—provided rhythmic and harmonic support. One of the greats of New Orleans jazz was Louis "Satchmo" Armstrong (trumpet).

Armstrong was unquestionably the most important single force in the development of early jazz styles. He was a great improviser who used a variety of mutes to expand the capacities of his trumpet in range of tone color. To distinguish his unique melodic-rhythmic style of performance, his admirers coined the term "swing," which became a standard description of jazz. His 1926 recording of *Heebie Jeebies* introduced **scat singing**, in which syllables without meaning (*vocables*) are set to an improvised vocal line.

In jazz, a **chorus** is a single statement of melodic-harmonic pattern, like a twelve-bar blues progression (see chart, above). Armstrong's style of jazz introduced a number of new features, including solo rather than ensemble choruses. In his solos, only hints of the original tune are recognizable. Through such innovations, jazz was transformed into a solo art that presented improvised fantasias on chord changes. Armstrong's instrumental-like approach to singing, his distinctive inflections, and his improvisatory style were highly influential to jazz vocalists, including Billie Holiday, one of the leading female singers in jazz history.

 **iMusic**

*When the Saints Go Marching In*

Scat singing

Chorus

# The Jazz Singer Billie Holiday

"I can't stand to sing the same song the same way two nights in succession, let alone two years or ten years. If you can, then it ain't music; it's close-order drill or exercise or yodeling or something, not music."

Billie Holiday had a unique talent that was immediately recognized by other musicians. "You never heard singing so slow, so lazy, with such a drawl," one band leader reminisced. Although her voice was untrained, she had a remarkable sense of pitch and a flawless delivery—a style she learned from listening to her two idols, Bessie Smith and Louis Armstrong.

We will hear a blues that Billie wrote and recorded in 1936, and which she performed regularly throughout her career. It is a twelve-bar blues, with a short

# The Roots of Jazz

Singer B. B. King has been dubbed "King of the Blues."

Jazz draws together traditions from West Africa, Europe, and the Americas. The African origins of jazz evoke an earlier episode of American history: the slave trade from Africa. Many of the slaves brought to America came from the west coast of Africa, often called the Ivory or Gold Coast, and their musical traditions came with them. These include singing styles (call-and-response patterns and various vocal inflections) and storytelling techniques, traits that have remained alive for several centuries through oral tradition.

Black music in nineteenth-century America included dancing for ritual and ceremonial purposes and the singing of work songs (communal songs that synchronized the rhythm of group tasks; see HTTN 1, p. 64) and spirituals (a kind of religious folk song, often with a refrain). West African religious traditions mingled freely with Protestant Christianity adopted by some slaves. The art of storytelling through music, and praise singing (glorifying deities or royalty) were other traditions retained by slaves that would contribute to spirituals and blues.

The city of New Orleans fueled the early sounds of jazz. There, in Congo Square, slaves met in the pre–Civil War era to dance to the accompaniment of all sorts of instruments, including drums, gourds, mouth harps, and banjos. Their music featured a strong underlying pulse with syncopations and polyrhythmic elaborations. Melodies incorporated African-derived techniques such as rhythmic interjections, vocal glides, and percussive sounds made with the tongue and throat, and were often set in a musical scale with blue notes (lowered scale degrees on the third, fifth, or seventh of a major scale).

In the years after the Civil War and the Emancipation Proclamation (1863), a new style of music arose in the South, especially in the Mississippi Delta—country, or rural, blues, performed by a raspy-voiced male singer and, by the turn of the century, accompanied by a steel-string guitar. This music voiced the difficulties of everyday life. The vocal lines featured melodic pitch bending, or blue notes, sung over repeated bass patterns. Among the greatest blues singers were Charlie Patton (1891–1934), Bessie Smith (1894–1937), and the legendary B. B. King (aka "King of the Blues").

This expressive musical genre has also permeated modern popular culture through a variety of media. These pop-culture icons include blues-rock artists Janis Joplin and Jimi Hendrix (whose posthumous studio album *Valleys of Neptune* [2010] contains several blues covers), and The White Stripes' guitarist Jack White

---

**iMusic**

*Swing Low, Sweet Chariot* (spiritual)
*When the Saints Go Marching In* (New Orleans jazz)

introduction and six choruses, some of which are instrumental (see Listening Guide 51). The first text-verse is a typical three-line strophe (as shown in the chart on p. 349), but as the work progresses, the form becomes freer. In the vocal verses, Billie demonstrates her masterful rhythmic flexibility and talent for jazz embellishments (scoops and dips on notes). In this performance, we hear Artie Shaw's creative clarinet improvisations and Bunny Berigan's earthy, "gutbucket" trumpet playing (this refers to an unrestrained, raspy quality of tone). Shaw remembered this 1936 recording session some years later, saying that Billie was "already beginning to develop that distinctive style of hers."

## LISTENING GUIDE 51

ⓢ | DVD | CD 7 (79–85) | CD 4 (40–46)

# Holiday: *Billie's Blues*

2:38

**DATE:** Recorded 1936

**GENRE:** 12-bar blues

**WHAT TO LISTEN FOR:**

| | |
|---|---|
| Melody | Syncopated melodies with pitch inflections (bent notes, blue notes); free improvisations |
| Rhythm/ Meter | Slow tempo, 4/4 meter; steady rhythmic accompaniment under more complex, flexible solo lines |
| Harmony | Repeated harmonic progressions for each chorus (I-IV-I-V-I) |
| Texture | Polyphonic, with countermelodies against solo voice or instrument |
| Form | 12-bar blues (introduction and 6 choruses; choruses 2, 3, 6 are vocal) |

| | |
|---|---|
| Expression | Laid-back feeling, earthy character; different moods created by varied improvisational styles of solos |
| Performing Forces | Billie Holiday, vocal<br>Bunny Berigan, trumpet<br>Artie Shaw, clarinet<br>Joe Bushkin, piano<br>Dick McDonough, guitar<br>Pete Peterson, string bass<br>Cozy Cole, drums |
| Text | Chorus 1 = typical blues text (see p. 349); others more free |

| | | |
|---|---|---|
| **40** | 0:00 | **Introduction** (4 bars)—bass and piano. |
| **41** | 0:07 | **Chorus 1**—ensemble (12 bars). |
| **42** | 0:32 | **Chorus 2**—vocal (12 bars): |

> Lord, I love my man, tell the world I do,
> I love my man, tell th' world I do,
> But when he mistreats me, makes me feel so blue.

Opening of first vocal chorus, showing syncopated line, with slide at the end:

| | | |
|---|---|---|
| **43** | 0:56 | **Chorus 3**—vocal (12 bars): |

> My man wouldn' gimme no breakfast,
> Wouldn' gimme no dinner,
> Squawked about my supper 'n put me outdoors,
> Had the nerve to lay a matchbox on my clothes;
> I didn't have so many but I had a long, long ways to go.

| | | |
|---|---|---|
| **44** | 1:21 | **Chorus 4**—solo clarinet improvisation (12 bars): |

*Continued on following page*

| 45 | 1:45 | **Chorus 5**—solo trumpet improvisation (12 bars). |
| 46 | 2:11 | **Chorus 6**—vocal (12 bars): |

> Some men like me 'cause I'm happy,
> Some 'cause I'm snappy,
> Some call me honey, others think I've got money,
> Some tell me, "Baby you're built for speed,"
> Now if you put that all together,
> Makes me ev'rything a good man needs.

🔊 **Now try the Listening Quiz.**

---

## Meet the Performers

### Billie Holiday

**"I don't think I'm singing. I feel like I'm playing a horn."**

Known as Lady Day, **Billie Holiday** (1915–1959) was the daughter of a guitar player with the Fletcher Henderson Band. Little is known of her youth (the account she gives in her autobiography, *Lady Sings the Blues*, is inaccurate). In 1928, with barely any formal education, she went to New York, where she probably worked as a prostitute. Around 1930, Billie began singing at clubs in Brooklyn and Harlem, and was discovered in 1933 by a talent scout who arranged for her to record with the white clarinetist Benny Goodman. This first break earned her thirty-five dollars.

By 1935, Billie was recording with some of the best jazz musicians of her day. As her popularity increased, she was featured with several prominent big bands—making her one of the first black singers to break the color barrier and sing in public with a white orchestra. Billie recorded one of her most famous songs in 1939—*Strange Fruit*, about a Southern lynching. With its horrible images of blacks dangling from trees, the song resonated with blacks and whites alike and became a powerful social commentary on black identity and equality. Billie's delivery of the macabre lyrics is cold and factual, but her voice is not.

By the 1940s, Billie's life had deteriorated, the result of alcohol, drug abuse, and ill-chosen relationships with abusive men. She began using opium and heroin, and was jailed on drug charges in 1947. Her health—and her voice—suffered because of her addictions, although she still made a number of memorable recordings. In May 1959, she was diagnosed with cirrhosis of the liver and died several months later, at the age of forty-four.

**Check out these recordings by Billie Holiday:** *God Bless the Child* and *Billie's Blues* (on CD set and 🔊), both songs on *Lady Day: The Best of Billie Holiday; Fine & Mellow* and *Strange Fruit*, on the album *Strange Fruit*

---

# The Swing Era and Beyond

Big band jazz   In the 1930s and '40s, the highly creative era of early jazz gave way to the *swing*, or *big band*, era. By then, jazz was America's voice in popular music. This was also the time of the Great Depression (see p. 343), the most severe economic slowdown in American history, which cost many musicians their livelihood but also provided an opening for new performers, and particularly black musicians. Among those who ascended to stardom in this era was Edward Kennedy "Duke" Ellington (1899–1974). His unique big-band style of jazz won over a wide audience—both black and white—who danced away its cares in clubs and hotel ballrooms across the country.

Duke Ellington (piano) and his band in a movie still from the Metro Goldwin Mayer musical *Cabin in the Sky* (1943).

One of the theme songs for Ellington's orchestra was *Take the A Train*, written by composer/arranger Billy Strayhorn (1915–1967) and first recorded in 1941. Ellington and Strayhorn collaborated for many years. *Take the A Train* is one of the few works solidly credited to Strayhorn, and it epitomizes the swing style. (The "A" train in the title refers to one of the subway lines that runs through Manhattan to Harlem.)

*Take the A Train*

Ellington's orchestral palette was much richer than that of the New Orleans band. It included two trumpets, one cornet, three trombones, four saxophones, two string basses, guitar, drums, vibraphone, and piano. The jazz standard has a tight structure: a thirty-two-bar song form, with four phrases of eight measures for each chorus in the scheme **A-A-B-A**. The introduction features Ellington at piano followed by three choruses (see Listening Guide 52). In the first chorus, the saxophones present the memorable tune in unison, answered by muted trumpets and trombones in call-and-response fashion. The second chorus stars a

## Meet the Performers

### Duke Ellington

**"Somehow I suspect that if Shakespeare were alive today, he might be a jazz fan himself."**

Edward Kennedy "Duke" Ellington was born in Washington, DC, in 1899, and was playing in New York jazz clubs—including the Harlem Cotton Club— in the 1920s with his group The Washingtonians. The advent of the big band era brought a greater need for arranged and composed music—that is, written down—and Ellington played a major role in its development. He was not only a gifted jazz pianist but also had an unrivaled talent for jazz orchestration. In 1939, Ellington began his collaboration with Billy Strayhorn, who served as an arranger and composer for the band; together they achieved an unparalleled success in their performances and recordings. Ellington continued as a soloist, touring as well as composing suites, tone poems, ballets, and even sacred music. He scored music for film, including for *Anatomy of a Murder* (in which he also acted, 1959). Among his most famous compositions are *Black and Tan Fantasy* (1927), *Mood Indigo* (1930), *Sophisticated Lady* (1933), *Ko-Ko*

(1940), and *Black, Brown, and Beige* (1943); his most famous recording is *Take the A Train*. Today he is remembered as a composer who brought the jazz art to new heights; as an arranger who left a rich legacy of works for jazz groups; as a band leader who served as a teacher and model to several generations of jazz musicians; and as a major artistic figure in the Harlem Renaissance movement (see p. 326).

**Check out these recordings by Duke Ellington:** *Best of The Duke Ellington Centennial Edition* (1999; available for download), which includes *Black and Tan Fantasy, East Saint Louis Toodle-O, Take the A Train,* and *Sophisticated Lady*

## LISTENING GUIDE 52

☉ | DVD | **CD 7 (86–90)** | CD 4 (47–51)

# Strayhorn: *Take the A Train*, by the Duke Ellington Orchestra

2:54

**DATE:** Recorded February 15, 1941

**GENRE:** Big band jazz

### WHAT TO LISTEN FOR:

| | | | |
|---|---|---|---|
| Melody | Disjunct, syncopated themes with call-and-response exchanges between instruments | Expression | Animated movement with special jazz effects (bent notes, shakes, glissandos) |
| Rhythm/Meter | Broad quadruple meter, at moderate tempo; syncopated rhythms, short riffs | Timbre | Big band sound, with reed, brass, and percussion sections |
| Harmony | Complex, advanced harmonies; chromatic; modulates to another key | Performing Forces | Jazz big band (trumpets, trombones, saxophones, piano, guitar, bass, drums); soloists: Duke Ellington, piano; Ray Nance, (trumpet) |
| Form | 32-bar pop song form (**A-A-B-A**) for each of 3 choruses, with introduction and coda | | |

**47** 0:00 **Introduction**—4 measures, piano (Ellington), with syncopated, chromatic motive idea.

**Chorus 1 (A-A-B-A)**

**48** 0:06 **A**—unison saxophones state disjunct melody, in key of C, in interjections from muted trumpets and trombones (8 bars) against steady rhythm accompaniment:

0:17 **A**—repeated (8 bars).

0:28 **B**—contrasting episode in saxophones; syncopated melody with low brass and rhythm.

0:39 **A**—saxophones restate main melody with new rhythmic figure from brass; rippling piano figures.

**49** 0:50 **Chorus 2 (A-A-B-A)**
Features Ray Nance on muted trumpet, accompanied by saxes and rhythm section;
trumpet solo in 2nd phrase, with bent pitches:

1:35 **Interlude**—4 measures, sustained accents as though in triple rather than quadruple meter.

**50** 1:41 **Chorus 3 (A-A-B-A)**
**A**—Saxophones play version of main theme (4 measures); followed by unmuted trumpet solo (Nance).

1:52 **A**—trumpet solo continues, with sustained chords in saxophones.

2:04 **B**—trumpet solo with countermelodies in saxes and trombones; closes with fanfare without rhythm accompaniment; punctuated by cymbal crash.

2:14 **A**—original theme played by saxophones in new key (E flat); brass interjects, alternating with muted and open notes.

**51** 2:26 **Coda**—two repetitions of **A** (8 bars each), first *mezzo piano*, then softer, with final closing sax riff.

☉ **Now try the Listening Quiz.**

new band member, Ray Nance, on muted trumpet, with an underlying conversation in the reeds. Nance's masterful improvisation, complete with bent notes, *shakes* (shaking the lips to fluctuate between pitches), and glissandos, has literally become a part of the score that is imitated by trumpet players everywhere. An energetic four-measure interlude that feels like triple meter suddenly intervenes, followed by the third chorus—another trumpet solo (this one open, or unmuted). The coda is a big-band signature closing: it repeats the opening eight bars of the piece twice, each time more softly. Like many jazz tunes, *Take the A Train* was built on the changes (the harmonic progression) of an earlier song, but it is enhanced with playful tunes, complex harmonies, and rich orchestration. This famed jazz standard is the result of one of the most productive collaborations in jazz history, its compositional concept the work of two giants in the field.

## Bebop and Later Jazz Styles

"It's taken me all my life to learn what not to play."

—*Dizzy Gillespie*

By the end of the 1940s, musicians were rebelling against big band jazz and developing new styles: first bebop, then cool jazz. *Bebop* (also known as *bop*) was an invented word mimicking the two-note trademark phrase of this style. Trumpeter Dizzy Gillespie, saxophonist Charlie Parker, and pianist Thelonious Monk were among the leaders of the bebop movement in the 1940s. Over the next two decades, the term "bebop" came to include a number of substyles such as *cool jazz* (the "cool" suggesting a restrained, unemotional manner), West Coast jazz, hard bop, and soul jazz. Trumpeter Miles Davis was the principal exponent of cool jazz, a laid-back style characterized by lush harmonies, lowered levels of volume, moderate tempos, and a new lyricism. *West Coast jazz* is a small-group, cool-jazz style featuring mixed timbres (one instrument for each color, often without piano) and contrapuntal improvisations. Among the important West Coast ensembles that sprang up in the 1950s are the Dave Brubeck Quartet (with Paul Desmond on saxophone) and the Gerry Mulligan Quartet (with Chet Baker on trumpet).

Latin American music has been highly influential in the development of jazz, chiefly its dance rhythms and percussion instruments (conga drum, bongos, and cowbells). In the 1930s and 1940s, Latin bandleaders such as Xavier Cugat brought Latin dance music—especially the rumba—into the mainstream. Duke Ellington's band recorded two hit Latin numbers: *Caravan* (1937, featuring Puerto Rican trombonist Juan Tizol) and *Congo Brava* (1940). Latin elements were integral to the bebop style of the late 1940s, and the next decades saw a strong Brazilian, as well as Cuban, influence on jazz.

In a 1957 lecture, composer and jazz historian Gunther Schuller coined the term *third stream*, holding that the first stream was classical music, the second jazz, and the third a combination of the other two, in which jazz performers' adopted classical forms

### In His Own Words

What's swinging in words? If a guy makes you pat your foot and if you feel it down your back, you don't have to ask anybody if that's good music or not. You can always feel it.

—*Miles Davis*

### By the way . . .

#### How Do Jazz Performers Stay Together?

Jazz is an improvisational art that can be mystifying to the listener: how is it that each musician seems to know exactly what to do and when to do it, yet the results are never the same in any subsequent performance? Despite the complexity of the music, each player in the group has a role that is understood by the others, almost like being an actor in a play. In addition, any good jazz musician knows the standard tunes and the underlying chord structure of each tune. The fact that many of these tunes fall into set forms—like 12-bar blues or 32-bar song form—is also key to understanding how the performers can stay together. For an accomplished jazz musician, these structures are so completely understood that each knows when the next chorus or section is coming up. The order in which the soloist performs might be prearranged, or not—just a nod of a head can trade the solo off to another performer for the next chorus. As a jazz performance progresses, the improvised solos tend to move away from, or not even refer to, the original tune—you might well have lost it in your ear—but the familiar melody generally reappears near the end in some version that reminds you where they started. These unwritten traditions are what make each jazz performance unique, spontaneous, and so magical.

Jazz greats Charlie Parker (saxophone) and Dizzy Gillespie (trumpet), performing ca. 1960.

and tonal idioms. Schuller's idea was picked up by a number of jazz musicians, among them pianist John Lewis (b. 1920), who formed the Modern Jazz Quartet in answer to the growing demand for jazz on college campuses across the country. More recently, trumpeter Wynton Marsalis demonstrated his mastery of both jazz and classical styles in his Pulitzer Prize–winning jazz oratorio *Blood on the Fields* (1996) and his Stravinsky-inspired *A Fiddler's Tale* (1998).

By the 1960s, new experiments were in the making. A free-style **avant-garde jazz** emerged, with tenor saxophonist John Coltrane as its leading exponent. At the same time, a hybrid style known as **fusion** arose that combined jazz improvisation with amplified instruments and the rhythmic pulse of rock. Trumpeter Miles Davis was an important catalyst in the advent of this style, and performers such as guitarist Jerry Garcia (1942–1995, of the Grateful Dead; see p. 377) and vibraphone player Gary Burton became proponents of the fusion sound.

In the last several decades, jazz styles have taken conflicting turns. Modern bebop arose as a contemporary **Neoclassical style** of the 1980s, characterized by expanded tonalities, modal improvisation, and new forms merged with bebop's disjunct lines. Wynton Marsalis is one of the new voices of this Neoclassicism. **Free jazz**, founded by saxophonist Ornette Coleman in the 1960s, has developed alongside the more mellow, contemplative strains of **new-age jazz**, the latter best exemplified by saxophonist Paul Winter. Technologies such as MIDI (see Chapter 46) and interactive performance between musicians and computers have opened a world of creative possibilities and sounds; meanwhile, other performers are looking back to the fundamentals of jazz, reinventing it for today's listeners.

## Critical Thinking

1. What were some of the African-American traditional and musical genres that led to the development of jazz?
2. What elements give ragtime its universal appeal?
3. How does New Orleans jazz differ from big band jazz?
4. How have jazz and classical musical idioms been combined, and by whom?

# 41 Musical Theater

*"The hills are alive with the sound of music."*
—**Oscar Hammerstein II**

## KEY POINTS

> **StudySpace** wwnorton.com/enjoy

- American musical theater has roots in European *operetta*, which was brought to America by immigrant composers.

- Musicals feature romantic plots (some taken from novels), comic moments, appealing melodies, and large ensembles and dance numbers.

- Known for his Tin Pan Alley songs and musical theater productions, George Gershwin sought to unite elements of jazz and classical music. His masterpiece is his folk opera *Porgy and Bess*.

- The great composer/lyricist teams include Rodgers and Hammerstein (*The Sound of Music*), Lerner and Lowe (*My Fair Lady*); other well-known composers are Stephen Sondheim (*Into the Woods*), Andrew Lloyd Webber (*Phantom of the Opera*), and Claude-Michel Schonberg (*Les Misérables*).

- Leonard Bernstein is remembered as a conductor and composer of symphonic and choral music, film music, and musical theater. His *West Side Story*, set in New York City amid turf wars of rival street gangs, updates the Romeo and Juliet legend.

## The Development of American Musical Theater

The American musical theater of today developed from the comic opera, or *operetta*, tradition of late-nineteenth-century European composers such as Johann Strauss Jr., and the team of Gilbert and Sullivan (*Pirates of Penzance*, 1879; *The Mikado*, 1885). The genre was revamped to suit American tastes, first by immigration composers like Victor Herbert (*Babes in Toyland*, 1903) but was soon taken up by American musicians like Jerome Kern (*Showboat*, 1927). In the ensuing decades, the musical established itself as America's unique contribution to world theater.

**Operetta**

While plots for early musicals were often silly and contrived—and depended on romantic plots in picturesque settings enlivened by comedy, appealing melodies, choruses and dances—this changed when composers looked to sophisticated literary sources (*Show Boat*, for example, is based on the Edna Ferber novel, and Lerner and Loewe's *My Fair Lady,* 1956, is based on George Bernard Shaw's play *Pygmalion*). A few works were ahead of their time in both serious subject matter and in compositional technique. One such case was George Gershwin's *Porgy and Bess* (1935), which was so far ahead of its time that it did not become a success until the 1950s. This work paved the way for Leonard Bernstein's *West Side Story* (1957), one of the first musical theater pieces to end tragically.

**Early musicals**

As in opera, a successful musical is often a collaboration between lyricist and composer. Several great teams have produced many of America's most beloved musicals: among these are Lerner and Loewe (*My Fair Lady*, 1956; *Camelot*, 1960) and Rodgers and Hammerstein (*Oklahoma!* 1943; *South Pacific*, 1949; *The King and I*, 1951;

Glinda, the "good" witch (Kristen Chenoweth, top) and Elphaba, the "bad" witch (Idina Menzel, bottom) from the musical *Wicked* (2004).

*The Sound of Music*, 1959). Other noted composers of musicals include Stephen Sondheim (*Sweeny Todd*, 1979; *Into the Woods*, 1988), who brought the genre to new levels of sophistication; Andrew Lloyd Webber (*Cats*, 1981; *Phantom of the Opera*, 1986), who combined song and dance with dazzling scenic effects; and Claude-Michel Schonberg (*Les Misérables*, 1987), who brought history alive with memorable songs. Over the last few decades, we have seen revivals of "classic" musicals like *The Sound of Music* and *South Pacific* as well as the rock musical *Hair* (1968) by Galt MacDermot. A new category of musicals has recently swept the Broadway stage, all based on animated films (*Beauty and the Beast*, 1994; *The Lion King*, 1997). Still others musicals have found their sources in older stories or even classical operas. Jonathan Larsen's hit show *Rent* (1996) is a modern rock opera based on Puccini's opera *La bohème*. The Broadway hit *Wicked* (2004) derives from the classic book *The Wizard of Oz* (1901) as well as the well-known movie (1937), featuring Judy Garland. Dance too has inspired a new type of musical in which choreography takes precedence over story line (*Riverdance,* 1994; *Billy Elliot*, 2005, with music by Elton John). Many "jukebox" musicals, featuring songs by a popular artist or group, have opened in recent years. The most successful were *Mamma Mia!* (1999), based on the songs of the Swedish pop group ABBA; and *Jersey Boys* (2006), which tells the story of the 1960s rock group The Four Seasons, starring Frankie Valli.

We will look at two of the classics from the musical theater repertory: George Gershwin's masterpiece *Porgy and Bess*, which focuses on African-American folk idioms; and Leonard Bernstein's *West Side Story*, which aptly incorporates Latin American and jazz styles with classical orchestrations and a timeless story. Both *Porgy and Bess* and *West Side Story* have now achieved worldwide success, and both would have been unthinkable twenty years earlier because of the serious elements in their plots.

# George Gershwin and the Merger of Classical and Jazz Styles

George Gershwin was one of the most gifted American composers of the twentieth century. Drawn to vernacular music styles, he was able to span the gap between jazz, pop, and classical genres, and he managed to bring jazz into the concert hall with some of the most enduring and appealing works of all time.

## Gershwin's *Porgy and Bess*

*Porgy and Bess* opens to a lively scene in Catfish Row, a black tenement in Charleston, South Carolina, where people are dancing, men are playing craps (a dice game), and Clara is singing the lullaby *Summertime* to her baby. The crippled beggar Porgy arrives along with Bess and her man Crown, who is drunk. Crown joins the game, and he kills the winner Robbins in a fit of rage, then flees. The dope dealer Sportin' Life tries to entice Bess to go to New York with him but she refuses. Porgy then takes in Bess as his woman. The mourners sing a spiritual over Robbins's body, and they search for a way to bury him soon.

In Act 2, the fishermen of Catfish Row prepare to head out to sea despite a storm warning. Although Clara asks her husband Jake not to go, he must, as they desperately need money. Leaving Porgy alone, Bess goes off on a picnic excursion to Kittiwah Island; there she finds the murderer Crown hiding and, after spending the night with him, returns home and confesses to Porgy. When the hurricane hits, Clara rushes into the storm to find Jake, leaving her baby with Bess. Crown calls

## George Gershwin (1898–1937)

**Gershwin** grew up in Manhattan, where he worked as a song plugger for a Tin Pan Alley publisher (see p. 342). A pianist, he pitched new releases by playing and singing them for customers. "This is American music," he told one of his teachers, "This is the kind of music I want to write." He had his first big hit in 1920, with the song *Swanee,* sung by Al Jolson.

During the 1920s, Gershwin launched his career as a composer of concert music: he won international acclaim with his beloved *Rhapsody in Blue*, premiered in 1924 by the Paul Whiteman Orchestra. This was followed by his Concerto in F (1925) and the tone poem *An American in Paris* (1928). He also had a string of hit musicals, beginning with *Lady, Be Good* (1924), his first collaboration with his brother Ira, who wrote many of his song lyrics. *Of Thee I Sing* (1931) was the first musical to win a Pulitzer for drama; however, Gershwin was not recognized because the music was not viewed as central to a drama. Gershwin also wrote enduring film scores, including *Shall We Dance* (1937), starring the dance team of Fred Astaire and Ginger Rogers. His folk opera *Porgy and Bess* is clearly his masterpiece; it falls somewhere between opera and musical theater, having continuous music and recurring themes similar to Wagner's use of leitmotifs and a new seriousness never before heard on the Broadway stage. George Gershwin died of a brain tumor in 1937, at only thirty-nine.

In Gershwin's music, he achieves an appealing rhythmic vitality through the use of syncopation, blue notes, and an "oom-pah" accompaniment typical of jazz piano style. His harmonic language is diverse, extending from diatonic to very chromatic, with sudden shifts in tonality. His melodies range from declamatory to highly lyrical, and his forms are typical blues and song structures. No master has achieved this union of styles—popular and classical, vernacular and art—more successfully than George Gershwin.

**Major Works:** Orchestral works, including *Rhapsody in Blue* (1924, for piano and jazz orchestra), Concerto in F (1925), and *An American in Paris* (1928, tone poem) • Piano music • More than 30 stage works, including *Strike Up the Band* (1927), *Girl Crazy* (1920), *Of Thee I Sing* (1931), and *Porgy and Bess* (1935) • Songs for films, including *Shall We Dance* (1937) • Other songs.

*In His Own Words*

Jazz has contributed an enduring value to America in the sense that it has expressed ourselves.

—*George Gershwin*

---

the other men cowards and rushes out to sea himself hoping to save the men. In Act 3, the women mourn all those lost in the storm, including Clara and Jake. Crown appears to claim Bess as his own, and Porgy kills him in a fight. Sportin' Life tells Bess that Porgy will never return from jail. Freed just a week later, Porgy comes home to find Bess gone to New York. The tragic story ends with Porgy, asking "Which way New York?"

The opening aria, *Summertime*, is a melancholy song that evokes an African-American spiritual, with its relaxed tempo, swaying intervals, gentle syncopations, blue notes, and expressive microtonal dips in pitch. It unfolds in a straightforward strophic form, set in a poignant minor key that anticipates the tragedy to come (see Listening Guide 53). The song is reprised several times throughout the opera, and notably near the end, when it is sung by Bess before she abandons the baby and heads to New York. *Summertime* is by far the most famous song from *Porgy and Bess*. The secret to its success is its utter simplicity as it sets up the languid world of Catfish Row.

In *Porgy and Bess*, Gershwin realized his dream of uniting jazz and classical music. His success lit a beacon for later composers like Leonard Bernstein, who claimed that, for later generations of composers, "jazz entered their bloodstream, became part of the air they breathed, so that it came out in their music . . . [They] have written music that is American without even trying."

The lullaby *Summertime* is heard in a scene from the 1959 movie version of Gershwin's *Porgy and Bess*, starring Dorothy Dandridge as Clara and Sammy Davis, Jr., as Sportin' Life.

**LISTENING GUIDE 53**

DVD | CD 7 (97–98) | CD 4 (52–53)

# Gershwin: *Summertime*, from *Porgy and Bess*

2:26

| | |
|---|---|
| **DATE:** | 1935 |
| **GENRE:** | Aria from folk opera |

**CHARACTERS:**

| | |
|---|---|
| Porgy, a crippled beggar (bass-baritone) | Jake, a fisherman (baritone) |
| Bess, Crown's girl (soprano) | Sportin' Life, a dope peddler (baritone) |
| Crown, a stevedore (baritone) | Robbins (tenor) |
| Clara, Jake's wife (soprano) | |

**WHAT TO LISTEN FOR:**

| | | | |
|---|---|---|---|
| Melody | Languid melody, plays on interval of 3rd; regular phrasing; high pitch on last chord, then downward slide | Form | Strophic (2 verses), with variations, brief introduction, interlude, and closing |
| Rhythm/ Meter | Rhythmic subtleties and gentle syncopation | Expression | Vocal inflections (dips, slides, blue notes) |
| | | Performing Forces | Soprano and orchestra; backup chorus on our recording |
| Harmony | Minor key, with rich chromaticism | Text | By librettist DuBose Heyward |
| Texture | Homophonic, with instrumental lines alternating with voice | | |

| | | |
|---|---|---|
| 52 | 0:00 | Orchestral introduction. |
| | | Gently syncopated *Summertime* vocal line; opens with interval of a 3rd: |

Sum - mer time____ an' the liv - in' is eas - y,____

| | | |
|---|---|---|
| | 0:21 | Summertime an' the livin' is easy, |
| | | Fish are jumpin', an' the cotton is high. |
| | | Oh, yo' daddy's rich, an yo' mamma's good lookin', |
| | | So hush, little baby, don't you cry. |
| 53 | 1:21 | One of these mornin's you goin' to rise up singin'; |
| | | Then you'll spread yo' wings an' you'll take to the sky |
| | | But till that mornin' there's a' nothin' can harm you |
| | | With Daddy and Mamma standin' by. |

**Now try the Listening Quiz.**

# Leonard Bernstein and the Broadway Musical

*"Any composer's writing is the sum of himself, of all his roots and influences."*

No figure in American music history has done more than composer/conductor Leonard Bernstein to promote classical music to the general public, both through his accessible compositions and his far-reaching educational efforts. Following in the footsteps of George Gershwin, Bernstein saw that freely mixing classical music

### Leontyne Price

*"For a long time the only time I felt beautiful—in the sense of being complete as a woman, as a human being—was when I was singing."*

African-American opera singer Leontyne Price was born in Mississippi in 1927, during the years of racial segregation in the South. She attended The Juilliard School in New York City, and from there her career soared. She earned the role of Bess in a revival of Gershwin's folk opera *Porgy and Bess* (we hear her sing the opening aria *Summertime*) and went on to great triumph with the title role of Verdi's *Aida*. Price sang this, and many other roles, in the leading opera houses of Europe. Although she expanded her repertory to include Monteverdi, Mozart, and Puccini. *Aida* remained a favorite with Price, who wrote a children's version of the story that gave birth to the Broadway musical *Aida* by Elton John and Tim Rice. Leontyne Price's voice has been described as full and dusky, and large enough to fill an opera house. Price was active throughout her career as a concert artist as well, singing German Lieder,

arias, and spirituals. She writes with great dignity about being a black artist, noting proudly that "the color of my skin . . . has nothing to do with what you are listening to." Now retired, Price gave a rare performance at Carnegie Hall in October 2001 in honor of those killed in the September 11 attacks: she closed the show with her very moving rendition of *God Bless America*.

**Check out these recordings by Leontyne Price:** "He's Got the Whole World in His Hands" from *The Essential Leontyne Price* (1997); "I Loves You, Porgy" and "I Got Plenty o' Nuttin'" from *Porgy and Bess: High Performance* (1999; *Summertime*, on our CD set)

---

techniques and jazz styles was a viable means of expression—the result was *West Side Story*, a stage work now revered as a classic.

## Bernstein's *West Side Story*

In *West Side Story*, Bernstein realized a dream: to create a musical based on the Romeo and Juliet story. This updated tale, with a book by playwright Arthur Laurents and lyrics by Stephen Sondheim (his first job as a lyricist), sets the saga amid turf wars of two rival street gangs in New York City. The hostility between the Jets (led by Riff) and their Puerto Rican rivals, the Sharks (led by Bernardo), is a modern-day counterpart of the feud between the Capulets and the Montagues in Shakespeare's *Romeo and Juliet*. In the musical's tragic tale, Tony, a former Jet, and Maria, Bernardo's sister, meet at a dance and immediately fall in love. Riff and Bernardo bring their two gangs together for a fight. When Tony tries to stop them, Riff is stabbed by Bernardo, and Tony in turn kills Bernardo. Tony begs Maria for forgiveness, but the gang warfare mounts to a final rumble in which Tony is killed. This story of star-crossed lovers unfolds in scenes of great tenderness, with memorable songs such as *Maria, Tonight*, and *Somewhere* alternating with electrifying dance sequences choreographed by Jerome Robbins.

Rival gangs (the Sharks and the Jets) dance in a 2007 production of Bernstein's *West Side Story*, performed in Paris.

We will hear first *Mambo*, a part of the dance scene (see illustration, right) where Tony meets Maria (see Listening Guide 54). When the lively Latin beat starts, the Jets and Sharks are on opposite sides of the hall. At the climax of the dance, Tony and Maria catch a glimpse of each other across the room. A *mambo* is an Afro-Cuban dance with a fast and highly syncopated beat; in Bernstein's score, the bongos and cowbells keep the

## Leonard Bernstein (1918–1990)

As a composer, conductor, educator, pianist, and television personality, **Bernstein** enjoyed a spectacular career. He was born in Lawrence, Massachusetts, the son of Russian-Jewish immigrants. He entered Harvard at seventeen, attended the prestigious Curtis Institute in Philadelphia, and then became a disciple of the conductor Serge Koussevitzky. When he was twenty-five, Bernstein was appointed assistant conductor of the New York Philharmonic. A few weeks later, a guest conductor, Bruno Walter, was suddenly taken ill. With only a few hours' notice, Bernstein took over the Sunday afternoon concert, which was broadcast coast to coast, and led a stunning performance. Overnight he became famous. Fifteen years later, he was himself named director of the New York Philharmonic, the first American-born conductor to occupy the post.

As a composer, Bernstein straddled the worlds of serious and popular music. He wrote several symphonies: he explored his Jewish background in his Third Symphony (*Kaddish*, 1963) and also tried his hand at serial composition. But he was rooted in tonality, as he demonstrated in his choral masterwork *Chichester Psalms*.

Bernstein is best known for his stage works. He had a genuine flair for orchestration; his harmonic idiom is spicily dissonant, his jazzy rhythms have great vitality, and his melodies soar.

Bernstein's feeling for the urban scene—specifically that of New York City—is vividly projected in his theater music. In *On the Town, Wonderful Town*, and *West Side Story*, he created a sophisticated kind of musical theater that explodes with movement, energy, and sentiment. His death in October 1990 aroused universal mourning in the music world.

**Major Works:** Orchestral music, including 3 symphonies (*Kaddish*, 1963) • Choral works, including *Chichester Psalms* (1965) • Operas, including *A Quiet Place* (1983) • Musicals, including *On the Town* (1944), *Wonderful Town* (1953), *Candide* (1956), and *West Side Story* (1957) • Other dramatic stage works, including the ballet *Fancy Free* (1944), the film score *On the Waterfront* (1954), and a staged Mass (1971) • Chamber and instrumental music • Solo vocal music.

◎ **iMusic:** *Tonight*, from *West Side Story*

### In His Own Words

Music. . . can name the unnamable and communicate the unknowable.

—*Leonard Bernstein*

frenetic pulse under the shouts of the gang members and the jazzy riffs of the woodwinds and brass. The music dies away as Maria and Tony walk toward each other on the dance floor.

The *Tonight* Ensemble is set later the same day, after a fire-escape version of Shakespeare's famous balcony scene, where Tony and Maria first sing their love duet. As darkness falls, the two gangs anxiously await the expected fight, each vowing to cut the other down to size. Underneath the gang music, an ominous three-note ostinato is heard throughout. Tony's thoughts are only of Maria as he sings the lyrical ballad *Tonight* (an **A-A'-B-A″** form we have seen in jazz works) over an animated Latin rhythmic accompaniment. The gang music returns briefly, after which Maria, and later Tony, repeat their love song, their voices soaring above the complex dialogue in an exciting climax to the first act.

*West Side Story* remains, fifty years after its production, a timeless masterpiece of musical theater; its dramatic content, stirring melodies, colorful orchestration, and vivacious dance scenes continue to delight audiences of today.

### Critical Thinking

1. How did George Gershwin and Leonard Bernstein both straddle the worlds of Classical and popular music?

2. What is the literary basis for *Porgy and Bess*? How does this story differ from other musicals written at the same time?

3. What is the literary basis for *West Side Story*? What does this story share with *Porgy and Bess*?

**LISTENING GUIDE 54**  ⓢ | DVD | **CD 8 (1–9)** | CD 4 (54–62)

# Bernstein: *West Side Story*, excerpts          5:26

**DATE:** 1957

**GENRE:** Musical theater

**CHARACTERS:** Maria, Puerto Rican girl, sister of Bernardo    Riff, leader of the Jets
Tony, former member of the Jets    Bernardo, leader of the Sharks
Anita, Puerto Rican girlfriend of Bernardo

---

### Act I: The Dance at the Gym, *Mambo*          1:48

**WHAT TO LISTEN FOR:**

| | | | |
|---|---|---|---|
| Melody | Disjunct, syncopated riffs (short ideas) | Expression | Frenetic Latin dance with excited voices and handclapping |
| Rhythm/Meter | Fast-paced Afro-Cuban dance; highly rhythmic with much syncopation | Timbre | Brass and Latin rhythm instruments (bongo drums, cowbells) featured |
| Harmony | Sweetly dissonant | Text | Libretto by Stephen Sondheim |
| Texture | Dense and polyphonic | | |

---

**54**  0:00  Percussion introduction, 8 bars, with bongos and cowbells; very fast and syncopated.

0:07  Brass, with accented chords; Sharks shout, "Mambo!"; followed by quieter string line, accompanied by snare drum rolls; accented brass chords return; Sharks shout, "Mambo!" again.

0:28  High dissonant woodwinds in dialogue with rhythmic brass.

0:33  Trumpets play riff over *fff* chords:

Woodwinds and brass alternate in highly polyphonic texture.

1:00  Rocking 2-note woodwind line above syncopated low brass:

**55**  1:13  Solo trumpet enters in high range above complex rhythmic accompaniment:

Complex *fortissimo* polyphony until climax; rhythm slows as music dies away at close.

---

### Act I: *Tonight* Quintet          3:38

**WHAT TO LISTEN FOR:**

| | | | |
|---|---|---|---|
| Melody | Speechlike exchanges; soaring lines in love duet | Texture | Complex and polyphonic; simultaneous lines |
| Rhythm/Meter | Fast, accented, and rhythmic dialogue; ominous 3-note ostinato; duple-meter love song in regular phrases, with gentle, offbeat accompaniment | Form | 32-bar popular song form (8-bar sections, **A-A'-B-A''**) |
| | | Expression | Breathless gang dialogue |
| Harmony | Some unison singing; tonal but modulating | Performing Forces | Men's chorus as gangs; Maria (soprano) and Tony (tenor), with orchestra |
| | | Text | Stephen Sondheim |

*Continued on following page*

Setting: The neighborhood, 6:00–9:00 p.m. Riff and the Jets, Bernardo and
the Sharks, Anita, Maria, and Tony all wait expectantly for the coming of night.

| 56 | 0:00 | Short, rhythmic orchestral introduction featuring brass and percussion; based on 3-note ostinato: |

**TEXT**                                              **DESCRIPTION**

0:07    **RIFF AND THE JETS**                         Gangs sing in alternation:
        The Jets are gonna have their day
        Tonight.

        **BERNARDO AND THE SHARKS**
        The Sharks are gonna have their way
        Tonight.

        **RIFF AND THE JETS**
        The Puerto Ricans grumble: "Fair fight."
        But if they start a rumble,
        We'll rumble 'em right.

0:24    **BERNARDO AND THE SHARKS**
        We're gonna hand 'em a surprise
        Tonight.

        **RIFF AND THE JETS**
        We're gonna cut then down to size
        Tonight.

        **BERNARDO AND THE SHARKS**
        We said, "O.K., no rumpus,
        No tricks."
        But just in case they jump us,
        We're ready to mix.
        Tonight

        **ALL**

| 57 | 0:43 | We're gonna rock it tonight, | Unison chorus, more emphatic and |

        We're gonna jazz it up and have us a ball!      accented; with accented brass
        They're gonna get it tonight;                   interjections.
        The more they turn it on, the harder they'll fall!

                        *Alternating exchanges between gangs*

        **RIFF AND THE JETS**
        Well, they began it!

        **BERNARDO AND THE SHARKS**
        Well, they began it!

        **ALL**
        And we're the ones to stop 'em once and for all,
        Tonight!

        **ANITA**

| 58 | 1:09 | Anita's gonna get her kicks | Opening melody now in uneven triplet rhythm; |

        Tonight.                                        sung sexily:
        We'll have our private little mix
        Tonight.
        He'll walk in hot and tired,
        So what?

Don't matter if he's tired,
As long as he's hot,
Tonight!

|59| 1:26 **TONY**
Tonight, tonight,
Won't be just any night,
Tonight there will be no
morning star.

**A section** (8 bars):

Tonight, tonight,
I'll see my love tonight,
And for us, stars will stop
where they are.

**A′ section** (8 bars); higher range, more emotional.

|60| 1:52 Today the minutes seem like hours,
The hours go so slowly,
And still the sky is light . . .

**B section** (8 bars); strings in canon with voice.

Oh moon, grow bright,
And make this endless day
endless night!

**A″ section** (8 bars); reaches climax, then cuts off.

2:15

Instrumental interlude.

**RIFF (to Tony)**
I'm counting on you to be there
Tonight.
When Diesel wins it fair and square
Tonight.
That Puerto Rican punk'll
Go down
And when he's hollered "Uncle,"
We'll tear up the town!

Return to opening idea, sung more vehemently.

**Ensemble finale:** Maria sings *Tonight* in high range, against simultaneous dialogue and interjections over the same syncopated dance rhythm that accompanied Tony's solo; dramatic climax on last ensemble statement of "Tonight!"

|61| 2:41 **MARIA (warmly)**
[A] Tonight, tonight

**RIFF**
So I can count on you, boy?

**TONY (abstractedly)**
All right.

**RIFF**
We're gonna have us a ball.

Won't be just any night,

**TONY**
All right.

**RIFF**
Womb to tomb!

Tonight there will be no morning star,

*Continued on following page*

TONY
Sperm to worm!

RIFF
I'll see you there about eight.

TONY
Tonight . . .

JETS
We're gonna jazz it tonight!

SHARKS
We're gonna rock it tonight!

[A′] Tonight, tonight,

ANITA
Tonight, tonight,
Late tonight,
We're gonna mix it tonight.

I'll see my love tonight,

SHARKS
They're gonna get it tonight!
They began it,
They began it,

And for us, stars will stop where they are.

62   3:07   TONY AND MARIA
[B] Today the minutes seem like hours,

⌈ ANITA
Anita's gonna have her day,
Anita's gonna have her day,
Bernardo's gonna have his way
Tonight, Tonight,
Tonight, this very night,
We're gonna rock it tonight.

SHARKS
⌊ They began it . . .

The hours go so slowly,

⌈ JETS
Tonight!
They began it,
And we're the ones to stop 'em once
      and for all!
The Jets are gonna have their way,
The Jets are gonna have their day,
We're gonna rock it tonight.
Tonight!

And still the sky is light.

SHARKS
They began it,
We'll stop 'em once and for all.
The Sharks are gonna have their way,
The Sharks are gonna have their day,
We're gonna rock it tonight,

[A″] Oh moon, grow bright,

⌊ Tonight!

And make this endless day endless night, tonight!

◎ **Now try the Listening Quiz.**

# 42 Music for Films

"A film is a composition and the musical composition is an integral part of the design."

—H. G. Wells

## KEY POINTS

StudySpace wwnorton.com/enjoy

- Film music sets the mood and helps establish the characters and a sense of place and time.
- There are two principal types of music in a film— *underscoring* and *source music*.
- The film music of John Williams marks a return to full orchestral resources and the use of *leitmotifs* (recurring themes) associated with characters or situations.

Music has helped to create some of the most memorable moments in film history. The opening of *2001: A Space Odyssey*, the Paris montage from *Casablanca*, and the shower scene in *Psycho* are all accompanied by music that has become an integral part of American culture.

The most important function of music in film is to set a mood. Choices of musical style, instrumentation, and emotional quality are critical in creating the director's vision. Even the absence of music in a scene or an entire movie (Hitchcock's *Lifeboat*, 1944) can contribute to the overall tone of a film.

**Setting the mood**

Most Hollywood films use music to reflect the emotions of a given scene. John Williams, for example, guides the viewer's emotions at the end of *E.T.: The Extra-Terrestrial* (1982) from sorrow at the apparent death of E.T. through joy at his recovery, excitement at the chase scene, to sadness at his final farewell. Howard Shore's scores to *The Lord of the Rings* trilogy play a major role in creating the dark, brooding mood surrounding Frodo's quest, but it also brings out the contrasting moments of humor and tenderness. But music does not necessarily need to mirror every emotion or action on the screen. In some films, the composer will establish a single dominant mood for the entire narrative, which is sustained no matter what happens on screen.

Elijah Wood as the heroic hobbit Frodo Baggins in *The Lord of the Rings* trilogy (2001–03).

Composers can sometimes create irony by supplying music that contradicts what is being shown on the screen. This technique is called *running counter to the action*. Perhaps the best-known musical/visual contradiction is the chilling climactic scene of *The Godfather* (1972). While the audience hears Bach organ music during a baptism, it sees the brutal and systematic murders of Michael Corleone's enemies. A number of action films since the 1990s, including Quentin Tarantino's *Pulp Fiction* (1994) and *Kill Bill, Vol. 1* and *Vol. 2* (2003–2004), contain scenes of graphic violence accompanied by lighthearted rock music.

The high-society deck on the Titanic from the 1997 movie epic; here, the privileged Rose (Kate Winslet) is courted by a lower class American (Jack, played by Leonardo DiCaprio).

This jarring contrast produces a sense of black comedy and raises questions about the superficial treatment of violence in today's media.

In addition to setting moods, music can play an important role in establishing character. The appearance of a dashing romantic hero might be accompanied by a passionate melody; and a worldly woman might be shown with a sultry saxophone melody. In *Titanic* (1997), music helps delineate the social levels of the principal characters (see illustration). A string quartet plays elegant chamber music to the upper-deck aristocrats while Irish dance music energizes the lower levels occupied by the common people.

Music can also help create a sense of place and time. The bagpipes in *Braveheart* (1995) and the guitar in *Brokeback Mountain* (2005) help transport the viewer to different locales. The musical instruments do not have to be authentic but merely suggest a time period. Indeed, in the movie *Avatar* (2009) a small choir sings in the Na'vi language—a language developed exclusively for the movie—that compliments the film's setting in a future utopia.

**Underscoring**

**Source music**

There are two principal types of music in a film. **Underscoring**, which is what most people think of as film music, occurs when music comes from an unseen source, often an invisible orchestra. But music can also function as part of the drama itself; this is referred to as *source music*. For example, someone may turn on a radio, or a character may be inspired to sing. Source music can be a fascinating part of the drama. In *Rear Window* (1954), Hitchcock employs only source music, which emanates from the various apartments on the block. Source music can also tell us a great deal about a character. In *Boyz 'N the Hood* (1991), source music of classical jazz, Motown, and rap helps define the principal figures of the story.

In an attempt to create musical unity within an ongoing dramatic flow, many film composers use the techniques of leitmotifs (see p. 260) and thematic transformation (see p. 232). In *Jaws* (1975), John Williams creates a two-note oscillating leitmotif that warns the audience of the shark's presence. Perhaps inspired by Wagner's *Ring Cycle*, Williams also introduces a multitude of leitmotifs for the *Star Wars* trilogy (see illustration, opposite). Each motif—the opening fanfare (which becomes the theme for Luke Skywalker), Yoda's gentle melody, and Darth Vader's intense march—supports the general nature of the character. Yet these musical motives can also be transformed to reflect totally different events. The theme for Luke Skywalker can sound sad or distorted when he is in trouble, triumphant when he is victorious. One of the finest musical moments of the trilogy occurs in *The Return of the Jedi* (1983). At the death of Darth Vader, his once terrifying theme is transformed into a gentle tune played by the woodwinds and harp (symbolizing the character's death).

# *Star Wars* and Beyond

It is difficult to underestimate the importance of American composer John Williams to film music. *Star Wars* (1977) revolutionized the movie industry with spectacular visual effects and a brilliant, colorful score. John Williams is often credited with the revival of the grand symphonic film score, writing unforgettable themes set in an accessible, neo-Romantic idiom. His first big hits—*Jaws* and then *Star Wars*—led to a string of major successes, including the venerated *Indiana Jones* films, from which we will hear the widely known *Raider's March*.

## John Williams's *Raiders March*

Most people recall the music for the box-office hit *Raiders of the Lost Ark* (1981), if not the film itself, in which the adventuring hero Indiana Jones is introduced. As in many of his films, Williams uses leitmotifs (see p. 260) throughout the film as a means to define the characters—notably here, for archaeologist Professor Jones and for his love interest, Marion Ravenwood. *The Raider's March*, first heard in its entirety during the closing credits of the film, presents the hero's music first, recalling Aaron Copland's style with its disjunct theme and stuttering accompaniment. Featuring brass and percussion, it projects our courageous and confident protagonist well. This strong idea is contrasted in the

Yoda advises the hero Luke Skywalker (Mark Hamill) in the *Star Wars* sequel, *The Empire Strikes Back* (1980), with a score by John Williams.

### John Williams (b. 1932)

A native of Long Island, **John Williams** moved to Los Angeles as a youth, where he studied at UCLA. He then attended New York's Juilliard School of Music, after which he worked as a jazz pianist. He began composing for television in the 1950s, writing for shows such as *Gilligan's Island*. Shifting to the big screen in the 1960s, he wrote a series of disaster film scores for movies like *Jaws*. By the end of the 1970s, he had established himself as Hollywood's foremost composer and had three blockbusters to his name: *Star Wars*, *Close Encounters of the Third Kind*, and *Superman*. During the 1980s, Williams scored many box-office hits including the two *Star Wars* sequels, the *Indiana Jones* trilogy, and *E.T.*, and in the 1990s, he wrote winning movie scores for *Home Alone*, *Jurassic Park*, and *Schindler's List*, among many others. You will remember his engaging scores to the first three *Harry Potter* films and the sequel *Indiana Jones and the Kingdom of the Crystal Skull*, which brings back many of the familiar themes of the trilogy.

In addition to this amazing lineup of film scores, John Williams has also written classical works, including fanfares for the Olympics and inauguration music for President Barack Obama (*Air and Simple Gifts*). He has maintained an active conducting career as well, serving as the director of the Boston Pops Orchestra from 1980 to 1993, and won more awards than we could possibly list, holding the record for the most Oscar nominations.

His film music explores the Wagnerian ideas of extended chromatic harmony and the use of leitmotifs—themes that represents a person, object, or idea—throughout a work. His writing is highly lyrical, providing us with eminently memorable themes that capture our imagination.

**Major Works:** Orchestral works, including *Winter Games Fanfare* (1989), *Summon the Heroes* (1996), and concertos for various solo instruments • Chamber music, including *Air and Simple Gifts* (2010) • More than 90 film scores, including *Jaws* (1975, and sequels), *Close Encounters of the Third Kind* (1977), *Star Wars* (1977, trilogy, and further sequels), *Superman* (1978, and sequels), *Raiders of the Lost Ark* (1981, and sequels), *E.T.: The Extra-Terrestrial* (1982), *Jurassic Park* (1993, and sequels), *Schindler's List* (1993), *Harry Potter and the Sorcerer's Stone* (2001, and sequels), *The Adventures of Tintin: Secret of the Unicorn* (2011) • Television series and themes, including *Gilligan's Island* (1957–60).

*In His Own Words*

So much of what we do is ephemeral and quickly forgotten . . . so it's gratifying to have something you have done linger in people's memories.

# John Williams: *Raiders March*, from *Raiders of the Lost Ark*

5:11

**DATE:** 1981

**GENRE:** Film score (orchestrated by Herbert Spencer)

## WHAT TO LISTEN FOR:

| | |
|---|---|
| **Melody** | Opening disjunct march theme; lyrical trio theme; both linked to movie |
| **Rhythm/ Meter** | Regular quadruple meter, with syncopations and triplets for variety |
| **Harmony** | Occasional dissonant harmonies |

| | |
|---|---|
| **Form** | Overall **A-B-A'** form (March-Trio-March), with sectional divisions and repeats |
| **Expression** | Contrasting moods set by vigorous march and romantic love theme |
| **Timbre** | Brass and percussion featured, typical of a march |

### March: A Section (a-b-a')

| | | |
|---|---|---|
| **63** | 0:00 | Introduction; stuttering rhythmic ostinato setup. |
| | 0:07 | **a section**—Disjunct march theme, with insistent dotted rhythm; played by trumpet. |
| | 0:21 | March tune repeated, with fuller accompaniment; offbeats on cymbals. |
| **64** | 0:36 | **b section**—strings present a contrasting idea with triplet figure. Closes with abrupt, disjunct rhythmic figure. |
| | 0:52 | **b section**—contrasting idea repeated in brass with extended cadential section. |
| **65** | 1:17 | **a' section**—opening march returns with a more vigorous accompaniment. |
| | 1:36 | Modulates up a half step; imitative answer in trombones. |
| | 1:52 | Cadential figure (from **b**) brings the March section to a close. |

### Trio: B Section (c-d-c')

| | | |
|---|---|---|
| **66** | 2:08 | **c section**—lyrical melody in low strings, ascending leap, then broad, flowing line. Trio theme repeated and developed. |
| **67** | 2:41 | **d section**—violins and cellos in dialogue with phrases of **c section**. |
| **68** | 3:08 | **c' section**—soaring violins play trio theme; slows to cadence. |

### March Reprise: A Section (b-a')

| | | |
|---|---|---|
| **69** | 3:32 | **b section**—accompaniment of opening returns; theme played by French horn, with extended cadence in brass. |
| **70** | 4:12 | **a″ section**—accompaniment pattern intensifies with louder dynamics and fuller orchestration; march theme stated, then repeated with answering phrases in the trombones. |
| | 4:47 | **Coda**—reiterates rhythmic ideas from march tune, leading to a loud and dissonant closing. |

ⓢ **Now try the Listening Quiz.**

march with Marion's love theme, in a lush setting that evokes their once-tender, now stormy, relationship.

The contrasting moods of the two melodies help delineate the **A-B-A'** march structure (see Listening Guide 55). In the **A** section, the Indiana Jones theme is divided into several component parts. The principal melody is heard four times, growing in intensity with each repetition. Marion's theme, heard primarily in the strings, projects a passionate songlike character and functions as the march's trio section. Typical of many **A-B-A** structures, the reprise of the **A** section is somewhat abbreviated. The playful quality of the march is emphasized by strong closing dissonances. This thoroughly delightful adventure film, in which our hero pursues, and finds, the legendary Ark of the Covenant, comes to life through the highly imaginative musical score by John Williams.

The adventurer Indiana Jones (Harrison Ford) attempts to recover a sacred idol in the jungles of South America, in *Raiders of the Lost Ark* (1981). The music of John Williams accompanies all the movies in the series.

The history of film music is now over a century old. During this time, the medium has attracted many of the world's best-known composers, including Aaron Copland, George Gershwin, Leonard Bernstein, Silvestre Revueltas, Sergei Prokofiev, Tan Dun, and Philip Glass. The Hollywood industry also supported a number of specialists, such as Max Steiner, Miklós Rózsa, Elmer Bernstein, and John Williams, who composed film music almost exclusively. While each composer brought an individual approach to his art, three general tendencies can be observed: the incorporation of the principles established by Wagner's music dramas, the assimilation of the ever-changing trends in popular music, and the constant search for fresh, new sounds. After one hundred years, film music remains a strong, vibrant medium and an integral part of the art of filmmaking.

### Critical Thinking

**1.** How does the music for film contribute to the drama of the story?

**2.** How does John Williams unify his films through the music?

# 43 The Many Voices of Rock

"You know my temperature's risin',
The juke box's blowin' a fuse,
My heart's beatin' rhythm,
My soul keeps singin' the blues—
Roll over, Beethoven,
Tell Tchaikovsky the news."

**—Chuck Berry**

## KEY POINTS

StudySpace wwnorton.com/enjoy

- The rise of **rock and roll** in the 1950s is one of the most significant phenomena in twentieth-century music history.

- Rock had its origins in **rhythm and blues**, country-western, pop and gospel; early rock crossed racial lines, featuring white and black performers.

- The Beatles, first heard live in the United States in 1964, were highly influential because of their expressive experiments in various musical styles (including non-Western ones).

- California groups contributed to the expressiveness of rock, particularly to the emergence of **folk rock**.

- The 1960s and 1970s saw the rise of many eclectic musical styles, including **acid rock, art rock, Latin rock, heavy metal, punk rock, disco, reggae,** and **new wave**.

- Music videos and MTV were important media for the dissemination of rock in the 1980s; other developments led to the emergence of rap.

- **Rap**, an element of **hip hop** culture, is one of the most popular forms of African-American music; like earlier rock styles, it has crossed racial lines and been adopted by performers of all ethnic backgrounds.

- In the 1990s and beyond, **grunge rock, alternative rock,** and **global pop** have captured the listening audience, along with numerous revivals by well-known artists and groups.

The rise of rock and roll and its offspring rock is the most important music phenomenon of the past sixty years. Economically, rock music has become a multibillion-dollar industry; socially, it has had a far-reaching impact on fashion, language, politics, and religion; musically, it has dominated the popular scene for some fifty years and influenced virtually every other style of music—classical, jazz, country-western, and contemporary global pop.

*Rock and roll*, which first emerged in the 1950s, was born of a union of African-American rhythm and blues with country-western. *Rhythm and blues*, a genre of dance music with roots in swing jazz, was popular from the late 1940s through the early 1960s. It is a predominantly vocal genre, featuring a solo singer accompanied by a small group often including piano, guitar (acoustic or electric), acoustic bass, drums, and tenor saxophone. Its harmonies and structure are clearly drawn from twelve-bar blues and thirty-two-bar pop song form (we heard these in Chapter 40). As the name implies, the style is characterized by a strong, driving

**Rhythm and blues**

rhythm, usually in a quadruple meter, with an emphasis on the second and fourth beats of the measure, known as **backbeat**. Of the great early rhythm and blues performers, almost all were African Americans—for example, Louis Jordan, Ruth Brown, Bo Diddley, and "Big" Joe Turner.

In the mid-1950s, the term "rock and roll" was coined to describe a form of rhythm and blues that crossed racial lines. White singers like Bill Haley, Elvis Presley, and Jerry Lee Lewis combined "hillbilly" country music with the sounds of rhythm and blues. This style became known as **rockabilly**, which featured twelve-bar blues progressions and boogie rhythms (in triplet patterns). At the same time, African Americans like Chuck Berry, Fats Domino, and Little Richard caught the attention of a white audience. The style of Little Richard clearly derived from gospel music, while Chuck Berry and Elvis Presley borrowed songs from the country-western repertory and played them with a rhythm-and-blues intensity. The new sounds of rock and roll, and the outrageous look and behavior that accompanied them, revolutionized the music industry's concept of markets, appealing to young audiences amid a flurry of anti–rock-and-roll propaganda.

Meanwhile, black America was listening to the sound of **soul**, a blend of gospel, pop, and rhythm and blues. Ray Charles is often considered to be the "father" of soul. Many of the top soul artists—James Brown and Aretha Franklin—came from the American South. **Motown** (from Motortown, or Detroit), one of the first and most successful black-owned record labels, represented the soul sound of the industrial North. The label's many hit acts took black and white listeners by storm and included Diana Ross and the Supremes, and Smokey Robinson and the Miracles.

In the mid-1960s, rock and roll was revitalized with the emergence of new groups, notably the Beach Boys in the United States, the Beatles, and the Rolling Stones in Britain. It was the Beatles, inspired by Motown and rock and roll, who provided direction amid a variety of styles. In 1964, this group from Liverpool, England, took America by storm, performing on television's highly popular *Ed Sullivan Show*. That year the Beatles also starred in a hit movie (*A Hard Day's Night*) and held the top five spots on the *Billboard* chart. This foursome—Paul McCartney on electric bass, George Harrison on lead guitar, John Lennon on rhythm guitar and harmonica, and Ringo Starr on drums—had a tight ensemble sound, featuring a strong backbeat and jangling guitars. John, Paul, and George had a distinctive vocal sound as well, singing unison and two- and three-part vocals in a high range, occasionally falsetto.

The Beatles' success was largely due to their creative experiments with other types of music. With Paul McCartney's lyrical ballads *Yesterday* (1965) and *Eleanor Rigby* (1966), the Beatles combined pop songwriting with a string quartet; and their albums *Rubber Soul* (1965) and *Revolver* (1966) introduced a new style, with poetic lyrics, complex harmonies, and sophisticated recording techniques. George Harrison took up the Indian sitar

Two rock-and-roll icons: Chuck Berry (top) and Elvis Presley (bottom).

Motown artist Diana Ross and the Supremes.

The Beatles (Paul, George, Ringo, John) on stage at the *Ed Sullivan Show* in February 1964.

for the 1965 song *Norwegian Wood*, helping to spark a surge of interest in non-Western music in the pop marketplace. With these new sounds, the old rock and roll was gone, and the more complex style known as **rock** emerged.

In 1966, the Beatles retired from live performance and dedicated themselves to mastering the recording studio. The albums *Sgt. Pepper's Lonely Hearts Club Band* (1967) and *Abbey Road* (1969) were both stunning musical achievements that showcased their various songwriting abilities and confirmed that the **concept album**—an album that was unified thematically—was here to stay. Notable among the selections on these albums are John Lennon's *A Day in the Life*, Paul McCartney's *When I'm Sixty-Four*, and George Harrison's *Here Comes the Sun*. In 1970, the group broke up, its members going on to establish successful solo careers. John Lennon was shot and killed in 1980, and George Harrison died of cancer in 2001, cutting short their creative lives.

The success of the Beatles in America had sparked a British invasion of rock groups—Herman's Hermits and especially the Rolling Stones (*Satisfaction*). Drawing from the American blues style of Muddy Waters, the Stones became the "bad boys" of rock: their lyrics, most by Mick Jagger, and their public behavior condoned sexual freedom, drugs, and violence. Sexual innuendo (*Let's Spend the Night Together*) and tales of violence (*Gimme Shelter*) are subjects typical of their songs.

## Meet the Performers

### Mick Jagger

"I believe there can be no evolution without revolution. Why should we try to fit in?"

Singer/songwriter Mick Jagger (b. 1943) is best known for his role as lead vocalist of the British rock band the Rolling Stones, which he founded in 1962 with Keith Richards. Although the band started by performing covers, Jagger and Richards soon formed a songwriting team that would make history. Their best-known collaboration was *(I Can't Get No) Satisfaction* (also 1965), which contributed much to the band's shocking "bad boy" image. Jagger was not immune to the band members' problems with drugs nor from the perception that he led a shocking lifestyle. Jagger's several high-profile marriages—first to Bianca Jagger, then to American model/actress Jerry Hall—contributed to his rebellious image. Jagger began a solo career in 1985, although with mixed success, but his third solo album, *Wandering Spirit* (1993), is considered a personal highpoint. In 2003, Jagger was knighted by the Prince of Wales for his "service to music." In recent years, Sir Mick Jagger has taken on new roles, as an actor, composer of sound tracks, and, as head of his own film production company. The generations of musicians who came after Jagger could not help but be influenced by his distinctive vocal style and stage persona.

**Check out these recordings by Mick Jagger:** *(I Can't Get No) Satisfaction*, from album *Out of Our Heads* (1965); *Get Off of My Cloud* (1965); *19th Nervous Breakdown* (1966); *Sweet Thing*, from album *Wandering Spirit* (1993); *Visions of Paradise*, from album *Goddess in the Doorway* (2001).

## Meet the Performers

### Bob Dylan

"They're just songs . . . songs that are transparent so you can see every bit through them."

American songwriter/singer Bob Dylan (b. 1941) has been on the music scene since the early 1960s. He dropped out of college after his freshman year and moved to New York, where he played in Greenwich Village and met his idol, folk singer Woody Guthrie. Dylan soon began making a name for himself as a songwriter and singer of protest songs. His first notable song was *Blowin' in the Wind*, which hit the charts in a cover by Peter, Paul, and Mary. Dylan's personal style—a raspy voice accompanied by acoustic guitar—changed in 1965 when he went electric. The next decade marked an era of experimentation and alienation from the mainstream, in which he, a second-generation Russian-Jew, became a born-again Christian. Since then, Dylan has edged his way back into the main current with his hectic international touring schedule and new protest songs: he won a Grammy Lifetime Achievement Award in 1991 concurrent with his release of *Masters of War*, about the beginnings of war with the Middle East. In recent years, Bob Dylan has enjoyed a renewed popularity; his 2006 album *Modern Times* was nominated for three Grammys, and his 2009 album *Together through Life* won wide acclaim as well. Dylan is a force to be reckoned with, viewed by many as one of the most important cultural and musical figures of the twentieth century.

**Check out these recordings by Bob Dylan:** *Mr. Tambourine Man*, from *Bringing It All Back Home* (1965) and CD set; *Blowin' in the Wind* and *Masters of War*, from *The Freewheelin' Bob Dylan* (1963/2004); *Beyond Here Lies Nothin'*, from *Together through Life* (2009).

Despite the negative image they acquired, the Rolling Stones opened the path for styles that would emerge in the 1970s and 1980s, such as punk rock and heavy metal. *19th Nervous Breakdown* (1965; see Listening Activity, p. 383), like many of their early selections, looks back to rhythm-and-blues style, notably to the guitar style of R & B legend Bo Diddley.

America's answer to this British invasion was to be found in a new generation of California bands. The Beach Boys (*Good Vibrations*, 1966), led by Brian Wilson, introduced new harmonic and melodic possibilities to rock songwriting and significantly raised the standard for studio production. Another important California group was the Byrds, whose music combined the folk style of protest singers Bob Dylan and Joan Baez with the new sounds of rock, thereby creating *folk rock*. Their first release was their biggest hit: *Mr. Tambourine Man* (1965), a rock setting of words and music by Bob Dylan. We will hear Dylan's own version of *Mr. Tambourine Man* (see Listening Activity, p. 376) and will see later how this poem inspired contemporary composer John Corigliano, who set it and other Dylan texts in an evocative song cycle (see p. 416).

**The Beach Boys**

**Folk rock**

Bob Dylan introduced his own electric rock group at the 1965 Newport (Rhode Island) Folk Festival to the boos and catcalls of folk music purists. The fusion of folk protest songs with rock music proved to be a potent element in a growing political movement concerned with free speech, civil rights, and America's involvement in the Vietnam War (1961–75).

American rock maintained its rebellious image with *acid rock* (or *psychedelic rock*)—a style focusing on drugs, instrumental improvisations, and new sound technologies. The music represented a countercultural movement, with Utopian ideals, based in the San Francisco Haight-Ashbury district. The Jefferson Airplane featuring female lead singer Grace Slick, made no pretense about their politically and socially radical lyrics, and the Grateful Dead, with lead guitarist Jerry Garcia,

**Acid rock**

## LISTENING ACTIVITY: THE INFLUENCE OF BOB DYLAN

Let's consider one of the most famous folk songs of modern times, Bob Dylan's *Mr. Tambourine Man,* which he recorded in 1965 after hearing the electrified version by The Byrds. You will need to locate a recording of the song (performed by Bob Dylan) on your own. Listen to it, first noting the regular verse/chorus structure of *Mr. Tambourine Man*

Guitar introduction
**Chorus** ("Hey, Mr. Tambourine Man")
**Verse 1** ("Though I know the evenin's empire")
**Chorus**
**Verse 2** ("Take me on a trip")
**Chorus**
**Verse 3** ("Though you might hear laughin'")
**Chorus**
Instrumental verse/chorus
**Verse 4** ("Then take me disappearin'")
**Chorus**

Answer the following questions about the song's style:

_____ **1.** Which best describes the melodic phrases?
    **a.** the chorus has irregular phrasing    **b.** the verses have irregular phrasing

_____ **2.** Which meter do you hear in this song?
    **a.** duple    **b.** triple

_____ **3.** Which best describes the main instrument heard?
    **a.** acoustic guitar    **b.** electric guitar

_____ **4.** Which instrument is featured in the instrumental verse (played by Dylan himself)?
    **a.** accordion    **b.** harmonica

_____ **5.** Which best describes Dylan's vocal quality in this song?
    **a.** velvety    **b.** raspy

Now let's compare Dylan's song to two others: the famous recording by The Byrds (you will need to find this one on your own as well) and a setting by composer John Corigliano, who wrote a song cycle on texts by Dylan (this is a Playlist selection). Note that you may give as many answers as are appropriate for each question below.

**a.** Bob Dylan: *Mr. Tambourine Man*
**b.** The Byrds: *Mr. Tambourine Man*
**c.** John Corigliano: *Prelude: Mr. Tambourine Man*

_____ **6.** Which setting(s) makes many tempo and mood changes?

_____ **7.** Which setting(s) features tambourine in the performance?

_____ **8.** Which setting(s) remains in the same meter throughout?

_____ **9.** Which setting(s) presents Dylan's four text verses?

_____ **10.** Which setting(s) features electric guitar?

_____ **11.** Which setting(s) features voices in harmony?

_____ **12.** In which setting(s) does the voice begin with the chorus?

_____ **13.** True/False: Corigliano's song is based on the music of Dylan's.

performed lengthy improvisational "jams" enhanced by elaborate lighting and sound effects.

The culminating event for rock music of the 1960s was the Woodstock Festival, held in upstate New York in August 1969, as a celebration of "peace, love, and brotherhood." The festival featured memorable performances by already iconic musicians and introduced many new faces and sounds to the music world (see Btw, p. 378).

The Grateful Dead, with guitarist and pop culture idol Jerry Garcia, at RFK Stadium, in Washington, DC, in a 1993 concert.

In 1970–71, the music world was shaken by the alcohol- and drug-related deaths of three superstars: the brilliantly innovative guitarist Jimi Hendrix, the soulful Janis Joplin, and the brooding lead singer of the Doors, Jim Morrison. Each was only twenty-seven years old. Acid rock seemed destined to become a short-lived style, but the Grateful Dead remained one of the world's top-grossing concert acts until the death of Garcia in 1995. The British group Pink Floyd has also exhibited great longevity: their 1973 album *Dark Side of the Moon*, with its ageless themes of madness and death, remained on the Top-200 charts for a record 751 weeks. Their operatic, two-album concept-piece, *The Wall* (1980), ensured them a place in the annals of rock. Both Pink Floyd and the Grateful Dead helped to spawn a new generation of improvisational *jam bands* and psychedelic *trance music* in the 1990s.

Many bands are not easily categorized, such as the Velvet Underground, whose music challenged the establishment with their nihilistic attitude and their free experimentation. Their first album, *The Velvet Underground and Nico* (1967), with explicit songs about drugs and sex, remains one of the greatest of all time (it is also famous for its Andy Warhol "banana" cover). This antiestablishment group is viewed as an early forerunner to both punk and alternative rock (see pp. 378 and 380).

Jam bands and trance music

# The Eclecticism of the 1970s

Eclectic styles of rock were developing in the early 1970s that furthered the artistic ambitions found in acid rock. *Art rock* (sometimes called *progressive rock*), which used large forms, complex harmonies, and occasional quotations from classical music, was largely a British style, pioneered by the Moody Blues with their 1968 album *Days of Future Passed*, recorded with the London Symphony Orchestra. The Who experimented with rock's narrative possibilities, and the result was the first rock opera, *Tommy*, written by Peter Townshend and premiered in 1969. One American who experimented with many genres, including art rock's large forms, was Frank Zappa (1940–1993). Zappa, who counted the composers Bartók and Varèse among his influences.

Jazz was also an important influence on rock in the '70s. The Californian group Santana started out as an electric blues-rock band to which Carlos Santana, the son of a Mexican mariachi musician, fused Latin jazz. The resulting style, called *Latin rock*, electrified the audience at Woodstock. Santana's unique sound came from their use of Latin and African percussion instruments—conga drums (of Afro-Cuban origin, played with bare hands), maracas (Latin-American rattles), and timbales (small kettledrums of Cuban origin)—their tight, Latin-style polyrhythms, and Carlos Santana's distinctive, and much-imitated, guitar tone.

### Why Is Woodstock So Important?

No rock festival has been so defining a cultural moment as the event of August 1969, where some 500,000 people found their way to a dairy farm in upstate New York for three days of peace, love, drugs, and music. Despite pouring rain, technical problems, and poor scheduling, Woodstock is notable for the peaceful nature of the gathering and for some important musical moments: The Who performed their new rock opera *Tommy* (just after Pete Townshend hit Abbie Hoffman over the head with his guitar); Mexican rock guitarist Santana rose to fame after his group performed, including an eleven-minute instrumental work (*Soul Sacrifice*); and Jimi Hendrix upstaged most groups with his over-the-top anti-war rendition of *The Star-Spangled Banner*, complete with explosions, gunfire, and a quotation of *Taps*, in memory of those killed in the Vietnam war. Woodstock was a turning point in the careers of Richie Havens (with a memorable improvisation on *Motherless Child*) and Crosby, Stills, and Nash, whose recording of Joni Mitchell's *Woodstock* song helped immortalize the festival. The media has kept Woodstock a part of musical and cultural history; in addition to the 1970 documentary film and soundtrack release, you may recall the recent Ang Lee film *Taking Woodstock* (2009).

The legendary guitarist/singer Jimi Hendrix at the Woodstock Festival (1969), flashing a peace sign to the audience.

The 1970s and 1980s saw the fragmentation of rock into many musical subgenres, and a continual procession of new groups. West Coast rock had a relaxed sound that evoked California, represented by groups like the Eagles and the Doobie Brothers. The British invaded once again, this time with **heavy metal**, featuring exaggerated displays of virtuosity in the form of loud, distorted instrumental solos, coupled with complex harmonies and melodies. Heavy metal, like art rock, was influenced by Western classical composers such as Mahler and Wagner but differed in its use of gothic, pagan, and satanic imagery. Led Zeppelin and Black Sabbath were among the most influential heavy metal bands of the 1970s. **Glam rock** (also known as **glitter rock**) was a showy, theatrical style of performance, represented by Britain's outrageous David Bowie and the American band KISS, known for their trademark face paint. The outlandish costumes of glitter rock were quickly adopted by mainstream artists like the talented pianist Elton John (*Bennie and the Jets*, 1973).

The ultimate rebellion came in the form of **punk rock**, a return to the basics of rock and roll—simple, repetitive, and loud—coupled with provoking lyrics and shocking behavior. The Ramones, a group from New York with a street-tough attitude and an arsenal of two-minute songs that were fast yet melodic, were the first punk group to make an impact. After touring England in 1976, they inspired many imitators, including the politically radical Sex Pistols, featuring lead singer Johnny Rotten.

Other reactions to the difficult times of the 1970s included the commercial dance music known as **disco** as well as **reggae**. Fostered in gay dance clubs, disco was characterized by repetitive lyrics, often sung in a high range, and a thumping, mechanical beat, exemplified by acts such as the Bee Gees. In disco, the producer reached an equal level with the artist in making the music. Reggae is a Jamaican style with offbeat rhythms and chanted

Heavy metal artist Ozzy Osbourne with Black Sabbath, in 1978.

vocals that reflected the beliefs of a religious movement known as Rastafarianism. By far, the most famous reggae group was Bob Marley and the Wailers.

**New wave**, a commercially accessible offshoot of punk rock with electronic enhancements (especially the synthesizer), has been popular among British and American groups since the late 1970s. In Britain, the new wave scene was home to Elvis Costello and the Police, with lead singer/bassist Sting. Arguably, America's most influential new wave group was the Talking Heads, whose lyrics (by singer-songwriter David Byrne) expressed the alienation and social consciousness of punk rock; their style embraced various world musics as well.

# The 1980s and Beyond

"Music allowed me to eat. But it also allowed me to express myself.
I played because I had to play. I rid myself of bad dreams and rotten memories."

— *Prince*

The single most important development in the 1980s was the music video. Now, instead of the radio, the visual medium (and especially MTV, or Music Television, which premiered in August 1981) was the principal means of presenting the latest music to the public. One giant in the video arena was Michael Jackson (1958–2009), who had gained early fame as lead singer of the Jackson Five and who then became a superstar in the 1980s. Jackson's album *Thriller* (1982–83), broke all previous sales figures; its hit songs included *The Girl Is Mine* (sung with Paul McCartney) and *Beat It* (Jackson's version of the rumble scene from Bernstein's *West Side Story*). Jackson's trend-setting dance style, together with his talent as a ballad singer, helped to make him a worldwide celebrity. Other superstars of the 1980s include Bruce Springsteen (*Born in the USA*, 1984), Prince (*Purple Rain*, 1984), and Madonna, who launched her first big hit with *Like a Virgin* (1984). She has achieved great success based not only on her carefully developed image as a sex object, but also her versatile sound and her ability to anticipate and set trends.

The 1980s saw many stars contributing their energies to social causes. The Irish group U2 sounded a unified voice of political activism and personal spirituality in their collection *The Unforgettable Fire* (1984). Following a series of concerts for Live Aid and Amnesty International, the group achieved stardom with the 1987 Grammy-winning album *The Joshua Tree*. U2 continues to represent the social conscience of rock, with lead singer Bono actively working with international politicians on global causes such as debt relief and AIDS.

The technological developments of the late 1970s and early 1980s paved the way for **rap**. This highly rhythmic style of musical patter emerged in New York during the 1970s as part of a cultural movement known as **hip hop**. The typical rap group consists of a DJ (disc jockey), who uses turntables to mix prerecorded sounds and beats, and MCs (master of ceremonies), who rhythmically rhyme over the DJ's musical backdrop. The group Run DMC (*Raising Hell*, 1986) was largely responsible for the commercialization of rap; their collaboration with Aerosmith, covering the 1974 hit song *Walk This Way*, introduced the style to mainstream white audiences. Public Enemy, a politically oriented group from Long Island, New York, produced several highly influential rap albums, and female rapper Queen Latifah made a strong case against the genre's frequent female bashing in *All Hail the Queen* (1989).

Rap in its diversified forms has continued as one of the most popular types of

*In His Own Words*

When I'm onstage, I feel this incredible, almost spiritual experience . . . lost in a naturally induced high. Those great rock-'n'-roll experiences are getting harder and harder to come by, because they have to transcend a lot of drug-induced stupor. But when they occur, they are sacred.

—*Peter Townshend*

Music video

Michael Jackson

Michael Jackson announces his concert series *This Is It* just before his untimely death in June 2009.

U2 in a 2009 performance at Giants Stadium, in East Rutherford, New Jersey.

African-American music and has been successfully adapted by white performers such as the Beastie Boys and Eminem. **Gangsta rap** of the 1990s has further disseminated the style through graphic descriptions of inner-city realities. This style was pioneered by the Compton, California, group N.W.A. (Niggaz with Attitude), whose album *Efil4zaggin* ("Niggaz 4 Life" spelled backward) hit the top of the charts in 1991. Former N.W.A. member Ice Cube and fellow West Coast rappers Snoop Doggy Dogg and Ice-T have all made a successful transition from gangsta rap to film and television acting.

Hip-hop culture has become the "alternative" lifestyle of choice for many young people, urban and suburban. The riveting rhythms of hip hop have transcended racial boundaries. Today, minority groups from around the world have chosen this form of expression to air their grievances and concerns.

The more mellow sounds of soul and rhythm and blues have changed with the times but are still extremely popular. The 1990s saw the rise of "divas," like Whitney Houston and Mariah Carey, both of whom utilize a heavily melismatic singing style, which has come to represent the new R & B (rhythm and blues) sound. Today, collaboration and "crossover" between the stars of hip hop and R & B has become one of the most marketable pop styles.

**Grunge rock**

The late 1980s and early 1990s also witnessed the success of a Seattle-based hybrid of punk and 1970s metal known as **grunge rock**. Popular groups to come out of the grunge scene were Soundgarden, Nirvana, and Pearl Jam. Pearl Jam's *Ten* and Nirvana's *Nevermind* (both from 1991) were huge hits, tapping into a young audience looking for passion and authenticity in a world of slick, theatrical acts. We will hear Nirvana's first and biggest single hit, *Smells Like Teen Spirit* (see Listening Activity, p. 383). Singer/guitarist Kurt Cobain (1967–1994) readily acknowledged his band's debt to the Pixies for their use of wide-ranging dynamics as an expressive device (see Meet the Performers, p. 381). The song has all the trademarks of the grunge sound. While the title might refer to a popular line of deodorant (Teen Spirit), Cobain claims the song was his attempt to "describe what I felt about my surroundings and my generation and my people."

Rapper Snoop Dogg performs at the SXSW 2010 Music Festival in Austin, Texas.

The "alternative" rock of the late 1990s exhibits a surprising breadth of styles. Beck combined 1990s hip hop, 1960s soul, 1930s country music, and even a bit of Schubert's *Unfinished* Symphony to create a fresh and futuristic sound. The Icelandic singer Björk has also been extremely innovative, moving from punk to jazz to electronic dance music to an elaborately conceived and arranged album consisting entirely of vocals (*Medulla*, 2005). The English alternative rock band Radiohead, known for its collaborative songwriting and experimental music has had a loyal following since the release of its first album (*Pablo Honey*, 1993). They returned to the spotlight with their 2007 release of *In Rainbows*, which was first released as a digital download and subsequently won them the Grammy for Best Alternative Music Album.

More and more women are finding success in popular music. Confessional piano-playing singers-songwriters like Tori Amos, who also did a great cover of *Smells Like Teen Spirit*, and Fiona Apple have garnered much critical praise for their complex compositions and introspective lyrics.

## Meet the Performers

### Nirvana

*"In Webster's, 'Nirvana' means freedom from pain, suffering and the external world; that's pretty close to my definition of punk rock."*

The rock band Nirvana, formed in 1987 by guitarist Kurt Cobain and bassist Krist Novoselic, soon had a strong following in the Seattle grunge scene. The 1991 release of Nirvana's second album, *Nevermind* (including the opening track *Smells Like Teen Spirit*), launched the group to stardom, despite Cobain's rejection of the rock-star image. This album was formative to the emerging alternative rock movement, which sought a return to simplicity. In 1992, Kurt Cobain married Courtney Love, the provocative lead singer with the alternative rock band Hole. Just as the band was at the height of its popularity, Cobain committed suicide; his untimely death in 1994 at twenty-seven—the same age that signaled the end for Jimi Hendrix, Janis Joplin, and Jim Morrison—promoted sales of their last album, *Unplugged in New York* (1994). A gifted guitarist and songwriter, Kurt Cobain's music, with its guitar distortions and guttural singing, had great appeal to a generation of young people who found themselves alienated from mainstream values. His death turned him into a cultural icon for generations to come.

**Check out these recordings by Nirvana:** *Smells Like Teen Spirit*, on the album *Nevermind* (1991); *About a Girl*, from the live album *Unplugged in New York* (1994); *You Know You're Right*, posthumously released demo recording (2002)

Neo-folk singers like Ani DiFranco have helped to redefine the role of the female "folk" singer. Women have brought new ideas to punk, ranging from the catchy pop-punk of Avril Lavigne to the powerful social commentary of Sleater-Kinney. The country pop group the Dixie Chicks broke into the mainstream with their number-one album *Fly* (2000). Even in the male-dominated world of rap, female artists like Missy "Misdemeanor" Elliot and Li'l Kim have claimed their share of the pop audience.

Among the hottest female stars today is theatrical dance-pop performer Lady Gaga, whose debut single *Just Dance* (2008) hit the *Billboard* charts and got the dance floor rocking. Borrowing from glam rock stars like Elton John and David Bowie and from pop sensations like Madonna and Michael Jackson, Lady Gaga (a stage name she borrowed from the Queen song *Radio Ga-Ga*) has created her own style that mixes dance-pop, electro-pop, and rock with wild fashions. She has already been recognized with six Grammy nominations for her first album *The Fame* (which won for the Best Dance Recording). Named by several news agencies as one of the most fascinating people to watch, Lady Gaga's tours are drawing sold-out crowds worldwide.

(Left) Beyoncé performing at the 2010 Grammy Awards ceremony in Los Angeles.

(Right) The outrageous Lady Gaga in London at the Brit Awards, February 16, 2010.

Older musical styles have been updated for twenty-first-century audiences. At the forefront is a melodic style of pop punk, represented by the northern California band Green Day, and the ska-influenced southern California group No Doubt, with their charismatic lead singer Gwen Stefani. Other groups

The original *American Idol* judges Randy Jackson, Paula Abdul, and Simon Cowell, in a 2005 show.

are mining even more venerable strains of American music. For example, the White Stripes is a drum and guitar duo that plays raw electric blues and country music evoking the 1930s and '40s, and Alicia Keys is a Grammy-winning singer-keyboardist who reinterprets the 1960s soul style of Aretha Franklin.

The world of popular music has changed radically with the introduction of reality TV shows like *American Idol*, which can make one an overnight superstar. Unlike the old days of the *Ed Sullivan Show*, where the Beatles were first seen in America, viewers can participate in the selection of the big winners on *Idol*. Among those *Idol* contestants who have gone on to fame are singer/songwriter Kelly Clarkson (from season one), country singer Carrie Underwood (season four), and pop artist Adam Lambert (season eight).

Many pop music singers today are also actors, such as Justin Timberlake, whose first two albums were huge hits and who has starred in numerous TV shows and films; and R & B artist Beyoncé, who was named by *Billboard* as the most successful female artist of the first decade of the twenty-first century and nominated for ten Grammys in 2010 (she won three). Beyoncé has starred in many films, including the successful movie adaptation of *Dreamgirls* (2006). She and her husband, rapper Jay-Z, may be the hottest couple on the current pop music scene.

The popularity of music video games, like the *Guitar Hero* series (introduced in 2005) and *Rock Band* series (2007) has been a key factor in the longevity of certain bands and songs. In particular, the 2009 game *Beatles Rock Band* ensures that the music of this legendary group will be revered for many years to come.

In this overview of the many styles of rock and pop music, we have highlighted a mere handful of music groups and individual artists whose influences have been considerable. Today, more than ever, it is difficult to categorize a musician's style, because popular music is moving in so many directions. Only time will tell which of the current stars will be tomorrow's legends.

## Critical Thinking

**1.** From which diverse musical styles did rock originate?

**2.** How is the Woodstock Festival significant to the history of rock?

**3.** Which could be considered "classic" rock groups, and why?

## LISTENING ACTIVITY: COMPARING STYLES 7 POP ROCK TO GRUNGE

Let's consider two of the greatest rock songs of all time: the Rolling Stones' hit, *19th Nervous Breakdown* (1965) and Nirvana's first and biggest single hit, *Smells Like Teen Spirit* (1991). You will need to locate recordings or videos of these well-known works on your own. Listen to both, focusing on song structure, laid out below, as well as the musical elements in the questions below.

### *19th Nervous Breakdown*, by the Rolling Stones

Mick Jagger, vocals

Keith Richards and Brian Jones, guitar

Bill Wyman, bass

Charlie Watts, drums

**Introduction**: 4-measure, syncopated guitar line
**Verse 1:** 16 measures, with driving backbeat; Jagger sings solo ("You're the kind of person")
**Chorus**: 16 measures, with repeated text (Here it comes"), rising line
**Verse 2**: 16 measures ("When you were a child")
**Chorus**: 16 measures ("Here it comes")
**Bridge**: 16 measures ("Oh, who's to blame") with breaks in drum beat
**Verse 3:** 16 measures ("You were still in school")
**Chorus**: 16 measures ("Here it comes")
**Bridge**: Instrumental passage (8 measures) then vocal ("Oh, who's to blame")
**Verse 2** repeated: ("When you were a child")
**Coda** (=shortened Chorus): Repeated text on song title

### *Smells Like Teen Spirit*, by Nirvana

Kurt Cobain, vocal and guitar          Krist Novaselic, bass          David Grohl, drums

**Introduction:** Solo guitar played softly, with a 2-measure phrase heard twice, followed by the full band playing loudly, then a return to the softer style
**Verse 1:** Cobain sings softly ("Load up on guns"), with strong beat and rising guitar riff
**Chorus 1**: First part ("Hello, hello") sung softly with 2-note riff
              Second part ("With the lights out") is loud and distorted closing instrumental section
**Verse 2:** Solo vocal ("I'm worse at what I do best"), sung softly
**Chorus 2**: Soft, then loud sections
**Instrumental Verse/Chorus**: Loud guitar solo, then closing soft section
**Verse 3**: High sustained pitch accompanied vocal ("And I forget just why I taste")
**Chorus 3**: Soft, then loud sections
**Coda**: Text changes from chorus; frenzied repetition on "a denial"; sustained chord dies out.

Now let's try to compare the styles of these songs by matching each selection with the musical traits below that best suit it—note that you can answer both songs for a trait, when appropriate.

> **a.** *19th Nervous Breakdown*
> **b.** *Smells Like Teen Spirit*

**1.** ___ Alternation of loud and soft sections as an expressive device

**2.** ___ Relatively even dynamic level

**3.** ___ Prominent rising 4th interval as 2-note guitar riff

**4.** ___ Basic chorus/verse structure, with instrumental introductions and bridges

**5.** ___ Ambiguous harmonic progression

**6.** ___ Regular phrasing over repeated chord progression (3 chord: I-IV-V) in major key

**7.** ___ Distorted guitar effects

**8.** ___ Distorted vocal quality

**9.** ___ Raucous, hard-driving chorus

**10.** ___ Exclusively solo singing on verse

**11.** ___ Lyrics easy to hear

**12.** ___ Frenzied ending, with much text repetition

**13.** ___ Grunge, or alternative, rock

**14.** ___ Classic hard rock

# World War II and Beyond

## COMPOSERS AND WORKS

**(1912–1982)** John Cage (*Sonatas and Interludes*)

**(b. 1928)** John Corigliano (*Prelude: Mr. Tambourine Man*)

**(b. 1929)** George Crumb (Madrigals)

**(b. 1935)** Arvo Pärt (*Cantate Domino canticum novum*)

**(b. 1947)** John Adams (*Doctor Atomic*)

**(b. 1952)** Tod Machover (*Begin Again Again . . .*)

**(b. 1955)** Bright Sheng (*China Dreams*)

**(b. 1962)** Jennifer Higdon (*blue cathedral*)

## EVENTS

**1917** U.S. enters World War I

**1941** Pearl Harbor attack by Japan

**1963** Assassination of President John F. Kennedy

**1965** First walk in space

**1968** Assassination of Martin Luther King, Jr.

**1974** First home computers

**1975** End of Vietnam War

**1991** Soviet Union dissolved

**2001** Terrorists attack World Trade Center

**2003** Iraq War begins

**2008** U.S. enters economic recession

**2009** Barack Obama elected first African-American U.S. president

# World War II and Beyond

Roy Lichtenstein (1923–1997).
*The Melody Haunts My Reverie* (1965).

# New Directions in the Arts

"From Schoenberg I learned that tradition is a home
we must love and forgo."

—**Lukas Foss**

- Post–World War II artists embraced new postmodern ideas that rejected the restrictions of modernism.

- *Postmodernist art* embraces neoclassical, minimalist, and feminist ideals, and exponents also explore environmental works, collage, ethnic expressions, and the mixture of popular and serious idioms.

- Exponents of multimedia and performance art include singer/violinist Laurie Anderson and composer John Cage; he also experimented with *chance*, or *aleatoric, music* in which certain elements are left up to the performer or to chance.

- The globalization of society has prompted composers to investigate the sound worlds of non-Western cultures.

- Other postmodern musical techniques include *quotation*—citing well-known works in a new composition—and the introduction of *electronic instruments* into live performance.

- Like artists, composers have blurred the lines between popular and elite music, enabling new works to be more immediately accessible to the general public.

*In His Own Words*

An artist is somebody who produces things that people don't need to have.

—*Andy Warhol*

Just as early-twentieth-century artists, writers, and musicians rebelled against the extremes of Romanticism, developing innovative approaches to form, color, and sound, so too did mid-twentieth-century artists strive to find new means of expression that turned against the principles of modernism, hoping to draw the general public back to the arts.

The increasing social turmoil since the Second World War has been reflected in the arts, which passed through a period of violent experimentation with new media, new materials, and new techniques. Artists unchained themselves from every vestige of the past in order to explore new areas of thought and feeling

A trend away from objective painting led to abstract expressionism in the United States during the 1950s and 1960s. In the canvases of painters such as Robert Motherwell (see illustration, p. 388) and Jackson Pollock, space, mass, and color were freed from the need to imitate objects in the real world. The urge toward abstraction was felt equally in sculpture, as is evident in the work of artists such as Henry Moore and Barbara Hepworth (see illustration, opposite).

At the same time, a new kind of realism appeared in the art of Jasper Johns (see illustration, p. 389), Robert Rauschenberg, and their colleagues, who owed some of their inspiration to the Dadaists of four decades earlier. Rauschenberg's aim, as

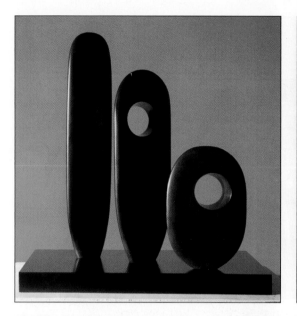

*Three Standing Forms* (1964), by English sculptor **Barbara Hepworth** (1903–1975), is an abstraction representing the relationship between nature and humankind.

The Walt Disney Concert Hall in Los Angeles, designed by **Frank Gehry** (b. 1929) and completed in 2003, is considered a masterpiece of postmodern architecture.

he put it, was to work the "gap between life and art." This trend culminated in pop art, which drew its themes and techniques from modern urban life: machines, advertisements, comic strips, movies, commercial photography, and familiar objects connected with everyday living. A similar aim motivated Andy Warhol's *32 Campbell's Soup Cans* (see illustration, p. 31) and the comic-strip art of Roy Lichtenstein (see illustration, p. 385).

Today the term "postmodernism" is applied to a variety of styles that represent a move away from modernism. No one agrees on how to define postmodernism, but this movement encompasses a number of ideas that promote the introduction of popular elements into art; that emphasize combinative techniques like collage, pastiche, or quotation in artworks; and that revive traditional and classical elements in art. In short, these ideas open broad possibilities for artistic expression, and consider all art—highbrow or lowbrow—to have equal potential for greatness. In architecture, for example, the trend is away from sleek, glass rectangular skyscrapers, embracing instead a neo-eclectic approach. Robert Venturi, a leader in the postmodern movement in architecture, parodied designer Mies van der Rohe's statement "less is more" with his idea that "less is a bore," suggesting that buildings were more interesting if they had some decorative elements. One stunning architectural example is Frank Gehry's design for the Walt Disney Concert Hall in Los Angeles, the interpretation of which has ranged from a blossoming flower to a sailing ship (see illustration, above).

Subcategories of postmodern art include new classicism, minimalism, as well as performance and multimedia art, among others. Artists have explored ecological and natural issues through environmental art, or earthworks, which advocates a bare and simple approach akin to that in minimalism. Bulgarian artists Christo, in collaboration with his wife Jeanne-Claude (both use only their first names), exploit installation art as a new way to view old landscapes and to draw attention to form through concealing it. Their projects have included wrapping the Pont Neuf Bridge (1985; see illustration, p. 388) over the Seine River in Paris and the Reichstag government building in Berlin (1995); one of their largest projects was

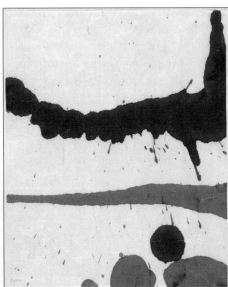

(Left) Artists **Christo** (b. 1935) and **Jeanne-Claude** (1935–2009) were allowed to wrap the Pont Neuf Bridge in Paris with sand-colored fabric (1985).

(Right) In abstract expressions, space and mass are independent, liberated from any need to express reality. Untitled, from *Lyric Suite* series, by **Robert Motherwell** (1915–1991).

The Gates (2005), in which they placed 7,503 gates with orange-colored fabric in New York's Central Park.

Postmodernism embraces a pluralistic approach to gender, sexual orientation, and ethnicity in art. One creative artist whose expression is distinctively feminist is Judy Chicago, known for *The Dinner Table* (1979), a triangular table with thirty-nine place settings that pay tribute to important women throughout history. Varied cultural expressions within America's diverse ethnic communities are welcomed, such as the work of Faith Ringgold, one of the leading African-American artists today. Known for her "storybook" quilts that feature narrative paintings with quilted borders, Ringgold's *Jazz Series* depicts black musicians in the context of life in the 1920s and '30s (see below).

Artists have also focused on recognizable images in their work, sometimes employing the technique of collage, which involves assembling images or forms to make a unified whole, or quotation from a literary, musical, or visual source. Jasper Johns's work focused on common symbols—flags, numbers, letters. He wrote that

African-American artist **Faith Ringgold** (b. 1930) celebrates jazz in *Groovin High* (1986), with couples dancing at the Savoy Ballroom in Harlem. Acrylic on canvas, tied-dyed, with fabric border.

using the flag "took care of a great deal for me because I didn't have to design it," giving him room to focus on the makeup and technique of the work. We have already heard how Charles Ives used quotation in his *Country Band March*, again focusing on the known and familiar to create something unique.

Postmodern ideas were easily extended to the medium of film, beginning with the "new wave" movement of the 1950s and '60s, epitomized in the works of Jean-Luc Godard (*Breathless*, 1959), Federico Fellini (*La Strada*, 1959; *8½* 1963), and Michelangelo Antonioni (*Blowup*, 1966; *The Passenger*, 1975). More recent film directors who explore postmodernism include Jane Campion (*Two Friends*, 1986, a saga of two schoolgirls that is arranged in reverse order); and Quentin Tarantino's *Kill Bill* films (2003–2004), which pay homage to the Italian spaghetti western, Kung Fu movies, and other familiar stereotypes; his *Pulp Fiction* (1994), which has a nonlinear storyline, and his recent, genre-bending *Inglourious Basterds* (2009). Visual collage is effective in films as well, such as in Godfrey Reggio's non-narrative *Koyaanisqatsi* (1982) and *Powaqqatsi* (1988), both of which set soundtracks by minimalist composer Philip Glass (see below).

Postmodern literature takes many forms and approaches as well. Among the writers you might know are E. L. Doctorow, whose book *Ragtime* (1975) has received many awards—including a Pulitzer Prize nomination—and has been made into a popular musical (1998; revival, 2009) that was nominated for twelve Tony Awards, and Gabriel García Márquez, whose novel *One Hundred Years of Solitude* explores the fluidity of time. A classic novelist on many required reading lists

**Jasper Johns'** (b. 1930) collage *Three Flags* (1958) superimposes three canvasses to play with how the viewer perceives a familiar image.

A hyperkinetic scene of urban life, from **Godfrey Reggio's** film *Koyaanisqatsi* (1982), for which Philip Glass wrote the minimalist musical score.

**Laurie Anderson**

"I see and write things first as an artist, second as a woman, and third as a New Yorker. All three have built-in perspectives that aren't neutral."

Performance artist Laurie Anderson (b. 1947) is an innovative postmodernist who uses a combination of popular music, storytelling, comic routines, and high-tech equipment to address social issues in her works. Anderson was educated at Mills College, in Oakland, California, and at Barnard College, in New York City. She also holds a master's degree in sculpture from Columbia University. Her instrument was the violin, but she is also a singer, poet, actress, and storyteller. Her first well-known work, the pop music-inspired *O Superman* (1981), is half-spoken, half-sung, drawing on an aria by French opera composer Jules Massenet (1842–1912) and using voices from answering machines to make a social commentary on communication and technology. The minimalist background in the song—just two alternated chords—is typical of her rock-influenced music; she has worked with a number of rock musicians, including Peter Gabriel of *Genesis*. Anderson has created several unique electronic devices for her performances: one is the "talking stick," a long, batonlike MIDI controller that replicates different sounds. She holds the distinction of being the first NASA artist-in-residence, for which she wrote *The End of the Moon*, a series for violin and electronics that is part travelogue, part personal history and dreams. Her latest endeavor, *Delusion,* premiered in February 2010 at the Vancouver Olympic Games. It is a series of short mystery plays that jump between real life and the mythic. In 2003, Laurie Anderson received the Dorothy and Lillian Gish Prize for her creativity and for her "outstanding contributions to the beauty of the world and to humankind's enjoyment and understanding of life."

**Check out these recordings by Laurie Anderson:** *Sharkey's Day* and *Excellent Birds,* with Peter Gabriel, both on album *Mister Heartbreak* (1984, 1990); *O Superman* and *Big Science,* both on album *Big Science;* (1982, 1990); new album *Homeland* (2010)

is Kurt Vonnegut, whose works (*Cat's Cradle,* 1963; *Slaughterhouse Five,* 1969) create a chaotic, fictional universe. Many recent authors have explored their identity through their writings, including African-American writers Maya Angelou (*I Know Why the Caged Bird Sings,* 1969) and Toni Morrison (*The Bluest Eye,* 1970; *Beloved,* 1987) as well as Chinese-American Amy Tan (*The Joy Luck Club,* 1989). Indeed, even popular works such as J. K. Rowling's Harry Potter books spin out postmodern themes that establish the mythic Harry among our superheroes of today.

# Postmodernism in Music

While a few composers continued the path set out by Schoenberg toward ever stricter organization in music, many others looked toward freer forms and procedures. The antirational element in art—drawing on intuition, change, and improvisation—was favored by composers such as John Cage, who wrote **chance,** or **aleatoric, music** that left decisions determining overall shape to the performer or to chance (see p. 399). Just as in the visual arts, the distinctions between elite and popular music are shrinking—we will hear, for example, how composer John Corigliano uses the popular poetry of folk singer Bob Dylan (see p. 375) as the starting point for his own song cycle (see p. 416); we have already noted how the film scores of John Williams have entered the realm of art music (see p. 369). The globalization of society has hugely impacted musical composition, opening up a world of expression that draws on non-Western music, as in the works of John Cage (see Chapter 45), and on the rich heritage of African-American and Latin-

American styles, as we have noted in the works of Copland, Ravel, and Gershwin, among others. Composers like William Grant Still and Bright Sheng (see p. 402) freely explore their ethnic identities through music while championing oppressed cultures. American composer George Crumb experiments with radical approaches to form and sound, while, at the same time, looking back to earlier influences. Others, like John Adams and the Estonian Arvo Pärt (both featured in Chapter 47), have reverted to a minimalist musical style built on small, repetitive ideas—a concept shared by various styles of popular music, especially rock.

Multimedia and performance art draw together various modes of expression—visual, aural, spoken, and dramatic—to challenge our notions of any one discipline or genre. The term "happening" was coined in the 1960s to describe a semi-improvised multimedia event that often depended on audience participation. The experimental composer John Cage was intrigued by this art form, as is contemporary performance artist Laurie Anderson (see Btw, across). It is important to note that electronic instruments figure prominently, sometimes alongside traditional acoustic ones, in modern performances; composers like Tod Machover often ask the performer to interact or improvise with the electronic devices (see p. 411). Collage, mentioned as a genre of art (see p. 388), was also explored in music: Lukas Foss (1922–2009) juxtaposed or overlapped fragments of Bach, Handel, and Scarlatti in his *Baroque Variations*, just as John Lennon created a sound collage of special effects and vocals in *Revolution 9* (*The Beatles*, 1968). A similar device involves the use of quotation—citing the work of another within a new composition as a parody or in homage. One could point as well to ambiguity in art as a postmodern expressive device: we will hear an otherworldly composition by contemporary composer Jennifer Higdon that bathes the listener in elusive washes of orchestral color (see p. 413). All these techniques, and many more, make up the palette of the modern composer. We will hear the individuality of each musical voice as we try to comprehend the expressive and eclectic language of today's music.

## Critical Thinking

1. Why did artists turn away from earlier twentieth-century approaches and search for newer, simpler expressions?
2. What makes postmodernism so difficult to define?
3. How have the distinctions between popular and art music broken down in recent years?

## By the way . . .

### "Who cares if you listen?"

In the years following World War II, composers explored how far they could take serial (twelve-tone) procedures in music, and in doing so, alienated audiences who neither understood nor appreciated what they were hearing. American composer Milton Babbitt (b. 1916) further distanced himself from audiences with a now infamous essay he published in *High Fidelity* magazine (1958) with the title "Who cares if you listen?" Although the title was the editor's rather than the composer's, the essay proposes an ever-widening gulf between serious contemporary music and its listeners. Babbitt insists that neither the general public nor the performer has any interest in his music, and he questions the power of the layperson and the critic in deciding the value of an artwork. A simple "I didn't like it" can ruin the reputation of a composer's creation. According to Stravinsky, critics "are not even equipped to judge one's grammar." Should composers surrender their creativity to write only what is immediately listenable? Or should they forge on, as did many artists before them who were misunderstood during their lifetimes? Stravinsky's *Rite of Spring* was written, so he claimed, for future generations, and Charles Ives's modernist music continues to challenge listeners; he asserted that "beauty in music is too often confused with something that lets the ears lie back in an easy chair." Babbitt's provocative article still resounds with modern composers, but as we will hear, many composers wish to draw in audiences and thereby preserve the future of contemporary art music.

# 44 The New Virtuosity of the Modern Age

---

**KEY POINTS**

⑤ **StudySpace** wwnorton.com/enjoy

- Contemporary music often calls for innovative and highly virtuosic instrumental or vocal effects that challenge performers to new expressive and technical levels.

- In his four books of madrigals, which use the voice as a virtuosic instrument, American composer George Crumb set texts by the Spanish poet Federico García Lorca.

---

**Avant-garde techniques and effects**

Avant-garde musical styles call for a new breed of instrumentalists and vocalists to cope with the music's technical demands. We have only to attend a concert of avant-garde music to realize how far the art of piano playing or singing has moved from the world of Chopin or Schubert. Pianists, wind players, and vocalists have developed a new arsenal of unusual techniques to meet modern performance demands (see HTTN 14, p. 395).

We will consider here the work of one creative mind whose music demands heightened levels of expression and virtuosity from performers: the American George Crumb, an original voice in the diverse world of avant-garde music.

*In His Own Words*

I have sought musical images that enhance and reinforce the powerful yet strangely haunting imagery of Lorca's poetry. I feel that the essential meaning of this poetry is concerned with the most primary things: Life, death, love, the smell of the earth, the sounds of the wind and the sea.

# George Crumb and Avant-Garde Virtuosity

"Music [is] a system of proportions in the service of a spiritual impulse."

---

The music of American composer George Crumb draws from many sources, including art music traditions, folk themes, and non-Western sounds. He has a talent for turning ordinary instruments, including the voice, into the extraordinary. His imaginative music resounds with extramusical and symbolic content that infuses it with a deep meaning waiting to be unlocked.

## Crumb's *Caballito negro*

*Caballito negro* (*Little Black Horse*) is the last of three songs in Crumb's second book of madrigals. All are set to poetry by Federico García Lorca (see p. 333), and scored for soprano with metallic percussion instruments and a flute (the first uses alto flute, and the last uses piccolo). The first madrigal invites one to "Drink the tranquil

**392**

## George Crumb (b. 1929)

**George Crumb** studied at Mason College of Fine Arts in Charleston, West Virginia, and earned graduate degrees at the University of Illinois and University of Michigan. He taught composition at University of Colorado and State University of New York at Buffalo before he was appointed to the University of Pennsylvania, where he remained until he retired in 1999. Crumb has shown a special affinity for the poetry of Federico García Lorca, the great poet killed by the Fascists during the Spanish Civil War (see p. 333). Among Crumb's works based on García Lorca's poetry is his song cycle *Ancient Voices of Children*, which abounds in a number of unusual effects, many inspired by musics of distant cultures. He also set García Lorca's poetry in his four books of madrigals, in which he explores Sprechstimme, quarter tones, and a "white" tone (without vibrato) for the voice.

Crumb's music is focused on creating new sonorities as well as exploring theatrical concepts involving staging and unusual performance demands. In *Echoes of Time and the River,* for which he won a Pulitzer Prize in 1968, performers whisper and shout as they move around the stage.

The music of George Crumb is charged with emotion, which derives from his highly developed sense of the dramatic. His use of contemporary techniques for expressive ends is extremely effective with audiences.

**Major Works:** Orchestral music, including *Echoes of Time and the River* (1967) • Vocal music set to García Lorca poetry, including 4 books of madrigals (1965–69) and *Ancient Voices of Children* (1970) • Chamber music, including *Black Angels* (for electrified string quartet, 1970), *Lux aeterna* (*Eternal Light*, for voice and chamber ensemble, with sitar, 1971), *Vox balaenae* (*The Voice of the Whales*, for amplified instruments, 1971) • Music for amplified piano, including 2 volumes of *Makrokosmos* (1972–73), *Music for a Summer Evening* (1974), *Zeitgeist* (1988), and *Otherworldly Resonances* (2 pianos, 2003) • Other piano music.

water of the antique song," the second is a dark lament ("Death goes in and out of the tavern"), and the last song, *Caballito negro,* presents a hair-raising image of death. Here, Crumb extracts only the two refrains from the poem, alternating between them: "Little black horse, where are you taking your dead rider? Little cold horse. What a scent of knife-blossom." Most phrases end with a downward melodic line, on ominous words like *muerto* (dead), *negro* (black), *frio* (cold), and *cuchillo* (knife). The rhythmic treatment might remind you of the galloping horse in Schubert's equally chilling *Elfking* (see p. 212), and the vocalist is even asked to whinny like a horse (see Listening Guide 56). This miniature is a companion to several other works by Crumb—*Song of the Rider* and *Songs, Drones, and Refrains of Death*—all imaginative musical elaborations of García Lorca's preoccupation with death.

This Italian stamp celebrates the centenary of the Spanish poet Federico García Lorca. The background depicts the Andalusian countryside with horsemen and Gypsy women.

## Critical Thinking

1. What kinds of new techniques have modern musicians needed to learn in order to perform avant-garde music (see HTTN 14, p. 395)?
2. What imaginative new sounds does George Crumb explore in his work?

**LISTENING GUIDE 56** ⑨ | DVD | CD 8 (30–32) | CD 4 (71–73)

# Crumb: *Caballito negro* (*Little Black Horse*)    1:32

**DATE:** 1965

**GENRE:** Song, from Madrigals, Book II

## WHAT TO LISTEN FOR:

| | | | |
|---|---|---|---|
| Melody | Highly disjunct, using extended technique (flutter tonguing, glissandos, whispering) | Expression | Grimly playful; very animated |
| Rhythm/Meter | Regular pulsations with no firm sense of meter | Timbre | Bright, hard, metallic quality |
| Harmony | Atonal idiom | Performing Forces | Soprano voice, piccolo, percussion (marimba, glockenspiel, antique cymbals) |
| Form | 3-part (**A-B-A′**) | Text | Refrains from poem by Federico García Lorca |

| | | TEXT | TRANSLATION |
|---|---|---|---|
| 71 | 0:00 | Caballito negro. | Little black horse. |
| | | ¿Dónde llevas tu jenete muerto? | Where are you taking your dead rider? |
| 72 | 0:30 | Caballito frío. | Little cold horse. |
| | | ¡Qué perfume de flor de cuchillo! | What a scent of knife-blossom! |
| 73 | 0:55 | Caballito negro . . . | Little black horse. . . |
| | | Caballito frío . . . | Little cold horse . . . |
| | | Caballito negro . . . | Little black horse . . . |

Opening of song, with pounding rhythm in piccolo and percussion, disjunct vocal line, and flutter tonguing in piccolo:

Return of opening line, with vocalist neighing like a horse:

⑨ **Now try the Listening Quiz.**

**14  Here & There, Then & Now**

# Modern Performers Say "Yes, We Can!"

David Tudor and John Cage (head in bell) experimenting with new sound effects in Japan, 1962.

As composers made increasingly virtuosic demands on performers in the twentieth century, some musicians chose to specialize in avant-garde music, thereby carving out a unique niche for themselves. Pianists might be asked to slam the keyboard with the fingers, fists, or forearms; to reach inside the piano and twang the strings; or even to insert bits of foreign substances under the piano's strings, creating a prepared piano (see p. 399). Among those who achieved fame in this realm was pianist David Tudor (1926–1996), who premiered and recorded works by some of the most experimental composers of the 1950s and '60s, including John Cage (see p. 397).

Tudor's particular talents included a highly developed finger independence, the ability to move agilely between the piano's most distant registers, and a willingness to devise new, nontraditional techniques as needed. He was closely associated with the innovative and eccentric John Cage, giving the premiere of his indeterminate, or chance, work *Music of Changes*, in which the performer makes decisions about tempo, dynamics, note durations, and timbre using the classic Chinese *I Ching* (*Book of Changes*). Tudor also premiered Cage's *4'33"* —a work that redefines music by instructing the performer not to play anything for 4 minutes and 33 seconds (hence the title); rather the "music" is the silence and sounds heard in the concert environment. Ironically, *4'33"* was first performed in Woodstock, New York, where it met with an uproar from the audience. As you might imagine, this infamous "performance" catapulted Tudor to fame.

A handful of vocalists—largely sopranos—found fame through their ability to do the near impossible with their voices, including singing microtonal intervals that most others could not hear, much less reproduce accurately, and using their voices as instruments to produce all manner of nonvocal sounds. Like pianist David Tudor, singer Cathy Berberian (1925–1983) also premiered works by John Cage, including his *Aria,* in which she had to create her own melody from the composer's purposely vague indications, singing in five languages and changing between widely varied vocal styles. Another extraordinary singer of avant-garde music was Jan DeGaetani (1933–1989), whose professional debut in New York in 1958 demonstrated her amazing vocal flexibility, precise sense of pitch, and clear crystalline tone. DeGaetani developed her ability to perform wide, "unsingable" leaps as well as microtonal intervals. Her talents attracted the attention of composer George Crumb, who wrote a number of works expressly for her, including his song cycle *Ancient Voices of Children* (1970), which asks for many unusual expressive devices (trills, clicks, buzzing, and flutter tonguing) and his first two books of madrigals, including *Caballito negro* (*Little Black Horse*), in which we will hear the singer whinny like a horse (see p. 394). DeGaetani explains her approach to singing contemporary music: "Quite often you must take time to learn a new skill. . . . The newness, the freshness comes . . . in the variety of articulations one must use, the sense of exact rhythmic proportion, the eloquent use of silence, the passing from singing speech to vocal percussion sounds." Among modern singers with extraordinary flexible vocal talents is Cecilia Bartoli (b. 1966), an Italian mezzo-soprano known for her flashy pyrotechnical technique that allows her to sing virtually anything with inexhaustible breath control, an exuberant expressivity, and a machine-gun-like delivery. Her revivals of little-known Baroque-era repertory that featured the virtuosic skills and range of the castrato singer is particularly notable (see p. 110).

Today, the demands on performers continue to increase; each musician's special skills can inspire a composer toward a new technique, and conversely, with each new, innovative work, performers will push their technique to meet and exceed the demand. The focus and training necessary to excel in avant-garde music is similar to how Olympic athletes push themselves beyond what seems humanly possible. Who can imagine where and when this trend will go next?

# 45

# Contemporary Composers Look to World Music

"I believe composers must forge forms out of the many influences that play upon them and never close their ears to any part of the world of sound."

—Henry Cowell

## KEY POINTS

> **StudySpace** wwnorton.com/enjoy

- Composer John Cage invented the **prepared piano** to simulate the sound of the Javanese gamelan.

- The **gamelan** is an ensemble of metallic percussion instruments played in Indonesia (on the islands of Java and Bali, in particular).

- The music of Chinese-American composer Bright Sheng merges Eastern and Western sound material and concepts.

- Traditional Chinese music is often performed on the **erhu** (a two-string fiddle).

- Improvisation, where the performer takes a role in the compositional process, is common not only in jazz but also in the solo genres of various Asian countries, including China, India, and Iran (see HTTN 15).

Throughout the course of history, the West has felt the influence of other cultures. Twentieth-century composers, as we have seen, found inspiration in the strong rhythmic features of songs and dances from the borderlands of Western culture—southeastern Europe, Asiatic Russia, the Near East, and parts of Latin America (see the world map at the back of this book). We have also noted how American musicians combined the powerful rhythmic impulse of African styles with the major-minor tonality of Western art music to produce a rich literature of spirituals, work songs, and shouts—and ultimately ragtime, blues, jazz, swing, and rock.

A number of contemporary composers have also responded to the philosophy of the Far East, notably Zen Buddhism and Indian thought. Among them are three Californians whose work has attracted much notice in the avant-garde scene: Henry Cowell, Harry Partch, and especially John Cage, whom we will consider.

## Important Experimenters

Henry Cowell (1897–1965) was drawn toward a variety of non-Western musics. His studies of the music of Japan, India, and Iran led him to combine Asian instruments with traditional Western ensembles. Cowell also experimented with foreign scales, which he harmonized with Western chords. The piano provided a medium for several of his innovations, including **tone clusters** (groups of adjacent notes that are sounded with the fist, palm, or forearm) and the plucking of the piano strings directly with the fingers.

The piano also lent itself to experiments with new tuning systems. One of the first to attempt microtonal music for the piano was Charles Ives (see p. 322), who wrote for pianos tuned a quarter tone apart. But perhaps the most serious proponent of this technique was Harry Partch (1901–1974), who single-mindedly pursued the goal of a microtonal music. In the 1920s, he developed a scale of forty-three microtones to the octave and adapted Indian and African instruments to fit this tuning. Among his original idiophones are cloud-chamber bowls (made of glass), the diamond marimba (made of wood), cone gongs (made of metal), and tree gourds (see illustration). Such instruments make melody and timbre, rather than harmony, the focus of his music. Partch's experiments helped shape the pioneering genius of John Cage.

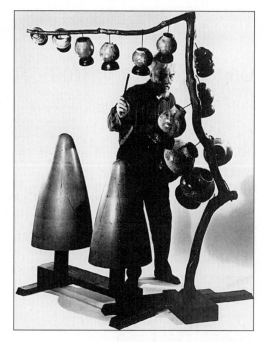

Composer Harry Partch, with his experimental gourd tree and cone gongs.

# The Music of John Cage

"I thought I could never compose socially important music. Only if I could invent something new, then would I be useful to society."

John Cage represents the type of eternally questing artist who no sooner solves one problem than presses forward to another. His works explore new sounds, approaches, and concepts that challenge the notion of what makes up music; his experimental compositions and writings have placed him as a leader in the postwar avant-garde scene.

## Cage's *Sonatas and Interludes*

*Sonatas and Interludes* represents Cage's crowning achievement for the prepared piano. In this set of works, he approximates the subtle sounds of the Javanese gamelan and preserves the effect of music floating above time. The pieces are free from the accents and dynamism of the West, and they capture the meditative character of East Asian thought.

There are sixteen Sonatas in this set, ordered in four groups of four Sonatas, and separated by Interludes (see Listening Guide 57). Cage provides detailed instructions at the beginning of the score, indicating that forty-five of the piano's eighty-eight keys should be prepared by inserting various types of materials consisting of nails, bolts, nuts, screws, and bits of rubber, wood, or leather at distances carefully specified by the composer. The effect is varied, depending upon the material inserted, its position, and whether the soft pedal is depressed. Some strings produce a nonpitched, percussive thump while others produce tones whose pitch and timbre are altered. This music is not concerned with the simultaneous sounding of pitches (harmony) but with the timbral effects and the rhythmic groupings of sounds.

Sonata V is short but highly structured; its overall shape is binary, with each section repeated (**A-A-B-B**). The sonority of the prepared piano is almost ethereal, remarkably like the gamelan orchestra of pitched and nonpitched instruments

**iMusic**

*Tabuh Kenilu Sawik*
(Indonesia)

Sonata V

# Cage: Sonata V, from *Sonatas and Interludes*                    1:23

**DATE:** 1946 (first performed 1949)

**OVERALL STRUCTURE:** 16 Sonatas, in 4 groups of 4, each group separated by an Interlude

**WHAT TO LISTEN FOR:**

| | | | |
|---|---|---|---|
| **Melody** | Irregular phrases, small-range, undulating chromatic line; 2nd section more disjunct | **Texture** | Focus on linear movement |
| | | **Form** | Binary structure (**A-A-B-B**) |
| **Rhythm/ Meter** | Opening with regular movement, then changing rhythmic flow, seemingly without a clear meter | **Expression** | Evokes ethereal, other-worldly sounds |
| | | **Timbre** | Piano produces percussive effects, both pitched and nonpitched; varied tone quality and pitches |
| **Harmony** | Minimal sense of harmony; dissonant ending | | |

---

**74**   0:00   **A section**—18 measures, grouped in irregular phrases (4 + 5 + 4 + 5 = 18).

Opening of Sonata V, with regular rhythmic movement and 2-voice texture:

*(una corda pedal)*

Irregular sense of meter develops.

0:12   Upper line sustained over moving, lower line (in last 9 measures).

0:20   **A section** repeated.

**75**   0:38   **B section**—22½ measures, in irregular phrases (4 + 5 + 4 + 5 + 4½ = 22½).

Rests break movement into sections.

0:46   Quicker tempo, lines more disjunct and accented.

Second half of **B section**, with more disjunct lines and accents:

0:55   Sustained dissonance at closing.

1:00   **B section** repeated.

ⓢ **Now try the Listening Quiz.**

## John Cage (1912–1992)

Born in Los Angeles, **Cage** exhibited an early interest in non-Western scales, which he learned from his mentor, Henry Cowell. His abiding fascination with rhythm led him to explore the possibilities of percussion instruments. He soon realized that the traditional division between consonance and dissonance had given way to a new opposition between music and noise, as a result of which the boundaries of the one were extended to include more of the other.

In 1938, Cage invented what he called the "prepared piano," in which various foreign substances were inserted at crucial points in the strings of an ordinary grand piano. From this instrument came a myriad of sounds whose overall effect resembled that of a Javanese *gamelan*. Cage wrote a number of works for the prepared piano, notably the set of *Sonatas and Interludes* (1946–48; we will consider Sonata V).

Cage's interest in indeterminacy, or chance, led him to compose works in which performers make choices by throwing dice. These experiments established him as a decisive influence in the artistic life of the era.

Cage maintained an intense interest in exploring the role of silence, which led to his composition entitled *4'33"*, without any musical content at all, consisting of four minutes and thirty-three seconds of "silence." The piece was first "performed" by the pianist David Tudor in 1952 (see HTTN 14, p. 395). He came onstage, placed a score on the piano rack, sat quietly for the duration of the piece, then closed the piano lid and walked off the stage. Cage viewed *4'33"* as one of the most radical statements he had made against the traditions of Western music, one that raised profound questions. What is music, and what is noise? And what does silence contribute to music? In any case, *4'33"*, which can be performed by anyone on any instrument, always makes us more aware of our surroundings.

**Major Works:** Orchestral music • Piano music, including *Book of Changes* (1951) • Prepared piano works, including *Bacchanale* (1940) and *Sonatas and Interludes* (1948) • Percussion works, including *First, Second, Third Construction* (1938, 1940, 1941) • Vocal works, including *Aria* (1958) • Electronic music, including *Fontana Mix* (1958), *Cartridge Music* (1960), and *HPSCHD* (for harpsichord and tapes, 1969) • Indeterminate works, including *4'33"* (for any instrument, 1952) • Writings, including *Silence* (1961), *Notations* (1969), *Themes and Variations* (1982), and *I-VI* (1990).

### In His Own Words

Once in Amsterdam, a Dutch musician said to me, "It must be very difficult for you in America to write music, for you are so far away from the centers of tradition." I had to say, "It must be very difficult for you in Europe to write music, for you are so close to the centers of tradition."

and far removed from the timbre we associate with the piano. Cage's music for prepared piano is made of wholly original sounds that delight the ears and, according to the composer, "set the soul in operation." We will consider here the gamelan orchestra that inspired Cage to create these new timbres.

John Cage's prepared piano works call for screws and nails to be inserted between the strings.

# The Javanese Gamelan

*"Simply said, gamelan music is the most beautiful music in the world,
and I for one see no reason to do any other kind of music ever again."*

—*Lou Harrison*

Indonesia, a highly populated country in Southeast Asia, has many diverse cultures and musical traditions. One of the most important traditions is the **gamelan**, an orchestra of metallic percussion played on the Indonesian islands of Java, Bali, and Sunda. A gamelan is composed of melodic-percussive instruments, each with its own function within the orchestra. The music is generally played from memory, passed as an oral tradition from master musician to apprentice. It is only in recent years that a notational method has been devised.

Gamelan music is often heard in ritual ceremonies, including court performances (there are four courts in central Java alone) and **wayang**, or shadow-puppet theater. Two tunings are used: **sléndro**, a pentatonic tuning, and **pélog**, a heptatonic (or seven-note) tuning. While court music often combines gamelans with these divergent tunings, the use of *sléndro* tuning for the puppet theater is a centuries-old practice. The instruments used in the puppet theater include soft and loud **metallophones** (instruments with tuned metal bars that are struck with a mallet), gongs of various sizes, wooden xylophones, drums, and voice.

The performance of a shadow-puppet theater would normally begin in the early evening with the overture, and continue for many hours, until dawn. A master puppeteer operates the puppets from behind a screen, and also narrates and sings the songs. The gamelan plays when signaled by the puppeteer, who leads the group in the drama. The story may be a written one, but it is more likely an elaborated version of a legend that is the puppeteer's own. We will hear a Javanese gamelan work in the accompanying Listening Activity (see p. 401), and consider how John Cage adapted these timbres to the piano.

This exotic sound has fascinated Western musicians and listeners alike, from their first exposure. Remember that Debussy, after hearing Javanese music for the first time at the Paris World Exhibition of 1889 (see HTTN 10, p. 293), said that the gamelan "contained every nuance of meaning, even unmentionable shades, and makes our tonic and dominant seem like empty phantoms for the use of unwise children."

(Left) A gamelan, with metallophones, playing for a meeting of OPEC (Organization of Petroleum Exporting Countries) in Jakarta. (Right) Javanese shadow-drama puppets of the King Rama, hero of the Hindu epic *Ramayama,* and his wife Sinta (left), who is kidnapped and later recovered.

**LISTENING ACTIVITY:**
**EXPLORING THE JAVANESE GAMELAN**

We will hear a kind of overture (called *Patalon*) for a shadow-puppet play (*wayang*) performed by a gamelan orchestra from Central Java (StudySpace, Chapter 45). The ensemble includes various sizes of gongs, drums, and wood xylophones. The music introduces an episode from the great Hindu epic, the *Ramayana*, and tells of the kidnapping of King Rama's wife Sinta by the evil king Rahwana, and how she is recovered. In this play, the evil king's brother Wibisana is cast out of the kingdom for suggesting that Sinta be returned to her husband. You will hear how the various instruments present interlocking melodies within complex recurring rhythmic patterns (called a *colotomic structure*). Note that the scale on which the music is built is different from a Western major or minor scale, and how the singer elaborates on the melody in quite a different way from the instruments. The different sections of *Patalon* are marked by changes in dynamic levels and tempos. This work sets the stage for the entrance of the dancers and puppet characters, and for the much-loved story.

For each element, select the trait that best fits *Patalon:*

**Melody**

_____ **1.** Scale          **a.** diatonic scale, or          **b.** pentatonic scale

**Rhythm/Meter**

_____ **2.** Rhythm          **c.** regular rhythmic flow,  or          **d.** changing rhythmic flow

_____ **3.** Rhythm          **e.** polyrhythmic, or          **f.** simple rhythmic treatment

_____ **4.** Meter          **g.** clear sense of meter, or          **h.** no clear sense of meter

**Texture**

_____ **5.** Polyphony/Homophony          **i.** complex, linear polyphony, or  **j.** vertically oriented homophony

**Instruments**

_____ **6.** Which two world instrument          **k.** aerophones          **m.** chordophones
          groups are prominently          **l.** idiophones          **n.** membranophones
          featured (excluding the voice)?

Compare this gamelan example with the Cage, Sonata V, which we just studied. For each characteristic below, match it to the Cage work, the gamelan selection, or both.

          **o.** Cage, Sonata V          **p.** *Patalon*          **q.** both

_____ **7.** drums marked the change of sections          _____ **11.** chromatic melodic line

_____ **8.** short sections, with exact repeats          _____ **12.** widely contrasting dynamics

_____ **9.** linear, rather than vertical, focus          _____ **13.** timbres produced by inserting various
          substances into the instrument
_____ **10.** irregular sense of meter

          _____ **14.** complex polyrhythms

# Multicultural Influences in Contemporary Society

The impulse toward a world music sound has continued beyond John Cage with composers such as Lou Harrison (1917–2003), Philip Glass, Terry Riley, and Steve Reich (on the last three composers, see p. 420). Also in this category are several composers who drew on their Asian heritage as well as the traditions of the West; these include Toru Takemitsu (1930–1996), Tan Dun (b. 1957; see p. 404), and Bright Sheng , whose blend of Pan-Asian idioms in Western contexts give his work a distinctive sound.

## Bright Sheng (b. 1955)

Born and raised in Shanghai, **Sheng** began studying piano at the age of four. But at the onset of the Cultural Revolution in 1966, schools were shut down, and Sheng, along with many other youths, was sent to Qinghai province, formerly part of Tibet. There, his talents allowed him to work as a musician, and he taught himself to play other instruments and began gathering folk songs as well. When the Revolution ended in 1976, he entered the Shanghai Conservatory of Music, where he studied composition. He came to New York in 1982 to study at Queens College and then at Columbia University.

Since coming to the United States, Sheng has won many awards—including the coveted MacArthur Foundation "Genius" Fellowship for "exceptional originality and creativity"—and has received numerous commissions from orchestras and from solo performers, including Yo-Yo Ma. Sheng currently holds the Leonard Bernstein Distinguished Professor Chair at the University of Michigan.

Much like the Hungarian composer Béla Bartók, to whom Sheng acknowledges a great debt, Bright Sheng writes music that transcends national boundaries. His compositional approach merges what he finds most important in Western music—its emphasis on harmony and counterpoint—with the Chinese affinity for linear sounds, played by a soloist or a traditional ensemble playing in unison.

Sheng's first important commission, which won him a Pulitzer nomination, was *H'un (Lacerations): In Memoriam 1966–75*, a dramatic orchestral portrait of the Cultural Revolution that tells the composer's story as a "victim, witness, and survivor." Generally his music is highly lyrical, often evoking elements of Chinese folk songs. Several of his concertos combine Chinese solo instruments (*pipa*, a kind of lute; and *sheng*, a mouth organ) with the Western orchestra. In his *Spring Dreams*, Sheng writes for solo cello accompanied by traditional Chinese orchestra.

**Major Works:** Orchestral music, including *H'un (Lacerations: In Memoriam, 1966–75,* [1988]), *China Dreams* (1995) • Concertos for Western and Asian instruments, including *Nanking! Nanking! A Threnody* (pipa and orchestra, 2000), *Red Silk Dance* (piano and orchestra, 2000) • Chamber music, including *Seven Tunes Heard in China* (for solo cello, 1995) • Operas, including *Madame Mao* (2003) • Vocal works, including *Two Folk Songs from Qinghai* (chorus and orchestra, 1989).

*In His Own Words*

Am I Chinese? Am I American? Am I Chinese-American? I have lived in the United States since my mid-twenties. The other part of me is Chinese, a person who grew up in China and whose outlook was formed there . . . I am a mixture. Identity cannot be decided by political boundaries. . . . I enjoy the fact that I can live in and appreciate two different cultures.

# Bright Sheng and the Meeting of Musical Cultures

"People acknowledge artistic license; I embrace cultural license."

Bright Sheng is one of the most innovative composers on the contemporary scene. He blends two different musical cultures—Western and Asian—into a new soundscape that respects the essence of each. Even his name crosses cultures: his official Chinese name is Sheng Song-Liang (Liang means "bright lights"), so he uses Bright as his Anglicized first name.

## Sheng's *China Dreams*

Sheng's symphonic suite *China Dreams* is a nostalgic work—he admits being homesick for China. The suite, set in four movements, is scored for a large orchestra, in the Western tradition. We will hear the opening *Prelude*, which is evocative of Chinese folk music, particularly from the northwest region where Sheng lived for seven years. Hauntingly lyrical pentatonic melodies in the woodwinds and upper strings are punctuated by rough, dissonant figures in the brass and low strings.

**LISTENING GUIDE 58**    Ⓢ | DVD | CD 8 (45–50) | CD 4 (76–81)

# Sheng: *China Dreams, Prelude*    4:55

**DATE:** 1995

**GENRE:** Symphonic suite

| | |
|---|---|
| ***Prelude*** | *The Stream Flows* |
| *Fanfare* | *The Three Gorges of the Long River* |

**WHAT TO LISTEN FOR:**

| Melody | Lyrical Asian-inspired pentatonic melodies, flow over barlines | Form | 3-part structure |
|---|---|---|---|
| Rhythm/ Meter | Subtle syncopations obscure the meter | Expression | Highly evocative of Asian music; ethereal quality |
| Harmony | Gentle, then dissonant figures punctuating the work | Timbre | Brilliant orchestration; brass and harp used percussively; juxtaposition of instrument families |
| Texture | Predominantly linear movement; some countermelodies | Performing Forces | Orchestra, with piano, celesta, and diverse percussion instruments |

---

76  0:00    Oboe and English horn, with haunting pentatonic melody with grace notes, accompanied by viola line and plucked low strings:

0:26    Melody taken over by clarinets, interrupted by quick flourishes in double reeds and trumpets; punctuated by harp and percussion; very Asian sound.

1:04    Melody passed to bass clarinet, closes on held note (fermata).

77  1:19    Pace slackens (*meno mosso*); new version of melody in violas:

Sharp, percussive notes plucked in violins and harp; crescendos to *fortissimo*.

78  2:03    Loud motive in French horns interrupts piccolo melody; more animated, then *decrescendo*.

2:18    Quieter section; flute has long melody, with active harp line and trombone glissandos:

2:31    Shift of timbre; violins have lyrical melody.

2:42    Flute melody accompanied by repeated notes in flute/piccolo.

*Continued on following page*

| 79 | 3:00 | Rich string section takes over with new theme; brass interjection. |
| | | Texture becomes more polyphonic; builds to climax. |
| | 3:40 | Loud timpani and low brass intrude on melody, *fortissimo*; timpani and trombones with glissandos. |
| 80 | 3:55 | Brass dominate with quick inverted dotted idea; rising then falling; very loud climax; trombones and timpani sliding in intervals. |
| | | Decrescendo to *ppp*. |
| 81 | 4:31 | Return to English horn melody, accompanied by high piccolo and pizzicato strings; soft dissonance fades out. |

Ⓢ **Now try the Listening Quiz.**

Sliding glissando figures suggest Asian melodic styles, as does the overall linear flow of the music (see Listening Guide 58). In this and his other compositions, Sheng's merger of Eastern and Western ideas does much to enrich the listener's understanding of both cultures.

# Chinese Traditional Music and Instruments

We have already explored the sounds of Chinese opera (see p. 279) and heard how instruments were used to accompany the vocal line. Here, we will consider several of the most popular instruments used in Chinese traditional music, some of which have been featured in Western works by Asian-American composers such as Bright Sheng.

Among the most important and oldest instruments in China are the **pipa**, a four-string plucked lute (see p. 57), and the **erhu**, a two-stringed violin (see illustration, top left). Western and Asian composers alike have written modern classical works for these instruments: Tan Dun arranged music from his film score to *Crouching Tiger, Hidden Dragon* (2000) into a concerto for erhu and orchestra, and Bright Sheng wrote a concerto for pipa and orchestra entitled *Nanking! Nanking! A Threnody* (2000) as well as several chamber works for pipa and erhu. Both instruments have long been used in traditional music performance as well. In our Listening Activity, we will hear a now-famous erhu piece entitled *Er quan ying yue* (*The Moon Reflected on the Second Springs*) by a street musician named Abing. This work is viewed as traditional music because it was created, like much music of Asia, through improvisation and thus took shape gradually, and because it has been disseminated orally in different versions—much like folk music. Abing's music is high revered; it forms part of the standard repertory at music conservatories for both erhu and pipa players, further blurring the lines between art and traditional music. Since first recorded by Abing in 1950, this work has been shaped by generations of musicians.

(Top) Man playing the erhu.

(Bottom) Master yangqin player in performance.

## LISTENING ACTIVITY:
## THE SOUNDS OF TRADITIONAL CHINESE MUSIC

*The Moon Reflected on the Second Springs* (StudySpace, Chapter 45) was written by a gifted Chinese street musician named Abing who left us a recording of the song before he died. Originally conceived for solo erhu by Abing, our recording adds the **yangqin**, a hammered dulcimer with a trapezoidal sound box and metal strings that are struck (see illustration, p. 404). Despite the yangqin accompaniment, the melodic line is the focus, built in regular phrases that are subjected to many types of embellishments in a kind of variations procedure. The ornamentation, known as "adding flowers" (*Jia hua*), features trills, slides, glissandos, grace notes, bent notes, and tremolos. Listen for how the melodic outline returns with newly invented ornamentation at each appearance and for the ethereal, "singing" quality of the erhu.

Consider the musical style of this Chinese work, answering the questions below.

### Melody

|  |  |  |
|---|---|---|
| _____ **1.** Scale | **a.** built on a diatonic (major) scale, or | **b.** built on a pentatonic scale |
| _____ **2.** Phrasing | **c.** regular phrases, or | **d.** highly irregular phrase lengths |
| _____ **3.** Range | **e.** remains in same range throughout, or | **f.** grows in range as melody proceeds |

### Rhythm/Meter

|  |  |  |
|---|---|---|
| _____ **4.** Pulse | **g.** weak or no pulse, or | **h.** regular sense of pulse |
| _____ **5.** Meter | **i.** feeling of duple meter, or | **j.** no sense of Western meter |

### Instruments

|  |  |  |
|---|---|---|
| _____ **6.** Melody Instrument | **k.** plucked, or | **l.** bowed |
| _____ **7.** Accompanying Instrument | **m.** plucked, or | **n.** struck |
| _____ **8.** Interplay | **o.** instruments equally balanced, or | **p.** melody instrument dominates |
| _____ **9.** Texture | **q.** linear movement, or | **r.** chordal, vertical focus |

### Expression

|  |  |  |
|---|---|---|
| _____ **10.** Form (at 1:15 into selection) | **s.** exact repeat of main melody | **t.** varied version of main melody |

Compare this Chinese music example with the *Prelude* to Bright Sheng's *China Dreams* we just studied. For each characteristic below, match it to the Sheng work, the Chinese selection, or both.

**u.** Sheng: *Prelude* to *China Dreams*      **v.** *The Moon Reflected on the Second Springs*      **w.** both

| | |
|---|---|
| _____ **11.** pentatonic melodies | _____ **15.** highly dissonant harmonies |
| _____ **12.** string and woodwind timbres | _____ **16.** two string-instruments only |
| _____ **13.** focus on melody and linear movement | _____ **17.** structured on variation procedure |
| _____ **14.** uses embellishments in melody | _____ **18.** uses slides between pitches |

## Critical Thinking

**1.** What are some of the ways in which modern composers have been influenced by world music?

**2.** What makes Cage's Sonata V sound like a gamelan? How does Bright Sheng evoke an Asian flavor in his *China Dreams*?

**3.** What is the role of the composer versus that of the performer in relation to improvisation (see HTTN 15, p. 406)?

# Improvisation as Compositional Process

Bahram Osqueezadeh plays the Iranian santur.

We have already seen how some modern Western art compositions and especially jazz tunes allow performers the freedom to "compose" a work on the spot, through improvisation. This practice is also found in other cultures around the world, especially in the solo genres of various Asian countries. But whether it is Eastern or Western music, improvisation shares the same concept worldwide: the musician starts with something definable—be it a scale, a mode, a tune, or a set of rules—and then creates the music through a series of specific performance conventions unique to that musical style—a style that is understood by both practitioner and audience. Let us examine various methods and styles of improvisation.

The Chinese piece *The Moon Reflected on the Second Springs* (*Er quan ying yue*, p. 405) provides the performer some freedom in interpretation to shape melodic lines, rhythmic flow, articulations (plucked vs. bowed, for example), ornamental notes, and pitch inflections. Much like a jazz standard, however, the work retains its overall shape and melodic familiarity.

In contrast, the classical music of India features the performer in the role of composer. The starting point is the *raga* (from the Sanskrit word "to

color"), which is much more than a scale. It sets the mood of a piece while providing material for endless variations. In addition, each raga has an overriding rhythmical structure determined by the *tala*, a complex cycle of beats and subbeats.

The *tabla* (a set of hand drums) sets up the rhythm—played slowly at first, then accelerating—giving a sense of climax to the work. We can hear how these melodic and rhythmic traits function in our excerpt from a North Indian (Hindustani) piece performed by the esteemed sitar player Ravi Shankar. (A *sitar* is a plucked string instrument—a long-necked lute—with six main strings and many side and sympathetic strings; see illustration on p. 41.) He uses the *Bhimpalási* raga, which evokes a mood of tenderness and suggests a restrained but deeply felt longing. We hear microtonal pitches when the strings are pulled sideways to inflect a note, making the sound dip lower.

A similar kind of melodic development occurs in the classical music of Iran. In this style, based on the ancient music of Persia, there is again no distinction between the performer and composer. Musicians think in terms of short melodic units that form a *dastgāh*, or melody type and mode, which is introduced and then expanded

through an organic process. Our example is unmeasured and is performed on the *santur*—a hammer dulcimer popular in Iran today. In *Avaz of Bayate Esfahan*, a unique scale is presented in the rhapsodic introduction that employs microtonal pitches not heard in the well-tempered Western system. This music features ornamental grace-notes as well as tremolos to extend and enhance the sound of the instrument.

In all these examples of improvisation, each performer's interpretation relies on the basic elements of repetition, contrast, and variation. Since much Asian music is conceived linearly, it is the melodic rather than harmonic development that captures the ear. Therefore tension and release is achieved by the fluctuations in the pacing—the acceleration and the slowing down—and in the rise and fall of the melodic line. In the end, it is the inventiveness of the performer that makes a work successful and comprehendible to the listener, regardless of the building materials and creative processes from which it is fashioned.

Opening of *Avaz of Bayate Esfahan* (iMusic), showing microtonal notes and ornamental effects (transcription by Bahram Osqueezadeh).

🔘 **iMusic**

India: *Bhimpalási* (sitar, tambura, tabla)

Iran: *Avaz of Bayate Esfahan* (santur)

# 46 Technology and Music

"I have been waiting a long time for electronics to free music from the tempered scale and the limitations of musical instruments. Electronic instruments are the portentous first step toward the liberation of music."

—Edgard Varèse

## KEY POINTS

> ⓢ **StudySpace** wwnorton.com/enjoy

- *Musique concrète*, which began in the late 1940s, used natural sounds recorded on magnetic tape as a new medium for composition.

- In the early 1950s, the German school of *electronische Musik* created compositions using electronically generated sounds.

- By the late 1960s, smaller, cheaper synthesizers were available to many musicians and composers.

- *Digital technology*, beginning with the invention of FM synthesis in the 1970s, revolutionized the world of electronic music.

- Computers can generate sounds, create compositions, and interact with synthesizers via the *Musical Instrument Digital Interface (MIDI)*.

- One of the most innovative composers of interactive music is Tod Machover, who writes for electronically enhanced *hyperinstruments*.

- Modern composers are moving toward *interactive performances* involving a live audience, either directly or via the Internet.

## The Technological Revolution

The most important development in art music during the last fifty years was the emergence of electronic music. New instruments such as the theremin, an eerie-sounding device often heard in film scores (see illustration, p. 408) and the Hammond organ—both of which produce sounds electronically—predicted a future that was quickly realized by the booming revolution of technology.

Two trends emerged simultaneously in the late 1940s and early 1950s: *musique concrète* in France and *electronische Musik* in Germany. *Musique concrète*, based in Paris, relied on sounds made by any natural source, including musical instruments, that were recorded onto magnetic tape and then manipulated by various means. For example one could change the speed of the playback, reverse the direction of the tape, or process the sounds through external devices such as filters. Many forward-looking composers experimented with *musique concrète*.

*Musique concrète*

The manifestations of natural sounds gave way to artificially generated ones, and a wide variety of sound equipment came into use. Studios for the production of **tape music** (an extension of *musique concrète*) sprang up in many musical centers of Europe and America. With the raw sound (either naturally or electronically produced) as a starting point, the composer could isolate its components, alter its pitch, volume, or other dimensions, play it backward, add reverberation (echo),

(Top) The theremin, an early electronic instrument, has been used in film music and by psychedelic rock bands as well as in concert art music.

(Bottom) Robert Moog, creator of the Moog synthesizer.

filter out some of the overtones (the series of tones naturally produced by a resonating body that sound above the fundamental frequency), or add other components by splicing and overdubbing.

*Electronische Musik* originated in the early 1950s, in Cologne, Germany, and was explored by Karlheinz Stockhausen among others. The heart of this German system was the oscillator, which could generate several waveforms, each capable of a different timbre. This electronically generated waveform could be subjected to filters, reverberation, amplifiers, and other devices. Eventually, these many components would be packaged together in a single console with a piano keyboard interface to become our modern-day *synthesizer*.

Two of the most important devices for sound generation were the RCA music synthesizer, completed in 1955, and a second version delivered to the Columbia-Princeton's Electronic Music Center in 1959. Unfortunately, the size and cost of this equipment prohibited other institutions from purchasing synthesizers of their own, and very few composers had the luxury of being able to work at the Electronic Music Center.

By the 1960s, more compact and affordable synthesizers suited for mass production were developed by Robert Moog and Donald Buchla. These newer synthesizers capitalized on the transistor technology developed in the late 1950s and the more efficient voltage-controlled oscillator as developed by Moog. Morton Subotnick's *Silver Apples of the Moon* (1967) was realized on one of these newer synthesizers and has the distinction of being the first electronic music composition commissioned by a record company. But it was a recording called *Switched-On Bach*, made in 1968 by Walter Carlos (who later became Wendy Carlos, through a sex change), that catapulted the synthesizer and the genre of electronic music to instant fame. The Moog synthesizer was quickly adopted by many musicians in the world of popular music and for film scores, including Stanley Kubrick's *A Clockwork Orange* (1971) and *The Shining* (1980).

This initial wave of commercially available synthesizers marked the era of **analog synthesis**. But by the late 1960s, a new wave of technology known as **digital frequency modulation synthesis** had already been developed by John Chowning at Stanford University. Synthesis by means of frequency modulation (FM) depends on a series of sine-wave generators interacting to produce new, more complex, waveforms. Chowning had perfected his new technique by the early 1970s and sold his rights to a company named Yamaha. It took nearly ten years before Yamaha turned Chowning's discovery of FM synthesis into a commercially feasible product. In 1983, the Yamaha DX7, one of the best-selling synthesizers of all time, was unveiled and retailed for slightly under $2,000. During that same year, a standardized communications protocol known as the **Musical Instrument Digital Interface** (**MIDI**) was officially adopted and incorporated into all new music synthesizers. MIDI allows synthesizers to communicate not only with one another, but with other devices such as computers, signal processors, drum machines, and even mixing boards. Specially designed software allows composers to record MIDI data (such as pitch, duration, volume, etc.) on the computer for playback on one or more synthesizers. By the mid-1980s, digital sampling synthesizers, capable of digitizing short audio samples, became affordable to the average musician. Digital samplers allow performers and composers to recreate a realistic sounding grand piano, trumpet, violin, bird call, car crash, or any other sound that can be sampled. With the affordability of digital synthesizers and personal computers, and their ability to communicate with one another, the digital revolution took the world of electronic music by storm.

Computer music, however, did not wait for the invention of MIDI to become integrated with the world of electronic music. Research in this field had already begun with the pioneering work of Max Mathews at Bell Laboratories in the 1950s. While Mathews explored the idea of using a computer to synthesize sounds via his series of MUSIC software programs, other composers used the computer to generate music compositions. Most early work in automated composition was done by Lejaren Hiller. In collaboration with Leonard Isaacson, Hiller developed a software program in 1956 that subsequently "composed" the *Illiac Suite for String Quartet* (see Btw, at right).

# Important Figures in Electronic Music

One of the pioneers of electronic music was the French composer Edgard Varèse (1883–1965). His composition *Poème electronique* (1956–58), commissioned for a sound-and-light show at Philips Pavilion at the Brussels World's Fair, consisted of both electronic and *concrète* sounds recorded onto multichannel tape. Varèse combined natural sounds (for example, the human voice) with electronically generated sounds and subjected them to tape music techniques such as altering the tape speed, using filters, and adding reverberation. The result was recognizable sounds—voices, bells, a flying airplane—along with pulse-generated percussion sounds and synthetic tones. The pavilion design by Le Corbusier called for music to accompany both the projected images and the lighting effects in order to provide a complete audio-visual experience.

Electronic music has two novel aspects. The most immediately obvious one, the possibility to create new sounds, has impelled many musicians to use the medium. Equally important, the composer of electronic music can work directly with the sounds and produce a finished work without the help of an intermediary performer.

Combining electronic sounds with live

Edgar Varèse's *Poème électronique* was composed as part of a multimedia show for the Philips Pavilion, designed by **Le Corbusier**, at the 1958 Brussels World's Fair.

Astronaut Dr. Dave Bowman (Keir Dullea) dismantles the "brains" of the supercomputer HAL-9000 aboard Discovery One, in the sci-fi classic film *2001: A Space Odyssey* (1968).

(Top) Cellist Yo-Yo Ma performing Tod Machover's *Begin Again Again* . . . .

(Bottom) English watercolorist **William Blake** (1757–1827) portrays the eighth circle of Hell from Dante's *Divine Comedy*, which also inspired Tod Machover's music. Here the pope is being dangled in a well of fire because of his corruptions in the Church. *The Simoniac Pope* (1824–1827).

music has also proved fertile, especially since many composers had worked in both media. Works for soloist and recorded tape became common, even "concertos" for tape recorder (or live-performance synthesizer or computer) and orchestra. One important composer who has worked in this mixed medium is Mario Davidovsky (b. 1934), whose works for tape and live performer include a series known as *Synchronisms* (1963–88), dialogues for solo instrument and prerecorded tape.

Another important voice in the field of electronic music is that of Milton Babbitt (b. 1916), whose early electronic works, composed at the Columbia-Princeton Electronic Music Center, reflect his interest in assuming total control of the final musical result. But it was never his intention that the synthesizer should replace the live musician. "I know of no serious electronic composer who ever asserts that we are supplanting any other form of music. . . . We're interested in increasing the resources of music."

Pauline Oliveros (b. 1932), one of the more experimental contemporary composers, helped found the San Francisco Tape Center and became its director in 1966. She has explored mixed media and the possibilities of multichannel tape interacting with live performers and theatrical forms. Oliveros is also known for her experiments with live electronic music, in which sounds are generated and manipulated during the performance. A forerunner in the field of electronic music, Oliveros has influenced younger generations of composers, including the very imaginative Tod Machover, whose work we will consider in a Listening Activity (see p. 412).

Electronic music has permeated the commercial world of music-making in a big way. Much of the music we hear today as movie and TV soundtracks is electronically generated, although some effects resemble the sounds of conventional instruments so closely that we are not always aware of the new technology. Popular music groups have been "electrified" for some years, but now most of them regularly feature synthesizers and samplers that both simulate conventional rock band instruments and produce altogether new sounds.

Tod Machover's work for solo hypercello, *Begin Again Again* . . . was written for the virtuoso Yo-Yo Ma (see illustration, left) and premiered at the Tanglewood Festiva. Machover conceived the piece as the first in a trilogy based on Dante's epic medieval poem

## Tod Machover

"The technique we invented [of hyperinstruments] is a fantastic way not only to extend virtuosic instruments but to break down boundaries and open doors to musical experiences for ordinary music lovers."

Meet Tod Machover (b. 1953), one of the most creative minds in the modern world of music technology. While studying at The Juilliard School, he experimented with amplifying his cello and manipulating its sound. He explains his early fascination with the computer, embracing "the idea of being able to go straight from the imagination to programming this machine to produce anything I want." Machover spent five years in Paris as director of IRCAM, the French center for contemporary music, and has since been appointed professor of music and media at the Massachusetts Institute of Technology. His development of hyperinstruments places him in the forefront of music technology, creating machines that "augment and expand performance virtuosity in real time."

Machover has composed many works that combine acoustic instruments with live computer electronics. Among his most important are *Bug-Mudra* (1990), in which the conductor wears an electronic glove that cap-tures hand gestures and turns them into musical controls; and *Begin Again Again . . .* (1991; rev. 2004), for solo cello (see below). Machover's more recent compositions seek a seamless combination of acoustic instruments with electronics. Notable are *his Brain Opera* (1996) and *Toy Symphony* (2003), both of which provide opportunity for the audience and children to interact with the compositional process. His newest opera, *Death and the Powers* (2010), features a robotic, animatronics stage that "comes alive" during the work.

**Check out these works by Tod Machover:** *Begin Again Again . . .* for hypercello, on album *Hyperstring Trilogy* and on video at StudySpace.

the *Divine Comedy*. Exploring the possibility of renewal after suffering, *Begin Again Again . . .* represents the rolling inferno of Dante's poem, with the hypercello plunging musical depths. The hypercello line gravitates toward the middle D pitch on the instrument, trying to ascend from it but constantly being pulled lower. "This serves as a metaphor for change in our lives," the composer writes, "of breaking with the past while retaining what is dearest to us; of opening doors to unknown possibilities; and finally, of renewed hope and affirmation."

According to the composer, the music is "a whirlwind alternating between tormented questions ('Where am I? Where am I going? How am I going to get out of here?') and frenzied, disco-like assertions." The electronic accompaniment takes on various timbres throughout the work, but the cellist is in control of an array of devices for producing and transforming sound. In turn, the computer responds to the performer's nuances, including bow angle and pressure, as well as finger and wrist positions—thereby extending, but in no way controlling, the sound world of the soloist (see Listening Activity, p. 412). The piece is so virtuosic that the composer asked Yo-Yo Ma, after a rehearsal for the premiere, "Is there any hair left on your bow?"

A cellist himself, Machover writes of his love affair with the instrument: "I wanted my instrument to be able to sing, expressing as much between the notes as on them." He notes the "human" qualities of the cello as well: it is the size of the human body, has the range of the male and female voice combined, and has vibrations that are felt throughout the performer's body, from head to toe. In *Begin Again Again . . .*, Machover explores the full possibilities of this expressive instrument.

## LISTENING ACTIVITY: HYPERINSTRUMENTS AND MUSICAL INTERACTIVITY

At StudySpace, watch the video entitled *The Hypercello: Tod Machover and Yo-Yo Ma*, in which they discuss the compositional process for this solo cello piece and work out some of the performance details. The following outline provides a guide to the basic sections of the video:

| | |
|---|---|
| 0:00 | Introduction to hyperinstruments and *Begin Again Again* . . . |
| 0:53 | Introduction to Yo-Yo Ma in performance (see also Meet the Perfomers, p. 45) |
| 2:13 | Composer Tod Machover at work |
| 3:09 | Discussion of the meaning and interpretation of the composition |
| 5:01 | Explanation of how the hypercello works |
| 6:15 | Introduction to the conductor's glove for *Bug-mudra* |
| 7:00 | Yo-Yo Ma demonstrating the hypercello |
| 8:06 | Yo-Yo Ma on the interactive process |
| 8:55 | The compositional process |
| 11:28 | The Bach Sarabande as basis for the work |
| 13:51 | Premiere of the work at Tanglewood (various sections heard) |

As you listen (beginning at 13:51), note the changes in style from one section to the next. Follow the timings as you listen, selecting the most appropriate musical description at each point.

____ **1.** 13:51   **a.** big chords, played *fortissimo* and *sforzando*

____ **2.** 14:30   **b.** free and rhapsodic, with growing accompaniment

____ **3.** 14:59   **c.** fast, descending idea

____ **4.** 15:35   **d.** long tremolo on a single pitch

____ **5.** 15:55   **e.** fast and rhythmic, disjunct line, glissandos and repeated pitches

____ **6.** 16:14   **f.** slow and lyrical, arpeggiated line

____ **7.** 16:20   **g.** reaches high-pitch climax

### Critical Thinking

**1.** How has technology changed the approach to composing music?

**2.** How has the role of the performer changed with new technologies?

# 47

# Some Current Trends

"Now that things are so simple, there's so much to do."
—Morton Feldman

- The recent trends of **Neoromanticism** and **minimalism** speak to audiences alienated by highly intellectual approaches to contemporary music.

- **Neoromanticism** favors the lush harmonic language of the late Romantic era: the music is often tonal, chromatic, and highly virtuosic with innovative timbral combinations, as in Jennifer Higdon's tone poem *blue cathedral*.

- Some Neoromantic works feature references to well-known compositions. John Corigliano's song cycle *Mr. Tambourine Man: Seven Poems of Bob Dylan* sets poetry by the iconic Dylan.

- **Minimalist music** is based on repetitive melodic, rhythmic, or harmonic patterns with few or slowly changing variations. The music can sound hypnotic or motor-driven and frenzied.

- **Spiritual minimalism** emanates from deep religious convictions and results in a simple, nonpulsed music. Estonian composer Arvo Pärt's music embodies this trend.

- American composer John Adams's eclectic approach combines elements of minimalism with traits of Neoromanticism, forging a **post-minimalist style** (in his recent opera, *Doctor Atomic*).

**M**odern composers have tried various means to reconnect with their audiences. One postmodern approach—*Neoromanticism*—embraces an eclecticism that mixes styles from the past with contemporary ones. Often a work uses a familiar and accessible musical vocabulary that is reminiscent of post-Romantic masters. We will consider two contemporary works that can be viewed as Neoromantic: the first is a powerfully emotional and richly colored orchestral tone poem by Jennifer Higdon, and the second, a song cycle by John Corigliano that sets the familiar texts of Bob Dylan.

## Jennifer Higdon and Romantic Ideals

"Can music reflect colors and can colors be reflected in music? . . . I often picture colors as if I were spreading them on a canvas, except I do so with melodies, harmonies, and through the peculiar sounds of the instruments themselves."

Jennifer Higdon is one of the most widely performed living American composers. Her music is richly Neoromantic with an innovative sound palette that has been described as "very American." We will consider her orchestral work *blue cathedral*, which is already garnering status as a "classic."

**413**

## Jennifer Higdon (b. 1962)

Born in Brooklyn, New York, **Jennifer Higdon** pursued music studies at Bowling Green State University and then completed graduate degrees in composition at the University of Pennsylvania, where she studied with George Crumb (see p. 392). She claims that "the sheer number of Beatles' tunes I listened to helped me to realize the ability of music to communicate."

Higdon has been recognized with prestigious awards: she received the coveted Pulitzer Prize in 2010 for her Violin Concerto, written to show off Hilary Hahn's talents. Since 1994, she has taught at the Curtis Institute of Music in Philadelphia, where she holds the Milton L. Rock Chair in Composition Studies.

Higdon's extensive output spans most genres, including much orchestral music and compositions for her own instrument, the flute. Her "American" sound harkens back to that of Aaron Copland on which she imposes her own highly colorful timbral palette as well as dense textures and wide-ranging dynamics. Some works, like *blue cathedral*, which we will hear, exude a rich lyricism and shimmering beauty, while others, like her *Fanfare Ritmico* and Percussion Concerto, are more propulsive. Her rooting in tonality as well as the familiar quality in her music helps mark her as a Neoromantic. Jennifer Higdon has a remarkable output of compositions to her credit—she is clearly someone to watch.

**Major Works:** Orchestral music, including *Fanfare Ritmico* (2000), *blue cathedral* (2000), *Concerto for Orchestra* (2002) • Concertos for oboe (2005), percussion (2009), and violin (2009 • Works for wind groups, including soprano saxophone concerto (with wind ensemble, 2009) • Chamber music, including *Amazing Grace* (for string quartet, 2002) • Choral works, including *Southern Grace* (1998) • Vocal works, including *Dooryard Bloom* (for baritone and orchestra, 2004).

## Higdon's *blue cathedral*

Jennifer Higdon's *blue cathedral* has already won its way into the hearts of listeners and critics alike. Written in 2000 to commemorate the anniversary of the Curtis Institute in Philadelphia, the work is a lush orchestral tone poem with a subtext of personal grief over the untimely death from skin cancer of the composer's younger brother, Andrew Blue Higdon. Despite the circumstances of its composition, there is a transcendent quality to this work. Higdon explains that she was contemplating the remarkable journey of life. The title refers to her brother's name, but she provides us with rich imagery to assist in understanding her composition.

Jennifer Higdon's *blue cathedral* evokes colorful Impressionist images like *Cathedral of Rouen: full sunlight, blue harmony and gold* (1894), by **Claude Monet** (1840–1926).

> Blue . . . like the sky. Where all possibilities soar. Cathedrals . . . a place of thought, growth, spiritual expression . . . serving as a symbolic doorway into and out of this world. I found myself imagining a journey through a glass cathedral in the sky. . . . The listener would float down the aisle, moving slowly at first and then progressing at a quicker pace, rising towards an immense ceiling which would open to the sky. . . . I wanted to create the sensation of contemplation and quiet peace at the beginning, moving toward the feeling of celebration and ecstatic expansion of the soul, all the while singing along with that heavenly music.

The tone poem opens to shimmering bell-like timbres (known as **tintinnabulation**; see p. 421) sounded over softly muted strings (see Listening Guide 59). An intimate dialogue ensues between an ethereal solo flute (the composer's instrument) and solo clarinet (her brother's instrument).

**LISTENING GUIDE 59**                      ⊚ | DVD | **CD 8 (59–61)** | CD 4 (82–84)

# Higdon: *blue cathedral*, excerpt                          6:18

**DATE:**  2000

**GENRE:**  Orchestral tone poem

## WHAT TO LISTEN FOR:

| | | | |
|---|---|---|---|
| Melody | Languorous, lyrical lines; ascending ideas | Expression | Transcendent mood, with several climaxes |
| Rhythm/ Meter | Mostly in 5/4 with veiled sense of barlines; some shifting meters | Timbre | Juxtaposes instrument families: features metallic percussion, solo woodwinds, dark instruments, brass chorales |
| Harmony | Prominent use of major triads but with no strong sense of key center | Performing Forces | Large orchestra with many percussion instruments (crotales, celesta, marimba, vibraphone, bell tree, chimes, triangle, tuned glasses, Chinese reflex balls) |
| Texture | Homophonic with focus on individual lines and duets | | |
| Form | Sectional, with rondo-like structure | | |

### A section

82  0:00   Gentle bell-like tintinnabulation, then muted lower strings, with 2-note descending motive.

0:47   Solo flute with rising line, accompanied by muted string chords; no sense of pulse.

1:14   Solo clarinet answers, with harp and string accompaniment.

1:30   Duet between flute and clarinet in overlapping high-range lines:

2:18   Violin solo joins with ascending lines; builds to large *crescendo* into next section.

### B section

83  3:07   Wavering horn chords alternating with open high strings; more rhythmic and syncopated:

Builds to loud climax as strings ascend, punctuated by brass.

4:12   *Fortissimo* climax, then fades quickly.

4:23   **A section** returns briefly; falling motive in strings.

*Continued on following page*

**C section**

84    4:50    Sustained pitch and rhythmic percussion chords introduce solo instruments;
plaintive English horn accompanied by harmonics on harp and percussion in open fifths:

Other solo instruments enter one at a time (viola, piccolo, cello, oboe, bassoon) over now-syncopated
accompaniment; crotales (antique cymbals) add bell-like timbre.

6:13    Builds to gentle climax, with syncopated chords continuing; our recording fades out.

ⓢ **Now try the Listening Quiz.**

A solo violin leads the way for other instruments to take part. Throughout, there
is a sense of continual expansion and ascent as the work builds toward several stirring climaxes. The open string sonority is very "American," while plaintive solos
are heard from darker instruments, like the English horn, viola, and cello. Higdon
notes she is "hyper-aware of color." The work garners energy from percussion,
and the horns sound a chorale that builds to a full orchestral declamation, after
which the contemplative opening idea returns briefly. Near the end, more soothing colors appear, including pitched crystal glasses (a finger is run around the rims)
and the "chiming" of some fifty Chinese reflex balls, played by most of the orchestra's musicians. This imaginative tone poem exudes an appealing lyricism, a transparent orchestration, and an inspired, uplifting quality that draws the listener into
her personal narrative.

# John Corigliano and the Contemporary Song Cycle

"I always conceive a piece as a different set of challenges."

One of the most lauded composers of our day, John Corigliano writes highly
imaginative scores that are rooted in the language of the past but at the same time
redefine traditional orchestral genres like the symphony and the concerto. His
music is widely performed by the premier ensembles and artists of our time.

## Corigliano's *Mr. Tambourine Man*

John Corigliano was commissioned by singer Sylvia McNair to write a song cycle
for her recital at New York's Carnegie Hall. Her only stipulation was that the text
be by an American writer. Corigliano wanted a poet who spoke universally across
generations: he decided to investigate the works of songwriter Bob Dylan. He

## John Corigliano (b. 1938)

**Corigliano** was born into a musical family: his father was the concertmaster of the New York Philharmonic and his mother was an accomplished pianist. After his studies at Columbia University and the Manhattan School of Music, he worked as a producer for the famous Leonard Bernstein *Young People's Concert Series*. A New Yorker all his life, he has held university teaching positions at the Manhattan School, The Juilliard School of Music, and at Lehman College of the City University of New York. Corigliano has won every distinguished award possible for his music, including an Academy Award for the film score to *The Red Violin* (1999); and a Grammy Award for his song cycle *Mr. Tambourine Man*, which we will consider.

Like Higdon's works, his early ones owe much to the "American" sound of Aaron Copland. But throughout his career he has drawn on diverse styles, including atonality, serialism, microtonality, and even aleatoric music. He has written concertos for luminary performers such as violinist Joshua Bell (*The Red Violin*), flutist James Galway (*Pied Piper Fantasy*, see p. 47), and percussionist Evelyn Glennie (*Conjurer,* see p. 51). His stage works include *The Naked Carmen* (1970), an eclectic rock opera fashioned after Bizet, and *The Ghosts of Versailles*, which, using contemporary serial language, looks back to Mozart's operas and presents various ghosts in the French royal palace at Versailles (see p. 106).

**Major works:** Orchestral music, including *Pied Piper Fantasy* (for flute and orchestra, 1981 • Concertos, including Concerto for Violin and Orchestra: *The Red Violin* (2005) • Choral music, including *A Dylan Thomas Trilogy* (a choral symphony, 1960–76) • Vocal music, including *Mr. Tambourine Man: Seven Poems of Bob Dylan* (2000) • Wind ensemble music • Stage works, including *The Naked Carmen* (1970) and *The Ghosts of Versailles* ( (1987) • Film music, including *The Red Violin* (1997) • Chamber music.

found Dylan's poems beautiful, immediate, and imminently suitable to his musical style. But he had no intention of using any of Dylan's familiar melodies, nor did he wish to suggest a popular or rock style; he wrote "I wanted to take poetry I knew to be strongly associated with popular art and readdress it in terms of concert art." He first wrote the song cycle for voice and piano, but then orchestrated it to add color and dimension.

Corigliano selected seven poems for the song cycle, which begins with a *Prelude: Mr. Tambourine Man* that Corigliano describes as "fantastic and exuberant." This is followed by five more reflective songs that take the listener on an emotional journey, starting with innocence (in *Clothes Line*), then developing an awareness of the world (in *Blowin' in the Wind)*, followed by political fury (*Masters of War*) and a premonition of an apocalypse (*All Along the Watchtower*), culminating in a victory of ideas (*Chimes of Freedom.*). The cycle closes with a Postlude set to *Forever Young*, which Corigliano calls a "folksong benediction." The songs are unified by recurring motives; each song introduces a short idea in the accompaniment that is picked up as important melodic material in the next song.

We will hear the *Prelude* to the song cycle, a quirky and wonderfully effervescent setting of *Mr. Tambourine Man*. After the dreamy opening that presents the first verse, the line moves along athletically, with disjunct, angular lines, asymmetrical phrasing, and a Broadway-style delivery of the text. Only the words and the prominent tambourine connect this dramatic setting to the Dylan original. The same mysterious mood returns to close off the song, and swirling instrumental lines produce effective word-painting (see Listening Guide 60).

**Milton Glaser** (b. 1929) paid homage to songwriter Bob Dylan in this famous 1967 silhouette featuring psychedelic hair.

# Corigliano: *Prelude,* from *Mr. Tambourine Man: Seven Poems of Bob Dylan:*

4:22

**DATE:** 2000 (voice and piano); orchestrated 2003

**GENRE:** Song cycle

**MOVEMENTS:** ***Prelude: Mr. Tambourine Man***      *All Along the Watchtower*
*Clothes Line*                                *Chimes of Freedom*
*Blowin' in the Wind*                   *Postlude: Forever Young*
*Masters of War*

## WHAT TO LISTEN FOR:

| | | | |
|---|---|---|---|
| **Melody** | Speechlike delivery; very disjunct with asymmetrical phrases; jazzy, "natural" vocal style with slides between pitches | **Form** | Modified verse-chorus structure, with introduction and coda |
| **Rhythm/Meter** | Alternates slow, free, and quick rhythmic sections with syncopation, shifting meters, and accents; jazzy feel | **Expression** | Dreamy, mysterious mood at opening and closing; quirky and frenetic; increasing dynamic level; various special effects; word painting (tambourine) |
| **Harmony** | Chromatic and spicily dissonant | **Performing Forces** | Orchestra, including harp, piano, alto and baritone saxophones, and tambourine |
| **Texture** | Largely homophonic | **Text** | Poems by Bob Dylan (1964) in verse/chorus form |

| | | | |
|---|---|---|---|
| **85** | 0:00 | Instrumental introduction. | Undulating winds with sustained strings punctuated by harp. |
| | | **Verse 1** | |
| | 0:15 | Though I know that evenin's empire has returned into sand, Vanished from my hand, Left me blindly here to stand but still not sleeping. | Sung freely, like recitation; rushing upward. Slower, leading to long note. Recitation-like. |
| | 0:42 | My weariness amazes me, I'm branded on my feet, I have no one to meet And the ancient empty street's too dead for dreaming. | Long vocal slide upwards; sustained chords. Slows, with repeated text ("dreaming"); low chords, then undulating accompaniment. |

Opening speechlike vocal line:

Though I know that eve-nin's em-pire    has re-turned__ in-to sand,__

| | | | |
|---|---|---|---|
| **86** | 1:27 | Instrumental introduction. | Quick and rhythmic; high woodwinds with tambourine; dissonant. |
| | | **Chorus** | |
| | 1:43 | Hey! Mr. Tambourine Man, play a song for me, I'm not sleepy and there is no place I'm going to. Hey! Mr. Tambourine Man, play a song for me, In the jingle jangle morning I'll come followin' you. | Fast and highly syncopated; disjunct, wide-ranging line; tambourine is prominent. Momentum grows. |

Opening of chorus; disjunct, syncopated, with shifting meters:

Hey!  Mis - ter  Tam-bou-rine Man,  play  a song for⎯⎯⎯ me,⎯⎯

### Verse 2

**87**    1:58    Take me on a trip upon your magic swirlin' ship,
My senses have been stripped, my hands can't feel to grip,
My toes too numb to step, wait only for my boot heels
To be wanderin'.
I'm ready to go anywhere, I'm ready . . . to fade
Into my own parade, cast your dancing spell my way,
I promise to go under it.

Louder, with rising instrument lines; wide leaps in vocal line; prominent brass and percussion.

Energetic and *fortissimo*.

Syncopated figure moves into chorus.

Excited melodic line for Verse 1, with swirling accompaniment (in piano reduction):

Take    me on    a    trip    up-on your ma - gic    swir - lin ship,

### Chorus

2:20    Hey! Mr. Tambourine Man, play a song for me,
I'm not sleepy and there is no place I'm going to.
Hey! Mr. Tambourine Man, play a song for me,
In the jingle jangle morning I'll come followin' you.

**Chorus** repeated; much syncopation.

### Verse 3

2:37    Though you might hear laughin', spinnin', swingin'
    madly across the sun
It's not aimed at anyone, it's just escapin' on the run . . .
And if you hear vague traces of skippin' reels of rhyme
To your tambourine in time, it's just a ragged clown behind,
I wouldn't pay it any mind, it's just a shadow you're
Seein' that he's chasing.

More dramatic; shrieking vocal quality; hard sonority, vibraphone and piano; instruments with running passages.
Softer, high woodwinds and tambourine.
Tambourine rolls.

### Verse 4 (partial)

**88**    2:58    . . . Yes, to dance beneath the diamond sky with one hand
    waving free,
Silhouetted by the sea, circles by the circus sands,
With all the memory and fate driven deep beneath
    the waves,
Let me forget about today until tomorrow.

Loud and dramatic again, with running instrumental lines; voice has wide leaps.

Suddenly quieter and slower.
Undulating woodwinds, like opening; repeated text ("until tomorrow").

3:52    Instrumental interlude.

Brief instrumental passage, quick and syncopated.

4:03    . . . I'm not sleepy and there is no place I'm going to . . .

Vocal line slow and free over rhythmic accompaniment; dies out with woodblock beats.

ⓒ **Now try the Listening Quiz.**

# Minimalism and Post-Minimalism

The other major compositional trend today is **minimalism**, a style that strips compositions down to bare essentials, focusing on a few basic details. The urge toward

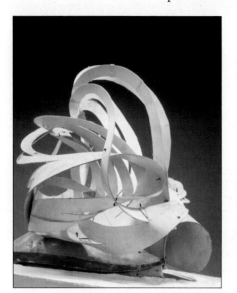

a minimalist art first found expression in painting and sculpture and, since the 1970s, has been a significant force in music. The salient feature of minimalism is the repetition of melodic, rhythmic, and harmonic patterns with very little variation. The music changes so slowly that it can have a hypnotic effect, and indeed the term "trance music" has attached itself to some of these works.

By simplifying melody, rhythm, and harmony within an unwavering tonality, the minimalists have turned away from the complex, highly intellectual style of Schoenberg and Berg. Instead, they open themselves to new modes of thought: the contemplative art of India, the quasi-obsessive rhythms of some African cultures, as well as jazz, pop, and rock.

There are several kinds of minimalist music. In some works, the pulse is repeated with numbing regularity. Others are very busy on the surface, though the harmonies and timbres change very slowly. Terry Riley (b. 1935) introduced the concept of tiny motivic cells that repeat to a hypnotic pulse in his ninety-minute masterwork *In C* (1964).

**Frank Stella**'s (b. 1939) minimalist sculpture *The Chapel of the Holy Ghost* radiates a mystical spiritualism.

Two widely known minimalists are Steve Reich (b. 1936), whose music achieves a trancelike quality that derives from his study of non-Western—especially African—music, and Philip Glass (b. 1937) whose style draws on the musical traditions of India and Africa as well as the techniques of rock and progressive jazz. In this chapter, we will consider the music of John Adams, who infuses the minimalist style with traits of Neoromanticism, thereby forging a **post-minimalist** style, illustrated in his recent opera, *Doctor Atomic*.

A European branch of minimalism involves a nonpulsed music inspired by religious beliefs and expressed in deceptively simple—and seemingly endless—chains of lush modal or tonal progressions. Representatives of this deeply meditative music, often referred to as **spiritual**, or **holy, minimalism**, include the Polish composer Henryk Górecki (b. 1933); and John Tavener (b. 1944). Tavener's powerful choral work *Song for Athene* was heard by millions at the close of the funeral service for Princess Diana on September 6, 1997; its text, "Alleluia. May flights of angels sing thee to thy rest," is drawn from Shakespeare's *Hamlet* and from the Orthodox Vigil Service. We will consider a sacred choral work by the most noted advocate of spiritual minimalism, the Estonian composer Arvo Pärt.

# Arvo Pärt and Spiritual Minimalism

"Arvo Pärt's music accepts silence and death, and thus reaffirms the basic truth of life, its frailty compassionately realised, its sacred beauty observed and celebrated."

—*Paul Hillier*

The music of Arvo Pärt (b. 1935) combines the fervent mysticism of Russian Orthodox rituals with elements of Eastern European folk music and reminiscences of Gregorian chant. His musical voice is unique among contemporary composers, evoking transcendence to another world.

## Arvo Pärt (b. 1935)

**Pärt** was born and raised in Estonia, formerly a republic of the Soviet Union (USSR). As a youth, Pärt studied piano, but his first acquaintance with orchestral music was as a teenager, when he met his friends in the town square and listened to music piped over loudspeakers. He served as a snare drummer in an army band, after which he studied music at the Tallinn Conservatory.

In his early compositions, Pärt explored both Neoclassical and serial techniques. An interest in the music of J. S. Bach led him to use a tone row that incorporated the B-A-C-H motive (which, in German, translates as the pitches of B flat, A, C, B natural). In *Collage sur B-A-C-H* (1964), Pärt transcribes a Bach dance and then distorts it nearly beyond recognition, and his *Credo* (1968), for piano, chorus and orchestra, distorts a quote from the C-major Prelude of Bach's *Well-Tempered Clavier* (Book 1).

There have been several notable periods of compositional silence from Pärt; in the early 1970s, he studied medieval and Renaissance music, while at the same time working with an Estonian early music ensemble. When he returned to composition in 1976, there was a new-found spiritualism at the root of his music. He shunned serialism in favor of a style all his own—**tintinnabulation** (after the Latin word for ringing of bells). Three works from 1977 catapulted Pärt, and his tintinnabular sound, to international fame: *Fratres,* a chamber work that explores the interval of open fifths; *Cantus in memoriam Benjamin Britten,* for string orchestra and bells; and *Tabula Rasa,* a kind of Baroque concerto for two violins.

In 1980 he and his family left the Soviet Union, eventually settling in what was then West Berlin. Since 1980, Pärt has focused his creative efforts on Latin and Orthodox choral music, including a *Te Deum* that evokes—but does not use—Gregorian chant; a Magnificat; and *Kanon Pokajanen* (on Russian Orthodox texts).

**Major Works:** Orchestral music, including 4 symphonies and *Cantus in memoriam Benjamin Britten* (1977) • Concertos, including *Tabula rasa* (for 2 violins, string orchestra, and prepared piano, 1977) and *Frates* (violin, string orchestra, and percussion, 1992) • Chamber works, including *Collage für B-A-C-H* (1964) • Sacred choral music, including *Cantate Domino* (for chorus and organ, 1977, revised 1996), Seven Magnificat Anthems (1988), and *Berlin Mass* (1992).

### In His Own Words

Tintinnabulation is an area I sometimes wander into when I am searching for answers—in my life, my music, my work. . . . Here I am alone with silence. I have discovered that it is enough when a single note is beautifully played. This one note, or a silent beat, or a moment of silence, comforts me. I work with very few elements—with one voice, with two voices.

## Pärt's *Cantate Domino*

Pärt's choral work on the psalm *Cantate Domino canticum novum* (O sing to the Lord a new song), is a captivating example of his tintinnabular style that evokes the ringing of bells with voices (see Listening Guide 61). Here, the composer returns to the simplicity of medieval chant with conjunct lines that move freely, following the Latin text. At the same time, the work seems to dance along lightly, interrupted by brief moments of silence. Pärt does not use traditional notation; instead, he provides only black note-heads to indicate pitch, adding dashes to lengthen a note at the end of a phrase. This notation is very similar to notating Gregorian chant today; you can see an example in Listening Guide 2, on page 79.

Each section of Pärt's work begins with a fluid, monophonic line to which is joined a second line, or countermelody, and then expands to four-part choir, still in strict homorhythmic movement. The full choir (SATB) proclaims "his glory among all the nations," and, near the end, announces that "all the trees of the wood sing for joy." The tintinnabular, or bell-like, style is achieved by weaving together two melodic lines that hover around a central pitch (B flat) and by triadic pitches in the organ that seem to ring throughout. Pärt's serenely religious music rejects the sounds of modernity, returning to a purity and simplicity that reopens communication with the listener.

# Pärt: *Cantate Domino canticum novum* (*O sing to the Lord a new song*)   2:50

**DATE:**   1977 (rev. 1996)

**GENRE:**   Psalm motet

## WHAT TO LISTEN FOR:

| | | | |
|---|---|---|---|
| Melody | Chantlike, wavy lines, in repeated patterns; contrary motion between voices | Expression | Evocative of Gregorian chant and of ringing bells |
| Rhythm/ Meter | Fluid, nonmetric movement | Timbre | Tintinnabular, or bell-like, style in voices and organ |
| Harmony | Occasional dissonances (intervals of 2nds) | Performing Forces | SATB chorus and organ |
| Texture | Changing from 1 voice part (monophonic), to 2, to 4 (homophonic) | Text | Psalm 96 |
| Form | 3 sections, each beginning with a monophonic line | | |

| | | TEXT | TRANSLATION | VOICES (WITH ORGAN) |
|---|---|---|---|---|
| 89 | 0:00 | Cantate Domino canticum novum: Cantate Domino omnis terra. | O sing to the Lord a new song: Sing to the Lord, all the earth. | Sopranos |
| | | Cantate Domino, et benedicite nomini ejus: | Sing to the Lord, bless his name; | Sopranos and Altos |
| | | Annuntiate de die in diem salutare ejus. Annuntiate inter gentes gloriam ejus, In omnibus populis mirabilia ejus. | Tell of his salvation from day to day. Declare his glory among the nations. His marvelous works among all the peoples. | SATB |
| 90 | 0:35 | Quoniam magnus Dominus, et laudabilis nimis: Terribilis est super omnes deos. | For great is the Lord, and greatly to be praised. He is to be feared above all gods. | Tenors |
| | | Quoniam omnes dii gentium daemonia: Dominus autem coelos fecit. Confessio et pulchritudo in conspectu ejus: | For all the gods of the people are idols; But the Lord made the heavens. Honor and majesty are before him; | Tenors and Basses |
| | | Sanctimonia et magnifcentia in sanctificatione ejus. | Strength and beauty are his salvation. | |
| 91 | 1:09 | Afferte Domino patriae gentium, | Ascribe to the Lord, o families of the peoples. | Sopranos |
| | | Afferte Domino gloriam et honorem: Afferte Domino gloriam nomini ejus. | Ascribe to the Lord glory and strength; Ascribe to the Lord the glory due his name. | |
| | | Tollite hostias, et introite in atria ejus: | Bring an offering, and come into his courts. | Sopranos and Altos |
| | | Adorate Dominum in atria sancto ejus. Commoveatur a facie ejus universa terra: | Worship the Lord in holy array. Tremble before him, all the earth; | SATB |
| | | Dicite in gentibus quia Dominus regnavit. | Say among the nations, "The Lord reigns. | |

| | | | | |
|---|---|---|---|---|
| **92** | 1:52 | Etenim corexit orbem terrae qui non commovebitur: | Yea, the world is established, it shall never be moved. | Tenors |
| | | Judicabit populus in aequitate. | He will judge the peoples with equity." | |
| | | Laetentur caeli, et exsultet terra: | Let the heavens be glad, and let the earth rejoice; | Tenors and Basses |
| | | Commoveatur mare, et plenitudo eius: | Let the sea roar, and all that fills it; | |
| | | Gaudebunt campi, et omnia quae in eis sunt. | Let the field exult, and every thing in it. | |
| | | Tunc exsultabunt omnia ligna silvarium | Then shall all the trees of the wood sing for joy | SATB |
| | | A facie Domini, quia venit: | Before the Lord, for he comes; | |
| | | Quoniam venit iudicare terram. | For he comes to judge the earth. | |
| | | Judicabit orbem terrae in aequitate, | He will judge the world with righteousness, | |
| | | Et populos in veritate sua. | And the peoples with his truth. | |

Duet between sopranos and altos, moving in contrary motion, showing free rhythmic notation (arrows mark stressed dissonances of intervals of a 2nd):

◉ **Now try the Listening Quiz.**

# John Adams and Post-Minimalism

"Whenever serious art loses track of its roots in the vernacular, then it begins to atrophy."

A composer who would respond to the emotional impulses of the Neoromantics by seeking to expand the expressive gamut of minimalist music was bound to appear. John Adams, the best known minimalist composer, answered this call.

## The Opera *Doctor Atomic*

For his third opera, John Adams chose as his subject the awe-inspiring creation of the atomic bomb by a team of scientists, headed up by physicist J. Robert Oppenheimer, working at the Los Alamos Laboratory in New Mexico. Peter Sellars's fascinating libretto draws on the memoirs of the project's scientists, some declassified government documents, as well as the poetry of John Donne, Baudelaire, and the sacred Hindu scripture *Bhagavad Gita* (Song of God), the last three all literary texts well known to Oppenheimer. Adams's rich and dark score is as complex texturally as are his very human and well-developed characters.

The opera focuses on the last days and hours before the first test on June 16, 1945. In Act I, chorus members sing of their hopes and fears about the invention—a twenty-one kiloton atomic weapon. We learn here from Oppenheimer that Japan is on the list of projected targets for the first bomb. A touching love duet intervenes between the lead scientist and his wife, Kitty. Meanwhile, at the test site, military commander General Leslie Groves presses to carry out the test as scheduled, despite concerns that poor weather might spread dangerous radiation. At the end of Act I,

Gerald Finley as physicist J. Robert Oppenheimer in the San Francisco Opera production of *Doctor Atomic*.

# Murder, Monsters, and Mayhem in Modern Opera

A scene from the 2008 opera *The Fly,* by Canadian composer Howard Shore, during a dress rehearsal in Paris.

Today's opera composers have set stories to music that at first seem unlikely choices for musical dramas. We have noted that all of John Adams's operas are based on actual historical events: *Nixon in China* documents the first visit by a U.S. president to the People's Republic of China in 1972, where he met Chairman Mao Zedong; *The Death of Klinghoffer* recounts the hijacking of a luxury liner by the Palestinian Liberation Front and the murder of a Jewish-American passenger, stressing a violent theme that continues today between Israelis and Palestinians; and *Doctor Atomic*, which we will see, focuses on the tormented atomic scientist J. Robert Oppenheimer and his creation. Who would have thought these significant moments in history could make such compelling sung drama?

Classic novels have always served up good stories for opera; this is no different today. In 1990, Libby Larsen set Mary Shelley's landmark horror novel *Frankenstein*, focusing on the monster's view of the events; and composer Jake Heggie presents Herman Melville's beloved novel *Moby-Dick*, through music, in a new 2010 production. You might ask how one can cram a 700-page book into a three-hour opera, and what about all the boats, not to mention the whale?

Shorter literary works have also provided inspiration to composers and librettists, who can extend and develop a story through music. One example is the gruesome short story of "The Fly" by George Langelaan, about a mad scientist who tries out his matter-transmitting machine and transforms himself into a fly by mistake (see illustration). This is the basis for a 2008 opera by Canadian film composer Howard Shore. (He also wrote the music for the 1986 film *The Fly.*)

The fascination many have for the supernatural inspired John Corigliano's opera *The Ghosts of Versailles* (1980), which is set in the afterlife at the French court of Louis XVI, outside of Paris. Marie Antoinette is quite upset about having been beheaded, and the ghost of the librettist Beaumarchais tries to cheer her up. The title of this opera draws on an "actual" supernatural event from 1901, when two women professors visiting Versailles got off the beaten tourist path near the Petit Trianon on the castle grounds and reportedly "time-slipped" back to the eighteenth century, where they saw Marie Antoinette and others from this era. Both women wrote accounts of the event and published their story anonymously—some made fun of the tale, but others, like J. R. R. Tolkien, were fascinated by it. All these contemporary operas demonstrate that almost any good story—no matter how macabre, hideous, or just plain weird—can be made into a successful dramatic musical work that can capture the imaginations of the young and old alike.

**Video**

Oppenheimer, struggling with his conscience, looks upon his creation with trepidation and sings the stunning aria "Batter my heart," set to a sonnet by the English metaphysical poet John Donne (1572–1631). The powerful yet elegiac aria takes us to the depths of Oppenheimer's soul as he looks with awe at his creation.

In Act II, we learn that the test will go on while scientists worry about fallout: no one really knows what to expect, but one team member speculates that the atmosphere itself might catch on fire. Tension mounts as the chorus sings "At the sight of this," a dramatic text from the *Bhagavad Gita* describing the moment when Krishna, an avatar (or incarnation) of Vishnu, reveals himself as the Supreme God, the all-powerful creator and destroyer of the world (see Listening Guide 62 and illustration, p. 426). Adams's spine-chilling chorus aptly conveys the apprehension and terror of those about to witness the historic blast. The fearsome text is declaimed on repeated notes in short phrases, punctuated with offbeat brass and percussion accents. An unsettling refrain ("O master") recurs with even shorter, more dissonant tones. The phrase "When I see you Vishnu" presents

## John Adams (b. 1947)

**Adams** was educated at Harvard University and thus was steeped in serialism. In his dorm room, he preferred to listen to rock: "I was much inspired by certain albums that appeared to me to have a fabulous unity to them, like . . . *Abbey Road* and *Dark Side of the Moon*." In 1971, he drove his VW Beetle cross-country to San Francisco, where he began teaching at the San Francisco Conservatory of Music in 1972. Adams quickly became an advocate for contemporary music in the Bay Area.

Strongly influenced by Steve Reich, Adams's music is marked by warm sonorities, a high energy level, and a more personal approach. He first gained notice with two hypnotic, minimalist works—*Phrygian Gates* (for piano, 1977) and *Shaker Loops* (for string septet, 1978)—and earned a national reputation with *Harmonium* (1980–81) and *Harmonielehre* (1984–85), both written for the San Francisco Symphony. In both *Harmonielehre* and Chamber Symphony (1992) he paid homage to Arnold Schoenberg.

Adams attracted much attention with his opera *Nixon in China* (1987), on the historic visit of former President Nixon in November 1972. The works that followed show Adams increasingly aware of the sumptuous orchestration and expressive harmonies of Neoromanticism, including his next opera, *The Death of Klinghoffer* (1991), based on the 1985 hijacking of the cruise liner *Achille Lauro* by Palestinian terrorists. In 2000, he wrote *El Niño*, a Nativity oratorio modeled on Handel's *Messiah*, with texts drawn from English, Spanish, and Latin sources. Both these recent stage works were collaborations with Peter Sellars.

Adams won a Pulitzer Prize for his composition *On the Transmigration of Souls* (2002), commissioned to mark the first anniversary of the destruction of the World Trade Towers on September 11, 2001 and setting texts based on victim's names. His latest stage work, *Doctor Atomic*, may be his most dramatic work yet.

**Major Works:** Stage works, including *Nixon in China* (1986), *The Death of Klinghoffer* (1990–91), *El Niño* (2000), and *Doctor Atomic* (2005) • Orchestral works, including *Short Ride in a Fast Machine* (1986), *Tromba lontana* (1986), and *City Noir* (2009) • Chamber music, including *Phrygian Gates* (1977), *Shaker Loops* (1978), and Chamber Symphony (1992) • Vocal works, including *On the Transmigration of Souls* (In Memory of September 11, 2001, for chorus, children's chorus, and orchestra, 2002) • Tape and electronic works

*In His Own Words*

[I am] a very emotional composer, one who experiences music on a very physical level. My music is erotic and Dionysian, and I never try to obscure those feelings when I compose.

---

contrast, with more sustained chords against a flickering and confused accompaniment. At the close, the crowd responds to the immense buildup of tension with mere utterances over distorted electronic sounds. The effect is highly dramatic and thoroughly compelling.

The opera's last scene depicts the moments before the detonation, when a rocket sends out a two-minute warning, and Oppenheimer sings "Lord, these affairs are hard on the heart." The scientist recalls the Hindu text again to describe the explosion: "If the radiance of a thousand suns were to burst at once into the sky, that would be like the splendor of the mighty one."

*Doctor Atomic* has been hailed as John Adams's most masterful work yet. In it, he has taken a hugely complex subject that draws together science and art, and presented it in a multilayered, eclectic score that offers much to the imagination as well as to the ears.

### Critical Thinking

1. What are the qualities that make an artwork Neoromantic or minimalist?
2. How do contemporary composers strive to attract audiences for their new works?
3. What literary sources and historical events have inspired contemporary composers in choosing their opera plots?

## LISTENING GUIDE 62

Video | DVD | CD 8 (70–75) | CD 4 (93–95)

# Adams: *Doctor Atomic*, excerpts

4:05

**DATE:**  2005

**GENRE:**  Opera

**SETTING:**  Los Alamos, NM, 1945

**LIBRETTIST:**  Peter Sellars

**CHARACTERS:**  J. Robert Oppenheimer, a physicist (baritone)
Kitty Oppenheimer, his wife (mezzo-soprano)
General Leslie Groves, U.S. army engineer (bass)
Edward Teller, a physicist (baritone)
Robert R. Wilson, a physicist (tenor)
Jack Hubbard, chief meteorologist (baritone)
Captain James Nolan, an army officer (tenor)
Pasqualita, the Oppenheimer's maid (mezzo-soprano)

Krishna displayed in his universal form as Vishnu, from the Sri Srinivasa Perumal Temple in Singapore.

### Act II, Scene 3, Chorus: "At the sight of this"

**WHAT TO LISTEN FOR:**

| | |
|---|---|
| Melody | Short, choppy phrases with declaimed text, much repetition of ideas |
| Rhythm/ Meter | Syncopated, with many offbeat accents |
| Harmony | Sharply dissonant |
| Form | Verse/refrain structure with repeated sections and text |

| | |
|---|---|
| Expression | Fiery mood; mysterious electronic sounds |
| Timbre | Prominent timpani and brass |
| Performing Forces | Chorus and orchestra |
| Text | *Bhagavad Gita*, chapter 11 |

---

**A section**

| 93 | 0:00 | At the sight of this, your Shape stupendous, Full of mouths and eyes, terrible with fangs, | Loud, fiery mood; offbeat horn accents. Chorus with short phrases, recitative style. |

Opening of *Bhagavad G ita* chorus, with text declaimed together:

**Refrain**

0:27  O O O O O    Regular harsh chords on main beats against syncopated accompaniment.

**A section elongated**

0:41   At the sight of this, your Shape stupendous, Full of mouths and eyes, feet, thighs and bellies, All the worlds are fear-struck, even just as I am.    **A section** repeated with harsh, offbeat, accented dissonances.

**Refrain**

1:06    O O O O Master.                                    Single chords again on main beats.

Choral refrain, invoking Vishnu:

**B section**

**94**   1:19    When I see you, Vishnu, when I see you omnipresent,    Connected chords, descending and chromatic,
         Shouldering the sky, in hues of rainbow,              against syncopated accompaniment.

**Refrain**

1:35    O O O O Master                                      Single chord interjections again; active accompa-
                                                            niment leads back to **A section.**

**A section**

**95**   1:48    At the sight of this, your Shape stupendous,          Repeated choral section; dissonant string chords.
         With your mouth agape and flame-eyes staring—
         All my peace is gone; O, my heart is troubled.

**Refrain**

2:13    O O O O Master.

**B section**

2:26    When I see you, Vishnu, omnipresent, flame-eyes    Connected chords as in last **B section.**
         staring—
         All my peace is gone, is troubled.

**B section**, with sustained chords:

**Coda**

2:43                                                        Disjunct high woodwinds, with agitated,
                                                            accented accompaniment.

3:00    Vocables:  ee ee (women)/Do (men).                 Electronically generated sounds accompany
                                                            vocables.

⊚ **Now try the Listening Quiz.**

## LISTENING ACTIVITY: COMPARING STYLES 8 CONTEMPORARY CHORAL MUSIC

In this last Listening Activity, let's review three choral works that we have studied to see how choral styles and genres have evolved from the early twentieth century until the present. Match each of these powerful works with the trait that best suits it below (StudySpace, Chapter 47).

    **a.** Adams: "At the Sight of This," from *Doctor Atomic*
    **b.** Orff: *O fortuna*, from *Carmina burana*
    **c.** Pärt: *Cantate Domino canticum novum*

**1.** Melody      ___ short, speechlike ideas      ___ wavy, chantlike lines      ___ opening lyrical lines

**2.** Rhythm/Meter      ___ nonmetric      ___ rhythmic, with regular accompaniment      ___ rhythmic, with complex textures for accompaniment

**3.** Form      ___ simple verse-chorus structure      ___ strophic, with 3 verses      ___ structured around changing textures and voices

**4.** Expression      ___ bell-like effect      ___ primitive, dramatic lines      ___ breathless text delivery

**5.** Genre      ___ opera chorus      ___ secular cantata chorus      ___ psalm motet

**6.** Text      ___ biblical      ___ medieval Latin      ___ Hindu

**7.** Arrange these three choruses in the order in which they were written: _____
    _____
    _____

# Coda

"Just listen with the vastness of the world in mind.
You can't fail to get the message."
—*Pierre Boulez*

These pages have included a variety of facts—cultural, historical, biographical, and analytical—that have entered into the making of music and that we must consider if we seek to listen intelligently to music. Like all books, this one belongs to the domain of words, and words have no power over the domain of sound. They are helpful only insofar as they lead us to enjoy the music.

The enjoyment of music depends on perceptive listening, which (like perceptive anything) is achieved gradually, with practice and effort. By studying the circumstances out of which a musical work issued, we prepare ourselves for its multiple meanings; we open ourselves to that exercise of mind and heart, sensibility and imagination, that makes listening to music a unique experience. But in building up our musical perceptions—that is, our listening enjoyment—let us always remember that the ultimate wisdom rests neither in dates nor in facts. It is to be found in one place only: the sounds themselves.

# Appendix I

## Musical Notation

### The Notation of Pitch

Musical notation presents a kind of graph of each sound's duration and pitch. These are indicated by symbols called **notes**, which are written on the **staff**, a series of five parallel lines separated by four spaces:

**Staff**

The positions of the notes on the staff indicate the pitches, each line and space representing a different degree of pitch.

A symbol known as a **clef** is placed at the left end of the staff to determine the relative pitch names. The **treble clef** (&) is used for pitches within the range of the female singing voices, and the **bass clef** (9:) for a lower group of pitches, within the range of the male singing voices.

**Clefs**

Pitches are named after the first seven letters of the alphabet, from A to G. (From one note named A to the next is the interval of an **octave**.) The pitches on the treble staff are named as follows:

**Pitch names**

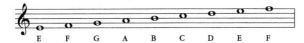

E   F   G   A   B   C   D   E   F

And those on the bass staff:

**Octave**

G   A   B   C   D   E   F   G   A

For pitches above and below these staffs, short extra lines called **ledger lines** can be added:

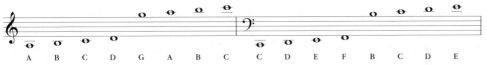

A   B   C   D   G   A   B   C       C   D   E   F   B   C   D   E

Middle C—the C that, on the piano, is situated approximately in the center of the keyboard—comes between the treble and bass staffs. It is represented by either the first ledger line above the bass staff or the first ledger line below the treble staff, as the following example makes clear. This combination of the two staffs is called the **great staff** or **grand staff**:

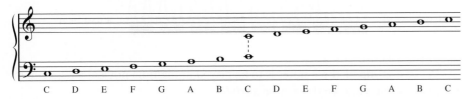

C   D   E   F   G   A   B   C   D   E   F   G   A   B   C

**Accidentals**    Signs known as **accidentals** are used to alter the pitch of a written note. A **sharp** (♯) before the note indicates the pitch a half step above; a **flat** (♭) indicates the pitch a half step below. A **natural** (♮) cancels a sharp or flat. Also used are the **double sharp** (✕) and **double flat** (♭♭), which respectively raise and lower the pitch by two halftones—that is, a whole tone.

In many pieces of music, where certain sharped or flatted notes are used consistently throughout, these sharps or flats are written at the beginning of each line **Key signature**    of music, in the **key signature,** as seen in the following example of piano music. Notice that piano music is written on the great staff, with the right hand usually playing the notes written on the upper staff and the left hand usually playing the notes written on the lower:

Beethoven: *Für Elise*

## The Notation of Rhythm

The duration of each musical tone is indicated by the type of note placed on the **Note values**    staff. In the following table, each note represents a duration, or **value,** half as long as the preceding one:

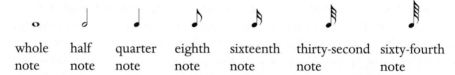

| whole note | half note | quarter note | eighth note | sixteenth note | thirty-second note | sixty-fourth note |

In any particular piece of music, these note values are related to the beat of the music. If the quarter note represents one beat, then a half note lasts for two beats, a whole note for four; two eighth notes last one beat, as do four sixteenths. The following chart makes this clear:

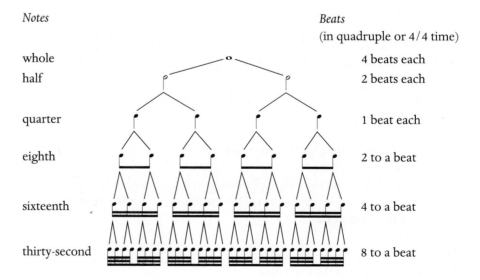

When a group of three notes is to be played in the time normally taken up by **Triplet**    only two of the same kind, we have a **triplet:**

If we combine successive notes of the same pitch, using a curved line known as a *tie*, the second note is not played, and the note values are combined:

**Tie**

beats:   4 + 4 = 8          2 + 4 = 6          $1 + \frac{1}{2} = 1\frac{1}{2}$

A *dot* after a note enlarges its value by half:

**Dot**

beats:   2 + 1 = 3          $1 + \frac{1}{2} = 1\frac{1}{2}$          $\frac{1}{2} + \frac{1}{4} = \frac{3}{4}$

Time never stops in music, even when there is no sound. Silence is indicated by symbols known as *rests*, which correspond in time value to the notes:

**Rests**

| whole rest | half rest | quarter rest | eighth rest | sixteenth rest | thirty-second rest | sixty-fourth rest |
|---|---|---|---|---|---|---|

The metrical organization of a piece of music is indicated by the **time signature**, which specifies the meter: this appears as two numbers written as in a fraction. The upper numeral indicates the number of beats within the measure; the lower one shows which note value equals one beat. Thus, the time signature 3/4 means that there are three beats to a measure, with the quarter note equal to one beat. In 6/8 time, there are six beats in the measure, each eighth note receiving one beat. Following are the most frequently encountered time signatures:

**Time signature**

| duple meter | 2/2 | 2/4 | |
|---|---|---|---|
| triple meter | 3/2 | 3/4 | 3/8 |
| quadruple meter | | 4/4 | |
| sextuple meter | | 6/4 | 6/8 |

The examples below demonstrate how the music notation system works. The notes are separated into measures, shown by a vertical line (called a **bar line**).

Mozart: *Ah! vous dirai-je, maman* (= Twinkle, Twinkle, Little Star *and the* Alphabet Song)

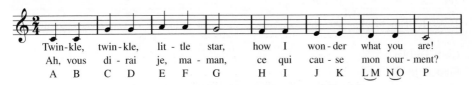

| Twin-kle, | twin-kle, | lit - tle | star, | how I | won-der | what you | are! |
| Ah, vous | di - rai | je, ma - man, | ce qui | cau - se | mon tour - ment? |
| A B | C D | E F | G | H I | J K | LM NO | P |

Clef: Treble
First pitch: C
Key signature: none (key of C major)
Meter: Duple (2/4)
◎ iMusic: This is the original piano version of the tune, composed by Mozart. Notice how turns decorate the familiar melody.

Brahms: *Lullaby (Wiegenlied)*

Clef: Treble

First pitch: A

Key signature: 1 flat (B♭) = 5 key of F major

Meter: Triple (3/4)

Other features: Begins on an upbeat, after two rests

◎ **iMusic:** This is the original vocal version by Brahms, sung in German. You probably know the English lyrics.

*Battle Hymn of the Republic* (Civil War song)

Clef: Treble

First pitch: G

Key signature: none = key of C major

Meter: Quadruple (4/4)

Other features: Many dotted rhythms

◎ **iMusic:** This is a nineteenth-century brass band version of the tune from the Civil War era. They play only the familiar chorus.

*Greensleeves* (English traditional song)

Clef: Treble

First note: E

Key signature: 1 sharp (F♯) = key of E minor

Meter: Sextuple (6/8)

Other features: Pick-up note, dotted rhythms, added accidentals

◎ **iMusic:** This Elizabethan-era song is played here on classical guitar.

# Appendix II

## Glossary

**absolute music** Music that has no literary, dramatic, or pictorial program. Also *pure music*.

**a cappella** Choral music performed without instrumental accompaniment.

**accelerando** Getting faster.

**accent** The emphasis on a *beat* resulting in its being louder or longer than another in a measure.

**accompagnato** Accompanied; also a *recitative* that is accompanied by orchestra.

**accordion** A musical instrument with a small keyboard and free-vibrating metal *reeds* that sound when air is generated by pleated *bellows*.

**acid rock** Genre of American *rock* that emerged in the late 1960s, often associated with psychedelic drugs. Its style featured heavy amplification, instrumental improvisation, new sound technologies, and light shows.

**acoustic guitar** A *guitar* designed for performance without electronic amplification.

**acoustic music** Music produced without electronics, especially amplifiers.

**active chords** In the *diatonic* system, chords which need to resolve to the *tonic chord*. These include the *dominant chord* and the *subdominant chord*.

**adagio** Quite slow.

**additive meter** Patterns of *beats* that subdivide into smaller, irregular groups (e.g., 2 + 3 + 2 + 3 = 10); common in certain Eastern European musics.

**ad libitum** Indication that gives the performer the liberty to omit a section or to improvise.

**aerophone** Instruments such as a *flute*, whistle, or *horn* that produce sound by using air as the primary vibrating means.

**agitato** Agitated or restless.

**Agnus Dei** A section of the *Mass*; the last musical *movement* of the *Ordinary*.

**aleatoric music** See *aleatory*.

**aleatory** Indeterminate music in which certain elements of performance (such as *pitch*, *rhythm*, or *form*) are left to choice or chance.

**alla breve** See *cut time*.

**allegro** Fast, cheerful.

**Alleluia** An item from the *Proper* of the *Mass* sung just before the reading of the Gospel; *neumatic* in style with a long *melisma* on the last syllable of the word "Alleluia."

**allemande** German dance in moderate duple time, popular during the Renaissance and Baroque periods; often the first *movement* of a Baroque *suite*.

**alternative rock** A broad term denoting any of several subgenres of *rock and roll* that emerged since the late 1980s. These styles, such as *grunge rock* and *indie rock*, often incorporate elements of *punk rock*.

**alto** Lowest of the female voices. Also *contralto*.

**amplitude** See *volume*.

**analog synthesis** Synthesis of waveforms by way of analog circuits.

**andante** Moderately slow or walking pace.

**answer** Second entry of the *subject* in a *fugue*, usually pitched a fourth below or a fifth above the *subject*.

**anthem** A religious choral composition in English; performed liturgically, the Protestant equivalent of the *motet*.

**antiphonal** Performance style in which an ensemble is divided into two or more groups, performing in alternation and then together.

**antique cymbals** Small disks of brass, held by the player (one instrument in each hand), that are struck together gently and allowed to vibrate.

**arabesque** Decorative musical material or a composition based on florid *embellishment*.

**aria** Lyric song for solo voice with orchestral accompaniment, generally expressing intense emotion; found in *opera*, *cantata*, and *oratorio*.

**arioso** Short, *aria*-like passage.

**arpeggio** Broken chord in which the individual tones are sounded one after another instead of simultaneously.

**Ars antiqua** *Polyphonic* musical style, usually French, from the period c. 1160–1320.

**Ars nova** Fourteenth-century French *polyphonic* musical style whose themes moved increasingly from religious to secular.

**art rock** Genre of *rock* that uses larger forms and more complex harmonies than other popular styles; occasionally quotes examples from classical music. Also *progressive rock*.

**a tempo** Return to the previous *tempo*.

**atonality** Total abandonment of *tonality* (centering in a *key*). Atonal music moves from one level of *dissonance* to another, without areas of relaxation.

**attaca** "Attack," proceed without a pause between *movements*.

**augmentation** Statement of a *melody* in longer note values, often twice as slow as the original.

**aulos** *Double-reed* pipe; played for public and religious functions in ancient Greece.

**avant-garde jazz** A free-style *jazz* that developed in the 1960s; John Coltrane was a major proponent.

**backbeat** In *rock and roll* and related *genres*, the second and fourth *beats* of the measure.

**bagpipe** Wind instrument popular in Eastern and Western Europe that has several tubes, one of which plays the melody while the others sound the *drones*, or sustained notes; a windbag is filled by either a mouth pipe or a set of *bellows*. See also *uilleann pipes*.

**balalaika** *Guitar*-like instrument of Russia with a triangular body, fretted neck, and three strings; often used in traditional music and dance.

**ballad** A form of English street song, popular from the sixteenth through the eighteenth centuries. Ballads are characterized by narrative content and *strophic form*.

**ballade** French poetic form and *chanson* type of the Middle Ages and Renaissance with courtly love texts. Also a Romantic genre, especially a lyric piano piece.

**ballad opera** English comic opera, usually featuring spoken dialogue alternating with songs set to popular tunes; also called dialogue opera.

**ballet** A dance form featuring a staged presentation of group or solo dancing with music, costumes, and scenery.

**ballet de cour** Courtly French *ballet* of the sixteenth and seventeenth centuries.

**banjo** Plucked-string instrument with round body in the form of a single-headed drum and a long, fretted neck; brought to the Americas by African slaves.

**bar form** Three-part **A-A-B** form, frequently used in music and poetry, particularly in Germany.

**baritone** Male voice of moderately low range.

**baritone horn** See *euphonium*.

**bas** Medieval category of soft instruments, used principally for indoor occasions, as distinct from *haut*, or loud, instruments.

**bass** Lowest of the male *voices*.

**bass clarinet** Woodwind instrument, with the lowest range, of the *clarinet* family.

**bass drum** *Percussion instrument* played with a large, soft-headed stick; the largest orchestral drum.

**basse danse** Graceful court dance of the early Renaissance; an older version of the *pavane*.

**basso continuo** Italian for "continuous bass." See *figured bass*. Also refers to performance group with a bass, chordal instrument (*harpsichord*, *organ*), and one bass melody instrument (*cello*, *bassoon*).

**bassoon** *Double-reed* woodwind instrument with a low range.

**bass viol** See *double bass*.

**baton** A thin stick, usually painted white, used by *conductors*.

**beat** Regular pulsation; a basic unit of length in musical time.

**bebop** Complex *jazz* style developed in the 1940s. Also *bop*.

**bel canto** "Beautiful singing"; elegant Italian vocal style characterized by florid melodic lines delivered by voices of great agility, smoothness, and purity of tone.

**bell** The wide or bulbed opening at the end of a wind instrument.

**bell tree** Long stick with bells suspended from it, adopted from *Janissary music*.

**bellows** An apparatus for producing air currents in certain wind instruments (*accordion*, *bagpipe*).

**bent pitch** See *blue note*.

**big band** Large *jazz* ensemble popular in 1930s and 1940s, featuring sections of *trumpets*, *trombones*, *saxophones* (and other *woodwinds*), and rhythm instruments (*piano*, *double bass*, drums, and *guitar*).

**big band era** See *swing era*.

**binary form** Two-part (**A-B**) form with each section normally repeated. Also *two-part form*.

**biwa** A Japanese *lute*, similar to the Chinese *pipa*.

**bluegrass** *Country-western* music style characterized by quick *tempos*, improvised instrumental solos, and high-range vocal harmonies.

**blue note** A slight drop of pitch on the third, fifth, or seventh tone of the scale, common in *blues* and *jazz*. Also *bent pitch*.

**blues** African-American form of secular *folk music*, related to *jazz*, that is based on a simple, repetitive poetic-musical structure.

**bodhran** Hand-held frame drum with a single goatskin head; used in Irish traditional music.

**bongo** A pair of small drums of differing pitches; held between the legs and struck with both hands; of Afro-Cuban origin.

**bop** See *bebop*.

**bossa nova** Brazilian dance related to the *samba*, popular in the 1950s and 1960s.

**bourrée** Lively French Baroque dance type in *duple meter*.

**bow** A slightly curved stick with hair or fibers attached at both ends, drawn over the strings of an *instrument* to set them in motion.

**bowed fiddle** Any of a variety of medieval bowed string instruments.

**branle** Quick French group dance of the Renaissance, related to the *ronde*.

**brass instrument** Wind instrument with a cup-shaped mouthpiece, a tube that flares into a bell, and slides or valves to vary the pitch. Most often made of brass or silver.

**brass quintet** Standard chamber ensemble made up of two *trumpets*, horn, trombone, and *tuba*.

**break** *Jazz* term for a short improvised solo without accompaniment that "breaks" an ensemble passage or introduces an extended solo.

**bridge** Transitional passage connecting two sections of a composition; also *transition*. Also the part of a string instrument that holds the strings in place.

**Broadway musical** A work of *musical* theater that is performed in New York City's major theater district (Broadway).

**buffo** In *opera*, a male singer of comic roles, usually a *bass*.

**bugle** *Brass instrument* that evolved from the earlier military, or field, *trumpet*.

**cadence** Resting place in a musical *phrase*; music punctuation.

**cadenza** Virtuosic solo passage in the manner of an improvisation, performed near the end of an *aria* or a *movement* of a *concerto*.

**Cajun music** Eclectic Louisiana traditional style that draws from French *folk music* as well as from music of Southern whites and blacks; *fiddle* is used as a solo instrument, sometimes accompanying itself with a *drone*.

**cakewalk** *Syncopated*, strutting dance of nineteenth-century origin; developed among Southern slaves in a parody of white plantation owners.

**call-and-response** Performance style with a singing leader who is imitated by a *chorus* of followers. Also *responsorial singing*.

**calypso** A style of music and dance developed in Trinidad, but also popular elsewhere in the Carribean. Calypso is strongly associated with *Carnival* celebrations.

**camerata** Literally, Italian for salon; a gathering for literary, artistic, musical, or philosophical discussions, notably the Florentine Camerata at the end of the sixteenth century.

**canon** Type of *polyphonic* composition in which one musical line strictly imitates another at a fixed distance throughout.

**cantabile** Songful, in a singing style.

**cantata** Vocal genre for solo singers, *chorus*, and instrumentalists based on a lyric or dramatic poetic narrative. It generally consists of several *movements*, including *recitatives*, *arias*, and ensemble numbers.

**cantor** Solo singer or singing leader in Jewish and Christian liturgical music.

**cantus firmus** "Fixed melody," usually of very long notes, often based on a fragment of *Gregorian chant* that served as the structural basis for a *polyphonic* composition, particularly in the Renaissance.

**canzona** Late-sixteenth- and early-seventeenth-century instrumental *genre* featuring contrasting sections, with *contrapuntal* versus *homophonic textures* and *changing meters*.

**capriccio** Short lyric piece of a free nature, often for piano.

**Carnival** The festive season just before Lent in the Christian calendar, which has historically been a vibrant time for music-making. Regions known for Carnival music are Venice, Brazil, the Caribbean Islands, and New Orleans.

**carol** English medieval *strophic* song with a *refrain* repeated after each stanza; now associated with Christmas.

**cassation** Classical instrumental genre related to the *serenade* or *divertimento* and often performed outdoors.

**castanets** *Percussion instruments* consisting of small wooden clappers that are struck together. They are widely used to accompany Spanish dancing.

**castrato** Male singer who was castrated during boyhood to preserve the soprano or alto vocal register, prominent in seventeenth- and early-eighteenth-century *opera*.

**celesta** *Percussion instrument* resembling a miniature upright *piano*, with tuned metal plates struck by hammers that are operated by a keyboard.

**cello** See *violoncello*.

**celtic harp** See *Irish harp*.

**chachacha** A Cuban dance developed in the 1950s, it derives its name from the characteristic rhythmic pattern.

**chaconne** Baroque form similar to the *passacaglia*, in which the *variations* are based on a repeated chord progression.

**chamber choir** Small group of up to about twenty-four singers, who usually perform *a cappella* or with piano accompaniment.

**chamber music** Ensemble music for up to about ten players, with one player to a part.

**chamber sonata** See *sonata da camera*.

**chance music** See *aleatory*.

**changing meter** Shifting between *meters*, sometimes frequently, within a single composition or *movement*; also called *shifting meter*.

**chanson** French *monophonic* or *polyphonic* song, especially of the Middle Ages and Renaissance, set to either courtly or popular poetry.

**chart** Colloquial or *jazz* term for a score or arrangement.

**chimes** *Percussion instrument* of definite pitch that consists of a set of tuned metal tubes of various lengths suspended from a frame and struck with a hammer. Also *tubular bells*.

**Chinese block** *Percussion instrument* made from a hollowed rectangular block of wood that is struck with a beater.

**choir** A group of singers who perform together, usually in parts, with several on each part; often associated with a church.

**chorale** Congregational hymn of the German Lutheran church.

**chorale prelude** Short Baroque *organ* piece in which a traditional *chorale* melody is embellished.

**chorale variations** Baroque *organ* piece in which a *chorale* is the basis for a set of *variations*.

**chord** Simultaneous combination of three or more *tones* that constitute a single block of *harmony*.

**chordal** *Texture* comprised of *chords* in which the *pitches* sound simultaneously; also *homorhythmic*.

**chordophone** Instrument that produces sound from a vibrating string stretched between two points; the string may be set in motion by bowing, striking, or plucking.

**chorus** Fairly large group of singers who perform together, usually with several on each part. Also a choral *movement* of a large-scale work. In *jazz*, a single statement of the melodic-harmonic pattern.

**chromatic** *Melody* or *harmony* built from many if not all twelve semitones of the *octave*. A *chromatic scale* consists of an ascending or descending sequence of *semitones*.

**church sonata** See *sonata da chiesa*.

**cimbalom** A type of Hungarian *dulcimer* with strings that are struck. Related to the *zither*.

**clarinet** *Single-reed* woodwind instrument with a wide range of sizes.

**classic country** *Country-western* music style of the 1960s and '70s in which performers remained connected to their southern roots.

**clavecin** French word for *harpsichord*.

**claves** A Cuban clapper consisting of two solid hardwood sticks; widely used in Latin American music.

**clavichord** Stringed *keyboard instrument* popular in the Renaissance and Baroque that is capable of unique expressive devices not possible on the *harpsichord*.

**clavier** Generic word for *keyboard instruments*, including *harpsichord*, *clavichord*, *piano*, and *organ*.

**climax** The high point in a melodic line or piece of music, usually representing the peak of intensity, *range*, and *dynamics*.

**closed ending** Second of two endings in a secular medieval work, usually cadencing on the final.

**coda** The last part of a piece, usually added to a standard form to bring it to a close.

**codetta** In *sonata form*, the concluding section of the *exposition*. Also a brief *coda* concluding an inner section of a work.

**collage** A technique drawn from the visual arts whereby musical fragments from other compositions are juxtaposed or overlapped within a new work.

**collegium musicum** An association of amateur musicians, popular in the Baroque era. Also a modern university ensemble dedicated to the performance of early music.

**col legno** *String instrument* technique in which the strings are hit with the wood of the bow.

**colotomic structure** Cyclic, interlocking rhythmic structure in Javanese gamelan music.

**comic opera** See *opéra comique*.

**commedia dell'arte** Type of improvised drama popular in sixteenth- and seventeenth-century Italy; makes use of stereotyped characters.

**common time** See *quadruple meter*.

**compound meter** *Meter* in which each beat is subdivided into three rather than two.

**computer music** A type of electro-acoustic music in which computers assist in creating works through sound synthesis and manipulation.

**con amore** With love, tenderly.

**concept album** In popular music, an LP or CD that is unified by a theme.

**concertante** Style based on the principle of opposition between two dissimilar masses of sound; *concerto*-like.

**concert band** Instrumental ensemble ranging from forty to eighty members or more, consisting of wind and *percussion* instruments. Also *wind ensemble*.

**concertina** Small, free-reed, *bellows*-operated instrument similar to an *accordion*; hexagonal in shape, with button keys.

**concertino** Solo group of instruments in the Baroque *concerto grosso*.

**concertmaster** The first-chair violinist of a symphony *orchestra*.

**concerto** Instrumental genre in several *movements* for solo instrument (or instrumental group) and *orchestra*.

**concerto form** Structure commonly used in first *movements* of *concertos* that combines elements of Baroque *ritornello* procedure with *sonata-allegro form*. Also *first-movement concerto form*.

**concerto grosso** Baroque *concerto* type based on the opposition between a small group of solo instruments (the *concertino*) and *orchestra* (the *ripieno*).

**concert overture** Single-movement concert piece for *orchestra*, typically from the Romantic period and often based on a literary program.

**conductor** Person who, by means of gestures, leads performances of musical ensembles, especially *orchestra*, bands, or *choruses*.

**con fuoco** With fire.

**conga** Afro-Cuban dance performed at Latin American *Carnival* celebrations. Also a single-headed drum of Afro-Cuban origin, played with bare hands.

**conjunct** Smooth, connected *melody* that moves principally by small *intervals*.

**con passione** With passion.

**consonance** Concordant or harmonious combination of *tones* that provides a sense of relaxation and stability in music.

**continuous bass** See *basso continuo*.

**continuous imitation** Renaissance *polyphonic* style in which the *motives* move from line to line within the *texture*, often overlapping one another.

**contour** The overall shape of a melodic line. It can move upward, downward, or remain static.

**contrabass** See *double bass*.

**contrabassoon** *Double-reed* woodwind instrument with the lowest *range* in the woodwind family. Also *double bassoon*.

**contralto** See *alto*.

**contrapunctus** A composition using imitative *counterpoint*.

**contrapuntal** *Texture* employing *counterpoint*, or two or more melodic lines.

**contrary motion** Motion in opposite directions between individual parts in a *polyphonic* work.

**contrast** Use of opposing musical elements to emphasize difference and variety.

**cool jazz** A substyle of *bebop*, characterized by a restrained, unemotional performance with lush harmonies, moderate volume levels and tempos, and a new lyricism; often associated with Miles Davis.

**cornet** Valved *brass instrument* similar to the *trumpet* but more mellow in sound.

**cornetto** Early instrument of the brass family with woodwind-like finger holes. It developed from the cow horn but was made of wood.

**Council of Trent** A council of the Roman Catholic Church that convened in Trent, Italy, from 1543 to 1565 and dealt with Counter-Reformation issues, including the reform of liturgical music.

**countermelody** An accompanying *melody* sounded against the principal *melody*.

**counterpoint** The art of combining in a single *texture* two or more melodic lines.

**Counter-Reformation** A reform movement within the Roman Catholic Church that began in the mid-sixteenth century, in reaction to the Protestant Reformation.

**countersubject** In a fugue, a secondary theme heard against the *subject*; a countertheme.

**country rock** A hybrid of *country-western* and *rock* music, fusing the themes and sound of *country-western* with the driving rhythms and instrumentation of *rock*.

**country-western** Genre of American popular music derived from traditional music of Appalachia and the rural South, usually vocal with an accompaniment of *banjos*, *fiddles*, and *guitar*.

**courante** French Baroque dance, a standard *movement* of the *suite*, in *triple meter* at a moderate *tempo*.

**courtesan** An educated, refined woman who entertained men intellectually and sexually.

**cover** Recording that remakes an earlier, often successful, recording with the goal of reaching a wider audience.

**cowbell** Rectangular metal bell that is struck with a drumstick; used widely in Latin American music.

**Credo** A section of the *Mass*; the third musical *movement* of the *Ordinary*.

**crescendo** Growing louder.

**crossover** Recording or artist that appeals primarily to one audience but becomes popular with another as well (e.g., a *rock* performer who makes *jazz* recordings).

**crotales** A pair of small pitched cymbals mounted on a frame; also made in *chromatic* sets.

**crumhorn** Early *woodwind instrument*, whose sound is produced by blowing into a capped *double reed* and whose lower body is curved.

**Cubism** Early-twentieth-century art movement begun in Paris, characterized by fragmentation of forms into abstract or geometric patterns.

**cut time** A type of *duple meter* interpreted as 2/2 and indicated as c | ; also called *alla breve*.

**cyclical form** Structure in which musical material, such as a *theme*, presented in one *movement* returns in a later *movement*.

**cymbals** *Percussion instruments* consisting of two large circular brass plates of equal size that are struck sidewise against each other.

**da capo** An indication to return to the beginning of a piece.

**da capo aria** Lyric song in *ternary*, or **A-B-A**, form, commonly found in *operas, cantatas*, and *oratorios*.

**dastgāh** The modal structure in Persian music. The dastgāh comprises not only a *diatonic* scale, but also melodic *motives* and an ascribed character.

**decibel** A unit of measurement of *amplitude* or *volume*.

**decrescendo** Growing softer.

**development** Structural reshaping of thematic material. Second section of *sonata-allegro form*; it moves through a series of foreign *keys* while *themes* from the *exposition* are manipulated.

**dialogue opera** See *ballad opera*.

**diatonic** *Melody* or *harmony* built from the seven tones of a *major* or *minor scale*. A diatonic scale encompasses patterns of seven *whole tones* and *semitones*.

**Dies irae** Chant from the *Requiem Mass* whose text concerns Judgment Day.

**digital frequency modulation synthesis (FM)** A form of audio synthesis whereby the *frequency* of the waveform is modulated, creating a more complex waveform and a different *timbre*.

**digital technology** A recording process in which sound waves are converted to and stored as numbers, as opposed to *analog synthesis*.

**diminuendo** Growing softer.

**diminution** Statement of a melody in shorter note values, often twice as fast as the original.

**disco** Commercial dance music popular in the 1970s, characterized by strong percussion in a *quadruple meter*.

**disjunct** Disjointed or disconnected melody with many leaps.

**dissonance** Combination of tones that sounds discordant and unstable, in need of resolution.

**divertimento** Classical instrumental genre for chamber ensemble or soloist, often performed as light entertainment. Related to *serenade* and *cassation*.

**divertissement** Grand entertainment of the French Baroque, characterized by spectacle and grandeur, intended for light entertainment or diversion.

**Divine Offices** Cycle of daily services of the Roman Catholic Church, distinct from the *Mass*.

**dizi** Traditional Chinese *flute* made of bamboo.

**doctrine of the affections** Baroque doctrine of the union of text and music.

**dodecaphonic** Greek for "twelve-tone"; see *twelve-tone music*.

**dolce** Sweetly.

**dolente** Sad, weeping.

**dominant** The fifth scale step, *sol*.

**dominant chord** *Chord* built on the fifth scale step, the V chord.

**double** To perform the same *notes* with more than one *voice* or *instrument*, either at the same *pitch* level or an *octave* higher or lower.

**double bass** Largest and lowest-pitched member of the bowed string family. Also called *contrabass* or *bass viol*.

**double bassoon** See *contrabassoon*.

**double exposition** In the *concerto*, twofold statement of the themes, once by the *orchestra* and once by the soloist.

**double reed** A *reed* consisting of two pieces of cane that vibrate against each other.

**double-stop** Playing two notes simultaneously on a string instrument.

**doubles** *Variations* of a dance in a French keyboard suite.

**downbeat** First *beat* of the *measure*, the strongest in any *meter*.

**drone** Sustained sounding of one or several tones for harmonic support, a common feature of some *folk musics*.

**drum chimes** A set of drums tuned to a musical scale, common in Africa and South and Southeast Asia.

**dulcimer** Early folk instrument that resembles the *psaltery*; its strings are struck with hammers instead of being plucked.

**duo** An ensemble of two players.

**duo sonata** A chamber group comprised of a soloist with piano. Also, in the Baroque period, a *sonata* for a melody instrument and *basso continuo*.

**duple meter** Basic metrical pattern of two *beats* to a *measure*.

**duplum** Second voice of a *polyphonic* work, especially the medieval *motet*.

**duration** Length of time something lasts; e.g., the vibration of a musical sound.

**dynamics** Element of musical expression relating to the degree of loudness or softness, or volume, of a sound.

**electric guitar** A *guitar* designed for electronic amplification.

**electronic music** Generic term for any composition created by electronic means; see also *musique concrète, analog sythesis, synthesizer, MIDI*, and *hyperinstrument*.

**electronische Musik** Electronic music developed in Germany in the 1950s that uses an oscillator to generate and alter waveforms.

**embellishment** Melodic decoration, either improvised or indicated through *ornamentation* signs in the music.

**embouchure** The placement of the lips, lower facial muscles, and jaws in playing a wind instrument.

**Empfindsamkeit** German "sensitive" style of the mid-eighteenth century, characterized by melodic directness and *homophonic* texture.

**encore** "Again"; an audience request that the performer(s) repeat a piece or perform another.

**English horn** *Double-reed* woodwind instrument, larger and lower in *range* than the *oboe*.

**English madrigal** English secular *polyphonic* song (for two to six *voices*) developed from the Italian *madrigal*; often lighter and less serious, featuring *refrain* syllables (fa-la); largely cultivated by amateurs.

**entenga** Tuned drum from Uganda; the royal drum ensemble of the former ruler of Buganda.

**episode** Interlude or intermediate section in the Baroque *fugue* that serves as an area of relaxation between statements of the *subject*.

**equal temperament** Tuning system based on the division of the *octave* into twelve equal *half steps*; the system used today.

**erhu** Bowed, two-string fiddle from China, with its bow hairs fixed between the strings; rests on the leg while playing.

**espressivo** Expressively.

**estampie** A dance form prevalent in late medieval France, either with voice or purely instrumental.

**ethnomusicology** Comparative study of musics of the world, with a focus on the cultural context of music.

**étude** Study piece that focuses on a particular technical problem.

**euphonium** Tenor-range brass instrument resembling the *tuba*. Also *baritone horn*.

**exoticism** Musical style in which *rhythms*, *melodies*, or instruments evoke the color and atmosphere of far-off lands.

**exposition** Opening section. In the *fugue*, the first section in which the voices enter in turn with the *subject*. In *sonata-allegro form*, the first section in which the major thematic material is stated. Also *statement*.

**Expressionism** A style of visual art and literature in Germany and Austria in the early twentieth century. The term is sometimes also applied to music, especially composers of the *Second Viennese School*.

**falsetto** Vocal technique whereby men can sing above their normal *range*, producing a lighter sound.

**fantasia** Free instrumental piece of fairly large dimensions, in an improvisational style; in the Baroque, it often served as an introductory piece to a *fugue*.

**fantasy** See *fantasia*.

**fiddle** Colloquial term for *violin*; often used in traditional music. Also a bowed medieval string instrument.

**fife** A small wooden transverse *flute*, with fewer holes than a *piccolo*, traditionally associated with the military.

**figured bass** Baroque practice consisting of an independent bass line that often includes numerals indicating the harmony to be supplied by the performer. Also *thorough-bass*.

**film music** Music that serves either as background or foreground for a film.

**first-movement concerto form** See *concerto form*.

**first-movement form** See *sonata-allegro form*.

**fixed forms** Group of forms, especially in medieval France, in which the poetic structure determines musical repetitions. See also *ballade, rondeau, virelai*.

**flat sign** Musical symbol (♭) that indicates lowering a pitch by a *semitone*.

**fluegelhorn** Valved brass instrument resembling a bugle with a wide bell, used in *jazz* and commercial music.

**flute** Soprano-range woodwind instrument, usually made of metal and held horizontally.

**flutter tonguing** Wind instrument technique in which the tongue is fluttered or trilled against the roof of the mouth.

**folk music.** See *traditional music*.

**folk rock** Popular music style that combines *folk music* with amplified instruments of *rock*.

**form** Structure and design in music, based on repetition, contrast, and variation; the organizing principle of music.

**formalism** Tendency to elevate formal above expressive value in music, as in *Neoclassical* music.

**forte** (*f*) Loud.

**fortepiano** Forerunner of the modern *piano* (also *pianoforte*).

**fortissimo** (*ff*) Very loud.

**four-hand piano music** Chamber music genre for two performers playing at one or occasionally two *pianos*, allowing home or *salon* performances of orchestral arrangements.

**free jazz** Modern *jazz* style developed in the 1960s by Ornette Coleman.

**French horn** See *horn*.

**French overture** Baroque instrumental introduction to an *opera, ballet,* or *suite*, in two sections: a slow opening followed by an *Allegro*, often with a brief reprise of the opening.

**frequency** Rate of vibration of a string or column of air, which determines *pitch*.

**fugato** A fugal passage in a nonfugal piece, such as in the *development* section of a *sonata-allegro form*.

**fuging tune** *Polyphonic*, imitative setting of a *hymn* or *psalm*, popular in Great Britain and the United States from the eighteenth century.

**fugue** *Polyphonic* form popular in the Baroque era in which one or more themes are developed by imitative *counterpoint*.

**fusion** Style that combines *jazz* improvisation with amplified instruments of *rock*.

**gagaku** Traditional court music of Japan.

**galliard** Lively, *triple meter* French court dance.

**gamelan** Musical ensemble of Java or Bali, made up of *gongs, chimes, metallophones,* and drums, among other instruments.

**gangsta rap** A particularly violent style of rap, with lyrics depicting gangs and street life.

**gavotte** *Duple-meter* French Baroque dance type with a moderate to quick *tempo*.

**geisha** In Japan, a woman professionally trained in conversation, dancing, and music in order to entertain men.

**genre** General term describing the standard category and overall character of a work.

**Gesamtkunstwerk** German for "total artwork"; a term coined by Richard Wagner to describe the synthesis of all the arts (music, poetry, drama, visual spectacle) in his late operas.

**gigue** Popular English Baroque dance type, a standard *movement* of the Baroque *suite*, in a lively *compound meter*.

**gioioso** Joyous.

**glam rock** See *glitter rock*.

**glee club** Specialized vocal ensemble that performs popular music, college songs, and more serious works.

**glissando** Rapid slide through *pitches* of a *scale*.

**glitter rock** Theatrical, flamboyant *rock* style popular in the 1970s.

**global pop** Collective term for popular third-world musics, ethnic and traditional musics, and eclectic combinations of Western and non-Western musics. Also *world beat*.

**glockenspiel** *Percussion instrument* with horizontal, tuned steel bars of various sizes that are struck with mallets and produce a bright metallic sound.

**Gloria** A section of the *Mass*; the second musical *movement* of the *Ordinary*.

**Goliard song** Medieval Latin-texted secular song, often with corrupt or lewd lyrics; associated with wandering scholars.

**gong** *Percussion instrument* consisting of a broad circular disk of metal, suspended in a frame and struck with a heavy drumstick. Also *tam-tam*.

**gospel music** Twentieth-century sacred music style associated with Protestant African Americans.

**grace note** Ornamental note, often printed in small type and not performed rhythmically.

**Gradual** Fourth item of the *Proper* of the *Mass*, sung in a *melismatic* style, and performed in a *responsorial* manner in which soloists alternate with a choir.

**grand opera** Style of Romantic *opera* developed in Paris, focusing on serious, historical plots with huge choruses, crowd scenes, elaborate dance episodes, ornate costumes, and spectacular scenery.

**grave** Solemn; very, very slow.

**Gregorian chant** *Monophonic* melody with a freely flowing, unmeasured vocal line; liturgical chant of the Roman Catholic Church. Also *plainchant* or *plainsong*.

**griot** West African poet or musician who is responsible for preserving and transmitting the history, stories, and poetry of the people.

**ground bass** A repeating *melody*, usually in the bass, throughout a vocal or instrumental composition.

**grunge rock** Seattle-based *rock* style characterized by harsh guitar chords; hybrid of *punk rock* and *heavy metal*.

**guijira** In music from the Basque region, the alternation between 3/4 and 6/8 meters.

**güiro** An idiophone of Latin American origin, comprised of a hollow gourd with notches, across which a stick is scraped.

**guitar** Plucked-string instrument originally made of wood with a hollow resonating body and a fretted fingerboard; types include *acoustic* and *electric*.

**guitarra moresca** A strummed string instrument introduced to Spain by the Moors.

**guitarrón** A large, six-stringed bass *guitar*, common in *mariachi* ensembles.

**habanera** Moderate *duple meter* dance of Cuban origin, popular in the nineteenth century; based on characteristic rhythmic figure.

**half step** Smallest *interval* used in the Western system; the *octave* divides into twelve such *intervals*; on the *piano*, the distance between any two adjacent keys, whether black or white. Also *semitone*.

**hammered dulcimer** Metal-stringed *instrument* with a trapezoidal sound box, struck with small hammers; an *idiophone*.

**Hammond organ** An early type of electronic *organ*, developed by Laurens Hammond.

**hard-core rock** A subgenre of *punk rock*; features violent behavior and sounds.

**harmonica** Mouth *organ*; a small metal box on which free reeds are mounted, played by moving back and forth across the mouth while breathing into it.

**harmonics** Individual pure sounds that are part of any musical tone; in string instruments, crystalline tones in the very high *register*, produced by lightly touching a vibrating string at a certain point.

**harmonic variation** The procedure in which the *chords* accompanying a *melody* are replaced by others. Often used in *theme and variations* form.

**harmonium** *Organ*-like instrument with free metal reeds set in vibration by a *bellows*; popular in late-nineteenth-century America.

**harmony** The simultaneous combination of notes and the ensuing relationships of *intervals* and *chords*.

**harp** Plucked-string instrument, triangular in shape with strings perpendicular to the soundboard.

**harpsichord** Early Baroque *keyboard instrument* in which the strings are plucked by quills instead of being struck with hammers like the *piano*. Also *clavecin*.

**haut** Medieval category of loud instruments, used mainly for outdoor occasions, as distinct from *bas*, or soft, instruments.

**heavy metal** *Rock* style that gained popularity in the 1970s, characterized by simple, repetitive ideas and loud, distorted instrumental solos.

**heptatonic scale** Seven-note *scale*; in non-Western musics, often fashioned from a different combination of *intervals* than *major* and *minor scales*.

**Hertz** (Hz.) In acoustics, a measurement of *frequency*.

**heterophonic** *Texture* in which two or more voices (or parts) elaborate the same melody simultaneously, often the result of *improvisation*.

**hillbilly music** An early style of *country-western* music featuring traditional music of the rural South, commercialized by such performers as the Carter family and Jimmie Rogers.

**hip hop**  Black urban art forms that emerged in New York City in the 1970s, encompassing *rap* music, break dancing, and graffiti art as well as the fashions adopted by the artists. The term comes from the strings of *vocables*, or nonsense syllables, used by rap artists.

**historical period**  A relatively distinct era, with unique artistic characteristics different from those of other eras, and shared by many works.

**homophonic**  *Texture* with principal *melody* and accompanying *harmony*, as distinct from *polyphony*.

**homorhythmic**  *Texture* in which all *voices*, or lines, move together in the same *rhythm*.

**honkytonk**  A genre of *country-western* music developed in the 1950s that was heavily influenced by *rock and roll*.

**horn**  Medium-range valved brass instrument that can be played "stopped" with the hand as well as open; also French horn.

**hornpipe**  Country dance of British Isles, often in a lively *triple meter*; optional dance movement of solo and orchestral Baroque suite; a type of *duple meter* hornpipe is still popular in Irish traditional dance music.

**hymn**  Song in praise of God; often involves congregational participation.

**hyperinstrument**  Interactive electronic instruments designed to expand the possibilities of human expressivity and virtuosity. Developed by Tod Machover at MIT.

**idée fixe**  "Fixed idea"; term coined by Berlioz for a recurring musical idea that links different movements of a work.

**idiophone**  Instrument that produces sound from the substance of the instrument itself by being struck, blown, shaken, scraped, or rubbed. Examples include bells, rattles, xylophones, and cymbals.

**imitation**  Melodic idea presented in one *voice* and then restated in another, each part continuing as others enter.

**Impressionism**  A French movement developed by visual artists who favored vague, blurry images intended to capture an "impression" of the subject. Impressionism in music is characterized by exotic *scales*, unresolved *dissonances*, parallel *chords*, rich orchestral *tone color*, and free *rhythm*.

**improvisation**  Creation of a musical composition while it is being performed, seen in Baroque *ornamentation*, *cadenzas* of *concertos*, *jazz*, and some non-Western musics.

**incidental music**  Music written to accompany dramatic works.

**inflection**  Small alteration of the *pitch* by a microtonal *interval*. See also *blue note*.

**instrument**  Mechanism that generates musical vibrations and transmits them into the air.

**interactive performance**  Computer-supported, collaborative music-making that includes live performers interacting with computers, interconnected performance networks, and online improvisation.

**interlude**  Music played between sections of a musical or dramatic work.

**intermedio**  In the Italian Renaissance, a work performed between the acts of a play.

**intermezzo**  Short, lyric piece or *movement*, often for *piano*. Also a comic *interlude* performed between acts of an eighteenth-century *opera seria*.

**Internet radio**  Radio stations that convert their signal into digital format and transmit it over the worldwide Web.

**interval**  Distance and relationship between two *pitches*.

**inversion**  Mirror or upside-down image of a *melody* or pattern, found in *fugues* and twelve-tone compositions.

**Irish harp**  Plucked-string instrument with about thirty strings; used to accompany Irish songs and dance music (also *celtic harp*).

**irregular meter**  An atypical metric scheme, often based on an odd number of *beats* per *measure* (5/4, 7/8, 11/4).

**isorhythmic motet**  Medieval and early Renaissance *motet* based on a repeating rhythmic pattern throughout one or more voices.

**Italian overture**  Baroque *overture* consisting of three sections: fast-slow-fast.

**jam band**  A group that focuses on live performance rather than commercial recordings. Jam bands, such as the Grateful Dead and Phish, combine many different musical traditions, most notably *folk*, *jazz*, *rock*, and *country-western*, in a highly improvisational and expressive style.

**Janissary music**  Music of the military corps of the Turkish sultan, characterized by *percussion instruments* such as triangle, cymbals, bell tree, and bass drum as well as *trumpets* and *double-reed* instruments.

**jarabe**  Traditional Mexican dance form with multiple sections in contrasting *meters* and *tempos*, often performed by *mariachi* ensembles.

**jazz**  A musical style created mainly by African Americans in the early twentieth century that blended elements drawn from African musics with the popular and art traditions of the West.

**jazz band**  Instrumental ensemble made up of reed (*saxophones* and *clarinets*), brass (*trumpets* and *trombones*), and rhythm sections (*percussion*, *piano*, *double bass*, and sometimes *guitar*).

**jia hua**  Literally, "adding flowers"; an embellishment style in Chinese music using various ornamental figures.

**jig**  A vigorous dance developed in the British Isles, usually in *compound meter*; became fashionable on the Continent as the *gigue*; still popular as an Irish traditional dance genre.

**jongleurs**  Medieval wandering entertainers who played instruments, sang and danced, juggled, and performed plays.

**jongleuresses**  Female *jongleurs*, or wandering entertainer/minstrels.

**jota**  A type of Spanish dance song characterized by a quick *triple meter* and *guitar* and *castanet* accompaniment.

**karaoke**  "Empty orchestra"; popular nightclub style from Japan where customers sing the melody to accompanying pre-recorded tracks.

**kettledrums**  See *timpani*.

**key**  Defines the relationship of *tones* with a common

center or *tonic*. Also a lever on a keyboard or woodwind instrument.

**keyboard instrument** Instrument sounded by means of a keyboard (a series of keys played with the fingers).

**keynote** See *tonic*.

**key signature** Sharps or flats placed at the beginning of a piece to show the *key* of a work.

**Klangfarbenmelodie** Twentieth-century technique in which the notes of a melody are distributed among different instruments, giving a pointillistic *texture*.

**koron** In Persian music, a *pitch* in between the natural pitch and a flat, notated as a flat sign with a triangular head.

**koto** Japanese plucked-string instrument with a long rectangular body, thirteen strings, and movable bridges or frets.

**kouta** A short Japanese song traditionally sung by a *geisha* for private or theatrical entertainment.

**Kyrie** The first item of the *Ordinary* in the Roman Catholic *Mass*. Its construction is threefold, involving three repetitions of "Kyrie eleison" (Lord, have mercy), three of "Christe eleison" (Christ, have mercy), and again three of "Kyrie eleison."

**lamellophone** Plucked *idiophone* with thin metal strips; common throughout sub-Saharan Africa.

**lamentoso** Like a lament.

**largo** Broad; very slow.

**Latin** Ancient language of the Roman empire; the language of learning in the Middle Ages and Renaissance; also the exclusive language of the Roman Catholic liturgy until the mid-twentieth century.

**Latin jazz** A *jazz* style influenced by Latin American music, which includes various dance rhythms and traditional *percussion instruments*.

**Latin rock** Subgenre of *rock* featuring Latin and African *percussion instruments* (maracas, conga drums, timbales).

**legato** Smooth and connected; opposite of *staccato*.

**Leitmotif** "Leading motive," or basic recurring *theme*, representing a person, object, or idea, commonly used in Wagner's operas.

**librettist** The author of a *libretto*.

**libretto** Text or script of an *opera, oratorio, cantata,* or *musical* (also call the "book" in a musical), written by a *librettist*.

**Lied** German for "song"; most commonly associated with the solo art song of the nineteenth century, usually accompanied by *piano*.

**Lieder** Plural of *Lied*.

**lining out** A *call-and-response* singing practice prevalent in early America and England; characterized by the alternation between a singer leader and a *chorus* singing heterophonically.

**liturgy** The set order of religious services and the structure of each service, within a particular denomination (e.g., Roman Catholic).

**lute** Plucked-string instrument of Middle Eastern origin, popular in western Europe from the late Middle Ages to the eighteenth century.

**lyre** Ancient plucked-string instrument of the *harp* family, used to accompany singing and poetry.

**lyric opera** Hybrid form combining elements of *grand opera* and *opéra comique* and featuring appealing melodies and romantic drama.

**madrigal** Renaissance secular work originating in Italy for voices, with or without instruments, set to a short, lyric love poem; also popular in England.

**madrigal choir** Small vocal ensemble that specializes in *a cappella* secular works.

**madrigalism** A striking effect designed to depict the meaning of the text in vocal music; found in many *madrigals* and other *genres* of the sixteenth through eighteenth centuries. See also *word painting*.

**maestoso** Majestic.

**Magnificat** Biblical text on the words of the Virgin Mary, sung polyphonically in church from the Renaissance on.

**mainstream country** A commercialized style of *country-western* music influenced by pop.

**major-minor tonality** A harmonic system based on the use of *major* and *minor scales*, widely practiced from the seventeenth to the late nineteenth century. See also *tonality*.

**major scale** Scale consisting of seven different tones that comprise a specific pattern of *whole* and *half steps*. It differs from a *minor scale* primarily in that its third degree is raised half a step.

**mambo** Dance of Afro-Cuban origin with a characteristic highly syncopated *quadruple-meter* rhythmic pattern.

**mandolin** Plucked-string instrument with a rounded body and fingerboard; used in some *folk musics* and in *country-western* music.

**maracas** Latin-American rattles *(idiophones)* made from gourds or other materials.

**march** A style incorporating characteristics of military music, including strongly accented *duple meter* in simple, repetitive rhythmic patterns.

**marching band** Instrumental ensemble for entertainment at sports events and parades, consisting of wind and *percussion instruments*, drum majors/majorettes, and baton twirlers.

**mariachi** Traditional Mexican ensemble popular throughout the country, consisting of *trumpets, violins, guitar,* and bass *guitar*.

**marimba** *Percussion instrument* that is a mellower version of the *xylophone*; of African origin.

**masque** English *genre* of aristocratic entertainment that combined vocal and instrumental music with poetry and dance, developed during the sixteenth and seventeenth centuries.

**Mass** Central service of the Roman Catholic Church.

**mazurka** Type of Polish folk dance in *triple meter*.

**mbube** "Lion"; *a cappella* choral singing style of South African Zulus, featuring *call-and-response* patterns, close-knit harmonies, and *syncopation*.

**measure** Rhythmic group or metrical unit that contains a fixed number of *beats*, divided on the musical staff by bar lines.

**measure lines** Vertical lines through the *staff* that separate metric units, or *measures*. Also called barlines.

**medium** Performing forces employed in a certain musical work.

**Meistersinger** A German "master singer," belonging to a professional guild. The Meistersingers flourished from the fourteenth through the sixteenth centuries.

**melismatic** Melodic style characterized by many notes sung to a single text syllable.

**melodic variation** The procedure in which a melody is altered while certain features are maintained. Often used in *theme and variations* form.

**melody** Succession of single *tones* or *pitches* perceived by the mind as a unity.

**membranophone** Any instrument that produces sound from tightly stretched membranes that can be struck, plucked, rubbed, or sung into (setting the skin in vibration).

**meno** Less.

**mesto** Sad.

**metallophone** *Percussion instrument* consisting of tuned metal bars, usually struck with a mallet.

**meter** Organization of rhythm in time; the grouping of *beats* into larger, regular patterns, notated as *measures*.

**metronome** Device used to indicate the *tempo* by sounding regular beats at adjustable speeds.

**mezzo forte** *(mf)* Moderately loud.

**mezzo piano** *(mp)* Moderately soft.

**mezzo-soprano** Female voice of middle range.

**micropolyphony** Twentieth-century technique encompassing the complex interweaving of all musical elements.

**microtone** Musical interval smaller than a *semitone*, prevalent in some non-Western musics and in some twentieth-century art music.

**MIDI** Acronym for Musical Instrument Digital Interface; technology standard that allows networking of computers with electronic musical instruments.

**minimalism** Contemporary musical style featuring the repetition of short melodic, rhythmic, and harmonic patterns with little variation. See also *post-minimalism* and *spiritual minimalism*.

**Minnesingers** Late medieval German poet-musicians.

**minor scale** *Scale* consisting of seven different *tones* that comprise a specific pattern of *whole* and *half steps*. It differs from the *major scale* primarily in that its third degree is lowered half a step.

**minuet** An elegant *triple-meter* dance type popular in the seventeenth and eighteenth centuries; usually in *binary form*. See also *minuet and trio*.

**minuet and trio** An **A-B-A** form (**A**= minuet; **B** = trio) in a moderate *triple meter*; often the third *movement* of the Classical *multimovement cycle*.

**misterioso** Mysteriously.

**modal** Characterizes music that is based on *modes* other than major and minor, especially the early church *modes*.

**mode** *Scale* or sequence of notes used as the basis for a composition; major and minor are modes.

**Modernism** Early-twentieth-century movement in the arts and literature that explored innovative, nontraditional forms of expression. See also *Post-Modernism*.

**moderato** Moderate.

**modified sonata-allegro** A statement (*exposition*) and restatement (*recapitulation*) of *themes* without the *development* section typical in *sonata-allegro form*.

**modified strophic form** Song structure that combines elements of *strophic* and through-composed forms; a variation of *strophic form* in which a section might have a new *key*, *rhythm*, or varied melodic pattern.

**modulation** The process of changing from one *key* to another.

**molto** Very.

**monody** Vocal style established in the Baroque, with a solo singer(s) and instrumental accompaniment.

**monophonic** Single-line *texture*, or *melody* without accompaniment.

**monothematic** Work or *movement* based on a single *theme*.

**morality play** Medieval drama, often with music, intended to teach proper values.

**motet** *Polyphonic* vocal *genre*, secular in the Middle Ages but sacred or devotional thereafter.

**motive** Short melodic or rhythmic idea; the smallest fragment of a *theme* that forms a melodic-harmonic-rhythmic unit.

**Motown** A record company, originally from Detroit, that moved to Los Angeles in 1971. Also the associated musical style—a fusion of *gospel*, *rock and roll*, and *rhythm and blues*.

**movement** Complete, self-contained part within a larger musical work.

**mp3** A file-compression format applied to audio files; term is short for Moving Pictures Expert Group 1 Layer 3.

**MTV** Acronym for music television, a cable channel that initially presented nonstop *music videos*.

**multimovement cycle** A three- or four-*movement* structure used in Classical-era instrumental music—especially the *symphony*, *sonata*, *concerto*—and in *chamber music*; each *movement* is in a prescribed *tempo* and *form*; sometimes called *sonata cycle*.

**multiphonic** Two or more *pitches* sung or played simultaneously by the same voice or instrument.

**muses** Nine daughters of Zeus in ancient mythology; each presided over one of the arts.

**musical** Genre of twentieth-century musical theater, especially popular in the United States and Great Britain; characterized by spoken dialogue, dramatic plot interspersed with songs, ensemble numbers, and dancing.

**Musical Instrument Digital Interface** See *MIDI*.

**musical saw** A handsaw that is bowed on its smooth edge; *pitch* is varied by bending the saw.

**musical sound** See *tone*.

**music drama** Wagner's term for his operas.

**music video** Video tape or film that accompanies a recording, usually of a popular or *rock* song.

**musique concrète** Music made up of natural sounds and sound effects that are recorded and then manipulated electronically.

**mute** Mechanical device used to muffle the sound of an instrument.

**nakers** Medieval *percussion instruments* resembling small *kettledrums*, played in pairs; of Middle Eastern origin.

**Nashville sound** A style of *country-western* influenced by record producers centered in Nashville. These producers had a broad knowledge of music and the industry, and cultivated a more mainstream style.

**Neoclassical jazz** A modern *jazz* style characterized by expanded *tonalities*, modal improvisations, and new forms; Wynton Marsalis is a proponent of this style.

**Neoclassicism** A twentieth-century style that combined elements of Classical and Baroque music with modernist trends.

**neumatic** Melodic style with two to four notes set to each syllable.

**neumes** Early musical notation signs; square notes on a four-line staff.

**new age** Style of popular music of the 1980s and 1990s, characterized by soothing *timbres* and repetitive forms that are subjected to shifting variation techniques.

**new-age jazz** A mellow, reflective *jazz* style exemplified by Paul Winter and his ensemble.

**New Orleans jazz** Early *jazz* style characterized by multiple improvisations in an ensemble of *cornet* (or *trumpet*), *clarinet* (or *saxophone*), *trombone, piano, double bass* (or *tuba*), *banjo* (or *guitar*), and drums; repertory included *blues, ragtime*, and popular songs.

**New Romanticism** A contemporary style of music that employs the rich harmonic language and other elements of Romantic and post-Romantic composers.

**new wave** Subgenre of *rock* popular since the late 1970s, highly influenced by simple 1950s-style *rock and roll*; developed as a rejection of the complexities of *art rock* and *beauty metal*.

**ninth chord** Five-tone *chord* spanning a ninth between its lowest and highest *tones*.

**nocturne** "Night piece"; introspective work common in the nineteenth century, often for *piano*.

**Noh drama** A major form of Japanese theater since the late fourteenth century; based on philosophical concepts from Zen Buddhism.

**noise** Sounds without a distinct *pitch*.

**nonmetric** Music lacking a strong sense of *beat* or *meter*, common in certain non-Western cultures.

**non troppo** Not too much.

**note** A musical symbol denoting *pitch* and *duration*.

**nuevo tango** A form of tango, developed in the 1950s by Astor Piazzola, that incorporates *fugue*, chromaticism, *dissonance*, and elements of *jazz*.

**oblique motion** Polyphonic voice movement in which one *voice* remains stationary while the others move.

**oboe** Soprano-range, *double-reed* woodwind instrument.

**octave** *Interval* between two tones seven diatonic pitches apart; the lower note vibrates half as fast as the upper and sounds an octave lower.

**octet** *Chamber music* for eight *instruments* or voices.

**ode** Secular composition written for a royal occasion, especially popular in England.

**offbeat** A weak *beat* or any pulse between the beats in a measured rhythmic pattern.

**Office** See *Divine Offices*.

**open ending** First ending in a medieval secular piece, often

cadencing on a *pitch* other than the final, which was generally the most prominent note in an early church mode.

**open form** Indeterminate contemporary music in which some details of a composition are clearly indicated, but the overall structure is left to choice or chance.

**opera** Music drama that is generally sung throughout, combining the resources of vocal and instrumental music with poetry and drama, acting and pantomime, scenery and costumes.

**opera buffa** Italian comic *opera*, sung throughout.

**opéra comique** French comic *opera*, with some spoken dialogue.

**opera seria** Tragic Italian *opera*.

**operetta** A small-scale operatic work, generally light in tone, with spoken dialogue, song and dance.

**ophicleide** A nineteenth-century *brass instrument* (now obsolete) with *woodwind* fingering holes; used by Berlioz, among others; the parts are generally played today on *tuba*.

**opus number** (op.) A number, often part of the title of a piece, designating the work in chronological relationship to other works by the same composer.

**oral tradition** Music that is transmitted by example or imitation and performed from memory.

**oral transmission** Preservation of music without the aid of written notation.

**oratorio** Large-scale dramatic genre originating in the Baroque, based on a text of religious or serious character, performed by solo voices, *chorus*, and *orchestra*; similar to *opera* but without scenery, costumes, or action.

**orchestra** Performing group of diverse instruments in various cultures; in Western art music, an ensemble of multiple strings with various *woodwind, brass*, and *percussion instruments*.

**orchestral bells** See *chimes*.

**orchestration** The technique of setting instruments in various combinations.

**Ordinary** Sections of the Roman Catholic *Mass* that remain the same from day to day throughout the church year, as distinct from the *Proper*, which changes daily according to the liturgical occasion.

**organ** Wind instrument in which air is fed to the pipes by mechanical means; the pipes are controlled by two or more keyboards and a set of pedals.

**organal style** *Organum* in which the Tenor sings the melody (original chant) in very long notes while the upper voices move freely and rapidly above it.

**organum** Earliest kind of *polyphonic* music, which developed from the custom of adding voices above a *plainchant*; they first ran parallel to it at the interval of a fifth or fourth and later moved more freely.

**ornamentation** See *embellishment*.

**ostinato** A short melodic, rhythmic, or harmonic pattern that is repeated throughout a work or a section of one.

**overture** An introductory *movement*, as in an *opera* or *oratorio*, often presenting melodies from *arias* to come. Also an orchestral work for concert performance.

**pan band** An ensemble comprised of a variety of *steel drums* and a percussion section known as the "engine room."

**panharmonicon** An automatic instrument designed to simulate a whole *orchestra* using *organ* pipes and mechanical percussion-devices. Beethoven's *Battle Symphony*, also known as *Wellington's Victory*, was originally written for the panharmonicon.

**panpipes** Wind instrument consisting of a series of small vertical tubes or pipes of differing length; sound is produced by blowing across the top.

**pantomime** Theatrical *genre* in which an actor silently plays all the parts in a show while accompanied by singing; originated in ancient Rome.

**part song** Secular vocal composition, unaccompanied, in three, four, or more parts.

**partita** See *suite*.

**pas de deux** A dance for two that is an established feature of classical ballet.

**paso doble** Marchlike Spanish dance in *duple meter*.

**passacaglia** Baroque form (similar to the *chaconne*) in moderately slow *triple meter*, based on a short, repeated base-line melody that serves as the basis for continuous variation in the other voices.

**passepied** French Baroque court dance type; a faster version of the *minuet*.

**Passion** Musical setting of the Crucifixion story as told by one of the four Evangelists in the Gospels.

**pastorale** Pastoral, country-like.

**patalon** An overture from a Javanese shadow-puppet play; performed by *gamelan*.

**patron (patroness)** A person who supports music or musicians; a benefactor of the arts. See also *patronage*.

**patronage** Sponsorship of an artist or a musician, historically by a member of the wealthy or ruling classes.

**pavane** Stately Renaissance court dance in duple meter.

**pedal point** Sustained *tone* over which the *harmonies* change.

**pélog** Heptatonic (7-note) tuning used in Javanese *gamelan* music.

**penny whistle** See *tin whistle*.

**pentatonic scale** Five-note pattern used in some African, Far Eastern, and Native American musics; can also be found in Western music as an example of exoticism.

**percussion instrument** Instrument made of metal, wood, stretched skin, or other material that is made to sound by striking, shaking, scraping, or plucking.

**perfect pitch** The innate ability to reproduce any *pitch* without hearing it first.

**performance art** Multimedia art form involving visual as well as dramatic and musical elements.

**period-instrument ensemble** Group that performs on historical instruments or modern replicas built after historical models.

**perpetuum mobile** Type of piece characterized by continuous repetitions of a rhythmic pattern at a quick *tempo*; perpetual motion.

**phasing** A technique in which a musical pattern is repeated and manipulated so that it separates and overlaps itself, and then rejoins the original pattern; getting "out of phase" and back "in sync."

**phrase** Musical unit; often a component of a *melody*.

**phrygian** One of the church *modes* often associated with a somber mood; built on the pitch E using only white keys.

**pianissimo (pp)** Very soft.

**piano (p)** Soft.

**piano** Keyboard instrument whose strings are struck with hammers controlled by a keyboard mechanism; pedals control dampers in the strings that stop the sound when the finger releases the key.

**pianoforte** Original name for the *piano*.

**piano quartet** Standard chamber ensemble of *piano* with *violin*, *viola*, and *cello*.

**piano quintet** Standard chamber ensemble of *piano* with *string quartet* (two *violins*, *viola*, and *cello*).

**piano trio** Standard chamber ensemble of *piano* with *violin* and *cello*.

**piccolo** Smallest *woodwind instrument*, similar to the *flute* but sounding an *octave* higher.

**pipa** A Chinese *lute* with four silk strings; played as solo and ensemble instrument.

**pipe** A medieval *flute* with three holes that is blown at one end through a mouthpiece.

**pitch** Highness or lowness of a *tone*, depending on the *frequency*.

**pizzicato** Performance direction to pluck a string of a bowed instrument with the finger.

**plainchant** See *Gregorian chant*.

**plainsong** See *Gregorian chant*.

**plectrum** An implement made of wood, ivory or another material used to pluck a *chordophone*.

**pluck** To sound the strings of an instrument using fingers or a *plectrum* or pick.

**poco** A little.

**polka** Lively Bohemian dance; also a short, lyric *piano* piece.

**polonaise** Stately Polish processional dance in *triple meter*.

**polychoral** Performance style developed in the late sixteenth century involving the use of two or more *choirs* that alternate with each other or sing together.

**polychord** A single *chord* comprised of several *chords*, common in twentieth-century music.

**polyharmony** Two or more streams of *harmony* played against each other, common in twentieth-century music.

**polymeter** The simultaneous use of several *meters*, common in twentieth-century music and certain African musics.

**polyphonic** Two or more melodic lines combined into a multivoiced *texture*, as distinct from *monophonic*.

**polyrhythm** The simultaneous use of several rhythmic patterns or *meters*, common in twentieth-century music and in certain African musics.

**polytextual** Two or more texts set simultaneously in a composition, common in the medieval *motet*.

**polytonality** The simultaneous use of two or more *keys*, common in twentieth-century music.

**portative organ** Medieval *organ* small enough to be carried or set on a table, usually with only one set of pipes.

**positive organ** Small single-manual *organ*, popular in the Renaissance and Baroque eras.

**post-minimalism** Contemporary style combining lush harmonies of New Romanticism with high-energy rhythms of minimalism; John Adams is a major exponent.

**Post-Modernism** A movement in the arts and literature that reacts against early modernist principles through the use of classical and traditional elements. See *Modernism*.

**Post-Romanticism** A trend at the turn of the twentieth century in which nineteenth-century musical characteristics like *chromatic* harmony and expansive *melodies*, are carried to the extreme.

**prelude** Instrumental work preceding a larger work.

**prelude and fugue** Paired *movements*, the *prelude* in a free form, the *fugue* in a strict, imitative form.

**prepared piano** *Piano* whose sound is altered by the insertion of various materials (metal, rubber, leather, and paper) between the strings; invented by John Cage.

**presto** Very fast.

**program music** Instrumental music endowed with literary or pictorial associations, especially popular in the nineteenth century.

**program symphony** Multimovement programmatic orchestral work, typically from the nineteenth century.

**progressive rock** See *art rock*.

**Proper** Sections of the Roman Catholic *Mass* that vary from day to day throughout the church year according to the particular liturgical occasion, as distinct from the *Ordinary*, in which they remain the same.

**Psalms** Book from the Old Testament of the Bible; the 150 psalm texts, used in Jewish and Christian worship, are often set to music.

**psaltery** Medieval plucked-string instrument similar to the modern *zither*, consisting of a sound box over which strings were stretched.

**psychedelic rock** See *acid rock*.

**punk rock** Subgenre of *rock*, popular since the mid-1970s; characterized by loud volume levels, driving rhythms, and simple forms typical of earlier *rock and roll*; often contains shocking lyrics and offensive behavior.

**pure music** See *absolute music*.

**quadrivium** Subdivision of the seven liberal arts; includes the mathematical subjects of music, arithmetic, geometry, and astronomy.

**quadruple meter** Basic metrical pattern of four beats to a measure. Also *common time*.

**quadruple stop** Playing four notes simultaneously on a string instrument.

**quadruplum** Fourth voice of a *polyphonic* work.

**quartal harmony** *Harmony* based on the *interval* of the fourth as opposed to a third; used in twentieth-century music.

**quarter tone** An *interval* halfway between a *half step*.

**quintet** *Chamber music* for five *instruments* or voices. See also *brass quintet*, *piano quintet*, *string quintet*, and *woodwind quintet*.

**quotation music** Music that parodies another work or works, presenting them in a new style or guise.

**rabab** Any of a variety of bowed string instruments from the Islamic world, most held upright. The medieval *rebec* was derived from these instruments.

**raga** Melodic pattern used in music of India; prescribes *pitches*, patterns, *ornamentation*, and extramusical associations such as time of performance and emotional character.

**ragtime** Late-nineteenth-century *piano* style created by African Americans, characterized by highly syncopated melodies; also played in ensemble arrangements. Contributed to early *jazz* styles.

**range** Distance between the lowest and highest *tones* of a *melody*, an instrument, or a voice.

**rap** Style of popular music in which rhymed lyrics are spoken over rhythm tracks; developed by African Americans in the 1970s and widely disseminated in the 1980s and 1990s; the style is part of the larger culture of *hip hop*.

**rebec** Medieval bowed-string instrument, often with a pear-shaped body.

**recapitulation** Third section of *sonata-allegro form*, in which the thematic material of the *exposition* is restated, generally in the *tonic*. Also *restatement*.

**recitative** Solo vocal declamation that follows the inflections of the text, often resulting in a disjunct vocal style; found in *opera*, *cantata*, and *oratorio*. Can be *secco* or *accompagnato*.

**recorder** End-blown *woodwind* instrument with a whistle mouthpiece, generally associated with early music.

**reed** Flexible strip of cane or metal set into a mouthpiece or the body of an instrument; set in vibration by a stream of air. See also *single reed* and *double reed*.

**reel** Moderately quick dance in *duple meter* danced throughout the British Isles; the most popular Irish traditional dance type.

**refrain** Text or music that is repeated within a larger form.

**regal** Small medieval reed *organ*.

**reggae** Jamaican popular music style characterized by offbeat rhythms and chanted vocals over a strong bass part; often associated with the religious movement Rastafarianism.

**register** Specific area in the range of an instrument or voice.

**registration** Selection or combination of stops in a work for *organ* or *harpsichord*.

**relative key** The major and minor key that share the same *key signature*; for example, D minor is the relative minor of F major, both having one flat.

**repeat sign** Musical symbol (‖: :‖) that indicates repetition of a passage in a composition.

**repetition** A compositional technique whereby a passage or section is restated.

**Requiem Mass** Roman Catholic *Mass* for the Dead.

**resolution** Conclusion of a musical idea, as in the progression from an *active chord* to a rest chord.

**response** Short choral answer to a solo *verse*; an element of liturgical dialogue.

**responsorial singing** Singing, especially in *Gregorian chant*, in which a soloist or a group of soloists alternates with the choir. See also *call-and-response*.

**rest chord** A *chord* that achieves a sense of *resolution* or completion, normally the *tonic*.

**restatement** See *recapitulation*.

**retrograde** Backward statement of melody.

**retrograde inversion** Mirror image and backward statement of a *melody*.

**rhyme scheme** The arrangement of rhyming words or corresponding sounds at the end of poetic lines.

**rhythm** The controlled movement of music in time.

**rhythm and blues** Popular African-American music style of the 1940s through 1960s featuring a solo singer accompanied by a small instrumental ensemble (*piano, guitar, double bass,* drums, tenor *saxophone*), driving rhythms, and *blues* and pop song forms.

**rhythmic modes** Fixed rhythmic patterns of long and short notes, popular in the thirteenth century.

**rhythmic variation** The procedure in which note lengths, *meter,* or *tempo* is altered. Often used in *theme and variations* form.

**riff** In *jazz,* a short melodic *ostinato* over changing harmonies.

**ring shout** Religious dance performed by African-American slaves, performed with hand clapping and a shuffle step to *spirituals.*

**ripieno** The larger of the two ensembles in the Baroque *concerto grosso.* Also *tutti.*

**ritardando** Holding back, getting slower.

**ritornello** Short, recurring instrumental passage found in both the *aria* and the Baroque *concerto.*

**rock** A style of popular music with roots in *rock and roll* but differing in lyric content, recording technique, song length and form, and range of sounds. The term was first used in the 1960s to distinguish groups like the Beatles and the Rolling Stones from earlier artists.

**rockabilly** An early style of *rock and roll,* fusing elements of *blues, rhythm and blues,* and *country-western* music.

**rock and roll** American popular music style first heard in the 1950s; derived from the union of African-American *rhythm and blues, country-western,* and pop music.

**rock band** Popular music ensemble that depends on amplified strings, percussion, and electronically generated sounds.

**rocket theme** Quickly ascending rhythmic melody used in Classical-era instrumental music; the technique is credited to composers in Mannheim, Germany.

**Rococo** A term from the visual arts that is frequently applied to eighteenth-century French music, characterized by simplicity, grace, and delicate *ornamentation.*

**romance** Originally a *ballad;* in the Romantic era, a lyric instrumental work.

**ronde** Lively Renaissance "round dance," associated with the outdoors, in which the participants danced in a circle or a line.

**rondeau** Medieval and Renaissance fixed poetic form and *chanson* type with courtly love texts.

**rondo** Muscial form in which the first section recurs, usually in the *tonic.* In the Classical *multimovement cycle,* it appears as the last *movement* in various forms, including **A-B-A-B-A, A-B-A-C-A,** and **A-B-A-C-A-B-A.**

**rosin** Substance made from hardened tree sap, rubbed on the hair of a bow to help it grip the strings.

**round** Perpetual *canon* at the *unison* in which each voice enters in succession with the same *melody* (for example, *Row, Row, Row Your Boat*).

**rounded binary** Compositional form with two sections, in

which the second ends with a return to material from the first; each section is usually repeated.

**rubato** "Borrowed time," common in Romantic music, in which the performer hesitates here or hurries forward there, imparting flexibility to the written note values. Also *tempo rubato.*

**rumba** Latin American dance of Afro-Cuban origin, in *duple meter* with syncopated *rhythms.*

**rural blues** American popular singing style with raspy-voiced male singer accompanied by acoustic steel-string *guitar;* features melodic *blue notes* over repeated bass patterns.

**sackbut** Early *brass instrument,* ancestor of the *trombone.*

**sacred music** Religious or spiritual music, for church or devotional use.

**salon** A gathering of musicians, artists, and intellectuals who shared similar interests and tastes, hosted by a wealthy aristocrat.

**salsa** "Spicy"; collective term for Latin American dance music, especially forms of Afro-Cuban origin.

**saltarello** Italian "jumping dance," often characterized by triplets in a rapid 4/4 time.

**samba** Afro-Brazilian dance, characterized by *duple meter, responsorial* singing, and *polyrhythmic* accompaniments.

**sampler** Electronic device that digitizes, stores, and plays back sounds.

**Santería** A pantheistic Afro-Cuban religion combining elements of traditional Yoruban beliefs with Catholicism.

**santur** A Middle Eastern hammer dulcimer, with a trapezoidal sound box and 12 to 18 sets of metal strings.

**Sanctus** A section of the *Mass;* the fourth musical *movement* of the *Ordinary.*

**sarabande** Stately Spanish Baroque dance type in *triple meter,* a standard *movement* of the Baroque *suite.*

**SATB** Abbreviation for the standard voices in a *chorus* or choir: *Soprano, Alto, Tenor, Bass;* may also refer to instrumental *ranges.*

**saxophone** Family of *single-reed* woodwind instruments commonly used in the concert and *jazz* band.

**scale** Series of tones in ascending or descending order; may present the notes of a *key.*

**scat singing** A *jazz* style that sets syllables without meaning *(vocables)* to an improvised vocal line.

**scherzo** Composition in **A-B-A** form, usually in *triple meter;* replaced the *minuet and trio* in the nineteenth century.

**secco** *Recitative* singing style that features a sparse accompaniment and moves with great freedom.

**Second Viennese School** Name given to composer Arnold Schoenberg and his pupils Alban Berg and Anton Webern; represents the first efforts in *twelve-tone* composition.

**secular music** Nonreligious music; when texted, usually in the vernacular.

**semitone** Also known as a *half step,* the smallest *interval* commonly used in the Western musical system.

**septet** *Chamber music* for seven *instruments* or voices.

**sequence** Restatement of an idea or *motive* at a different *pitch* level.

**serenade** Classical instrumental *genre* that combines

elements of *chamber music* and *symphony*, often performed in the evening or at social functions. Related to *divertimento* and *cassation*.

**serialism** Method of composition in which various musical elements (*pitch, rhythm, dynamics, tone color*) may be ordered in a fixed series. See also *total serialism*.

**sesquialtera** In Spanish and Latin American music, an unequal *meter* based on the alternation of duple and triple time within groups of six beats.

**seventh chord** Four-note combination consisting of a *triad* with another third added on top; spans a seventh between its lowest and highest tones.

**sextet** *Chamber music* for six *instruments* or voices.

**sextuple meter** Compound metrical pattern of six *beats* to a *measure*.

**sforzando (sf)** Sudden stress or accent on a single *note* or *chord*.

**shake** A *jazz* technique in which brass players shake their lips to produce a wide vibrato.

**shakuhachi** A Japanese end-blown *flute*.

**shamisen** Long-necked Japanese *chordophone* with three strings.

**shape-note** Music notation system originating in nineteenth-century American church music in which the shape of the note heads determines the *pitch*; created to aid music reading.

**sharp sign** Musical symbol (♯) that indicates raising a pitch by a *semitone*.

**shawm** Medieval wind instrument, the ancestor of the *oboe*.

**sheng** A reed mouth *organ* from China.

**shifting meter** See *changing meters*.

**side drum** See *snare drum*.

**simple meter** Grouping of *rhythms* in which the *beat* is subdivided into two, as in duple, triple, and quadruple meters.

**sinfonia** Short instrumental work, found in Baroque *opera*, to facilitate scene changes.

**single reed** A *reed* consisting of one piece of cane vibrating against another part of the instrument, often a mouthpiece.

**Singspiel** Comic German drama with spoken dialogue; the immediate predecessor of Romantic German *opera*.

**sitar** Long-necked plucked *chordophone* of northern India, with movable frets and a rounded gourd body; used as solo instrument and with *tabla*.

**ska** Jamaican urban dance form popular in the 1960s, influential in *reggae*.

**sléndro** *Pentatonic* tuning used in Javanese *gamelan* music; a gapped *scale* using tones 1, 2, 3, 5, 6.

**slide** In bowed string instruments, moving from one *pitch* to another by sliding the finger on the string while bowing.

**slide trumpet** Medieval *brass instrument* of the *trumpet* family.

**snare drum** Small cylindrical drum with two heads stretched over a metal shell, the lower head having strings across it; played with two drumsticks. Also *side drum*.

**soca** A style of music and dance derived from *calypso*, mixing elements of *soul*, funk, *ska* and *calypso*.

**soft rock** Lyrical, gentle *rock* style that evolved around 1960 in response to hard-driving *rock and roll*.

**solo concerto** See *concerto*.

**son** A genre of traditional Mexican dances that combine compound duple with triple meters.

**sonata** Instrumental genre in several *movements* for soloist or small ensemble.

**sonata-allegro form** The opening *movement* of the *multi-movement cycle*, consisting of themes that are stated in the first section (*exposition*), developed in the second section (*development*), and restated in the third section (*recapitulation*). Also *sonata form* or *first-movement form*.

**sonata cycle** See *multimovement cycle*.

**sonata da camera** Baroque *chamber sonata*, usually a suite of stylized dances. Also *chamber sonata*.

**sonata da chiesa** Baroque instrumental work intended for performance in church; in four *movements*, frequently arranged slow-fast-slow-fast. Also *church sonata*.

**sonata form** See *sonata-allegro form*.

**song cycle** Group of songs, usually *Lieder*, that are unified musically or through their texts.

**son jalisciense** A *son* in the style that originated in the Mexican State of Jalisco.

**soprano** Highest-ranged voice, normally possessed by women or boys.

**soul** A black American style of popular music, incorporating elements of *rock and roll* and *gospel*.

**source music** A film technique in which music comes from a logical source within the film and functions as part of the story.

**sound** Vibrations perceived by the human ear; a musical sound is described by its *pitch* and its *duration*.

**sousaphone** *Brass instrument* adapted from the *tuba* with a forward bell that is coiled to rest over the player's shoulder for ease of carrying while marching.

**spiritual** Folklike devotional *genre* of the United States, sung by African Americans and whites.

**spiritual minimalism** Contemporary musical style related to *minimalism*, characterized by a weak pulse and long chains of lush progressions—either *tonal* or *modal*.

**Sprechstimme** A vocal style in which the melody is spoken at approximate *pitches* rather than sung on exact *pitches*; developed by Arnold Schoenberg.

**staccato** Short, detached *notes*, marked with a dot above them.

**statement** See *exposition*.

**steamroller effect** A drawn-out *crescendo* heard in Classical-era instrumental music; a technique credited to composers in Mannheim, Germany.

**steel drum** A *percussion instrument* made from an oil drum, developed in Trinidad during the 1930s and 1940s.

**stile concitato** Baroque style developed by Monteverdi, which introduced novel effects such as rapid repeated notes as symbols of passion.

**stile rappresentativo** A dramatic *recitative* style of the Baroque period in which melodies moved freely over a foundation of simple *chords*.

**stopping** On a string instrument, altering the string length by pressing it on the fingerboard. On a *horn*, playing with the bell closed by the hand or a *mute*.

**strain** A series of contrasting sections found in rags and marches; in *duple meter* with sixteen-measure themes or sections.

**streaming audio** Music that is played directly from the Web, in real time, and does not require downloading.

**stretto** In a *fugue*, when entries of the *subject* occur at faster intervals of time, so that they overlap forming dense, imitative *counterpoint*. Stretto usually occurs at the climactic moment near the end.

**string instruments** Bowed and plucked instruments whose sound is produced by the vibration of one or more strings. Also *chordophone*.

**string quartet** *Chamber music* ensemble consisting of two *violins*, viola, and cello. Also a multimovement composition for this ensemble.

**string quintet** Standard chamber ensemble made up of either two *violins*, two *violas*, and *cello* or two *violins*, viola, and two *cellos*.

**string trio** Standard chamber ensemble of two *violins* and *cello* or of *violin*, viola, and *cello*.

**strophic form** Song structure in which the same music is repeated with every stanza (strophe) of the poem.

**Sturm und Drang** "Storm and stress"; late-eighteenth-century movement in Germany toward more emotional expression in the arts.

**style** Characteristic manner of presentation of musical elements (*melody, rhythm, harmony, dynamics, form*, etc.).

**subdominant** Fourth scale step, *fa*.

**subdominant chord** *Chord* built on the fourth scale step, the IV chord.

**subject** Main idea or *theme* of a work, as in a *fugue*.

**suite** Multimovement work made up of a series of contrasting dance movements, generally all in the same *key*. Also *partita* and *ordre*.

**suona** Traditional Chinese instrument with a *double reed*, similar to the Western *oboe*.

**Surrealism** Early-twentieth-century artistic movement that explored the subconscious, often through fantastic imagery.

**swing** *Jazz* term coined to described Louis Armstrong's style; more commonly refers to *big band* jazz.

**Swing Era** The mid-1930s to the mid-1940s, when *swing* was the most popular music in the United States. The most important musicians of the swing era were Duke Ellington, Louis Armstrong, and Benny Goodman.

**syllabic** Melodic style with one note to each syllable of text.

**Symbolism** Literary movement that paralleled *Impressionism*, in which poetic images were invoked through suggestion or symbol rather than literal description.

**symphonic poem** One-*movement* orchestral form that develops a poetic idea, suggests a scene, or creates a mood, generally associated with the Romantic era. Also *tone poem*.

**symphony** Large work for *orchestra*, generally in three or four *movements*.

**symphony orchestra** See *orchestra*.

**syncopation** Deliberate upsetting of the *meter* or pulse through a temporary shifting of the *accent* to a weak *beat* or an *offbeat*.

**synthesizer** Electronic instrument that produces a wide variety of sounds by combining sound generators and sound modifiers in one package with a unified control system.

**Syrinx** See *panpipes*.

**tabla** Pair of single-headed, tuned drums used in north Indian classical music.

**tabor** Cylindrical medieval drum.

**tag** *Jazz* term for a *coda*, or a short concluding section.

**tala** Fixed time cycle or *meter* in Indian music, built from uneven groupings of *beats*.

**tambourine** *Percussion instrument* consisting of a small round drum with metal plates inserted in its rim; played by striking or shaking.

**tam-tam** See *gong*.

**tango** A Latin American dance involving couples in tight embrace; characterized by abrupt movements and syncopated rhythms.

**tape music** Type of *electronic music* in which sounds are recorded on tape and then manipulated and mixed in various ways. See also *musique concrète*.

**Te Deum** Song of praise to God; a text from the Roman Catholic rite, often set *polyphonically*.

**tempo** Rate of speed or pace of music.

**tempo rubato** See *rubato*.

**tenor** Male voice of high *range*. Also a part, often structural, in *polyphony*.

**tenor drum** *Percussion instrument*, larger than the *snare drum*, with a wooden shell.

**ternary form** Three-part (**A-B-A**) form based on a statement (**A**), contrast or departure (**B**), and repetition (**A**). Also *three-part form*.

**tertian harmony** *Harmony* based on the *interval* of the third, particularly predominant from the Baroque through the nineteenth century.

**texture** The interweaving of melodic (horizontal) and harmonic (vertical) elements in the musical fabric.

**thematic development** Musical expansion of a *theme* by varying its melodic outline, *harmony*, or *rhythm*. Also *thematic transformation*.

**thematic transformation** See *thematic development*.

**theme** Melodic idea used as a basic building block in the construction of a composition. Also *subject*.

**theme and variations** Compositional procedure in which a *theme* is stated and then altered in successive statements; occurs as an independent piece or as a *movement* of a *multimovement cycle*.

**theme group** Several *themes* in the same *key* that function as a unit within a section of a form, particularly in *sonata-allegro form*.

**theremin** An early electronic instrument from the 1920s, named after its inventor Leon Theremin.

**third** *Interval* between two *notes* that are two *diatonic* scale steps apart.

**third stream** *Jazz* style that synthesizes characteristics and techniques of classical music and *jazz*; term coined by Gunther Schuller.

**thirty-two-bar song form** Popular song structure that subdivides into four sections (A-A-B-A) of eight measures each.

**thorough-bass** See *figured bass*.

**three-part form** See *ternary form*.

**throat singing** A vocal technique in which more than one *tone* is produced simultaneously: a deep fundamental *pitch* with reinforced harmonics above the fundamental.

**through-composed** Song structure that is composed from beginning to end, without repetitions of large sections.

**timbales** Shallow, single-headed drums of Cuban origin, played in pairs; used in much Latin American popular music.

**timbre** The quality of a sound that distinguishes one voice or instrument from another. Also *tone color*.

**timbrel** Ancient *percussion instrument* related to the *tambourine*.

**timpani** *Percussion instrument* consisting of a hemispheric copper shell with a head of plastic or calfskin, held in place by a metal ring and played with soft or hard padded sticks. A pedal mechanism changes the tension of the head, and with it the *pitch*. Also *kettledrums*.

**Tin Pan Alley** Nickname for the popular music industry centered in New York from the nineteenth century through the 1950s. Also the style of popular song in the United States during that period.

**tintinnabulation** A bell-like style developed by Estonian composer Arvo Pärt, achieved by weaving conjunct lines that hover around a central *pitch*; from the Latin word for bell.

**tin whistle** Small metal end-blown *flute* commonly used in Irish traditional music.

**toccata** Virtuoso composition, generally for *organ* or *harpsichord*, in a free and rhapsodic style; in the Baroque, it often served as the introduction to a *fugue*.

**tom-tom** Cylindrical drum without snares.

**tone** A sound of definite *pitch*.

**tonal** Based on principles of major-minor *tonality*, as distinct from *modal*.

**tonality** Principle of organization around a *tonic*, or home, *pitch*, based on a major or minor *scale*.

**tone cluster** Highly dissonant combination of *pitches* sounded simultaneously.

**tone color** See *timbre*.

**tone poem** See *symphonic poem*.

**tone row** An arrangement of the twelve *chromatic* tones that serves as the basis of a *twelve-tone* composition.

**tonic** The first note of the *scale* or *key*, do. Also *keynote*.

**tonic chord** *Triad* built on the first scale *tone*, the I chord.

**total serialism** Extremely complex, totally controlled music in which the twelve-tone principle is extended to elements of music other than *pitch*.

**traditional music** Music that is learned by *oral transmission* and is easily sung or played by most people; may exist in variant forms. Also *folk music*.

**tragédie lyrique** French serious *opera* of the seventeenth and eighteenth centuries, with spectacular dance scenes and brilliant choruses on tales of courtly love or heroic adventures; associated with J.-B. Lully.

**trance music** A style of dance music fusing techno and house music. The name derives from the throbbing *beats* designed to put the listener in a trance-like state.

**transition** See *bridge*.

**tranposed row** A tone row whose notes are shifted in order to start at a different pitch level. See *twelve-tone row* and *transpostion*.

**transposition** Shifting a piece of music to a different pitch level.

**tremolo** Rapid repetition of a *tone*; can be achieved instrumentally or vocally.

**triad** Common *chord* type, consisting of three *pitches* built on alternate *tones* of the *scale* (e.g., steps 1-3-5, or *do-mi-sol*).

**triangle** *Percussion instrument* consisting of a slender rod of steel bent in the shape of a triangle, struck with a steel beater.

**trill** Ornament consisting of the rapid alternation between one *tone* and the next or sometimes the *tone* below.

**trio** An ensemble of three players.

**trio sonata** Baroque *chamber sonata* type written in three parts: two melody lines and the *basso continuo*; requires a total of four players to perform.

**triple meter** Basic metrical pattern of three beats to a *measure*.

**triple-stop** Playing three notes simultaneously on a string instrument.

**triplet** Group of three equal-valued notes played in the time of two; indicated by a bracket and the number 3.

**triplum** Third voice in early *polyphony*.

**tritonic** Three-note scale pattern, used in the music of some sub-Saharan African cultures.

**trobairitz** Female *troubadours*, composer-poets of southern France.

**trombone** Tenor-range brass instrument that changes *pitch* by means of a movable double slide; there is also a bass version.

**troubadours** Medieval poet-musicians in southern France.

**trouser role** In Classical *opera*, the part of a young man, written for a soprano or alto singer.

**trouvères** Medieval poet-musicians in northern France.

**trumpet** Highest-pitched *brass instrument* that changes *pitch* through valves.

**tuba** Bass-range *brass instrument* that changes *pitch* by means of valves.

**tubular bells** See *chimes*.

**Turkish Janissary band** See *Janissary Music*.

**turn** A *bridge*, or alternate phrase, in Cajun dance music.

**tutti** "All"; the opposite of solo. See also *ripieno*.

**twelve-bar blues** Musical structure based on a repeated harmonic-rhythmic pattern that is twelve *measures* in length (I-I-I-I-IV-IV-I-I-V-V-I-I).

**twelve-tone music** Compositional procedure of the twentieth century based on the use of all twelve chromatic tones (in a *tone row*) without a central tone, or *tonic*, according to prescribed rules.

**two-part form** See *binary form*.

**underscoring** A technique used in films in which the music comes from an unseen source.

**union pipes** See *uilleann pipes*.

**unison** Interval between two *notes* of the same *pitch*; the simultaneous playing of the same *note*.

**upbeat** Last *beat* of a *measure*, a weak *beat*, which anticipates the *downbeat*.

**vamp** Short passage with simple *rhythm* and *harmony* that introduces a soloist in a *jazz* performance.

**variation** The compositional procedure of altering a pre-existing musical idea. See also *theme* and *variations*.

**vaudeville** A light comedic variety show with music featuring popular song, dance, comedy, and acrobatics; flourished in the late nineteenth and early twentieth centuries.

**verismo** Operatic "realism," a style popular in Italy in the 1890s, which tried to bring naturalism into the lyric theater.

**vernacular** The common language spoken by the people as distinguished from the literary language, or language of the educated elite.

**verse** In poetry, a group of lines constituting a unit. In liturgical music for the Catholic Church, a phrase from the Scriptures that alternates with the *response*.

**Vespers** One of the *Divine Offices* of the Roman Catholic Church, held at twilight.

**vibraphone** A *percussion instrument* with metal bars and electrically driven rotating propellers under each bar that produces a *vibrato* sound, much used in *jazz*.

**vibrato** Small fluctuation of *pitch* used as an expressive device to intensify a sound.

**vielle** Medieval bowed-string instrument; the ancestor of the *violin*.

**Viennese School** Title given to the three prominent composers of the Classical era: Haydn, Mozart, and Beethoven.

**vihuela** A type of Mexican *guitar* with a rounded back, common in *mariachi* ensembles.

**villancico** Spanish vernacular musical and poetic form consisting of several stanzas (coplas) and a *refrain* (estribillo) at the beginning and end. Can be *monophonic* or *polyphonic*; sacred or secular.

**viola** Bowed-string instrument of middle *range*; the second-highest member of the *violin* family.

**viola da gamba** Family of Renaissance bowed-string instruments that had six or more strings, was fretted like a *guitar*, and was held between the legs like a modern *cello*.

**violin** Soprano, or highest-ranged, member of the bowed-string instrument family.

**violoncello** Bowed-string instrument with a middle-to-low range and dark, rich sonority; lower than a *viola*. Also *cello*.

**virelai** Medieval and Renaissance fixed poetic form and *chanson* type with French courtly texts.

**virtuoso** Performer of extraordinary technical ability.

**vivace** Lively.

**vocable** Nonlexical syllables, lacking literal meaning.

**vocalise** A textless vocal melody, as in an exercise or concert piece.

**voice** In a *fugue*, a melodic line. Keyboard *fugues* of the late Baroque period, such as those by J. S. Bach, commonly have four distinct *voices* even though they are played by a single musician.

**volume** Degree of loudness or softness of a sound. See also *dynamics*.

**waltz** Ballroom dance type in *triple meter*; in the Romantic era, a short, stylized *piano* piece.

**Wayang** Javanese shadow-puppet theater.

**West Coast jazz** *Jazz* style developed in the 1950s, featuring small groups of mixed *timbres* playing contrapuntal improvisations; similar to *cool jazz*.

**whole step** Interval consisting of two *half steps*, or *semitones*.

**whole-tone scale** Scale pattern built entirely of *whole-step* intervals, common in the music of the French Impressionists.

**wind ensemble** See *concert band*.

**woodwind** Instrumental family made of wood or metal whose tone is produced by a column of air vibrating within a pipe that has holes along its length.

**woodwind quintet** Standard chamber ensemble consisting of one each of the following: *flute, oboe, clarinet, bassoon,* and *horn* (not a *woodwind instrument*).

**word painting** Musical pictorialization of words from the text as an expressive device; a prominent feature of the Renaissance madrigal.

**work song** Communal song that synchronized group tasks.

**xylophone** *Percussion instrument* consisting of tuned blocks of wood suspended on a frame, laid out in the shape of a keyboard and struck with hard mallets.

**yangqin** A Chinese hammered *dulcimer* with a trapezoidal sound box and metal strings that are struck with bamboo sticks.

**zither** Family of string instruments with sound box over which s trings are stretched; they may be plucked or bowed. Zithers appear in many shapes and are common in traditional music throughout Europe, Asia, and Africa.

**zortziko** Basque dance in *compound meter* with many dotted rhythms.

# Appendix III

## Answers to Listening Activities

**Listening Activity: Melody (p. 12)**
1. b        4. a, b
2. b        5. c
3. a, c      6. b

**Listening Activity: Rhythm (p. 16)**
1. a        4. b
2. a        5. b
3. b

**Listening Activity: Harmony (p. 19)**
1. b        3. a
2. a        4. a

**Listening Activity: Musical Scales and Key (p. 25)**
1. b        4. b
2. a        5. c
3. a        6. d

**Listening Activity: Texture (p. 29)**
1. b        3. b
2. a

**Listening Activity: Musical Form (p. 34)**
1. b        4. b
2. a, c, d    5. a, b, c
3. b

**Listening Activity: Tempo and Dynamics (p. 38)**
1. b        4. a
2. b        5. a
3. b

**Listening Activity: Voices (p. 42)**
1. c        5. c
2. a        6. c
3. b        7. a
4. b        8. b, c
           9. a, c

**Listening Activity: Western Instruments (p. 52)**
1. c        3. a
2. d        4. b

**Listening Activity: Reviewing Ensembles (p. 62)**
1. strings, woodwinds, brass
2. trumpets, French horns, oboes, bassoons, violins, violas, cellos, double basses
3. woodwinds, brass, percussion
4. tuba, trombone, trumpet, drums, cymbals, clarinet
5. flute, oboe, clarinet, bassoon, French horn
6. a        9. b
7. b        10. a, b
8. c        11. c, d

**Listening Activity: Comparing Styles 1: Historical Periods (p. 67)**
1. Melody: b, a
   Rhythm: b, a
   Form: a, b
   Meter: b, a
   Texture: a, b
   Performing Forces: b, a
2. Melody: c, d
   Harmony: d, c
   Timbre: c, d
   Melody: d, c
   Meter: c, d
   Expression: d, c
3. Meter: f, e
   Melody: e, f
   Timbre: f, e
   Expression: f, e
4. Rhythm: h, g
   Performing Forces: h, g
   Meter: h, g
   Function: h, g
   Special Effects: g, h

**Listening Activity: Comparing Styles of Sacred Music (p. 81)**
Left column: b, a, a, b
Middle column: b, a, b
Right column: b, a, a

**Listening Activity: Comparing Styles 2: Medieval, Renaissance, and Baroque (p. 102)**
1. a, b, c
2. duple meter: b, c; triple meter: none; nonmetric: a
3. b, a, c
4. b, c, a
5. b, a, c
6. syllabic: b, c; melismatic: a
7. a cappella: a, b; concerted performance: c

**Listening Activity: Reviewing Baroque Vocal Genres (p. 129)**
1. a, c, b
2. c, b, a
3. c, b, a
4. c, b, a
5. court: a; church: b, c

**Listening Activity: Comparing Styles 3: Baroque to Classical (p. 147)**
1. c, d        6. n, p
2. a, d        7. l, q
3. b, e        8. m, p
4. f, i, j      9. n, p
5. g, h, k

**Listening Activity: Thematic Development (p. 157)**
1. T        6. T
2. T        7. T
3. T        8. F
4. T        9. F
5. F        10. F

**Listening Activity: Hearing Larger Forms (p. 162)**
1. b        6. b
2. a        7. b
3. b        8. b
4. a        9. c
5. c        10. a

**Listening Activity: Mozart and the Concerto (p. 185)**

1. a, c, b
2. b, c, a
3. c, b, a
4. pizzicato: b; bowed: a, c
5. piano

**Listening Activity: Comparing Styles 4: Classical to Romantic (p. 201)**

1. b, a        7. d, c
2. a, b        8. c, d
3. b, a        9. f, e
4. a, b       10. f, e
5. c, d       11. e, f
6. d, c       12. e, f

**Listening Activity: Romantic-Era Orchestral Music (p. 251)**

1. a, b        5. d, c
2. b, a        6. c, d
3. a, b        7. d, c
4. a, b

**Listening Activity: Opera in China and the West (p. 279)**

1. b, a        5. a, b
2. a, b        6. b, a
3. b, a        7. a, b
4. b, a

**Listening Activity: Comparing Styles 5: Romantic to Twentieth Century (p. 281)**

1. a          9. c
2. b         10. c
3. b         11. d
4. a         12. c
5. b         13. c
6. b         14. d
7. a         15. d
8. d         16. c

**Listening Activity: Music at the 1889 World's Fair (p. 294)**

1. b         10. g
2. a         11. a
3. c         12. a
4. e         13. b
5. d         14. b
6. f         15. a
7. h         16. b
8. i         17. a
9. j

**Listening Activity: Previewing Early-20th-Century Styles (p. 299)**

1. b          7. b
2. a          8. a
3. a          9. a
4. a         10. b
5. b         11. b
6. b         12. a

**Listening Activity: The Sounds of the Mariachi Tradition (p. 338)**

1. b          5. j
2. c          6. l
3. f          7. n, p, r
4. h

**Listening Activity: Comparing Styles 6: Early to Later Twentieth Century (p. 339)**

1. b, a        6. d, c
2. a, b        7. c, d
3. b, a        8. d, c
4. b, a        9. d, c
5. b, a       10. d, c

**Listening Activity: The Influence of Bob Dylan (p. 376)**

1. b          8. a, b
2. a          9. a, c
3. a         10. b
4. b         11. b
5. b         12. a, b
6. a         13. F
7. b, c

**Listening Activity: Comparing Styles 7: Pop Rock to Grunge (p. 383)**

1. b          8. b
2. a          9. b
3. b         10. b
4. a, b       11. a
5. b         12. b
6. a         13. b
7. b         14. a

**Listening Activity: Exploring the Javanese Gamelan (p. 401)**

1. b          8. o
2. d          9. q
3. e         10. q
4. h         11. o
5. i         12. p
6. l, n       13. o
7. p         14. p

**Listening Activity: The Sounds of Traditional Chinese Music (p. 405)**

1. b         10. t
2. c         11. w
3. f         12. u
4. h         13. w
5. j         14. w
6. l         15. u
7. n         16. v
8. p         17. v
9. q         18. w

**Listening Activity: Hyperinstruments and Musical Interactivity (p. 412)**

1. e          5. a
2. b          6. c
3. g          7. d
4. f

**Listening Activity: Comparing Styles 8: Contemporary Choral Music (p. 428)**

1. a, c, b     5. a, b, c
2. c, b, a     6. c, b, a
3. a, b, c     7. b, c, a
4. c, b, a

# Credits

Every effort has been made to contact the rights holders for each image. Please contact W. W. Norton & Company with any updated information.

London/The Bridgeman Art Library; **126 (bottom)** Snark/Art Resource, NY; **130** Scala/Art Resource, NY; **131** Réunion des Musées Nationaux/Art Resource, NY; **132** National Gallery, Prague, Czech Republic. Photo: Bridgeman-Giraudon/Art Resource, NY; **134 (top)** Scala/Art Resource, NY; **134 (bottom)** Victoria & Albert Museum, London./Bridgeman Art Library; **137** Civico Museo Bibliografico Musicale Rossini, Bologna, Italy. Photo: Scala/Art Resource, NY; **139** Alte Pinakothek, Munich, German. Photo: Erich Lessing, Art Resource, NY; **140** Image copyright © The Metropolitan Museum of Art/Art Resource, NY; **141 (top)** Dave Bartruff/Corbis; **141 (bottom)** Öffentliche Kunstsammlung, Basel, Junstmuseum. Photo: Öffentliche Kunstsammlung Basel, Martin Buhler. © 2010 The Josef and Anni Albers Foundation/Artists Rights Society (ARS), New York; **145** © National Gallery, London/Art Resource, NY; **148** *Madame Henriette de France (1727–52) in Court Costume Playing a Bass Viol*, 1754 (oil on canvas), Nattier, Jean-Marc (1685–1766)/Chateau de Versailles, France/Lauros/Giraudon/The Bridgeman Art Library; **151 (top)** Charles O'Rear/Corbis; **151 (bottom)** Joseph Sohm/Visions of America/Corbis; **152** Bildarchiv Preussischer Kulturbesitz/Art Resource, NY; **154** Réunion des Musées Nationaux/Art Resource, NY; **156** Tate Gallery, London/Art Resource, NY; **158** The M.C. Escher Company-Holland/Art Resource, NY; **164 (top)** Historisches Museum der Stadt, Vienna, Austria/The Bridgeman Art Library; **164 (bottom)** Lebrecht Musc & Arts Photo Library; **167 (top)** Courtesy of the Ibusz-Hungarian Travel Company; **167 (bottom)** Apic/Getty Images; **171** Casa Goldoni, Venice, Italy/The Bridgeman Art Library; **174 (top)** Erich Lessing/Art Resource, NY; **174 (bottom)** Roger-Viollet/The Image Works; **180 (top)** The Guevara Lock of Beethoven's Hair (from the collection of the Ira F. Brilliant Center for Beethoven Studies, San Jose State University); **180 (bottom)** Erich Lessing/Art Resource, NY; **181** AP Photo/Eric Bouvet; **182** International Stiftung, Mozarteum, Salzburg; **183** Musée Conde, Chantilly, France. Photo: Erich Lessing/Art Resource, NY; **185** akg-images; **186** Bibliothèque Nationale, Paris; **188** Beethoven-Haus, Bonn. H.C. Bodmer Collection. Photo: Beethoven-Haus/akg-images; **191(top)** Historisches Museum der Stadt, Vienna, Austria/Bridgeman Art Library; **191 (bottom)** Marina Henderson Gallery/The Bridgeman Art Library; **192** Beatriz Schiller/Time Life Pictures/Getty Images; **197** Johan Elbers/Time Life Pictures/Getty Images; **198** The Nelson-Atkins Museum of Art, Kansas City, Missouri. Bequest of Milton McGreevy, 81-30/108; **203** De Agostini Picture Library/Getty Images; **205 (top)** The Louvre, Paris, France. Photo: Bridgeman-Giraudon/Art Resource, NY; **205 (bottom)** Erich Lessing/Art Resource, NY; **206 (top)** Phillips Collection, Washington DC, USA/The Bridgeman Art Library; **206 (bottom)** Courtesy of Les Hutchins; **207** Adam Woolfitt/Corbis; **209 (top)** Lebrecht Music & Arts/Corbis; **209 (bottom)** Phillips Collection; **210** Freies DeutschesHochstift-Goethemuseum, Frankfurt; **212** Archives Charmet/The Bridgeman Art Library; **213 (top)** Erich Lessing/Art Resource, NY; **213 (bottom)** Schack-Galerie, Munich; **216** Hideo Haga/HAGA/The Image Works; **217** Robert Schumann Haus; **219** The Metropolitan Museum of Art/Art Resource, NY; **220** Staatliche Kunstsammulungen Dresden/Deutsche Fotothek Dresden; **221** Manchester Art Gallery, UK/Bridgeman Art Library; **222 (top)** Bob Thomas/Popperfoto/Getty Images; **222 (bottom)** Erich Lessing/Art Resource, NY; **225** The Granger Collection, New York; **228 (top)** Hinata Haga/HAGA/The Image Works; **228 (bottom)** New York Public Library/Art Resource, NY; **230** Tate Gallery, London, Great Britain/Art Resource, NY; **231** Wallace Collection, London, UK/The Bridgeman Art Library; **232 (top)** Lebrecht Music & Arts Photo Library; **232 (bottom)** *Harriet Smithson (1800–54) as Miss Dorillon*, c.1822 (oil on panel), Clint, George (1770–1854)/Yale Center for British Art, Paul Mellon Collection, USA/The Bridgeman Art Library; **234** The Granger Collection, New York; **236** Collection Archiv f. Kunst & Geschichte/AKG-images; **237 (top)** The Art Archive/Corbis; **237 (bottom)** Wolfgang Kaehler/Corbis; **240 (top)** *Edvard Hagerup Grieg (1843–1907)* (oil on canvas), Italian School (19th century)/Conservatory of St. Peter, Naples, Italy/Giraudon/The Bridgeman Art Library; **240 (bottom)** Mary Evans Picture Library/Arthur Rackman/The Image Works; **242 (a & b)** from *Ivan Bilibin*, Aurora Art Publishers, Leningrad; **243 (bottom)** The Granger Collection, New York; **245** Private Collection/Bridgeman Art Library; **247** Erich Lessing/Art Resource, NY; **250** Stefan M. Prager/Redferns/Getty Images; **251** Lebrecht Music & Arts Photo Library/Colouriser. AL; **253** Private Collection/Lebrecht/The Image Works; **254 (top)** © akg-images/The Image Works; **254 (bottom)** Courtesy of Giovanni Christen and Opera Glass; **255** Bettmann/Corbis; **261** Scala/Art Resource, NY; **262** Courtesy of the Archives of the Richard Wagner Museum, Bayreuth; **266** Private Collection/Lebrecht Music & Arts Photo Library; **268** Stefano Bianchetti/Corbis; **269** Scala/Art Resource, NY; **271** Chris Pancewicz/Alamy; **272 (top)** Lebrecht Music & Arts/The Image Works; **272 (bottom)** Elliott Franks/ArenaPal/The Image Works; **274** Martha Swope; **275** Photograph © 2010 Museum of Fine Arts, Boston. 1951 Purchase Fund, 56.147; **276 (top)** Popperfoto/Getty Images; **276 (bottom)** Private Collection/Bridgeman Art Library; **278** Private Collection/The Stapleton Collection/The Bridgeman Art Library; **279** Österreichische Galerie, Vienna. Erich Lessing/Art Resource, NY; **283** CNAC/MNAM/Dist. Réunion des Musées Nationaux/Art Resource, NY; **285 (top)** Musée Marmottan, Paris, France/Giraudon-Bridgeman Art Library; **285 (bottom)** Musée de Quai Branly, Paris, France. Photo: Giraudon/Art Resource, NY; **286 (top)** Hermitage, St. Petersburg, Russia. Photo: Scala/Art Resource, NY; **286 (bottom)** © The Museum of Modern Art/Licensed by Scala/Art Resource, NY. © 2010 Succession Miro/Artists Rights Society (ARS), New York/ADAGP, Paris; **287** Photograph by Sally Ritts © The Solomon R. Guggenheim Foundation, New York. © 2010 Artists Rights Society (ARS), New York/Pro Litteris, Zurich;

## MUSIC

# Index

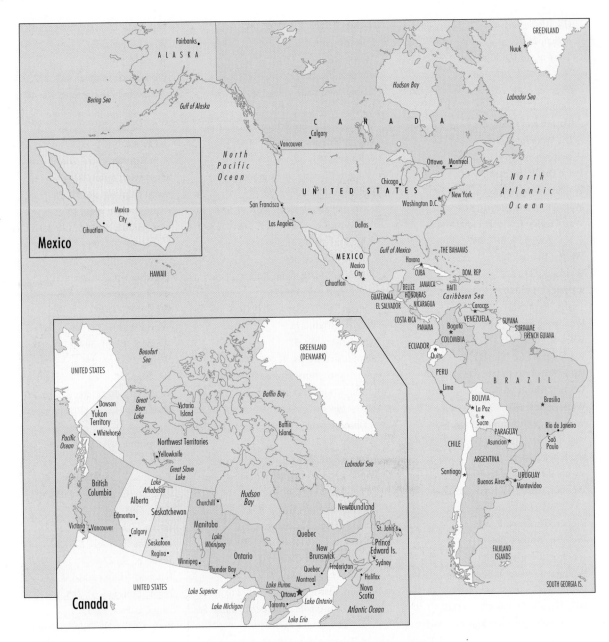

**Mexico**

**Canada**

**United States**

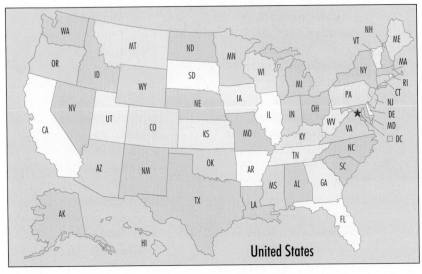

ICELAND

SWEDEN
FINLAND
NORWAY
St. Petersburg
ESTONIA
North Sea
DENMARK
Baltic Sea
LATVIA
LITHUANIA
IRELAND
U.K.
NETH.
BELGIU
GERMANY
POLAND
BYELARUS
English Channel
LU
FRANCE
UKRAINE
Volgograd
Moscow
Omsk
Novosibirsk
R  U  S  S  I  A
Sea of Okhotsk

See detail
at bottom
of page

PORTUGAL
SPAIN
ALBANIA
GREECE
TUNISIA
Mediterranean Sea
TURKEY
Black Sea
GEORGIA
ARMENIA
AZERBAIJAN
Caspian Sea
TURKMENISTAN
UZBEKISTAN
KYRGYZSTAN
TAJIKISTAN
KAZAKHSTAN
MONGOLIA
Vladivostok
Beijing
NORTH KOREA
SOUTH KOREA
Sea of Japan
East China Sea
JAPAN
Wuxi
C  H  I  N  A
TAIWAN

MOROCCO
WESTERN SAHARA
ALGERIA
LIBYA
EGYPT
CYPRUS
LEBANON
ISRAEL
SYRIA
IRAQ
I R A N
JORDAN
KUWAIT
QATAR
U.A.E.
SAUDI ARABIA
Red Sea
OMAN
Arabian Sea
AFGHANISTAN
PAKISTAN
NEPAL
BHUTAN
BANGLADESH
MYANMAR
I N D I A
LAOS
THAILAND
KAMPUCHEA
VIETNAM
South China Sea
Philippine Sea
PHILIPPINES
PALAU

MAURITANIA
MALI
NIGER
CHAD
SUDAN
ERITREA
YEMEN
DJIBOUTI
SOMALIA
ETHIOPIA
Bay of Bengal
SRI LANKA
Indian Ocean
Phnom Penh
BRUNEI
MALAYSIA
SUMATRA
PAPUA NEW GUINEA

SENEGAL
GAMBIA
GUINEA
BISSAU
GUINEA
BURKINA
SIERRA LEONE
IVORY COAST
BENIN
NIGERIA
CAMEROON
CENTRAL AFRICAN REPUBLIC
UGANDA
KENYA
Kampala
I N D O N E S I A
Java Sea
JAVA
BALI
Timor Sea

GHANA
TOGO
LIBERIA
GABON
REP. OF THE CONGO
DEMOCRATIC REP. OF THE CONGO
RWANDA
BURUNDI
TANZANIA
COMOROS

South Atlantic Ocean
ANGOLA
ZAMBIA
ZIMBABWE
MALAWI
MOZAMBIQUE
MADAGASCAR
NAMIBIA
BOTSWANA
SWAZILAND
SOUTH AFRICA
LESOTHO
AUSTRALIA

North Sea
SWEDEN
DENMARK
Copenhagen
Baltic Sea
ESTONIA
Riga
LATVIA
LITHUANIA
Vilnius
Minsk
RUSSIA
Dublin
IRELAND
Cork
U. K.
London
NETH.
Berlin
Gdansk
POLAND
Warsaw
BYELARUS
English Channel
BELGIUM
LUX.
GERMANY
CZECH REP.
Kraków
SLOVAKIA
Lvov
Kiev
UKRAINE
Paris
Nantes
FRANCE
SWITZ.
AUSTRIA
HUNGARY
SLOVENIA
CROATIA
MOLDOVA
Bay of Biscay
ITALY
BOSNIA & HERZEGOVINA
SERBIA
R O M A N I A
Bucharest
Constanta
Black Sea
Bayonne
Toulouse
MONTENEGRO
BULGARIA
Madrid
Barcelona
Rome
Naples
ALBANIA
F.Y.R.O.M.
Ankara
PORTUGAL
S P A I N
Lisbon
Sevilla
GREECE
TURKEY
Gibraltar
Athens

Europe